lonely pla

Vietnam

**Northern
Vietnam**
p93

⭐ Hanoi
p50

**Central
Vietnam**
p144

**Siem Reap & the
Temples of Angkor**
p399

**Southwest
Highlands**
p270

**Southeast
Coast**
p217

Ⓗ **Ho Chi
Minh City**
p294

**Mekong
Delta**
p347

THIS EDITION WRITTEN AND RESEARCHED BY

Iain Stewart,

Brett Atkinson, Damian Harper, Nick Ray

915.97
LON
2014

PLAN YOUR TRIP

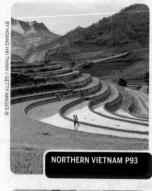

BY HOANG HAI THINH / GETTY IMAGES ©

NORTHERN VIETNAM P93

DAN HERRICK / GETTY IMAGES ©

VIETNAMESE CUISINE P448

ON THE ROAD

Contents

Welcome to Vietnam

Astonishingly exotic and utterly compelling, Vietnam is a country of breathtaking natural beauty with an incredible heritage that quickly becomes addictive.

Sensory Overload

Unforgettable experiences are everywhere in Vietnam. There's the sublime: gazing over a surreal seascape of limestone islands from the deck of a Chinese junk in Halong Bay. The ridiculous: taking 10 minutes just to cross the street through a tsunami of motorbikes in Hanoi. The inspirational: exploring the world's most spectacular cave systems in Phong Nha-Ke Bang National Park. The comical: watching a moped loaded with oinking pigs weave a wobbly route along a country lane. And the contemplative: witnessing a solitary grave in a cemetery of tens of thousands of war victims.

A Culinary Superpower

The Thais may grumble, but in Southeast Asia nothing really comes close: Vietnamese food is *that* good. Incredibly subtle in its flavours and outstanding in its diversity, Vietnamese cooking is a fascinating draw for travellers – the dozens of cooking schools in Hoi An are testament to this. Geography plays a crucial role, with Chinese flavours influencing the soups of northern Vietnam, spices sparking up southern cuisine and myriad herbs and complex techniques typifying the central region, rightly renowned as Vietnam's epicurean epicentre.

Thrills & Chills

If you've got the bills, Vietnam's got the thrills and chills. Some activities require a little physical effort, like motorbiking switchback after switchback up the jaw-dropping Hai Van Pass in central Vietnam. Others require even more sweat: kitesurfing the tropical waters off Mui Ne or hiking the evergreen hills around Bac Ha or Sapa. And when you're done with all that adrenalin stuff, there's plenty of horizontal 'me time' to relish. Vietnam has outstanding spas – from marble temples of treatments, to simple family-run massage salons with backpacker-friendly rates.

Meet the Locals

Vietnamese people are energetic, direct, sharp in commerce and resilient by nature. The locals love a laugh and you'll have plenty of opportunities to socialise with them and hear their tales. Generally the rule is the more uncomfortable the (always tiny) seats in the bar or cafe, the more fun you'll have. Poor in parts but never squalid, Vietnam is developing at an astonishing pace and inevitably there are some issues to consider (including a few minor scams). However, on the whole this is an extremely safe (apart from the traffic!) and wonderfully rewarding country to explore.

Why I Love Vietnam

By Iain Stewart, Author

I know of few more driven, purposeful people on earth than the Vietnamese. Back in 1991 when I first arrived, the country was broke – one of the poorest on earth – but not broken. The streets were swept, the cuisine was outstanding and visitors (yes, even Americans) were welcomed. Over the years I've returned to enjoy the same simple pleasures: chatting with friends over a glass of *bia hoi* (draught beer), soaking up the street scenes in Hanoi's Old Quarter, biking lonely mountain roads, and marvelling at the locals' sheer lust for life. And then I start planning a return trip.

For more about our authors, see page 512

Above: H'mong woman, Sinho market (p128)

Vietnam

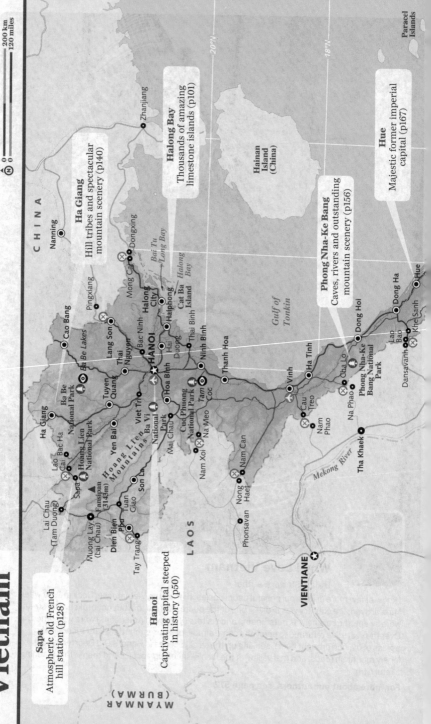

Sapa
Atmospheric old French hill station (p128)

Ha Giang
Hill tribes and spectacular mountain scenery (p140)

Halong Bay
Thousands of amazing limestone islands (p101)

Hue
Majestic former imperial capital (p167)

Phong Nha-Ke Bang
Caves, rivers and outstanding mountain scenery (p156)

Hanoi
Captivating capital steeped in history (p50)

200 km
120 miles

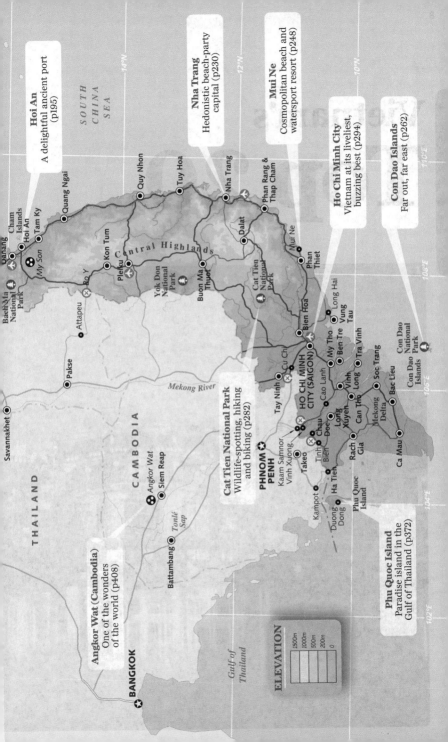

Hoi An
A delightful ancient port (p195)

Nha Trang
Hedonistic beach-party capital (p230)

Mui Ne
Cosmopolitan beach and watersport resort (p248)

Ho Chi Minh City
Vietnam at its liveliest, buzzing best (p294)

Con Dao Islands
Far out, far east (p262)

Angkor Wat (Cambodia)
One of the wonders of the world (p408)

Cat Tien National Park
Wildlife-spotting, hiking and biking (p282)

Phu Quoc Island
Paradise island in the Gulf of Thailand (p372)

SOUTH CHINA SEA

14°N
12°N
10°N

THAILAND

CAMBODIA

Mekong River

Tonlé Sap

Gulf of Thailand

BANGKOK

Battambang

Angkor Wat
Siem Reap

PHNOM PENH

Takeo

Kampot

Pakse

Savannakhet

Attapeu

Duong Dong

Phu Quoc Island

Ha Tien

Rach Gia

Ca Mau

Bac Lieu

Soc Trang

Can Tho

Long Xuyen

Chau Doc

Tinh Bien

Kaam Samnor
Vinh Xuong

Tay Ninh

Cu Chi

HO CHI MINH CITY (SAIGON)

Cao Lanh

Long Xuyen

Vinh Long

Tra Vinh

Ben Tre

My Tho

Mekong Delta

Bien Hoa

Vung Tau

Long Hai

Phan Thiet

Mui Ne

Phan Rang & Thap Cham

Nha Trang

Dalat

Buon Ma Thuot

Cat Tien National Park

Central Highlands

Yok Don National Park

Pleiku

Kon Tum

BO Y

Tuy Hoa

Quy Nhon

Quang Ngai

Tam Ky
Hoi An
Cham Islands

Danang

My Son

Bach Ma National Park

ELEVATION

	1500m
	1000m
	500m
	200m
	0

102°E
104°E
106°E
108°E
110°E

Vietnam's
Top 20

Hoi An

1 Vietnam's most cosmopolitan and civilised town, this beautiful, ancient port (p195) is bursting with gourmet Vietnamese restaurants, hip bars and cafes, quirky boutiques and expert tailors. Immerse yourself in history in the warren-like lanes of the Old Town, shop till you drop, tour the temples and pagodas, and dine like an emperor on a peasant's budget (and even learn how to cook like the locals). Then hit glorious An Bang Beach, wander along the riverside and bike the back roads. Yes, Hoi An has it all. Japanese Covered Bridge (p198)

Food

2 Perhaps Asia's greatest culinary secret, Vietnamese food is on the radar but hardly a global phenomenon. Essentially it's all about the freshness of the ingredients – chefs shop twice daily to source just-picked herbs from the market. The result? Incomparable texture and flavour combinations. For the Vietnamese, a meal should balance sour and sweet, crunchy and silky, fried and steamed, soup and salad. Wherever you are, you'll find exquisite local specialities – the 'white rose' of Hoi An, the *canh chua* of the Mekong Delta or the good ol' *pho* of the north. *Cao lau* (p206), Hoi An

Mui Ne

3 Perhaps the adrenalin epicentre of Vietnam, the relaxed, prosperous beach resort of Mui Ne (p248) is a kite-surfing capital with world-class wind and conditions, and excellent schools for professional training. For those who prefer dry land, sandboarding and golf are popular alternatives. The resort itself has more than 20km of palm-fringed beachfront that stretches invitingly along the shores of the South China Sea. From guesthouses to boutique resorts, designer bars to fine-value spas, Mui Ne has a broad appeal.

Sapa & the Tonkinese Alps

4 Dubbed the Tonkinese Alps by the French, the spectacular Hoang Lien Mountains soar skywards along the rugged edges of northwest Vietnam towards the Chinese border. Shape-shifting banks of cloud and mist ebb and flow in the mountainous area around Sapa (p128), parting to reveal a glimpse of Fansipan, Vietnam's highest peak. From the sinuous and spidery ridges, rice terraces cascade down into river valleys, home for several centuries to ethnic minority villages of H'mong, Red Dzao and Giay peoples. Rice fields, Sapa

Hue

5 The nation's capital for 150 years in the 19th and early 20th centuries, Hue (p167) is perhaps the easiest Vietnamese city to love. Its situation on the banks of the Perfume River is sublime, its complex cuisine is justifiably famous and its streets are relatively traffic free. And that's without the majesty of the Hue Citadel, with its royal residences and elegant temples, formidable walled defences and gateways. On the city's fringes are some of Vietnam's most impressive pagodas and royal tombs, many in wonderful natural settings. Hue Citadel (p171)

Halong Bay

6 A stunning combination of karst limestone peaks and sheltered, shimmering seas makes Halong Bay (p101) one of Vietnam's top tourist draws, but with more than 2000 different islands there's plenty of superb scenery to go around. Definitely book an overnight cruise and make time for your own special moments on this World Heritage wonder – rising early for an ethereal misty dawn, or piloting a kayak into grottoes and lagoons. If you're hankering for more karst action, move on to the less touristy but equally spectacular Lan Ha Bay.

WWW.JETHUYNH.COM / GETTY IMAGES ©

Ho Chi Minh City

7 Increasingly international but still unmistakably Vietnamese, the former Saigon's visceral energy will delight big-city devotees. HCMC (p294) doesn't inspire neutrality: you'll either be drawn into its thrilling vortex, hypnotised by the perpetual whir of its orbiting motorbikes, or you'll find the whole experience overwhelming. Dive in and you'll be rewarded with a wealth of history, delicious food and a vibrant nightlife that sets the standard for Vietnam. The heat is always on in Saigon; loosen your collar and enjoy.

Phong Nha-Ke Bang National Park

8 Picture jungle-crowned hills, rainforest, turquoise streams and traditional villages. Then throw in the globe's most impressive cave systems – river-created Phong Nha Cave, the ethereal beauty of Paradise Cave and the cathedral-like chambers of Hang Son Doong, the world's largest cave – and you can see why Phong Nha-Ke Bang (p156) is Vietnam's most rewarding national park to explore. It's a great place to experience rural Vietnam at its most majestic. Hang Son Doong (p158)

Angkor Wat

9 One of the world's most magnificent sights, the temples of Angkor (p408) lie just over the border in Cambodia. Choose from Angkor Wat, the world's largest religious building; Bayon, the world's weirdest; or Ta Prohm, where nature runs amok. Siem Reap is the base for exploring Angkor and it's a buzzing destination with a superb selection of restaurants and bars. Beyond the temples lie floating villages on the Tonlé Sap Lake, adrenalin-filled activities such as quad biking, and cultured pursuits such as cooking classes and bird-watching.

Biking the North

10 Saddle up for the ride of a lifetime into the mountains of Vietnam's deep north (p120). From Hanoi, journey through sleepy Mai Chau and the historic battlefields of Dien Bien Phu before crossing the 1900m Tram Ton Pass to the stunning scenery and cascading rice terraces around Sapa. Continue east to the mosaic of ethnic minorities around Bac Ha before pushing on to challenging Ha Giang province, Vietnam's hugely spectacular destination for intrepid travellers. In all parts of the north, look forward to the road trip of your life.

Ha Giang province (p140)

HOANG GIANG HAI / GETTY IMAGES ©

Cat Tien National Park

11 One of the most accessible and impressive protected areas in Vietnam, Cat Tien (p282) lies conveniently midway between Ho Chi Minh City and Dalat. Popular activities include trekking, cycling and wildlife-spotting. The park is home to the Dao Tien Endangered Primate Species Centre, where gibbons and langurs are coaxed back into their natural environment. The Wild Gibbon Trek is a must, one of the wildlife highlights of Vietnam. Dong Nai River, Cat Tien

Phu Quoc Island

12 Lapped by azure waters and edged with the kind of white-sand beaches that make sun seekers sink to their weak knees, Phu Quoc (p372) – way down in the south of Vietnam – is ideal for slipping into low gear, reaching for a seaside cocktail and toasting a blood-orange sun as it dips into the sea. And if you want to notch it up a gear, grab a motorbike and hit the red-dirt roads to your heart's content: the island's the size of Singapore. Sao Beach (p373)

DAN J DIXON / GETTY IMAGES ©

PETER STUCKINGS / GETTY IMAGES ©

ROMANA CHAPMAN / GETTY IMAGES ©

HHH IMAGES / GETTY IMAGES ©

Hanoi's Old Quarter

13 Don't worry, it happens to everyone when they first get to Hanoi. Get agreeably lost in the city's centuries-old Old Quarter (p51), a frantic commercial labyrinth where echoes of the past are filtered and framed by a thoroughly 21st-century energy. Discover Vietnam's culinary flavours and aromas at street level, perched on a tiny chair eating iconic Hanoi dishes like *pho bo, bun cha* and *banh cuon*. Later at night, join the socialising throngs enjoying refreshingly crisp *bia hoi* at makeshift street-corner bars.

Coffee Time

14 Starbucks may have opened its first branch here in 2013, but in Vietnam, cafes and coffee culture (p459) run deep. Virtually every neighbourhood in every town (and most villages) will have a little cafe where locals go to de-stress from the office, the family or simply the traffic (most are located on quiet side streets with copious greenery to promote relaxation). Vietnamese coffee can be served hot or iced (a real treat in summer), either treacle thick, or with milk (usually sweetened and condensed) for a double-whammy caffeine-sugar kick. Vietnamese coffee with condensed milk

Con Dao Islands

15 The furious energy that characterises Vietnamese cities can be intoxicating, but when you need an urban detox these idyllic tropical islands (p262) make the perfect escape. Once hell on earth for a generation of political prisoners, Con Dao is now a heavenly destination of remote beaches, pristine dive sites and diverse nature (including nesting sea turtles). It's a wonderful place to explore by bike in search of that dream beach, and the main settlement of Con Son is one of Vietnam's most charming towns.

Ba Be National Park

16 Detour from the regular tourist trail to visit Ba Be National Park (p96), an essential destination for active and intrepid travellers, with towering limestone mountains, plunging valleys and evergreen forests. Waterfalls, caves and lakes combine in a landscape that sustains over 550 different plants and hundreds of bird and animal species. Explore Ba Be's natural spectacle by boat or on trekking and mountain-biking excursions, before relaxing and recharging in the villages and homestays of the local Tay ethnic minority. Ba Be Lake

Nha Trang

17 First things first: Nha Trang (p230) must boast one of the finest municipal beaches in Asia, a breathtaking strip of fine, golden sand lapped by the balmy waters of the South China Sea. But there's much more to the town than beach appeal, with river and island boat trips, ancient Cham towers to explore, natural mud-bath spas and a great dining scene. Nha Trang is also a party mecca for backpackers, for whom the bar and club scene is legendary. Nha Trang Beach

Bia Hoi

18 One of the great pleasures of travelling in Vietnam, *bia hoi* (fresh draught beer) is brewed daily, without additives or preservatives, to be drunk within hours. Incredibly cheap and widely available, *bia hoi* places offer a very local experience. Park (or attempt to park) your rear on one of the tiny plastic stools and get stuck in. Bites to eat are often sold too. Said to have been introduced to Hanoi by Czech brewers, every town now has a *bia hoi* place, often with a street terrace. Hanoi's Old Quarter

Ethnic Minority Markets

19 Use the dusty town of Bac Ha (p137) as a convenient base to explore and discover a colourful variety of local ethnic minority markets. Dzao, Flower H'mong, Tay and Nung people all visit Tuesday's Coc Ly market, and on Saturday mornings the Can Cau market is the place to meet Blue H'mong people over a robust shot of *ruou,* local wine made from corn. Further afield, in remote Ha Giang province, Dong Van and Meo Vac both have vibrant Sunday markets (p142). Flower H'mong women, Bac Ha

Dalat

20 Dalat (p272) is the queen of the southwest highlands and has been popular with international tourists since the days of the French colonialists. Grand Gallic villas are dotted amid pine groves and the whole town is centred on a pretty lake, with numerous nearby waterfalls adding to its natural appeal. Dalat is also fast becoming one of Vietnam's key adventure-sport centres, with abseiling, canyoning, mountain biking, hiking and rafting all on offer. The benign climate here will be a relief if you've been suffering in HCMC. Highlands around Dalat

Need to Know

For more information, see Survival Guide (p468)

Currency
Dong (d)

Language
Vietnamese

Visas
Most nationalities need a visa, which must be arranged in advance. If you're arriving by air, online visa agents (www. vietnamvisachoice.com) are more efficient than embassies.

Money
ATMs widely available, except well off the beaten track. Credit cards accepted in most midrange and luxury hotels, but rarely in restaurants or stores.

Mobile Phones
To avoid roaming charges, local SIM cards can be used in most European, Asian and Australian (and many North American) phones.

Time
Vietnam is seven hours ahead of GMT/UTC.

When to Go

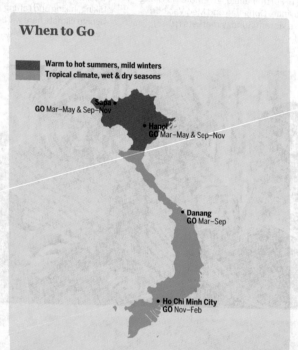

Warm to hot summers, mild winters
Tropical climate, wet & dry seasons

Sapa
GO Mar–May & Sep–Nov

Hanoi
GO Mar–May & Sep–Nov

Danang
GO Mar–Sep

Ho Chi Minh City
GO Nov–Feb

High Season
(Jul–Aug)

➡ Prices increase by up to 50% by the coast; book hotels well in advance.

➡ All Vietnam, except the far north, is hot and humid, with the summer monsoon bringing downpours.

Shoulder
(Dec–Mar)

➡ During the Tet festival, the whole country is on the move and prices rise.

➡ North of Nha Trang can get cool weather. Expect cold conditions in the far north.

➡ In the south, clear skies and sunshine are the norm.

Low Season
(Apr–Jun, Sep–Nov)

➡ Perhaps the best time to tour the whole nation.

➡ Typhoons can lash the central and northern coastline until November.

Websites

Vietnam Coracle (http://vietnamcoracle.com) Excellent independent travel advice from a long-term resident.

The Word (www.wordhcmc.com) This comprehensive magazine has excellent features.

Thanh Nien News (www.thanhniennews.com) Government-approved news, but includes diverse and interesting content.

Lonely Planet (www.lonelyplanet.com/vietnam) Destination information, hotel bookings, traveller forum and more.

The Economist (www.economist.com/topics/vietnam) Analytical and provocative articles.

Vietnam Online (www.vietnamonline.com) Good all-rounder.

Important Numbers

To call Vietnam from outside, drop the initial 🖉0 from the area code. Mobile numbers begin with 🖉09 or 🖉01.

Country Code	🖉84
International Access Code	🖉00
Directory Assistance	🖉116
Police	🖉113
General Information Service	🖉1080

Exchange Rates

Australia	A$1	20,301d
Canada	C$1	20,305d
Euro	€1	29,070d
Japan	¥100	21,678d
New Zealand	NZ$1	17,676d
UK	£1	34,093d
US	US$1	21,085d

For current exchange rates see www.xe.com.

Daily Costs

Budget:
Less than US$40

➡ Glass of *bia hoi*: from US$0.50

➡ One hour on a local bus: US$1–1.50

➡ Cheap hotel: US$10–15 a night, dorms less

➡ Local meal of noodles: US$1.50–2.50

Midrange: US$40–100

➡ Comfortable double room: US$20–50

➡ Meal in a smart restaurant: from US$5

➡ One-hour massage: US$6–20

➡ Ten-minute taxi ride: US$4

Top End: More than US$100

➡ Luxury hotel room: from US$70

➡ Gourmet restaurant: from US$15

➡ Most internal flights: US$30–75

Opening Hours

Opening hours vary very little throughout the year.

Restaurants 11.30am–9pm

Banks 8am–3pm weekdays, 8am–11.30am Saturday

Offices and museums 7am or 8am to 5pm or 6pm. Museums generally close on Monday.

Temples and pagodas 5am–9pm

Shops 8am–6pm

Arriving in Vietnam

Tan Son Nhat International Airport (Ho Chi Minh City; p478) Taxis to central districts cost 175,000d and around 30 minutes. There's also an air-conditioned bus (Route 152) to the centre (5000d, every 15 minutes, 6am–6pm, around 40 minutes).

Noi Bai Airport (Hanoi; p478) Taxis to the centre cost 400,000d and take around one hour. The Vietnam Airlines minibus costs 60,000d and runs every 30 minutes. Route 17 public bus from airport to Long Bien bus station (walking distance to the Old Quarter) is 5000d.

Getting Around

Buses are the main mode of transport for locals in Vietnam, but travellers tend to prefer planes, trains and automobiles.

Train Reasonably priced and comfortable enough if you score an air-conditioned carriage (and a sleeper on overnight routes). But note there are no real express trains.

Plane Very cheap if you book ahead (often less than the equivalent bus fare) and the network is pretty comprehensive. However, cancellations are quite common.

Car Very useful for travelling at your own pace or for visiting regions with minimal public transport. Cars always come with a driver as part of the rental deal.

Bus On the main highways services are quite good, although it's not a particularly relaxing way to travel. In remote areas things deteriorate rapidly. Open-tour buses are very inexpensive and worth considering.

For much more on **getting around**, see p478

First Time Vietnam

For more information, see Survival Guide (p468)

Checklist

➡ Apply for your visa in advance (p476)

➡ Make sure your passport is valid for at least six months past your arrival date

➡ Check your immunisation history

➡ Arrange appropriate travel insurance (p471)

➡ Inform your debit-/credit-card company

➡ Pre-book internal flights and trains

What to Pack

➡ Good footwear – Vietnam's streets are bumpy and lumpy

➡ Mosquito repellent with DEET

➡ Rain jacket

➡ Electrical adapter

➡ Torch (flashlight)

➡ Flip-flops or sandals

➡ Binoculars

Top Tips for Your Trip

➡ Prepare yourself for the crazy driving: traffic can come at you every which way, and in the cities swarms of motorbikes reach biblical proportions. Try to keep calm and consider arranging a massage after a long journey.

➡ Be aware that Vietnam has more than its fair share of scams; most concern overcharging. Though very rare, there are some more serious dangers (like unexploded ordnance) to also be aware of. Relevant warnings are given in destinations throughout this guide.

➡ In towns like Hue and Sapa, and beaches popular with tourists, expect plenty of hustle from street vendors, *cyclo* drivers and the like. Off the beaten track there's little or no hassle.

➡ Load your bargaining head before you arrive.

What to Wear

There are no serious cultural concerns about wearing inappropriate clothing in Vietnam. In temples, pagodas and government offices (or if attending a formal dinner), legs should be covered and singlets avoided.

Yes, Vietnam is in the tropics, but visit anywhere north of Hoi An between October and March and it can be cool, so pack some layers (a fleece or two). The rest of the year, and in the south, flip-flops or sandals, a T-shirt and shorts are likely to be your daily uniform.

Sleeping

Tourism is booming in Vietnam so it's usually best to book your accommodation a day or two in advance, or several weeks ahead in the high season (the Tet Lunar New Year holiday, July to August, and around Christmas). See p468 for more information.

➡ **Hotels** Range from simple functional minihotels to uber-luxurious spa hotels.

➡ **Hostels** Popular in the main tourism centres, but not that widespread elsewhere.

➡ **Guesthouses** Usually family run and less formal than hotels.

Money

ATMs can be found throughout the country, even in small towns, though charges for withdrawals are quite steep. In general, cash is king in Vietnam, but credit and debit cards are accepted in many hotels.

For more information, see p472.

Bargaining

Bargaining is essential in Vietnam, but not for everything. Sharpen your haggling skills when shopping in marketplaces and in some small shops (that sell souvenirs and the like), and when arranging local transport like *cyclos* (bicycle rickshaws) and *xe om* (motorbike taxis).

Many hotels will also offer a discount if you ask for one. In restaurants prices are fixed.

Some bus drivers try to overcharge foreigners, so it's worth bargaining if you're certain the fare is overpriced.

Tipping

➡ **Hotels** Not expected. Leave a small gratuity for cleaning staff if you like.

➡ **Restaurants** Not expected; 5% to 10% in smart restaurants or if you're very satisfied. Locals don't tip.

➡ **Guides** A few dollars on day trips is sufficient, more for longer trips if the service is good.

➡ **Taxis** Not necessary, but a little small change is appreciated, especially at night.

➡ **Bars** Never expected.

Halong Bay (p101)

Language

English is not widely spoken in Vietnam. In the tourist areas most staff at hotels and restaurants will speak a little, but communication issues are common. A few key phrases of Vietnamese go a long way. See Language (p493) for more information.

Etiquette

➡ **Meals** When dining with Vietnamese people, it's customary for the most senior diner to pay for everyone.

➡ **Homes** Remove your shoes when entering a private house.

➡ **Heads** Don't pat or touch an adult (or child) on the head.

➡ **Feet** Avoid pointing your feet at people or sacred objects (eg Buddhas).

Eating

➡ **Local restaurants** Vietnamese restaurants tend to have purely functional decor and even look scruffy, but if they're busy the food will usually be fresh and delicious.

➡ **International restaurants** In tourist areas many restaurants serve up Western and Asian food. Often the local food is 'toned down' and not that authentic in these places.

➡ **Street food** Pavement kitchens offer cheap and often incredibly tasty local grub.

What's New

The World's Biggest Cave
Finally, after years of speculation, the Vietnamese government has granted (strictly regulated) access to Hang Son Doong, the world's biggest cave. Sign up for the trip of a lifetime. (p158)

Imperial Citadel, Hanoi
The nexus of Vietnamese military power for more than 1000 years, Hanoi's World Heritage–listed Imperial Citadel has recently been opened for public viewing. It's a right royal history lesson. (p61)

Phong Nha Fun
Phong Nha-Ke Bang National Park continues to open up. Superb new hiking and caving excursions are now possible deep inside Paradise Cave to remote Hang En, and the Tu Lan river-cave system. (p156)

Zone 9, Hanoi
Filling a former pharmaceutical factory with bars, galleries and art spaces, Hanoi's Zone 9 precinct is the city's hippest and most vibrant new destination. (p78)

Hill Station Signature Restaurant
In chic surroundings in Sapa, learn how to cook H'mong cuisine at the Hill Station Signature Restaurant. Wash it all down with a tasting set of delicious *ruou* (traditional rice wine). (p131)

Independent Tours in Ho Chi Minh City
A bevy of entertaining and inspiring tours is now up for grabs, taking visitors on a wild carousel ride of street food, night sights, bars and more. (p316)

A Tribal Base
High in the hills above Hoi An, this spectacular, unexpectedly comfortable new guesthouse is located in Bho Hoong, a traditional Co Tu minority village. (p212)

An Bang Beach
This beach goes from strength to strength with hip new accommodation choices, like the delightful An Bang Seaside Village, and chic new restaurants, like the effortlessly relaxed, ocean-facing Le Banyan Bar. (p212)

Cham Homestays
Such is its fame these days that the main Cham island settlement of Bai Lang can get crowded, but pretty Bai Huong remains totally tranquil, and has a great new homestay program. (p213)

Cat Ba Island Hotels
New hotels are opening up on private islands in the Cat Ba area, including Cat Ong Beach Cottages, which has its own private beach and chic bungalows. (p111)

Phu Thuan Beach
A short cruise from the cultural capital of Hue, lovely Phu Thuan Beach offers a perfect vision of the tropics, with ocean-washed clean sands, a shack-bar and beautifully crafted, great-value accommodation. (p183)

For more recommendations and reviews, see lonelyplanet.com/vietnam

If You Like...

Fabulous Food

Hoi An Try herb-rich dishes and unique creations like *banh bao* and *banh xeo*, then take a cooking course. (p206)

Hanoi An endlessly tasty street-food scene including *bun cha*, sticky rice creations and crab noodle soup. (p72)

Ho Chi Minh City Foodie paradise: roadside stalls, swish gourmet restaurants, to-die-for Vietnamese eateries and international cuisine. (p323)

Minority Flavours Taste H'mong, Tay and Muong ethnic minority food at specialist restaurants like Quan Kien and The Hill Station. (p76; p134)

Hue This city is famous for its complex imperial cuisine tradition, but is also great for a casual bite. (p178)

Markets

Bac Ha One of the most colourful markets in Southeast Asia where you can see the unique costumes of the Flower H'mong. (p138)

Mekong Delta's Floating Markets Early birds get to catch the delta's panoply of river markets, selling everything from durian to dog meat. (p364)

Sinho Experience an authentic minority market in this isolated highland town, which now has a good new hotel. (p128)

Ben Thanh Market HCMC's most famous and most central market is a hive of activity. (p333)

Remote & Hidden

Ha Giang Crammed with jaw-dropping scenery, this rugged area abuts Vietnam's northern border with China. (p140)

HCMC Tours Sample food from the backstreets, speed on Vespas along alleys and dig out the city's hidden pockets. (p316)

Ganh Da Dia An isolated coastline boasting empty beaches, lonely fishing villages and impressive sand dunes. (p229)

Phu Dien Buried in sand dunes for centuries, this small Cham temple is surrounded by magnificent coastal scenery. (p183)

Bai Dram Trau A half-moon crescent of pale sand, bookended by forest-topped rocky promontories on the Con Dao Islands. (p266)

Tombs & Temples

Hue Vietnamese emperors built dazzling monuments around this city. Don't miss the tombs of Tu Duc and Minh Mang. (p181; p182)

My Son Unquestionably the most impressive Cham site; the forested hilltop location is very special too. (p214)

Hanoi Come face-to-face with history in Ho Chi Minh's austere mausoleum. (p59)

Cao Dai Great Temple A brightly coloured, magnificent hybrid of Chinese temple, Islamic mosque and Christian cathedral. (p344)

Jade Emperor Pagoda Taoism and Buddhism achieve a notable fusion at HCMC's most famous temple. (p300)

Beautiful Beaches

Mui Ne Squeaky sands along the shore, towering sand dunes nearby and expanses of empty beaches up the coast. (p248)

Quan Lan Island Join friendly Vietnamese families for beer

IF YOU LIKE... CAVES

Phong Nha-Ke Bang National Park is simply in a class of its own. It contains the world's largest cave. (p156)

and seafood on sleepy Minh Chau beach. (p114)

Nha Trang Flop on the inviting sands, then explore the bay's islands by boat. (p230)

Con Dao Islands We suggest a self-imposed exile of at least three nights. (p262)

Phu Quoc Island Long Beach is the natural choice, but Sao Beach has beautiful sand, sapphire waters and fewer people. (p372)

Lan Ha Bay Kayak to hidden sandy coves amid the karst labyrinths of this spectacular bay. (p106)

Road Trips

Mai Pi Leng Pass Negotiate this mountainous route from Dong Van to Meo Vac cut into a narrow pass high above the Nho Que River. (p140)

Phu Quoc Island Straddle a motorbike to tame the red-dirt distances of this island. (p372)

Mekong Delta Whiz about the delta, hopping aboard the occasional ferry when you run out of road. (p349)

Ho Chi Minh Highway Forgo Hwy 1 for a while: this inland route is light on traffic and big on scenery. (p285)

Spectacular Treks

Hang Son Doong For the ultimate finale, hike through pristine mountain and valley trails to the world's largest cave. (p158)

Sapa Join chatty H'mong guides to explore the ethnic minority villages around Sapa, framed by cascades of verdant rice terraces. (p128)

Mai Chau Take-it-easy trekking in spectacular scenery around sleepy Mai Chau. (p121)

(Top) Terraced rice fields, Ha Giang province (p140)
(Bottom) Children in traditional ethnic minority clothing, Sapa (p128)

Month by Month

TOP EVENTS
....

Tet, January–February

Hue Festival, June (Biennial)

Wandering Souls Day, August

Danang Fireworks Festival, April

Buddha's Birth, Enlightenment and Death, May

January

Winter temperatures can be bitterly cold in the far north, with snow possible. The further south you go, the milder the weather. Tet occurs at the end of the month (or in February).

✿ Dalat Flower Festival

Held early in the month, this is always a wonderful occasion, with huge elaborate displays and the whole town involved. It's become an international event, with music and fashion shows and a wine festival.

February

North of Danang, chilly 'Chinese winds' usually mean grey, overcast conditions. Conversely, sunny hot days are the norm in the southern provinces.

✿ Tet (Tet Nguyen Dan)

The Big One! Falling in late January or early February, Vietnamese Lunar New Year is like Christmas, New Year and birthdays all rolled into one. Travel is difficult at this time, as transport is booked up and many businesses close.

March

Grey skies and cool temperatures can affect anywhere north of Hoi An, but towards the end of the month the thermometer starts to rise. Down south, the dry season is ending.

✿ Buon Ma Thuot Coffee Festival

Caffeine cravers should make for the highlands during March, as Buon Ma Thuot plays host to an annual coffee festival. Growers, grinders, blenders and addicts rub shoulders in the city's main park, and local entertainment is provided.

☆ Saigon Cyclo Challenge

On your marks...get pedaling. Ho Chi Minh City's fastest rickshaw drivers battle it out in their three-wheeled chariots to raise funds for charity. Takes place in mid-March every year.

April

Generally an excellent time to cover the nation, as the winter monsoon rains should have subsided and there are some excellent festivals. Flights are usually moderately priced (unless Easter falls in this month).

✿ Holiday of the Dead (Thanh Minh)

It's time to honour the ancestors with a visit to graves of deceased relatives to tidy up and sweep tombstones. Offerings of flowers, food and paper are presented. It's held on the first three days of the third moon.

✿ Hue Festival (Biennial)

Vietnam's biggest cultural event (www.huefestival.com) is held every two years, with events in 2014 and 2016. Most of the art, theatre, music, circus and dance performances are held inside Hue's Citadel.

✨ Danang Fireworks Festival

Danang's riverside explodes with sound, light and colour during this spectacular event, which features competing pyrotechnic teams from the USA, China, Europe and Vietnam. Held in the last week of the month.

May

A fine time to tour the centre and north, with a good chance of clear skies and warm days. Sea temperatures are warming up nicely and it's a pretty quiet month for tourism.

✨ Buddha's Birth, Enlightenment and Death (Phong Sinh)

A big celebration at Buddhist temples with lively street processions and lanterns used to decorate pagodas. Complexes including Chua Bai Dinh near Ninh Binh and HCMC's Jade Emperor Pagoda host lavish celebrations. Fifteenth day of the fourth lunar month. (p151; p300)

✨ Nha Trang Sea Festival

Falls at the end of May (and the beginning of June) and includes a street festival, photography exhibitions, embroidery displays and kite-flying competitions.

(Top) Tet (Tet Nguyen Dan) decorations
(Bottom) Traditional dress for Hue Festival

June

A great time to tour Vietnam as it's just before the peak domestic season. Humidity can be punishing at this time of year, so plan to spend some time by the coast.

★☆ Summer Solstice Day (Tet Doan Ngo)

Keep epidemics at bay with offerings to the spirits, ghosts and the God of Death on the fifth day of the fifth moon. Sticky rice wine *(ruou nep)* is consumed in industrial quantities.

August

The peak month for tourism with domestic and international tourists. Book flights and accommodation well ahead. Weather-wise it's hot, hot, hot.

★☆ Wandering Souls Day (Trung Nguyen)

Second in the pecking order to Tet is this ancient Vietnamese tradition. Huge spreads of food are left out for lost spirits who, it's believed, wander the earth on this day. Held on the 15th day of the seventh moon.

★☆ Children's (or Mid-Autumn) Festival, Hoi An

This is a big event in Hoi An, when citizens celebrate

the full moon, eat moon cakes and beat drums. The lion, unicorn and dragon dance processions are enacted, and children are fully involved in the celebrations.

October

A good time to visit the far north, with a strong chance of clear skies and mild temperatures. Winter winds and rain begin to affect the centre, but down south it's often dry.

★☆ Mid-Autumn Festival (Trung Thu)

A fine time for foodies with moon cakes of sticky rice filled with lotus seeds, watermelon seeds, peanuts, the yolks of duck eggs, raisins and other treats. It's celebrated across the nation on the 15th day of the eighth moon and can fall in September or October.

★☆ CAMA Festival, Hanoi

Hanoi's Club for Art and Music Appreciation (www.camavietnam.org) promotes this annual one-day festival. It's an excellent opportunity to experience the best of Hanoi's emerging music scene.

★☆ Cham New Year (Kate)

This is celebrated at Po Klong Garai Cham Towers in Thap Cham on the

seventh month of the Cham calendar. The festival commemorates ancestors, Cham national heroes and deities, such as the farmers' goddess Po Ino Nagar. (p245)

★☆ Khmer Oc Bom Boc Festival

The Mekong Delta's Khmer community celebrates on the 15th day of the 10th moon of the lunar calendar (late October or November) with colourful boat races at Ba Dong Beach in Tra Vinh Province and on the Soc Trang River.

December

The month begins quietly, but from mid-December the popular tourist resorts get increasingly busy and you should book well ahead to secure a room over the Christmas break. It's still steamy in the south but can get chilly up north.

★☆ Christmas Day (Giang Sinh)

This is not a national holiday, but it is celebrated throughout Vietnam, particularly by the sizeable Catholic population. It's a special time to be in places like Phat Diem and HCMC, where thousands attend midnight Mass.

Plan Your Trip
Itineraries

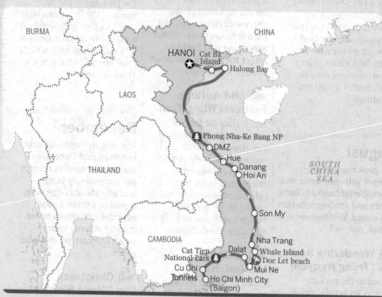

BURMA

CHINA

HANOI — Cat Ba Island

Halong Bay

LAOS

Phong Nha-Ke Bang NP

DMZ

Hue

THAILAND

Danang
Hoi An

SOUTH CHINA SEA

Son My

CAMBODIA

Nha Trang

Cat Tien National Park

Dalat

Whale Island
Doc Let beach

Cu Chi Tunnels

Mui Ne

Ho Chi Minh City (Saigon)

From South to North

Making the most of Vietnam's spectacular coastline, this route hugs the shore for much of the time and is bookended by the country's two greatest cities. You'll have ample opportunity to indulge in some serious beach time, and be able to hit the cultural sights and explore two national parks en route.

The adventure begins in the cauldron of commerce that is **Ho Chi Minh City**. Spend three days hitting the markets,
browsing museums and eating some of the globe's best cuisine. Take a day trip to discover wartime history at the **Cu Chi Tunnels**. Head north into the central highlands via **Cat Tien National Park**, home to gibbons, crocodiles and bountiful birdlife. Next up is the romantic hill station of **Dalat** for a tour of its quirky sights, and the opportunity to get stuck into some adventure sports such as canyoning, mountain biking or kayaking.

Then it's a stunning road trip down to the beach at **Mui Ne**, a tropical idyll with towering dunes and crazy kitesurfing. Continue up the coast to the big brash

Mui Ne (p248)

resort of **Nha Trang**, where party people will love the hedonistic bar scene. On the way, be sure to explore the largely undeveloped coastline, perhaps stopping at **Doc Let Beach**, **Whale Island** and the moving war memorial at **Son My**.

Cultured charmer and culinary mecca **Hoi An** is the next essential stop. This town certainly warrants three days, such is its allure. Then it's a quick look at booming **Danang** and on to the old imperial capital of **Hue** and its citadel, tombs and pagodas. From here pause to tour the **DMZ** (Demilitarised Zone) and its famous war sites before hitting the truly remarkable **Phong Nha-Ke Bang National Park**, the world's greatest caving region, with towering limestone mountains and cobalt jungle rivers.

Next it's a long journey by road or train towards **Halong Bay**, with more than 2000 limestone outcrops dotting the ocean. Stop for a couple of days on rugged **Cat Ba Island**, an important adventure-sports centre, before heading to the capital. Budget for at least a couple of days in **Hanoi** to sample its evocative Old Quarter and to view the city's elegant architecture and memorable museums. Make the most of your last day, perhaps munching street food and sampling *bia hoi* (fresh draught beer).

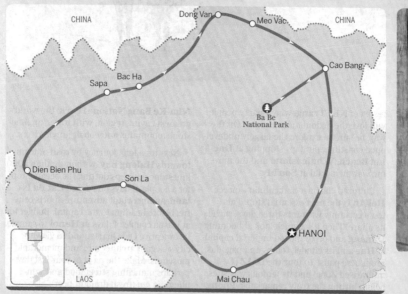

Northern Mountains

3 WEEKS

Northern Vietnam is a world unto itself: a land of brooding mountains, overwhelming beauty and a mosaic of ethnic minorities. It's ideal terrain to cover on two wheels, with light traffic and breathtaking views, though most of the region can be tackled by public transport with a patient attitude.

Visit **Hanoi** to explore its Old Quarter and visit the museums. Then head west to **Mai Chau**, home to the White Thai people, for your first two nights; it's a perfect introduction to ethnic minority life. Northwest where the road begins to climb into the Tonkinese Alps, a logical overnight stop is **Son La**.

Continue on for two nights at **Dien Bien Phu**, a name that resonates with history as it was here that the French colonial story ended with defeat. Tour the military sights and then continue north through stunning scenery up the Tram Ton Pass.

Sapa is the premier destination in the northwest, thanks to the infinite views (on a clear day!), and an amazing array of minority peoples. Explore the area on two feet or two wheels for around four days before heading to **Bac Ha** for three nights to experience the best of the region's markets. Most colourful are the Flower H'mong people.

From Bac Ha move east to Ha Giang province, taking it slowly through stunning scenery and towns including Yen Minh, Dong Van and Meo Vac. Explore remote destinations like the Lung Cu flag tower and the Vuong Palace from **Dong Van**, before negotiating the vertiginous Mai Pi Leng Pass to **Meo Vac**. From Meo Vac, there's no public transport further south, so you'll need to hire a *xe om* (motorbike taxi) or car to get to the riverside junction town of Bao Lac.

Local buses run from Bao Lac to **Cao Bang** and on to **Ba Be National Park**. Spend about three nights around Ba Be, staying at local Tay ethnic minority homestays, and exploring the park by trekking or kayaking. From Ba Be travel back to Cao Bang for the trip south to Hanoi.

Top: Rice paddies, Mai Chau (p121)
Bottom: Red Dzao woman, Ta Phin (p129)

BRUNO DE HOGUES / GETTY IMAGES ©

KIMBERLEY COOLE / GETTY IMAGES ©

Off the Beaten Track: Vietnam

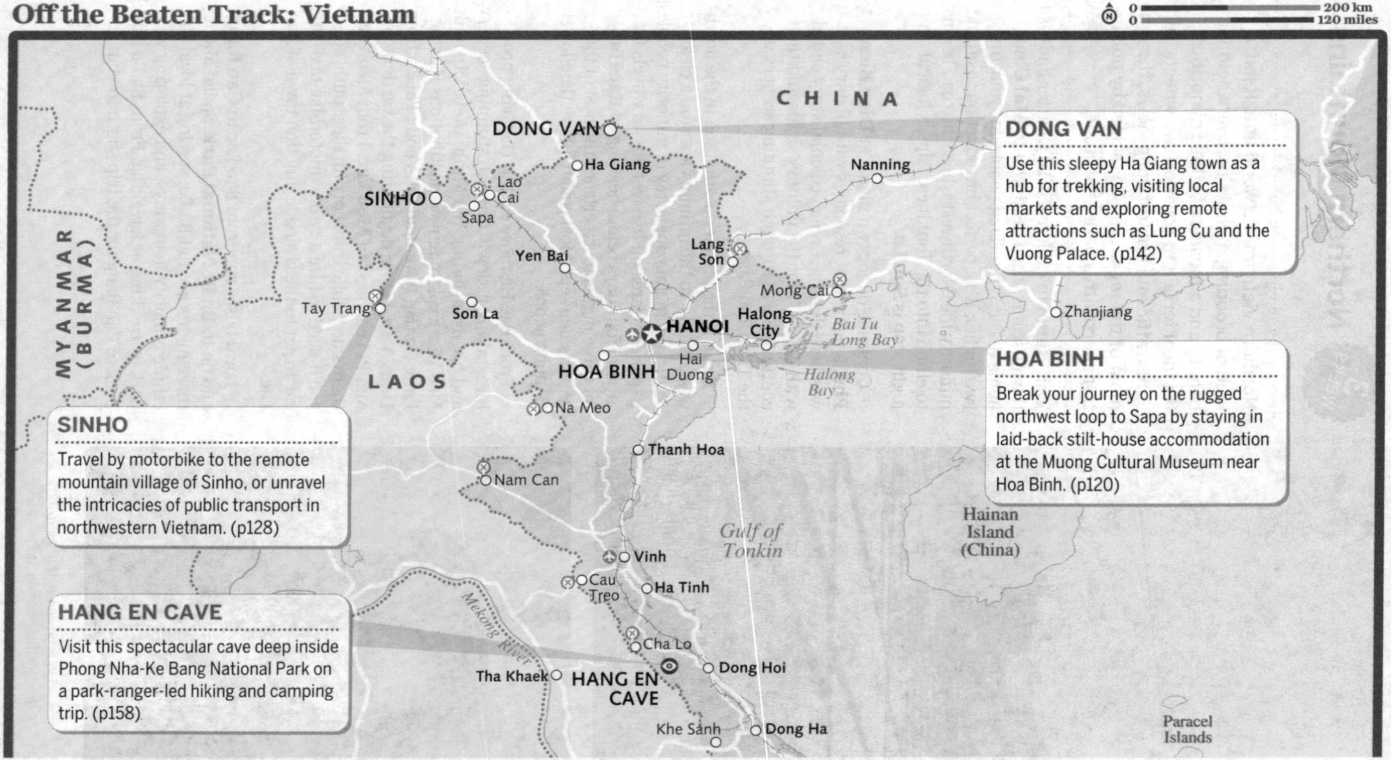

DONG VAN

Use this sleepy Ha Giang town as a hub for trekking, visiting local markets and exploring remote attractions such as Lung Cu and the Vuong Palace. (p142)

HOA BINH

Break your journey on the rugged northwest loop to Sapa by staying in laid-back stilt-house accommodation at the Muong Cultural Museum near Hoa Binh. (p120)

SINHO

Travel by motorbike to the remote mountain village of Sinho, or unravel the intricacies of public transport in northwestern Vietnam. (p128)

HANG EN CAVE

Visit this spectacular cave deep inside Phong Nha-Ke Bang National Park on a park-ranger-led hiking and camping trip. (p158)

CHINA

MYANMAR (BURMA)

LAOS

Nanning

Zhanjiang

Hainan Island (China)

Parcel Islands

Mong Cai

Bai Tu Long Bay

Halong Bay

Halong City

Lang Son

HANOI

Hai Duong

Gulf of Tonkin

Thanh Hoa

Ha Giang

DONG VAN

Lao Cai

Sapa

SINHO

Yen Bai

Son La

HOA BINH

Na Meo

Nam Can

Vinh

Ha Tinh

Cau Treo

Mekong River

Tha Khaek

Cha Lo

Dong Hoi

HANG EN CAVE

Khe Sanh

Dong Ha

Tay Trang

200 km
120 miles

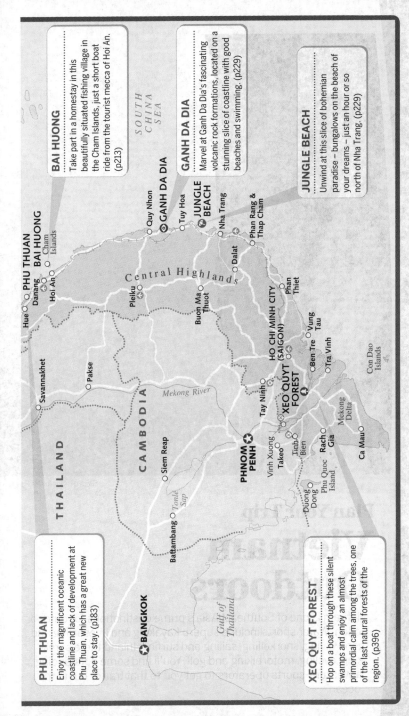

BAI HUONG

Take part in a homestay in this beautifully situated fishing village in the Cham Islands, just a short boat ride from the tourist mecca of Hoi An. (p213)

GANH DA DIA

Marvel at Ganh Da Dia's fascinating volcanic rock formations, located on a stunning slice of coastline with good beaches and swimming. (p229)

JUNGLE BEACH

Unwind at this slice of bohemian paradise – bungalows on the beach of your dreams – just an hour or so north of Nha Trang. (p229)

PHU THUAN

Enjoy the magnificent oceanic coastline and lack of development at Phu Thuan, which has a great new place to stay. (p183)

XEO QUYT FOREST

Hop on a boat through these silent swamps and enjoy an almost primordial calm among the trees, one of the last natural forests of the region. (p396)

Rock climbing (p108), Halong Bay

Plan Your Trip
Vietnam Outdoors

Vietnam is one of Southeast Asia's prime destinations for outdoor action. Water sports include superb kayaking and kitesurfing and good diving, snorkelling, sailing and surfing. Inland there's trekking, cycling, motorbiking and golf. You'll find some outstanding adventure-sports operators to get you to that trail or out in the ocean.

COLIN BRYNN / GETTY IMAGES ©

Best Outdoors

Best Trekking

Sapa Superlative views but can be crowded.

Dong Van New routes through spectacular mountain scenery.

Moc Chau An emerging hiking-and-homestay destination in the northwest.

Mai Chau Sublime landscapes and tribal villages.

Best Surfing & Kitesurfing

Mui Ne Southeast Asia's kitesurfing capital.

China Beach When it rolls, it rolls.

Bai Dai South of Nha Trang, this beach break is great for beginners.

Best Diving & Snorkelling

Con Dao Islands Remote, but the best.

Phu Quoc Visibility can be a challenge, but some nice coral gardens.

Nha Trang Professional scuba schools and many dive sites.

Best Cycling

Dalat Base camp for the dramatic two-day descent to Mui Ne.

Hoi An Flat terrain to explore craft villages and cut across rice paddies.

Mekong Delta Back roads beside waterways under the shade of coconut palms.

Planning

Whether you're a committed kitesurfer or a genteel golfer, some careful planning is essential – Vietnam's climate is extremely variable and monsoon-dependent.

Best Times to Go

Surfers should be aware that the wave action peaks in winter (November to April). Kitesurfing also excels at this time of year. Divers take note that water visibility is best in the calm months of June, July and August.

Times to Avoid

It would be foolish to attempt an ascent of Fansipan in the height of the rainy season, from May to September. Snorkelling and diving is virtually impossible between November and April when the winter winds blow and visibility drops.

Trekking

Vietnam offers excellent trekking and less-strenuous walks. The scenery is often remarkable – think plunging highland valleys, tiers of rice paddies and soaring limestone mountains. Anything is possible, from half-day hikes to assaults on Fansipan (3143m), Vietnam's highest mountain. Even if you're somewhere like An Bang Beach near Hoi An, you can stroll along the sands for an hour or two and experience a near-pristine coastal environment.

Generally northern Vietnam is your best bet: its dramatic mountain paths and fascinating minority culture are a huge draw. Elsewhere, national parks and nature reserves have established trails (and usually guides available to keep you on them).

Northern Vietnam

The region north of Hanoi is truly spectacular. Sapa is Vietnam's trekking hub, full of hiking operators and hire stores (renting out sleeping bags, boots and waterproof gear). Maps detailing trails are available, as are guides. The scenery is remarkable, with majestic mountains, impossibly green rice paddies and some fascinating tribal villages. But prepare yourself – the main trails are incredibly popular and some villagers see hiking groups on an hourly basis. To trek remote paths you'll have to find an expert local guide.

At a lower elevation is Bac Ha. It's less rainy and the trails are not heavily trampled. It's very picturesque, but it lacks Sapa's jaw-dropping mountain scenery. However, you will find great hikes to waterfalls and to Flower H'mong and Nung villages.

High-altitude Ha Giang province, in the extreme north of Vietnam, is the nation's Tibet. Hikers can hook up with guides in Ha Giang city, or head out to Dong Van where there are new trekking opportunities.

The Moc Chau plateau is famous for its limestone karsts, plum orchards, tea plantations and dairy products. Thanks to new accommodation options, hiking routes are now opening up here. The nearby Mai Chau region is far more established and popular with tourists, offering great walking in an idyllic valley setting.

Other key destinations include Ba Be, with its network of beautiful trails amid spectacular karst scenery, and Cat Ba, which has a popular 18km hike as well as shorter alternatives such as Butterfly Valley.

Central Vietnam

The most spectacular hiking in this region is on offer at Phong Nha-Ke Bang National Park, and numerous new trails between the limestone hills are being developed. Most combine trekking with some caving, including, most famously, the hike to the world's largest cave, Hang Son Doong.

You'll find excellent trails inside Cuc Phuong National Park through superb forest and past ancient trees and caves to a minority village.

Close to Danang, Bach Ma National Park has some good trails while the Ba Na Hill Station has short trails and awesome views. Adventure tour operators in Hoi An also offer some intriguing treks in the tribal areas west of town.

Southern Vietnam

With a bit of luck you might glimpse one of the dozens of mammals present in Yok Don National Park near Buon Ma

Surfboards, Mui Ne (p248)

Thuot. You'll need to hire a guide to see the best of Cat Tien National Park, where crocodiles can be seen and night hikes are possible. The Wild Gibbon Trek here is proving a big hit. Over in Dalat, several adventure tour operators offer hiking trips: one rewarding area is the Bidoup Nui Ba National Park.

Further south there's little for hikers to get excited about – the climate is perennially hot and humid and landscape largely flat. Con Son is one curious exception, an island with cooling sea breezes and hikes through rainforest and mangroves.

Diving & Snorkelling

Vietnam is not a world-class dive mecca but it does have some fascinating dive sites. If you've experienced reefs in Indonesia or Australia, prepare yourself for less sea life and reduced visibility. The most popular scuba-diving and snorkelling is around Nha Trang where there are several reputable dive operators with equipment and training up to international standards. Hoi An's two dive schools

Hiking (p109), Halong Bay

head to the Cham Islands where macro life can be intriguing. Phu Quoc Island is another popular spot. One-off discover diving experiences cost around US$60 to US$80, with two fun dives running around US$70 to US$80. Expect to pay between US$30 and US$42 for a snorkelling day trip.

The Con Dao Islands offer unquestionably the best diving and snorkelling in Vietnam, with bountiful marine life, fine reefs and even a wreck dive. However, expect to pay more than you would elsewhere in Vietnam (around US$160 for two fun dives).

It is also possible to hire snorkelling gear and scuba equipment at several beach resorts along the coast, including Cua Dai Beach, Ca Na and China Beach.

Note that Vietnam is home to several dodgy dive shops, some of which have fake PADI credentials. Nha Trang in particular has an excess of such places. Stick to reputable, recommended dive schools with good safety procedures, qualified instructors and well-maintained equipment. PADI Open Water courses cost around US$350 to US$500.

Surfing

There's surf most times of year in Vietnam, though it isn't an acclaimed destination – the wave scene in *Apocalypse Now* was shot in the Philippines. Dedicated surf shops are rare, though the odd guesthouse and adventure-sport tour operator have boards for hire.

The original GI Joe break, China Beach is a 30km stretch of sand, which can produce clean peaks of over 2m, though watch out for pollution after heavy rains.

In season, head to Bai Dai beach, 27km south of Nha Trang, where's there's a good left-hand break up to 2m during stormy conditions. There's also powerful body surfing on Nha Trang's main beach.

Beginners can head to Mui Ne, with multiple breaks around the bay, including short right- and left-handers. Further south, Vung Tau is inconsistent, but offers some of Vietnam's best waves when conditions are right.

Surf's up between November and April when the winter monsoon blows from the north. Several typhoons form in the South China Sea each year, and these produce the

CHRISTER FREDRIKSSON / GETTY IMAGES ©

Kitesurfing, Mui Ne (p248)

The best conditions in Mui Ne are in the dry season from November to April. Mornings are ideal for beginners, while in the afternoon wind speeds regularly reach 35 knots. Nha Trang and Vung Tau are also best at this time of year.

Kayaking

Kayaking has exploded in popularity around Halong Bay in the past few years. Many standard Halong Bay tours now include an hour or so of kayaking through the karsts, or you can choose a kayaking specialist and paddle around majestic limestone pinnacles, before overnighting on a remote bay.

Other kayaking destinations include Cat Ba Island, the Con Dao Islands, Phong Nha, Dalat and rivers in the Hoi An region. You can also rent sea kayaks on beaches including Nha Trang.

Operators include Blue Swimmer (p109), Asia Outdoors (p109), Cat Ba Ventures (p109) and Marco Polo Travel (p83).

biggest wind swells, though the action is usually short lived.

Anyone searching for fresh waves in remote locations should be extremely wary of unexploded ordnance, which litters the countryside, particularly near the Demilitarised Zone (DMZ). Garbage, stormwater run-off and industrial pollution are other hazards, particularly near cities. Rip tides can be powerful, so use a leash on your board.

White-Water Rafting

Rafting is in its infancy in Vietnam. Several outfits in Dalat offer trips around the town, including Phat Tire Ventures (p276), which runs a day trip down the Langbian River with Class II, III or IV rapids, depending on the season; prices start at US$62. Companies based in Nha Trang also offer trips.

Kitesurfing & Windsurfing

Windsurfing and kitesurfing are taking off. Mui Ne Beach is fast becoming a wind-chasers' hot spot in Asia with competitions and a real buzz about the place. Nha Trang and Vung Tau are other possibilities.

If you've never kitesurfed, have a taster lesson (US$80 to US$100) before enrolling in lengthy training – a three-day course costs from US$275 to US$385. It's tough to get your head around all the basics (and also tough on your body!).

Cycling

Cycling is a popular mode of transport in Vietnam, and it's an excellent way to experience the country. Basic bicycles can be rented for US$1 to US$3 per day, and good-quality mountain bikes for US$7 to US$12.

The flat lands of the Mekong Delta region are ideal for long-distance rides down back roads. The entire coastal route along Hwy 1 has allure, but the insane traffic makes it tough going and dangerous. Consider the inland Ho Chi Minh Highway (Hwys 14, 15 and 8), which offers stunning scenery and little traffic. There's flat terrain around Hoi An, which is an

Above: Cycling,
Dalat (p272)

Right:
Windsurfing,
Mui Ne (p248)

CHRISTER FREDRIKSSON / GETTY IMAGES ©

ALT HIGHWAY 1

Hwy 1's heavy traffic and trucks don't make for great motorbiking or bicycling. It's possible, with some careful planning, to loop off Hwy 1 at regular intervals and use coastal back roads. East of Hue between Thuan An and Vin Hien; between Chi Thanh and the Hon Gom peninsula; south of Nha Trang to the Cam Ranh airport; and between Phan Thiet and Vung Tau are perfect examples.

excellent base for exploring craft villages and country lanes. Hue is also a great place for cycling, with temples, pagodas and the Perfume River.

In the southwest highlands, Dalat has lots of dirt trails and is the base camp for the dramatic two-day descent to Mui Ne.

Motorbiking

Motorbiking through Vietnam is an unforgettable way to experience the nation. It's the mode of transport for most Vietnamese, so you'll find repair shops everywhere. Two wheels put you closer to the countryside – its smells, people and scenery – compared with getting around by car or bus. For those seeking true adventure there is no better way to go.

If you're not confident riding a motorbike, it's comparatively cheap to hire someone to drive one for you. Easy Riders (p277) is one such scheme.

Unless you relish getting high on exhaust fumes and barged by trucks, avoid too much time on Hwy 1. The inland Ho Chi Minh Highway running the spine of the country from north to south is one alternative, though of course you miss out on the ocean. The stretch from Duc Tho to Phong Nha offers wonderful karst scenery, forests, little traffic and an excellent paved road. For outstanding ocean views, try coastal Hai Van Pass, which features hairpin after hairpin.

Further north, there's glorious mountain scenery, river valleys and tribal villages around Sapa and Dien Bien Phu. The route through Ha Giang province through Ha Giang, Dong Van and Bao Lac is the

ultimate, with superlative vistas and stupendous mountain roads.

The spectacular new road between Nha Trang and Dalat cuts through forests and takes in a 1700m pass.

Caving

There are amazing cave trips at Phong Nha-Ke Bang National Park, many of which involve some hiking, swimming (there are a lot of river caves) and a short climb or two.

Specialist Oxalis (p158) is the only operator licensed to take you to the wonders of Hang Son Doong, the world's largest cave, but if your budget won't stretch to this there are other options. You can now trek 7km inside Paradise Cave, do a remarkable two-day hike to Hang En Cave and Ban Doong village and there's the lovely swim-through Tu Lan cave system. It may be touristy, but the Phong Nha river cave trip by boat is still a great excursion.

Rock Climbing

It's early days, but with the sheer range of limestone karsts found up and down the country, it is only a matter of time before Vietnam becomes a climbing mecca. The pioneers, and acknowledged specialists, are Asia Outdoors (p109), a highly professional outfit based in Cat Ba Town that has instruction for beginners and dedicated trips for rock addicts. In Dalat there are a couple of good adventure tour operators offering climbing and canyoning too. And in Hoi An, Phat Tire Ventures (p203) offers climbing and rappelling (from US$48) on a marble cliff.

Golfing

Most Vietnamese golf clubs will allow you to pay a guest fee. The best golf courses in Vietnam include those around Dalat and Phan Thiet, but there are also plenty of courses in and around Hanoi and HCMC.

Golfing package deals are offered by **Luxury Travel** (www.luxurytravelvietnam.com) and UK-based **Vietnam Golf** (www.vietnam golf.co.uk).

Hoi An (p195)

Eat & Drink Like a Local

Showcasing fresh and vibrant flavours, excellent street food and elegant restaurants in restored colonial architecture, Vietnam is packed with superb opportunities for eating and drinking. Cookery classes, market visits and walking tours all make it easy to get to the authentic heart of the country's culinary heritage.

A Day in Hanoi

Surrounded by an array of eating and drinking opportunities, this is how a resident of the Vietnamese capital might fill a tasty day.

Early Morning

A local breakfast speciality is *bun rieu cua*, noodle soup made with a hearty broth using tiny crabs from rice paddies.

Mid-Morning

Simple cafes and coffee stalls dot Hanoi, and catching up with friends over deliciously strong *caphe* is virtually mandatory. During summer, *tra chanh* (iced lemon tea) is equally popular.

Lunch

Bun cha (grilled pork with crab spring rolls, fresh herbs and vermicelli) is the classic Hanoi midday meal.

Mid-Afternoon

Hanoi is a city that's perfect for snacking. Popular on-the-go options include *banh ghoi*, deep-fried pastries with pork, vermicelli and mushrooms.

Evening

After dark Hanoi's footpaths come alive with simple *bia hoi* (fresh draught beer) stalls; popular drinking snacks include roast duck and dried squid.

Food & Drink Experiences

Plan your travel around these tasty recommendations and understand the essence of Vietnamese cuisine

First-Night Dining

Welcome to your first night in Vietnam in Ho Chi Minh City, Hoi An or Hanoi. Here's where to go to get quickly up to speed with the country's cuisine.

➡ **Nha Hang Ngon** Street-food classics served in a stylish garden setting in Ho Chi Minh City. (p323)

➡ **Morning Glory Street Food Restaurant** The country's diverse dishes are served around a lively open kitchen; Hoi An. (p206)

➡ **Quan An Ngon** Bustling showcases of Vietnamese food in restored colonial buildings in the nation's capital. (p75)

Street-Food Tours

Pull up a squat plastic stool and discover what makes Vietnam's street food exceptional, usually in the company of a knowledgeable local foodie.

➡ **Saigon Street Eats** Ho Chi Minh City (p316)

➡ **Taste of Hoi An Food Tour** Hoi An (p203)

➡ **Danang Food Tour** Danang (p189)

➡ **Hanoi Cooking Centre** Hanoi (p65)

➡ **Hanoi Street Food Tours** Hanoi (p66)

Best Fusion Restaurants

Discover the culinary intersection between Western flavours and Vietnamese cuisine at these elegant and innovative big-city restaurants.

➡ **Pots 'n Pans** Modern spins on traditional Vietnamese cuisine; Hanoi. (p76)

➡ **La Badiane** French flavours blend with Vietnamese in this leafy colonial villa, also in Hanoi. (p76)

➡ **Xu** Stylish HCMC restaurant-lounge with an inventive Vietnamese-inspired fusion menu. (p324)

Beyond Bia Hoi

Downing a few leisurely glasses of inexpensive *bia hoi* (fresh draught beer) is an essential Vietnamese experience, but also popular is *ruou* (traditional liquor made from fruit, corn or rice).

➡ **Quan Ly** Robust options include rice wine infused with ginseng, snake and gecko; Hanoi. (p78)

➡ **House of Son Tinh** Elegant Hanoi bar featuring cocktails crafted from high-quality *ruou*. (p77)

➡ **Quan Kien** Serves interesting *ruou* crafted from apricots, apples and limes; Hanoi. (p76)

➡ The Hill Station Signature Restaurant
Tasting sets of corn and rice wine are partnered with traditional H'mong cuisine and superb views in Sapa. (p134)

Vegetarian & Vegan Food

Com chay (vegetarian) restaurants serving vegan food can be found across Vietnam, and around the first and fifteenth days of the Buddhist calendar month, some food stalls substitute tofu in their dishes.

➡ Chay Nang Tam Tasty variations on tofu and tempeh; Hanoi. (p76)

➡ ...hum Vegetarian Cafe & Restaurant
Excellent salads in an elegant HCMC space. (p327)

➡ Com Chay Phuoc Around five different daily dishes star at this simple roadside spot in Mui Ne. (p253)

➡ Lien Hoa Featuring flavour-packed dishes with eggplant and jackfruit; Hue. (p178)

➡ Au Lac Simple vegetarian food in a destination (Nha Trang) more known for seafood. (p240)

Minority Flavours

Curious travellers should seek out the food of Vietnam's ethnic minority groups, especially in the north of the country. Look forward to occasionally challenging but always interesting dishes.

➡ Chim Sao Try the ethnic minority sausages, served with a zingy mint and coriander dipping sauce (Hanoi; p76)

Street-food stall, Hanoi's Old Quarter (p73)

PLAN YOUR TRIP EAT & DRINK LIKE A LOCAL

➡ Quan Kien Dishes inspired by H'mong, Thai and Muong cuisine (Hanoi; p76)

➡ The Hill Station Signature Restaurant
Chic and modern decor combines with dishes influenced by traditional H'mong cuisine (Sapa; p134)

TABLE ETIQUETTE

➡ Have your bowl on a small plate, chopsticks and a soup spoon at the ready.

➡ Each place setting will include a small bowl at the top right-hand side for *nuoc nam* (fish sauce) and other dipping sauces.

➡ Don't dip your chopsticks into the central bowls of shared food, but use the communal serving spoons instead.

➡ Pick up your bowl with your left hand, bring it close to your mouth and use the chopsticks to manoeuvre the food. If you're eating noodles, lower your head till it hangs over the bowl and slurp away.

➡ If you're dining in a private home, it is polite for the host to offer more food than the guests can eat, and it's also polite for guests not to eat everything.

➡ Remember not to leave chopsticks standing in a V-shape in your bowl as this is a sign of death.

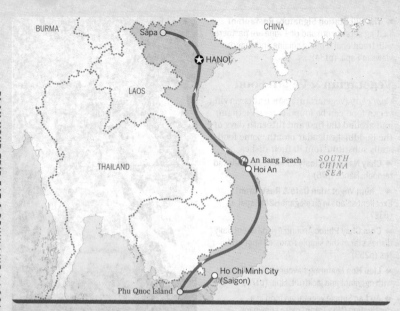

The Ultimate Vietnamese Food Tour

Start in **Ho Chi Minh City**, Vietnam's energetic southern hub, and negotiate the city's street-food scene on two wheels with Back of the Bike Tours (p316) or XO Tours (p316). Discover local dishes like *banh xeo* (filled savoury pancakes) before exploring produce markets and trying a cooking class with Cyclo Resto (p316). Consider a southern sojourn on **Phu Quoc Island**, taking in excellent grilled seafood at the Dinh Cao Night Market (p380).

Heading north to the riverside town of **Hoi An**. Once one of Asia's most cosmopolitan ports with traders from around the world, Hoi An now hosts an international collection of visitors at the town's many cookery schools. Learn the secrets of local cuisine at the Morning Glory Cooking School (p203) or Red Bridge Cooking School (p204), and uncover more street-food secrets with the original Taste of Hoi An (p203) food tour. Detour to nearby **An Bang Beach** for more seafood, and try Hoi An's signature dish *cao lau* (Japanese-style noodles with herbs, salad greens, bean sprouts and roast pork) at Mermaid Restaurant (p206).

Continue north to **Hanoi**, renowned as one of Asia's great cities for street food, and negotiate the bustling labyrinth of the Old Quarter with Food on Foot (p66) or Hanoi Street Food Tours (p66). Iconic Hanoi dishes to try while in the city include cha ca (grilled fish with turmeric and dill) at Cha Ca Thang Long (p72), and pho bo (beef noodle soup) at Pho Thin (p73). Learn about northern Vietnamese cuisine at the Hanoi Cooking Centre (p65), and try dishes inspired by Vietnam's ethnic minorities at Quan Kien (p76) or Chim Sao (p76).

Next, catch the train north to **Sapa**, the heartland region of minority groups including the H'mong and the Red Dzao. Experience H'mong-inspired dishes at The Hill Station Signature Restaurant (p131), book in for its cooking class, and toast your new knowledge of Vietnamese cuisine with a *ruou* tasting set.

Cao lau (p206), Hoi An

Authentic Coffee

Try these places for an authentic coffee experience.

➡ **Café Duy Tri** Dripping with heritage, and virtually unchanged for more than 75 years; Hanoi. (p77)

➡ **Cafe Pho Co** Negotiate your way to a hidden balcony overlooking Hanoi's Hoan Kiem Lake. (p77)

Cooking Courses

Cooking courses in Vietnam can range from a simple set-up in someone's back-yard to purpose-built schools.

➡ **Green Bamboo Cooking School** A charming and accomplished chef offers personalised cooking courses in Hoi An. (p203)

➡ **Hanoi Cooking Centre** Excellent interactive cooking classes in Hanoi that include a visit to the market and cooking classes for kids. (p65)

➡ **Saigon Cooking Class** Learn from the chefs at Hoa Tuc restaurant as they prepare a mouth-watering three-course meal in HCMC. (p316)

How to Eat & Drink

When to Eat

Generally Vietnamese eat three meals per day, beginning with a bowl of noodles or *chao* (rice porridge) for breakfast. Lunch is usually a social affair, often eaten in the company of workmates at a local restaurant or food stall, and dinner is a leisurely meal, usually shared with friends and family. Throughout the day, snacking opportunities also abound, especially in bigger cities.

Where to Eat

Throughout Vietnam, food stalls often specialise in just one dish; simple *com* (literally 'rice') restaurants serve the staple along with vegetables and meat or seafood. Vietnamese-style food courts like Quan An Ngon (p75) in Hanoi serve dishes from around the country, and more expensive eateries offer Vietnamese classics and Vietnamese-French fusion food, often in restored colonial buildings.

Regions at a Glance

Occupying a slender slice of the east Asian landmass, Vietnam combines jagged alpine peaks in the north, a pancake-flat river delta in the south, cave-riddled limestone hills in its central provinces and dense rainforest along its western border with some of the world's most productive rice-growing terrain. And that's just the countryside.

Climatically the northern half of the nation experiences a much cooler winter, and the cuisine, lifestyle and character of the people reflect this. As you head south, the country has more of a tropical feel, with coconut trees outnumbering bamboo plants and fish sauce replacing soy sauce on the menu. The southern provinces are always humid, hot and sticky, their food sweet, spicy, aromatic and complex.

Hanoi

Food
History
Culture

Spectacular Street Food

Dine in elegantly restored colonial villas, or pull up a stool and chow down on street food classics like *pho bo* (beef noodle soup) or *bun cha* (barbecued pork with rice vermicelli).

A Millennium of History

Immerse yourself in Hanoi's heady combination of history and culture. The tumultuous events of over one thousand years are showcased in fascinating detail at the city's excellent museums.

Traditional & Cutting Edge

Hanoi's eclectic cultural scene includes storied musical traditions like *Ca tru* and *Hat tuong*, and newer visual arts on display at hip galleries like Manzi and Zone 9.

p50

Northern Vietnam

Landscapes
Trekking
Adventure

Soaring Limestone Peaks

Halong Bay's majesty is best observed shrouded in ethereal morning mist, and to the north the sublime mountainous scenery of Ha Giang province is arguably even more spectacular.

Meeting the Locals

The cascading rice paddies around Sapa and Bac Ha are a spectacular hub for trekking and homestays with ethnic minorities, including the colourful Dzao and Flower H'mong people.

Active Adventures

Adventurous detours in northern Vietnam include rock climbing on Cat Ba Island or kayaking to hidden coves and sandy beaches in nearby Lan Ha Bay.

p93

Central Vietnam

Food
History
Landscapes

Imperial Cuisine

Hoi An is a foodie capital, with outstanding restaurants and delicious local dishes. While in Hue, sample its incredibly intricate imperial cuisine.

Historic Gems

At Hue's citadel, you'll see a unique collection of palaces, temples, gateways and towers, despite wartime bombing. Other gems include the Perfume River's royal tombs, pagodas and Hoi An's Old Town.

Stunning Scenery

The area around Ninh Binh is typified by sublime limestone mountains. Further south, Phong Nha-Ke Bang National Park offers more of the same, plus several immense cave systems.

p144

Southeast Coast

Beaches
Temples
Food

Empty Coastlines

Vietnam's coastline at its most voluptuous. Mui Ne and Nha Trang are the big hitters, but there are hundreds of kilometres of empty beaches to discover, including on the Con Dao Islands.

Ancient Temples

The Kingdom of Champa once held sway over much of this region. The legacy is still visible in a host of ancient brick temples, including the Po Nagar towers (Nha Trang) and the Po Klong Garai towers (Thap Cham).

Fresh Seafood

Vietnamese cuisine is always a delight, but in this region fresh seafood stands out. Choose from succulent prawns, soft squid or juicy crabs, grilled on a barbecue at your table.

p217

Southwest Highlands

Adventure
Wildlife
Culture

Ride Around

Get off the trail with a motorbike trip into the hinterlands. Self-drive on a Minsk, Vespa or Honda Cub, or hook up with the Easy Riders to experience a Vietnam less travelled on the back roads between Dalat and Hoi An.

National Parks

Explore some of Vietnam's leading national parks where the wild things are. Cat Tien is home to endangered primates and the innovative Gibbon Trek. Yok Don, easily accessible from Buon Ma Thuot, is where elephants roam.

Meet the Locals

Leave the lowlanders behind on the coast and meet the high-ground minority people. Get to know them better with a traditional village homestay around Kon Tum.

p270

Ho Chi Minh City

War History
Nightlife
Food

Military History

The fall/liberation of Saigon was one of the late 20th century's defining moments. Explore sites associated with the American War, from the tunnels at Cu Chi to the War Remnants Museum and Reunification Palace.

Bars & Clubs

From late-night bars to full-on clubs, Saigon's sizzling nightlife keeps things hopping till the wee hours. The tireless Pham Ngu Lao backpacker strip is virtually 24/7.

Foodie Tours

Chefs here have more than a few tricks up their sleeves. Even if you stick purely to Vietnamese cuisine, there's a bewildering array of choice, along with a juicy menu of foodie tours to choose from.

p294

Mekong Delta

Beaches
Boat Trips
Pagodas

White Sands

The white sands of gorgeous Sao Beach and graceful Long Beach on Phu Quoc Island are Mekong Delta trump cards. The island's a world away from the muddy riverbanks of the delta. Don't forget your beach gear.

Floating Markets

Boat trips are essential for grasping how water defines this part of Vietnam, a region where children swim all day and the river can get so wide that you almost lose sight of either bank.

Sacred Sites

The delta's constant religious undercurrent percolates most visibly in Vietnamese Buddhist sites, such as Sam Mountain, and a wealth of Khmer temples, where young monks in saffron robes read Sutras.

p347

Siem Reap & the Temples of Angkor

Temples
Dining
Activities

Khmer Kingdoms

Many think that it's all about Angkor Wat. True, the 'city that is a temple' is one of the world's most iconic buildings, but nearby are the enigmatic faces of the Bayon, the jungle temple of Ta Prohm and the inspirational carvings of Banteay Srei.

Foodie Heaven

Contemporary Khmer, spiced-up street food, fine French and a whole host more, plus legendary Pub St – Siem Reap is where it's happening.

Cultural Immersion

Take to the skies by hot-air balloon or helicopter to see Angkor from a different angle. Learn the secrets of Cambodian cuisine with a cooking class or indulge in a massage at a spa.

p399

On the Road

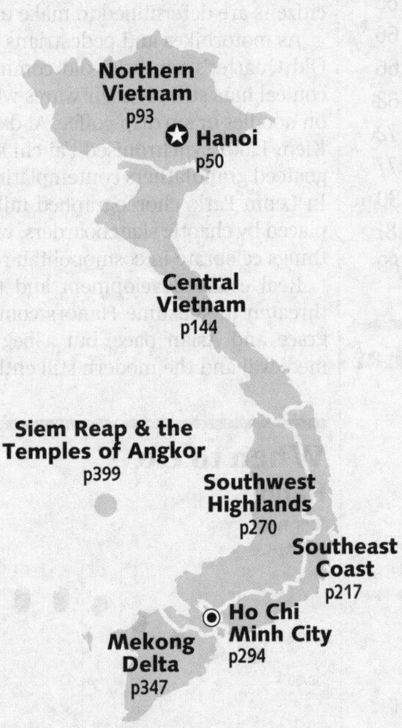

Northern Vietnam
p93

⭐ **Hanoi**
p50

Central Vietnam
p144

Siem Reap & the Temples of Angkor
p399

Southwest Highlands
p270

Southeast Coast
p217

Mekong Delta
p347

⦿ **Ho Chi Minh City**
p294

Hanoi

POP 6.8 MILLION

Best Places to Eat

➡ Chim Sao (p76)

➡ Quan Kien (p76)

➡ Nha Hang Ngon (p76)

➡ La Badiane (p76)

➡ Hanoi's street food (p73)

Best Places to Stay

➡ Sofitel Metropole Hotel (p71)

➡ Art Trendy Hotel (p70)

➡ Hanoi Elite (p69)

➡ 6 on Sixteen (p70)

➡ Calypso Legend Hotel (p69)

Why Go?

Showcasing sweeping boulevards, tree-fringed lakes and ancient pagodas, Hanoi is Asia's most atmospheric capital. It's an energetic city on the move, and Hanoi's ambitious citizens are determined to make up for lost time.

As motorbikes and pedestrians ebb and flow through the Old Quarter's centuries-old commercial chaos, hawkers in conical hats still ply their wares while other locals breakfast on noodles or sip drip-coffee. At dawn on the shores of Hoan Kiem Lake, synchronised t'ai chi sessions take place beside goateed grandfathers contemplating their next chess moves. In Lenin Park, choreographed military drills have been replaced by chaotic skateboarders, while Hanoi's bright young things celebrate in cosmopolitan restaurants and bars.

Real estate development and traffic chaos increasingly threaten to subsume Hanoi's compelling blend of Parisian grace and Asian pace, but a beguiling coexistence of the medieval and the modern still enthrals.

When to Go
Hanoi

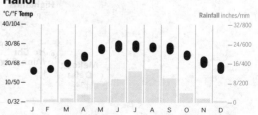

Jan–Apr Expect cooler days and the energy and colour of the annual Tet New Year Festival.

May Experience the region's alternative arts and music scenes at the CAMA Asean music festival.

Oct–Dec Clear, sunny days and low humidity make this the best time to visit Hanoi.

History

The site where Hanoi stands today has been inhabited since the neolithic period. Emperor Ly Thai To moved his capital here in AD 1010, naming it Thang Long (City of the Soaring Dragon). Spectacular celebrations were held in honour of the city's 1000th birthday in 2010.

The decision by Emperor Gia Long, founder of the Nguyen dynasty in 1802, to rule from Hue relegated Hanoi to the status of a regional capital for a century. The city was named Hanoi (The City in a Bend of the River) by Emperor Tu Duc in 1831. From 1902 to 1953, Hanoi served as the capital of French Indochina.

Hanoi was proclaimed the capital of Vietnam after the August Revolution of 1945, but it was not until the Geneva Accords of 1954 that the Viet Minh, driven from the city by the French in 1946, were able to return.

During the American War, US bombing destroyed parts of Hanoi and killed hundreds of civilians. One of the prime targets was the 1682m-long Long Bien Bridge. US aircraft repeatedly bombed this strategic point, yet after each attack the Vietnamese managed to improvise replacement spans and return road and rail services. It is said that the US military ended the attacks when US POWs were put to work repairing the structure. Today the bridge is renowned as a symbol of the tenacity and strength of the people of Hanoi.

As recently as the early 1990s, motorised transport was rare; most people got around on bicycles and the only modern structures were designed by Soviet architects. Today Hanoi's conservationists fight to save historic structures, but the city struggles to cope with a booming population, soaring pollution levels and an inefficient public transport system.

◉ Sights

Note that some museums are closed on Mondays and take a two-hour lunch break on other days of the week. Check the opening hours carefully before setting off.

◉ Old Quarter

Steeped in history, pulsating with life, bubbling with commerce, buzzing with motorbikes and rich in exotic scents, the Old Quarter is Hanoi's historic heart. The streets are narrow and congested, and crossing the road is an art form, but remember to look up as well as down, as there is some elegant old architecture amidst the chaos. Hawkers pound the streets with sizzling and smoking baskets hiding cheap meals, and *pho* stalls and *bia hoi* dens resonate with the sound of gossip and laughter. Modern yet medieval, there is no better way to spend time in Hanoi than walking the streets, soaking up the sights, sounds and smells.

HANOI IN...

One Day
Rise early for a morning walk around misty Hoan Kiem Lake before a classic Hanoi breakfast of *pho bo* (beef noodle soup) at Pho Thin. Pay your respects at the Ho Chi Minh Mausoleum, before checking out the museum and stilt house. Wander back down P Dien Bien Phu to the Vietnam Military History Museum. Have a coffee at funky Cong Caphe before visiting the cultural treasures of the Fine Arts Museum. Grab a cab to lunch at La Badiane before continuing to the peaceful Temple of Literature. Catch another cab to the chaotic Old Quarter, browsing the ancient neighbourhood's buildings, shops and galleries. Make time to stop for a well-earned and refreshing glass of *bia hoi* (draught beer). Catch a performance of the water puppets before heading south of the lake to the atmospheric Nha Hang Ngon for dinner.

Two Days
Head into the suburbs to the excellent Vietnam Museum of Ethnology to discover the ethnic mosaic that makes up modern Vietnam. Back in the city have lunch at Chim Sao before exploring the Museum of the Vietnamese Revolution and the adjacent National Museum of Vietnamese History. The architecture at the latter is stunning, and the contents a fine introduction to 2000 years of highs and lows. After dinner at Highway 4, head for drinks at Manzi Art Space or Bar Betta.

Hanoi Highlights

1 Experience Asia at its raw, pulsating best in the labyrinthine streets of the **Old Quarter** (p51).

2 Step into history, and a spiritual retreat from the busy streets, at the **Temple of Literature** (p58).

3 Get an authentic taste of the city while exploring Hanoi's intoxicating **street food** scene (p73).

4 Wake at dawn to ease peacefully into another Hanoi day with the t'ai chi buffs along **Hoan Kiem Lake** (p57).

5 Piece together the country's ethnic mosaic at the wonderful **Vietnam Museum of Ethnology** (p63).

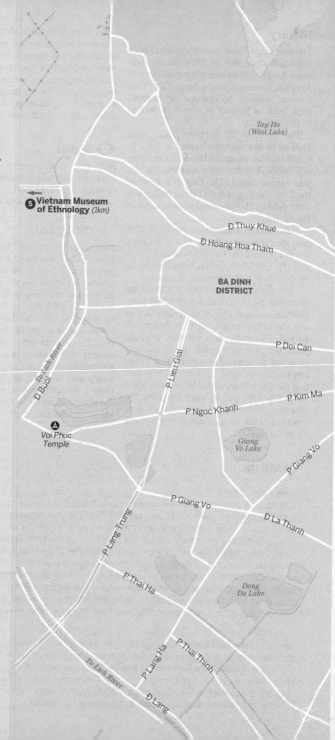

5 Vietnam Museum of Ethnology *(1km)*

Tay Ho (West Lake)

Đ Thuy Khue

Đ Hoang Hoa Tham

BA DINH DISTRICT

P Doi Can

To Lich River

Đ Buoi

P Lieu Giai

P Kim Ma

P Ngoc Khanh

Voi Phuc Temple

Giang Vo Lake

P Giang Vo

P Giang Vo

Đ La Thanh

P Lang Trung

Dong Da Lake

P Thai Ha

P Thai Thinh

To Lich River

P Lang Ha

Đ Lang

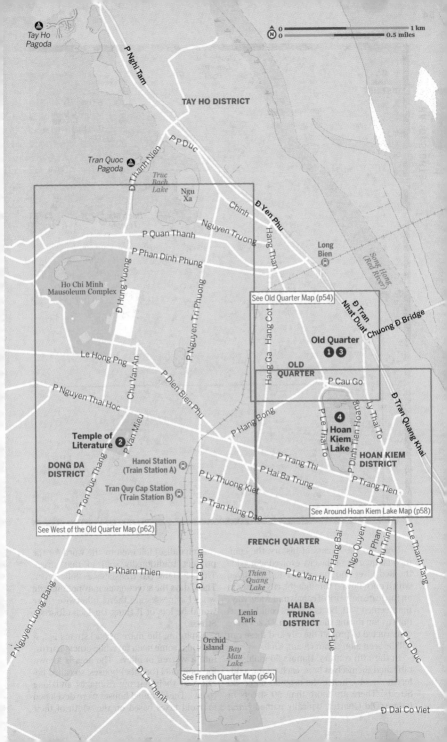

Old Quarter

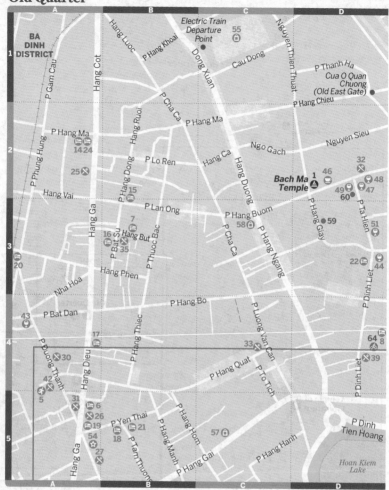

Home to 1000 years of history, the commercial quarter of the city evolved alongside the Red River and the smaller To Lich River, which once flowed through the city centre in an intricate network of canals and waterways that teemed with boats. Waters could rise as high as 8m during the monsoon. Dykes were constructed to protect the city and these can still be seen along Tran Quang Khai.

In the 13th century, Hanoi's 36 guilds established themselves here, each taking a different street – hence the original name '36 Streets'. There are more than 50 streets in today's Old Quarter, typically named *Hang*

(merchandise) followed by the word for the product traditionally sold in that street. Thus, P Hang Gai translates as 'Silk Street'. These days the street name may not indicate what businesses are there; otherwise there would be lots of P Hang Du Lich (Tourism Streets).

Exploring the maze of backstreets is fascinating: some open up while others narrow into a warren of alleys. The area is known for its tunnel (or tube) houses, so called because of their narrow frontages and long rooms. These tunnel houses were developed to avoid taxes based on the width of their

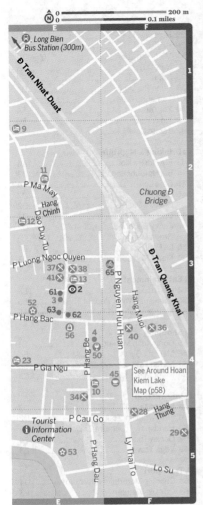

boxes, flags and temple items; and the more glamorous P Hang Gai, with its silk, embroidery, lacquerware, paintings and water puppets. Finally, no trip to the Old Quarter would be complete without a visit to the Dong Xuan Market (p82), rebuilt after a fire in 1994.

A stroll through the historic Old Quarter can last anywhere from an hour to the better part of a day, depending on your pace. However long, or whatever detours you might take, our walking tour will provide you with a heady dose of Vietnamese culture, lots of shopping opportunities and some insight into the city's long history.

Along the western periphery of the Old Quarter is the ancient Imperial Citadel (p61), which was originally constructed by Emperor Gia Long. Most of the ancient buildings were destroyed by French troops in 1894, and US bombers also did considerable damage, but the citadel has recently been opened for public viewing after significant restoration.

★ **Bach Ma Temple**   BUDDHIST TEMPLE
(Map p54; cnr P Hang Buom & P Hang Giay; ⊙8-11am & 2-5pm Tue-Sun) FREE In the heart of the Old Quarter, the small Bach Ma Temple is said to be the oldest temple in the city, though much of the current structure dates from the 18th century and a shrine to Confucius was added in 1839. It was originally built by Emperor Ly Thai To in the 11th century to honour a white horse that guided him to this site, where he chose to construct his city walls.

Pass through the wonderful old wooden doors of the pagoda to see a statue of the legendary white horse, as well as a beautiful red-lacquered funeral palanquin.

Memorial House   HISTORICAL BUILDING
(Map p54; 87 P Ma May; admission 5000d; ⊙8.30am-5pm) One of the Old Quarter's best-restored properties, this traditional merchants' house is sparsely but beautifully decorated, with rooms set around two courtyards and filled with fine furniture. Note the high steps between rooms, a traditional design incorporated to stop the flow of bad energy around the property.

There are crafts and trinkets for sale here, including silver jewellery, basketwork and Vietnamese tea sets, and there's usually a calligrapher or other craftsperson at work too.

street frontage. By feudal law, houses were also limited to two storeys and, out of respect for the king, could not be taller than the royal palace. These days there are taller buildings, but no real high-rises.

Opportunities to dispense with your Vietnamese dong are endless. As you wander, you'll find clothes, cosmetics, fake sunglasses, bootleg DVDs and software, T-shirts, musical instruments, plumbing supplies, herbal medicines, jewellery, religious offerings, spices, woven mats and much, much more.

Some of the specialised streets include P Hang Quat, with its red candlesticks, funeral

Old Quarter

◎ Around Hoan Kiem Lake

★**National Museum of Vietnamese History**   MUSEUM
(Map p58; www.nmvnh.org.vn; 1 P Trang Tien; adult/student 20,000/10,000d; ◎8am-noon & 1.30-5pm, closed first Mon of the month) The wonderful architecture of the history museum was formerly home to the École Française d'Extrême Orient in Vietnam. It is an elegant, ochre-coloured structure built between 1925 and 1932. French architect Ernest Hebrard was among the first in Vietnam to incorporate a blend of Chinese and French design elements. Highlights include bronzes from the Dong Son culture (3rd century BC to 3rd century AD), Hindu statuary from the Khmer and Champa kingdoms, and beautiful jewellery from imperial Vietnam.

More recent history includes the struggle against the French and the story of the Communist Party. The breezy garden cafe is a lovely spot for a drink.

★**Hoa Lo Prison**
Museum   HISTORICAL BUILDING
(Map p58; ☑04-3824 6358; cnr P Hoa Lo & P Hai
Ba Trung; admission 15,000d; ☺8am-5pm) This
thought-provoking site is all that remains
of the former Hoa Lo Prison, ironically
nicknamed the 'Hanoi Hilton' by US POWs
during the American War. Most exhibits relate to the prison's use up to the mid-1950s,
focusing on the Vietnamese struggle for independence from France. A gruesome relic
is the ominous French guillotine, used to
behead Vietnamese revolutionaries. There
are also displays focusing on the American
pilots who were incarcerated at Hoa Lo
during the American War.

These include Pete Peterson (the first US
ambassador to a unified Vietnam in 1995),
and Senator John McCain (the Republican
nominee for the US presidency in 2008).
McCain's flight suit is displayed, along with
a photograph of Hanoi locals rescuing him
from Truc Bach Lake after he was shot down
in 1967.

The vast prison complex was built by the
French in 1896. Originally intended to house
around 450 inmates, records indicate that by
the 1930s there were close to 2000 prisoners.
Hoa Lo was never a very successful prison,
and hundreds escaped over the years, many
by squeezing out through sewer grates.

★**Hoan Kiem Lake**   LAKE
(Map p58) Legend claims in the mid-15th century Heaven sent Emperor Le Thai To (Le
Loi) a magical sword which he used to drive
the Chinese from Vietnam. After the war a giant golden turtle grabbed the sword and disappeared into the depths to restore the sword
to its divine owners, inspiring the name Ho
Hoan Kiem (Lake of the Restored Sword).
Every morning at around 6am local residents
practise traditional t'ai chi on the shore.

Ngoc Son Temple sits on an island in
Hoan Kiem Lake. The ramshackle Thap Rua
(Turtle Tower), on an islet near the southern
end, is topped with a red star and is often
used as an emblem of Hanoi.

★**Museum of the**
Vietnamese Revolution   MUSEUM
(Map p58; 216 Đ Tran Quang Khai; adult/student
20,000/10,000d; ☺8am-noon & 1.30-5pm, closed
first Mon of the month) A must for all budding
revolutionaries, this museum enthusiastically presents a history of the Vietnamese
Revolution.

Ngoc Son Temple   BUDDHIST TEMPLE
(Jade Mountain Temple; Map p58; Hoan Kiem Lake;
adult/student 20,000/10,000d; ☺7.30am-5.30pm)
Hanoi's most visited temple sits pretty on a
delightful little island in the northern part of
Hoan Kiem Lake. An elegant scarlet bridge,
Huc (Rising Sun) Bridge, constructed in classical Vietnamese style and lined with flags,
connects the island to the lake shore. The
nearby Martyrs' Monument was erected
as a memorial to those who died fighting for
Vietnam's independence.

Surrounded by water and shaded by
trees, the small temple is dedicated to
General Tran Hung Dao (who defeated the
Mongols in the 13th century), La To (pa-
tron saint of physicians) and the scholar
Van Xuong. Inside you'll find some fine
ceramics, a gong or two, some ancient
bells and a glass case containing a stuffed
lake turtle, which is said to have weighed
a hefty 250kg.

Vietnamese Women's Museum   MUSEUM
(Map p58; www.baotangphunu.org.vn; 36 P Ly
Thuong Kiet; admission 30,000d; ☺8am-5pm)
This excellent museum showcases women's
role in Vietnamese society and culture.
Labelled in English and French, it's the
memories of the wartime contribution by
individual heroic women that are most
poignant. There is a stunning collection of
propaganda posters, as well as costumes,
tribal basketware and fabric motifs from Vietnam's ethnic minority groups. Check the
website for special exhibitions.

St Joseph Cathedral   CHURCH
(Map p58; P Nha Tho; ☺main gate 5am-noon &
2-7.30pm) FREE The striking neo-Gothic St
Joseph Cathedral was inaugurated in 1886,
and boasts a soaring facade that faces a little plaza. Its most noteworthy features are
its twin bell towers, elaborate altar and
fine stained-glass windows. Mass times are
listed on a sign on the gates to the left of
the cathedral. The main gate is open during
Mass.

Guests are welcome at other times of the
day, but must enter via the compound of the
Diocese of Hanoi, the entrance to which is
a block away at 40 P Nha Chung. Walking
through the gate, go straight and then turn
right. When you reach the side door to the
cathedral, ring the small bell high up to the
right-hand side of the door.

Around Hoan Kiem Lake

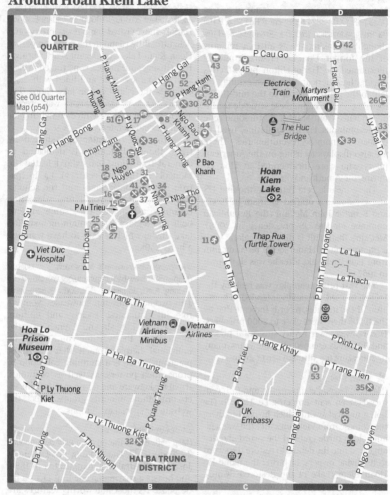

See Old Quarter Map (p54)

West of the Old Quarter

★ **Temple of Literature**   CONFUCIAN TEMPLE
(Map p62; ☎ 04-3845 2917; Quoc Tu Giam;
adult/student 20,000/10,000d; ☺ 8am-5pm)
About 2km west of Hoan Kiem Lake, the
Temple of Literature is a rare example of
well-preserved traditional Vietnamese architecture. Founded in 1070 by Emperor
Ly Thanh Tong, the temple is dedicated
to Confucius (Khong Tu) and honours Vietnam's finest scholars and men of literary
accomplishment. Vietnam's first university

was established here in 1076. At this time
entrance was only granted to those of noble
birth, but after 1442 a more egalitarian approach was adopted and gifted students
from all over the nation headed to Hanoi
to study the principles of Confucianism, literature and poetry.

In 1484 Emperor Le Thanh Tong ordered
that stelae be erected to record the names,
places of birth and achievements of exceptional scholars: 82 stelae remain standing.
The imposing tiered gateway (on P Quoc Tu
Giam) that forms the main entrance is pre-

★ **Ho Chi Minh Mausoleum Complex**   HISTORICAL SITE

(Map p62; entrance cnr P Ngoc Ha & P Doi Can) This is a special place for many Vietnamese. To the west of the Old Quarter, the Ho Chi Minh Mausoleum Complex is an important place of pilgrimage. A traffic-free area of botanical gardens, monuments, memorials and pagodas, it's usually crowded with groups of all ages, from all over the nation, who have come to pay their respects. Within the complex are Ho Chi Minh's Mausoleum, Ho Chi Minh's Stilt House and the Presidential Palace, and the Ho Chi Minh Museum.

➤ **Ho Chi Minh's Mausoleum**

(Map p62; admission free; ⊙ 8-11am Tue-Thu, Sat & Sun Dec-Sep, last entry 10.15am) In the tradition of Lenin, Stalin and Mao, Ho Chi Minh's Mausoleum is a monumental marble edifice. Contrary to his desire for a simple cremation, the mausoleum was constructed from materials gathered from all over Vietnam between 1973 and 1975. Set deep in the bowels of the building in a glass sarcophagus is the frail, pale body of Ho Chi Minh. The mausoleum is closed for about two months each year while his embalmed body goes to Russia for maintenance.

The roof and peristyle are said to evoke either a traditional communal house or a lotus flower, though to many tourists it looks like a concrete cubicle with columns.

The queue, which moves quite quickly, usually snakes for several hundred metres to the mausoleum entrance itself. Inside, adopt a slow but steady pace as you file past Ho's body. Guards, in snowy-white military uniforms, are posted at intervals of five paces, giving an eerily authoritarian aspect to the slightly macabre spectacle of the body with its wispy white hair.

Note that wearing shorts and tank tops is not permitted so dress modestly, and maintain a respectful demeanour at all times; no talking. It's also forbidden to put your hand in your pockets. Hats must be taken off, and you may also be requested to store day packs, cameras and phones before you enter. Photography is strictly prohibited in the mausoleum.

Most of the visitors are Vietnamese and it's interesting to watch their reactions. Most show deep respect for Ho Chi Minh, who is honoured for his role as the liberator of the Vietnamese people from colonialism, as much as for his communist ideology. This

ceded by a curious plaque, whose inscription requests that visitors dismount their horses before entering.

Paths then lead through formal gardens to the Khue Van pavilion, constructed in 1802, beyond which is a large square pond known as the Well of Heavenly Clarity.

The northern side of this courtyard is marked by a low-slung pagoda housing an extraordinary statue of a majestic-looking Confucius, depicted with a goatee and bearing scarlet robes, flanked by four of his disciples.

Around Hoan Kiem Lake

Top Sights
1 Hoa Lo Prison Museum A4
2 Hoan Kiem Lake C2
3 Museum of the Vietnamese Revolution F4
4 National Museum of Vietnamese History F4

Sights
5 Ngoc Son Temple C2
6 St Joseph Cathedral B3
7 Vietnamese Women's Museum C5

Activities, Courses & Tours
8 Explore Indochina B2
9 Hanoi Foreign Language College F5
Hash House Harriers .... (see 55)
La Siesta Spa .... (see 19)
10 MOD Palace Hotel F5
11 QT Anam Spa C3

Sleeping
12 6 on Sixteen B2
13 Central Backpackers Hanoi B2
14 Church Hotel B3
15 Cinnamon Hotel B3
16 Especen Hotel B2
17 Golden Lotus Hotel B2
18 Hanoi Backpackers Hostel B2
19 Hanoi Elegance Diamond Hotel D1
20 Heart Hotel C1
21 Hilton Hanoi Opera F5
22 Hong Ha Hotel F3
23 Hotel L'Opera E5
24 Hotel Thien Trang B3
25 Impressive Hotel A3
26 Jasmine Hotel D1
27 Joseph's Hotel B3
28 Madame Moon Guesthouse C1
29 Sofitel Metropole Hotel E4

Eating
30 Apple Tart B1
31 Banh Ghoi B2
32 Fanny Ice Cream B5
33 Fivimart D2
34 Hanoi House B2
35 Kem Dac Diet Trang Tien D4
36 La B2
37 La Place B2
38 Madame Hien B2
39 Pho Thin D2
40 Spices Garden E4
41 The Cart B2

Drinking & Nightlife
Angelina .... (see 29)
42 Blah Blah D1
43 Cafe Pho Co C1
44 GC Pub C2
45 Legend Beer C1
46 Nha Hang Lan Chin E1

Entertainment
47 Centre Culturel Français de Hanoi E4
48 Cinematheque D5
49 Hanoi Opera House F5

Shopping
50 Hanoi Moment B1
Indigenous .... (see 15)
51 Mosaique B2
52 Tan My Design B1
53 Thang Long D4
54 Things of Substance B2
Three Trees .... (see 54)

Information
55 American Club D5

view is reinforced by Vietnam's educational system, which emphasises Ho's deeds and accomplishments.

If you're lucky, you'll catch the changing of the guard outside Ho's mausoleum – the pomp and ceremony displayed here rivals the British equivalent at Buckingham Palace.

➡ Ho Chi Minh's Stilt House

(Nha San Bac Ho; Map p62; admission 25,000d; ⏲summer 7.30-11am & 2-4pm, winter 8-11am & 1.30-4pm, closed Mon, closed Fri afternoon) This humble stilt house is where Ho lived intermittently from 1958 to 1969. Set in a well-tended garden, the house is an interpretation of a traditional rural dwelling, and has been preserved just as Ho left it. Just how much time he actually spent here is questionable, as the house would have been a tempting target for US bombers. In an adjacent building a sign proclaims, 'Ho Chi Minh's Used Cars' – in reality, automobiles he used during his life.

➡ Presidential Palace

(Map p62; admission 25,000d; ⏲summer 7.30-11am & 2-4pm, winter 8-11am & 1.30-4pm, closed Mon, closed Fri afternoon) This restored colonial building was constructed in 1906 as the Palace of the Governor General of Indochina. It is now used for official receptions and isn't open to the public. There is a combined entrance gate to the stilt house and Presidential Palace grounds on P Ong Ich Kiem inside the mausoleum complex. When the main mausoleum entrance is closed, enter from Đ Hung Vuong near the palace building.

➡ Ho Chi Minh Museum

(Map p62; ☑ 04-3846 3757; www.baotanghochiminh.vn; admission 25,000d; ☺ 8-11.30am daily & 2-4.30pm Tue-Thu, Sat & Sun) The huge concrete Soviet-style Ho Chi Minh Museum is a triumphalist monument dedicated to the life of the founder of modern Vietnam and to the onward march of revolutionary socialism. Mementos of Ho's life are showcased, and there are some fascinating photos and dusty official documents relating to the overthrow of the French and the rise of communism. Photography is forbidden and you may be asked to check your bag at reception.

An English-speaking guide costs around 100,000d, and given the quite surreal nature of the exhibition it's a worthwhile investment.

➡ One Pillar Pagoda

(Map p62; P Ong Ich Kiem; admission 25,000d; ☺ summer 7.30-11am & 2-4pm, winter 8-11am & 1.30-4pm, closed Mon, closed Fri afternoon; 🚻) The One Pillar Pagoda was originally built by the Emperor Ly Thai Tong who ruled from 1028 to 1054. According to the annals, the heirless emperor dreamed that he met Quan The Am Bo Tat, the Goddess of Mercy, who handed him a male child. Ly Thai Tong then married a young peasant girl and had a son and heir by her. As a way of expressing his gratitude for this event, he constructed a pagoda here in 1049.

Built of wood on a single stone pillar, the pagoda is designed to resemble a lotus blossom, the symbol of purity, rising out of a sea of sorrow. One of the last acts of the French before quitting Hanoi in 1954 was to destroy the original One Pillar Pagoda; the structure was rebuilt by the new government.

★ Vietnam Military History Museum   MUSEUM

(Map p62; ☑ 04-3823 4264; www.btlsqsvn.org.vn; P Dien Bien Phu; admission 30,000d, camera 20,000d; ☺ 8-11.30am & 1-4.30pm, closed Mon & Fri) Easy to spot thanks to a large collection of weaponry out front, the Military Museum displays Soviet and Chinese equipment alongside French- and US-made weapons captured during years of warfare. The centrepiece is a Soviet-built MiG-21 jet fighter, triumphant amid the wreckage of French aircraft downed at Dien Bien Phu, and a US F-111.

Adjacent is the hexagonal Flag Tower, one of the symbols of Hanoi. Access is possible to a terrace overlooking a rusting collection of war *matériel* (equipment and supplies used by soldiers). Opposite the museum is a small park with a commanding statue of Lenin.

★ Fine Arts Museum   MUSEUM

(Map p62; www.vnfam.vn; 66 P Nguyen Thai Hoc; adult/concession 20,000/7,000d; ☺ 8.30am-5pm) Hanoi's excellent Fine Arts Museum is housed in two buildings that were once the French Ministry of Information. Artistic treasures from Vietnam abound, including ancient Champa stone carvings and some astonishing effigies of Guan Yin, the thousand-eyed, thousand-armed goddess of compassion. Reproductions of antiques are available, but ask for a certificate to clear these goods through customs when you leave Vietnam.

Look out too for the remarkable lacquered-wood statues of robed Buddhist monks from the Tay Son dynasty. There's also a large collection of contemporary art and folk-naive paintings.

Imperial Citadel   HISTORICAL SITE

(Map p62; www.hoangthanhthanglong.vn; 19C P Hoang Dieu, main entrance; ☺ 8.30-11.30am & 2-5pm, closed Mon & Fri) FREE Added to Unesco's World Heritage List in 2010 and reopened in 2012, Hanoi's Imperial Citadel was the hub of Vietnamese military power for over 1000 years. Ongoing archeological digs of ancient palaces, grandiose pavilions and imperial gates are complemented by fascinating military command bunkers from the American War – complete with maps and 1960s communications equipment – used by the legendary Vietnamese General Vo Nguyen Giap.

The citadel's leafy grounds are also an easygoing and quiet antidote to Hanoi's bustle.

Ambassadors' Pagoda   BUDDHIST TEMPLE

(Map p62; ☑ 04-3825 2427; 73 P Quan Su) The official centre of Buddhism in Hanoi, the Ambassadors' Pagoda attracts quite a crowd on holidays. During the 17th century there was a guesthouse here for the ambassadors of Buddhist countries; today there are about a dozen monks and nuns based here. Next to the pagoda is a shop selling Buddhist ritual objects.

Quan Thanh Temple   BUDDHIST TEMPLE

(Map p62; P Quan Thanh) Shaded by huge trees, Quan Thanh Temple was established during the Ly dynasty (1010–1225) and was dedi-

West of the Old Quarter

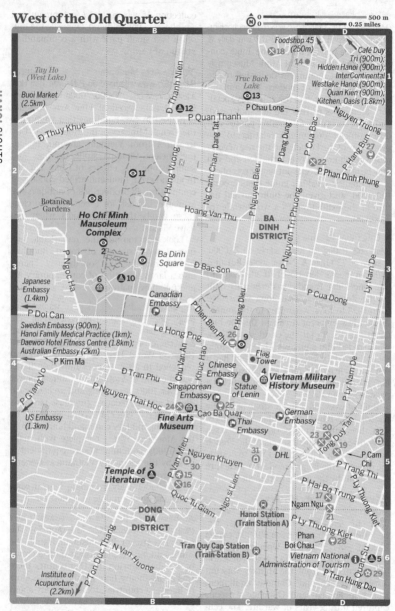

N

0 — 500 m
0 — 0.25 miles

Tay Ho
(West Lake)

Buoi Market
(2.5km)

Đ Thuy Khue

Foodshop 45
(250m)
18
14

Café Duy
Tri (900m);
Hidden Hanoi (900m);
InterContinental
Westlake Hanoi (900m);
Quan Kien (900m);
Kitchen, Oasis (1.8km)

Truc Bach
Lake

Đ Thanh Nien

13

P Chau Long

Nguyen Truong

12

P Quan Thanh

Đ Hung Vuong

Ng Canh Chan

Dang Tat

P Nguyen Bieu

P Dang Dung

P Cua Bac

P Hang Bun

27

11

Hoang Van Thu

P Phan Dinh Phung

22

8

Botanical
Gardens

Ho Chi Minh
Mausoleum
Complex

2

7

Ba Dinh
Square

Đ Bac Son

BA
DINH
DISTRICT

P Nguyen Tri Phuong

Ly Nam De

6

10

P Ngoc Ha

Japanese
Embassy
(1.4km)

Canadian
Embassy

P Dien Bien Phu

P Cua Dong

Swedish Embassy (900m);
Hanoi Family Medical Practice (1km);
Daewoo Hotel Fitness Centre (1.8km);
Australian Embassy (2km)

P Doi Can

Le Hong Png

P Hoang Dieu

26

9

Flag
Tower

P Kim Ma

Đ Tran Phu

Chu Van An

Khuc Hao

Chinese
Embassy

4

Vietnam Military
History Museum

P Ly Nam De

P Giang Vo

P Nguyen Thai Hoc

Singaporean
Embassy

Statue
of Lenin

24

1

Cao Ba Quat

US Embassy
(1.3km)

Fine Arts
Museum

25

Thai
Embassy

German
Embassy

20

23

19

32

P Van Mieu

Nguyen Khuyen

31

DHL

Tong Duy Tan

P Cam
Chi

P Trang Thi

Temple of
Literature

3

30

15

16

Quoc Tu Giam

Ngo si Lien

P Hai Ba Trung

17

P Ly Thuong Kiet

DONG
DA
DISTRICT

N Van Huong

Tran Quy Cap Station
(Train Station B)

Hanoi Station
(Train Station A)

21

Ngam Ngu

P Ly Thuong Kiet

Phan
Boi Chau

28

Đ Ton Duc Thang

Vietnam National
Administration of Tourism

5

29

Institute of
Acupuncture
(2.2km)

P Tran Hung Dao

cated to Tran Vo (God of the North), whose symbols of power were the tortoise and the snake. A bronze statue and bell date from 1677. The temple is on the shores of Truc Bach Lake, near the intersection of Đ Thanh Nien and P Quan Thanh.

French Quarter

★ **Hai Ba Trung Temple**   BUDDHIST TEMPLE
(Map p64; P Tho Lao) Two kilometres south of Hoan Kiem Lake, this temple was founded in 1142. A statue shows the two Trung

West of the Old Quarter

sisters (from the 1st century AD) kneeling with their arms raised in the air. Some say the statue shows the sisters, who had been proclaimed the queens of the Vietnamese, about to dive into a river. They are said to have drowned themselves rather than surrender in the wake of their defeat at the hands of the Chinese.

⊙ Greater Hanoi

★**Vietnam Museum of Ethnology** MUSEUM
(☎04-3756 2193; www.vme.org.vn; Đ Nguyen Van Huyen; admission 40,000d, guide 100,000d, camera fee 50,000d; ☺8.30am-5.30pm Tue-Sun) Occupying a modern structure, the terrific collection here features well-presented tribal art, artefacts and everyday objects gathered from across the nation. Displays are well labelled in Vietnamese, French and English. For anyone with an interest in Vietnam's minorities, it's an essential visit – though it is located way out in the suburbs. The museum is in the Cau Giay district, about 7km from the city centre and around 200,000d each way in a taxi.

Local bus 14 (3000d) departs from P Dinh Tien Hoang on the east side of Hoan Kiem Lake and passes within a couple of blocks (around 600m) of the museum – get off at the Nghia Tan bus stop and head to Đ Nguyen Van Huyen.

In the grounds are examples of traditional village houses – a Tay stilt house, an impressive Bahnar communal structure and a Yao home. Don't miss the soaring, thatch-roofed Giarai tomb, complete with risqué wooden statues.

A fair-trade craft shop sells books, beautiful postcards, and arts and crafts from ethnic communities.

Tay Ho (West Lake) LAKE
The city's largest lake, Tay Ho is 15km in circumference and ringed by upmarket suburbs. On the south side, along Đ Thuy Khue, are seafood restaurants, and to the east, the Xuan Dieu strip is lined with restaurants, cafes, boutiques and luxury hotels. You'll also find two temples on its shores; the Tay Ho and Tran Quoc pagodas. A pathway circles the lake, making for a great bicycle ride. For bike rental contact the Hanoi Bicycle Collective (p88).

Two legends explain the origins of Tay Ho, which is also known as the Lake of Mist and the Big Lake. According to one legend, Tay Ho was created when the Dragon King drowned an evil nine-tailed fox in his lair, in a forest on this site. Another legend relates that in the 11th century a Vietnamese Buddhist monk, Khong Lo, rendered a great service to the emperor of China, who rewarded him with a vast quantity of bronze. The monk cast the bronze into a huge bell,

French Quarter

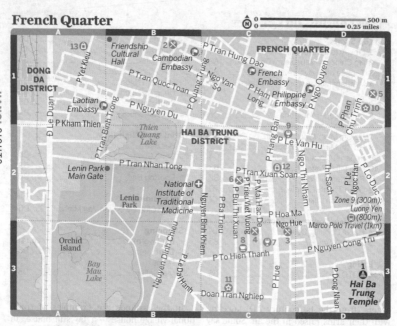

0 ───── 500 m
0 ───── 0.25 miles

the sound of which could be heard all the way to China, where the Golden Buffalo Calf, mistaking the ringing for its mother's call, ran southward, trampling on the site and turning it into a lake.

The geological explanation is that it was created when Song Hong (Red River) over-

flowed its banks. The flood problem has been partially controlled by building dykes – the highway along the eastern side of Tay Ho is built upon one.

Tay Ho Pagoda   BUDDHIST TEMPLE
(P Tay Ho) Jutting into West Lake, beautiful Tay Ho Pagoda is perhaps the most popular place of worship in Hanoi. Throngs of people come here on the first and 15th day of each lunar month in the hope of receiving good fortune from the Mother Goddess, to whom the temple is dedicated.

Tran Quoc Pagoda   BUDDHIST TEMPLE
One of the oldest pagodas in Vietnam, Tran Quoc Pagoda is on the eastern shore of Tay Ho, just off Đ Thanh Nien, which divides this lake from Truc Bach Lake. A stela here, dating from 1639, tells the history of this site. The pagoda was rebuilt in the 15th century and again in 1842.

Truc Bach Lake   LAKE
(Map p62) Separated from Tay Ho only by Đ Thanh Nien, this lake is lined with flame trees. During the 18th century the Trinh lords built a palace on the lakeside; it was later transformed into a reformatory for wayward royal concubines, who were condemned to spend their days weaving pure white silk.

🏃 Activities

Sports & Swimming

Daewoo Hotel Fitness Centre
GYM

(☑04-3835 1000; www.hanoidaewoohotel.com. vn; 360 Đ Kim Ma) Situated 5km west of Hoan Kiem Lake along Đ Kim Ma, the Daewoo Hotel Fitness Centre has a day-use fee of US$25 for all facilities, including the pool. There's also a good spa.

Hash House Harriers
RUNNING

(Map p58; www.hanoih3.com; ⊙ from 1.30pm Sat) For the uninitiated, these are drinkers with a running problem. The 'hash' meets at the American Club (Map p58; ☑04-3824 1850; www.facebook.com/AmClubHanoi; 19-21 P Hai Ba Trung).

MOD Palace Hotel
SWIMMING POOL

(Map p58; ☑04-3825 2896; 33C P Pham Ngu Lao; admission 65,000d; ⊙6am-8pm) In central Hanoi, the MOD Palace offers day use of its pool, which is big enough for laps and open all year. It gets very busy with children in the afternoon. Buy a ticket at the hotel's reception first.

Hanoi Water Park
SWIMMING POOL

(☑04-3753 2757; ⊙9am-9pm Wed-Mon Apr-Nov) Hanoi Water Park is around 5km north of the city centre and has pools, slides and a lazy river. Entry costs 120,000d for those over 110cm tall, and 70,000d for shorter people, translating roughly to adults and children. Again, it gets extremely busy on hot summer afternoons. It's a 15-minute taxi ride from central Hanoi on the northern edge of Tay Ho.

King's Island
GOLF

(☑04-3772 3160; www.kingsislandgolf.com; weekday/weekend from US$90/130) King's Island, 45km west of Hanoi, close to the base of Ba Vi Mountain, is north Vietnam's first 36-hole golf course. The course offers lakeside or mountain-view play. There is also a popular course at Tam Dao Hill Station.

Zenith Yoga
YOGA

(Map p54; ☑0904 356 561; www.zenithyogavietnam.com; 16 P Duong Thanh; one-off class 250,000d) Yoga, Pilates and meditation classes are all available at this centrally located studio. Downstairs is the Zenith Cafe (p72) with lots of soothing teas and healthy vegetarian food. Check the website for the schedule of classes. There's also another Zenith Yoga branch (Map p62; ☑0904 356 561; www.zenithyogavietnam.com; 111 P Xuan Dieu) near Tay Ho.

Massage & Spa

Hanoi has many spas and massage centres. Rates are less than in the West, so it's a great place for a little indulgence.

La Siesta Spa
SPA

(Map p58; ☑04-3935 1632; www.zenspa.vn/lasiesta; 32 P Lo Su) Spa, massage and beauty treatments across two floors of the Hanoi Elegance Diamond Hotel.

QT Anam Spa
SPA

(Map p58; ☑04-3928 6116; www.qtanamspa.com; 26-28 P Le Thai To) Excellent spa, massage and beauty treatments near Hoan Kiem Lake.

🍴 Courses

Hanoi Cooking Centre
COOKING

(Map p62; ☑04-3715 0088; www.hanoicookingcentre.com; 44 P Chau Long; per class US$55) Excellent interactive classes including market visits and a special Kids' Club – handy if your children are aspiring chefs. The Hanoi Cooking Centre also runs a highly recommended walking tour exploring Hanoi's street-food scene, and cookery classes conclude with a shared lunch in its elegant restaurant.

HANOI FOR CHILDREN

Hanoi is a fun city for children thanks to the all-action Old Quarter and the city's many parks and lakes. Wandering the Old Quarter can be tiring for young ones, and you'll have to maintain a watchful eye for motorbikes, but there are enough diversions to keep them entertained, and plenty of ice-cream shops and fruit markets for those little treats along the way. If they like to cook their own food, book them in for a special Kids' Club session at the Hanoi Cooking Centre (p65).

Boating is a fun family activity and there is the choice of bigger boats on Tay Ho or pedal-powered boats in Lenin Park. Hanoi Water Park (p65) is a great place to take children to cool off, but it is only open half the year. Come evening, there is only one place for any self-respecting child to be in Hanoi and that is at a water-puppet show – a Punch and Judy pantomime on water.

Hidden Hanoi
COOKING, LANGUAGE

(☑0912 254 045; www.hiddenhanoi.com.vn; 147 P Nghi Tam, Tay Ho; per class without/with market tour US$45/55) Offers cooking classes from its kitchen near the eastern side of Tay Ho. Options include seafood and village food menus. Walking tours (per person US$20 to US$25) exploring the Old Quarter and Hanoi street food are available. Hidden Hanoi also offers a language study program (per person from $US200), including two field trips.

Highway 4
COOKING

(Map p54; ☑04-3715 0577; www.highway4.com; 3 Hang Tre; per class US$50) Classes begin at its Old Quarter eatery, incorporate a *cyclo* ride and market tour, and continue on to Highway 4's Tay Ho restaurant, the House of Son Tinh (p77). And yes, you can learn how to make its signature catfish spring rolls. Also on offer are cocktail-making classes using Highway 4's traditional Son Tinh liquors.

Hanoi Foreign Language College
LANGUAGE

(Map p58; ☑04-3826 2468; 1 P Pham Ngu Lao) Housed in the History Museum compound, this is a branch of Hanoi National University where foreigners can study Vietnamese for about US$15 per lesson.

Hanoi Language Tours
LANGUAGE

(☑0901 352 2605; www.hanoilanguagetours.com; per person from US$150) Courses from two to 10 days focusing on language and cultural essentials for travellers, expats and business-people.

☞ Tours

Hidden Hanoi and the Hanoi Cooking Centre also offer interesting tours with a foodie slant, visiting markets and eating street food.

Bloom Microventures
CULTURAL TOUR

(☑04-387 6594; www.bloom-microventures.org/vietnam) Tours an ethnic minority village in Hoa Binh province, around 70km west of Hanoi. It's a good opportunity to see how micro-loans are funding rural entrepreneurs, and is an excellent insight into Vietnamese rural life. Most tours run on a Saturday. Check the website for timings.

Food on Foot
WALKING TOUR

(Map p54; ☑04-3990 1733; www.vietnamawesometravel.com; 19B P Hang Be; US$25) Excellent-value, street-food walking tours around the Old Quarter. Look forward to around four hours of tasty eating and drinking, including beer and rice wine.

Hanoi Kids
WALKING TOUR

(☑0978 162 283; www.hanoikids.org; by donation) This volunteer organisation partners visitors with Hanoi teens and young adults wishing to improve their English-language skills. Tours are customised to the needs of visitors and can include Hanoi sights like the Temple of Literature and Hoa Lo Prison Museum, or street food and market visits. It's best to arrange tours online a couple of weeks before you arrive in Hanoi.

Hanoi Street Food Tours
WALKING TOUR

(☑0904 517 074; www.streetfoodtourshanoi.blogspot.com) Exploring Hanoi's street food, with tours run by a couple of passionate Hanoi foodies so you're guaranteed the best the city can offer. Full-day tours run to six hours, and evening tours with *bia hoi*, snacks and noodles are also great. Tours can be customised to different interests. Check the website for occasional blog posts from co-owner Tu.

Vietnam in Focus
PHOTOGRAPHY TOUR

(☑0122 435 1929, 0121 515 0522; www.vietnaminfocus.com; per person US$80) Journalists Colm Pierce and Alex Sheal run photographic tours exploring Hanoi life, including the Old Quarter, markets and the Long Bien Bridge. Tours usually include a meal and can be customised to photographers of all levels, even beginners. Check the website for details of longer tours to more remote destinations like Moc Chau, Ha Giang and Ba Be National Park.

★ Festivals & Events

Tet
CULTURE

(Tet Nguyen Dan, Vietnamese Lunar New Year; ☑04-3928 2618; ⊙late Jan or early Feb) During the week preceding Tet, there is a flower market on P Hang Luoc. There's also a colourful, two-week flower exhibition and competition, beginning on the first day of the new year, that takes place in Lenin Park near Bay Mau Lake.

Quang Trung Festival
CULTURE

(⊙Feb/Mar) Wrestling competitions, lion dances and human chess take place on the 15th day of the first lunar month at Dong Da Mound, site of the uprising against the Chinese led by Emperor Quang Trung (Nguyen Hué) in 1788.

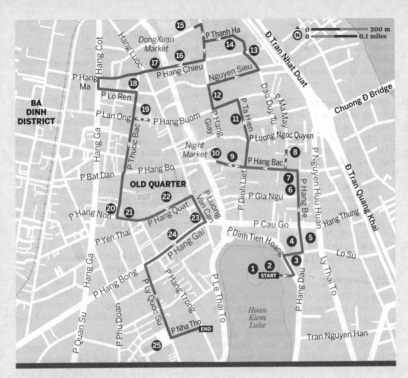

Walking Tour
Old Quarter

START NGOC SON TEMPLE
END P NHA THO
LENGTH 3.5KM; MINIMUM TWO HOURS

Start at the **1 Ngoc Son Temple** (p57) on Hoan Kiem Lake. Return over the red **2 Huc Bridge**, to the **3 Martyrs' Monument**. Follow P Dinh Tien Hoang to the **4 Water Puppet Theatre**. Head north on P Hang Dau to Hanoi's **5 shoe shops**. Cross P Cau Go to P Hang Be and the local **6 market** on P Gia Ngu.

Back on P Hang Be, continue north to P Hang Bac. Look out for the artisans hand-carving intricate **7 gravestones**. Next head up P Ma May to the **8 Memorial House** (p55) at No 87.

Return to P Hang Bac, passing **9 jewellery shops**, to **10 house 102**, which includes a fully functioning temple. Retrace your steps and head up narrow **11 P Ta Hien**, popular for after-dark bars. Turn left on P Hang Buom to the **12 Bach Ma Temple** (p55), and continue to **13 Cua O Quan**

Chuong, the well-preserved Old East Gate. Continue north on P Thanh Ha to a **14 street market**. Veer right to **15 Dong Xuan Market** (p82).

Backtrack south on Nguyen Thien Thuat and turn right on to P Hang Chieu, past **16 shops** selling straw mats and rope. This becomes **17 P Hang Ma** where imitation 'ghost money' is sold for burning in Buddhist ceremonies. Follow your ears to the **18 blacksmiths** near the corner of P Lo Ren and P Thuoc Bac. Continue along Lan Ong to the pungent fragrances of **19 herb merchants**.

Double back to P Thuoc Bac and head south past the **20 tin-box makers**, opposite the **21 mirror shops** on P Hang Thiec. Continue left towards shops selling **22 Buddhist altars and statues** along P Hang Quat.

Head south past P Luong Van Can's **23 toy shops**, and continue along P Hang Gai for elegant **24 silk shops**. Head south on P Ly Quoc Su to **25 St Joseph Cathedral** (p57), and the cafes on P Nha Tho and P Au Trieu.

Vietnam's National Day
CULTURE

(⊙ 2 Sep) Celebrated with a rally and fireworks at Ba Dinh Sq, in front of Ho Chi Minh's Mausoleum. There are also boat races on Hoan Kiem Lake.

CAMA Festival
MUSIC

(www.camafestival.com; ⊙ Oct) Hanoi's Club for Art and Music Appreciation (CAMA) brings an eclectic bunch of performers to the city for an annual one-day music festival at the American Club. Festival-goers can look forward to electronica, Laotian DJs and rowdy-as-hell Burmese punk – anything goes. It's also a good chance to see local bands and DJs, and catch up with the city's expat crew.

In May CAMA also hosts a festival of music from ASEAN countries, and throughout the year different edgy and arty events are held at the Cama ATK (p78) bar.

🛏 Sleeping

Much of Hanoi's cheap accommodation is located in or around the Old Quarter. We receive numerous complaints about budget-hotel owners pressuring guests to book tours with them. Some travellers have even been turfed out into the street for not complying, while others have found mysterious taxes added to their bills. In addition, Old Quarter traffic is oppressive, particularly around Hang Be, Hang Bac and Ma May.

Emerging areas for good-value accommodation include around St Joseph Cathedral, and on and around P Hang Dieu on the western edge of the Old Quarter.

Expect to pay US$25 to US$30 for a decent budget room. For around US$30 to US$50, rooms are loaded with gadgets and facilities including air-con, satellite TV, wi-fi, a computer and minibar. Hanoi has several efficiently run hostels, and dorm beds range from US$5 to US$9.

Contemporary boutique hotels are also emerging, with tariffs around US$50 to US$75 a night. Above US$100, you're looking at luxury hotels with pools, fitness centres and restaurants.

Most budget and midrange hotels include free internet access, while top-end hotels levy a charge. Always check whether tax and service is included in the quoted price.

🛏 Old Quarter

May De Ville Backpackers
HOSTEL $

(Map p54; ☑ 04-3935 2468; www.maydevilleback-packershostel.com; 1 Hai Tuong, P Ta Hien; dm US$6, d US$30-35; ❋ @ 🛜) A short walk from Ta Hien's bars, May De Ville is one of Hanoi's best hostels. Dorms are spotless and it also has a movie room. Doubles are good value.

Hanoi Backpackers 2
HOSTEL $

(Map p54; ☑ 04-3935 1890; www.hanoibackpacker-shostel.com; 9 Ma May; dm US$7.50, tw & d US$25; ❋ @ 🛜) Options range from spotless dorms to designer doubles, and there's a restaurant and bar downstairs. The relaxed team at reception arranges well-run tours including excursions to Halong Bay and Sapa.

Hanoi Hostel 1
HOSTEL $

(Map p54; ☑ 0972 844 804; www.vietnam-hostel.com; 91C P Hang Ma; dm/d/tr US$6/16/21; 🛜) Well-run and clean with lots of tours on tap and plenty of information about onward travel to China or Laos. Look forward to a more local location outside of Hanoi's backpacker scrum.

Hanoi Hostel 2
HOSTEL $

(Map p54; ☑ 0972 844 804; www.vietnam-hostel.com; 32 P Hang Vai; dm/d/tr US$6/18/21; 🛜) It's same, same but not really different at the Hanoi Hostel's second Old Quarter location. Still clean and well-run, and with the option of a private family room for four people (US$25).

Hanoi Rendezvous Hotel
HOTEL $

(Map p54; ☑ 04-3828 5777; www.hanoiren-dezvoushotel.com; 31 Hang Dieu; dm/s/d/tr US$7.50/25/30/35; ❋ @ 🛜) Deliciously close to several brilliant street-food places, Hanoi Rendezvous features spacious rooms, friendly staff and well-run tours to Halong Bay, Cat Ba Island and Sapa.

Camel City Hotel
GUEST HOUSE $

(Map p54; ☑ 04-3935 2024; www.camelcityhotel.com; 8/50 Dao Duy Tu; r $17-30; ❋ @ 🛜) A family owned operation in a quiet lane just a short walk from the after-dark attractions on P Ta Hien. Rooms are trimmed with Asian design touches and service is friendly.

Hanoi Lucky Guesthouse
GUEST HOUSE $

(Map p54; ☑ 04-3824 5732; www.hanoiluckyguest-house.com; 14 P Bat Su; r $24; @ 🛜) Tucked away on quiet P Bat Su, the Hanoi Lucky Guesthouse is a bustling little spot with an eager young English-speaking crew on reception. Rooms are simple but very clean.

Thuy Nga Guesthouse
GUEST HOUSE $

(Map p54; ☑ 04-3826 6053; thuyngahotel@hotmail.com; 10D P Dinh Liet; r US$12; ❋ @ ☏) This homely little place is run by an accommodating family and has six rooms with natural light, a TV and fridge. Pop outside for lots of good bars.

Serenity Hotel
HOTEL $

(Map p54; ☑ 04-3923 3549; www.hanoiserenityhotel.com; 1B P Cua Dong; s/d from US$18/20; ❋ @ ☏) Spacious rooms and a quieter location outside of Hanoi's backpacker hub add up to one of Hanoi's best budget sleeps. Be prepared to tackle up to six flights of stairs.

Thu Giang Guesthouse
GUEST HOUSE $

(Map p54; ☑ 04-3828 5734; www.thugianggh.com; 5A P Tam Thuong; dm US$5, r US$7-17; ❋ @ ☏) Hidden at the end of a narrow alley, this modest place is owned and run by a hospitable family that understands travellers' needs. There's a second branch for overspills at 35A P Hang Dieu.

Manh Dung Guesthouse
GUEST HOUSE $

(Map p54; ☑ 04-3826 7201; lethomhalong@yahoo.com; 2 P Tam Thuong; r US$12-18; ❋ @ ☏) Slightly more salubrious than other nearby guesthouses; has a lift but most rooms are on the small side.

★ Hanoi Elite
BOUTIQUE HOTEL $$

(Map p54; ☑ 04-3828 1711; www.hanoielitehotel.com; 10/5032 Dao Duy Tu; r US$50-55; ❋ @ ☏) It's surprising what you can find in the most narrow and hidden-away of lanes in the Old Quarter. Hanoi Elite features cool and classy decor, top-notch staff and the kind of touches – rainforest shower-heads, breakfasts cooked to order and in-room computers – you'd expect only from more expensive accommodation.

★ Art Trendy Hotel
HOTEL $$

(Map p54; ☑ 04-3923 4294; www.arttrendyhotel.com; 6 Hang But; r US$45-70; ⊖ ❋ @ ☏) One of Hanoi's newer hotels, Art Trendy enjoys a quiet location on the western edge of the Old Quarter. Rooms are stylish and relatively spacious, and there's a real can-do attitude and friendly style from all the exceptional staff. Each room has a laptop, and breakfast includes warm baguettes, omelettes and fresh fruit.

★ Calypso Legend Hotel
BOUTIQUE HOTEL $$

(Map p54; ☑ 04-3935 2751; www.calypsolegendhotel.com; 11A Trung Yen, P Dinh Liet; r US$50-58, ste US$80-85; ⊖ ❋ @ ☏) Tucked away in a small lane, it's a bit of a mission to find the Calypso Legend, but definitely worth it. Red and white combines for romantic decor, and the reception team is unfailingly friendly and helpful. To find the hotel, walk up P Dinh Liet away from the lake, and turn right into Trung Yen, a quiet lane with no traffic.

DO THE HUSTLE

Hanoi is not only the political capital of Vietnam, it is also the capital of hotel hustles. Copycat and fly-by-night hotels abound. These will rent a building, appropriate the name of another hotel, and then work with touts to bring unwitting tourists to their 'chosen' accommodation. Visitors who question the alternative location are told the hotel has moved and it is not until they check the next day that they realise they have been had. These hotels overcharge on anything they can, often giving a price for the room on check-in and a price per person on check out. The best way to avoid this is to prebook a room by phone or email. This way, you know the hotel is still open, still in the same location and not full.

Airport taxis and minibuses often work in partnership with these copycat hotels, as they give the biggest commissions, and there have even been reports of desperate Westerners working in tandem with these hotels, steering backpackers their way. Confirm an airport transfer with your first night's accommodation to avoid this hassle.

If you come across any dodgy hotels, guesthouses, travel companies or other business, report them to the **Vietnam National Administration of Tourism** (Map p62; ☑ 04-3942 3760; www.vietnamtourism.gov.vn; 80 Quan Su) to hopefully pressure the cowboys into cleaning up their act.

Tirant Hotel
HOTEL $$

(Map p54; 04-6269 8899; www.tiranthotel.com; 38 Gia Ngu; s/d from US$55/65; ✷@⑨) Trendy decor, switched-on staff who speak excellent English, and spacious bedrooms all conspire to make this one of central Hanoi's best hotels. The buffet breakfast is definitely worth lingering for, and the huge Grand Suite (US$145) is quite possibly the Old Quarter's best room.

Art Hotel
HOTEL $$

(Map p54; 04-3923 3868; www.hanoiarthotel.com; 65 P Hang Dieu; s/d from US$30/45; ✷@⑨) The young, friendly and welcoming crew at the Art Hotel make this well-located spot really stand out. Rooms are spacious with spotless bathrooms and wooden floors, and within a 30m radius you'll find some of Hanoi's best opportunities for partaking in the city's great street food.

Nova Hotel
HOTEL $$

(Map p54; 04-3923 3366; www.hanoinovahotel.com; 75 P Hang Dieu; US$25-48; ✷@⑨) On the western edge of the Old Quarter, P Hang Dieu has good-value midrange hotels. The Nova exemplifies what any place in this part of town needs to offer: spacious bedrooms, balcony views and spotless modern bathrooms.

Tu Linh Palace
HOTEL $$

(Map p54; 04-3923 0154; www.tulinhpalace-hotels.com; 2B P Hang Ga; s/d from US$25/28; ✷@⑨) Clean and spacious rooms in a less busy area of the Old Quarter. Wooden floors and modern Asian design add up to a chic ambience; the bathrooms in the deluxe rooms are especially stylish.

Classic Street Hotel
HOTEL $$

(Map p54; 04-3825 2421; www.classicstreet-phocohotel.com; 41 P Hang Be; r US$32-45; ✷⑨) This place on ever-busy Hang Be has cosy rooms with large beds and satellite TV. Plenty of paintings and ceramics brighten up the communal spaces and corridors.

Hanoi Guesthouse
HOTEL $$

(Map p54; 04-3935 2572; www.hanoiguesthouse.com; 85 P Ma May; d/tr from US$26/38; ✷@⑨) Recently relocated to bustling P Ma May, the Hanoi Guesthouse has newly decorated rooms, and a very central location right in the middle of all the action, with bars, restaurants, travel agencies and shopping right outside.

🛏 Around Hoan Kiem Lake

Madame Moon Guesthouse
GUEST HOUSE $

(Map p58; 04-3938 1255; www.madam-moonguesthouse.com; 17 Hang Hanh; r US$23-27; ✷@⑨) Keeping it simple just one block from Hoan Kiem Lake, Madame Moon has surprisingly chic rooms and a (relatively) traffic-free location in a street filled with local cafes and bars.

Hanoi Backpackers Hostel
HOSTEL $

(Map p58; 04-3828 5372; www.hanoibackpackershostel.com; 48 P Ngo Huyen; dm US$7.50, r US$25; ✷@⑨) An efficient, perennially popular hostel now occupying two buildings on a quiet lane. It's impressively organised, with custom-built bunk beds and lockers, and the dorms all have en-suite bathrooms.

Central Backpackers Hanoi
HOSTEL $

(Map p58; 04-3938 1849; www.centralbackpackershostel.com; 16 P Ly Quoc Su; dm US$5; @⑨) This well-run hostel is in close proximity to good cafes and street eats. It's a pretty social spot, possibly due to the free beer every night from 8pm to 9pm.

Especen Hotel
HOTEL $

(Map p58; 04-3824 4401; www.especen.vn; 28 P Tho Xuong & 41 P Ngo Huyen; r $22-25; ✷@⑨) This budget hotel near St Joseph Cathedral has spacious and light rooms in an almost tranquil location (by Old Quarter standards anyway). A second branch is nearby.

Hotel Thien Trang
GUEST HOUSE $

(Map p58; 04-3826 9823; thientranghotel24@hotmail.com; 24 P Nha Chung; r US$12-22; ✷@⑨) This place enjoys a quiet location in the stylish Nha Tho area. Its spacious rooms retain a degree of period character alongside somewhat less pleasing modern additions.

★ 6 on Sixteen
BOUTIQUE HOTEL $$

(Map p58; 04-6673 6729; www.sixonsixteen.com; 16 P Bao Khanh; r US$72; ✷@⑨) Adorned with designer textiles, ethnic art and interesting locally made furniture, 6 on Sixteen has a welcoming ambience. There are just six concisely decorated rooms, but lots of shared areas to encourage guests to mingle and share travel tips. Breakfast includes freshly baked pastries and robust Italian coffee. Book a balcony room, as rooms at the back have tiny windows.

Cinnamon Hotel
BOUTIQUE HOTEL $$

(Map p58; ☑ 04-3938 0430; www.cinnamonhotel. net; 26 P Au Trieu; r US$58-65; ◉ ※ @ ☎) A hip hotel overlooking St Joseph Cathedral in the Old Quarter's smartest enclave. The design is outstanding, combining the historic features of the building – wrought-iron and window shutters – with Japanese-influenced interiors and modern gadgetry. Of the six rooms, all with balcony and tropical names, 'Lime' has a commanding perspective of the cathedral. There's also a small bar-restaurant.

Joseph's Hotel
HOTEL $$

(Map p58; ☑ 04-3939 1048; www.josephshotel. com; 5 P Au Trieu; r from US$40; ※ @ ☎) Tucked away in a quiet lane behind St Joseph Cathedral, this compact 10-room hotel features pastel tones, mod-Asian decor and breakfasts cooked to order. Try to secure a room with views of the church's nearby towers. It's a laid-back location if the speed and scale of Hanoi's traffic doesn't appeal.

Golden Lotus Hotel
HOTEL $$

(Map p58; ☑ 04-3938 0901; www.goldenlotushotel. com.vn; 32 P Hang Trong; r $65-100; ※ @ ☎) An elegant, polished lobby sets the tone at this atmospheric little hotel, which blends Eastern flavours and Western chic. All rooms have wooden floors, silk trim, art aplenty and broadband internet connections, though most rooms at the rear do not enjoy any natural light. Breakfast is included.

Jasmine Hotel
HOTEL $$

(Map p58; ☑ 04-3926 4420; www.thejasminehotel. com; 57 Lo Su; s/d US$45/55; ※ @ ☎) Caution: must like carved dark wood. The Jasmine's decor is slightly ostentatious, but this hotel is handily near Hoan Kiem Lake and good restaurants. Standard rooms are a touch dark, and there's some road noise from the front rooms with balconies, but it's still good value for such a central location.

Hanoi Elegance Diamond Hotel
HOTEL $$

(Map p58; ☑ 04-3935 1632; www.hanoielegance-hotel.com; 32 Lo Su; s/d from US$55/65; ※ @ ☎) With large rooms, each kitted out with a computer, wooden floors, modern furniture and cable TV, this is a solid choice.

Impressive Hotel
BOUTIQUE HOTEL $$

(Map p58; ☑ 04-3938 1590; www.impressive-hotel.com; 54-56 P Au Trieu; r US$40-60; ※ @) Impressive both in name and in nature, with clean and cosy rooms and a top-notch location.

Heart Hotel
HOTEL $$

(Map p58; ☑ 04-3928 6682; www.heart-hotel.com; 11B P Hang Hanh; r US$30-35; ※ @) Popular little hotel with 10 neat rooms, some with lake views.

★ Sofitel Metropole Hotel
HOTEL $$$

(Map p58; ☑ 04-3826 6919; www.sofitel.com; 15 P Ngo Quyen; r from US$220; ※ @ ☎ ☒) A refined place to stay, the Metropole boasts an immaculately restored colonial facade, with mahogany-panelled reception rooms and well-regarded restaurants. The accommodation in the old wing offers unmatched colonial style, while the modern Opera Wing has sumptuous levels of comfort but not quite the same heritage character. Even if you're not staying here, pop in for a drink at the Bamboo Bar.

Hilton Hanoi Opera
HOTEL $$$

(Map p58; ☑ 04-3933 0500; www.hanoi.hilton. com; 1 P Le Thanh Tong; r from US$135; ※ @ ☎ ☒) Built in 1998, this impressive neoclassical edifice blends in well with its surroundings, especially the adjacent Opera House. Rooms are spacious and plush, and both business and leisure facilities – including a gym and a pool – are impressive.

Church Hotel
BOUTIQUE HOTEL $$$

(Map p58; ☑ 04-3928 8118; www.churchhotel.com. vn; 9 P Nha Tho; r US$80-140; ※ @ ☎) Classy mini-hotel with real boutique appeal. Some rooms are smallish, but all have stylish furnishings, and there's an elegant dining room for your complimentary breakfast. Location-wise this is as good as it gets, on Nha Tho's epicentre of Old Quarter chic. Two other openings by the Church Hotel in the Old Quarter are equally classy.

Hotel L'Opera
HOTEL $$$

(Map p58; ☑ 04-6282 5555; www.mgallery.com; 29 P Trang Tien; r from US$140; ※ @ ☎) The Hotel L'Opera effortlessly combines French colonial style with a sophisticated design aesthetic. Rooms are trimmed in silk and Asian textiles, and splurge-worthy features include a spa and the hip late-night vibe of the La Fée Verte (Green Fairy) bar. If you're wondering, Green Fairy is a reference to absinthe, the infamous alcoholic beverage.

Greater Hanoi

InterContinental Westlake Hanoi HOTEL $$$

(☎04-6270 8888; www.intercontinental.com/
hanoi; 1A P Nghi Tam, Tay Ho; d from US$155;
★❋@☎✉) The most luxurious address
in the north of the city, this hotel features a
contemporary Asian-design theme, and the
whole complex juts out into the lake. Many
of the stunning rooms (all with balconies)
are set on stilts above the water. The hotel's
signature Sunset Bar celebrates some of the
city's best cocktails; sitting on its own man-
made island, it's quite probably the most romantic spot in town.

Eating

Hanoi is an international city, and whatever
your budget (or tastes), it's available here. If
you've just flown in, get stuck into the local
cuisine, which is wonderfully tasty, fragrant-
ly spiced and inexpensive. Don't miss the
experience of dining on Hanoi's street food.

If you've been up in the hills of northern
Vietnam subsisting on noodles and rice, the
capital's cosmopolitan dining, including
Japanese, French, Italian and Indian, will be
a welcome change.

Old Quarter

Zenith Cafe CAFE $

(Map p54; www.zenithyogavietnam.com; 16 P Duong
Thanh; mains 45,000-100,000d; ☺9am-6pm; ✐)
Relaxing and peaceful haven under a yoga
studio with excellent juices, salads and vegetarian mains, including falafel and hummus,
goat-cheese pizzas and healthy breakfasts
like homemade muesli.

New Day VIETNAMESE $

(Map p54; 72 P Ma May; mains 70,000-100,000d;
☺8am-late) New Day attracts locals, expats
and travellers. The eager staff always find
space for new diners, so look forward to
sharing a table with some like-minded fans
of Vietnamese food.

Nola CAFE $

(Map p54; 89 P Ma May; snacks 30,000-60,000d;
☺9am-midnight) Retro furniture is mixed and
matched in this bohemian labyrinth tucked
away from Ma May's tourist bustle. Pop in
for a coffee and banana bread, or return after dark for one of Hanoi's best little bars.

Highway 4 VIETNAMESE $$

(Map p54; ☎04-3926 0639; www.highway4.com; 3
P Hang Tre; mains 125,000-275,000d; ☺noon-late)
This is the original location of a family of restaurants pioneering the development of Vietnamese cuisine. Try bite-sized snacks like
nem ca xa lo (catfish spring rolls) or meatier
dishes like *da dieu nuong sate* (spicy satay
grilled ostrich). There's another branch (Map
p54; 25 P Bat Su) in the Old Quarter.

Yin & Yang VIETNAMESE $$

(Map p54; 78 P Ma May; mains 100,000-130,000d;
☺8am-late; ☎) This atmospheric spot along
touristy Ma May stands out with well-priced
versions of Vietnamese classics like *bun
cha* and banana flower salad. Compared
to heaving *bia hoi* corner, it's also a great
spot for a quieter drink in the Old Quarter.
Don't leave town without having a Yin &
Yang mojito.

Cha Ca Thang Long VIETNAMESE $$

(Map p54; ☎04-3824 5115; 21 P Duong Thanh; cha
ca fish 180,000d; ☺10am-3pm & 5-10pm) Bring
along your DIY cooking skills here and grill
your own succulent fish with a little shrimp
paste and plenty of herbs. *Cha ca* is an iconic
Hanoi dish, and while another nearby more-
famous *cha ca* eatery gets all the tour-bus
traffic, the food here is actually better.

Foodshop 45 INDIAN $$

(Map p54; www.foodshop45.com; 32 P Hang Buom;
meals 100,000-150,000d; ☺10am-10.30pm) A new
Old Quarter location now showcases Hanoi's
best Indian food. This spot is definitely convenient, but the lakeside location of the original Foodshop 45 (p76) is more atmospheric.
Either way, the curries are great, and the
beers are exceedingly well-chilled.

Quan Bia Minh VIETNAMESE $$

(Map p54; 7A P Dinh Liet; mains 90,000-130,000d;
☺8am-late) This *bia hoi* joint has evolved
into an Old Quarter favourite with well-
priced Vietnamese food and excellent service led by the eponymous Mrs Minh. Grab
an outdoor table and a cold beer and watch
the beautiful chaos unfold below.

Green Mango MEDITERRANEAN $$

(Map p54; ☎04-3928 9917; www.greenmango.
vn; 18 P Hang Quat; meals 200,000-250,000d;
☺noon-late) This hip restaurant-cum-lounge
has a real vibe as well as great cooking. The
stunning dining rooms, complete with rich
silk drapes, evoke the feel of an opium den,
while the huge rear courtyard comes into its
own on summer nights. Menu-wise there's
everything from pizza and pasta to mod-
Asian fusion creations.

LOCAL KNOWLEDGE

TOP 10 STREET FOOD EXPERIENCES

Deciphering Hanoi's Old Quarter street-food scene can be bewildering, but it's worth persevering and diving in. The city's best food definitely comes from the scores of vendors crowding the city's pavements with smoking charcoal burners, tiny blue plastic stools and expectant queues of canny locals. Many of the stalls have been operating for decades, and often they offer just one dish. After that long perfecting their recipes, it's little wonder the food can be sensational. Note that opening hours may be somewhat flexible. Around 40,000d to 60,000d should be sufficient per person.

Bun Cha Nem Cua Be Dac Kim (Map p54; 67 P Duong Thanh; ⊙11am-7pm) Visiting Hanoi and not eating *bun cha* (barbecued pork with rice vermicelli) should be classed as a capital offence. This is an excellent spot to try this street-food classic.

Banh Cuon (Map p54; 14 P Hang Ga; ⊙8am-3pm) Don't even bother ordering here; just squeeze in and a plate of gossamer-light *banh cuon* (steamed rice crêpes filled with minced pork, mushrooms and shrimp) will be placed in front of you.

Pho Thin (Map p58; 61 Dinh Tien Hoang; ⊙6am-3pm) Negotiate your way to the rear of this narrow, rustic establishment and sit down to some excellent *pho bo* (beef noodle soup). A classic Hanoi experience that hasn't changed in decades.

Banh Ghoi (Map p58; 52 P Ly Quoc Su; ⊙10am-7pm) Nestled under a banyan tree near St Joseph Cathedral, this humble stall turns out *banh ghoi*, moreish deep-fried pastries crammed with pork, vermicelli and mushrooms.

Bun Oc Saigon (Map p54; cnr P Nguyen Huu Huan & Hang Thung; ⊙11am-11pm) Look closely at the plastic buckets and you'll see more than a few unfamiliar shellfish species. Try the *bun oc* (snail noodle soup) with a hearty dash of tart tamarind, or *so huyet xao toi* (blood cockles fried with garlic).

Bun Bo Nam Bo (Map p54; 67 P Hang Dieu; ⊙11am-10pm) *Bun bo nam bo* (dry noodles with beef) is a dish from southern Vietnam, but it's certainly travelled north well. Mix in bean sprouts, garlic, lemongrass and green mango for a filling treat.

Xoi Yen (Map p54; cnr P Nguyen Huu Huan & P Hang Mam; ⊙7am-11pm) Equally good for breakfast or as a hangover cure, Xoi Yen specialises in sticky rice topped with goodies, including sweet Asian sausage, gooey fried egg and slow-cooked pork.

Mien Xao Luon (Map p54; 87 P Hang Dieu; ⊙7am-2pm) Head to this humble stall trimmed with mini-mountains of fried eels for three different ways of eating the crisp little morsels. Try them stir-fried in vermicelli with egg, bean sprouts and shallots.

Bun Rieu Cua (Map p54; 40 P Hang Tre; ⊙7-9am) Get to this incredibly popular spot early, as its sole dish of *bun rieu cua* (crab noodle soup) is only served for a couple of hours from 7am. A Hanoi classic.

Che (Map p54; 76 P Hang Dieu; ⊙7am-3pm) In winter try *che banh troi tau* (sweet mung beans with sesame and ginger) or in summer *che thap nam* (with coconut milk, crushed peanuts, lotus seeds and dried apples).

Tamarind Café VEGETARIAN **$$**
(Map p54; ☑04-3926 0580; 80 P Ma May; mains 80,000-140,000d; ⊙8am-late; 🛜🍴) A relaxed cafe-restaurant with lounge-around cushioned seating and plenty of space. Offers an eclectic menu but is best for tabouli, eggplant claypot and salads. Drinks include lassis, zesty juices and wine by the glass. A specialist Indian menu is available upstairs. We're not sure about the 1980s power ballads though.

Green Tangerine FUSION **$$**
(Map p54; ☑04-3825 1286; www.greentangerinehanoi.com; 48 P Hang Be; mains US$12-20; ⊙noon-late; 🍴) Experience the mood and flavour of 1950s Indochine at this elegant restaurant located in a beautifully restored colonial house with a cobbled courtyard. The fusion French-Vietnamese cuisine is not always entirely successful, but it's still worth popping in for coffee or a drink. Two-course lunches (218,000d) are good value.

🍴 Around Hoan Kiem Lake

Hanoi House
CAFE $

(Map p58; www.thehanoihouse.com; 48A P Ly Quoc Su; snacks 40,000-60,000d; ⊗8.30am-11pm; 🛜) A chic and bohemian cafe with superb upstairs views of St Joseph Cathedral. Chill out on the impossibly slim balcony with excellent juices and Hanoi's best ginger tea.

The Cart
CAFE $

(Map p58; www.thecartfood.com; 10 Tho Xuong; snacks & juices 40,000d-80,000d; ⊗7.30am-5pm; 🛜🖬) Superlative pies, excellent juices and smoothies, and interesting baguette sandwiches feature at this little haven of Western comfort food tucked away near St Joseph Cathedral.

La Place
CAFE $

(Map p58; 🖉04-3928 5859; 4 P Au Trieu; meals from 70,000d; ⊗7.30am-10.30pm; 🛜) This stylish, popular little cafe adjacent to St Joseph Cathedral has walls covered in propaganda art and an East-West menu. Plenty of wine by the glass is on offer and the coffee has a real kick.

Apple Tart
BAKERY $

(Map p58; 11 Ngo Bao Khanh; snacks from 40,000d; ⊗8am-7pm) Tiny hole-in-the-wall spot serving eat-on-the-run French baked goods like *créme caramel* and apple *tartine*. Pop next door and combine your still-warm baked goodies with a robust espresso.

Fanny Ice Cream
ICE CREAM $

(Map p58; 51 P Ly Thuong Kiet; ice cream from 38,000d; ⊗8am-9pm) The place for French-style ice creams and sorbets in Hanoi. During the right season try the *com,* a delightful local flavour extracted from young sticky rice; other innovative flavours include ginger and green tea.

Kem Dac Diet Trang Tien
ICE CREAM $

(Map p58; 35 P Trang Tien; ice cream from 10,000d; ⊗8am-10pm) It's barely possible to walk down the road to get to this parlour on hot summer nights, such is its popularity.

Fivimart
SELF-CATERING $

(Map p58; 27A Ly Thai Tho; ⊗9am-5pm) One of the best-stocked supermarkets in the centre of town.

Hanoi Social Club
CAFE $$

(www.facebook.com/TheHanoiSocialClub; 6 Hoi Vu; mains 95,000-160,000d; ⊗8am-11pm) On three funky levels with retro furniture, the Hanoi Social Club is the city's most cosmopolitan cafe. Dishes include potato fritters with chorizo for breakfast, and pasta, burgers

---

SPECIALITY FOOD STREETS

To combine eating with exploration, head to these locations crammed with interesting restaurants and food stalls.

➡ **Pho Cam Chi** This narrow lane is packed with local eateries turning out cheap, tasty food for a few dollars. Cam Chi translates as 'Forbidden to Point' and dates from centuries ago. It is said that the street was named as a reminder for the local residents to keep their curious fingers in their pockets when the king and his entourage went through the neighbourhood. Cam Chi is about 500m northeast of Hanoi train station. Adjoining Tong Duy Tan is also crammed with good eating.

➡ **Đuong Thuy Khue** On the southern bank of Tay Ho, Đ Thuy Khue features dozens of outdoor seafood restaurants with a lakeside setting. The level of competition is evident by the daredevil touts who literally throw themselves in front of oncoming traffic to steer people towards their tables. You can eat well here for about 150,000d per person.

➡ **Truc Bach** A quieter waterfront scene is around the northeast edge of Truc Bach Lake. Many *lau* (hotpot) restaurants are huddled together in an almost continuous strip for a few hundred metres. Grab a few friends and settle in at one of the dinky lakeside tables for a DIY session of fresh seafood, chicken or beef. It's perfect on a cool Hanoi night.

➡ **Pho Nghi Tam** About 10km north of central Hanoi, P Nghi Tam has a 1km-long stretch of about 60 dog-meat restaurants: keep an eye out for the words *thit cho*. Hanoians believe that eating dog meat in the first half of the month brings bad luck, so the restaurants are deserted. On the last day of the lunar month, however, they're packed with locals.

and wraps for lunch or dinner. Vegetarian options feature a tasty mango curry, and the quiet laneway location is a good spot for an end-of-day coffee, beer or wine.

The Hanoi Social Club also hosts regular gigs and events. Check its Facebook page for what's on.

La   INTERNATIONAL $$
(Map p58; ☑04-3928 8933; 49 P Ly Quoc Su; mains 125,000-255,000d; ☺noon-late) An intimate, modest-looking and yet atmospheric bistro with a creative menu that includes lamb shank braised in orange, sweet pepper and espresso. Regular seasonal specials include Dalat strawberries, and La also offers wines by the glass.

Madame Hien   VIETNAMESE $$$
(Map p58; ☑04-3938 1588; www.verticale-hanoi. com; 15 Chan Cam; mains US$10-15; ☺11am-10pm) Housed in a restored 19th-century villa, Madame Hien is a tribute to French chef Didier Corlu's Vietnamese grandmother. Look forward to more elegant versions of traditional Hanoi street food, with the '36 Streets' fixed menu (535,000d) a good place to kick off your culinary knowledge of the city. A good-value lunch (147,000d) is also available.

Spices Garden   VIETNAMESE $$$
(Map p58; ☑04-3826 6919; www.sofitel-legend. com; Sofitel Metropole Hotel, 15 P Ngo Quyen; tasting platter 460,000d, mains 500,000-800,000d; ☺11.30am-2.30pm & 6-10.30pm) Here's where to go to try a stunning range of street food from across Vietnam, all with the 5-star ambience of the Sofitel Metropole Hotel. You'll obviously be paying way more than if you were sitting on a squat plastic stool in the Old Quarter, but the food is authentic and good, and the heritage vibe unmatched.

✕ West of the Old Quarter

Net Hue   VIETNAMESE $
(Map p62; cnr P Hang Bong & P Cam Chi; snacks & mains from 35,000d; ☺11am-9pm) Net Hue is well-priced for such comfortable surroundings. Head to the top floor for the nicest ambience and enjoy Hue-style dishes like *banh nam* (steamed rice pancake with minced shrimp).

Quan An Ngon   VIETNAMESE $
(Map p62; www.ngonhanoi.com.vn; 15 Phan Boi Chau; dishes 60,000-120,000d; ☺11am-11pm) A number of small kitchens turn out street-food specialities from across Vietnam. Try

and visit just outside the busy lunch and dinner periods, or consider Quan An Ngon's newest branch (Map p62; www.ngonhanoi.com. vn; 34 P Phan Đinh Phung; dishes 60,000-120,000d; ☺11am-11pm) in a lovely French villa just north of the Old Quarter.

KOTO   CAFE $$
(Map p62; ☑04-3747 0338; www.koto.com.au; 59 P Van Mieu; meals 120,000-160,000d; ☺7.30am-10pm, closed dinner Mon; ➋) Stunning four-storey modernist cafe-bar-restaurant overlooking the Temple of Literature, where the interior design has been taken very seriously, from the stylish seating to the fresh flowers by the till. Daily specials are chalked up on a blackboard and the short menu has everything from excellent Vietnamese food to yummy pita wraps and beer-battered fish 'n' chips.

KOTO is a not-for-profit project providing career training and guidance to disadvantaged children and teens.

Southgate   FUSION $$
(Map p62; ☑04-3938 1979; www.southgatehanoi. com; 28 Tong Duy Tan; tapas 90,000-120,000d, mains 150,000-275,000d; ☺11.30am-midnight Sun-Wed, to 2am Thu-Sat) Tempting fusion tapas and superb desserts, including thyme, honey and yoghurt pannacotta, feature at this stylish restaurant and bar in a wonderfully restored colonial villa. Excellent cocktails hint at a hip vibe transplanted from New York or Sydney. A lazy brunch including omelettes and eggs Benedict (120,000d to 220,000d) is a great way to start the day.

The Matchbox   EUROPEAN, VIETNAMESE $$
(Map p62; ☑04-3734 3098; www.thematchbox.vn; 40 Cao Ba Quat; mains 100,000-290,000d; ☺8am-10.30pm) In an elegant courtyard beside the Fine Arts Museum, the Matchbox delivers well-priced food with a Mediterranean spin. Pop in for a plate of pasta and a glass of wine, or linger longer over excellent steaks and Australian red wine. Vietnamese meals are also available, and there's a good-value steak-and-wine deal (199,000d) on Monday nights.

Puku   CAFE $$
(Map p62; 18 Tong Duy Tan; mains 70,000-125,000d; ☺24hr; ➋➌) A little slice of Kiwi cafe culture – *puku* means 'stomach' in New Zealand's indigenous Maori language – with great burgers, Mexican wraps and all-day eggy breakfasts. The coffee is terrific and it's a five-minute walk from the Hanoi railway

station, ideal for a restorative brunch after the overnight train back from Sapa. Upstairs shows big-screen live sports.

★ **La Badiane**   INTERNATIONAL $$$
(Map p62; ☑ 04-3942 4509; www.labadiane-hanoi. com; 10 Nam Ngu; mains from US$17; ☺ noon-11pm) This stylish bistro is set in a restored whitewashed French villa arrayed around a breezy central courtyard. French cuisine underpins the menu – La Badiane translates to 'star anise' – but Asian and Mediterranean flavours also feature. Menu highlights include sea bass tagliatelle with smoked paprika, and prawn bisque with wasabi tomato bruschetta. Three-course lunches for 325,000d are excellent value.

French Quarter

★ **Chim Sao**   VIETNAMESE $$
(Map p64; www.chimsao.com; 63-65 Ngo Hue; salads 50,000-65,000d, mains 80,000-130,000d; ☺ 11am-11pm) Sit at tables downstairs or grab a more traditional spot on the floor upstairs and discover excellent Vietnamese food, with some dishes inspired by the ethnic minorities of Vietnam's north. Definite standouts are the hearty and robust sausages, zingy and fresh salads, and duck with starfruit. Try and come with a group so you can explore the menu fully.

★ **Nha Hang Ngon**   VIETNAMESE $$
(Map p64; 26A Tran Hung Dao; mains 80,000-130,000d; ☺ 11am-11pm) If you find the food-court ambience of Quan An Ngon a little frenetic, consider detouring to this similar establishment. There's the same focus on authentic street-food flavours from around Vietnam, but the courtyard ambience in a restored French villa is more romantic. Weekends are very busy with locals.

Izakaya Yancha   JAPANESE $$
(Map p64; ☑ 04-3974 8437; 121 P Trieu Viet Vuong; meals 120,000-250,000d; ☺ 1am-11pm) Surrounded by local cafes on 'Coffee St', Izakaya Yancha serves *izakaya* – think Japanese tapas – in a buzzy and friendly atmosphere. Secure a spot near the open kitchen and work your way through lots of Osaka-style goodies, including excellent tuna sashimi and miso with udon noodles.

Chay Nang Tam   VEGETARIAN $$
(Map p64; 79A P Tran Hung Dao; meals from 100,000d; ☺ 11am-11pm; ☑) Dishes of vegeta-

bles that look like meat, reflecting an ancient Buddhist tradition designed to make carnivore guests feel at home.

Pots 'n Pans   FUSION $$$
(Map p64; ☑ 04-3944 0204; www.potsnpans. vn; 57 P Bui Thi Xuan; mains 295,000-620,000d; ☺ 11.30am-late) In a chic modern space, Pots 'n Pans specialises in innovative fusion dishes blending Vietnamese and European influences. Service is professional from graduates of KOTO, a training organisation for disadvantaged teens. An excellent wine list partners dishes like crispy skin seabass with a prawn and ginger boudin, black sesame noodles, mushrooms, chilli jam and tamarind-and-coconut sauce.

Greater Hanoi

Oasis   SELF-CATERING $
(24 P Xuan Dieu; ☺ 8am-6pm) Italian-owned deli with excellent bread, cheese and salami, as well as homemade pasta and sauces. It's north of central Hanoi in the Tay Ho restaurant strip on P Xuan Dieu.

★ **Quan Kien**   VIETNAMESE $$
(☑ 0983 430 136; www.quankien.com; 143 P Nhgi Tam; mains 80,000-130,000d; ☺ 11am-11pm) An interesting spot for cuisine from the H'mong, Muong and Thai ethnic minorities – try the grilled chicken with wild pepper – traditional Vietnamese *ruou* (wine) made from apricots or apples, and more challenging snacks like grilled ants' eggs and crickets. If insects aren't your thing, it's still a fun night sitting at the low tables eating excellent Vietnamese dishes.

Mâu Dich 37   VIETNAMESE $$
(Map p62; 37 Nam Trang, Truc Bach; snacks 35,000-55,000d, mains 90,000-180,000d; ☺ 10am-10pm) Styled after a government-run food shop from the impoverished period after 1976, Mâu Dich 37 in a unique exercise in nostalgia. Waiters are dressed as state workers, and diners queue to 'purchase' coupons that can be exchanged for food. The menu focuses on robust northern flavours, and features a few challenging dishes like braised frog and snails with ginger leaves.

Foodshop 45   INDIAN $$
(☑ 04-3716 2959; www.foodshop45.com; 59 P Truc Bach; meals 100,000-150,000d; ☺ 10am-10.30pm) Hanoi's best Indian flavours fea-

ture at this cosy lakeside spot sandwiched between the *lau* (hotpot) restaurants on Truc Bach Lake. The ambience is more authentic at the rustic downstairs tables, and menu standouts include a superb *kadhai* chicken that will definitely have you ordering a second beer.

House of Son Tinh VIETNAMESE **$$**
(☏04-3715 0577; www.highway4.com; 31 P Xuan Dieu, Tay Ho; meals 100,000-200,000d; ☺10am-11.30pm) This showcase for the Highway 4 empire features the Son Tinh Lounge Bar, an intimate, downstairs cocktail bar specialising in delicious concoctions made from the award-winning Son Tinh liquors. Upstairs the elegant Highway 4 restaurant offers a diverse range of Vietnamese dishes. Definitely worth the short taxi ride out to the Tay Ho area.

Kitchen CAFE **$$**
(7A/40 P Xuan Dieu, Tay Ho; snacks & meals 90,000-180,000d; ☺7am-9.30pm; ☎) This West Lake terrace cafe with a Mexican tinge ticks all the right boxes with a mellow buzz and a creative, healthy menu of delicious sandwiches and salads sourced from organic ingredients. Also great for breakfast or a juice (try the ginger and watermelon tonic) if you've been cycling around the lake.

🍷 Drinking

Hanoi's eclectic drinking scene features grungy dive bars, a Western-style pub or two, sleek lounge bars, cafes and hundreds of *bia hoi* joints.

However, as the no-fun police supervise a strict curfew, and regularly show up to enforce the closure of places that flout this law, there's minimal action after midnight. Lock-

---

HANOI'S COFFEE CULTURE

Western-style cafes and coffee shops are becoming increasingly common in Vietnamese cities, but most of them pale in comparison to the traditional cafes dotted around central Hanoi. Here's where to go and what to order for an authentic local experience. Most cafes are open from around 7am to 7pm, but hours sometimes vary. On the eastern edge of the Old Quarter, P Nguyen Huu Huan is lined with good cafes, most with free wi-fi.

Café Duy Tri (43A P Yen Phu) In the same location since 1936, this caffeine-infused labyrinth is a Hanoi classic. You'll feel like Gulliver as you negotiate the tiny ladders and stairways to reach the 3rd-floor balcony. Order the delicious *caphe sua chua* (iced coffee with yoghurt), and you may have discovered your new favourite summertime drink. You'll find P Yen Phu a couple of blocks east of Truc Bach Lake north of the Old Quarter.

Cafe Pho Co (Map p58; 11 P Hang Gai) One of Hanoi's best-kept secrets, this place has plum views over Hoan Kiem Lake. Enter through the silk shop, and continue through the antique-bedecked courtyard up to the top floor for the mother of all vistas. You'll need to order coffee and snacks before tackling the final winding staircase. For something deliciously different, try the *caphe trung da*, coffee topped with a silkily smooth beaten egg white.

Cafe Lam (Map p54; 60 P Nguyen Huu Huan) Another classic cafe that's been around for yonks – long enough to build up a compact gallery of paintings left behind by talented patrons who couldn't afford to pay their tabs during the American War. These days, you're just as likely to spy Converse-wearing and Vespa-riding bright young things refuelling on wickedly strong *caphe den* (black coffee).

Cong Caphe (Map p64; 152 P Trieu Viet Vuong) An essential pilgrimage for coffee fiends is P Trieu Viet Vuong, around 1km south of Hoan Kiem Lake. This street is lined with scores of cafes – some modern spots with iPad-toting teens and others more old school. Settle in to the eclectic beats and kitsch Communist memorabilia at Cong Caphe with a *caphe sua da* (iced coffee with condensed milk). There's another branch (Map p62; 32 P Dien Bien Phu) near the Military History Museum en route to Ho Chi Minh's Mausoleum.

Cafe Linh (Map p54; 65 P Hang Buom) Step out of the chaos of the Old Quarter into this fascinating cafe decorated with military memorabilia from the American War. Light boxes display the detritus of war, mortars and grenades are fashioned into lamps, and khaki parachutes billow from the ceiling. Factor in the music – often classic 1960s and 1970s soul and rock – and it's a happening scene.

in action after midnight does occur though; ask around in Hanoi's hostels to find out which bars are currently staying open beyond the witching hour.

The best places for a bar crawl include traveller-friendly P Ta Hien in the Old Quarter, and Ngo Bao Khanh near the northwest edge of Hoan Kiem Lake. An alternative scene, popular with expats, is in the Tay Ho Lake area on P Xuan Dieu.

Hanoi is definitely not a clubbers' paradise, and the often-enforced midnight curfew means dancing is pretty much confined to bar-clubs in and around the Old Quarter.

Bar Betta
BAR, CAFE

(Map p62; www.facebook.com/barbetta34; 34 Cao Ba Quat; ☺9am-midnight) Retro decor and a jazz-age vibe combine with good cocktails, coffee and cool music in this breezy French colonial villa. Two-for-one beers are available from 3pm to 7pm, and the rooftop terrace (from 8pm) is essential on a sultry Hanoi night.

Manzi Art Space
BAR, CAFE

(Map p62; www.facebook.com/manzihanoi; 14 Phan Huy Ich, Ba Dinh; ☺cafe 9am-midnight, shop 10am-6pm) Part cool art gallery and part chic cafe and bar, Manzi is worth seeking out north of the Old Quarter. A restored French villa hosts diverse exhibitions of painting, sculpture and photography, and the compact courtyard garden is perfect

for a coffee or glass of wine. There's also a small shop selling works by contemporary Vietnamese artists.

Summit Lounge
BAR

(20th fl, Sofitel Plaza, 1 Đ Thanh Nien; ☺4.30pm-late) It's official. The best views in town are from this 20th-floor lounge bar. Order a (pricey) cocktail or beer, grab a spot on the outside deck, and take in Truc Bach Lake and great vistas of the city. And if you do blow your budget on flash drinks, you can still eat bargain-priced and delicious street food for the rest of the week.

Cama ATK
BAR

(Map p64; www.cama-atk.com; 73 P Mai Hac De; ☺6pm-midnight Wed-Sat) Make the trek south of Hoan Kiem Lake to this bohemian bar run by CAMA (Hanoi's Club for Art and Music Appreciation). Check the website for what's on, which includes everything from Japanese funk and dancehall DJs through to experimental short films and reggae sound systems.

Quan Ly
BAR

(Map p64; 82 P Le Van Hu; ☺10am-9pm) Owner Pham Xuan Ly has lived on this block since 1950, and now runs one of Hanoi's most traditional *ruou* (Vietnamese liquor) bars. Kick off with the ginseng one, and work your way up to the gecko variation. An English-language menu makes it easy to choose, and there's also cheap beer and good Vietnamese food on offer.

DON'T MISS

BIA AHOY!

'Tram phan tram!' Remember these words, as all over Vietnam, glasses of *bia hoi* are raised and emptied, and cries of *tram phan tram* ('100%' or 'bottoms up') echo around the table.

Bia hoi is Vietnam's very own draught beer or microbrew. This refreshing, light-bodied pilsener was first introduced to Vietnam by the Czechs in a display of Communist solidarity. Brewed without preservatives, it is meant to be enjoyed immediately and costs as little as 5000d a glass.

Hanoi is the *bia hoi* capital of Vietnam and there are microbars on many Old Quarter street corners. A wildly popular place is '**bia hoi junction** (Map p54)' in the heart of the Old Quarter, where P Ta Hien meets P Luong Ngoc Quyen. It's now packed with backpackers and travellers though, and has really lost most of its local charm. Did you really come all this way to drink Heineken and talk to boozed neighbours from Jersey City or Johnsonville?

An alternative, more local *bia hoi* junction is where P Nha Hoa meets P Duong Thanh on the western edge of the Old Quarter. For something to go with the beer, **Bia Hoi Ha Noi** (Map p54; 2 P Duong Thanh) also does the best spare ribs in town. You'll also have a great night at **Nha Hang Lan Chin** (Map p58; cnr P Hang Tre & P Hang Thung) on the corner of P Hang Tre and P Hang Thung. Order the *vit quay* (roast duck).

Blah Blah BAR

(Map p58; 59B P Hang Be; ⊗ 7am-late) The unpretentious Blah Blah is Hanoi's cosiest bar, so you'll definitely have to chat to other fellow travellers. The music's decent and we're big fans of the Friday night pub quiz at 8pm. Rustle up a team at your hostel to win a bottle of whiskey. No Googling answers on your phone, OK?

Cheeky Quarter BAR

(Map p54; ☑ 0936 143 3999; 1 P Ta Hien; ⊗ noon-4am) This sociable bar comes complete with patterned wallpaper and intriguing framed portraits (that look vaguely like they're depicting some eccentric titled family). Table footy (foosball) is taken very seriously, and the tunes are contemporary: drum 'n' bass or house music.

Le Pub PUB

(Map p54; ☑ 04-3926 2104; 25 P Hang Be; ⊗ 7am-late) Le Pub is a great place to hook up with others, as there's always a good mix of travellers and Hanoi expats. There's a cosy, tavern-like interior (with big screens for sports fans), a street-facing terrace and a rear courtyard. Bar snacks are served, the service is slick and the music usually includes tunes you can sing along to.

Mao's Red Lounge BAR

(Map p54; 5 P Ta Hien; ⊗ noon-late) One of Ta Hien's most popular bars, this place is a classic dive bar with dim lighting and air thick with tobacco smoke. Drinks are well priced and the music's usually good. If you don't like what's playing, just ask if you can hook up your own tunes to the sound system.

Funky Buddha BAR

(Map p54; 2 P Ta Hien; ⊗ noon-late) Crowd around the L-shaped bar and enjoy some of Hanoi's better cocktails. Once the techno and house beats kick in, it's more of a nightclub than a bar. Cheap drinks make it a favourite for travellers from nearby backpacker hostels.

Angelina BAR

(Map p58; Sofitel Metropole Hotel, 15 P Ngo Quyen; ⊗ noon-2am) Flash hotel bar with glitzy decor and a late licence. DJs spin funky house and chill-out tunes here on weekend nights. Also in the Sofitel Metropole is the poolside **Bamboo Bar**, dripping in chic, heritage cool.

Legend Beer PUB

(Map p58; ☑ 04-3557 1277; 109 P Nguyen Tuan; ⊗ 11am-late) Yes, it's a tad touristy, but as every beer comes with fine balcony views

GAY & LESBIAN HANOI

There are very few gay venues in Hanoi, but plenty of places that are gay-friendly. However official attitudes are still fairly conservative and Hanoi is home to these official attitudes. Police raids in the name of 'social reform' aren't unknown and that tends to ensure the gay and lesbian community keeps a low profile.

The GC Pub (below) is one of the more-established gay bars in Hanoi, and it's a good place to find out about the most happening new places in town. Accommodation-wise, the Art Hotel (p70) and Art Trendy Hotel (p69) are gay-friendly.

The website www.utopia-asia.com has up-to-date information about gay Hanoi. See also the Vietnam information section on www.cambodiaout.com.

of Hoan Kiem Lake, it's still worth dropping by for a cold one. Bring your electronic device of choice to capture essential video views of the incessant ebb and flow of Hanoi traffic around the city's busiest roundabout.

Green Mango BAR

(Map p54; 18 P Hang Quat; ⊗ noon-11pm) This hotel-restaurant also has a great lounge bar, with stylish seating, a tempting cocktail list and plenty of beautiful people enjoying the relaxed vibe.

Dragonfly BAR

(Map p54; 15 P Hang Buom; ⊗ 4pm-late) Bar-club with a handy Old Quarter location, it draws a (very) young crowd and the music is pretty mainstream.

Rooftop Bar BAR

(Map p62; 19th fl, Pacific Place, 83B P Ly Thuong Kiet; ⊗ noon-midnight) Another place to come for views of the city – pop in for an expensive beer or cocktail and enjoy the vista. It's very popular with a glittering array of Hanoi's bright young things.

GC Pub PUB

(Map p58; ☑ 04-3825 0499; 7 P Bao Khanh; ⊗ noon-midnight) This pub looks pretty run down from the street but it gets very lively on weekend nights. Popular with gay Hanoians and has pool tables.

☆ Entertainment

Cinemas

Centre Culturel Français de Hanoi   CINEMA
(Map p58; www.ifhanoi-lespace.com; 24 P Trang Tien) Set in the sublime L'Espace building near the Opera House, it offers a regular program of French flicks. Musical events are also staged; check the website for what's on.

Cinematheque   CINEMA
(Map p58; ☑04-3936 2648; 22A P Hai Ba Trung) This Hanoi institution is a hub for art-house film lovers, and there's a great little cafe-bar here too. It's nominally 'members only', but a 50,000d one-off membership usually secures visitors an always-interesting themed double bill.

Megastar Cineplex   CINEMA
(Map p64; ☑04-3974 3333; www.megastar.vn; 6th fl, Vincom Tower, 191 Ba Trieu) Multiplex cinema with quality screen and audio, and comfy seats. Here's your chance to see blockbuster movies a few days before they're on sale as cheap DVDs in the Old Quarter.

Music

Traditional music is usually performed daily at the Temple of Literature. Upmarket Vietnamese restaurants in central Hanoi are also good places to catch traditional Vietnamese music; try **Cay Cau** (Map p64; ☑04-3824 5346; 17A P Tran Hung Dao; ⊙7.30-9.30pm) in the De Syloia Hotel. Other venues for modern music include the Cama ATK (p78) bar and Zone 9 (p78).

Hanoi Opera House   OPERA
(Map p58; ☑04-3993 0113; 1 P Trang Tien) This French-colonial 900-seat venue was built in 1911. On 16 August 1945 the Viet Minh–run Citizens' Committee announced from a balcony on this building that it had taken over the city. Performances of classical music and opera are periodically held here in the evenings. Most weekends you'll see Hanoi wedding couples getting photographed on the elegant front steps.

Check the website www.ticketvn.com for upcoming performances.

Ca Tru   LIVE MUSIC
(Map p54; 42 P Hang Bac; admission 220,000d; ⊙8pm Wed, Fri & Sat) Concerts of traditional Vietnamese music held in the intimate surroundings of a restored courtyard house in the Old Quarter. *Ca tru* is indigenous to the north of Vietnam, and concerts feature a selection of the 100 or so *ca tru* melodies. The art form has also been recognised as an endangered 'intangible cultural heritage' by Unesco.

Vietnam National Tuong Theatre   OPERA
(Map p54; www.vietnamtuongtheatre.com; 51 P Duong Thanh; admission 100,000d; ⊙6.30pm Thu-Sun) *Hat tuong* is a uniquely Vietnamese variation of Chinese opera that enjoyed its greatest popularity under the Nguyen dynasty in the 19th century. Until 2007, performances at this theatre were by invitation only. Now performances are open to locals and visitors, and a night watching *hat tuong* is an interesting traditional alternative to Hanoi's wildly popular water puppets.

Expect highly stylised acting, wonderfully elaborate costumes, and comedy and tragedy with characters from Vietnamese folklore.

Hanoi Rock City   LIVE MUSIC
(www.hanoirockcity.com; 27/52 To Ngoc Van, Tay Ho) Hanoi Rock City is tucked away down a residential lane about 7km north of the city near Tay Ho, but it's a journey well worth taking for an eclectic mix including reggae, Hanoi punk and regular electronica nights. A few international acts swing by, so check the website or www.newhanoian.xemzi.com for listings.

Jazz Club By Quyen Van Minh   LIVE MUSIC
(Map p62; www.minhjazzvietnam.com; 65 Quan Su; ⊙performances 9-11.30pm) This atmospheric venue is the place in Hanoi to catch some live jazz. There's a full bar, food menu and high-quality gigs featuring father-and-son team Minh and Dac, plus other local and international jazz acts. Check the website for listings.

Water Puppets

This fascinating art form originated in northern Vietnam, and Hanoi is the best place to catch a show. Performances are held at the **Municipal Water Puppet Theatre** (Map p54; ☑04-3824 9494; www.thanglongwaterpuppet.org; 57B P Dinh Tien Hoang; admission 60,000-100,000d, camera fee 20,000d, video fee 60,000d; ⊙performances 3.30pm, 5pm, 6.30pm, 8pm & 9.15pm daily, 10.30am Sat, 9.30am Sun). Multilingual programs allow the audience to read up on each vignette as it's performed. Try to book ahead.

DON'T MISS

PUNCH & JUDY IN A POOL

The ancient art of water puppetry (roi nuoc) was virtually unknown outside northern Vietnam until the 1960s. It originated with rice farmers who worked the flooded fields of the Red River Delta. Some say they saw the potential of the water as a dynamic stage; others say they adapted conventional puppetry during a massive flood. Whatever the real story, the art form is at least 1000 years old.

The farmers carved the puppets from water-resistant fig-tree timber (sung) in forms modelled on the villagers themselves, on animals from their daily lives and on fanciful mythical creatures such as the dragon, phoenix and unicorn. Performances were usually staged in ponds, lakes or flooded paddy fields.

Contemporary performances use a square tank of waist-deep water for the 'stage'; the water is murky to conceal the mechanisms that operate the puppets. The wooden puppets, up to 50cm long and weighing as much as 15kg, are decorated with glossy vegetable-based paints. Each lasts only about three to four months if used continually, so puppet production provides several villages outside Hanoi with a full-time livelihood.

Eleven puppeteers, each trained for a minimum of three years, are involved in the performance. The puppeteers stand in the water behind a bamboo screen and have traditionally suffered from a host of water-borne diseases – these days they wear waders to avoid this nasty occupational hazard.

Some puppets are simply attached to a long pole, while others are set on a floating base, in turn attached to a pole. Most have articulated limbs and heads, some also have rudders to help guide them. In the darkened auditorium, it looks as if they are literally walking on water.

The considerable skills required to operate the puppets were traditionally kept secret and passed only from father to son – never to daughters through fear that they would marry outside the village and take the secrets with them.

The music, which is provided by a band, is as important as the action on stage. The band includes wooden flutes (sao), gongs (cong), cylindrical drums (trong com), bamboo xylophones and the fascinating single-stringed zither (dan bau).

The performance consists of a number of vignettes depicting pastoral scenes and legends. One memorable scene tells of the battle between a fisherman and his prey, which is so electric it appears as if a live fish is being used. There are also fire-breathing dragons (complete with fireworks) and a flute-playing boy riding a buffalo.

The performance is a lot of fun. The water puppets are both amusing and graceful, and the water greatly enhances the drama by allowing the puppets to appear and disappear as if by magic. Spectators in the front-row seats can expect a bit of a splash.

🔖 Shopping

The area around St Joseph Cathedral has good-quality furnishing stores and stylish clothing boutiques. Both P Nha Tho and P Au Trieu are filled with interesting shops, and there are also several good cafes in the neighbourhood. For Vietnamese handicrafts, including textiles and lacquerware, head to the stores along P Hang Gai, P To Tich, P Hang Khai and P Cau Go.

For upmarket art galleries stroll along P Trang Tien, between Hoan Kiem Lake and the Opera House. It's also worth dropping by the Fine Arts Museum, which has a couple of interesting galleries. The stylish cafe and bar Manzi Art Space (p78) also has an interesting store showcasing local artists.

P Hang Gai and its continuation, P Hang Bong, are good places to look for embroidered tablecloths, T-shirts and wall hangings. P Hang Gai is also a fine place to buy silk and have clothes custom-made.

Bookworm BOOKSTORE
(Map p62; www.bookwormhanoi.com; 44 Chau Long; ⊙9am-7pm) Stocks over 10,000 new and used English-language books. There's plenty of fiction and it's good on South Asian history and politics.

Thang Long BOOKSTORE
(Map p58; 53-55 P Trang Tien; ⊙9am-6pm) One of the biggest bookshops in town with English and French titles, international newspapers and magazines, and a good selection of titles on the history of Hanoi.

Dome
HOMEWARES

(Map p62; ☑ 04-3928 7677; www.dome.com.vn; 71 P Yen The Trong; ⊗ 9am-6pm) An elegant emporium with stylish furniture, gorgeous curtains and cushions made from Vietnamese fabrics. Also has very high-quality basketry, lacquerware and gifts.

Hanoi Moment
HANDICRAFTS

(Map p58; www.hanoimoment.vn; 101 P Hang Gai; ⊗ 8am-9pm) An oasis of classier Vietnamese souvenirs, including lacquerware and jewellery, amidst the T-shirt overkill of nearby stores. Bamboo, stone and porcelain are also used to great effect.

Tan My Design
CLOTHING

(Map p58; www.tanmydesign.com; 61 P Hang Gai; ⊗ 8am-8pm) Stylish clothing, jewellery and accessories, with the added bonus of a funky cafe when you need a break from shopping. The homewares and bed linen are definitely worth a look.

Metiseko
CLOTHING, ACCESSORIES

(Map p54; www.metiseko.com; 71 P Hang Gai; ⊗ 8am-9pm) Lots of stylish, organic and eco-friendly spins on clothing, homewares and accessories. Both cotton and silk are harnessed for Metiseko's chic collections.

Things of Substance
CLOTHING

(Map p58; ☑ 04-3828 6965; 5 P Nha Tho; ⊗ 9am-6pm) Tailored fashions and some off-the-rack items at moderate prices. The staff are professional and speak decent English.

Three Trees
ACCESSORIES

(Map p58; ☑ 04-3928 8725; 15 P Nha Tho; ⊗ 9am-7pm) Stunning, very unusual designer jewellery, including many delicate necklaces, which make special gifts.

Mai Gallery
ART

(Map p62; ☑ 04-3828 5854; www.maigallery-vietnam.com; 113 P Hang Bong; ⊗ 9am-7pm) Run by resident artist Mai, this is a good place to learn more about Vietnamese art before making a purchase.

Viet Art Centre
ART

(Map p64; ☑ 04-3942 9085; www.vietartcentre.vn; 42 P Yet Kieu; ⊗ 9am-5pm) A fine place to browse contemporary Vietnamese art, including paintings, photography and sculpture.

Mekong Quilts
HANDICRAFTS

(Map p54; www.mekong-quilts.org; 13 P Hang Bac; ⊗ 8am-8pm) This store offers beautiful quilts handcrafted by rural women working in a not-for-profit community development program.

Craft Link
HANDICRAFTS

(Map p62; ☑ 04-3843 7710; www.craftlink.com.vn; 43 P Van Mieu; ⊗ 9am-6pm) This not-for-profit organisation near the Temple of Literature sells quality tribal handicrafts and weavings at fair-trade prices.

Mosaique
HOMEWARES

(Map p58; www.mosaiquedecoration.com; 6 P Ly Quoc Su; ⊗ 9am-8pm) Modern and chic updates of traditional lacquerware and silk. The ideal spot to pick up stylish cushion covers, linen and accessories.

Indigenous
HANDICRAFTS

(Map p58; 36 P Au Trieu; ⊗ 9am-6pm) A top spot for quirky ethnic-style gifts and excellent fair-trade coffee. There's a great little cafe too, so you can choose your favourite Vietnamese java before you buy.

Markets

Buoi Market
MARKET

(⊗ 6am-2pm) Located near the southwest edge of Tay Ho at the intersection of Duong Buoi and Lac Long Quan, this market sells live animals like chickens, ducks and pigs, but also features ornamental plants.

Dong Xuan Market
MARKET

(Map p54; ⊗ 6am-7pm) A large, nontouristy market located in the Old Quarter of Hanoi, about 900m north of Hoan Kiem Lake. There are hundreds of stalls here, and it's a fascinating place to explore if you want to catch a flavour of Hanoian street life. The area around the market also has loads of bustling shops.

Hom Market
MARKET

(Map p64; ⊗ 6am-5pm) On the northeast corner of P Hué and P Tran Xuan Soan, this is a good general-purpose market and excellent for local fabric, if you plan to have clothes made.

Night Market
MARKET

(Map p54; ⊗ 7pm-midnight Fri-Sun) This market runs north to south through the Old Quarter, from P Hang Giay to P Hang Dao. Content-wise it's something of a spillover for the area's shops, but at least the streets are closed to traffic. Keep an eye out for pickpockets.

ⓘ Information

DANGERS & ANNOYANCES

First the good news: Hanoi is generally a very safe city to explore, and crimes against tourists are extremely rare. Most visitors are thoroughly seduced by the city and leave captivated by its charm. Don't let your guard down completely though. While it's usually perfectly safe to walk around the streets of the Old Quarter at night, it's best to avoid the darker lanes after around 10pm. It's also sensible for solo women to take a metered taxi when travelling across the city at night. Do watch out for pickpockets around market areas and unwanted baggage 'helpers' in crowded transport terminals – particularly when boarding night trains.

Hanoi has more than its fair share of scam merchants and swindlers, so be sure to keep your antennae up. Most problems involve budget hotels and tours. Very occasionally things can get quite nasty and we've received reports of verbal aggression and threats of physical violence towards tourists who've decided against

NEGOTIATING HANOI'S TRAVEL AGENCY MAZE

Hanoi has hundreds of travel agencies, most of a pretty dubious quality, while a few are downright dodgy. Many of the sketchy agencies operate with pushy, ill-informed staff out of Old Quarter budget hotels. It's these fly-by-night operations we receive the most complaints about. Some cheap hotels have been known to kick out travellers who book tours elsewhere. When you book accommodation, check to make sure there are no strings attached and that it's not mandatory to book tours at the same business also.

Look out for clones of the popular agencies, as it's common for a rival business to set up shop close to a respected agency and attempt to cream off a slice of their business. Often these impostors are staffed by ill-informed workers adopting a very hard sell. Visit online forums like the Thorn Tree (www.lonelyplanet.com/thorntree) to check the latest travellers' buzz.

Some agencies have professional, knowledgeable staff and coordinate well-organised trips. These companies are inevitably more expensive, but offer a far greater degree of satisfaction. Look for companies that run small groups, use their own vehicles and guides, and offer trips away from the main tourist trail. The following are recommended.

Ethnic Travel (Map p54; ☑ 04-3926 1951; www.ethnictravel.com.vn; 35 P Hang Giay; ⊙ 9am-6pm Mon-Sat, 10am-5pm Sun) Off-the-beaten-track trips across the north in small groups. Some trips are low-impact using public transport and homestays, others are activity-based (including hiking, cycling and cooking). Offers Bai Tu Long Bay tours and also has an office in Sapa.

Free Wheelin' Tours (Map p54; ☑ 04-3926 2743; www.freewheelin-tours.com; 2 P Ta Hien, Hoan Kiem District, Hanoi; ⊙ 10am-7pm) Offers motorbike and 4WD tours around the north, including an eight-day trip to the northeast on Minsk bikes.

Handspan Adventure Travel (Map p54; ☑ 04-3926 2828; www.handspan.com; 78 P Ma May; ⊙ 9am-8pm) Sea-kayaking trips in Halong Bay and around Cat Ba Island, and jeep tours, mountain biking and trekking. Other options include remote areas such as Moc Chau and Ba Be National Park, community-based tourism projects in northern Vietnam, and the *Treasure Junk*, the only true sailing craft cruising Halong Bay. Handspan also has offices in Sapa and HCMC.

Marco Polo Travel (☑ 04-3997 5136; www.marcopoloasia.com; Room 107B, N14-49 Nguyen Khoai, Hanoi; ⊙ 9am-5pm) Runs kayaking trips around Halong Bay and Ba Be Lakes. Also good mountain-biking trips and hiking expeditions around the north of Vietnam.

Ocean Tours (Map p54; ☑ 04-3926 0463; www.oceantours.com.vn; 22 P Hang Bac, Hanoi; ⊙ 8am-8pm) Well-organised tour operator with Halong Bay and Ba Be National Park options, and 4WD road trips around the northeast.

Vega Travel (Map p54; ☑ 04-3926 2092; www.vegatravel.vn; cnr P Ma May & 24A P Hang Bac; ⊙ 8am-8pm) Family owned and operated company offering well-run tours around the north and throughout Vietnam. Excellent guides and drivers, and the company also financially supports ethnic minority kindergartens and schools around Sapa and Bac Ha. Good-value tours of Halong Bay.

a hotel room or a tour. Stay calm and back away slowly or things could quickly flare up.

Traffic and pollution are other irritants. The city's traffic is so dense and unrelenting that simply crossing the street can be a real headache, and weaving a path through a tide of motorbikes (two million and counting) can be a hairy experience. Our advice is to walk slowly and at a constant pace, allowing motorcyclists sufficient time to judge your position and avoid you. Don't try to move quickly as you'll just confuse them. Keep your wits about you as you explore the Old Quarter, as motorbikes come at you from all directions and pavements are obstructed by cooking stalls and more parked motorbikes.

Pollution levels are punishing and air quality is poor, with levels of some contaminants higher than in Bangkok.

Scams

Whilst there's no need to be paranoid, Hanoi is riddled with scams, many of them inextricably linked. The taxi and minibus mafia at the airport shuttle unwitting tourists to the wrong hotel. Invariably, the hotel has copied the name of another popular property and will then attempt to appropriate as much of your money as possible. Taxi swindles are also becoming increasingly common. Try to avoid the taxis loitering at Hanoi's bus stations; many have super-fast meters.

Some shoeshine boys and *cyclo* drivers attempt to add a zero or two to an agreed price for their services; stick to your guns and give them the amount you originally agreed.

Watch out for friendly, smooth-talking strangers approaching you around Hoan Kiem Lake. There are many variations, but sometimes these con-artists pose as students and suggest a drink or a meal. Gay men are also targeted in this way. Your new friend may then suggest a visit to a karaoke bar, snake-meat restaurant or some other venue and before you know it you're presented with a bill for hundreds of dollars. Be careful and follow your instincts, as these crooks can seem quite charming.

We've also heard reports of male travellers being approached by women late at night in the Old Quarter, and then being forced at gunpoint by the women's male accomplices to visit multiple ATMs and empty their accounts. Keep your wits about you, and try to stay in a group if you're returning from a bar late at night.

EMERGENCY

The emergency services should be able to transfer you to an English speaker.

Ambulance (☏115)

Fire (☏114)

Police (☏113)

INTERNET ACCESS

Most budget and midrange hotels offer free access to a computer and the internet: at fancier places in the rooms, at cheaper places in the lobby.

Free wi-fi access is virtually ubiquitous in the city's cafes and bars, but dedicated internet cafes are largely a thing of the past, so pack a tablet or smartphone.

MAPS

Hanoi city maps come in every size and scale. Some are freebies subsidised by advertising and others are precise works of cartography.

Leading maps include detailed ones at a scale of 1:10,000 or 1:17,500. Covit produces a couple of hand-drawn 3D maps of Hanoi, including a detailed Old Town map, which make nice souvenirs. Various maps, including those produced by Covit, are available at leading bookshops in Hanoi.

There is also an excellent bus map available: *Xe Buyt Ha Noi* (5000d).

MEDICAL SERVICES

Hanoi Family Medical Practice (☏04-3843 0748; www.vietnammedicalpractice.com; Van Phuc Diplomatic Compound, 298 P Kim Ma; ⊙24hr) Located a few hundred metres west of the Ho Chi Minh Mausoleum Complex, this practice includes a team of well-respected international physicians and dentists and has 24-hour emergency cover. Prices are high, so check that your medical travel insurance is in order.

L'Hopital Français de Hanoi (☏04-3577 1100, emergency 04-3574 1111; www.hfh.com. vn; 1 Phuong Mai; ⊙24hr) Long-established, international-standard hospital with accident and emergency, intensive care, dental clinic and consulting services. It's around 3km southwest of Hoan Kiem Lake.

SOS International Clinic (☏04-3826 4545; www.internationalsos.com; 51 Xuan Dieu; ⊙24hr) English, French, German and Japanese are spoken and there is a dental clinic. It's 5km north of central Hanoi near Tay Ho Lake.

Viet Duc Hospital (Benh Vien Viet Duc; Map p58; ☏04-3825 3531; 40 P Trang Thi; ⊙24hr) Old Quarter unit for emergency surgery; the doctors here speak English, French and German.

Traditional Medicine

Institute of Acupuncture (☏04-3853 3881; 49 P Thai Thinh; ⊙8-11.30am & 2-4.30pm) Offers effective holistic medicine; located around 4km southwest of Hoan Kiem Lake.

National Institute of Traditional Medicine (Map p64; ☏04-3826 3616; 29 P Nguyen Binh Khiem; ⊙7.30-11.30am & 1.30-4pm) For Vietnamese-style medical solutions.

MONEY

Hanoi has many ATMs, and on the main roads around Hoan Kiem Lake there are international banks where you can exchange currency and receive cash advances on credit cards. There is no black market exchange in Hanoi, and if someone offers to change money on the street, they're looking to rip you off. Note that some ATMs limit the amount you can withdraw to only 3,000,000d. ANZ and HSBC ATMs usually have higher limits.

POST

Domestic Post Office (Buu Dien Trung Vong; Map p58; ☑04-3825 7036; 75 P Dinh Tien Hoang; ☺7am-9pm) For internal postal services in Vietnam; also sells philatelic items.

International Postal Office (Map p58; ☑04-3825 2030; cnr P Dinh Tien Hoang & P Dinh Le; ☺7am-8pm) The entrance is to the right of the domestic office.

DHL (Map p62; ☑04-3733 2086; www.dhl.com.vn)

Federal Express (☑04-3824 9054; www.fedex.com/vn)

TELEPHONE

Guesthouses are convenient for local calls within Hanoi. For international services, Skype offers the cheapest rates, either via a wi-fi hotspot or on shared computers in guesthouses and hotels.

TOURIST INFORMATION

Tourist Information Center (Map p54; ☑04-3926 3366; P Dinh Tien Hoang; ☺9am-7pm) City maps and brochures, but privately run with an emphasis on selling tours. In the cafes and bars of the Old Quarter, look for the excellent local magazine *The Word*.

USEFUL WEBSITES

Hanoi Grapevine (www.hanoigrapevine.com) Information about concerts, art exhibitions and cinema.

Infoshare (www.infosharehanoi.com) Geared towards expats, this site also has useful content for visitors, and links to other worthwhile sites.

Sticky Rice (www.stickyrice.typepad.com) Foodie website, with the lowdown on everything from gourmet Vietnamese to Hanoi street kitchens.

The Word (www.wordhanoi.com) Online version of the excellent, free monthly magazine *The Word*.

TNH Vietnam (www.tnhvietnam.xemzi.com) Formerly dubbed The New Hanoian, TNH Vietnam is the premier online resource for visitors and expats; good for up-to-date restaurant and bar reviews.

❶ Getting There & Away

AIR

Hanoi has fewer direct international flights than Ho Chi Minh City, but with excellent connections through Singapore, Hong Kong or Bangkok you can get almost anywhere easily.

Vietnam Airlines (Map p58; ☑1900 545 486; www.vietnamair.com.vn; 25 P Trang Thi; ☺8am-5pm Mon-Fri) Links Hanoi to destinations throughout Vietnam. Popular routes include Hanoi to Dalat, Danang, Dien Bien Phu, HCMC, Hue and Nha Trang, all served daily.

Jetstar Airways (☑1900 1550; www.jetstar.com) Operates low-cost flights to Danang, HCMC and Nha Trang.

Vietjet Air (☑1900 1886; www.vietjetair.com) Launched in 2012, this low-cost airline has flights to Hanoi, Nha Trang, Danang, Dalat and Bangkok.

BUS & MINIBUS

Hanoi has four main long-distance bus stations of interest to travellers. They are fairly well organised, with ticket offices, fixed prices and schedules. Consider buying tickets the day before you plan to travel on the longer distance routes to ensure a seat. It's often easier to book through a travel agent, but you'll obviously be charged a commission.

Tourist-style minibuses can be booked through most hotels and travel agents. Popular destinations include Halong Bay and Sapa. Prices are usually about 30% to 40% higher than the regular public bus, but include a hotel pick-up.

Many open-ticket tours through Vietnam start or finish in Hanoi.

---

❶ CATCHING THE BUS TO CHINA

Two daily services (at 7.30am and 7.30pm) to Nanning, China (450,000d, eight hours) leave near the **Hong Ha Hotel** (Map p58; ☑04-3824 7339; 204 Đ Tran Quang Khai). Tickets should be purchased in advance, though little English is spoken at the hotel. You may be asked to show your Chinese visa. Most travel agencies also sell tickets.

The bus runs to the border at Dong Dang, where you pass through Chinese immigration. You then change to a Chinese bus, which continues to the Lang Dong bus station in Nanning. Reports from Nanning-bound travellers indicate that this route is less hassle and quicker than travelling by train.

Giap Bat Bus Station (☑04-3864 1467; Đ Giai Phong) Serves points south of Hanoi, and offers more comfortable sleeper buses. It is 7km south of the Hanoi train station.

Gia Lam Bus Station (☑04-3827 1569; Đ Ngoc Lam) Has buses to the northeast of Hanoi. It's located 3km northeast of the centre across the Song Hong (Red River).

Luong Yen Bus Station (☑04-3942 0477; cnr Tran Quang Khai & Nguyen Khoai) Located 3km southeast of the Old Quarter, it operates services to the east. Transport to Cat Ba Island is best organised here. Note that the taxis at Luong Yen are notorious for dodgy meters. Walk a couple of blocks and hail one off the street.

My Dinh Bus Station (☑04-3768 5549; Đ Pham Hung) This station 7km west of the city provides services to the west and the north, including sleeper buses to Dien Bien Phu for onward travel to Laos. It's also the best option for buses to Ha Giang and Mai Chau.

BUSES FROM HANOI

Giap Bat Bus Station

DESTINATION	DURATION (HR)	COST (D)	FREQUENCY
Ninh Binh	2	70,000	Frequent 7am-6pm
Dong Hoi	8	380,000	Frequent sleepers noon-6.30pm
Dong Ha	8	380,000	Frequent sleepers noon-6.30pm
Hue	10	380,000	Frequent sleepers noon-6.30pm
Danang	12	380,000	Frequent sleepers noon-6.30pm
Dalat	35	450,000	9am, 11am
Nha Trang	32	700,000	10am, 3pm, 6pm

Gia Lam Bus Station

DESTINATION	DURATION (HR)	COST (D)	FREQUENCY
(Bai Chay) Halong City	3½	120,000	Every 30min
Haiphong	2	70,000	Frequent
Lang Son	4	100,000	Every 45min
Mong Cai	8	260,000	Hourly (approx)
Lao Cai	9	250,000	6.30pm, 7pm (sleeper)
Sapa	10	300,000	6.30pm, 7pm (sleeper)
Ba Be	5	180,000	Noon

Luong Yen Bus Station

DESTINATION	DURATION (HR)	COST (D)	FREQUENCY
HCMC	40	920,000	7am, 10am, 2pm, 6pm
Haiphong	3	70,000	Frequent
Lang Son	3½	100,000	Frequent
Cat Ba Island	5	240,000	5.20am, 7.20am, 11.20am, 1.20pm

My Dinh Bus Station

DESTINATION	DURATION (HR)	COST (D)	FREQUENCY
Cao Bang	10	190,000	Every 45min
Dien Bien Phu	11	375,000	11am, 6pm
Hoa Binh	3	55,000	Frequent
Son La	7	170,000	Frequent to 1pm
Ha Giang	7	140,000	Frequent

CAR

Car hire is best arranged via a travel agency or hotel. Rates almost always include a driver, a necessity as many roads and turnings are not signposted. The roads in the north are in OK shape, but narrow lanes, potholes and blind corners equate to an average speed of 35km/h to 40km/h. During the rainy season, expect serious delays as landslides are cleared and bridges repaired. You'll definitely need a 4WD.

Rates start at about US$110 a day (including a driver and petrol). Make sure the driver's expenses are covered in the rate you're quoted.

MOTORBIKE

Hanoi has several good operators with well-maintained bikes. See also motorbike tours on p486.

Offroad Vietnam (Map p54; ☑0913 047 509; www.offroadvietnam.com; 36 P Nguyen Huu Huan; ☺8am-6pm Mon-Sat) For reliable Honda trail bikes (from US$20 daily) and road bikes (US$17). The number of rental bikes is limited, so booking ahead is recommended. Offroad's main business is running excellent tours, mainly dealing with travellers from English-speaking countries. Tours are either semi-guided excluding meals and accommodation, or all inclusive fully-guided tours.

Mr Anh at Offroad Vietnam is also a great source of information on the changing state of northern Vietnam's roads.

Cuong's Motorbike Adventure (Map p54; ☑0913 518 772; www.cuongs-motorbike-adventure.com; 46 P Gia Ngu; ☺8am-6pm) Also recommended with trips all around the north. Look out for the bright pink Minsk motorbike.

TRAIN

Southbound Trains to Hue, Danang, Nha Trang, HCMC

Trains to southern destinations go from the main **Hanoi Train Station** (Ga Hang Co; Train Station A; ☑04-3825 3949; 120 Đ Le Duan; ☺ticket office 7.30am-12.30pm & 1.30-7.30pm) at the western end of P Tran Hung Dao on Đ Le Duan. To the left of the main entrance is the ticket office with adjacent posters displaying train departure times and fares. Take a ticket and look out for your booth number on the screens. It's a good idea to write down your train number, departure time and preferred class in Vietnamese. Southbound trains depart at 6.15am, 9am, 1.15pm, 7pm and 11pm.

We recommend buying your tickets a few days before departure to ensure a seat or sleeper. Tickets can also be purchased from most travel agencies, and their commission for booking usually offsets the language hassle it can sometimes be to buy tickets directly from the railway station. They also often have preferential access to tickets to popular destinations like Hue, Ho Chi Minh City and Lao Cai (for Sapa).

Approximate journey times from Hanoi are as follows, but check when you book, as some trains are quicker than others: Hue (11 hours), Danang (13½ hours), Nha Trang (24½ hours), HCMC (31 hours). Approximate costs from Hanoi are shown in the Southbound Trains table, but note that different departures have different fare structures and available classes.

Northbound Trains to Lao Cai (for Sapa) & China

All northbound trains leave from a separate station (just behind Station A and known as

TRAINS FROM HANOI

Eastbound & Northbound Trains

DESTINATION	STATION	DURATION	HARD SEAT/ SLEEPER	SOFT SEAT/ SLEEPER	FREQUENCY
Beijing	Tran Quy Cap	18hr	US$224	US$328	6.30pm Tue & Fri
Haiphong	Gia Lam	2hr	55,000d	65,000d	6am
Haiphong	Long Bien	2½-3hr	55,000d	65,000d	9.20am, 3.30pm, 6.10pm
Nanning	Gia Lam	12hr	US$23	US$35	9.40pm

Southbound Trains

DESTINATION	HARD SEAT	SOFT SEAT	HARD SLEEPER	SOFT SLEEPER
Hue	From 364,000d	From 535,000d	From 665,000d	From 884,000d
Danang	From 418,000d	From 615,000d	From 773,000d	From 942,000d
Nha Trang	From 678,000d	From 996,000d	From 1,237,000d	From 1,607,000d
HCMC	From 776,000d	From 1,140,000d	From 1,300,000d	From 1,672,000d

Station B) called **Tran Quy Cap Station** (Train Station B; ☑ 04-3825 2628; P Tran Quy Cap; ⊙ ticket office 4am-6am & 4pm-10pm). This is accessed by an entrance on P Tran Quy Cap. Cross the tracks north of Station A and turn left to reach this station. There are separate ticket offices for northbound trains to Lao Cai (for Sapa) and China. If you've already booked for one of the private carriages to Sapa, you'll need to exchange your voucher for a ticket at the appropriate tour desk.

Once you're in China the train to Beijing is a comfortable, air-conditioned service with four-bed sleeper compartments and a restaurant.

Eastbound trains to Haiphong and China

Eastbound (Haiphong) trains depart from **Gia Lam Train Station** on the eastern side of the Song Hong (Red River), or **Long Bien** on the western (city) side of the river. Be sure to check which station. Trains to Nanning (China) also depart from here. Note that you cannot board international Nanning-bound trains in Lang Son or Dong Dang.

See www.seat61.com for the latest information on all trains in Vietnam.

ⓘ Getting Around

TO/FROM THE AIRPORT

Hanoi's Noi Bai International Airport is about 35km north of the city. The trip here takes 45 minutes to an hour, along a fast modern highway.

Bus

Public bus 17 (5000d) from outside the arrivals hall runs to/from **Long Bien bus station** (5000d; ⊙ 5am-9pm) on the northern edge of the Old Quarter. Luggage may be charged separately. Allow around 90 minutes' travelling time.

Taxi

Airport Taxi (☑ 04-3873 3333) charges US$20 for a taxi ride door-to-door to or from Noi Bai

airport. From the terminal, look out for the official taxi drivers who wear bright-yellow jackets. They do not require that you pay the toll for the bridge you cross en route. Some other taxi drivers do require that you pay the toll, so ask first. There are numerous airport scams involving taxi drivers and dodgy hotels. Don't use freelance taxi drivers touting for business – the chances of a rip-off are too high. If you've already confirmed accommodation, definitely book a taxi through your hotel.

Jetstar Airport Bus

Goes to Noi Bai (40,000d) from southeast of the lake at 206 Tran Quang Khai. Passengers must be at the city stop at least 2½ hours before their flight's scheduled departure time.

Vietnam Airlines Minibus

Links Hanoi and Noi Bai (US$3), leaving every half hour to/from the Vietnam Airlines office on P Trang Thi. It's best – though not essential – to book the day before.

BICYCLE

Many Old Quarter guesthouses and cafes rent bikes for about US$3 per day. Good luck with that traffic.

The Hanoi Bicycle Collective (www.thbc.vn; 44 Ngo 31, Xuan Dieu, Tay Ho; bike rental per day from 100,000d; ⊙ 8am-8pm Tue-Sun) Vietnamese bikes and mountain bikes (phone ahead one day prior to book) can be rented at this funky spot near Tay Ho that also doubles as a cafe and gin bar. Grab a Spanish-style *bocata* sandwich before setting off around the 15km lakeside path around Tay Ho. Check the website for regular rides around the city hosted by the Collective.

BUS

Hanoi has an extensive public bus system, though few tourists take advantage of the rock-bottom fares (3000d). If you're game, pick up the *Xe Buyt Ha Noi* (Hanoi bus map; 5000d) from the Thang Long (p81) bookstore.

MIND THE MAFIA

It happens all over the world and Hanoi is no exception. Many of the drivers who hang out at Noi Bai airport are working in cahoots with hotels and travel agencies in Hanoi. They know every trick in the book and usually carry the cards of all the popular budget hotels. 'It's full today' is popular, as is 'they have a new place, much nicer, number two'. Usually it's a bunch of lies. The best defence is to insist you already have a reservation. Even if the place does turn out to be full, you can plot your own course from there. When it comes to the Vietnam Airlines minibus, the best bet is to bail out at the Vietnam Airlines office, usually the first stop in the centre. Otherwise you will be dragged around endless commission-paying hotels in the Old Quarter. Another option to avoid the nonsense is to book a room in advance and arrange an airport pick-up. Someone will be waiting with a name board and you can wave to the taxi touts as you exit the airport.

CAR & MOTORBIKE

Getting around Hanoi by motorbike means relentless traffic, non-existent road manners and inadequate street lighting. Factor in possible theft, parking hassles and bribe-happy police, and it's not for the timid. Intrepid types can arrange mopeds for around US$5 per day in the Old Quarter.

CYCLO

A few *cyclo* drivers still frequent the Old Quarter, and if you're only going a short distance, it's a great way to experience the city (despite the fumes). Settle on a price first and watch out for overcharging – a common ploy when carrying two passengers is to agree on a price, and then *double* it upon arrival, gesturing 'no, no, no...that was per person'.

Aim to pay around 50,000d for a shortish journey; night rides are more. Few *cyclo* drivers speak English so take a map with you.

ELECTRIC TRAIN

Hanoi's eco-friendly **electric train** (Map p58; per car (six passengers), 250,000d; ⊙ 8.30am-10.30pm) is actually a pretty good way to get your bearings in the city. It traverses a network of 14 stops in the Old Quarter and around Hoan Kiem Lake, parting the flow of motorbikes and pedestrians like a slow-moving white dragon. Nothing really beats haphazardly discovering the nooks and crannies of the Old Quarter by foot, but if you're feeling a tad lazy, the train is worth considering. The main departure point is the northern end of Hoan Kiem Lake, and there's another departure point outside Dong Xuan Market. A full journey around the Old Quarter takes around an hour.

MOTORBIKE TAXI

You won't have any trouble finding a *xe om* (motorbike taxi) in Hanoi. An average journey in the city centre costs around 15,000d to 20,000d, while a trip further to Ho Chi Minh's Mausoleum is around 35,000d to 40,000d. For two or more people, a metered taxi is usually cheaper than a convoy of *xe om*.

TAXI

Several reliable companies offer metered taxis. All charge fairly similar rates. Flag fall is around 20,000d, which takes you 1km to 2km; every kilometre thereafter costs around 15,000d. Some dodgy operators have high-speed meters, so use the following more reliable companies.

Thanh Nga Taxi (☑ 04-3821 5215)
Van Xuan (☑ 04-3822 2888)

AROUND HANOI

The fertile alluvial soils of the Red River Delta nurture a rich rice crop, and many of the communities surrounding Hanoi are still engaged in agriculture. The contrast between modern Hanoi and the rural villages is stark. Many tour operators in Hanoi offer cycling tours to villages near Hanoi – a great way to discover a different world. Lotussia (☑ 04-2249 4668; www.vietnamcycling.com) specialises in cycling tours from Hanoi, some taking in the Thay and Tay Phuong pagodas and nearby handicraft villages. These tours also avoid having to struggle through Hanoi's ferocious traffic, as a minibus takes the strain through the suburbs.

Ho Chi Minh Trail Museum

The Ho Chi Minh Trail Museum (☑ 034-382 0889; Hwy 6; admission 20,000d; ⊙ 7.30-11.30am & 1.30-2.30pm Mon-Sat) is dedicated to the famous supply route from the Communist north to the occupied south of Vietnam. The displays, including an abundance of American ammunition and weaponry as well as some powerful photography, document all too clearly the extreme effort and organisation needed to keep the show on the road, and the death and destruction involved. Quite simply, defeat was not an option for the VC, whatever the odds. There's a model of the trail, which shows the nightmarish terrain through which it passed. It's located about 13km southwest of Hanoi and can be combined with Van Phuc handicraft village or the Perfume Pagoda.

Perfume Pagoda

North Vietnam's very own Marble Mountains, the Perfume Pagoda (Chua Huong; admission incl return boat trip 90,000d) is a striking complex of pagodas and Buddhist shrines built into the karst cliffs of Huong Tich Mountain (Mountain of the Fragrant Traces). Among the better-known sites here are Thien Chu (Pagoda Leading to Heaven); Giai Oan Chu (Purgatorial Pagoda), where the faithful believe deities purify souls, cure sufferings and grant offspring to childless families; and Huong Tich Chu (Pagoda of the Perfumed Vestige). It's very popular with Vietnamese domestic tourists.

Great numbers of Buddhist pilgrims come here during a festival that begins in the middle of the second lunar month and lasts until the last week of the third lunar month (usually corresponding to March and April). It's very busy during this period, especially on the even dates of the lunar month; you'll have a much easier time if you establish the lunar date and plan to visit on an odd date. Weekends tend to draw crowds year-round, with pilgrims and other visitors spending their time boating, hiking and exploring the caves. Litter and hawkers are part and parcel of the visit, and some hawkers are persistent enough to hassle visitors all the way to the top.

The Perfume Pagoda is about 60km southwest of Hanoi by road. Getting there requires a journey first by road, then by river, then on foot or by cable car.

Travel from Hanoi by car for two hours to My Duc, then take a small boat, usually rowed by women, for one hour to the foot of the mountain. This entertaining boat trip travels along scenic waterways between limestone cliffs. Allow a couple more hours to climb to the top and return. The path to the summit is steep in places and if it's raining the ground can get very slippery. There's also a cable car to the summit (one-way/return 80,000/120,000d), and a smart combination is to catch the cable car up and then walk down.

Most tour operators and some traveller cafes in Hanoi offer inexpensive tours to the pagoda for around US$20 (inclusive of transport, guide and lunch). Small-group tours cost around US$30. This is one of those places where it is easier to take a tour, as it's a pain by public transport.

Handicraft Villages

Numerous villages surrounding Hanoi specialise in cottage industries. Visiting these settlements can make a rewarding day trip, though having a good guide helps make the journey really worthwhile. Most Hanoi tour operators offer departures to these villages.

Bat Trang is known as the 'ceramic village'. Here, artisans mass-produce ceramic vases and other pieces in their kilns. It's hot, sweaty work, but the results are superb and very reasonably priced compared with the boutiques in town. There are masses of ceramic shops, but poke around down the lanes and behind the shops to find the kilns. Bat Trang is 13km southeast of Hanoi. Public bus 47 runs here from Long Bien bus station.

Van Phuc specialises in silk. Silk cloth is produced here on looms and lots of visitors like to buy or order tailor-made clothes. Many of the fine silk items you see on sale in Hanoi's P Hang Gai are made in Van Phuc. There's also a pretty village pagoda with a lily pond. Van Phuc is 8km southwest of Hanoi; take city bus 1 from Long Bien bus station.

Dong Ky was known as the 'firecracker village' until 1995, when the Vietnamese government banned firecrackers. With that industry now extinguished, the village survives by producing beautiful traditional furniture inlaid with mother-of-pearl. Dong Ky is 15km northeast of Hanoi. Buses 10 and 54 travel from Long Bien bus station passing around 2km from Dong Ky, from where you'll need to either walk or catch a motorbike taxi to the village.

Thay & Tay Phuong Pagodas

Stunning limestone outcrops loom up from the emerald-green paddy fields, and clinging to the cliffs are these two pagodas, about 20 minutes apart from each other by road.

The pagodas are about 30km west of Hanoi in Ha Tay province. Hanoi travel agents and tour operators offer day trips that take in both pagodas, from US$45 per person. Alternatively, hire a car and driver for about US$80 and plot a rewarding day trip that combines the pagodas and Ba Vi National Park.

◉ Sights

Thay Pagoda   BUDDHIST TEMPLE
(Master's Pagoda; admission 5000d) Also known as Thien Phuc (Heavenly Blessing), Thay Pagoda is dedicated to Thich Ca Buddha (Sakyamuni, the historical Buddha). To the left of the main altar is a statue of the 12th-century monk Tu Dao Hanh, the master in whose honour the pagoda is named. To the right is a statue of King Ly Nhan Tong, who is believed to have been a reincarnation of Tu Dao Hanh.

In front of the pagoda is a small stage built on stilts in the middle of a pond where water-puppet shows are staged during festivals. Follow the path around the outside of the main pagoda building and take a steep 10-minute climb up to a beautiful smaller pagoda perched high on the rock. Thay Pagoda is a big and confusing complex for non-Buddhists – consider hiring a guide.

The pagoda's annual festival is held from the fifth to the seventh days of the third lunar month (approximately March). Visitors enjoy watching water-puppet shows, hiking and exploring caves in the area.

Tay Phuong Pagoda   BUDDHIST TEMPLE

(Pagoda of the West; admission 5000d) Tay Phuong Pagoda, also known as Sung Phuc Pagoda, consists of three single-level structures built in descending order on a hillock that is said to resemble a buffalo. Figures representing 'the conditions of man' are the pagoda's most celebrated feature – carved from jackfruit wood, many date from the 18th century. The earliest construction dates from the 8th century.

Take the steep steps up to the main pagoda building, then find a path at the back that loops down past the other two pagodas and wander through the adjacent hillside village.

Ba Vi National Park

📁 034

Formerly a French hill station, the triple-peaked Ba Vi Mountain (Nui Ba Vi) has been attracting visitors for decades and remains a popular weekend escape for Hanoians. The limestone mountain is now part of the Ba Vi National Park (📁 034-388 1205; per person/ motorbike 10,000/5000d), which has several rare and endangered plants in its protected forest, as well as mammals including two species of rare 'flying' squirrel and bountiful bird life.

There's an orchid garden and a bird garden, and hiking opportunities through the forested slopes. A temple dedicated to Ho Chi Minh sits at the mountain's summit (1276m) – it's a difficult but beautiful 30-minute climb up 1229 steps through the trees. Fog often shrouds the peak, but despite the damp and mist it's eerily atmospheric – visit between April and December for the best chance of clear views down to the Red River valley and Hanoi in the distance.

🍴 Sleeping & Eating

Ba Vi Guesthouse   GUEST HOUSE $

(📁 034-388 1197; r weekdays 180,000-240,000d, weekends 220,000-300,000d; 🏊) Spreads over several blocks in the heart of the park and has a big swimming pool and a moderately priced restaurant (meals 60,000d). Go for one of the less noisy guesthouses away from the pool and restaurant area if you're here on a weekend. You'll need your passport to check in.

❶ Getting There & Away

Ba Vi National Park is about 65km west of Hanoi, and the only practical option for visiting is by hired vehicle from Hanoi. Travelling by motorbike, it is possible to visit Ba Vi before taking a beautiful riverside road down to Hoa Binh and onwards into the northwest.

There has been some confusion between attractions near Ba Vi town – which is well away from the park boundaries – and Ba Vi National Park. Make sure your driver knows you want the national park.

Co Loa Citadel

Dating from the 3rd century BC, Co Loa Citadel (Co Loa Thanh; admission per person/ car 10,000/20,000d; ⏰7.30am-5.30pm) was the first fortified citadel in Vietnamese history and became the national capital during the reign of Ngo Quyen (AD 939-44). Only vestiges of the ancient ramparts, which enclosed an area of about 5 sq km, remain.

In the centre of the citadel are temples dedicated to the rule of King An Duong Vuong (257-208 BC), who founded the legendary Thuc dynasty, and his daughter My Nuong (Mi Chau). Legend tells that My Nuong showed her father's magic crossbow trigger (which made him invincible in battle) to her husband, the son of a Chinese general. He stole it and gave it to his father. With this not-so-secret weapon, the Chinese defeated An Duong Vuong, beginning 1000 years of Chinese occupation.

Co Loa Citadel is 16km north of central Hanoi in Dong Anh district, and can be visited as a short detour while on the way to or from Tam Dao Hill Station. Public bus 46 (5000d) runs here every 15 minutes from My Dinh bus station in Hanoi. Buses run regularly from Hanoi's Luong Yen station to My Dinh. From the Co Loa bus station, cross the bridge, turn left and walk for around 500m.

Tam Dao Hill Station

📞 0211/ELEV 930M

Nestling below soaring forest-clad peaks, Tam Dao is a former French hill station in a spectacular setting northwest of Hanoi. Today it's a popular summer resort – a favoured weekend escape for Hanoians, who come here to revel in the temperate climate and make merry in the extensive selection of restaurants and bars. Founded in 1907 by the French, most of its colonial villas were destroyed during the Franco–Viet Minh War, only to be replaced with brutalist concrete architecture. Tam Dao is a useful base for hiking, but the town itself is an unattractive sprawl of hotel blocks.

Remember that it is cool up in Tam Dao, and this part of Vietnam has a distinct winter. Don't be caught unprepared.

The best time to visit is between late April and mid-October, when the mist sometimes lifts and the weather can be fine. Weekends can be packed but weekdays are far less busy.

◎ Sights & Activities

Tam Dao National Park　　NATURE RESERVE
(admission 20,000d) Tam Dao National Park was designated in 1996 and covers much of the area around the town. Tam Dao means 'Three Islands', and the three summits of Tam Dao Mountain, all about 1400m in height, are sometimes visible to the northeast of the hill station, floating like islands in the mist.

There are at least 64 species of mammal (including langurs) and 239 species of bird in the park, but you'll need a good local guide and be prepared to do some hiking to find them. Illegal hunting remains a big problem.

Hikes vary from half an hour return to the waterfall, to day treks taking in bamboo forest and primary tropical forest. A guide is essential for the longer hikes and can be hired from 400,000d; enquire at the Mela Hotel.

🛏 Sleeping & Eating

The town is easy to navigate, so look around and negotiate. There are also plenty of hotel restaurants and good *com pho* (rice-noodle soup) places. Try to avoid eating the local wildlife; you'll frequently see civet, squirrel, porcupine, fox and pheasant advertised, but most of these are endangered species.

Huong Lien Hotel　　HOTEL $
(📞 0211-382 4282; r weekday 250,000d, r weekend 350,000d; 🖥) Offering decent value for the price, most of the rooms here have balconies to make the most of those misty mountain views. There's a little restaurant as well (mains 120,000d to 200,000d).

Nha Khach Ngan Hang　　GUEST HOUSE $
(📞 0989 152 969; r 180,000-200,000d; 🖥) Opposite the Phuong Nam Quan restaurant, this spotless guesthouse sits beside a sprawling plot of *xu xu*, the local green vegetable. Try it with some garlic when you ask about accommodation.

Mela Hotel　　HOTEL $$
(📞 0211-382 4321; melatamdao@yahoo.com; weekday/weekend r from 850,000d/1,100,000d; ❄🖥🏊) A modern, attractive, European-managed hotel with 20 spacious, comfortable rooms (some include fireplaces) and most with balconies and wonderful valley views. The in-house Bamboo restaurant (meals 60,000d to 200,000d) has an eclectic menu that features everything from French food to burgers, sandwiches and spring rolls. Rack rates are a little silly, so come midweek and start negotiating.

❶ Getting There & Away

Tam Dao is 85km northwest of Hanoi in Vinh Phuc province. Buses to the town of Vinh Yen (50,000d, frequent 6am to 4pm) leave from Hanoi's Gia Lam bus station. From Vinh Yen hire a *xe om* (around 150,000d one-way) or a taxi (300,000d) to travel the 24km road up to Tam Dao.

On a motorbike from Hanoi, the journey takes around three hours, and the last part of the ride into the national park is beautiful.

Northern Vietnam

Best Places to Eat

➡ The Hill Station Signature Restaurant (p134)

➡ Thanh Lan Com Binh Dan (p117)

➡ Sapa Market (p133)

Best Places to Stay

➡ Ancient House Homestay (p110)

➡ Mai Chau Nature Lodge (p122)

➡ Hmong Mountain Retreat (p132)

Why Go?

Northern Vietnam's top ticket is the wildly popular Halong Bay, and nearby Cat Ba Island offers excellent hiking, biking and rock climbing. The karst connection continues into Cao Bang province – an essential detour are the sublime lakes of Ba Be National Park – and then west into Ha Giang, Vietnam's emerging destination for travellers, which hugs the Chinese border.

Further west the landscape segues into towering evergreen peaks and fertile river valleys. This is the heartland of hill-tribe culture with markets enlivened by the scarlet headdresses of the Dzao, the indigo fabrics of the Black H'mong and the brocaded aprons of the Flower H'mong.

Sapa is a great base for hiking and stunning vistas of Fansipan, Vietnam's highest peak. From this former French hill station, the fabled northwest loop road crosses high mountain passes to historic Dien Bien Phu, before crossing lush lowland valleys south to sleepy Mai Chau.

When to Go
Halong City

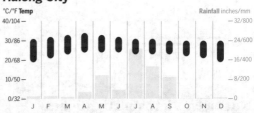

Jan–Mar Cool and drizzly; fog in Halong Bay and very cold overnight lows in Sapa.

May–Aug Tropical storms in the northeast, which may disrupt Halong Bay tours.

Oct–Dec The best time to be around Sapa and Halong Bay.

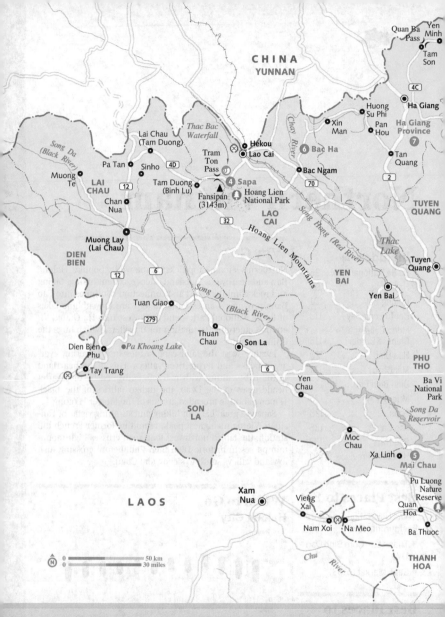

Northern Vietnam Highlights

1 Escape **Halong Bay's** tourist buzz by gently kayaking into hidden lagoons and grottoes (p103).

2 Hike, bike and climb your way around the great outdoors in Cat Ba Island's fascinating **national park** (p106).

3 Board a boat to glide through lakes and rivers, and spend the night with a local

Tay family in **Ba Be National Park** (p96).

4 Walk misty mountain trails through sublime scenery and hill-tribe villages around **Sapa** (p128).

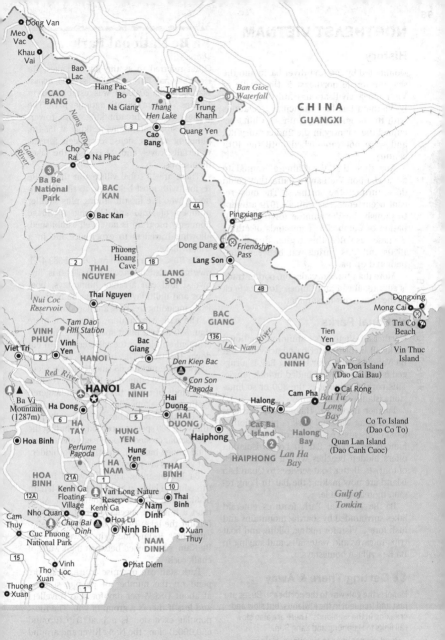

5 Escape from the noise and bustle of busy, busy Hanoi by trekking, kayaking and biking in the **Mai Chau** region (p121).

6 Make for the minority markets – a blaze of colour when the Flower H'mong are in town – around **Bac Ha** (p137).

7 Negotiate Vietnam's newest traveller frontier – the improbably scenic mountains and valleys of **Ha Giang Province** (p140).

NORTHEAST VIETNAM

History

Dominated by the Red River basin and the sea, the fertile northeast is the cradle of Vietnamese civilisation. Until very recently, Vietnam has had challenging relations with the neighbouring Chinese. China occupied the country in the 2nd century BC, and were not vanquished until the 10th century.

Any time that the Chinese wanted to advance upon Vietnam's affairs, they could do so through the northeast. The most recent occurrence was China's 1979 attempt to punish the Vietnamese for their occupation of Cambodia. Thousands of ethnic Chinese also fled this region during the 1970s and '80s during war between Vietnam and China.

More than three decades on, border trade is surging ahead and Chinese tourists flock to the region during summer.

National Parks

Northeast Vietnam's stunning national parks all involve water-based activities. Cat Ba National Park, near Halong Bay, is a rugged island liberally shrouded in lush jungle. This park also includes the 300 or so limestone islands of Lan Ha Bay.

Further northeast, Halong Bay becomes Bai Tu Long National Park, a procession of karst landscapes easily the equal to its more famous neighbour. Bai Tu Long's isolation offers hidden beaches with a relative lack of tourists. Better boat services to Quan Lan Island are now making the Bai Tu Long region more accessible.

Ba Be National Park features emerald lakes surrounded by soaring mountains and lush forest. Visit for hiking, biking and boat trips to caves and waterfalls, and staying in Ba Be's village homestays.

❶ Getting There & Away

Hanoi is the gateway to the northeast. Buses are fast and frequent in the lowlands, but slow and creaking in the highlands. There are also slow rail links to Haiphong and Lang Son.

Road connections to Haiphong, Halong City and Lang Son are fast, but as the terrain gets more mountainous, things slow down considerably.

Ba Be National Park

📋 0281

Often referred to as the Ba Be Lakes, Ba Be National Park (📋 0281-389 4014; admission per person 20,000d) was established in 1992 as Vietnam's eighth national park. The scenery here is breathtaking, with towering limestone mountains peaking at 1554m, plunging valleys, dense evergreen forests, waterfalls, caves and, of course, the lakes themselves.

There are 13 tribal villages in the Ba Be region, with most belonging to the Tay minority, who live in stilt homes, plus smaller numbers of Dzao and H'mong. A village homestay program is now well established, allowing travellers to experience life in a tribal village.

Ba Be Center Tourism (📋 0281-389 4721; www.babecentertourism.com; Bolu village) is Tay-owned and can arrange homestays, boat trips and multiday tours of Ba Be National Park, including trekking and kayaking.

The park is a rainforest area with more than 550 named plant species, and the government subsidises the villagers not to cut down the trees. The hundreds of wildlife species here include 65 (mostly rarely seen) mammals, 353 butterflies, 106 species of fish, four kinds of turtle, the highly endangered Vietnamese salamander and even the Burmese python. Ba Be birdlife is equally prolific, with 233 species recorded, including the spectacular crested serpent eagle and the oriental honey buzzard. Hunting is forbidden, but villagers are permitted to fish.

Ba Be (meaning Three Bays) is in fact three linked lakes, which have a total length of 8km and a width of about 400m. More than a hundred species of freshwater fish inhabit the lake. Two of the lakes are separated by a 100m-wide strip of water called Be Kam, sandwiched between high walls of chalk rock.

Park staff can organise tours. Costs depend on the number of people, starting at about US$35 per day for solo travellers and less if there's a group of you. The most popular excursion is a boat trip (around 650,000d) along the Nang River and around the lake – keep an eye out for kingfishers and raptors. The boats can accommodate up to 12 people and the tour usually takes in the tunnel-like Hang Puong (Puong Cave), which is about 40m high and 300m long, and completely passes through a mountain. As many as 7000 bats (belonging to 18 species) are said to live in this cave. Further stops can be made at the pretty Tay village of Cam Ha (where every timber house has a satellite dish) and the startling, circular, jungle-rimmed lagoon of Ao Tien, before finishing at An Ma Pagoda, situated on a little island in the middle of the lake.

The Thac Dau Dang (Dau Dang or Ta Ken Waterfall), consisting of a series of spectacular cascades between sheer walls of rock, is another possible destination. Just 200m below the rapids is a small Tay village called Hua Tang.

Other options include dugout-canoe tours or combination cycling, boating and walking possibilities. Longer treks can also be arranged.

The park entrance fee is payable at a checkpoint on the road into the park, about 15km before the park headquarters, just beyond the town of Cho Ra.

Sleeping & Eating

The only hotel rooms inside the park are in a government-owned complex (0281-389 4026; r from 220,000d, cabin 220,000d, bungalow 350,000d) next to the park headquarters. The best rooms here are in attractive semi-detached bungalows, each with two double beds, while the cabins are small and fairly basic. A few rooms are available too. The complex has two restaurants (meals from 50,000d), though you should place your order an hour or so before you want to eat. For a less formal setting, you'll find a line of cookshacks by the chalets that sell cheap meals and snacks and are run by local villagers.

It's also possible to stay in Pac Ngoi village, where a successful homestay (per person 60,000d) program has been established so visitors can stay in a stilt house. The park office usually organises this, but you can just show up and check in too. The very well kept Hoa Son Guesthouse (0281-389 4065) is one of the best, with a huge balcony and lake views, but there are at least a dozen other options, all of which have hot-water bathrooms. Meals (50,000d to 80,000d) are available, and can include fresh fish from the lake.

Another option is to use the nearby town of Cho Ra as a base. The Thuy Dung Guesthouse (0281-387 6354; 5 Tieu Khu; r 300,000d;

) is a friendly, family-run spot with balconies, wooden shutters and views of the nearby rice paddies. There's a good restaurant on site, and the staff can arrange onward transport by boat from Cho Ra (400,000d) into the heart of the national park. The journey takes you past waterfalls and minority villages.

Information

Only cash is accepted. The nearest ATM and internet access is in Cho Ra.

Getting There & Away

Ba Be National Park is 240km from Hanoi, 61km from Bac Kan and 18km from Cho Ra.

Most people visit Ba Be as part of a tour, or by chartered vehicle from Hanoi (a 4WD is not necessary). The one-way journey from Hanoi takes about six hours.

BUS & BOAT

By public transport, the most direct route is on a daily bus at noon from the Gia Lam bus station in Hanoi to Cho Ra (180,000d, six hours). This allows travellers to overnight in Cho Ra before continuing on to Ba Be by boat the following morning. A direct bus (90,000d, five hours) also departs Cao Bang for Ba Be Lakes at noon.

BUS & MOTORBIKE

Take a bus from Hanoi to Phu Thong (180,000d, five hours) via Thai Nguyen and/or Bac Kan, and from there take another bus to Cho Ra (7000d, one hour). In Cho Ra arrange a motorbike (about 100,000d) to cover the last 18km.

If you're heading northeast from Ba Be, it's best to get a local bus from Cho Ra to Na Phac and get a connection there to Cao Bang.

Con Son & Den Kiep Bac

Most appealing to domestic travellers, Con Son and Den Kiep Bac are potential diversions en route to Haiphong or Halong City.

Con Son was home to Nguyen Trai (1380–1442), the famed Vietnamese poet, writer and general. Nguyen Trai assisted Emperor Le Loi in his successful battle against the Chinese Ming dynasty in the 15th century. Con Son Pagoda (admission per person/vehicle 5000/15,000d) has a temple honouring Nguyen Trai. It's a strenuous 600-step climb. Alternatively, loop past a spring through pine forests, and return down the steps.

Nearby, Den Kiep Bac (Kiep Bac Temple; admission per person/vehicle 5000/15,000d) is dedicated to Tran Hung Dao (1228–1300). Founded in 1300, the temple sits where Tran Hung Dao is said to have died. Within the complex there's an exhibition on his exploits, but you'll need someone to translate. The annual **Tran Hung Dao Festival** is held from the 18th to the 20th day of the eighth lunar month, usually in October.

Den Kiep Bac and Con Son are in Hai Duong province, about 80km east of Hanoi. With your own wheels, it's easy to detour en route to Haiphong or Halong Bay.

Haiphong

📞 031 / POP 1,884,600

With graceful tree-lined boulevards, an impressive array of colonial-era buildings and an unhurried air, Haiphong is a very approachable city. It's an important seaport and industrial centre, but few visitors linger. If you do pass through, you'll find minimal hassles compared to Vietnam's main tourism centres, with barely a tout to be found. Cafe culture is very strong here and many central places have street tables – perfect for people-watching.

Haiphong is a major transport hub, and well connected to Cat Ba Island and Hanoi by bus, boat and train.

History

The French took possession of Haiphong in 1874 and the city developed rapidly, becoming a major port. Heavy industry evolved through the proximity to coal supplies.

The French bombardment of Haiphong in 1946 killed thousands and was a catalyst for the ensuing Franco-Viet Minh War. Between 1965 and 1972 Haiphong came under air and naval attack from the US, and the city's harbour was mined to disrupt Soviet military supplies. In the late 1970s and 1980s Haiphong experienced a mass exodus that included many ethnic Chinese refugees, who left taking much of the city's fishing fleet with them.

Today Haiphong is a fast-growing city, attracting investment from multinational corporations lured by its port facilities and transport links.

◉ Sights & Activities

★ **Haiphong Museum**　　MUSEUM

(66 P Dien Bien Phu; admission 5000d; ⊙8am-12.30pm & 2-4pm Mon-Fri, 7.30-9.30pm Wed & Sun) In a splendid colonial building, the

Haiphong Museum concentrates on the city's history. Some displays have English translations and the museum's garden harbours a diverse collection of war detritus.

★ **Queen of the Rosary Cathedral**　　CATHEDRAL

(P Hoang Van Thu; ⊙24hr) FREE Haiphong's elegant Roman Catholic cathedral was built in the 19th century and comprehensively restored in 2010. The building's grey towers are a local landmark, and the inner courtyard is spacious and relaxing – until friendly children from the adjacent primary school are let loose after classes.

★ **Opera House**　　HISTORICAL BUILDING

(P Quang Trung) With a facade embellished with white columns, Haiphong's neoclassical Opera House dates from 1904. Unfortunately it is usually not possible to view the interior.

Du Hang Pagoda　　BUDDHIST TEMPLE

(121 P Chua Hang; ⊙7am-10pm) Du Hang Pagoda was founded three centuries ago. It's been rebuilt several times, but remains a fine example of traditional Vietnamese architecture and sculpture. P Chua Hang is a narrow thoroughfare, bustling with Haiphong street life. The pagoda is around 1.5km southwest of Haiphong's main street, Dien Bien Phu.

Navy Museum　　MUSEUM

(P Dien Bien Phu; ⊙8-11am Tue, Thu & Sat) FREE The Navy Museum is interesting for visiting sailors and US Vietnam veterans.

🛏 Sleeping

Duyen Hai Hotel　　HOTEL $

(☑031-384 2134; 6 Đ Nguyen Tri Phuong; r 250,000-400,000d; ❄❀) With a recently renovated reception area and decent rooms, the Duyen Hai offers fair value and is handily near Lac Long bus station and Ben Binh harbour.

Bao Anh Hotel　　HOTEL $$

(☑031-382 3406; www.hotelbaoanh.com; 20 P Minh Khai; r 400,000-700,000d; ❄@❀) Refurbished in trendy minimalist style, the Bao Anh features a great location in a leafy street framed by plane tress and buzzy cafes. It's a short walk to good beer places if you're after something stronger. Reception is definitely open to negotiation.

Monaco Hotel　　HOTEL $$

(☑031-374 6468; www.haiphongmonacohotel.com; 103 P Dien Bien Phu; r US$30-50; ❄❀) This

Haiphong

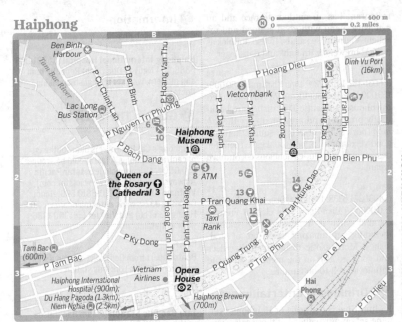

modern and central hotel has a real polish about it, including the smart lobby where the helpful reception staff speak some English. The spacious, spotless rooms come with two double beds, and the attractive bathrooms are well presented Breakfast is included.

Harbour View Hotel HOTEL **$$$**
(☑031-382 7827; www.harbourviewvietnam.com; 4 P Tran Phu; r US$95-125; ❈✳@🛜🏊) Built in replica-colonial style in 1998, this stately hotel has comfortable rooms and excellent facilities, including a gym, spa and restaurant. Breakfast is included, and the superfriendly team on reception can arrange tours around Haiphong in a vintage Citroën car. Be sure to try for a substantial discount off rack rates.

✗ Eating

Haiphong is noted for its fresh seafood. Visit P Quang Trung for seafood restaurants with point-and-cook tanks, as well as *bia hoi* (beer) joints. For more stylish cafes and restaurants, take a wander along P Minh Khai.

Com Vietnam VIETNAMESE **$**
(☑031-384 1698; 4A P Hoang Van Thu; mains 40,000-60,000d; ⊘11am-9pm) This restaurant hits the spot for its affordable local seafood

Haiphong

◎ Top Sights
1 Haiphong Museum B2
2 Opera House B3
3 Queen of the Rosary Cathedral B2

◎ Sights
4 Navy Museum C2

⌂ Sleeping
5 Bao Anh Hotel C2
6 Duyen Hai Hotel B1
7 Harbour View Hotel D1
8 Monaco Hotel B2

✗ Eating
9 Big Man Restaurant..............................C3
 BKK ....(see 5)
10 Com Vietnam..B2
11 Van Tue D1

◉ Drinking & Nightlife
12 Caffe Tra Cuc C2
13 Julie's Bar...C2
14 Vuon Dua C2

and Vietnamese specialities. Diminutive, unpretentious and with a small patio.

★ Big Man Restaurant RESTAURANT **$$**
(☑031-384 2383; 7 P Tran Hung Dao; mains from 100,000d; ⊘11am-11pm) This sprawling

restaurant has an outdoor terrace and an extensive menu with good seafood and excellent Vietnamese salads. It also doubles as a microbrewery, with light and dark lager.

BKK THAI $$

(☑031-382 1018; 22 P Minh Khai; mains 80,000-150,000d; ☺11.30am-10pm) At this restored townhouse, authentic Thai dishes are beautifully prepared and presented – try the *lab moo* (pork salad) or pepper squid; there are good vegetarian options too. Leave room for dessert, which includes delicious coconut ice cream.

Van Tue SEAFOOD $$

(☑031-374 6338; 1 P Hoang Dieu; mains 100,000-250,000d; ☺11am-11pm) This elegant French-colonial villa is renowned for seafood, including an amazing selection of crab dishes. More exotic dishes featuring deer and goat are also on the menu. A favourite with local well-to-do families.

 Drinking & Entertainment

P Minh Khai is the heart of Haiphong's caffeine action. Virtually all of these cafes have street terraces, serve beer and have a snack menu.

Haiphong Brewery BIA HOI

(16 Đ Lach Tray; ☺10am-8pm) The local brew is deservedly renowned around Vietnam, and the best place to try it is at the brewery's bustling beer hall. Lunchtimes get very crowded (the food is cheap and very good) but staff can always find room for a few more drinkers. Haiphong brewery is a short cab ride to the southeast of the city centre.

Vuon Dua BIA HOI

(5 P Tran Hung Dao; ☺11am-11pm) Boisterous beer garden with lots of cheap brews, and squid, chicken and pork prepared in many different ways. It's packed with locals every night enjoying a few (not so) quiet beers after work.

Julie's Bar BAR

(22C P Minh Khai; ☺11am-11pm; ☎) Cosy expat hang-out that's the ideal spot to get the low-down on the latest Haiphong gossip.

Caffe Tra Cuc CAFE

(46C P Minh Khai; ☺7am-11pm; ☎) The coffee, done loads of ways, and free wi-fi is lapped up by grizzled regulars and Haiphong trendies alike.

❶ Information

Cafes on P Minh Khai have free wi-fi. ATMs dot the city centre.

Haiphong International Hospital (☑031-395 5888; 124 Nguyen Duc Canh) Recently built and modern, with some English-speaking doctors.

❶ Getting There & Away

AIR

Haiphong's Cat Bi airport is 6km southeast of central Haiphong. A taxi should be around 150,000d. Airlines include **Jetstar Pacific Airways** (☑1900 1550; www.jetstar.com), **Vietnam Airlines** (☑031-3810 890, Hanoi 04-3832 0320; www.vietnamair.com.vn; 30 P Hoang Van Thu) and **VietJet** (☑1900 1886; www.vietjetair.com).

BOAT

Boats depart from Ben Binh Harbour, a short walk from the Lac Long bus station.

BUS

Haiphong has three long-distance bus stations: **Tam Bac Bus Station** (P Tam Bac) Buses to Hanoi (100,000d, two hours, every 10 minutes).

Niem Nghia Bus Station (Đ Tran Nguyen Han) Buses south of Haiphong, such as to Ninh Binh (120,000d, 3½ hours, every 30 minutes).

Lac Long Bus Station (P Cu Chinh Lan) Buses to Halong City (Bai Chay; 70,000d, 1½ hours, every 30 minutes), and regular connections to Mong Cai (120,000d, four hours, approximately every two hours) near the Chinese border. Lac Long also has buses to and from Hanoi (80,000d, two hours, every 10 minutes), convenient for those connecting with the Cat Ba boats at nearby Ben Binh Harbour.

CAR & MOTORBIKE

Haiphong is 103km from Hanoi on the expressway, Hwy 5.

TRAIN

A slow spur-line service travels daily to Hanoi's Long Bien station (48,000d, 2½ hours, 6.05am, 8.55am, 2.55pm, 6.40pm).

❶ Getting Around

Try **Haiphong Taxi** (☑031-383 8383) or **Taxi Mai Linh** (☑031-383 3833). A *xe om* (motorbike taxi) from the bus stations to the hotels should be around 30,000d.

Halong Bay

🎵 033

Imagine 2000 or more islands rising from the emerald waters of the Gulf of Tonkin and you have a vision of breathtaking beauty. *Halong* translates as 'where the dragon descends into the sea', and legend claims the islands of Halong Bay were created by a great dragon from the mountains. As it charged towards the coast, its flailing tail gouged out valleys and crevasses. When it finally plunged into the sea, the area filled with water, leaving only the pinnacles visible.

Designated a World Heritage site in 1994, this mystical landscape of limestone islets is often compared to Guilin in China or Krabi in southern Thailand. In reality, Halong Bay is more spectacular. The bay's immense number of islands are dotted with wind- and wave-eroded grottoes, and their sparsely forested slopes ring with birdsong.

Visitors to Halong also come to explore the caves. There are few real beaches in Halong Bay, but Lan Ha Bay has sandy coves a short boat hop from Cat Ba Town.

Sprawling Halong City is the bay's main gateway, but the raffish collection of high-rise hotels and karaoke bars is not a great introduction to this incredible site.

Most visitors sensibly opt for tours that include sleeping on a boat in the bay. Some travellers dodge Halong City and head straight for Cat Ba Town, from where trips to less-visited, equally alluring Lan Ha Bay are easily set up. Cat Ba Island can also be a good base for visiting Halong Bay itself.

As the number-one tourist attraction in the northeast, Halong Bay attracts visitors year-round. January to March is often cool and drizzly, and the ensuing fog can make visibility low, but also adds an ethereal air. From May to September tropical storms are frequent, and year-round, tourist boats sometimes need to alter their itineraries, depending on the weather. Some tour companies offer full or partial refunds if tours are cancelled; check when you book.

👁 Sights & Activities

Caves

Halong Bay's islands are peppered with caves, many now illuminated with technicolor lighting effects. Sadly, litter and trinket-touting vendors are also part of the experience.

NORTHERN VIETNAM HALONG BAY

DON'T MISS

CRUISING THE KARSTS: TOURS TO HALONG BAY

There are many ways to experience the ethereal beauty of Halong Bay. Unless you have a private yacht (or you're an Olympic kayaker), you'll have to take a tour of some kind.

For a serious splurge, cruising the karsts aboard a luxury Chinese-style junk is hard to beat. There's also a very luxurious paddle ship, based on a French craft from the early 20th century. But be aware that nearly all of these luxury trips operate on a fixed itinerary, taking in the well-known caves and islands, and simply do not have the time to stray far from Halong City. Many 'two-day' tours actually involve less than 24 hours on a boat (and cost hundreds of dollars per person).

At the other end of the scale, budget tours sold out of Hanoi start from a rock-bottom US$60 per person for a dodgy day trip, and rise to around US$220 for two nights on the bay with kayaking. For around US$100 to US$130, you should get a worthwhile overnight cruise.

We get many complaints about poor service, bad food and rats running around boats, but these tend to be on the ultrabudget tours. Spend a little more and enjoy the experience a whole lot more. It can be a false economy signing up for one of the budget tours, and it's also potentially a matter of safety.

Most tours include transport and meals, and sometimes include island hikes. Drinks are extra. Most of these trips follow a strict itinerary, with planned stops at illuminated caves often at the same time as many of the other boats operating out of Bai Chay.

If you have more time and want to experience Halong Bay without the crowds, consider Cat Ba Island. Here you'll find operators who concentrate on Lan Ha Bay, which is less frequented, relatively untouched and has a few sandy beaches.

Because of weather, boat tours are sometimes cancelled and you'll probably be offered a full or partial refund. Ascertain in advance what that will be.

Halong Bay & Bai Tu Long Bay

QUANG NINH

Nam Vap (1142m)

Dong Mung

Troi

Nga Hai

Mong Duong

Cam Pha

Cua Ong

18

Cai Rong

Van Don Island (Dao Cai Bau)

Dao Ha Loan

Bai Dai (Long Beach)

Bai Tu Long National Park

Dao Cao Lo

Dao Sau Nam

Co To Island (Dao Co To)

Gulf of Tonkin

Minh Chau

Minh Chau Ferry

Van Don Trading Port Ruins

Son Hao

Quan Lan

Quan Lan Town

Quan Lan Ferry

Quan Lan Island (Dao Canh Cuoc)

Tra Ban Island (Dao Tra Ban)

Van Hai Island (Cu Lao Mang)

Dao Thuong Mai

Dao Ha Mai

Dao The Vang

Dao Trao

Dao Phoung Hoang

Ngoc Vung

Beach Huts

Bai Tu Long Bay

Ha Tu

Dao Cong Dong

Dao Cong Do

World Heritage Zone

Halong Bay

Dao Titop

Hang Trong

Hang Sung Sot

Dao Hang Trai (Ile de l'Union)

Dao Dau Be

Hon Cat Dua

Ben Beo

Cat Ba

Lan Ha Bay

Halong City

Bai Chay

Dao Hang Dau Go & Hang Thien Cung

Dao Hang Dau Go (Ile des Merveilles)

Viet Hai Village

Whisper of Nature

Cat Ba National Park

Echo Lake

Hang Park Trung Trang

Cat Ba Eco Lodge

Hospital

Cai Vieng (Phu Long) Cave

Gia Luan harbour

Cat Ba Island

Dao Tuan Chau

Hoang Tan

Cat Hai

HAI PHONG

Haiphong (40km)

Haiphong (17km)

18

229

0 ___ 10 km
0 ___ 6 miles

Hang Dau Go (Cave of Wooden Stakes) is a huge cave consisting of three chambers that you reach via 90 steps. Among the stalactites of the first hall, scores of gnomes appear to be holding a meeting. The walls of the second chamber sparkle if a bright light is shone on them. The cave derives its name from its third chamber's role in Vietnamese history. Part of the same system, the nearby Hang Thien Cung has 'cauliflower' limestone growths as well as stalactites and stalagmites.

The popular Hang Sung Sot (Surprise Cave) has three vast chambers; in the second there's a pink-lit rock phallus, called the 'Cock Rock' by some guides. Not surprisingly it's regarded as a fertility symbol.

Hang Trong (Drum Grotto) is named because when the wind blows through its stalactites and stalagmites, the effect resembles the sound of distant drumbeats.

Which of the caves you'll visit depends on several factors, including the weather and the number of other boats in the vicinity.

Islands

Dao Titop (Titop Island) is a small island with a scruffy little beach. Make straight for the island's summit for superb panoramic views of Halong Bay.

Cat Ba Island is the most developed of Halong Bay's islands and Cat Ba Town is very close to the gorgeous Lan Ha Bay region.

Kayaking

A kayak among the karsts is an option on most Halong Bay tours. Count on about an hour's paddling, often including negotiating your way through karst grottoes and around lagoons, or to a floating village in the bay. The villagers here farm fish, which are caught offshore and fattened up in netted enclosures. Most tour operators include a visit as part of their Halong Bay itineraries. These are probably also where your evening meal will come from.

If you're really keen on kayaking, contact Handspan Adventure Travel (p83) in Hanoi, which runs professionally organised trips, has qualified guides and operates beach camps. Trips are operated from less touristed Lan Ha Bay.

ⓘ Information

All visitors must purchase entry tickets for the national park. Tickets for daytime visits are between 80,000d and 120,000d, and overnight stays are 320,000d. Note that visitors must

---

ⓘ WATCH THOSE VALUABLES!

Take real care with your valuables when cruising the waters of Halong Bay. Do not leave them unattended as they might grow legs and walk. Always try to ensure there is someone you know and trust watching your gear on a day cruise. When it comes to overnight cruises, most boats have lockable cabins.

---

also purchase additional tickets (30,000d to 50,000d) for separate attractions like caves, islands and fishing villages within the park. Most admission fees are included with organised tours, but check when you book.

The official **Halong Bay Tourist Information Centre** (☑ 033-384 7481; www.halong.org. vn; ⊘7am-4pm) is at Bai Chay tourist dock in Halong City.

ⓘ Getting There & Away

Taking a tour is certainly convenient, and many are pretty good value.

It's also possible to head here independently. The regular run is by bus from Hanoi to Bai Chay (Halong City), and then by xe om or taxi to Bai Chay harbour. At bustling Bai Chay, you can book a tour, but once you factor in getting there from Hanoi it's actually not much cheaper. These day-trip boats are also usually crowded, and often come with a soundtrack of Vietnamese karaoke.

There are also tour boats running from Bai Chay via Halong Bay to Cat Ba Island. Alternatively, head directly to Cat Ba Island from Hanoi and arrange a boat trip from there to explore Lan Ha Bay.

ⓘ Getting Around

Most boat tours leave from Bai Chay tourist dock in Halong City. Prices are officially regulated and depend upon the route, length of trip and class of boat. This dock is pretty chaotic, with hundreds of people embarking and disembarking from dozens of boats.

Hiring a one-star boat for a four-hour cruise costs around 2,000,000d, or it's around 3,000,000d for a six-hour cruise. On weekends, prices rise by around 20%. Costs are usually divided between the total number of people on board.

Halong City

☑ 033 / POP 193,700

Halong City (Bai Chay) is the main gateway to Halong Bay. Though the city enjoys a stunning position on the cusp of Halong

Halong City

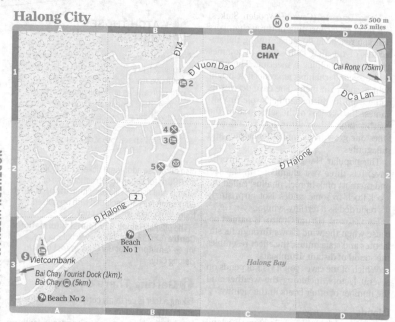

Halong City

😴 Sleeping
1 Novotel	....	A3
2 Thanh Hue Hotel	....	B1
3 Tung Lam Hotel	....	B2

🍴 Eating
4 Asia Restaurant	....	B2
5 Toan Huong	....	B2

Bay, developers have not been kind to it, and high-rise hotels dot the shoreline. However, the majority of food, accommodation and other Halong Bay services are found here.

Most travellers don't stay in town, preferring to spend a night out in Halong Bay itself. Increased competition for a dwindling clientele means budget hotel rates are some of the cheapest in Vietnam. Chinese and Korean visitors are now more prevalent, preferring to enjoy the terra firma attractions of casinos and karaoke after a day exploring the bay.

🛌 Sleeping

Most people stay on a boat in the bay but there are hundreds of hotels around Bai Chay, and prices are very reasonable outside the peak season (June to August) or during the Tet festival.

Virtually all budget accommodation is on the hotel alley of Ð Vuon Dao, home to around 50 near-identical minihotels. Comfortable doubles are around US$15. Midrange and top-end hotels are scattered along Ð Halong, many commanding great views.

Thanh Hue Hotel   HOTEL $
(☎ 033-384 7612; Ð Vuon Dao; r US$12-18; ❄ @ 🤖) Look for the powder blue paint job on this good-value hotel. Most rooms have cracking views of the bay from their balconies. It's a bit of a walk uphill after a seafood meal and a few beers, but well worth it.

Tung Lam Hotel   HOTEL $
(☎ 033-364 0743; 29 Ð Vuon Dao; r US$10-16; ❄ 🤖) This minihotel is making a little more effort than most on this strip. All rooms have two beds, a TV, a minibar and en suite. Those at the front are spacious and include a balcony.

Novotel   HOTEL $$$
(☎ 033-384 8108; www.novotelhalongbay.com; Ð Halong; r from US$110; ❄ ❄ @ 🤖 ≋) This hip hotel fuses Asian and Japanese influences with contemporary details. The rooms are stunning, with teak floors, marble bathrooms and sliding screens to divide living areas. Facilities include an oval infinity pool, an espresso bar and a great restaurant.

Eating

For cheap, filling food, there are modest places at the bottom of Đ Vuon Dao with English menus. Seafood lovers should head to the harbour-front Đ Halong.

Toan Huong VIETNAMESE $
(☑ 033-384 4651; 1 Đ Vuon Dao; mains from 50,000d; ⊙10am-10pm) A simple place with friendly staff, a street terrace and an extensive menu (in English) with a bit of everything: Western breakfasts, fresh seafood and imported wine.

Asia Restaurant VIETNAMESE $
(☑ 033-384 6927; 24 Đ Vuon Dao; mains 60,000-100,000d; ⊙10am-10pm) A clean, attractive place that's geared to travellers' tastes, with good Vietnamese food and a smattering of Western favourites.

ℹ Information

Main post office (Đ Halong) At the bottom of Vuon Dao.

Vietcombank (Đ Halong) Exchanges cash and has an ATM.

ℹ Getting There & Away

BUS

All buses leave Bai Chay bus station, 6km south of central Bai Chay, just off Hwy 18. Note that many long-distance buses will be marked 'Bai Chay' rather than 'Halong City'. The overnight bus to Sapa departing at 6.45pm is a good option if you don't wish to return to Hanoi. For Tam Coc, there are also direct buses to Ninh Binh.

For Cai Rong Pier (Cai Rong Pha) on the island of Van Don – where you can catch onward ferries to the islands of Bai Tu Long – either catch a direct bus to Van Don, or get off at the junction town of Cua Ong on any Mong Cai or Lang Son bus. Then catch a xe om or taxi to the pier. Not all Van Don buses continue to Cai Rong Pier, so check at the Bai Chay bus station.

Buses from Halong City:

DESTINATION	COST (D)	DURATION & FREQUENCY
Hanoi	100,000	4hr; frequent
Haiphong	50,000	2hr; frequent to 3pm
Mong Cai	90,000	4hr; every 40min to 3pm
Van Don	60,000	1½ hr; approx hourly
Lang Son	110,000	5½ hr; 11.45am & 12.45pm
Sapa	450,000	12hr; 6.45pm
Ninh Binh	130,000	4hr; 5.30am & 11.30am

CAR & MOTORBIKE

Halong City is 160km from Hanoi and 55km from Haiphong. The one-way trip from Hanoi to Halong City takes about three hours by private vehicle.

ℹ Getting Around

Bai Chay is quite spread out; **Mai Linh** (☑ 033-382 2226) is a reliable taxi option.

Cat Ba Island

☑ 031 / 13,500
Rugged, craggy and jungle-clad Cat Ba, the largest island in Halong Bay, is northern Vietnam's adventure-sport and ecotourism hub.

In recent years Cat Ba Town has experienced a hotel boom, and a chain of ugly concrete hotels now frames a once-lovely bay. But the rest of the island is largely untouched, and with idyllic Lan Ha Bay just offshore you'll soon overlook Cat Ba Town's overdevelopment.

Most of the year Cat Ba Town is a laid-back place, and an excellent base for activities around the island, or sailing and kayaking around Lan Ha Bay. On summer weekends Cat Ba turns into a roaring resort, filling up with vacationing Vietnamese. Hotel prices double or treble and there's an excess of karaoke joints and hubbub. Cars are banned from the promenade, which is taken over by a sea of strolling holidaymakers. Weekdays are saner, but still busy between June and August.

Ho Chi Minh paid a visit to Cat Ba Island on 1 April 1951 and there is an annual festival to commemorate the event. During this time, expect lots of waterfront karaoke and techno beats from 8am to midnight.

Almost half of Cat Ba Island (with a total area of 354 sq km) and 90 sq km of the adjacent waters were declared a national park in 1986 to protect the island's diverse ecosystems. Most of the coastline consists of rocky cliffs, but there are some sandy beaches and tiny fishing villages hidden away in small coves.

Lakes, waterfalls and grottoes dot the spectacular limestone hills, the highest rising 331m above sea level. The island's largest body of water is Ech Lake (3 hectares). Almost all of the surface streams are seasonal. Most of the island's rainwater flows into caves and follows underground streams to the sea, creating a shortage of fresh water during the dry season.

Cat Ba's best weather is from late September to November, when air and water temperatures are mild and the skies are mostly clear. December to February is cooler but pleasant. February to April is still good, but you can expect some rain. Summer (June to August) is hot and humid with occasional thunderstorms. This is peak season and the island is packed with Vietnamese tourists.

⊙ Sights

First impressions of Cat Ba Town are not great, but the mediocre vision of a low-rent mini-Manhattan only extends for a street or two behind the promenade. A **Ho Chi Minh monument** stands up on Mountain No 1, the hillock opposite the pier in Cat Ba Town. The **market** at the northern end of the harbour is a great local affair with twitching crabs, jumbo shrimp and pyramids of fresh fruit. Head out of the town for the island's best sights.

Lan Ha Bay   ISLAND
(admission 30,000d) The 300 or so karst islands of Lan Ha Bay are south and east of Cat Ba Town. Geologically they are an extension of Halong Bay, but these islands lie in a different province of Vietnam. The limestone pinnacles and scenery are just as beautiful as Halong Bay, but these islands have the additional attraction of numerous white-sand beaches.

Lan Ha Bay is a fair way from Halong City, so not so many tourist boats venture to this side of the bay. In short, Lan Ha Bay has a more isolated, off-the-beaten-track appeal (and far fewer visitors). There is an admission fee to the bay, but this is often incorporated into the cost of tours.

Around 200 species of fish, 500 species of mollusc, 400 species of arthropod and numerous hard and soft coral live in Lan Ha Bay. Larger marine animals in the area include seals and three species of dolphin.

Sailing and kayak trips here are best organised in Cat Ba Town. With hundreds of beaches to choose from, it's easy to find your own private patch of sand for the day. Camping is permitted on gorgeous Hai Pai Beach (also known as Tiger Beach), which is used as a base camp by the Cat Ba adventure-tour operators and also hosts occasional full-moon parties. Lan Ha Bay also offers superb rock climbing and is the main destination for trips run by Asia Outdoors.

Cat Ba National Park   NATURE RESERVE
(☎ 031-216 350; admission 30,000d; ⊙ sunrise-sunset) This accessible national park is home to 32 types of mammal and 70 bird species. To reach the park headquarters at Trung Trang, take a green QH public bus from the docks at Cat Ba Town (20,000d, 20 minutes). Buses leave at 8am and 11am. Another option is to hire a *xe om* for around 80,000d one way, or hire your own motorbike for the day.

Mammals in the park include langurs and macaques, wild boar, deer, civets and several species of squirrel, including the giant black squirrel. The golden-headed langur is officially the world's most endangered primate with around 65 remaining, most in this park. Birds include hawks, hornbills and cuckoos, and Cat Ba lies on a major migration route for waterfowl that feed and roost on the beaches in the mangrove forests. Over a thousand species of plants have been recorded here, including 118 trees and 160 plants with medicinal value.

CRUISES WITH A DIFFERENCE

If you're after something a little different with your Halong Bay cruise, consider one of the following more interesting (and more expensive) options. All are based in Hanoi.

Emeraude Classic Cruise (☎ 04-3934 0888; www.emeraude-cruises.com; d US$360-600) A 56m replica paddle steamer with 38 air-conditioned cabins, all with elegant wooden furniture and smart hot-water showers. Lavish buffet-style meals are served. It is pricey for a cruise that's less than 24 hours.

Handspan (☎ 04-3926 2828; www.handspan.com; d US$320-400) Handspan's *Treasure Junk* is the only true sailing ship operating on the bay. That means you get to meander peacefully through the karsts without the constant hum of a diesel engine. Crack open a cold Bia Hanoi and you'll be in heaven.

Indochina Sails (☎ 04-3984 2362; www.indochinasails.com; d US$896-1000) Cruise Halong on a traditional junk kitted out to a three-star standard. Indochina operates two 42m junks and one smaller craft; all have attractive wooden cabins and great viewing decks.

Cat Ba Town

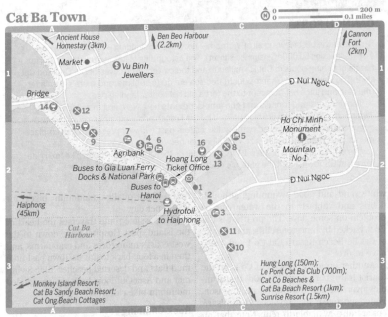

A guide is not mandatory but is definitely recommended to help you make sense of the verdant canopy of trees. The multichambered **Hang Trung Trang** (Trung Trang Cave) is easily accessible, but you will need to contact a ranger to make sure it's open. Bring a torch (flashlight).

There's a challenging 18km hike through the park and up to one of the mountain summits. Arrange a guide for this six-hour hike and organise a bus or boat transport to the trailhead and a boat to get back to town. This can be arranged with the rangers at the national park headquarters, or at Asia Outdoors or Cat Ba Ventures in Cat Ba Town. Be sure to take proper hiking shoes, a raincoat and a generous supply of water for this hike. Independent hikers can buy basic snacks at the kiosks in Viet Hai, which is where many hiking groups stop for lunch. This is not an easy walk, and is much harder and more slippery after rain. There are shorter hiking options that are less hardcore.

Many hikes end at **Viet Hai**, a remote minority village just outside the park boundary, from where taxi boats shuttle back to Ben Beo pier (about 200,000d per boat). A shared public boat (50,000d per person) departs Ben Beo at 6am on weekdays and 7am on weekends. There is also accommodation here at Whisper of Nature (p110).

Cat Co Cove   BEACH

A 15-minute walk southeast from Cat Ba Town, the three Cat Co Cove beaches boast

DON'T MISS

CANNON FORT

For one of the best views in all of Vietnam – no, we're not kidding – head to Cannon Fort (admission 50,000d; ⊙ sunrise-sunset). The astounding vistas include the colourful tangle of fishing boats in Cat Ba harbour, and the perfect little coves of Cat Co 1 and Cat Co 2. The views out to a karst-punctuated sea are quite sublime, and there's even a terrific cafe and juice bar adjacent to the fort's old helicopter landing pad.

The underground tunnels and gun emplacements here were first installed by the Japanese in WWII, but were also utilised by the French and Vietnamese during subsequent conflicts. Well-labelled paths guide visitors past two well-preserved gun emplacements, one 'manned' by life-size Viet Minh mannequins.

The entrance gate is a steep 10-minute walk or 15,000d *xe om* (motorbike taxi) ride from Cat Ba Town. From the gate, it's another stiff 20-minute walk.

white sand and good swimming, although debris and rubbish in the water can be problem on some days. The prettiest is Cat Co 2, backed by limestone cliffs, and the site of Cat Ba Beach Resort. Cat Co 1 and 3 also have resorts.

Another option to reach Cat Co is on the tourist train (per person 10,000d) that trundles over the hill during the peak season. Water-sport gear like kayaks and windsurfers are also available to rent. Note that on summer weekends the three beaches get packed with Vietnamese tourists, and litter can be a problem.

Other beaches on Cat Ba Island include Cai Vieng, Hong Xoai Be and Hong Xoai Lon.

Hospital Cave
HISTORICAL SITE

(☑ 031-368 8215; admission 15,000d; ⊙ 7am-4.30pm) Hospital Cave served both as a secret, bomb-proof hospital during the American War and as a safe house for Viet Cong (Vietnamese Communists; VC) leaders. Built between 1963 and 1965 (with assistance from China), this incredibly well-constructed three-storey feat of engineering was in constant use until 1975. The cave is about 10km north of Cat Ba Town on the road to the national-park entrance.

A guide (most know a few words of English) will show you around the 17 rooms, point out the old operating theatre and take you to the huge natural cavern that was used as a cinema (and even had its own small swimming pool).

🏃 Activities

Cat Ba is a superb base for adventure sports – on the island, and in, on and over the water.

Mountain Biking

Hotels can arrange Chinese mountain bikes (around US$6 per day). Blue Swimmer rents better-quality mountain bikes for US$15 per day.

One possible route traverses the heart of the island, past Hospital Cave down to the west coast's mangroves and crab farms, and then in a loop back to Cat Ba Town past tidal mud flats and deserted beaches. Blue Swimmer and Asia Outdoors both arrange guided mountain-bike rides.

Rock Climbing

Cat Ba Island and Lan Ha Bay's spectacular limestone cliffs make for world-class rock climbing.

Based on Cat Ba, Asia Outdoors pioneered climbing in Vietnam and uses fully licenced and certified instructors. Advanced climbers can hire gear here, talk shop and pick up a copy of *Vietnam: A Climber's Guide* (US$20) by Asia Outdoors' Erik Ferjentsik, which describes climbs and has some great tips about Cat Ba too. Full-day climbing trips include instruction, transport, lunch and gear. Longer trips by boat incorporate kayaking, beach stops and exploring the amazing karst landscape. Other less qualified Cat Ba operators also offer climbing trips, but Asia Outdoors is the authority on the island.

Sailing & Kayaking

Don't miss exploring the spectacular islands and beaches of Lan Ha Bay. Blue Swimmer offers sailing excursions to myriad islands around Cat Ba, often including kayaking and sleeping in a bamboo hut on a private beach.

Plenty of hotels in Cat Ba Town rent kayaks (half-day around US$8). Blue Swimmer also has good-quality kayaks (single/double per day US$12/25), ideal for exploring the Cat Ba coast independently.

Trekking

Most of Cat Ba Island consists of protected tropical forest. Asia Outdoors and Blue Swimmer both offer a great hike around Cat Ba Island that takes in Butterfly Valley.

☞ Tours

Tours of the island and boat trips around Halong Bay are offered by nearly every hotel in Cat Ba Town. Typical prices start at around US$20 per person for day trips and US$80 for two-day, one-night tours, but it is worth spending a bit more. We receive unfavourable feedback – cramped conditions and dodgy food – about some of these trips, but the following offer good prices and service.

If you're looking for a different experience, the following adventure-tour operators understand travellers' needs and will steer you away from the tourist trail to really special areas of Cat Ba, Lan Ha Bay and beyond.

Cat Ba Ventures   BOAT TOUR, KAYAKING
(✆0912 467 016, 031-388 8755; www.catbaventures.com; 223 Đ 1-4, Cat Ba Town) Locally owned and operated company offering boat trips to Halong Bay, kayaking and hiking. Excellent service from Mr Tung is reinforced by multiple reader recommendations.

Asia Outdoors   ROCK CLIMBING
(✆031-368 8450; www.asiaoutdoors.com.vn; Đ 1-4, Cat Ba Town) Climbing instruction is Asia Outdoors' real expertise, but it also offers excellent, well-structured boating, kayaking, biking and hiking trips. Rock up to its office in Noble House (at 6pm every night) to see what's planned. Note that Asia Outdoors was formerly known as Slo Pony Adventures.

Blue Swimmer   SAILING, KAYAKING
(✆0915 063 737, 031-368 8237; www.blueswimmersailing.com; Ben Beo harbour) A very well-organised, environmentally conscious outfit established by Vinh, one of the founders of respected tour operator Handspan. Superb sailing and kayak trips, trekking and mountain-biking excursions are offered. Check it out at Ben Beo harbour or at its booking office in Cat Ba Town at the Green Bamboo Forest restaurant.

Some of Blue Swimmer's trips also include staying at the Ancient House in a quiet location on the outskirts of Cat Ba Town.

CLIMBING THE KARSTS

If you've ever considered it, or been tempted to climb, Halong Bay is a superb place to go for it – the karst cliffs here offer exceptional climbing amid stunning scenery. Most climbers in Cat Ba are complete novices, but as the instruction is excellent, many leave Cat Ba completely bitten by the bug.

You don't need great upper-body strength to climb, as you actually use your legs far more. The karst limestone of Halong Bay is not too sharp and quite friendly on the hands, and as many of the routes are sheltered by natural overhangs that prevent the climbable portion of the rock from getting wet, climbing is almost always possible, rain or shine.

A few inexperienced locals may offer climbing excursions to new arrivals on Cat Ba, but beginners should sign up with the experienced crew at Asia Outdoors (above).

Climbing opportunities for beginners are located on walls inland on Cat Ba Island or out on beautiful Lan Ha Bay. You'll be kitted up with a harness and climbing shoes, given instruction and taught the fundamentals of the climbing and belaying techniques, then given a demonstration. Then it's over to you (with your climbing instructor talking you through each move and anchoring you, of course!). Most people are able to complete a couple of climbs at Hai Pai and Moody's Beach, which are both ideal for beginners.

The vertical cliffs of Halong and Lan Ha Bays are also perfect for deep-water soloing, which is basically climbing alone, without ropes or a harness, and using the ocean as a water bed in case you fall. This is obviously only for experienced climbers, and it's essential to know the depth of water and tidal patterns. We've heard reports of some climbers being injured falling into shallow waters, so it's vital to attempt deep-water soloing only with an experienced crew like Asia Outdoors. It's customary to finish a solo climb with a controlled free fall (or 'tombstone') into the sea and a swim back to the shore, or your boat.

🛏 Sleeping

Most basic hotels are situated on (or just off) the waterfront in Cat Ba Town, but the area's accommodation scene is quickly evolving. More interesting options have opened in other parts of Cat Ba, and there are some wonderfully isolated spots on other islands in Lan Ha Bay.

Room rates fluctuate greatly. In the high-season summer months (June to August) you can expect to pay a minimum of US$20 per room; rates sink to around US$12 for a decent room outside this time. The rates given here are for low season. Peak season rates are impossible to determine as hotel owners tend to pick a number out of their heads depending on demand. Note that from June to August, it's definitely worth booking ahead because of demand.

CAT BA TOWN

If the seafront hotels in Cat Ba Town are full, detour to Đ Nui Ngoc, which is lined with good-value accommodation.

Thu Ha
HOTEL $

(☑ 031-388 8343; Đ 1-4; r US$12-20; ❄ 🛜) With air-con, wi-fi and a seafront location, the Thu Ha offers great value. Negotiate hard for a front room and wake up to sea views.

Le Pont
HOSTEL $

(☑ 0165 662 0436; jim.lepontcatba@gmail.com; 62-64 Đ Nui Ngoc; dm US$5, d & tw US$15-20; @ 🛜) The best spot in town for budget-wise backpackers with cheap dorms and OK double and twin rooms. The rooftop bar and terrace is a handy place to meet fellow travellers.

Duc Tuan Hotel
HOTEL $

(☑ 031-388 8783; www.catbatravelservice.com; 210 Đ 1-4; r US$12-20; ❄ 🛜) Simple but colourfully furnished rooms feature at this main-drag, family-owned spot. The rooms at the back are quieter, but lack windows.

Cat Ba Dream
HOTEL $

(☑ 031-388 8274; www.catbadream.com.vn; 226 Đ 1-4; r US$15-25; ❄ @ 🛜) Slightly more expensive than Cat Ba's ultracheapies, Cat Ba Dream is a good addition to the town's seafront cavalcade of accommodation. Angle for a front room with sea views.

Phong Lan Hotel
HOTEL $

(☑ 031-388 8605; Đ 1-4; r US$12-20; ❄ 🛜) In the middle of the seafront strip; some rooms have balconies overlooking the harbour.

Hung Long
HOTEL $$

(☑ 031-626 9269; 268 Đ 1-4; d US$80) At the quieter southeastern end of Cat Ba Town, the Hung Long has very spacious rooms, many with excellent views.

CAT BA BEACHES & ISLANDS

Whisper of Nature
GUEST HOUSE $

(☑ 031-265 7678; www.vietbungalow.com; Viet Hai Village; dm/d US$12/28) Whisper of Nature's simple concrete-and-thatch bungalows are arrayed around a quietly flowing stream on the edge of the forest. Accommodation ranges from shared dorms to bungalows with private bathrooms. Getting there is an adventure in itself, with the final stage a bike ride through lush scenery. Ask about transport when you book, or hire a bamboo boat from Cat Ba Town to the Viet Hai village jetty (200,000d), and then a *xe om* (50,000d) for the final 5km to the village.

⭐ Ancient House Homestay
HOMESTAY $$

(☑ 0916 645 858, 0915 063 737; www.catba-homestay.com; Ang Soi village; shared house s/d US$17/25, private house d US$50; 🛜) Located around 3km from Cat Ba Town in the quiet village of Ang Soi, this beautiful heritage home was carefully moved here from the outskirts of Hanoi. Antiques fill the high-ceilinged interior and outside are well-tended gardens. A second adjacent house is available for more private use, and lunch and dinner set menus (180,000d per person) are available on request.

Activities such as cookery classes, biking, sailing and kayaking can all be arranged.

Cat Ba Eco Lodge
GUEST HOUSE $$

(☑ 031-368 8966; www.suoigoicatbaresort.vn; Xuan Dam village; s/d from US$35/45; ❄ 🛜) This eco-resort celebrates a wonderfully quiet village location 12km from Cat Ba Town. Spacious wooden stilt houses sit around a breezy bar and restaurant, and activities include trekking, and riding bicycles to a beach 2km away. Pick-ups can be arranged from the ferry or Cat Ba Town.

Cat Ba Beach Resort
RESORT $$

(☑ 031-388 8686; www.catbabeachresort.com; Cat Co 2 beach; bungalows from around US$80; ❄ 🛜) Recently opened on Cat Co 2 beach, Cat Ba Beach Resort has manicured tropical grounds and accommodation ranging from seafront bungalows to shared houses sleeping up to eight. Kayaking, windsurfing and a sauna are all on tap, and there's a breezy open-sided bar-restaurant with views over the water. Check online for good discounts.

Monkey Island Resort
RESORT $$

(☏ 04-3926 0572; www.monkeyislandresort.com; d US$60-100; ❇️) There's a nicely social vibe going down at Monkey Island with a nightly seafood buffet, cool R&B beats, and a bar with a pool table. Accommodation is in comfortable private bungalows, and beach barbecues, kayaks and volleyball keep the holiday spirit alive. The resort provides free transfers from Cat Ba Town.

Look online for good-value packages combining Halong Bay and Lan Ha Bay.

Cat Ba Sandy Beach Resort
RESORT $$

(☏ 0989 555 773; www.catbasandybeachresort.com; Nam Cat Island; d from US$45; ❇️) This island's prescription for relaxation includes a choice between simple bungalows and posher villas with private facilities – all located under looming, indigo limestone cliffs. Spend your days swimming and kayaking, and kick back with seafood barbecues and beach bonfires after dark. Sandy Beach Resort is included on itineraries arranged by Cat Ba Ventures, as well as Vega Travel in Hanoi.

Sunrise Resort
RESORT $$$

(☏ 031-388 7360; www.catbasunriseresort.com; Cat Co 3; r from US$110; ❇️ @ 🛜 ❇️) This beachfront resort is tastefully planned, with low-rise tiled-roofed blocks sitting below green cliffs. Rooms are spacious and smart, all with sea-view balconies, and facilities include a swimming pool, spa and kiddies' playground.

Cat Ong Beach Cottages
BUNGALOWS $$$

(☏ 0983 234 628; www.catongisland.com; Cat Ong Island; r US$75-150) Located on a private island a short ride from Cat Ba Town, these beautiful, traditionally-built cottages enjoy a wonderful beachfront location. A seafood barbecue is served on the sand every night and boat transfers are included.

Eating

There are a few good places dotted along Cat Ba Town's seafront strip, and the floating restaurants offshore are also worth a visit. For a cheaper feed, head to the food stalls in front of the market, or one block back from the watefront on the cross street that links the loop of Đ Nui Ngoc.

Green Bamboo Forest
VIETNAMESE $

(Đ 1-4; meals 80,000-120,000d; ⊙ 7am-11pm) Friendly and well-run waterfront eatery that also acts as a booking office for Blue Swimmer. Our pick of the restaurants along the seafront, and the quieter location is also a bonus.

Family Bakery
BAKERY $

(196 Đ 1-4, Cat Ba Town; dishes 80,000-120,000d; ⊙ 7am-4pm) Friendly spot that opens early for goodies like Turkish bread and almond pastries. Pop in for a coffee, crème caramel or croissant before the bus-ferry-bus combo back to Hanoi.

Phuong Nung
VIETNAMESE $

(184 Đ 1-4, Cat Ba Town; meals 45,000d; ⊙ 7-10am) Bustling breakfast spot that's the most popular place in town for a hearty bowl of *pho bo* (beef noodle soup) – just the thing you need before a day of climbing or kayaking.

FLOATING RESTAURANTS

There are numerous 'floating' seafood restaurants just offshore in Cat Ba harbour. We've heard reports of overcharging, so it's essential to confirm the price of the food in advance, as well as the cost of a boat to get you out there and back. Locals actually advise heading around the bay to the floating restaurants in Ben Beo harbour. They're less touristy and less likely to rip you off, but still check on the price of food upfront. A boat ride there and back, including waiting time, should cost around 140,000d. Hold off paying your boat fare until the return journey is completed, as we've also had reports of diners being left stranded on the restaurants. Ask your hotel to recommend a boat or catch a *xe om* (motorbike taxi; around 30,000d) over the hill to the harbour.

A recommended place at Ben Beo pier is Xuan Hong (☏ 031-388 8485). Choose your dinner from the floating pens and they'll be grilled, fried or steamed for your table in no time. Prices simply go by weight and type of seafood; you can eat your fill of a selection of fish for around 200,000d per person. Just make sure you establish the estimated price before you eat.

CT Mart
SELF-CATERING $

(18 Đ Nui Ngoc, Cat Ba Town; ☺8am-8pm) Handy supermarket at which to stock up before heading off trekking or on the boat trip back to the mainland.

Vien Duong
VIETNAMESE $$

(12 Đ Nui Ngoc, Cat Ba Town; meals from 120,000d; ☺11am-11pm) One of the most popular of the seafood spots lining Đ Nui Ngoc, and often heaving with Vietnamese tourists diving into local crab, squid and steaming seafood hotpots. Definitely not the place to come if you're looking for a quiet night.

Le Pont Cat Ba Club
SEAFOOD, ITALIAN $$

(meals 90,000-350,000d; ☺11am-late) At the southeastern edge of the bay and with great views, the spacious and stylish Le Pont is our pick for Cat Ba's best spot for a sunset cocktail or cold beer. The food's passable, but really it's the harbour vistas that are worth the walk from the centre of town. After dark it morphs into a nightclub.

Green Mango
INTERNATIONAL $$

(☑031-388 7151; Đ 1-4, Cat Ba Town; mains 150,000-220,000d; ☺8am-10pm; ☎) A good place for a glass of wine, cocktail or Cat Ba's best espresso, but the huge menu covering everything from pizza, pasta and occasional Asian flavours can tend towards mediocrity.

🍷 Drinking

Cat Ba Town has a few good bars, or you can head to the *bia hoi* stalls near the entrance to the fishing harbour.

Flightless Bird Café
BAR

(☑031-388 8517; Đ 1-4, Cat Ba Town; ☺noon-11pm; ☎) Discover your inner Kiwi at this friendly bar decorated with New Zealand memorabilia, including pictures of the mighty All Blacks rugby team and the beautiful Southern Alps. There's free wi-fi for customers, and even well-priced massage and manicure services on offer.

Rose Bar
BAR

(15 Đ Nui Ngoc; ☺noon-3am; ☎) With cheap (US$2) cocktails, loads of happy-hour specials and *shisha* (water pipes) on offer, Rose Bar ticks all the boxes for backpacker fun a long way from home. Bring along your MP3 player of choice, and you can usually hijack the sound system. Rose Bar often stays open after midnight during the busy season.

Good Bar
BAR

(Đ 1-4, Cat Ba Town; ☺noon-late) This upper-floor bar has a real vibe, and the drinking, flirting and storytelling goes on until late most nights. It comes fully equipped with pool tables and terrific harbour views.

ℹ️ Information

INTERNET ACCESS

Most accommodation, seafront cafes and restaurants offer wi-fi access.

MONEY

Agribank Has an ATM on the harbour, and a branch 1km north of town for changing dollars.

Vu Binh Jewellers (☑031-388 8641; Cat Ba market) Changes US dollars and offers credit-card cash advances at 5%.

TOURIST INFORMATION

The best impartial advice is at Asia Outdoors, where the helpful crew can bring you up to speed on everything from transport connections to the best family run restaurants. Cat Ba Ventures is also very helpful. Online, see www.asiaoutdoors.com.vn and www.catbaventures.com for local information.

ℹ️ Getting There & Away

Cat Ba Island is 45km east of Haiphong and 50km south of Halong City. Various boat and bus combinations make the journey, starting in either Hanoi or Haiphong.

It is possible to travel by boat from Halong City to Cat Ba Island, but it is a journey often blighted by scams.

TO/FROM HANOI

Departing from the Luong Yen bus station in Hanoi, **Hoang Long** (☑031-268 8008) operates a bus to Haiphong, followed by a minibus to Dinh Vu port near Haiphong, then a 40-minute boat trip to Cai Vieng harbour (also known as Phu Long) on Cat Ba Island. From there, another minibus whisks passengers around the coast road into Cat Ba Town. The complete bus-bus-boat-bus combo takes around three hours (240,000d) and is very efficiently run. Buses depart Hanoi at 5.20am, 7.20am, 11.20am and 1.20pm, and return from Cat Ba Town at 7.15am, 9.15am, 1.15pm and 3.15pm. If you're travelling from Hanoi, this is the most hassle-free way.

TO/FROM HAIPHONG

A fast hyrdofoil departs Haiphong's Ben Binh Harbour and goes straight to Cat Ba Town. This takes around 50 minutes (200,000d). Cat Ba–bound hydrofoils depart from Haiphong at 7am, 9am, 1pm and 3pm, and return from Cat Ba Town at 8am, 10am, 2pm and 4pm.

ⓘ HALONG BAY TO CAT BA (WITHOUT THE HASSLE)

Based on the map, it looks like an easy undertaking to travel by sea from Bai Chay in Halong City to Cat Ba Island. And while it's not very far in terms of distance, it can be a journey fraught with hassle for some travellers.

Tourist boats (around US$10) depart from Bai Chay in Halong City from around 1pm heading to Gia Luan harbour in the north of Cat Ba Island. The journey takes four hours, usually stopping for swimming and to visit a cave, but once you land at Gia Luan, you're actually still 40km from Cat Ba Town. We've heard many reports of travellers then being hassled by the local taxi and *xe om* (motorbike taxi) mafia who will demand up to US$50 for onward travel to Cat Ba Town. Despite their claims, there is a local bus (20,000d) – the QH Green Bus – that travels from Gia Luan to Cat Ba Town. Unfortunately the last bus of the day (5pm) usually departs Gia Luan before the boats arrive from Bai Chay. Funny that...

Some boat owners in Halong Bay are part of the scam, so if you do book a tour or boat transport from Bai Chay to Cat Ba Island, ask specifically if there will be onward transport provided to Cat Ba Town once the boat lands at Gia Luan. Onward bus transport is included by some recommended operators, including Cat Ba Ventures.

An alternative, and potentially hassle-free, way of getting from Halong Bay to Cat Ba is on the passenger and vehicle ferry (50,000d, one hour, departing around hourly 6am to 6pm May to September, and 7.30am, 9am, 11.30am, 1.30pm & 3pm October to April) that travels from the resort island of Tuan Chau to Gia Luan. From Halong City across the causeway to Tuan Chau by taxi is around 150,000d (50,000d by *xe om*). Once on Cat Ba Island, travellers can then catch the QH Green Bus into Cat Ba Town. Purchase your ticket from the driver. Note that these buses leave Gia Luan for Cat Ba Town at 6am, 9.30am, 1.10pm, 4pm and 5pm, and despite what the local *xe om* and taxi drivers will tell you, foreigners are definitely allowed to travel on these services. You might also be able to hitch a lift to Cat Ba Town from a private car off the ferry if you ask around.

To travel the other way – Cat Ba Island to Bai Chay in Halong City – on the above services, contact Cat Ba Ventures (p109) in Cat Ba Town for the latest information.

ⓘ Getting Around

BICYCLE & MOTORBIKE

Bicycle and motorbike rentals are available from most Cat Ba hotels (both around US$5 per day). If you're heading out to the beaches or national park, pay the parking fee for security.

A *xe om* from Cat Ba Town to Cat Co 2 beach or Ben Beo harbour is around 10,000d, and in summer a kitsch tourist train also runs from Cat Ba Town to the Cat Co beaches (10,000d per person).

BUS

Cat Ba's public **QH Green Bus** (20,000d) trundles between Cat Ba harbour and Gia Luan harbour in the north of the island, passing the national park headquarters en route.

Bai Tu Long Bay

🎵 033

There's way more to northeast Vietnam than Halong Bay. The sinking limestone plateau, which gave birth to the bay's spectacular islands, continues for some 100km to the Chinese border. The area immediately northeast of Halong Bay is part of Bai Tu Long National Park.

Bai Tu Long Bay is every bit as beautiful as its famous neighbour. In some ways it's actually more stunning, since it's only in its initial stages as a destination for travellers. Improved boat transport means it is quickly growing in popularity with domestic tourists, but the bay and its islands are still unpolluted and relatively undeveloped. For Western travellers, it's a laid-back alternative to the touristy bustle of Halong Bay.

Charter boats can be arranged to Bai Tu Long Bay from Halong Bay; rates start at around 300,000d per hour and the trip there takes about five hours. A cheaper, and more flexible alternative is to travel overland to Cai Rong and visit the outlying islands by boat from here. An increased frequency of ferry sailings definitely makes this a more viable alternative than in earlier years.

Hanoi travel agencies, including Ethnic Travel, run trips into the Bai Tu Long area.

Van Don Island

Van Don is the largest (around 30 sq km), most populated and most developed island in the Bai Tu Long archipelago. Now linked to the mainland by a series of bridges, it has a few places to stay, but more importantly it's the jumping off point to other islands.

Van Don's main town is Cai Rong (pronounced Cai Zong). Nearby, Bai Dai (Long Beach) runs along much of the island's southern side and has hard-packed sand with some mangroves. Just offshore there are stunning limestone rock formations.

Cai Rong Pier (Cai Rong Pha), about 8km north of the bridge to the mainland, is the key port for boats to other Bai Tu Long islands. It's a bustling port, full of karaoke bars and motorbikes, but there are decent hotels if you're forced to overnight before catching a morning ferry.

Hung Toan Hotel (☑ 033-387 4220; r 250,000d; ☀) is good value, while Viet Linh Hotel (☑ 033-379 3898; r 400,000d; ☀) is fancier. Both are around 300m north of the pier. Just opposite the Viet Linh Hotel is a simple, unnamed restaurant that does great seafood and pork dishes – try the pork with ginger, chilli and lemongrass.

Frequent buses run between Bai Chay (Halong City) and Cai Rong on Van Don Island (60,000d, 1½ hours). Alternatively catch a Mong Cai or Lang Son bus to the Cua Ong turn-off, and then catch a *xe om* or taxi to Cai Rong Pier.

Quan Lan Island

The main attraction on Quan Lan is the beautiful, 1km-long crescent-moon sweep of Minh Chau beach on the island's northeastern coast. The water is clear blue and the waves are suitable for surfing. Water-sports action includes kayaks for hire and there are lots of cheap eateries for beer and seafood. There are several other blissful beaches on the eastern seaboard, though water temperatures are a bit chilly between January and April.

The northeastern part of the island has some battered ruins of the old Van Don Trading Port. Other attractions include forest walks and a beautiful 200-year-old pagoda in Quan Lan Town. Apart from hanging out on the beaches, and cycling or motorcycling around this island, there's not much to do. It's a very laid-back place and a terrific detour off the usual tourist trail. There's no ATM on Quan Lan Island, so come armed with cash.

🍽 Sleeping & Eating

Quan Lan Town, the island's main town, features an improving array of accommodation, from simple guesthouses to new midrange hotels, and a few decent restaurants. Quan Lan's second-largest settlement is Minh Chau, just a short walk from gorgeous Minh Chau beach. It lacks the facilities of Quan Lan Town, but has a couple of good places to stay, both around 3km from the pier. Note that most accommodation and beachfront restaurants are only open from May to October, and that June and July are more expensive with the influx of Vietnamese domestic tourists.

Ngan Ha Hotel HOTEL $
(☑ 033-387 7296; Quan Lan Town; r 350,000d; ☀) This corner-front establishment in the heart of town has redecorated rooms and a good restaurant downstairs.

Ann Hotel HOTEL $$
(Quan Lan Town; r US$25; ☀) The newish Ann Hotel offers spacious rooms, gleaming bathrooms and balconies with ocean views. It's located around 200m from the centre of town towards the old pagoda.

Le Pont Hotel HOTEL $$
(www.leponttravel.com; Minh Chau; r weekend/weekday US$40/25; ☀) This hotel has newish rooms, a downstairs restaurant and also rents out bikes and motorcycles. Minh Chau beach is a short, forested walk away. For more information contact 'Mr Jim' at Le Pont (p110) in Cat Ba Town.

Minh Chau Resort RESORT $$$
(☑ 0904 081 868; Minh Chau; r US$80) Bai Tu Long's flashest accommodation, arrayed across two leafy locations and featuring a very good restaurant. Rates rise by around 15% on weekends.

ⓘ Getting There & Away

TO/FROM CAI RONG
Boats from Cai Rong dock at two places: the Quan Lan pier, 3km from the main township on the island's southern tip, and near Minh Chau beach, on the island's northeastern coast. Fast boats to Minh Chau (120,000d, 45 minutes) depart Cai Rong at 7.30am and 1.30pm. Fast boats to Quan Lan pier (100,000d to 120,000d, 1½ hours) depart Cai Rong at 8am and 2pm. A slower wooden boat (50,000d, 2½ hours) departs from Cai Rong to Quan Lan pier at 7am and 1pm.

An alternative route to Quan Lan pier is from the Hon Gai ferry terminal across the suspension bridge from Halong City. A speedboat leaves at 1.30pm (160,000d, 1½ hours). The Hon Gai ferry terminal is adjacent to the Vinashin bus station.

ⓘ Getting Around

Quan Lan Town has places to rent bicycles (US$4 per day) and motorcycles (US$6 per day). Most of Quan Lan is pretty flat, but it's a surprisingly large island, so maybe opt for something with an engine.

Tra Ban & Ngoc Vung Islands

One of Bai Tu Long's largest islands, Tra Ban offers some of the bay's most dramatic karsts. The southern part is blanketed in thick jungle and provides a habitat for many colourful butterflies. Boats leave from Van Don's Cai Rong Pier at 7am and 2pm (40,000d, one hour). There's no accommodation, so check on times for return boats.

Dao Ngoc Vung borders Halong Bay and has some dramatic limestone cliffs and a great beach on its southern shore with some basic beach huts (r 200,000d). Bring along your own food. Daily boats link Cai Rong to Ngoc Vung (60,000d, 2½ hours, 7am and 1.30pm).

Co To Island

In the northeast, Co To Island is the furthest inhabited island from the mainland. Its highest peak reaches a respectable 170m. There are numerous other hills, and a large lighthouse. The coastline is mostly cliffs and large rocks, but there's at least one sandy beach.

There are a couple of recently built hotels and guesthouses on Co To, including the Coto Lodge Hotel (www.coto.vn; d 500,000d; ❄ @ 🛜). The attached Jellyfish restaurant is surprisingly chic, and the hotel can arrange beach barbecues and island tours. Rates include breakfast. The hotel also rents out camping gear including tents and portable stoves.

Slow ferries bound for Dao Co To depart Cai Rong Pier at 7am daily (70,000d, three hours). There are also slow ferries departing Cai Rong at 1pm on Wednesday, Friday and Saturday.

A faster speedboat departs Cai Rong daily at 1pm (155,000d, 1½ hours). On Saturdays there's also a 6am departure from Cai Rong.

Mong Cai & the Chinese Border

Huge industrial zones are being created around Mong Cai, with plots being snapped up by Chinese and foreign corporations. Shopping malls dot the city centre. For the Vietnamese, the big draw is the chance to purchase low-priced (and low-quality) Chinese-made consumer goods. For the Chinese, the attraction is two huge casinos and new golf courses. Elsewhere in this border region, travellers' highlights include the stunning karst scenery around Cao Bang, historical caves and the thundering Ban Gioc Waterfall.

Mong Cai

🔊 033 / POP 103,000

A bustling border city, Mong Cai is an upwardly mobile place that thrives on trade with China. But other than as a border crossing, Mong Cai holds no interest for tourists.

🍽 Sleeping & Eating

There are plenty of food stalls on P Hung Vuong, including several good spots near the Nam Phong Hotel.

Nha Nghi Thanh Tam   GUEST HOUSE $
(📞033-388 1373; 71 Đ Trieu Duong; r 280,000d; ❄) Clean comfortable rooms with hot-water bathrooms. There are similar options on this street. Đ Trieu Duong runs south from Đ Tran Phu, two blocks before Mong Cai's main market.

> ### ⓘ GETTING TO CHINA: MONG CAI TO DONGXING
>
> **Getting to the border** The Chinese border at the Mong Cai–Dongxing border crossing is around 3km from the Mong Cai bus station; around 20,000d on a *xe om* (motorbike taxi) or 40,000d in a taxi.
>
> **At the border** The border is open daily between 7am and 10pm Vietnam time. Note that China is one hour ahead of Vietnam. You'll need to have a prearranged visa for China.
>
> **Moving on** Across the border in Dongxing, frequent buses run to Nanning in China's Guangxi province.

Nam Phong Hotel
HOTEL $

(☎ 033-388 7775; P Hung Vuong; r 320,000-450,000d; ※ @ 🛜) A more upmarket place featuring spacious, well-equipped rooms with satellite TV. There's a bar and restaurant serving good Chinese and Vietnamese dishes.

❶ Getting There & Away

Mong Cai is located 340km from Hanoi. The bus terminal is on Hwy 18, about 3km from the border.

Buses from Mong Cai:

DESTINATION	COST (D)	DURATION & FREQUENCY
Hanoi	230,000	8hr; frequent to 1pm
Halong City	100,000	4hr; every 30 minutes
Lang Son	110,000	7hr; 6.30am & 12.30pm

Lang Son

☎ 025 / POP 79,200

Very close to the Chinese border, Lang Son is a booming city. Surrounded by karst peaks, it is in an area populated largely by Tho, Nung, Man and Dzao tribal people, though their influence is not evident in the city.

The city was partially destroyed in February 1979 by Chinese forces, and the ruins of the town and the devastated frontier village of Dong Dang were shown to foreign journalists as evidence of Chinese aggression. Although the border is still heavily fortified, both towns have been rebuilt and Sino–Vietnamese trade is in full swing again.

Lang Son has a good night market, and there's a great local restaurant. Most travellers come to Lang Son when crossing between Vietnam and China; the border is 18km north, just outside Dong Dang.

❍ Sights & Activities

There are two large and beautiful caves around 1200m from central Lang Son. Both are illuminated and have Buddhist altars inside. **Tam Thanh Cave** (combined admission with Nhi Thanh 5000d; ⊘ 6am-6pm) is vast and seductive. There's an internal pool and natural 'window' offering a sweeping view of the surrounding rice fields. A few hundred metres up a stone staircase are the ruins of the **Mac Dynasty Citadel**. It's a lovely, deserted spot, with stunning rural views.

The Ngoc Tuyen River flows through **Nhi Thanh Cave** (combined admission with Tam Thanh 5000d; ⊘ 6am-6pm), 700m beyond Tam Thanh. The entrance has a series of carved poems written by the cave's 18th-century discoverer, a soldier called Ngo Thi San. There's also a carved stone plaque commemorating an early French resident of Lang Son, complete with his silhouette in European clothing.

Lang Son's huge **night market** (⊘ 5-11pm) is a bargain-basement delight, with cheap electrical goods and decent food stalls.

🛏 Sleeping & Eating

Van Xuan Hotel
HOTEL $

(☎ 025-371 0440; lsvanxuanhotel@yahoo.com.vn; 147 P Tran Dang Ninh; r 320,000-500,000d; ※ @ 🛜) All rooms are light and airy, but the family rooms (500,000d) are particularly enormous and extremely comfortable. The hotel is on the lake's eastern edge, around 50m from the market.

Hoa Binh Hotel
HOTEL $

(☎ 025-870 807; 127 Đ Thanh Tam; r 280,000d; ※ 🛜) A reliable cheapie close to the Lang Son market. Cane furniture, spacious rooms and spotless bathrooms add up to the best deal in town.

---

❶ GETTING TO CHINA: LANG SON TO NANNING

Getting to the border: The Friendship Pass at the Dong Dang–Pingxiang border crossing is the most popular crossing in the far north. The border post itself is at Huu Nghi Quan (Friendship Pass), 3km north of Dong Dang town. Frequent minibuses travel between Lang Son and Dong Dang. From Dong Dang a *xe om* to Huu Nghi Quan is around 30,000d and a taxi around 60,000d. From Lang Son count on about 140,000d for a taxi and 70,000d for a *xe om* (motorbike taxi).

At the border: The border is open from 7am to 7pm daily Vietnam time. Note that China is one hour ahead of Vietnam. To cross 500m to the Chinese side you'll need to catch one of the electric cars (10,000d). You'll also need a pre-arranged visa for China.

Moving on: On the Chinese side, it's a 20-minute drive to Pingxiang by bus or shared taxi. Pingxiang is connected by train and bus to Nanning (three hours).

⭐ **Thanh Lan Com Binh Dan**   VIETNAMESE $
(Tran Quoc Tran; meals 50,000-70,000d; ⊙11am-10pm) One block south of the market, the delightful Miss Lan serves around 20 different dishes for lunch and dinner. It's a point-and-pick affair – all seasonal and all local.

New Dynasty Restaurant   VIETNAMESE $$
(☑025-389 8000; Phai Loan Lake; hotpots 150,000d; ⊙noon-11pm) This bar-restaurant juts out into the lake. Everyone's here for the hotpots, but there's also a draught-beer emporium.

❶ Information

Vietin Bank (51 Đ Le Loi) has an ATM and changes money; the **post office** (Đ Le Loi) is adjacent. Both are around 300m from the lake on the road heading east towards Mong Cai.

❶ Getting There & Away

BUS
Buses to Hanoi leave from the terminal on Đ Le Loi, around 500m east of the post office. From the Vietin Bank and post office, turn right into P Tran Dang Ninh, and continue for 200m to the market, hotels and restaurants. Buses to Mong Cai and Cao Bang leave from a separate northern bus terminal around 3km north of the town centre.

Buses from Lang Son:

DESTINATION	COST (D)	DURATION & FREQUENCY
Hanoi	90,000	3hr; frequent to 6pm
Cao Bang	85,000	4hr; five from 5.15am to 1.45pm
Mong Cai	100,000	7hr; 11.30am

TRAIN
There are only very slow trains between Lang Son and Hanoi (100,000d, 5½ hours).

Cao Bang
☑026 / POP 48,200

Mountainous Cao Bang province is one of the most beautiful regions in Vietnam. Cao Bang itself is more prosaic, but it is a useful base to explore the surrounding countryside. The climate is mild here, and winter days can get chilly when a thick fog clings to the banks of the Bang Giang River.

◉ Sights

War Memorial   MONUMENT
(Cao Bang town) Climb the hill and head up the second lane off Đ Pac Bo, go under the en-

Cao Bang

◉ Sights
1 War Memorial................................B2

🛏 Sleeping
2 Duc Trung Hotel...........................A2
3 Thanh Loan Hotel A1

✖ Eating
4 Men Quyen Restaurant................A1
5 Night Market..............................A1
6 Thu Ngan..................................A1

🍸 Drinking & Nightlife
7 Coffee Pho.................................A1

trance to a primary school and you'll see the steps. There are great 360-degree views from the summit, and it's a very peaceful spot.

🛏 Sleeping

Thanh Loan Hotel   HOTEL $$
(☑026-385 7026; ThanhLoan_hotel@yahoo.com; 159 P Vuon Cam; r 400,000-550,000d; ✳@🛜) On a quiet street with cafes and restaurants, this efficient, spotless place features spacious rooms with high ceilings, dark-wood furniture and bathrooms with tubs. Rates include breakfast, and there's even a bar area for a nightcap.

Duc Trung Hotel   HOTEL $$
(☑026-385 3424; www.ductrunghotel.com.vn; 85 Đ Be Van Dan; d 430,000-630,000d) Wooden floors and spotless bathrooms stand out at this 2012 opening in a quiet residential neighbourhood just a short walk from Cao Bang's main drag. Big windows allow for lots

of sunshine, and there are good *banh mi* (filled baguettes) and *pho* stalls just across the road.

Eating & Drinking

You'll find cheap **food stalls** (meals from 15,000d) near the night market on P Vuon Cam near the Thanh Loan Hotel.

Men Quyen Restaurant VIETNAMESE **$**
(☏ 026-385 6433; Đ Kim Dong; meals 45,000-70,000d) Tucked away behind the market, this modest little place has a buffet-style set-up – just point to the dishes you want. Be sure to try the delicious *cha la lot* (cabbage rolls).

Thu Ngan VIETNAMESE **$**
(21 P Vuon Cam; mains 40,000-60,000d; ⊗8am-9pm) Good-value local eatery owned by a friendly family.

Coffee Pho CAFE
(☏ 026-395 0240; 140 P Vuon Cam) Good Vietnamese coffee, cappuccino, juices and beer, plus a snack or two.

ℹ Information

ATMs are in the centre of town, and internet cafes are on P Vuon Cam.

ℹ Getting There & Away

Cao Bang is 272km north of Hanoi, along Hwy 3. It's a fully sealed road, but a full day's drive through mountainous terrain. Buses depart Cao Bang for Hanoi (140,000d, seven hours, 12 daily) and Lang Son (90,000d, three hours, four daily before 2pm).

A direct bus (90,000d, five hours) departs Cao Bang for Ba Be Lakes at noon. Another option is to catch a local bus to Na Phuc and then another to Cho Ra, where you'll need to hire a *xe om* for the final stretch into the national park.

A direct bus (75,000d, 2½ hours) departs Cao Bang for Ban Gioc Waterfall most mornings at 7.30am and 9am. If you're heading northwest to Ha Giang, a daily bus (100,000d) leaves Cao Bang for Bao Lac. From there you'll need to arrange private transport to Meo Vac.

Hang Pac Bo (Water-Wheel Cave)

After 30 years of exile, Ho Chi Minh re-entered Vietnam in January 1941 and took shelter in a small cave in one of the most remote regions of Vietnam, 3km from the Chinese border. The cave itself, Hang Pac Bo (Water-Wheel Cave), and the surrounding area are sacred ground for Vietnamese revolutionaries – this is the base from which Ho launched the revolution he'd long been planning.

Even if you have little interest in the history of Vietnamese communism, the cave is in a beautiful location surrounded by evergreen forests filled with butterflies and birdsong, and overlooked by limestone mountains.

Ho Chi Minh lived in the cave for a few weeks in 1941, writing poetry and translating key texts by the fathers of socialism. He stuck close to China so that he would be able to flee across the border if French soldiers discovered his hiding place. Ho named the stream in front of his cave Lenin Creek and the jungle-clad mountain that overlooks this stream Karl Marx Peak.

There's a modest Uncle Ho **museum** (admission 20,000d; ⊗7.30-11.30am & 1.30-5pm Wed-Sun) at the entrance to the Pac Bo area. About 2km beyond this is a parking area. The **cave** is a 10-minute walk away along a shady stone path that follows the riverbank. You can step inside the mouth of the small cave, but not enter inside. The path then loops past various other points of interest, including a rock table that Ho is said to have used as a kind of jungle office for his translations and writing.

In a patch of forest about a 15-minute walk in the opposite direction is a **jungle hut**, another of Ho's hideouts. On the way to the hut is a rock outcrop used as a 'dead-letter box', where he would leave and pick up messages.

Hang Pac Bo is 58km northwest of Cao Bang. Allow three hours to make the return trip by road, plus an hour to look around. To do this as a return half-day trip by *xe om*, expect to pay around 200,000d. No permits are currently needed, despite the proximity to the Chinese border.

Ban Gioc Waterfall & Nguom Ngao Cave

Ban Gioc Waterfall (admission 15,000d; ⊗7.30am-5pm) is one of Vietnam's best-known waterfalls, and its image adorns the lobby of many a cheap guesthouse. The falls, fed by the Quay Son River that marks the border with China, are an impressive sight and in a highly scenic location.

The waterfall is the largest in the country, though not the highest. Its vertical drop is only around 30m, but it has an impressive 300m span; one side of the falls is in China, the other is in Vietnam. Water volume varies considerably between the dry and rainy seasons, and the sight is most impressive from May to September.

Boat owners will punt you on bamboo rafts (100,000d) close enough to the waterfall so you can feel the spray on your hair (bring shampoo!) and skin. Rafts on the Vietnamese side have green canopies, and on the Chinese side canopies are blue. You're allowed to swim in the large natural pool on the Vietnamese side, but not in the river or close to the main waterfall.

It's a picturesque 10-minute stroll through paddy fields to reach the base of the falls from the parking area. If you're here at harvest time in September or October, the farmers may encourage you to try out their pedal-powered threshing machines.

A police permit (200,000d for up to 10 people) is required to visit this region. The permit has to be organised in advance but any hotel in Cao Bang can sort it out for you. You'll need to show your passport.

About 4km from the waterfall, Nguom Ngao Cave (admission incl guide 30,000d; ☺7.30am-4.30pm) is one of the most spectacular cave systems in Vietnam. Created by an underground river, it extends for several kilometres underground; villagers sheltered here during the 1979 war with China. Visitors are permitted in one section, where a 1km-long concrete path and excellent lighting have been installed. A guide (speaking very few words of English) accompanies you on an hour-long tour of the cave network, past huge stalagmite and stalactite outcrops that resemble a waterfall and chandelier, and through a vast 100m chamber. The 10-minute walk from the parking lot to the cave is also very beautiful, threading through the limestone hills that characterise Cao Bang province, past fields of soya beans.

A second, even bigger branch of the cave system is said to extend almost all the way to the waterfall, though there's currently no visitor access to this section.

There are snack and drink stalls by the cave and waterfall, but the nearest accommodation is in Cao Bang.

❶ Getting There & Away

The journey to the falls and cave is absolutely stunning; the road follows a beautiful river valley and weaves through soaring karst peaks for much of the trip. It's an 87km journey along a decent paved road, and takes about 2½ hours.

BUS & BIKE

Buses (70,000d, two hours, 12 daily) connect Cao Bang with Trung Khanh, 27km short of the falls. Negotiate for a xe om in Trung Khanh to take you onward, which should come to around 200,000d including a two-hour wait. Another option is a direct bus (75,000d, 2½ hours) departing Cao Bang at 7.30am and 9am.

CAR & MOTORBIKE

Alternatively, hotels and guesthouses in Cao Bang can arrange a motorbike (self-drive) or vehicle (with driver).

NORTHERN VIETNAM MONG CAI & THE CHINESE BORDER

MINORITY MARKETS

In the province of Cao Bang, Kinh (ethnic Vietnamese) are a distinct minority. The largest ethnic groups are the Tay (46%), Nung (32%), H'mong (8%), Dzao (7%) and Lolo (1%). Intermarriage and mass education are gradually eroding tribal and cultural distinctions. Check out Tim Doling's *Mountains and Ethnic Minorities: North East Vietnam* for detailed accounts of tribal people in the region. It's available from the Vietnam Museum of Ethnology and bookshops in Hanoi.

Most of Cao Bang's minorities remain blissfully unaware about the ways of the outside world. Cheating in the marketplace, for example, is virtually unknown and even tourists are charged the same price as locals without bargaining. Whether or not this innocence can withstand the onslaught of even limited tourism remains to be seen. The following big markets in Cao Bang province are held every five days, according to lunar calendar dates. The Na Giang market, which attracts Tay, Nung and H'mong people, is one of the best and busiest in the provinces.

Nuoc Hai 1st, 6th, 11th, 16th, 21st and 26th day of each lunar month.

Na Giang 1st, 6th, 11th, 16th, 21st and 26th day of each lunar month.

Tra Linh 4th, 9th, 14th, 19th, 24th and 29th day of each lunar month.

Trung Khanh 5th, 10th, 15th, 20th, 25th and 30th day of each lunar month.

NORTHWEST VIETNAM

History

The history of the northwest differs to lowland Vietnam. The Vietnamese traditionally avoided mountains, believing the terrain was not suitable for large-scale rice production. For many centuries the area remained inhabited by scatterings of minority people, joined in the 19th century by migrants from Yunnan, China and Tibet. This was the 'badlands', a buffer zone of bandits between China and Vietnam. During Ho Chi Minh's leadership, the North Vietnamese experimented with limited autonomy in 'special zones', but these were abolished after reunification.

Life for the minorities has always been difficult. Their most profitable crop was opium, but the authorities have clamped down and very little is now produced. Educational opportunities were limited, but new schools in remote areas now provide most children with education. Economic prospects remain limited, so many highlanders move to cities in search of work.

ℹ Getting There & Away

The main airport is at Dien Bien Phu, but most travellers take the train from Hanoi to Lao Cai, the gateway to Sapa. On a public bus, the mountain roads can be unforgiving. Consider renting a private 4WD and driver, or riding a motorbike.

To undertake the northwest loop, most travellers head for Mai Chau, then Son La and Dien Bien Phu. Continue north to Lai Chau, Sapa and back to Hanoi. Allow a week for this journey, and more time if using local buses.

Travellers can cross from Laos into Vietnam at the Tay Trang–Sop Hun border crossing, 34km from Dien Bien Phu (see boxed text p127).

Hoa Binh

✆ 0218 / POP 112,000

Hoa Binh means 'peace' and this easygoing nature town is a relief after the traffic-plagued suburbs of Hanoi. The area is home to many hill-tribe people, including the H'mong and Thai. Hoa Binh is a handy pit stop en route to Mai Chau.

◎ Sights

Muong Cultural Museum   MUSUEM, ART GALLERY
(Khong Gian Van Hoa Muong; ✆ 0913 553 937; www.muong.vn; 202 Tay Tien; admission 50,000d; ⊙ 7.30am-5.30pm) Founded by Hanoi artist Vu Duc Hieu, this establishment showcases the art, culture and history of the local Muong ethnic minority. Sprawled across five verdant hectares, it also highlights the quirky art and sculpture of the owner and is worth visiting for the relaxed vibe and beautiful surroundings alone. There's also shared accommodation in simple stilt houses.

A *xe om* from Hoa Binh to the museum is around 50,000d and a taxi around 100,000d. Treks with local Muong ethnic minority guides can also be arranged (300,000d).

Museum   MUSEUM
(⊙ 8-10.30am & 2-4.30pm Mon-Fri) **FREE** A small museum showcasing war memorabilia, including an old French amphibious vehicle. It's on Hwy 6, after the turn-off to Cu Chinh Lan.

Dam Wall   LANDMARK
Cross the bridge towards Phu Tho and you'll see the dam wall of a vast Russian-built hydroelectric station. Across the river is a memorial to the 161 workers who died during its construction.

🛏 Sleeping & Eating

You'll find *com pho* (rice-noodle soup) places lining Hwy 6, and both the Hoa Binh hotels have restaurants.

Thap Vang Hotel   HOTEL $
(✆ 0218-385 2864; 810A Đ Cu Chinh Lan; r 160,000-300,000d; ❈ 🛜) Set just off the main street, this smart minihotel has neat rooms with fridge and satellite TV. It's worth paying slightly more for the larger rooms.

Muong Cultural Museum Homestay   HOMESTAY $
(✆ 0913 553 937; www.muong.vn; 202 Tay Tien; per person 100,000d) Simple shared accommodation in ethnic minority stilt houses. Breakfast is an additional 30,000d and other meals are also available. Longer-term residencies by artists are possible.

Hoa Binh Hotels I & II   HOTEL $$
(✆ 0218-385 2051; s/d US$30/35; ❈ 🛜) Heading west of the centre along Hwy 6, Hoa Binh Hotels I and II have comfortable accommodation in replica stilt houses. Rooms are showing some wear and tear, but the quiet, almost rural, location is a bonus.

ℹ Information

There are ATMs along Hwy 6. Internet access is at the **main post office** (per hour 3000d).

THE HIGH ROADS ON TWO WHEELS

With spectacular scenery and relatively minimal traffic, more travellers are choosing to go by motorcycle around the northwest loop from Hanoi up to Lao Cai, over to Dien Bien Phu and back to the capital. For the really intrepid, the roads venturing north towards China into the spectacular provinces of Ha Giang and Cao Bang are the newest frontier for travel in Vietnam.

Hanoi is the place to start making arrangements. Consider joining a tour or hiring a guide, who will know the roads and can help with mechanical and linguistic difficulties. Be sure to get acquainted with your bike first and check current road conditions and routes.

Most motorbikes in Vietnam are small capacity (under 250cc). For years the sturdy Minsk was the bike of choice for travellers. Today numbers have dwindled, as mopeds and Chinese off-road bikes have proliferated. Honda road bikes (such as the Honda GL160) and trail bikes are other good choices. These bikes have a good reputation for reliability and have decent shock absorbers.

Rental agencies will provide checklists, but essentials include a good helmet, local mobile phone for emergencies, rain gear, a spare parts and repair kit (including spark plugs, spanners, inner tube and tyre levers), air pump and decent maps. Knee and elbow pads and gloves are also a good idea.

Highways can be hell in Vietnam, so let the train take the strain on the long route north to Lao Cai. Load your bike into a goods carriage while you sleep in a berth. You'll have to (almost) drain it of petrol.

If you're planning on riding from Dien Bien Phu via Muong Lay and Lai Chau on Hwy 12 to Sapa, check with bike-rental places before you leave Hanoi. At the time of writing, the 40km after Muong Lay to Lai Chau was very rough with many roadworks, so the rental places will be able to provide updated information and advise about any recommended alternative routes. Hwy 12 was scheduled to be completed by August 2014, so it should be ready by the time you read this.

Take it slowly, particularly in the rain: smooth paved roads can turn into muddy tracks in no time. Do not ride during or immediately after heavy rainstorms as this is when landslides might occur; many mountain roads are quite new and the cliff embankments can be unstable. Expect to average about 35km/h. Only use safe hotel parking. Fill up from petrol stations where the petrol is less likely to have been watered down.

If running short on time or energy, remember that many bus companies will let you put your bike on the roof of a bus, but get permission first from your bike-rental company.

Recommended specialists in Hanoi include Cuong's Motorbike Adventure (p87) and Offroad Vietnam (p87).

Hoa Binh Tourism Company (☑ 0218-385 4374; www.hoabinhtourism.com; Hoa Binh Hotels I & II) Has offices at both hotels; regional tours are offered.

ⓘ Getting There & Away

BUS

Hoa Binh is 74km southwest of Hanoi and accessible by public bus (45,000d, two hours, frequent from 5am to 5pm) from My Dinh station. Buses (55,000d, 1½ hours) to Mai Chau leave around every two hours from 6am to 2pm.

CAR

Visit Ba Vi National Park en route from Hanoi, and follow a riverbank road to Hoa Binh.

Mai Chau

☑ 0218 / POP 12,000

In an idyllic valley, the Mai Chau area is a world away from the hustle and bustle of Hanoi. The small town of Mai Chau is unappealing, but nearby are Thai villages surrounded by lush paddy fields. There's minimal traffic, and the rural soundtrack is defined by gurgling irrigation streams and birdsong.

The villagers are mostly White Thai, distantly related to tribes in Thailand, Laos and China. Most no longer wear traditional dress, but the Thai women are masterful weavers producing plenty of traditional-style clothing and souvenirs. Locals do not

DON'T MISS

SLEEPING ON STILTS

If you are anticipating an exotic encounter – sharing a bowl of eyeball soup or entering a shamanic trance with the local medicine man – think again. Staying in Mai Chau's minority villages is a civilised experience. There's electricity, Western-style toilets and hot showers, and roll-up mattresses and mosquito nets are provided. While this is eminently more comfortable, it probably won't fulfil your rustic hill-tribe trekking expectations.

Despite – or maybe because of – the modern amenities, it's still a memorable experience, and many people end up staying longer than planned. The surrounding area is beautifully lush, the Thai villages are attractive and tidy, and locals are exceedingly friendly. Even with a TV on and the hum of the refrigerator, it is a peaceful place, and you're still sleeping in a thatched-roof stilt house on split-bamboo floors.

Reservations are not necessary. Just show up, but try and arrive before dark so you can get your bearings.

employ strong-arm sales tactics here: polite bargaining is the norm.

Mai Chau is a successful grassroots tourism project, though some find the experience too sanitised, and the villages are firmly on the tour-group agenda. Weekends are also increasingly popular with expats visiting from Hanoi, so try and come midweek if you can.

If you're looking for hardcore exploration, this is not the place, but for biking, hiking and relaxation, Mai Chau fits the bill nicely.

◉ Sights & Activities

This is one of the closest places to Hanoi where you can sleep in a stilt house in a tribal village. There's also fine **walking** past rice fields and **trekking** to minority villages. A typical trek further afield covers 7km to 8km; a local guide can be hired for about US$10. Most homestays also rent bikes to explore the village at your own pace.

A popular 18km trek is from **Lac village** (Ban Lac) in Mai Chau to **Xa Linh village**, near a mountain pass (elevation 1000m) on Hwy 6. Lac village is home to White Thai, while the inhabitants of Xa Linh are H'mong. The trek is strenuous in one day, so most people spend a night in a village. Arrange a guide and a car to meet you at the mountain pass for the journey back to Mai Chau. Note there's a 600m climb in altitude, and the trail is slippery after rain.

Ask around in Mai Chau about longer treks of three to seven days. Other options include **kayaking** and **mountain-biking** excursions; enquire at Mai Chau Lodge.

Many travel agencies in Hanoi run inexpensive trips to Mai Chau.

🛏 Sleeping & Eating

Most visitors stay in **Thai stilt houses** (per person incl breakfast around 200,000d) in the villages of Lac or Pom Coong, just a five-minute stroll apart.

Most people eat where they stay. Establish the price of meals first as some places charge up to 200,000d for breakfast and dinner. Everything from fried eggs to French fries is available, but the local food is best.

★**Mai Chau Nature Lodge**   BUNGALOW **$$**
(☑0946 888 804; www.maichaunatureplace.com; Lac Village; dm/d US$5/40) This friendly operation in Lac village offers private bungalows with bamboo furniture and local textiles. Dorms are also available, and there are free bikes to explore the surrounding countryside.

Mai Chau Lodge   HOTEL **$$$**
(☑0218-386 8959; www.maichaulodge.com; Mai Chau; r US$150; ❋@🛜☒) This tour-group favourite has contemporary rooms with wooden floors and designer lighting, all trimmed with local textiles. Most rooms have balconies with rice-paddy views. The thatched-roof restaurant overlooks a small lake and the pool. Activities on offer include visits to nearby markets, caves and handicraft villages, cookery classes, and guided walking, kayaking and mountain-biking excursions.

❶ Getting There & Away

Direct buses to Mai Chau (100,000d, 3¾ hours) leave Hanoi's My Dinh bus station at 6am, 8.30am and 11am.

If you want to stay in Lac village, just ask the bus driver to drop you off there. You may have to pay a 7000d entry fee to Mai Chau, but the toll booth is often unattended.

Son La
☎ 022 / POP 66,500

Son La has prospered as a logical transit point between Hanoi and Dien Bien Phu. It's not a must-see destination, but the surrounding scenery is impressive, and there are a few interesting diversions.

The region is one of Vietnam's most ethnically diverse and home to more than 30 different minorities including Black Thai, Meo, Muong and White Thai. Vietnamese influence was minimal until the 20th century, and from 1959 to 1980 the region was part of the Tay Bac Autonomous Region.

◉ Sights & Activities

Old French Prison & Museum　MUSEUM
(admission 10,000d; ⊙ 7.30-11am & 1.30-5pm) Son La's Old French Prison & Museum was a French penal colony where anticolonial revolutionaries were incarcerated. It was destroyed by the 'offloading' of unused ammunition by US warplanes after bombing raids, but is now partially restored. Rebuilt turrets stand guard over crumbling cells and a famous lone surviving peach tree, planted by To Hieu, a 1940s inmate.

Nearby the People's Committee office has a small museum, with local hill-tribe displays and good views of the prison.

Lookout Tower　LANDMARK
For an overview of Son La and the surrounding area, follow the stone steps to the left of the Trade Union Hotel. Look forward to a 20-minute walk to reach the lookout.

Craft Markets　MARKET
Thuan Chau is about 35km northwest of Son La. Take a local bus or *xe om* here early in the morning, when its daily market is full of colourful hill-tribe women.

You'll also find woven shoulder bags, scarves, silver buttons and necklaces, and other hill-tribe crafts at Son La's market.

🛏 Sleeping & Eating

Sao Xanh Hotel　HOTEL $
(☎ 022-378 9999; www.saoxanh.vn; 1 Đ Quyen Thang; r 280,000-380,000d) Excellent value with spotless rooms and a friendly vibe at reception. The hotel is just a short walk to good cafes and restaurants.

Viet Trinh　GUEST HOUSE $
(☎ 022-385 2263; 15 Đ 26/8; r 300,000d) Here's the best budget option for long-term

Southeast Asian travellers, with simple but clean rooms in a small family-owned guesthouse.

Hanoi Hotel　HOTEL $$
(☎ 022-375 3299; www.khachsanhanoi299.com; 228 Đ Truong Chinh; r US$35-47; ❋ @ 🛜) This gleaming main-drag edifice has spacious and modern rooms trimmed with colourful art, wooden furniture and surprisingly comfortable beds. Mod cons include a bar, restaurant and jacuzzi, and the massage chairs are definitely worth considering after a long bus journey. Bring along your negotiation A-game to get a good walk-in rate.

Long Phuong Restaurant　VIETNAMESE $
(☎ 022-385 2339; P Thinh Doi; mains 40,000-70,000d; ⊙ 11am-10pm) Located at one of the busier junctions in town, this restaurant features local minority dishes. Try sour *mang dang* (bamboo shoots) soup with sticky rice dipped in sesame-seed salt.

❶ Information

Agribank (8 Đ Chu Van Thinh) Has an ATM and changes dollars. The main post office is west of here.

❶ Getting There & Away

Son La is 340km from Hanoi and 140km from Dien Bien Phu. The bus station is 5km southwest of town.

Buses from Son La:

DESTINATION	COST (D)	DURATION & FREQUENCY
Dien Bien Phu	97,000	4hr; frequent 5.30am-1.30pm
Hanoi	150,000,000	8½hr; frequent 5am-1pm
Ninh Binh	from 135,000	9hr; 5.30am

Dien Bien Phu
☎ 0230 / POP 72,700

Around Dien Bien Phu on 7 May 1954, the French colonial forces were defeated by the Viet Minh in a decisive battle, and the days of their Indochina empire became numbered.

Dien Bien Phu (DBP) sits in the heart-shaped Muong Thanh Valley, surrounded by heavily forested hills. The scenery to or from DBP is stunning, with approach roads scything through thick forests and steep terrain. The city itself lies more prosaically on

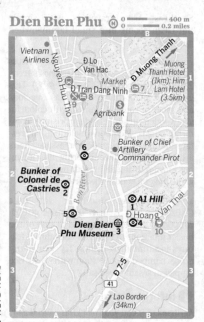

Dien Bien Phu

a broad dry plain. Thai, H'mong and Si La people live in the surrounding mountains, but the city and valley are mainly inhabited by ethnic Vietnamese.

Previously just a minor settlement, DBP only achieved town status in 1992. It became a city in 2003, and a year later was elevated to provincial capital. Expansive boulevards and civic buildings have been constructed, and the airport now receives daily flights from Hanoi. With the nearby Sop Hun–Tay Trang Vietnam–Laos border open to foreigners, more travellers are passing through the city.

History is the city's main attraction, with colonial-era bunkers and museums.

History

In early 1954 General Henri Navarre, commander of the French forces in Indochina, sent 12 battalions to occupy the Muong Thanh Valley in an attempt to prevent the Viet Minh from crossing into Laos and threatening the former Lao capital of Luang Prabang. The French units, of which 30% were ethnic Vietnamese, were soon surrounded by Viet Minh forces under General Vo Nguyen Giap. The Viet Minh outnumbered the French by five to one, and were equipped with artillery pieces and anti-aircraft guns, painstakingly carried by porters through jungles and across rivers. The guns were placed in carefully camouflaged concealed positions overlooking the French positions.

When the guns opened up, French Chief Artillery Commander Pirot committed suicide. He'd assumed there was no way the Viet Minh could get heavy artillery to the area. A failed Viet Minh human-wave assault against the French was followed by weeks of intense artillery bombardments. Six battalions of French paratroopers were parachuted into DBP as the situation worsened, but bad weather and the impervious Viet Minh artillery prevented sufficient French reinforcements from arriving. An elaborate system of trenches and tunnels allowed Viet Minh soldiers to reach French positions without coming under fire. The trenches and bunkers were overrun by the Viet Minh after the French decided against the use of US conventional bombers, and the Pentagon's proposal to use tactical atomic bombs. All 13,000 French soldiers were either killed or taken prisoner, and Viet Minh casualties were estimated at 25,000.

Just one day before the Geneva Conference on Indochina was set to begin in Switzerland, Viet Minh forces finally overran the beleaguered French garrison after a 57-day siege. This shattered French morale, and the French government abandoned all attempts to re-establish colonial control of Vietnam.

⊙ Sights

★ Dien Bien Phu Museum　MUSEUM
(☎0230-382 4971; Đ 7-5; admission 5000d; ⊙7-11am & 1.30-5pm) Commemorating the 1954 battle, this well-laid-out museum features an eclectic collection. Alongside weaponry and guns, there's a bath-tub that belonged to the French commander Colonel de Castries, a bicycle capable of carrying 330kg of ordnance, and photographs and documents, some with English translations. At the time of writing, a new modern structure to house the collection was under construction.

★ Bunker of Colonel de Castries　WAR MEMORIAL
(admission 5000d; ⊙7-11am & 1.30-5pm) Across the river the command bunker of Colonel Christian de Castries has been re-created. A few discarded tanks linger nearby, and you'll probably see Vietnamese tourists mounting the bunker and waving the Vietnamese flag, re-enacting an iconic photograph taken at the battle's conclusion.

★ A1 Hill　WAR MEMORIAL
(admission 3000d; ⊙7-11am & 1.30-5pm) There are more tanks and a monument to Viet Minh casualties on this former French position, known to the French as Eliane and to the Vietnamese as A1 Hill. The elaborate trenches at the heart of the French defences have also been re-created.

Cemeteries　WAR MEMORIAL
A formal French War Memorial, erected on the 30th anniversary of the 1954 battle, commemorates the 3000 French troops buried under the rice paddies. On the other bank of the Ron River, the immaculately maintained Dien Bien Phu Cemetery commemorates the Vietnamese dead, each gravestone bearing the gold star of the Vietnamese flag and a clutch of incense sticks.

Muong Thanh Bridge　BRIDGE
The old Muong Thanh Bridge is preserved and closed to four-wheeled traffic. Near the southern end of the bridge – though not much more than an overgrown crater – is the bunker where Chief Artillery Commander Pirot committed suicide.

NORTHERN VIETNAM DIEN BIEN PHU

WORTH A TRIP

CHOW DOWN IN MOC CHAU & YEN CHAU

Many travellers heading west enjoy the beautiful scenery around Mai Chau before kicking on to Laos via Dien Bien Phu, or heading north to Sapa. If you have a hankering for local flavours, especially if you've got a sweet tooth, it's worth stopping off at a couple of other towns along Hwy 6.

Around 200km west of Hanoi, Moc Chau boasts a pioneering dairy industry launched in the late 1970s with Australian and UN assistance. The dairy provides Hanoi with fresh milk, sweetened condensed milk and little tooth-rotting bars called *banh sua*, and the town is a good place to sample fresh milk and yoghurt. Moc Chau also produces some of Vietnam's best tea, and the surrounding area is home to ethnic minorities, including Green H'mong, Dzao, Thai and Muong. Vietnam in Focus (p66) offers annual photographic trips from Hanoi to Moc Chau's fascinating H'mong Love Market in late August/early September, and Handspan Adventure Travel (p83) runs two- and three-day trips to the area, staying in a Black Thai homestay in Ban Doi village.

A further 60km west, the agricultural Yen Chau district is known for its abundant fruit production. Apart from bananas, all fruits grown here are seasonal. Mangoes, plums and peaches are harvested from April to June, longans in July and August, and custard apples from August to September.

Yen Chau mangoes are renowned as Vietnam's tastiest, although travellers may initially find them disappointing, as they are small and green, rather than big, yellow and juicy like those of the tropical south. Most Vietnamese actually prefer the tart flavour of the green ones, especially dipped in *nuoc mam* (fish sauce) and sugar.

Both Moc Chau and Yen Chau can be reached on departures to either Son La or Dien Bien Phu from Hanoi's My Dinh bus station. Once on the road, travellers should find it relatively easy to flag down onward transport along Hwy 6 ranging from local minibuses to air-con coaches.

🛌 Sleeping

Viet Hoang 2   GUEST HOUSE **$**
(☑ 0989 797 988; 69 Đ Phuong Thanh Binh; r
250,000-350,000d; ✳ @ 🛜) Tucked away opposite the bus station, this guesthouse is the
newer (and much cleaner) offshoot of the
older, nearby Viet Hoang 1 (rooms 150,000d
to 200,000d). The extra dong are worth it.

Binh Long Hotel   GUEST HOUSE **$**
(☑ 0230-382 4345; 429 Đ Muong Thanh; d & tw
US$10; ✳ 🛜) Another small, friendly, family-
run place, but on a busy junction in the thick
of things. The twin rooms aren't exactly
huge, but the owners know about onward
transport to Sapa and Laos.

Muong Thanh Hotel   HOTEL **$$**
(☑ 0230-381 0043; www.muongthanhthanhn-
ien.com; Đ Muong Thanh; r US$50-80; ✳ 🛜 ≋)
Modern rooms include satellite TV, elegant
furniture and marble bathrooms. Added at-
tractions include a swimming pool watched
over by a not-so-scary concrete dragon.

Him Lam Hotel   RESORT HOTEL **$$**
(☑ 0230-381 1999; www.himlamhotel.com.vn; Hwy
279; r US$30-45; ✳ @ ≋) This resort-style ho-
tel is one of Vietnam's best government-run
places, with attractive wooden stilthouses
and modern rooms, and extensive grounds,
tennis courts, pools, and a bar and restaurant. Weekends might see your lakeside rev-
erie interrupted by a local wedding. A taxi
from the DBP bus station is around 60,000d.
Count on 30,000d for a *xe om*.

🍴 Eating & Drinking

Dining options are limited in DBP, though
the Muong Thanh Hotel has an OK restaurant. It's also worth considering eating at the
Him Lam Hotel.

Pho Stalls   VIETNAMESE **$**
(dishes around 30,000d; ⊙ 8am-10pm) There's
good-value eating at the inexpensive *pho*
stalls and simple restaurants opposite the
bus station; some serve delicious fresh sugar-
cane juice.

Bia Hoi   BIA HOI
(Đ Hoang Van Thai; ⊙ noon-10pm) You're probably only in town for a night so meet the
locals at the *bia hoi* gardens along Đ Hoang
Van Thai. There's decent and cheap grilled
food also if you're tired of rice and noodles.

ℹ️ Information

Agribank (☑ 0230-382 5786; Đ 7-5) Has an
ATM and changes US dollars.
Main post office (Đ 7-5)

ℹ️ Getting There & Away

AIR

Vietnam Airlines (☑ 0230-382 4948; www.
vietnamairlines.com; Nguyen Huu Tho; ⊙ 7.30-
11.30am & 1.30-4.30pm) operates one flight
daily between Dien Bien Phu and Hanoi. The
office is near the airport, about 1.5km from the
town centre, along the road to Muong Lay.

BUS

DBP's bus station is on Hwy 12, at the corner of
Đ Tran Dang Ninh.
  Buses from Dien Bien Phu:

DESTINATION	COST (D)	DURATION & FREQUENCY
Hanoi	375,000	11½hr; frequent 4.30am-9pm
Lai Chau	130,000	6-7hr; frequent 5am-1.15pm
Muong Lay	57,000	3-4hr: 6.30am, 2.30pm, 4pm
Son La	97,000	4hr; 4.30am, 8am, noon, 2pm

CAR & MOTORCYCLE

The 480km drive from Hanoi to Dien Bien Phu on
Hwys 6 and 279 takes around 11 hours.

Muong Lay
☑ 0231 / POP 8800

Formerly known as Lai Chau, the small
town of Muong Lay en route from Dien Bien
Phu to Sapa has undergone a massive trans-
formation in recent years.

  The former town of Lai Chau was perched
on the banks of the spectacular Da River valley, but has now been flooded to incorporate
the Song Da Reservoir, part of a massive
hydroelectricity scheme. The township's
been moved up the riverbank, and an expansive new bridge crosses the newly formed
lake. A couple of hotels are open high above
the lake, and it's envisaged that the new
body of water will have a future as a tourist
centre for boat trips and water sports. At the
time of writing though, it still resembles a
very big construction site.

ⓘ GETTING TO LAOS: DIEN BIEN PHU TO MUANG KHUA

Getting to the border Buses from Dien Bien Phu (DBP) to Muang Khua (110,000d) leave daily at 5.30am. It's advisable to book your ticket the day prior to travelling. This bus takes you through the Sop Hun/Tay Trang border crossing and drops you off in Muang Khua in Laos. The journey typically takes between seven and eight hours, but can be longer depending on the roads and border formalities. Other destinations in Laos from DBP include Luang Prabang (495,000d, 6am), Nam Tha (350,000d, 6.30am) and Udomxai (230,000d, 7.30am).

At the border The Lao border at Tay Trang, 34km from Dien Bien Phu, is open daily between 7am and 7pm. Crossing into Laos most travellers can get a 30-day visa on arrival (US$20 to US$42, depending on your nationality). Have photo ID and additional cash (around US$5) on hand for occasional local administrative fees.

Moving on From Muang Khua there are buses to Udomxai.

🛏 Sleeping & Eating

Lan Anh Hotel   HOTEL $$
(☑ 0231-385 2682; www.lananhhotel.com; r US$15-45; ❋ @) Relocated across the bridge onto a ridge overlooking the lake, the Lan Anh has rooms ranging from rustic stilt houses to VIP suites with flash marble bathrooms. Trekking to nearby minority villages and boat trips on the lake can be organised. Pick-ups can be arranged from Muong Lay's bus station on the opposite bank.

ⓘ Getting There & Away

At the time of writing, Muong Lay had a makeshift bus station on Hwy 12. If you can book ahead at Lan Anh Hotel, Muong Lay is worth a slightly surreal overnight stop, but given the town's current reinvention, a through bus from Dien Bien Phu to Lai Chau is probably the best option. If you're on a motorbike, note that at the time of writing, the road north of Muong Lay to Lai Chau was very rough, with many roadworks for around 40km. It was scheduled to be completed around August 2014, but could potentially take longer.

Buses from Muong Lay:

DESTINATION	COST (D)	DURATION & FREQUENCY
Dien Bien Phu	73,000	3hr; 6.15am, 7.15am, 1.45pm
Lai Chau	70,000	8hr; 7am
Sinho	80,000	2½; 8am

Lai Chau

☑ 0231 / POP 37,000

After passing through one of Vietnam's remotest regions, the new eight-lane boulevards and monumental government buildings of Lai Chau appear like some Vietnamese El Dorado. The reality is more prosaic.

Formerly known as Tam Duong, this remote town was renamed Lai Chau when a decision was made to flood 'old' Lai Chau (now called Muong Lay). 'New' Lai Chau is split between the old town, with its market full of hill-tribe people, and the concrete new town 3km to the southeast.

Despite its grandiose streets and upgrade to provincial-capital status, Lai Chau is still something of a one-horse town. Fortunately the surrounding scenery of verdant conical peaks is as beguiling as ever.

Most visitors stop for a lunch break between Dien Bien Phu, Muong Lay and Sapa. The drive from Lai Chau to Sapa along Hwy 4D, threading through the Fansipan Mountain Range near the Chinese border, is a beautiful stretch of road.

🛏 Sleeping & Eating

Cam Tu Hotel   HOTEL $
(☑ 0964 444 6555; 330 Đ Tran Phu; r 200,000-250,000d) Colourful decor and friendly dogs in reception give way to more prosaic but clean rooms, and the Cam Tu is well located, with good restaurants just across the road.

Phuong Tanh   HOTEL $$
(☑ 0231-387 5235; Main Sapa Rd; d US$27; ❋ 🛜) Part of a burgeoning mini-empire (the owners also run a nearby restaurant of the same name – mains cost around 150,000d) the Phuong Tanh overcomes a drab reception area with clean and well-lit rooms offering big bathrooms. On the 2nd floor, Café Phan Xi Pan is a brightly coloured oasis with wi-fi, cold beer and tasty variations on rice and noodles.

WORTH A TRIP

SINHO VILLAGE

Sinho is a scenic mountain village that's home to a large number of ethnic minorities. It should attract more tourists, but when you visit, there is a 'you ain't from around here' look on the faces of many locals.

However, a decent hotel and improving road access means it's an excellent detour if you're keen to see an authentic local market very different to the markets at Sapa and Bac Ha, which are now firmly on the tour-bus route.

Sinho has markets on Saturday and Sunday; the wildly colourful Sunday market is the more impressive of the two. Just don't expect trendy ethnic handicrafts: you're more likely to be confronted with a full-on mix of bovine moos and porcine squeals.

The best (only!) place in town that accepts foreign travellers is the welcoming **Thanh Binh Hotel** (0231-387 0366; Zone 5, Sinho; r US$25-27; @), a surprisingly comfortable spot comprised of 17 spotless rooms with mountain and rice-paddy views. Rates include breakfast, and lunch and dinner (120,000d) are on offer in cosy bamboo gazebos. Treks from 3km to 10km can be arranged to nearby White H'mong and Red Dzao villages.

Note there are no ATMs or banking services in Sinho, but there is internet access at the Thanh Binh Hotel.

A bus to Sinho leaves Dien Bien Phu daily (120,000d, six hours) at around 5.30am, transiting through Muong Lay around 8am. These times can be flexible, so check at the Dien Bien Phu bus station the day before you want to leave. From Sinho, buses then trundle downhill to Lai Chau (80,000d, three hours) at 7am and 1pm. Heading south from Lai Chau to Sinho, there are two buses per day at 6.30am and 12.30pm (80,000d, three hours), and a daily departure (120,000d, six hours) to Dien Bien Phu. Note that the road linking Sinho to Lai Chau was very poor at the time of writing, but major road-works were planned to be completed by around September 2014.

It's definitely slow getting to Sinho by public transport, but achievable with patience and a flexible attitude.

If you're travelling on two wheels, the turn-off uphill to Sinho is 1km north of Chan Nua on the main road from Muong Lay to Lai Chau. Definitely ask about the state of the road from Sinho to Lai Chau before you leave Hanoi.

ⓘ Information

There's an Agribank and ATMs in the old town's main street.

ⓘ Getting There & Away

The bus station is 1km out of town, on the road to Sapa. A xe om from the bus station to hotels is around 10,000d and a taxi around 20,000d.

Buses from Lai Chau:

DESTINATION	COST (D)	DURATION & FREQUENCY
Dien Bien Phu	150,000	7hr; frequent 5am–1pm
Hanoi	from 320,000	12hr; 5am, frequent 4–8pm
Sapa	100,000	2½hr; frequent 5am–6pm
Muong Lay	90,000	3hr; frequent 5am–1.30pm
Sinho	80,000	3hr; 6.30am, 12.30pm

Sapa

020 / POP 36,200 / ELEV 1650M

Established as a hill station by the French in 1922, Sapa is the one place in the northwest where tourism is booming. It's now firmly on the European and North American package-tour circuit, and well-equipped trekkers are a common sight around town.

The town is oriented to make the most of the spectacular views emerging on clear days. It overlooks a plunging valley of cascading rice terraces, with mountains towering above on all sides. Views of this epic scenery are often subdued by thick mist rolling across the peaks, but even if it's cloudy, Sapa is still a fascinating destination, especially when local hill-tribe people fill the town with colour.

The town's French-colonial villas fell into disrepair during successive wars with the French, Americans and Chinese, but following the advent of tourism, Sapa has experienced a renaissance. The downside is a hotel building boom, and because height restrictions are rarely enforced, the Sapa skyline is changing for the worse.

Inherent in this prosperity is cultural change for the hill-tribe people. The H'mong people are very canny traders, urging you to buy handicrafts and trinkets. Many have had little formal education, yet all the youngsters have a good command of English, French and a handful of other languages.

◉ Sights & Activities

Sapa Museum   MUSEUM
(103 Đ Xuan Vien; ⊙ 7.30-11.30am & 1.30-5pm) **FREE** Excellent showcase of the history and ethnology of the Sapa area including the colonial times of the French. Exhibitions demonstrate the differences between the various ethnic minority people of the area, so it's definitely worth visiting the muesum when you first arrive in town. Downstairs is a handicrafts and weaving demonstration with items for sale.

★ Sapa Market   MARKET
(⊙ 6am-2pm) Hill-tribe people from surrounding villages go to the Sapa market most days to sell handicrafts and ethnic-style clothing. Saturday is the busiest day, and every day the market's food stalls are popular for breakfast and lunch. The location of the town's market may change in the next few years.

Chieu Suong   MASSAGE
(☑ 020-387 1919; 16 P Thach Son; massages from 150,000d; ⊙ 7am-10pm) Hiking those mountain trails can be tough on your joints, so come to this humble spot for bona fide foot and body massages.

Victoria Spa   SPA
(☑ 020-387 1522; www.victoriahotels-asia.com; Victoria Sapa Resort & Spa, P Hoang Dieu; ⊙ 8am-10pm) This upmarket spa complex at the Victoria Sapa Resort has gorgeous massage and treatment rooms. The spa's pool is open to people not staying at the resort for US$10 per person.

Local Villages   HIKING
For overnight stays in villages and longer treks into the mountains, it's important to hook up with someone who knows the terrain and culture and speaks the language. We recommend using minority guides, as this offers them a means of making a living. Note it's illegal to stay overnight in villages that are not officially recognised as home-stays. Ignoring this could cause significant problems for your hosts and yourself.

Speak to travel agencies or guides (who'll probably approach you in the street), pick up a decent map and plot your course. The villages and the surrounding landscape are now part of Hoang Lien National Park.

The nearest village within walking distance is **Cat Cat** (admission 40,000d), 3km south of Sapa. It's a steep and beautiful hike down, and there are plenty of *xe om* for the return uphill journey.

Another popular hike is to **Ta Phin village** (admission 20,000d), home to Red Dzao and about 10km from Sapa. Most people take a *xe om* to a starting point about 8km from Sapa, and then make a 14km loop through the area, passing through Black H'mong and Red Dzao villages.

For spectacular valley views (if the mist and cloud gods relent), there's a beautiful hike along a high ridge east of Sapa through the Black H'mong settlements of **Sa Seng** and **Hang Da** down to the Ta Van River, where you can get transport back to Sapa.

There are also community-based tours to the nearby H'mong village of **Sin Chai**, with an overnight in the village to learn about textiles or music and dance. Other popular communities to visit include the Giay village of **Ta Van** and the H'mong village of **Matra**. Note that admission charges (between 20,000d and 40,000d) also apply to these other villages.

Fansipan   CLIMBING
Surrounding Sapa are the Hoang Lien Mountains, dubbed the Tonkinese Alps by the French. These mountains include the often cloud-obscured Fansipan (3143m), Vietnam's highest peak. Fansipan is accessible year-round to sensibly equipped travellers in good shape, but don't underestimate the challenge. It is very wet, and can be perilously slippery and generally cold. Don't attempt an ascent if Sapa's weather is poor, as limited visibility on Fansipan can be treacherous.

The summit of Fansipan is 19km from Sapa and can be reached only on foot. The terrain is rough and adverse weather is frequent. The round trip usually takes three days; some experienced hikers do it in two days, but you'll need to be fit. After walking through hill-tribe villages on the first morning, it's just forest, mountain vistas and occasional wildlife, including monkeys, mountain goats and birds.

Sapa

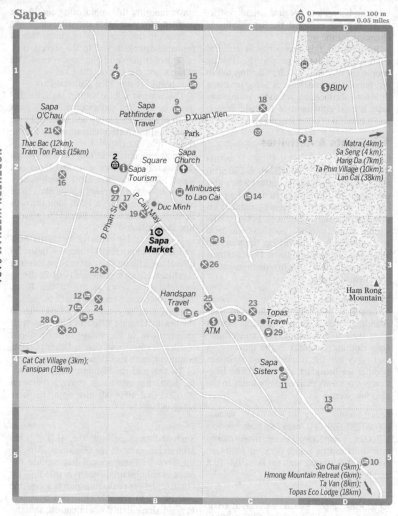

Sapa O'Chau

Thac Bac (12km);
Tram Ton Pass (15km)

Sapa Pathfinder Travel

Đ Xuan Vien

Park

Sapa Church

Sapa Tourism

Square

Minibuses to Lao Cai

Duc Minh

P Cau May

Đ Phan Si

Sapa Market

BIDV

Matra (4km);
Sa Seng (4km);
Hang Da (7km);
Ta Phin Village (10km);
Lao Cai (38km)

Handspan Travel

Topas Travel

ATM

Ham Rong Mountain

Cat Cat Village (3km);
Fansipan (19km)

Sapa Sisters

Sin Chai (5km);
Hmong Mountain Retreat (6km);
Ta Van (8km);
Topas Eco Lodge (18km)

No ropes or technical climbing skills are needed, just endurance. There are a few rudimentary shelters at a couple of base camps en route, but it's better to be self-sufficient with sleeping bag, waterproof tent, food, stove, raincoat or poncho, compass and other miscellaneous survival gear. It's vital to carry out all your garbage, as some of the camps are now impacted by trash. Hiring a reputable guide is vital, and porters are also recommended.

Through local operators, count on an all-inclusive rate of around US$150 per person for a couple, US$125 per person for a group of four and US$100 per person for the sensible maximum group size of six.

Weather-wise the best time is from mid-October to mid-December, and in March, when wildflowers are in bloom.

Tram Ton Pass   VIEWPOINT, HIKING
(loop track admission 3000d) The road between Sapa and Lai Chau crosses the Tram Ton Pass on the northern side of Fansipan, 15km from Sapa. At 1900m this is Vietnam's highest mountain pass, and acts as a dividing line between two weather fronts. Even if you're not touring the northwest, come up

Sapa

NORTHERN VIETNAM SAPA

here to experience the often-ferocious winds and the incredible views.

On the Sapa side, it's often cold and foggy, but drop a few hundred metres onto the Lai Chau side, and it can be sunny and warm. Surprisingly, Sapa is the coldest place in Vietnam, but Lai Chau can be one of the warmest.

Alongside the road, 12km from Sapa, is 100m-high **Thac Bac** (Silver Waterfall); the **loop track** is steep and scenic. The waterfall is sometimes included on tours offered by Sapa travel agencies and another option to get there is to rent a motorbike.

⊁ Courses

Indigo Cat   CRAFT
(http://indigocat.dznly.com; 46 Đ Phan Si; per person per project 100,000d; ⊙ 9am-7pm) Learn traditional H'mong weaving at this funky and friendly craft shop co-owned by a H'mong-Swiss couple. There's no time limit; just come back as many times as you need to finish your work. Bags and iPad covers are popular items for sale.

The Hill Station Signature Restaurant   COOKING
(⊉ 020-388 7112; www.thehillstation.com; 37 Đ Phan Si; per person US$29; ⊙ from 9am) Features five local dishes, and is conducted by an English-speaking H'mong chef. The class begins with a 30-minute market tour and includes local rice wine and dishes like smoked buffalo and homemade tofu.

Sapa Rooms   COOKING
(⊉ 020-650 5228; www.saparooms.com; Đ Phan Si; per person US$35; ⊙ from 9:30am) Pop into the Sapa Rooms cafe and ask about its cookery courses held at the Hmong Mountain Retreat. Classes kick off with a visit to Sapa market, just 10m from the cafe.

⊨ Sleeping

Sapa has accommodation ranging from bare-bones cheapies, through to boutique-style offerings, and a luxury hilltop resort. Most hotels listed have views, but Sapa's building boom can change that overnight; check when you book.

Prices are competitive, but often double on busy weekends with the influx of Vietnamese tourists. Note some midrange places also have excellent budget rooms.

Beware of hotels using old-style charcoal burners for heat, as the fumes can cause severe breathing problems if the room's not well ventilated. Most hotels have now switched over to electric heaters or open fireplaces for the winter.

Green Valley Hotel HOSTEL $
(☑ 0979 110 800; sapagreenvalleyhotel@gmail.
com; 45 Đ Muong Hoa; dm US$4, s US$7-10, d & tw
US$10-15; @ 🛜) Sapa's only true backpacker
hostel is this welcoming spot with great
views. Motorcycles can be rented for US$5
per day, and there's a cosy on-site bar with
pool table.

It's also a good source of information for
onward travel to Laos or China.

Casablanca Sapa Hotel BOUTIQUE HOTEL $
(☑ 0974 418 111; www.sapacasablanca.com; Đ Dong
Loi; r US$22-30; @ 🛜) One of Sapa's first bou-
tique hotels has a new lease on life thanks
to the friendly family owners. Look forward
to colourful decor and good hospitality from
Mr Tom.

**Luong Thuy
Family Guesthouse** GUEST HOUSE $
(☑ 020-387 2310; www.familysapa.com; 28 Đ
Muong Hoa; s/d US$15/18; @ 🛜) This friendly
guesthouse is slightly away from the hubbub of downtown Sapa. Motorcycles and
bikes can be rented, trekking and transport
arranged, and there are valley views from
front balconies.

⭐**Hmong Mountain Retreat** ECOLODGE $$
(☑ 020-650 5228; www.hmongmountainretreat.
com; 6 Ban Ho Rd, Lao Chai; d/f incl breakfast
US$59/120) 🌿 Accommodation in bunga-
lows or a restored H'mong house is simple,
but the real attraction is sleeping above a
cascade of rice paddies several kilometres
out of Sapa. Rates include breakfast, served
in the retreat's restaurant, crafted from an
80-year-old tribal house; up to 95% of in-
gredients are sourced within a 2km radius.
The grounds are dotted with the owner's
artworks.

Nam Cang Riverside House HOMESTAY $$
(www.topasecolodge.com; Nam Cang Village; d
US$60) Located in a valley 36km from Sapa,
this stylish wooden house with nine rooms
is a collaboration between a Red Dzao family and Topas Travel. Final access is across a
private bridge over a river and rates include
breakfast. Look forward to remote isolation
surrounded by stunning scenery. Enquire at
Topas Travel (p135) in Sapa town.

Thai Binh Hotel HOTEL $$
(☑ 0977 448 866; www.thaibinhhotel.com; 45 Đ
Ham Rong; d/f US$35/70) Run by a couple of
teachers, the Thai Binh enjoys a quiet loca-
tion near Sapa's church. Rooms are spotless
and decked out with crisp pine furniture
and cosy bedspreads. Rates include break-
fast, and the owners are well equipped with
information about onward travel to China.

Cha Pa Garden BOUTIQUE HOTEL $$
(☑ 020-387 2907; www.chapagarden.com; 23B
P Cau May; r US$65-82; ❄ @ 🛜) Cha Pa oc-
cupies a sensitively restored colonial villa
amid lush and private gardens in the heart
of Sapa. There are just four rooms, all presented in contemporary style, with wooden
floors, uncluttered lines and hip bathrooms.

Cat Cat View Hotel HOTEL $$
(☑ 020-387 1946; www.catcathotel.com; 46 Đ
Phan Si; s/d from US$30/35; @ 🛜) This excel-
lent spot has 40 rooms over nine floors,
many with great views. There's something
for every budget, with homely, comfortable
pine-trimmed accommodation, and even
a seriously spacious three-bedroom apart-
ment (US$180). The cheaper rooms are the
best value: bargain hunters should check
out the budget digs starting from US$10 for
a single.

BUILDING A STRONGER H'MONG FUTURE

Traditionally, the H'mong have been employees of Vietnamese-owned trekking compa-
nies, restaurants and accommodation, with many H'mong children kept out of school to
sell handicrafts or to be trekking guides, often walking up to 10km daily from their vil-
lages to Sapa to earn money. A new generation, including former handicraft peddler Shu
Tan's organisation Sapa O'Chau (p135), is now focused on securing a more independent
and positive future for their people.

Meaning 'thank you Sapa' in the H'mong language, Sapa O'Chau is focused on provid-
ing training and opportunities to H'mong children. The Sapa O'Chau Learning Centre is
a live-in school where up to 20 H'mong children can learn English and Vietnamese.

Sapa O'Chau is always interested to hear from travellers keen on volunteering as
English-language teachers, and the organisation also runs excellent walks and treks.
Their cafe (p133) in Sapa is also a cosy spot for a drink or a snack.

Boutique Sapa Hotel
BOUTIQUE HOTEL **$$**

(☑020-387 2727; www.boutiquesapahotel.com; 41 Đ Phan Si; s/d from US$30/40; @ 🛜) This hotel features classy furniture, flat-screen TVs and superb vistas from the terrace cafe, while the downstairs dining room does pizza and warming hotpots. Pay a little more for a room with valley views. Massage and cookery classes are both available.

Fansipan View Hotel
HOTEL **$$**

(☑020-387 3759; www.fansipanview.com; 45 Đ Xuan Vien; s/d from US$25/30; @ 🛜) Here you'll find cosy rooms tucked away in a quiet lane. Ask for a room at the front for views of the town. Downstairs is the good Sapa Cuisine restaurant. The owners were busy building a new hotel nearby when we last dropped by.

Sapa Rooms
BOUTIQUE HOTEL **$$**

(☑020-650 5228; www.saparooms.com; Đ Phan Si; d/f US$59/72; @ 🛜) Billing itself as a boutique hotel, this place is decorated in a highly quirky style and has an excellent lobby cafe. The rooms are more prosaic, but show some nice touches including fresh flowers. Prices include a good breakfast.

Sapa Luxury Hotel
HOTEL **$$**

(☑020-387 2771; www.sapaluxuryhotel.com; 36 Đ Phan Si; s/d/tr from US$28/28/35; @ 🛜) One of the newer openings on Đ Phan Si features spacious rooms with wooden floors and trendy Asian decor last seen at your local furniture superstore.

Sapa View
HOTEL **$$**

(☑020-387 2388; www.sapaview-hotel.com; 41 Đ Muong Hoa; s/d/ste from US$65/75/85; @ 🛜) Look forward to excellent valley views, especially from the attached Tam Tam restaurant. The decor is a winning combination of local tribal art and lots of Scandinavian-style wood.

★Topas Eco Lodge
ECOLODGE **$$$**

(☑020-387 2404; www.topasecolodge.com; bungalows US$115-140; @ 🛜) 🏊 Overlooking a plunging valley, this ecolodge has 25 lovely stone-and-thatch bungalows, each with front balconies to make the most of the magnificent views. The whole project is sustainable and environmentally friendly, with solar energy providing the power. Hiking, biking and market tours are all available, and romantic dinners (1,500,000d per couple) in a private hilltop pavillion can also be arranged.

The lodge is also open to outside guests for lunch (mains 120,000d to 200,000d), with a free shuttle bus departing from the Topas Travel office (9.30am Monday to Saturday) in Sapa.

Victoria Sapa Resort & Spa
RESORT HOTEL **$$$**

(☑020-387 1522; www.victoriahotels-asia.com; P Hoang Dieu; r from US$190; ✳ @ 🛜 ⛱) This alpine-style hilltop hotel is a well-maintained establishment, right down to the manicured lawns. Rooms aren't large, but they do feature hand-carved furniture and private balconies. Facilities include two bars, a heated swimming pool and a fitness centre. Get here in style from Hanoi on one of the resort's luxury *Victoria Express* train carriages.

✗ Eating

For Western and Vietnamese food in comfortable surroundings, there's a diverse scene along the main drag P Cau May. Most places in town open for breakfast, lunch and dinner.

For eating on a budget, humble Vietnamese restaurants huddle below the market on Đ Tue Tinh, and the night-market stalls south of the church can't be beaten for *bun cha* (barbecued pork).

Little Sapa
VIETNAMESE **$**

(18 P Cau May; mains 50,000-80,000d; ⊘8am-10pm) One of the better-value eateries along touristy P Cau May, Little Sapa also lures in locals. Steer clear of the largely medicore European dishes and concentrate on the Vietnamese menu.

Sapa O'Chau
CAFE **$**

(www.sapaochau.org; 8 Đ Thac Bac; snacks from 20,000d; ⊘6.30am-6.30pm) Cosy cafe that's also the best place to ask about trekking, homestays and volunteering opportunities with Sapa O'Chau. Don't miss warming up with a cup of ginger tea sweetened with Sapa mountain honey.

Sapa Market
VIETNAMESE **$**

(P Cau May; dishes around 30,000d; ⊘6am-1pm; ☺) Lots of local food stalls and a good alternative to another hotel breakfast or for a cheap and authentic lunch.

Baguette & Chocolat
CAFE **$**

(☑020-387 1766; Đ Thac Bac; cakes from 30,000d, snacks & meals 70,000-160,000d; ⊘7am-10pm) Head to this cafe in an elegant converted villa for one of their fine breakfasts, open sandwichs, baguettes or a tasty slab of gateau.

Barbecue Restaurants
VIETNAMESE $

(Ð Phan Si; meals around 70,000-120,000d; ⊘noon-11pm) Several easygoing spots along the northern end of Ð Phan Si specialise in expertly grilled meat and vegetables. Kick things off with a lazy session at *bia hoi* corner nearby.

Hotpot Stalls
VIETNAMESE $

(Ð Xuan Vien; hotpots around 50,000d; ⊘11am-11pm) Vietnamese-style *lau* hotpot (meat stew cooked with local vegetables, cabbage and mushroom) is a very popular local dish; try it at the hotpot stalls just south of the bus station.

★The Hill Station Signature Restaurant
H'MONG $$

(www.thehillstation.com; 37 Ð Phan Si; meals 90,000-180,000d; ⊘7am-10.30pm) Cool Zen decor and superb views showcase H'mong ethnic minority cuisine. Dishes include chicken with wild ginger, ash-baked trout in banana leaves, and traditional H'mong-style black pudding. Tasting sets of local rice and corn wine are also of interest to curious travelling foodies. Don't miss trying the delicate rainbow-trout rolls; think of them as 'Sapa sushi'.

The Village Noshery
CAFE $$

(www.saparooms.com/village_noshery; 42 P Cau May; tapas 60,000-80,000d, mains 70,000-110,000d; ⊘6.30am-11pm) Stylish cafe with decent Vietnamese food, including tapas-sized plates of interesting snacks like barbecued beef in betel leaves, and chicken and beef lemongrass satay sticks. Noodle dishes, soups and spring rolls are also available, and it's a top place for an end-of-day beer or cocktail. Coffee and cake is another post-trekking option. Upstairs are double rooms (US$30 including breakfast).

Nature View
VIETNAMESE $$

(51 Ð Phan Si; mains 90,000-150,000d; ⊘8am-10pm) You've got to love the photos of the owner's kids on the walls at this friendly spot with great valley views. Look forward to decent Vietnamese and European food and just maybe Sapa's best fruit smoothies. Those who aren't fans of tofu should try the sizzling tofu with lemongrass and be converted. Don't worry – it's not all vegetarian food.

The Hill Station Deli & Boutique
CAFE $$

(www.thehillstation.com; 7 Ð Muong Hoa; mains 125,000-165,000d; ⊘7am-10.30pm) With cheese and charcuterie plates, pork terrine and local smoked trout, the Hill Station Deli & Boutique is a stylish new addition to the Sapa dining scene. Factor in some of Sapa's best coffee and an interesting array of international beers and wines, and you've got cosmopolitan options if you've just arrived overland from Laos. It's also a top spot for breakfast.

Sapa Rooms
CAFE $$

(www.saparooms.com; Ð Phan Si; mains 60,000-120,000d; ⊘6.30am-10.30pm) This flamboyantly decorated cafe looks like it should be in New York or London rather than the highlands of northern Vietnam. It's great for a snack (think corn fritters or BLT baguette), decent burgers and soups, and great coffee and cake. Noodles are also available.

Viet Emotion
MEDITERRANEAN $$

(✆020-387 2559; www.vietemotion.com; 27 P Cau May; meals 70,000-150,000d; ⊘7am-11pm) This stylish and intimate bistro features a cosy fireplace and has bottles of wine hanging from the ceiling. Try the trekking omelette, homemade soup or something from the tapas menu, such as *gambas al ajillo* (garlic prawns). If the weather really sets in, there are books and magazines to browse, and games including chess.

🍷 Drinking

A bar crawl in Sapa will take in a maximum of three or four venues – this is not a party town.

Mountain Bar & Pub
BAR

(2 Ð Muong Hoa; ⊘noon-11pm) Dangerously strong cocktails, cold beer and ultracompetitive games of table football conspire to make this Sapa's go-to place for a great night out. Even if it's freezing outside, a *shisha* beside the open fire will soon perk up the chilliest of travellers. Try the warm apple wine for some highland bliss.

Color Bar
BAR

(www.facebook.com/colorbar; 56 Ð Phan Si; ⊘noon-11pm) Owned by a Hanoi artist, this rustic and atmospheric spot ticks all the boxes with reggae, table football, *shisha* and ice-cold Bia Lao Cai. A great local spot if your accommodation is nearby on Ð Phan Si, or as a refuelling option on the steep walk up from Cat Cat Village.

Hmong Sisters
BAR

(Đ Muong Hoa; ◑noon-late) This spacious bar with pool tables and an open fire has pretty decent music, but can feel a bit sparse if it's a quiet night. Bar prices are reasonable though, so it's always worth checking out.

Bia Hoi Corner
BIA HOI

(cnr 56 Đ Phan Si & P Cau May; ◑4-11pm) The cheapest beer in town and the occasional company of assorted locals and Sapa's small crew of expat residents. Adjacent are good barbecue restaurants for a cheap and tasty night out.

🔒 Shopping

Scour the stores on P Cau May and Đ Phan Si for clothing, accessories and jewellery produced by the area's minority peoples. Urban Vietnamese designers are also producing clothes and household furnishings inspired by tribal motifs.

Lots of the minority women and girls have gone into the souvenir business; the older women in particular are known for their strong-armed selling tactics. When negotiating prices, hold your ground, but avoid aggressive bargaining.

Note that on some cheaper clothing, the dyes used are not set, which can turn anything the material touches (including your skin) a muddy blue-green colour. Wash the fabric separately in cold salted water to stop the dye from running, and wrap items in plastic bags before packing them in your luggage.

If you've arrived in town with insufficient warm clothing, stores along P Cau May sell lots of 'brand-name' walking shoes, parkas and thermals. Some of it might even be authentic. Anyone for a North Fake daypack?

Indigo Cat
HANDICRAFTS

(http://indigocat.dznly.com; 46 Đ Phan Si; ◑9am-7pm) The only H'mong-owned handicrafts shop in Sapa offers a wonderful selection of interesting local crafts including bags, clothing, pillows and belts. Co-owner Pang speaks good English and her young son Sanji is a real charmer. Pop by and ask about joining in the H'mong weaving lessons.

ℹ️ Information

INTERNET ACCESS

Internet access – including complimentary wi-fi – is available at hotels, restaurants and cafes around town.

MONEY

There are two ATMs in Sapa, and many of the hotels and businesses will change US dollars and euros.

BIDV (🗹020-387 2569; Đ Ngu Chi Son) Has an ATM and will exchange cash.

POST

Main post office (Đ Ham Rong) International phone calls can also be made here.

TOURIST INFORMATION

The *Sapa Tourist Map* (20,000d) is an excellent 1:75,000 scale map of the walking trails and attractions around Sapa. The *Sapa Trekking Map* is a worthwhile hand-drawn map showing trekking routes and the town.

Sapa Tourism (🗹020-387 3239; www.sapa-tourism.com; 103 Đ Xuan Vien; ◑7.30-11.30am & 1.30-5pm) Helpful English-speaking staff offering details about transport, trekking and weather. Internet access is free for 15 minutes, and the organisation's website is also a mine of useful information.

TRAVEL AGENCIES

Duc Minh (🗹020-387 1881; www.ducminhtravel.com; 10 P Cau May) Friendly English-speaking operator organising transport, treks to hill-tribe villages and assaults of Fansipan.

Handspan Travel (🗹020-387 2110; www.handspan.com; Chau Long Hotel, 24 Dong Loi) Offers trekking and mountain-biking tours to villages and markets.

Sapa O'Chau (🗹020-377 1166; www.sapaochau.org; 8 Đ Thac Bac) Operating out of the Sapa O'Chau cafe and offering trekking, homestays and ascents of Fansipan. Check the website for different options.

Sapa Pathfinder Travel (🗹020-387 3468; www.sapapathfinder.com; 13 Đ Xuan Vien) Trekking, mountain biking, Fansipan and advice on transport.

Sapa Sisters (www.sapasisters.webs.com; Luong Thuy Family Guesthouse, 28 Đ Muong Hoa) Trekking and homestays with a group of savvy and knowledgable H'mong girls.

Topas Travel (🗹020-387 1331; www.topas-travel.vn; 21 Đ Muong Hoa) A Sapa-based operator that has high-quality trekking, biking and village encounters. Options include a stay in Topas Eco Lodge or the Nam Cang Riverside House.

ℹ️ Getting There & Away

The gateway to Sapa is Lao Cai, 38km away via a smooth, well-maintained highway.

BICYCLE & MOTORCYCLE

Motorcycling from Hanoi to Sapa is feasible, but it's a long 380km trip. Put your bike on the train to Lao Cai and save yourself the hassle. The 38km between Lao Cai and Sapa is all uphill – hell on a bicycle.

BUS

Sapa's bus station is in the north of town, but you can also check schedules at the tourist office or most travel agents. Direct sleeper buses for Hanoi (300,000d) also depart from Sapa's main square, and there's a 5pm direct sleeper bus to Bia Chay for Halong Bay (500,000d).

Buses from Sapa:

DESTINATION	COST (D)	DURATION & FREQUENCY
Dien Bien Phu	from 170,000	8hr; 7.30am
Hanoi	from 210,000	12hr; 7.30am, 5.30pm
Lai Chau	70,000	3hr; frequent 6am-4pm

MINIBUS

Minibuses to/from Lao Cai are frequent between 5am and 5pm (50,000d, one hour), leaving from outside the church. Hotels and travel agents offer direct minibus services to Bac Ha (from US$30 return) for the Sunday market. It's cheaper, but much slower, to go to Bac Ha by public minibus, changing buses in Lao Cai.

TRAIN

There's no direct train line to Sapa, but regular services from Hanoi to Lao Cai. Most hotels and travel agencies can book tickets back to Hanoi.

ⓘ Getting Around

The best way to get around compact Sapa is to walk. A bicycle can be hired, but you'll spend half your time pushing it up steep hills.

For excursions further afield, motorbikes are available from about US$5 a day. If you've never ridden a motorbike before, this is not the place to learn. The weather can be wet and treacherous at any time of the year, and roads are steep and regularly damaged by floods and heavy rain. Consider hiring a bike with a local driver (about US$15 a day).

Cars, 4WDs and minibuses are also available for hire.

Lao Cai

✆ 020 / POP 46,700

Lao Cai is right on the Vietnam–China border. The town was razed in the Chinese invasion of 1979, so most of the buildings are new. The border crossing here slammed shut during the 1979 war and only reopened

in 1993. Now it's a bustling spot fuelled by growing cross-border trade.

Today Lao Cai is also a destination for travellers journeying between Hanoi and Sapa, or further north to Kunming in China. With Sapa just an hour or so away, Lao Cai is no place to linger, but it offers everything China-bound travellers will need for an overnight stay.

🛏 Sleeping & Eating

Nga Nghi Tho Huong GUEST HOUSE $
(✆ 020-383 5111; 342A P Nguyen Hue; r 180,000-300,000d; ❄ ⓦ) On a corner opposite the train station, this family-run spot is slightly kitsch, but the rooms are clean and colourful, and there's a good tea house on the bottom floor.

Terminus Hotel & Restaurant HOTEL $
(✆ 020-383 5470; 342 P Nguyen Hue; r 250,000-300,000d; ❄ ⓦ) Right across the square from the train station, this is a good spot for an early breakfast or a filling meal. Rooms are very clean and tidy, with frilly decorative touches.

Pineapple CAFE $
(✆ 020-383 5939; Pha Dinh Phung; meals 80,000-125,000d; ⊙ 7am-10pm; ❄ ⓦ) A stylish Sapa-esque cafe. Try the full English breakfast or a salad, pizza or baguette. Walk down the street in front of the train station for around 100m.

Viet Emotion CAFE $
(65 Pha Dinh Phung; meals 65,000-180,000d; ⊙ 7am-10pm; ❄ ⓦ) Viet Emotion is an offshoot of the successful Sapa cafe, celebrating a handy spot midway between the train and bus stations. Good breakfasts, pizza and pasta are popular choices.

ⓘ Information

Be wary of being short-changed by black-market currency traders, especially on the Chinese side. If you do need to change money, just change a small amount.

There are two ATMs by the train station. **BIDV Bank** (Đ Thuy Hoa) on the west bank of the river changes cash.

ⓘ Getting There & Away

BUS & MINIBUS

Lao Cai is about 340km from Hanoi. Nine daily buses make the journey to Hanoi (250,000d, nine hours), leaving from outside the railway station. Most travellers still prefer taking the

NORTHERN VIETNAM BAC HA

> **GETTING TO CHINA: LAO CAI TO KUNMING**
>
> **Getting to the border** The Chinese border at the Lao Cai–Hekou border crossing is about 3km from Lao Cai train station, a journey done by *xe om* (motorbike taxi; around 25,000d) or taxi (around 50,000d).
>
> **At the border** The border is open daily between 7am and 10pm Vietnam time. Note that China is one hour ahead of Vietnam. You'll need to have a pre-arranged visa for China, and border-crossing formalities usually take around one hour. China is separated from Vietnam by a road bridge and a separate rail bridge over the Red River. Note that travellers have reported Chinese officials confiscating Lonely Planet *China* guides at this border, so you may want to try masking the cover.
>
> **Moving on** The new Hekou bus station is around 6km from the border post. There are regular departures to Kunming, including sleeper buses. Buses leave at 7.20pm and 7.30pm, getting into Kunming at around 7am. There are also earlier departures.

train, but the completion of a new road linking Lao Cai to Hanoi in a few years should increase the popularity of the bus option.

Minibuses for Sapa (50,000d, one hour) wait by the station for trains that arrive from Hanoi, and also run regularly from the minibus terminal next to the Red River bridge. Minibuses to Bac Ha (60,000d, 2½ hours) also leave from here; there are seven daily services at 6.30am, 8.15am, 9am, 11.30am, noon, 2pm and 3pm. There are also departures to Ha Giang, Haiphong and Bai Chay (for Halong Bay) from here if you're travelling further east.

TAXI

A taxi to Sapa costs about US$25; it's around US$50 to Bac Ha.

TRAIN

Virtually everyone travelling to and from Hanoi uses the train. There are several trains and also private rail carriages that hitch a ride on the main train. Hotels and travel agencies in Hanoi can book you tickets, or you can book at the station yourself. The journey takes around eight to nine hours. There are five daily departures in either direction, with prices ranging from 135,000d for a hard seat to 515,000d for a soft sleeper. Note that Thursday, Friday and Saturday departures from Hanoi, and Sunday, Monday and Tuesday depatures from Lao Cai are from 50,000d to 80,000d more expensive than prices quoted above.

Several companies operate special private carriages with comfortable sleepers, including affordable **ET Pumpkin** (www.et-pumpkin.com), midrange **Livitrans** (www.livitrantrain.com) and the luxurious and expensive **Victoria Express** (www.victoriahotels-asia.com), only available to guests at the Victoria Sapa Resort & Spa.

See www.seat61.com for the latest information on all trains between Hanoi and Lao Cai.

Bac Ha

☑ 020 / POP 7400

An unhurried and friendly town, Bac Ha makes a relaxed base to explore the northern highlands and hill-tribe villages. The atmosphere is very different to Sapa, and you can walk the streets freely without being accosted by hawkers. To experience a small, untouristy mountain town, Bac Ha is an excellent destination.

The town has a certain charm, though its stock of traditional old adobe houses is dwindling and being replaced by concrete structures. Wood smoke fills the morning air and chickens and pigs poke around the back lanes. For six days a week, Bac Ha slumbers, but its lanes fill up to choking point each Sunday when tourists and Flower H'mong flood in for the weekly market.

This Sunday market is a riot of colour and commerce, and while the influx of day trippers from Sapa is changing things fast, it's still a worthwhile and relatively accessible place to visit. The other markets around Bac Ha are also gradually becoming more visited by tourists, so if you're after a truly authentic experience try and head to the mountain town of Sinho instead.

Bac Ha is a good base to explore the surrounding highlands, as it has an improving choice of inexpensive hotels and the climate here is noticeably warmer than in Sapa. There are 11 hill-tribe groups that live around Bac Ha: the colourful Flower H'mong are the most visible, but other groups include Dzao, Giay (Nhang), Han (Hoa), Xa Fang, Lachi, Nung, Phula, Tay, Thai and Thulao.

Bac Ha

0 — 200 m
0 — 0.1 miles

Na Kheo (3.5km);
Ban Pho (3.5km)

Vua Meo
Lung Phin
Market (12km);
Can Cau
Market (20km)

Ngoc Uyen

Na Co River

Tran Bac

Agribank

Animal
Market

Market

Coc Ly
Market (35km);
Lao Cai (63km)

Bac Ha
Market

One of Bac Ha's main industries is the manufacture of alcoholic home brews (rice wine, cassava wine and corn liquor). The *ruou* corn hooch produced by the Flower H'mong is so potent it can ignite; there's an entire area devoted to it at the Sunday market.

⊙ Sights & Activities

There are several markets in and around Bac Ha. Organised trips to these can be booked in Bac Ha, and also at travel agencies in Sapa.

★ Bac Ha Market   MARKET
(☺ sunrise-2pm Sun) This Sunday market is Bac Ha's big draw. There's an increasing range of handicrafts for sale, but it's still pretty much a local affair. Bac Ha market is a magnet for the local hill-tribe people, above all the exotically attired Flower H'mong. If you can, stay overnight in Bac Ha on Saturday, and get here early before hundreds of day trippers from Sapa start arriving.

Flower H'mong women wear several layers of dazzling clothing. These include an elaborate collar-cum-shawl that's pinned at the neck and an apron-style garment; both are made of tightly woven strips of multicoloured fabric, often with a frilly edge. Highly ornate cuffs and ankle fabrics are also part of their costume, as is a checked headscarf (often electric pink or lime green).

Can Cau Market   MARKET
(☺ 6am-1pm Sat) This Saturday-morning market, 20km north of Bac Ha and 9km from the Chinese border, attracts a growing number of visitors. Some tours from Sapa now visit Can Cau on Saturday before moving on to Bac Ha for the Sunday market. A few Bac Ha stallholders also make the journey to Can Cau on Saturdays. It's still a mecca for the local tribal people though, including Flower H'mong and Blue H'mong (look out for the striking zigzag costume of the latter).

The Can Cau spills down a hillside with basic food stalls on one level and livestock at the bottom of the valley, including plenty of dogs. Locals will implore you to drink the local *ruou* with them. Some trips from Bac Ha include the option of an afternoon trek (for those still standing after *ruou* shots) to the nearby village of Fu La.

Lung Phin Market   MARKET
(☺ 6am-1pm Sun) Lung Phin market is between Can Cau market and Bac Ha, about 12km from town. It's less busy than other markets, with a really local feel, and is a good place to move on to once the tour buses arrive in Bac Ha from Sapa.

Coc Ly Market   MARKET
(☺ 6am-1pm Tue) The impressive Coc Ly market attracts Dzao, Flower H'mong, Tay and Nung people from the surrounding hills. It's about 35km southwest of Bac Ha along reasonably good roads. Tour operators in Bac Ha can arrange day trips here.

★ Vua Meo   NOTABLE BUILDING
('Cat King' House; ☺ 7.30-11.30am & 1.30-5pm)
FREE Don't miss the outlandish Vua Meo, a palace constructed in a kind of bizarre 'oriental baroque' architectural style on the northern edge of town. It was built in 1921 by the French to keep the Flower H'mong

chief Hoang A Tuong happy, and looks like a cross between an exotic church and a French chateau. A shop selling ethnic minority crafts is also here.

Thai Giang Pho Waterfall
WATERFALL

FREE There's a waterfall near Thai Giang Pho village, about 12km east of Bac Ha, which has a pool big enough for swimming.

Local Villages
HIKING

There's great hiking to remarkable hill-tribe villages around Bac Ha. The Flower H'mong village of Ban Pho is one of the nearest to town, from where you can walk to the Nung settlement of Na Kheo, then head back to Bac Ha. Other nearby villages include Trieu Cai, an 8km return walk, and Na Ang, a 6km return walk; it's best to set up a trip with a local guide.

Until very recently most of the minority people in these hills had no formal education, but the government has opened several schools in the last few years. Most hill-tribe children now receive an education (in the Vietnamese language). Boarding schools are favoured because the communities are so spread out, so children spend the week away from their families and sleep in dormitories. Tour guides in Bac Ha can arrange visits to rural schools as part of a motorbike or trekking day trip.

Mr Nghe
HIKING

(☑ 0912 005 952; www.bachatourist.com; Green Sapa Tour, Đ Tran Bac) Spend any time at all in Bac Ha and the irrepressible Mr Nghe will no doubt find you. This one-man cheerleader for the considerable charms of the Bac Ha area offers trekking and day trips to the best of the area's minority markets, longer two- to six-day adventures integrating village homestays, and more physically challenging mountain hiking.

If you're keen to set out on your own, he also rents motorbikes (US$5 to US$6 per day), and is hands down the best person in town to see to make sense of the intricacies of onward travel east to Ha Giang province.

🛏 Sleeping

Bac Ha offers simple guesthouses and a couple of more comfortable options. Room rates tend to increase by about 20% on weekends for the Sunday market; we've quoted the weekday rates here.

Hoang Vu Hotel
GUEST HOUSE $

(☑ 020-388 0264; www.bachatourist.com; 5 Đ Tran Bac; r from US$8) It's nothing fancy, but the spacious rooms offer good value (all have TV and fan). The best spot in town for budget travellers.

Sunday Hotel
HOTEL $

(☑ 020-384 1747; 1 Đ Vu Cong Mat; r 200,000-350,000d; ❈ ❀ ❁) Bac Ha's newest opening, on the edge of the market and main square, is colourful and bright. Look forward to good value and clean rooms.

Ngan Nga Bac Ha
HOTEL $

(☑ 020-380 0286; www.nganngabachahotel.com; 117 Ngoc Uyen; r US$18-20; ❁) This friendly place is above a popular restaurant that does a roaring trade in tasty steamboats for travellers and the occasional tour group. Tours to homestays and markets can be arranged.

Congfu Hotel
HOTEL $$

(☑ 020-388 0254; www.congfuhotel.com; 152 Ngoc Uyen; r US$30; ❈ @ ❁) This place has 21 attractive rooms and its restaurant (meals from 60,000d) is one of the best in town. Book rooms 205, 208, 305 or 308 for a floor-to-ceiling window overlooking Bac Ha Market. Excursions to the Can Cau and Coc Ly markets can also be booked.

🍴 Eating

Of Bac Ha's hotel restaurants, the Congfu has great views of the animal market area through huge plate-glass windows, while the Ngan Nga Bac Ha does great steamboats. Both get very busy for Sunday lunch on market day.

Note that tourists are often overcharged at the cafes near the market, so establish the cost of food and drink up front.

Hoang Yen Restaurant
VIETNAMESE $

(Đ Tran Bac; mains 60,000-100,000d; ⊙ 7am-10pm; ❁) Hoang Yen's menu includes good breakfast options and a good-value set menu for 140,000d. Cheap beer and wi-fi access are both available. You'll find it right on Bac Ha's main square.

Duc Tuan Restaurant
VIETNAMESE $

(mains 50,000-80,000d; ⊙ 7am-6pm) This place is handily near the market and has big portions of reliable Vietnamese food, plus it's usually largely free of tour groups.

ⓘ Information

There's an ATM at the Agribank, and wi-fi access at the Hoang Yen Restaurant.

Green Sapa Tour (www.bachatourist.com; Đ Tran Bac; ◷ 8am-6pm) The main booking office for Mr Nghe if you can't find him at the Hoang Vu Hotel or the Hoang Yen Restaurant, two other businesses he's involved with.

ⓘ Getting There & Away

BUS

Sleeper buses run to/from My Dinh bus station in Hanoi (US$20, 11 hours, 7pm daily) and normal buses head to Lao Cai (60,000d, 2½ hours, 6am, 8am, noon, 1pm, 2pm).

Tours to Bac Ha from Sapa cost from around US$20 per person; on the way back you can bail out in Lao Cai and catch the night train back to Hanoi.

If you're headed east to Ha Giang, there were two options at the time of writing, but we recommend checking the latest information with Mr Nghe. Option one is to catch a xe om from Bac Ha 35km northeast to Xin Man (US$15), and then a public bus (200,000d, five hours, 6am and 11am) to Ha Giang. Option two is the public bus south from Bac Ha to Bac Ngam (40,000d, 45 minutes, 6am), followed by another bus from Bac Ngam to Ha Giang (400,000d, five hours, 7am). Note this is a very tight connection.

MOTORCYCLE & TAXI

A motorbike/taxi to Lao Cai costs US$25/70, or to Sapa US$30/80.

Ha Giang Province

🕽 0219 / POP 79,000

Ha Giang is the final frontier in northern Vietnam, an amazing landscape of limestone pinnacles and granite outcrops. The far north of the province has some of the most spectacular scenery in the country, and the trip between Dong Van and Meo Vac across the Mai Pi Leng Pass is quite mind-blowing. Ha Giang should be one of the most popular destinations in this region, but its proximity to the Chinese border still keeps visitor numbers at a low level.

Travel permits are required to travel further north to Dong Van and Meo Vac, but these can now be arranged directly with accommodation in those towns, or ideally at your hotel in the gateway city of Ha Giang. Permits cost 300,000d and are for up to five people if you're travelling in a group.

The province is best managed with a car and driver or by motorbike, but public transport quality is improving now that years of roadworks are largely completed. You'll still need to arrange private transport to reach off-the-beaten-track attractions like Lung Cu and the Vuong Palace though.

It's relatively simple to complete a journey by public transport from Ha Giang city to Dong Van, but at the time of writing private transport was needed to continue via Meo Vac to Bao Lac for onward public transport southeast to the bigger centre of Cao Bang.

Whichever way you tackle Ha Giang, you'll be among only a handful of travellers to the area and experience some of Indochina's most jaw-dropping scenery.

Ha Giang

Ha Giang is somewhere to recharge the batteries on the long road north. This town, bisected by the broad river Lo, is a provincial capital with clean streets and an understated ambience. The main drag is P Nguyen Trai, which runs north–south paralleling the west bank of the Lo for 3km or so. You'll find hotels, banks and restaurants on this road.

Ha Giang is a mildly diverting town, but the spectacular limestone outcrops soaring skywards over the suburbs hint at the amazing scenery in the surrounding hinterland.

🖝 Tours

Johnny Nam Tram MOTORBIKE TOUR
(🕽 0917 797 269; www.rockyplateau.com) Highly experienced in the backroads and byways of northern Vietnam, Johnny Nam Tram is an excellent contact for motorbike rental or organised bike tours around Ha Giang province. Tours by car and including trekking can also be arranged.

🛏 Sleeping & Eating

You'll find several cheap restaurants scattered along P Nguyen Trai.

Cao Nguyen Hotel HOTEL $
(🕽 0219-386 6966; khachsannguyen@gmail.com; 297 P Nguyen Thai Hoc; r 350,000-400,000d; 🕸 @) Just a couple of years old, this newish hotel near the river has 40 spotless and spacious rooms. Breakfast isn't included but there are good *pho* stalls just a short walk away.

Huy Hoan Hotel HOTEL $
(🕽 0219-386 1288; P Nguyen Trai; r 200,000-500,000d; 🕾) This tall, slim place offers large, clean, well-kept rooms with dark fur-

niture and (very) firm beds. Newer rooms are overly chintzy, and the cheapest rooms don't have windows.

Truong Xuan Resort BUNGALOW **$$**
(☑0219-381 1102; www.hagiangresort.com; Km 5, P Nguyen Van Linh; d 400,000-520,000d; ❋ ﹖) An absolute riverside location has 13 spacious bungalows. There's a decent restaurant (mains 80,000d to 220,000d), and even kayaks for rent to explore the adjacent waterway. Red Dzao massages (60,000d) and herbal baths (80,000d) are on offer. It's 5km out of town, so from the bus station count on 40,000d for a *xe om,* or 100,000d in a taxi.

Bien Nho Thanh Thu Restaurant VIETNAMESE
(☑0219-328 2558; 17 P Duong Huu Nghi; meals from 120,000d; ☉ 11am-10pm) For something exotic, this place has crocodile, seafood, goose and traditional food from the ethnic minorities of Ha Giang.

ⓘ Information

Agribank (P Nguyen Trai) Has an ATM; internet cafes nearby.

ⓘ Getting There & Away

Ha Giang's most convenient bus station is centrally located just off P Nguyen Trai west of the Lo River. However, some buses from My Dinh bus station in Hanoi may arrive at a second bus station on the outskirts of the city. From Ha Giang, there is relatively frequent bus transport northeast to Dong Van or Meo Vac.

Note that no buses run directly to Bac Ha from Ha Giang. The route is very beautiful, but at the time of writing you needed to transit through Xin Man or Bac Ngam.

Buses from Ha Giang:

DESTINATION	COST (D)	DURATION & FREQUENCY
Dong Van	105,000	4½hr; around 3 daily
Hanoi	140,000	7hr; every 30 minutes to 9pm
Meo Vac	105,000	6hr; around 3 daily
Tam Son	35,000	1½hr; around 5 daily
Yen Minh	75,000	3hr; around 5 daily

Quan Ba Pass

Leaving Ha Giang, the road climbs over the Quan Ba Pass (Heaven's Gate) around 40km from the city. Poetic licence is a national pastime in Vietnam, but this time the romantics have it right. The road winds

WORTH A TRIP

PAN HOU VILLAGE

Pan Hou Village (☑0219-383 3565; www.panhou-village.com; s/d US$45/55; ❋ ﹖) is tucked away in a hidden river valley in the High Song Chau mountains, and its private bungalows are set in a riot of tropical gardens and rice paddies. This wonderfully isolated ecolodge is the base for trekking and ethnic-minority market visits. Rooms are smartly furnished with wooden furniture and tiled floors, and the restaurant pavilion (lunch US$10, dinner US$12) is spacious and social. Traditional spa treatments and baths are infused with medicinal healing herbs.

From Tan Quang village south of Ha Giang, Pan Hou is 36km west up a winding mountain road.

over a saddle and opens up on to an awesome vista of limestone towers.

At the top of Quan Ba Pass is an information centre and lookout with amazing views down into Tam Son. An English-language information board details the 2011 initiative to declare the Dong Van Karst Plateau part of the Unesco Global Network of National Geoparks. It's the first Unesco-recognised geopark in Vietnam and the second one in Southeast Asia, after Langkawi Geological Park in Malaysia.

Tam Son

From Quan Ba Pass you drop through pine forests into Tam Son, where it's worth stopping for a drink before the final leg into the incredibly surreal scenery near China. On Sundays there's a good market with ethnic minorities including White H'mong, Red Dzao, Tay and Giay. There's also good accommodation at the guesthouse **Nha Nghi Anh Hoat** (☑0219-651 0789; r 250,000d; ❋ ﹖), with eight spotless rooms, wi-fi and air-con. Around five buses per day trundle through Tam Son en route to Dong Van (100,000d).

From Tam Son to Dong Van

From Tam Son, the road – and the astounding scenery – continues through to the sleepy town of **Yen Minh**. There's decent accommodation here at the **Thao Nguyen**

Hotel (☑0219-385 2297; khachsanthaonguyen2011@gmail.com; r 300,000-400,000d), but it's worth pushing on to overnight in Dong Van. Around 5km east of Yen Minh a road meanders southeast to Meo Vac, but the recommended route is the northern fork to Dong Van taking in the astounding **Vuong Palace** (admission 10,000d; ⊙8am-5pm), a grandiose two-storey mansion built for a local H'mong king by the French. Set in a hidden valley near a quiet village, the building was renovated in 2006 and is a fascinating sight in such a remote region of the country. The Vuong Palace is at Sa Phin, around 15km west of Dong Van, and the scenery of countless conical peaks through to Dong Van is quite incredible.

Dong Van

Dong Van is mainly a dusty outpost, but the town has a great **Sunday market**, and makes a good base for day treks around nearby minority villages. It also features an interesting old quarter with traditional H'mong houses dating from French colonial times.

◉ Sights

Lung Cu   MONUMENT
(admission 10,000d; ⊙8am-5pm) Around 25km north of Dong Van and right on the Chinese border, Lung Cu is a massive flag tower erected in 2010 to mark the northernmost point of Vietnam. The summit is reached by almost 300 steps from a midlevel carpark, and the views across rural villages are stunning. You'll need to show your passport and Ha Giang permit twice – at the local tourist police and army checkpoint near the base of the tower – before ascending to the top.

☞ Tours

CND Travel   TOUR
(☑0219-388 8769; www.cndtravel.com; 124 Đ 3/2; 1-day tours per person around 800,000d) Minimal English is spoken here, but CND Travel is a good option if you've arrived by public transport and wish to organise a day trip to see the Vuong Palace and Lung Cu.

⌇ Sleeping & Eating

Nha Nghi Binh An   GUEST HOUSE $
(☑0219-385 6177; Đ 3/2; r 250,000-300,000d) Located on the right as you enter Dong Van from Yen Minh, this easygoing guesthouse

has three recently completed rooms and a warm welcome from the friendly family owners who always seem to be hanging out downstairs.

Hoang Ngoc Hotel   HOTEL $$
(☑0219-385 6857; www.hoangngochotel2.blogspot.com; Đ 3/2; r 300,000-400,000d; ❋☎) Popular with Western tour groups, the Hoang Ngoc features spacious rooms, some with balconies. There's a handy map in reception showing trekking trails around the area. Staff can arrange tours to the Vuong Palace, Lung Cu and Meo Vac, and can also usually rustle up motorbikes to rent to independent travellers.

Au Viet   VIETNAMESE $
(26 Đ 3/2; mains from 60,000d; ⊙7am-8pm) Opposite the Hoang Ngoc Hotel, the Au Viet is the only place in town with an English menu, and does a good line in robust hotpots and cold beer. Breakfast is also available.

ⓘ Information

Dong Van's only ATM is across the road from the market at the eastern end of town en route to Meo Vac.

ⓘ Getting There & Away

At the time of writing there were no buses linking Dong Van to Meo Vac. A *xe om* to Meo Vac should cost around 250,000d and a taxi around 400,000d. Note a private taxi is often hard to find in Dong Van, so a *xe om* journey may well be your only option.

Meo Vac

Beyond Dong Van the spectacular Mai Pi Leng Pass continues for 22km to Meo Vac. The road has been cut into the side of a cliff: far below are the distant waters of the Nho Que River.

Meo Vac is a district capital hemmed in by mountains and, like many towns in the northwest, it is steadily being settled by Vietnamese from elsewhere.

Don't be surprised if you're offered a slug of a local speciality, 'bee wine'. We're still trying to work out if it's made from bees and honey, or just '100% bees'. Either way, it's a bracing drink on a chilly Meo Vac night.

Like Dong Van, Meo Vac has a good **Sunday market**, and it's easy enough to combine the two by *xe om*.

🛏 Sleeping

Hoa Cuong Hotel HOTEL $

(📞 0219-387 2888; r US$15-20; ❋ @ 🛜) In an impressive spot opposite the market, this hotel has spacious rooms and flat-screen TVs. A couple of karaoke places nearby are more active on Saturday and Sunday nights.

Meo Vac Mountain Lodge HOMESTAY $$

(aubergemeovac@gmail.com; dm/d US$15/60) Located in a semi-rural neighbourhood around 500m from the town market, the Mountain Lodge is in a lovingly restored ethnic minority house dating from the 19th century. Look forward to clay walls, lots of natural timber and a spacious inner courtyard. Bathroom facilities are shared, and breakfast (US$5) and lunch (US$12) are available. Trekking to nearby villages can also be arranged.

ℹ Getting There & Away

At the time of research there was no public transport southeast to the transport hub of Cao Bang. Instead, travellers can catch a xe om (800,000d) or taxi (1,500,000d) to Bao Lac where there is accommodation and a daily bus to Cao Bang.

South to Bao Lac & Cao Bang

Foreigners are now permitted to travel from Meo Vac to Bao Lac in Cao Bang province. You must have your Ha Giang permit to do this spectacular trip. The road is now mostly paved, though it's still best on trail bikes or by 4WD.

Heading south from Meo Vac you'll pass through the town of Khau Vai after about 20km, which is famous for its annual love market, where the tribal minorities swap wives and husbands. Though it's undoubtedly a fascinating tradition, many busloads of Vietnamese tourists now gatecrash the dating scene, and this unique event has become something of a circus. It takes place on the 27th day of the third lunar month in the Vietnamese calendar, usually from late April to mid-May.

After Khau Vai, a new bridge crosses the Nho Que River, and the road continues south to Bao Lac. In Bao Lac, the Song Gam (📞 026-387 0269; Bao Lac; s/d from 200,000/250,000d; ❋ 🛜) guesthouse has a riverside location and is popular with motorbike tours. A daily bus (100,000d) leaves at 12.30pm for Cao Bang from where there is transport to Hanoi and Ba Be National Park.

NORTHERN VIETNAM HA GIANG PROVINCE

Central Vietnam

Why Go?

The cultural heart of the nation, central Vietnam is fully loaded with historical sights and cultural interest, and blessed with ravishing beaches and outstanding national parks. Marvel at Hue and its imperial citadel and royal tombs. Savour the unique grace of riverside jewel Hoi An. Tour the military sites of the Demilitarised Zone (DMZ). Check out Danang, fast-emerging as one of the nation's most dynamic cities. And don't neglect the extraordinary Phong Nha region, home to three gargantuan cave systems (including the world's largest cave). And when you've had enough of touring the sights, invest in some well-deserved hammock time on the golden sands of An Bang beach or learn to cook central Vietnamese cuisine, the nation's most complex. And now with improving highways, and upgraded international airports at Hue and Danang, access to this utterly compelling and diverse part of the nation has never been easier.

Best Places to Eat

➡ Morning Glory Street Food Restaurant (p206)

➡ Cargo Club (p206)

➡ Waterfront (p190)

➡ Les Jardins de La Carambole (p179)

Best Places to Stay

➡ An Bang Seaside Village (p212)

➡ Phong Nha Farmstay (p159)

➡ Hoi An Chic Hotel (p205)

➡ Beach Bar Hue (p183)

When to Go
Hue

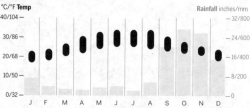

Late Apr
Danang's riverfront explodes with colour for the annual fireworks competition.

May Temperatures are on the rise and central Vietnam's beaches come into their own.

Sep Sticky summer heat relents, peak crowds are a memory and sea temperatures are balmy.

NORTH-CENTRAL VIETNAM

History

This region's seen it all: kings, warriors and occupiers and a history of warfare and conflict. The ancient kingdom of Champa began here in the 2nd century and flourished for more than a thousand years. It left its mark in the myriad towers and temples dotting the landscape; the most renowned are at My Son. The Vietnamese subdued Champa in the 15th century, and in subsequent centuries European, Japanese and Chinese traders established footholds in Hoi An.

In 1802 Vietnam's last royal dynasty, the Nguyens, set up court at Hue, which became the centre of political intrigue, intellectual excellence and spiritual guidance. Later emperors were subdued by expanding French ambitions in Vietnam, and by the time of independence the locus of national power had shifted back to Hanoi.

In 1954 Vietnam was partitioned into North and South, creating a DMZ that saw some of the American War's heaviest fighting. Thousands of lives were lost in bloody battles as entire cities, including Vinh and most of Hue's imperial enclosure, were flattened. Vast tracts of countryside around Dong Hoi and Dong Ha remain littered with lethal ordnance. Hoi An was one of the few places spared, and remains a magical exception.

Today, there's a burgeoning tourism sector around Hue and Hoi An, and the city of Danang goes from strength to strength. But the northern part of the region remains poor and undeveloped.

ⓘ Getting There & Away

The main north–south railway cuts directly through the region, as does Hwy 1 and the Ho Chi Minh Highway. Airports at Vinh and Dong Hoi run flights to Ho Chi Minh City (HCMC) and Hanoi.

Ninh Binh Province

A short hop south of Hanoi, Ninh Binh Province is blessed with breathtaking natural beauty, intriguing cultural sights and the wonderful Cuc Phuong National Park. That said, Ninh Binh has become a massive destination for domestic travellers, and many of its attractions are heavily commercialised. Expect plenty of hawkers and a degree of hassle at the main sights.

Central Vietnam Highlights

① Travel back in time in the historic old port of **Hoi An** (p195).

② **Phong Nha-Ke Bang National Park** (p156) is truly something else: the world's foremost caving destination.

③ Tread in the footsteps of emperors from the Forbidden Purple City to the imperial tombs of **Hue** (p167).

④ Learn a new culinary craft in a **Vietnamese cooking class** (p203) in Hoi An.

⑤ Head out for a nature ramble at delightful **Cuc Phuong National Park** (p152).

⑥ Wonder while you wander amid the enigmatic Cham ruins at **My Son** (p214).

⑦ Test your two-wheel prowess on a **motorbike tour** (p203) around the idyllic back roads of central Vietnam.

⑧ Go underground at the **Vinh Moc Tunnels** (p162) in the Demilitarised Zone (DMZ).

North-Central Vietnam

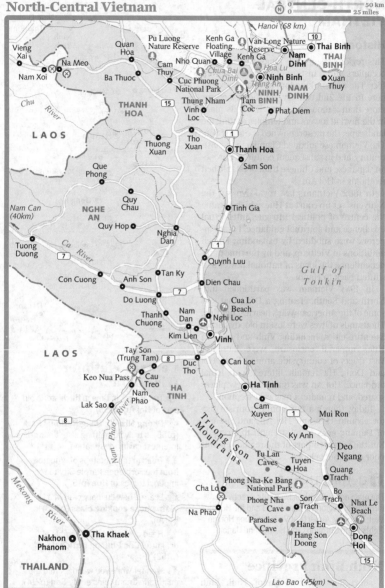

Ninh Binh

♪ 030 / POP 158,000

Ninh Binh is a resolutely provincial industrial city – not a destination in itself, but a good base for exploring some quintes- sentially Vietnamese limestone scenery. A steady trickle of Western tourists head here, but far larger numbers of holidaying Vietnamese flock to nearby sights that include the nation's biggest pagoda and the Trang An grottoes.

The region does have great natural allure, but insensitive development is a huge concern, with giant cement factories being constructed next to beautiful nature spots.

👉 Tours

Tours of the sights around Ninh Binh Province can be set up in hotels including Thanh Thuy's and Thuy Anh. Freelance guide **Truong** (📞 091 566 6211; truong_tour@yahoo.com) offers escorted trips on motorbikes around Ninh Binh using country backroads. and also sets up treks in Pu Luong Nature Reserve, a fairly undisturbed area spread across two mountain ridges, where you can stay in Thai and H'mong homestays.

🛏 Sleeping

Ninh Binh has some great value hotels and guesthouses, most of which can make tour arrangements, or rent you a bicycle or motorbike.

Thanh Thuy's Guest House & New Hotel   GUEST HOUSE $
(📞 030-387 1811; www.hotelthanhthuy.com; 53 Đ Le Hong Phong; r with fan/air-con from 150,000/250,000d; 🕸@🛜) Set well back from the road, this guesthouse's courtyard and restaurant are a great place to meet other travellers. Offers good-value, clean rooms, some with balcony; and tours.

Kinh Do Hotel   HOTEL $
(📞 030-389 9152; http://kinhdohotel.vn; 18 Đ Phanh Dinh Phung; s/d 140,000/250,000d; 🕸@🛜) The service here is excellent, as management goes the extra mile (even offering free pick-ups from the bus/train station) and the spacious, clean rooms with high ceilings represent fine value.

Thanh Binh Hotel   HOTEL $
(📞 030-387 2439; www.thanhbinhhotelnb.com.vn; 31 Đ Luong Van Tuy; s US$10-25, d US$15-30; 🕸@🛜) Popular place with a wide selection of rooms, from cheap 'n' cheerful to spacious and well equipped, all have air-conditioning. There's a small restaurant and inexpensive bicycle and motorbike rental.

⭐ Thuy Anh Hotel   HOTEL $$
(📞 030-387 1602; www.thuyanhhotel.com; 55A Đ Truong Han Sieu; r old wing US$15–25, r new wing US$25-35; 🌀🕸@🛜) This very well-run hotel sets very high standards with inexpensive, good-value rooms in the old wing and spotless, very well-equipped, tastefully furnished

and comfortable rooms in the new wing. You'll also find a top-floor bar and restaurant serving Western-style food (including hearty complimentary breakfasts).

Ninh Binh Legend Hotel   HOTEL $$$
(📞 030-389 9880; www.ninhbinhlegendhotel.com; Tien Dong Zone; r/ste from US$77/126; 🌀🕸@🛜) Landmark four-star hotel with stunning countryside views from its upper floors, all rooms boast hardwood floors, contemporary trim and luxury bedding while the suites are palatial. There's a small gym, spa, tennis courts and staff are well trained and welcoming. Located in the emerging 'new' city centre, 2km northwest of the old heart of town.

Emeralda Resort Ninh Binh   HOTEL $$$
(www.emeraldaresort.com; Van Long Nature Reserve; r US$119-140, ste US$184; 🌀🕸🛜) Built in a neo-traditional style this large resort hotel has commodious villas with elegant decor, a great pool area and a (pricey) spa. However, staff speak limited English and the location, though in lovely grounds, is 10km north of town and quite close to some cement factories.

🍴 Eating & Drinking

The town doesn't have much in the way of restaurants so plan to eat early as there's very little available after 9pm. The local speciality is *de* (goat meat), usually served with fresh herbs and rice paper to wrap it in – around 3km out of town, the road to the Trang An Grottoes is lined with dozens of **goat meat restaurants**.

Snails are another excellent local dish. The lanes north of Đ Luong Van Tuy, close to the stadium, have several **snail restaurants** serving delicious *oc luoc xa* (snails cooked with lemongrass and chilli); you'll also find a few casual bars in this area too.

In the warmer months, **bia hoi** places become very tempting. Try the streetside set-ups directly opposite Thanh Thuy or the riverside places near the local brewery.

For fresh fruit **Cho Bop market** (Truong Han Sieu) is the place to go.

Trung Tuyet   VIETNAMESE $
(14 Đ Hoang Hoa Tham; meals 25,000-65,000d; ⏰7am–9.45pm) Expect filling portions, rock-bottom rates and a warm welcome from the host family at this busy little place which is popular with travellers.

Ninh Binh

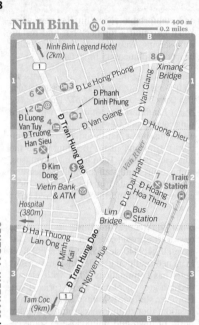

⊙ 0 ━━━━━ 400 m
0 ━━━━━ 0.2 miles

Ninh Binh

🛏 Sleeping
1	Kinh Do Hotel	A1
2	Thanh Binh Hotel	A1
3	Thanh Thuy's Guest House & New Hotel	A1
4	Thuy Anh Hotel	A1

🍴 Eating
5	Cho Bop market	A2
6	Huong Mai Restaurant	A1
7	Trung Tuyet	B2

🍸 Drinking & Nightlife
| 8 | Bia Hoi | B1 |

Huong Mai Restaurant VIETNAMESE $$
(12 Đ Tran Hung Dao; dishes 40,000-160,000d;
⊙7am-8.45pm) Little or no English is spoken,
but the food is good, if a little pricey. Try the
pork with green mustard, rice cakes and beef
broth or steamed chicken with lime leaves.

ℹ️ Orientation

The entire layout of the city of Ninh Binh is
steadily being changed. The city centre, cur-
rently plagued by heavy traffic (Hwy 1 thunders
right through it) is being shifted 2km to the west,
to around the present location of the Legend
Hotel. Here a slew of new municipal buildings, a

civic square, and a 27-storey hotel and mall are
rising from the wasteland. City planners aim to
redirect Hwy 1 by around 2015, so it will flow via
the new city centre.

ℹ️ Information

Hospital (Benh Vien Da Khoa Tinh; ☏030-387
1030; Đ Hai Thuong Lan; ⊙24hr)
Internet (Đ Luong Van Tuy; per hr 6000d;
⊙7am-10pm) There's a cluster of cybercafes
here.
Main Post Office (Đ Tran Hung Dao; ⊙7am-
6pm Mon-Fri, 8am-1pm Sat)
Vietin Bank & ATM (Đ Tran Hung Dao; ⊙7am-
2.30pm Mon-Fri, 7.30am-noon Sat) One of two
branches on this street.

ℹ️ Getting There & Away

BUS
Ninh Binh's **bus station** (Đ Le Dai Hanh) is
located near Lim Bridge. Public buses leave
almost every 15 minutes until 7pm for the
Giap Bat and Luong Yen bus stations in Hanoi
(72,000d, 2½ hours) and there are regular buses
to Haiphong (94,000d, three hours, every 1½
hours) and twice-daily connections to Halong
City (115,000d, 3½ hours).

Ninh Binh is also a stop for open-tour buses
between Hanoi (US$6, two hours) and Hue
(US$14, 10 hours); hotel pick-up and drop-offs
are offered.

TRAIN
The **train station** (Ga Ninh Binh; 1 Đ Hoang
Hoa Tham) is a scheduled stop on the main
north–south line, with destinations including
Hanoi (67,000d, two to 2½ hours, four daily),
Vinh (103,000d, six hours, four daily) and Hue
(285,000d, 12½ to 13½ hours, four daily).

ℹ️ Getting Around

Most hotels rent out bicycles (US$1 to US$2 per
day) and motorbikes (US$4 to US$8 per day).
Motorbike drivers charge around US$10 a day.

Tam Coc

This is what most travellers associate with
Ninh Binh: limestone outcrops sweeping up
from serene rice paddies, best appreciated on
a languorous row-boat ride down the river, to
the soundtrack of water lapping against the
oars. Unfortunately there are a lot of subsidi-
ary issues that detract from the experience,
including a glut of hawkers, so prepare your-
self if you do decide to go. A polite but firm
'no' and adopting a complete lack of interest
is the best way to combat the hassle.

PHAT DIEM

Home of a celebrated cathedral, remarkable for its vast dimensions and unique Sino-Vietnamese cum European architecture, Phat Diem makes an intriguing half-day excursion.

During the colonial era Phat Diem's bishop ruled the area with his private army, Middle Ages–style, until French troops took over in 1951. The cathedral (1891) featured prominently in Graham Greene's novel *The Quiet American,* and it was from the bell tower that the author watched battles between the North Vietnamese Army (NVA) and the French.

At busy times you have to steer a path through aggressive sellers and beggars to earn your entrance, but inside it's peaceful in a sepulchre-like way. The cathedral's largely wooden interior boasts a vaulted ceiling supported by massive columns (almost 1m in diameter and 10m tall). Above the granite altar Vietnamese-looking cherubs with golden wings swarm, while Chinese-style clouds drift across the blue ceiling. Beneath them are icons of the martyrs slaughtered by Emperor Tu Duc during the anti-Catholic purges of the 1850s.

Opposite the cathedral's main doors is the free-standing bell tower, with stone columns carved to look like bamboo. At its base lie two enormous stone slabs. Their purpose was to provide a perch for mandarins to sit and observe the rituals of the Catholic mass.

Between the tower and the cathedral is the tomb of the Vietnamese founder, Father Six, and a Lourdes-style grotto, with a somewhat spooky bust of Father Six beside it.

Hordes of Vietnamese tourists come to this place, few of them Catholic but many curious about churches and Christianity. Mass is celebrated daily at 5am and 5pm, when the massive bell is rung and the faithful stream into the cathedral, dressed in their finest.

Not far from this cathedral is a covered bridge dating from the late 19th century. Dong Huong Pagoda is the largest pagoda in the area, catering to the Buddhist community. Many of its congregation are from the minority Muong people. To find it, turn right at the canal as you're approaching town from the north and follow the small road alongside the water for 3km.

A Gothic counterpoint to Phat Diem is the cathedral at Ton Dao, along Route 10 about 5km from Phat Diem. It looks beatifically out over rice fields and, at the rear of the churchyard, a statue of the Virgin Mary keeps unexpected company with porcelain images of Quan Am.

Phat Diem, sometimes known by its former name Kim Son, is 26km southeast of Ninh Binh. There are direct buses here from Ninh Binh (15,000d, one hour); xe om (motorcycle) drivers charge about 140,000d (including waiting time) for a return trip.

◉ Sights & Activities

Bich Dong Pagoda
BUDDHIST TEMPLE

(Jade Grotto) FREE This charming cluster of cave temples is a couple of kilometres north of Tam Coc. The Lower Pagoda is located at the foot of the outcrop, from which it's a climb of about 100 steps to the Middle Pagoda, then a shorter but still steep ascent to the Upper Pagoda. Inside each cave temple, looming statues and the smoke of burning incense create an otherworldly atmosphere. Outside, there are some incredible views of the countryside.

Van Lan
VILLAGE

Near the entrance to Tam Coc, Van Lan village is famous for its embroidery. Local artisans make napkins, tablecloths, pillowcases and T-shirts, some of which you will undoubtedly encounter on the boat ride. Bargain hard if you're interested.

Tam Coc Boat Trips
BOAT RIDE

(per boat 1/2 people 110,000/140,000d; ⊙ 7am-3.30pm) Tam Coc (meaning 'three caves') covers a stretch of the Ngo Dong River and boasts a landscape of surreal beauty, but it's also immensely popular – the river's often filled with a procession of boats, with all the accompanying babble and noise.

Consider visiting in the early morning or late afternoon when things are quieter, and bring some sunscreen.

Each row boat carries two visitors. The route (around two hours) takes you through the three caves for which Tam Coc is named.

Rowers are adept at using their feet to propel the oars, which makes for a tourist-pleasing Kodak moment.

Unfortunately the whole area is now overshadowed by some giant cement factories. You can't see them from the river, but air quality and pollution are concerns.

ⓘ Getting There & Away

Tam Coc is 9km southwest of Ninh Binh. Ninh Binh hotels run tours, or you can make your own way by bicycle or motorbike. Hotel staff can advise you on some beautiful back roads.

Many Hanoi tour operators offer day trips here for around US$25.

Mua Cave

Tucked away at the end of a road running between rice paddies, this cave (Cave of Dance; admission 30,000d; ⓧ7am-4pm) is not terribly impressive, but the main attraction is the panoramic view from the peak above. A stone staircase beside the cave entrance zigzags up the side of the karst (beware the goat droppings). It's 450 steps to the top, where there's a simple altar to Quan Am (the Goddess of Mercy). Look west and you'll see Ngo Dong River winding through Tam Coc.

The climb is paved but steep in sections, so bring some water and allow an hour for the trip. Mua Cave is 5km from Ninh Binh and a popular stop on tours heading to Tam Coc.

Hoa Lu

Hoa Lu was the capital of Vietnam during the Dinh (AD 968–80) and early Le (AD 980–1009) dynasties. The Dinh chose the site to put some distance between them and China.

Most of the ancient citadel is in ruins, but Yen Ngua Mountain provides a scenic backdrop for two surviving temples (admission 10,000d). Dinh Tien Hoang is dedicated to the Dinh dynasty and has the stone pedestal of a royal throne. Inside are bronze bells and a statue of Emperor Dinh Tien Hoang with his three sons.

The second temple is dedicated to monarch Le Dai Hanh. It has the usual assortment of drums, gongs, incense burners, candle holders and weapons, as well as a statue

---

ⓘ GETTING TO LAOS

Thanh Hoa to Sam Neua

Getting to the border Those seeking a backwoods adventure can try the Na Meo/Nam Xoi border crossing. If at all possible take a direct bus and avoid getting onward transport on the Vietnamese side of the border where foreigners are seriously ripped off. There's a daily 8am bus from Thanh Hoa's western bus station (Ben Xe Mien Tay) to Sam Neua (310,000d), but expect overcharging.

At the border The border is open from 7am to 5pm. Lao visas are available here. Readers have reported no hassle from border officials, but they may try to offer you bad rates for all currencies – you'll get a better deal in Na Meo hotels. It's best not to get stuck on the Laos side of the border as transport is extremely irregular and there's no accommodation. Na Meo has several basic, serviceable guesthouses.

Moving on There's unbelievable overcharging on this route (unless you're on a direct bus). Vietnamese bus drivers demand up to US$50 for the trip to Thanh Hoa (it should cost about US$8).

Vinh to Phonsavan

Getting to the border The often mist-shrouded Nam Can/Nong Haet border crossing is 250km northwest of Vinh. Direct buses from Vinh's marketplace leave daily for Phonsavan in Laos (320,000d, 12 hours). It's possible to travel independently from Vinh to Muong Xen by bus and then take a motorbike (around 170,000d) uphill to the border, but we strongly recommend you take the direct option due to overcharging and hassle.

At the border The border post is open from 7am to 5pm. Vietnamese visas aren't available, but Lao visas are available for most nationalities for between US$30 and US$40.

of the king in the middle, his queen on the right and their son on the left. A modest **museum** here features part of the excavations of a 10th-century city wall.

For a great perspective of the ruins, take the 20-minute hike up to the **tomb of Emperor Dinh Tien Hoang**. The access path is via the hill opposite the ticket office.

Hoa Lu is 12km northwest of Ninh Binh; turn left 6km north of town on Hwy 1. There is no public transport available, but tours can easily be set up in Ninh Binh.

Chua Bai Dinh

Chua Bai Dinh (⊙ 7am-5.45pm) **FREE** is a bombastic Buddhist complex, built on a vast scale, that rises up a hillside near Ninh Binh. Building work started in 2003, and was mostly completed by 2010. It's quickly become a huge attraction.

From the (small) entrance gateway, turn right and you'll pass through cloister-like walkways past 500 stone *arhats* (enlightened Buddhists) that line the route up to the main triple-roofed **Phap Chu pagoda**. This contains a 10m, 100-tonne bronze

Buddha (surrounded by a gaudy collection of spinning lights and a pyramid or two for good measure), flanked by two more gilded Buddha figures.

Steps behind lead up to a viewpoint, a **13-storey pagoda** (still under construction at the time of research) and a giant Buddha. If you return via the central part of the compound you'll pass more temples, including one that harbours a 36-tonne bell – cast in 2006, it's the largest in Vietnam.

Chua Bai Dinh attracts thousands of Vietnamese visitors some days, including many day trippers, so think twice if you're after a spiritual experience – the numbers here don't facilitate feelings of peace. That said, the complex does have its merits. Commendably, most of the structures have been constructed from natural materials. Some of the bronzework, wood-detailing, lacquerwork and stone-carving is very impressive; much of it was crafted by artisans from local villages.

Chua Bai Dinh is 11km northwest of Ninh Binh; you'll pass dozens of goat meat restaurants en route.

Moving on Travellers not on the direct bus connection face numerous challenges. Firstly you'll have to haggle over a motorbike ride from the border to the nearest town, Muong Xen. The route is breathtaking but only 25km downhill and should cost around 100,000d; drivers may ask for up to 300,000d. From Muong Xen there are irregular buses to Vinh (125,000d, six hours). Note that some buses from Phonsavan claim to continue to Hanoi or Danang, but unceremoniously discharge all their passengers in Vinh.

Transport on the Laos side to Nong Haet is erratic, but once you get there you can pick up a bus to Phonsavan.

Vinh to Lak Sao

Getting to the border The Cau Treo/Nam Phao border crossing has a dodgy reputation with travellers who report chronic overcharging and hassle (such as bus drivers ejecting foreigners in the middle of nowhere unless they cough up extra bucks). Stick to direct services. Most transport to Phonsavan in Laos uses the Nong Haet–Nam Can border further north. Buses leave Vinh at 6am (on Mondays, Wednesdays, Fridays and Saturdays) for Vieng Khan in Laos (280,000d). There are also regular local buses from Vinh to Tay Son (70,000d, two hours) and then irregular services from Tay Son on to the border at Cau Treo. Otherwise *xe om* (motorbike taxi) ask for around 170,000d for the ride.

At the border The border is open from 7am to 6pm. Lao visas are available.

Moving on If you're not on a direct bus, expect rip-offs. Upon entering Vietnam bus drivers quote up to US$40 for the ride to Vinh. A metered taxi costs about US$50, a motorbike about 320,000d. Some buses from Lak Sao claim to run to Danang or Hanoi, but in fact terminate in Vinh. On the Laos side, a jumbo or *songthaew* (truck) between the border and Lak Sao runs to about 50,000 kip (bargain hard).

Kenh Ga

The village of Kenh Ga (Chicken Canal) gets its name, apparently, from the number of wild chickens that used to live here. Today it's the riverine way of life and stunning limestone formations that are its main draw.

The local people seem to spend most of their lives on or in the water; watching over their floating fish-breeding pens, harvesting river grass for fish feed or selling vegetables boat-to-boat. Even the children commute to school by river. This used to be largely a floating village, but as fortunes have improved, more and more houses have been built.

From the pier you can hire a motorboat (100,000d) for a 1½-hour ride along the river around the village.

Kenh Ga is 21km from Ninh Binh off the road to Cuc Phuong National Park. Follow Hwy 1 north for 11km, then it's a 10km drive west to the boat pier.

Van Long Nature Reserve

Set amid yet more glorious limestone pinnacles, this tranquil reserve (admission 15,000d, boat 90,000d; ⊙7am-4.45pm) comprises a reedy wetland ideal for bird-watching. Rare black-faced spoonbill, cotton pygmy goose and white-browed crake have been seen here.

The reserve is also one of the last refuges of the endangered Delacour's langur – the Frankfurt Zoology Association in Vietnam boosted numbers by releasing three captively reared animals here in August 2012.

Row-boat rides here (maximum two people per boat) are wonderfully relaxing.

Van Long is 2km east of Tran Me, a small town 23km from Ninh Binh along the road to Cuc Phuong.

Trang An Grottoes

A huge riverside development, Trang An (⊙7.30am-4pm) offers a similar experience to Tam Coc, though it's also very commercial. The sheer number of boats, proximity to the highway, vast parking lots and weekend traffic jams make it a bit of a tourist circus. Once you're actually on a row boat, bobbing along the Sao Khe River through a succession of limestone caves, obviously things improve considerably, but this is still an overdeveloped sight. Many of the caves have also been enlarged to accommodate boats, including the removal of the odd pesky stalactite.

Boat trips (100,000d for up to four people) take two hours to tour the caves and tunnels. Bring a hat and sunscreen as the boats lack shade.

Trang An is 7km northwest of Ninh Binh. You'll pass it on the way to the Chua Bai Dinh.

Thung Nham

A private ecopark fashioned in a gorgeous valley near Tam Coc, Thung Nham (⊙7.30am-4.30pm) consists of a pretty lagoon surrounded by the craggy limestone peaks that characterise the province of Ninh Binh. Fishing for snakehead fish, catfish and tilapia, row-boat trips and cave visits are activities offered.

It's certainly a scenic spot, but the park has been developed to Vietnamese tastes – why leave nature as it is when you can improve it? Nevertheless it's still a very pretty spot, and development (there are bungalows and a large restaurant) has been quite sensitive to the surroundings. The park is the end of a road, well away from highways, so it's tranquil (if you avoid weekends!) and the bird-watching is good: look out for storks, crane, teal and herons.

Thung Nham is 6km west of Tam Coc.

Cuc Phuong National Park
☑030 / ELEV 150-656M

This important national park (☑030-384 8006; www.cucphuongtourism.com; adult/child 40,000/20,000d) is home to diverse animal and plant life, making it one of Vietnam's most important protected areas. Some 307 bird species, 133 kinds of mammal, 122 reptiles and more than 2000 different plants have been recorded here.

The national park covers an area spanning two limestone mountain ranges, across three provinces. Its highest peak is Dinh May Bac (Silver Cloud Peak) at 656m. No less than Ho Chi Minh took time off from the American War in 1962 to declare this Vietnam's first national park, saying: 'Forest is gold.'

Despite the exhortations, poaching and habitat destruction plague the Cuc Phuong National Park. Improved roads have led to more illegal logging, and many native species – the Asiatic black bear, Siamese

SAVING MONKEYS & TURTLES

Cuc Phuong's conservation centres provide a glimpse of their work and the fascinating animals they're trying to help. Officially you're supposed to hire a guide (no charge) from the visitor centre to escort you to these two places, both about 2km from the park's accommodation.

The impressive **Endangered Primate Rescue Center** (☎030-384 8002; www.primatecenter.org; ☉9.30-11.30am & 1.30-4.30pm) is managed under the supervision of Frankfurt Zoological Society. Its large enclosures are home to around 150 monkeys: 12 kinds of langur, three species of gibbon and two loris. All the centre's animals were either bred here or rescued from illegal traders (in Asia, monkeys can fetch large sums for their perceived 'medicinal worth').

The centre has bred more than 100 offspring in all, from nine different species, including the world's first captive-born Cat Ba langur and grey-shanked douc langur. But it's incredibly difficult to rehabilitate primates once they've lived in cages; it's only been possible to release 30 or so gibbons and langurs into semi-wild areas (one site is adjacent to the centre) since the centre opened.

There's also a non-primate section housing nocturnal animals including civet and pangolins, which can only be visited with prior permission.

The **Turtle Conservation Center** (☎030-384 8090; www.asianturtlenetwork.org; ☉9-11am & 2-4.45pm) houses more than 1000 terrestrial, semi-aquatic and aquatic turtles representing 20 of Vietnam's 25 native species. Many have been confiscated from smugglers. It's China (and Vietnam) generating the demand – eating turtle is thought to aid longevity. Professional hunters and opportunistic collectors have decimated wild populations of turtles throughout Vietnam and Southeast Asia, with as many as 10 million turtles traded per year through the 1990s.

You'll find excellent information displays, and there are incubation and hatchling viewing areas. The centre successfully breeds and releases turtles from 11 different species including six native turtles. Around 60 turtles are released back into the wild each year.

crocodile, wild dog and tiger – have vanished from the area as a result of human activity. Other wildlife is notoriously elusive, so manage your expectations accordingly.

To learn more about the park's conservation efforts, visit the excellent Endangered Primate Rescue Center and Turtle Conservation Center on the fringes of the park.

The park is also home to the minority Muong people, whom the government relocated from the park's central valley to its western edge in the late 1980s.

The best time of year to visit the park is in the dry months from November to February. From April to June it becomes increasingly hot, wet and muddy, and from July to October the rains arrive, bringing lots of leeches. Visitors in April and May might see some of the millions of butterflies that breed here. Weekends can be busy with Vietnamese families.

The visitor centre near the entrance has informative English-speaking staff, and guides and tours can be organised here.

👁 Sights & Activities

Cuc Phuong offers excellent hiking. Short walks include a trail up to the **Cave of Prehistoric Man** via a 220-step stairway. Human graves and tools were found here that date back 7500 years, making it one of the oldest sites of human habitation in Vietnam.

Popular hikes include a 6km-return walk to the massive, 1000-year-old **'old tree'** (*Tetrameles nudiflora*) and a longer four-hour walk to **Silver Cloud Peak**. There's also a strenuous 15km (approximately five-hour) hike to **Kanh**, a Muong village. You can stay overnight here with local families and raft on the Buoi River (60,000d).

Park staff can provide you with basic maps, but a guide is recommended for day trips and mandatory for longer treks. Two-hour escorted **night hikes** to spot nocturnal animals, or the Silver Cloud Peak hike both cost US$22 (for up to five people). The Deep Jungle trek (US$50) gets into remote terrain where you might spot civets or flying squirrels.

🛏 Sleeping & Eating

There are three accommodation areas in the national park, and one new luxury resort close by.

The visitor centre (s/d with shared bathroom US$8/15, guesthouse US$25-30, bungalows US$35) beside the park entrance has a selection of options including dark, functional rooms, comfortable en-suite guesthouse rooms and one bungalow. Attractive cottages overlooking Mac Lake (r $US25), 2km inside the park, have been renovated and are tempting, though the location is quite isolated and the restaurant here often undersupplied. Camping (per person US$2, with a tent US$4) is also available at the visitor centre or by Mac Lake.

Close to the heart of the reserve, the main park centre (stilt house per person US$8, q $US25, bungalows US$32) at Bong, 18km from the entrance, is the best place to be for an early morning walk or bird-watching. Here you'll find simple rooms with no hot water in a pseudo-stilt house, a building with large four-bed rooms, and a few bungalows. Kanh village homestays (per person US$5) with Muong families are also available and can be organised by park staff.

You'll find restaurants (meals 25,000d to 50,000d) at the park centre, Mac Lake and visitor centre. The cooking is flavoursome and filling. It's important to book your order in advance for each meal (except breakfast).

The new resort hotel, Cuc Phuong Resort (☎ 030-384 8886; www.cucphuongresort.com; Dong Tam village; bungalow/villa from US$92/165; ❋ @ ⊛ ⊠ ⛲) has proximity to a natural spring, enabling a flow of mineral-rich water to be pumped into the lovely wooden bathtubs in each room. It also has (spring water–fed) indoor and outdoor pools, tennis courts, and an impressive spa, and breakfast is included. It's just 2km from the park entrance.

The park can get very busy at weekends and during school holidays, when you should make a reservation.

ℹ Getting There & Away

Cuc Phuong National Park is 45km from Ninh Binh. The turn-off from Hwy 1 is north of Ninh Binh and follows the road that runs to Kenh Ga and Van Long Nature Reserve.

Regular buses link Ninh Binh with Cuc Phuong (22,000d, 1½ hours, every 1½ hours). Lots of Hanoi tour companies also offer trips to Cuc Phuong, usually combined with sights in the Ninh Binh area.

Vinh

♪ 038 / POP 446,000

Practically obliterated during the American War, Vinh was hastily rebuilt with East German aid – hence the brutalist concrete architecture that dominates the downtown drag. Unlike other Vietnamese towns, it has wide boulevards and broad pavements.

Despite attempts to prettify the place with trees and parks, the city remains a resolutely bleak-looking industrial city, nicknamed 'grim Vinh' by some travellers. There are few reasons to stop here unless you are a Ho Chi Minh devotee (he was born in a nearby village) or heading to Laos.

History

Vinh came to prominence as the 'Phoenix Capital City' of the Tay Son Rebellion. A May Day demonstration in 1930 was suppressed by the police, who killed seven people. Nonetheless revolutionary fervour spread, with Vinh's Communist cells, trade unions and farmers' organisations earning it the appellation 'Red-Glorious City'.

In the early 1950s, the city was reduced to rubble by a three-punch whammy: French aerial bombing, the Viet Minh's scorched-earth policy and, finally, a huge fire. During the American War, the port of Vinh became a key supply point for the Ho Chi Minh Trail. The city was relentlessly pounded with bombs for eight years – until only two buildings were left standing. In 1972 its population was officially zero.

⊙ Sights

There's not a lot left to see of Vinh's citadel (1831) apart from the sludgy green moat and three gates: Left Gate (Cua Ta; Đ Dao Tan), Right Gate (Cua Huu; Đ Dao Tan) and Front Gate (Cua Tien; Khoi 5 Đ Dang Thai Than). The walk between the Left and Right Gates provides a pleasant interlude and passes the little-visited Xo Viet Nghe Tinh Museum (Đ Dao Tan; admission free; ⊙ 7-11am & 1-5pm), which memorialises local heroes. Outside, in true socialist-art style, is a large stone monument to those who perished at the hands of the French.

🛏 Sleeping

Thanh An Hotel HOTEL $
(☎ 038-384 3478; 156 Nguyen Thai Hoc; r 230,000-300,000d; ❋ @ ⊛) Enjoys a convenient

location 300m south of the bus terminal, and rooms have attractive wooden furniture and good beds. Near-zero English is spoken at reception, however.

Asian Hotel HOTEL $

(038-359 3333; 114 Tran Phu; r 270,000-360,000d; ❄ 🅰) This multistorey hotel was modern a couple of decades ago. Rooms remain in fair condition and there's a lift and restaurant. It's about 300m southeast of the central city park.

Hotel Muong Thanh HOTEL $$

(038-353 5666; http://muongthanh.vn; Phan Boi Chao; r 400,000-700,000d, ste from 1,200,000d; ❄ @ 🅰) Three-star hotel with good-value rooms in many price categories; all are aging but spacious enough. It's located a few steps from the train station.

Muong Thanh Dien Chau Hotel HOTEL $$

(038-353 5666; http://muongthanh.vn; Quang Trung; r US$50-84, ste from US$112; ❄ @ 🅰 ❄) New in May 2013, this 33-storey glass-and-concrete monument dominates central Vinh and is unquestionably the best address in town. The decor is a tad chintzy, but the lobby has a real 'wow' factor and rooms are certainly commodious, with plush carpets and all mod cons. Promotional rates can drop as low as US$45 a night.

✗ Eating & Drinking

Dining selections are very thin on the ground in Vinh. Street food options include the Central Market, **pho bo food stalls** (Beef Noodle Soup stalls; Đ Phan Dinh Phung; ⊙ 7am-7pm) and **bun bo Hue food stalls** (Hue-style Spicy Beef Noodle Soup stalls; off Đ Dinh Cong Trang; ⊙ 7am-6pm).

You'll find a group of **bars** along Đ Quang Trung and **pool halls** on Đ Nguyen Thai Hoc.

Left Gate Street Food VIETNAMESE $

(Đ Dao Tan; meals 25,000-50,000d; ⊙ 3pm-3am) Raucous, sociable evening hot spot just past the Left Gate where locals tuck into chicken and duck, served with noodles and salad on long dining tables.

Thuong Hai CHINESE, VIETNAMESE $

(144 Đ Nguyen Thai Hoc; meals 40,000-95,000d; ⊙ 11.30am-9pm) The bustling Thuong Hai's speciality is delicious Shanghai-style chicken, though it also has good Vietnamese seafood and vegetarian dishes.

ℹ Information

Main Post Office (Đ Nguyen Thi Minh Khai; ⊙ 7am-6pm Mon-Sat, 7.30am-1pm Sun)

Saigon Commercial Bank (25 Đ Quang Trang; ⊙ 7.30am-3.30pm Mon-Fri, 7.30am-12.30pm Sat) With ATM.

Vinh City Hospital (Benh Vien Da Khoa Thanh Pho Vinh; 383 5279; 178 Đ Tran Phu; ⊙ 24hr) Just southwest of the central city park.

ℹ Getting There & Away

AIR

Vietnam Airlines (359 5777; www.vietnamairlines.com; 2 Đ Le Hong Phong) flies from Vinh to HCMC twice daily and has daily flights to Hanoi, Danang and Buon Ma Thuot. **Jetstar Pacific** (355 0550; 46 Đ Nguyen Thi Min Khai) has two to three daily links to HCMC. The airport is 8km north of the city.

A new Vietnam Airlines international connection between Vinh and Vientiane, Laos was scheduled to start in December 2013.

BUS

Vinh **bus station** (Đ Le Loi) has a reasonably modern booking office (including departures board and price list) and is centrally located.

Buses for Hanoi leave very regularly until 4.30pm, and there are also 10 sleeper buses. Services go to all four Hanoi bus terminals. For

TRANSPORT FROM VINH

DESTINATION	AIR	BUS	TRAIN (SOFT SEAT)
Danang	from 930,000d, 1hr, 1 daily	220,000d, 10-11hr, 12 daily	274,000d, 9½–10½hr, 5 daily
Dong Hoi	-	120,000d, 5hr, 12 daily	149,000d, 4r, 6 daily
Hanoi	from 930,000d, 30min, 1 daily	170,000d, 7hr, frequent	217,000d, 5½–6½hr, 5 daily
HCMC	from 1,200,000d, 5 daily, 2hr	660,000d, around 30hr, 4 daily	857,000d, 24–27hr, 5 daily
Hue	n/a	180,000d, 8-9hr, 13 daily	232,000d, 6½–7½hr, 6 daily

Ninh Binh (75,000d, four hours) take a Hanoi-bound bus. There are also six daily buses to Dien Bien Phu (540,000d, 16 hours).

Open-tour buses pass through town between Hanoi and Hue, and while it's easy to ask to jump off here, it's harder to arrange a pick-up.

For Laos, buses leave at 6am (on Mondays, Wednesdays, Fridays and Saturdays) for Vieng Khan (280,000d, 10 hours). Buses also leave at 6am (on the same four days only) for Luang Prabang (600,000d, 22 hours) via Phonsavan (12 hours). We've also heard there is another 6am daily departure from Vinh's central market to Phonsavan.

TRAIN

Vinh train station (Ga Vinh; Đ Le Ninh) is on the northwestern edge of town. There are regular departures to all stations on the main north–south line.

Around Vinh

Cua Lo Beach

Cua Lo is pleasant enough, with white sand, clean water and a shady grove of pine trees – but the concrete, karaoke, massage parlours and litter won't suit all travellers. Still, it's an option for a cooling dip and seafood lunch at one of the many beach restaurants.

Huge government hotels face the beach and behind them are uninspired guest houses (r 200,000-250,000d). Most hotels offer 'massage' and karaoke; some with prostitutes. In summer, rooms can go for triple (or more) the usual price.

Cua Lo is 16km northeast of Vinh and can be reached easily by motorbike (130,000d including waiting time) or taxi (around 90,000d one way).

Kim Lien

Ho Chi Minh's birthplace in Hoang Tru, and the village of Kim Lien, where he spent some of his formative years, are 14km northwest of Vinh. For all that these are popular pilgrimage spots (⊘ 7-11.30am & 2-5pm Mon-Fri, 7.30am-noon & 1.30-5pm Sat & Sun) FREE for the party faithful, there's little to see other than re-created houses of bamboo and palm leaves, dressed (barely) with a few pieces of furniture.

Ho Chi Minh was born in Hoang Tru in 1890 and raised there till 1895, when the family moved to Hue. They returned in 1901, but it was to the house in Kim Lien, about 2km from Hoang Tru. Not far from this house is a shrine-like museum, and a shop packed with Ho memorabilia.

No English-language information is available at either site. From Vinh, xe om (motorbike) drivers charge 100,000d (including waiting time), taxis ask for around double that.

Phong Nha-Ke Bang National Park

☑ 052

Designated a Unesco World Heritage site in 2003, the remarkable Phong Nha-Ke Bang National Park contains the oldest karst mountains in Asia, formed approximately 400 million years ago. Riddled with hundreds of cave systems – many of extraordinary scale and length – and spectacular underground rivers, Phong Nha is a speleologists' heaven on earth.

Its collection of stunning dry caves, terraced caves, towering stalagmites and glistening crystal-edged stalactites represent nature on a very grand scale indeed, and are beginning to create a real buzz in Vietnam, as more and more riches are discovered.

Serious exploration only began in the 1990s, lead by the British Cave Research Association and Hanoi University. Cavers first penetrated deep into Phong Nha Cave, one of the world's longest systems. In 2005 Paradise Cave was discovered, and in 2009 a team found the world's largest cave – Son Doong. Huge caverns and unknown cave networks are being discovered each year.

Above the ground, most of the mountainous 885 sq km of Phong Nha-Ke Bang National Park is near-pristine tropical evergreen jungle, more than 90% of which is primary forest. It borders the biodiverse Hin Namno reserve in Laos to form an impressive, continuous slab of protected habitat. More than 100 types of mammal (including 10 species of primate, tigers, elephants, and the saola, a rare Asian antelope), 81 types of reptile and amphibian, and more than 300 varieties of bird have been logged in Phong Nha.

Until recently, access to the national park was very limited and strictly controlled by the Vietnamese military. Access is still quite tightly controlled for good reason (the park is still riddled with unexploded ordnance). Officially you are not allowed to hike here without a licensed tour operator.

You can however travel independently (on a motorbike or car) on the Ho Chi Minh Highway or Hwy 20 that cut through the park. Sights that can be visited include the astounding Paradise Cave, turquoise river, ecotrail of Nuoc Mooc and a war shrine known as Eight Lady cave.

The Phong Nha region is changing fast, with more and more accommodation options opening. Son Trach village (population 3000) is the main centre, but it's a tiny place – there's only one ATM and transport connections are poor.

◉ Sights & Activities

Paradise Cave   CAVE
(Thien Dong; Phong Nha-Ke Bang National Park; adult/child under 1.3m 120,000/60,000d; ⊙7.30am-4.30pm) Deep in the national park, surrounded by forest and karst peaks, this remarkable cave system extends for 31km, though most people only visit the first kilometre or so.

Once you're inside, the sheer scale of Paradise Cave is truly breathtaking, as wooden staircases descend into a cathedral-like space replete with colossal stalagmites and glimmering stalactites of white crystal that resemble glass pillars.

Paradise Cave has only been open to the public since 2011. Commendably, development has been sensitive: there's no litter and even the trees along the access tracks are labelled. But in the last few years, visitor numbers have soared and if you come at peak times (the early afternoon) you can expect tour guides shepherding their flocks using megaphones – spoiling the whole experience. Try to get here as early as you can to beat the crowds.

To really explore deep inside Paradise Cave, consider booking Phong Nha Farmstay's 7km Trekking trip (2,650,000d, minimum two people), which penetrates deep into the cave and includes a swim through an underground river and lunch under a light shaft.

There's a restaurant (meals 35,000d to 70,000d) next to the visitor centre and a cafe sells cold drinks near the cave entrance.

Paradise Cave is about 14km southwest of Son Trach.

Tu Lan Caves   CAVE
A spectacular excursion, the Tu Lan cave trip begins with a countryside hike then a swim (with headlamps and life jackets) through two spectacular river caves before emerging in an idyllic river valley. Then there's more hiking through dense forest to a 'beach' where rivers merge that's an ideal campsite. There's more wonderful swimming here in vast caverns.

Moderate fitness levels are necessary. Tu Lan is 65km north of Son Trach and can only be visited on a guided tour.

Howard and Deb Limbert, consultants to tour operator Oxalis (p158), discovered these caves in 2010. Oxalis in Son Trach offer everything from four-day treks to day trips to Tu Lan. The longer excursions penetrate deeper into the jungle, but as the region is so pristine even day hikes are very rewarding.

Phong Nha Caves & Boat Trip   CAVE
The spectacular boat trip through Phong Nha Cave (☎052-367 5110; adult/child 40,000/20,000d, boat 220,000d; ⊙7am-4pm) is a highly enjoyable, though quite touristy, experience beginning in Son Trach village. You cruise along the Son River past bathing buffalo, jagged limestone peaks and church steeples to the cave's gaping mouth – Phong Nha means 'Cave of Teeth', but the 'teeth' (stalagmites) by the entrance are long gone. Then the engine is cut and you're transported to another world as you're paddled through cavern after garishly illuminated cavern.

On the return leg you've the option to climb (via 330 steps) up to Tien Son Cave, a dry cave in the mountainside. Here there are remains of Cham altars and inscriptions that date back to the 9th century. The cave was used as a hospital and ammunition depot during the American War and consequently was heavily bombed.

The ticket office and jetty for boat departures are in Son Trach village. Allow two hours to see Phong Nha; add an hour

NUOC MOOC ECOTRAIL

A beautiful riverside retreat inside the national park, the wooden walkways and paths of the Nuoc Mooc Ecotrail (adult/child 6-16yr 50,000/30,000d; ⊙7am-5pm) extend over a kilometre through woods to the confluence of two rivers. It's a gorgeous place for a swim, where you can wallow hippo-style in turquoise waters with a limestone-mountain backdrop. Bring a picnic. Nuoc Mooc is 12km southwest of Son Trach.

HANG SON DOONG

Ho Khanh, a hunter from a jungle settlement close to the Vietnam–Laos border, would often take shelter in the caves that honeycomb his mountain homeland. He stumbled across gargantuan **Hang Son Doong** (Mountain River Cave) in the early 1990s, but the sheer scale and majesty of the principal cavern (more than 5km long, 200m high and, in some places, 150m wide) was only confirmed as the world's biggest cave when British explorers returned with him in 2009.

The expedition team's biggest obstacle was to find a way over a vast overhanging barrier of muddy calcite they dubbed the 'Great Wall of Vietnam' that divided the cave. Once they did, its true scale was revealed – a cave big enough to accommodate a battleship. Sections of it are pierced by skylights that reveal formations of ethereal stalagmites that cavers have called the Cactus Garden. Some stalagmites are up to 80m high. Colossal cave pearls have been discovered, measuring 10cm in diameter, formed by millennia of drips, as calcite crystals fused with grains of sand. Magnificent rimstone pools are present throughout the cave.

Hang Son Doong is one of the most spectacular sights in Southeast Asia, and the government only approved (very restricted) access to the cave system in June 2013. The only specialist operator permitted (by the Vietnamese president no less) to lead tours here is Son Trach–based Oxalis (p158). Son Doong is no day-trip destination, it's in an extremely remote area and the only way to visit is by booking a seven-day expedition with around 16 porters. It costs US$3000 per person, with a maximum of eight trekkers on each trip.

Is it worth it? Well, *National Geographic* photographer Carsten Peter, whose photographs first unveiled the majesty of the cave to the world (and has climbed Everest and K2), described it as the most impressive natural sight in the world.

Note that you may come across tour agencies professing to sell tours of Hang Son Doong on the internet. The only licensed operator with access is Oxalis. Other agencies promise to take you to Hang Son Doong but actually set up a trip to Hang En instead (which is mighty impressive, but not Son Doong).

for Tien Son. In November and December seasonal floods may mean Phong Nha Cave is closed. Weekends are extremely popular with Vietnamese visitors, whose presence is magnified by the spectacular echoes and unventilated cigarette smoke.

Hang En   CAVE

This gigantic cave is very close to Hang Son Doong, and featured in the same *National Geographic* photographic spread in 2011. Getting here involves a trek through dense jungle, valleys and the Ban Doong minority village, a very remote tribal settlement (with no electricity or roads). You stay overnight in the cave or minority village.

Tours (4,600,000d per person, minimum two people) here are run by the Phong Nha-Ke Bang National Park rangers, but can also be booked via Phong Nha Farmstay.

Tours

Tours of Phong Nha can be set up in Dong Hoi, but as the region has so much to offer, try to base yourself locally if you can.

The National Park office organises two-day trips to spectacular Hang En cave and remote Ban Doong minority villages.

★ Oxalis   ADVENTURE
(☏052-367 7678; www.oxalis.com.vn; Son Trach Village) Oxalis are unquestionably *the* experts in caving and trekking expeditions, and are the only outfit licensed to conduct tours to Hang Son Doong. Staff are all fluent English speakers, and trained by world-renowned British cavers Howard and Deb Limbert. All excursions, from day trips to Tu Lan to weeklong expeditions to the world's largest cave, are meticulously planned and employ local guides and porters, so the wider community benefits. There's a little cafe at their riverside office where you can discuss trips.

Phong Nha Farmstay Tours   ADVENTURE
(☏052-367 5135; www.phong-nha-cave.com; Cu Nam village) Tours to Paradise Cave and the National Park are highly recommended and cost 1,000,000d. They are extremely

popular, so groups can be large (as many as 20) but they are well organised, and include entrance fees and minibus transport. Bicycle and boat tours to Hang Toi (Dark Cave) and tubing and biking trips (600,000d) are also great. Guides are extremely well informed about the region's history.

🛏 Sleeping

There are around a dozen simple local guesthouses in Son Trach village, all charging the same rate (250,000d a double). You'll find several cheap dining options near Son Trach's tiny marketplace.

Easy Tiger   HOSTEL $
(☑052-367 7844; www.easytigerphongnha.com; Son Trach; dm 160,000d; ❄ @ 🛜) Owned by the Farmstay crew, this great new hostel has comfortable dorms, a great bar-resto area, pool table and excellent travel info. A swimming pool is planned.

Thanh Dat   GUEST HOUSE $
(☑052-367 7069; Son Trach; r 250,000d; ❄🛜) On the main drag in Son Trach, this is the most welcoming locally owned place. Rooms are clean and it's owned by a family who speak a little English.

Pepper House   HOSTEL $
(☑016-7873 1560; www.pepperhouse-homestay. com; Khuong Ha village, 6km east of Son Trach; dm incl breakfast 200,000d; 🛜) Run by long-term resident Dave and his local wife Diem, this simple welcoming and very rural homestay has dorms with deep-sleep mattresses, cold beer and cheap grub.

★ Phong Nha Farmstay   GUEST HOUSE $$
(☑052-367 5135; www.phong-nha-cave.com; Cu Nam village; r 500,000-900,000d; f 1,500,000d; ⊜❄@🛜❄) The place (and people) that really put Phong Nha on the map, the Farmstay goes from strength to strength. Views overlooking an ocean of rice paddies are unmatched. Rooms are smallish but neat, with high ceilings and shared balconies. The bar-restaurant with pool table is the engine room of the operation with tasty Asian and Western grub (meals 40,000d to 120,000d) and a gregarious vibe. Tours (trekking, kayaking, caving, tubing, biking and hiking) are outstanding. Note that there's no longer a dorm. It's in Cu Nam village, 9km east of Son Trach. Pick-ups can be arranged in Dong Hoi.

Phong Nha Lake House Resort   HOTEL $$
(☑052-367 5999; http://phongnhalakehouse.com; Khuong Ha; dm/d/villas US$10/35/50; ❄🛜) Impressive new lakeside resort owned by an Australian-Vietnamese couple with an excellent dorm (with quality beds, mozzie nets, en-suite bathroom and high ceilings), spacious and stylish rooms and lovely villas. A pool, jacuzzi and spa are planned. The huge wooden restaurant is a traditional structure from rural Vietnam. It's 7km east of Son Trach.

Phong Nha Homestay   HOMESTAY $$
(☑012-9959 7182; www.phong-nha-homestay.com; Son Tranch; r US$30-50; ❄❄🛜) How often do you get the chance to stay in the house of a Vietnamese legend? This homestay belongs to Ho Khanh, who discovered the world's largest cave. He's also a master carpenter, and his four wood-panelled rooms, with tiled floors and excellent beds with mozzie nets, are attractive and comfortable. There's a great riverside cafe, too.

🍴 Eating & Drinking

★ Jungle Bar   CAFE, BAR $
(Son Trach; meals 25,000-50,000d; ⊗7am-midnight; 🛜) Run by Hai, a switched-on, English-speaking local, this cool bar-cafe offers cheap grub (including breakfast and vegetarian choices), fresh juices, travel info, bike rental and a welcoming atmosphere. In the evening it's more of a bar, with lounge music, cocktails and an open mic some nights.

Pub with Cold Beer   BAR
(beer 20,000d, meals from 20,000d; ⊗8am-8pm) Up a dirt track in the middle of nowhere (but well-signposted) this excellent barn-cum-bar is owned by a local farming family and does what it says on the tin – the beer is ice cold. Bring your iPod and they'll let you play some tunes, too. Hungry? Order roast chicken with peanut sauce (all ingredients are farm-fresh). The Farmstay will provide you with a map to get here by bike. Rooms were under construction when we passed by.

ℹ Information

In Son Trach, head to the Jungle Bar where owner Hai (an ecologist) is a superb source of independent travel information on the park and region, can book train and bus tickets for a small commission, organise tours and rent bikes and motorbikes. The helpful staff at Phong Nha Farmstay and Easy Tiger hostel are also extremely well informed and can assist with information and transport.

There's a tourist office opposite the jetty in Son Trach, but staff are not well versed regarding independent travel. You'll find an ATM next to the tourist office.

It's possible to rent a bike and explore the region yourself, though bear in mind that most locals do not speak English and road signs are lacking. But with a sense of adventure, some wheels and a map (ask at Jungle Bar) it's perfectly do-able.

ⓘ Getting There & Around

Son Trach village is 50km northwest of Dong Hoi; from Dong Hoi head 20km north on Hwy 1 to Bo Trach, then turn west for another 30km.

Phong Nha-Ke Bang National Park abuts Son Trach village and spreads west to the Lao border. The region has only very recently opened up; until 2011 access was tightly controlled by the Vietnamese state. Things have been relaxed considerably but some areas remain off limits to independent travellers.

Hotels can organise lifts in private cars from Dong Hoi (400,000d to 500,000d); they work together so rides can be shared between travellers to cut costs.

BUS

Local buses (45,000d, two hours) offer irregular connections between Dong Hoi and Son Trach. There's also a bus connection (120,000d, 1hr 15min) between Dong Hoi train station, the Farmstay and Son Trach. It leaves Dong Hoi daily at 6.30am and 8am and returns from Son Trach (via Farmstay) at 6pm and 8pm.

A tour bus (500,000d, five hours) also links Son Trach, the Farmstay and Hue, stopping at the Ben Hai river museum and Vinh Moc Tunnels. It leaves Son Trach at 6.30am daily and returns from Hue at 1pm. Tickets on these buses to/from Hue and Dong Hoi can be booked via the Farmstay (p158), Easy Tiger (p159) or Hue Backpackers (p176).

Dong Hoi & Around

📞 052 / POP 116,000

Pleasantly untouristed, Dong Hoi is a port and seaside town with no souvenir shops and a lack of hassle. It enjoys an attractive location, clinging to the banks of the Nhat Le River, and has beaches to the north and south.

As the main staging area for the North Vietnamese Army (NVA), Dong Hoi suffered more than most during the American War. The town has since recovered as a congenial provincial capital.

⊙ Sights & Activities

The Nhat Le River, which divides the city from a beautiful sandy spit, boasts a landscaped riverside promenade that includes the haunting, ruined facade of the **Tam Toa Church** FREE, which was bombed in 1965.

All that remains of Dong Hoi Citadel (1825) are two restored gates, one close to the riverbank, the other on Đ Quang Trung.

As there's no nightlife or bar scene in town you may as well plan to get up early and check out the excellent **fish market** (Đ Me Suot; ⊙ 6am-2pm).

A2Z   TOUR OPERATOR
(📞 052-384 5868; www.atoztourist.com; 29 Đ Ly Thuong Kiet) Contact for tours to Phong Nha or open-tour bus tickets.

Nam Long Hotel Tours   TOUR OPERATOR
(📞 052-382 1851; sythang25@yahoo.com; 22 Đ Ho Xuan Huong) Day trips to Phong Nha cost 800,000d (minimum two people).

🛏 Sleeping & Eating

⭐**Nam Long Hotel**   HOTEL $
(📞 052-382 1851; sythang25@yahoo.com; 22 Đ Ho Xuan Huong; dm US$5, r US$12-15; ⊛ ❋ ⊛ 🛜) Simply excellent budget hotel run by Nga and Sy, a welcoming, ever-helpful, English-speaking couple. Rooms are bright and airy with enormous windows – book 301 for a river-view balcony. The new eight-bed dorm is superb, with two en-suite bathrooms and its own balcony with great views. Breakfast is available, and Phong Nha tours and onward buses can be organised.

Nam Long Plaza   HOTEL $
(nga_namlonghotel@yahoo.com; 28A Đ Phan Chu Trinh; dm US$7, s US$13-16, d US$18-26; ⊛ ❋ 🛜) Fine new eight-storey hotel, with 19 comfortable, spacious rooms all with city or river views. A free hot breakfast is included, service is good and tours can be arranged.

Sunshine Hotel   HOTEL $
(📞 052-381 1333; http://anhduonghotel.com.vn; 301 Đ Ly Thuong Kiet; r 240,000-400,000d; ❋ 🛜) A new minihotel renowned for its excellent service. Manager Cindy is a fluent English

Dong Hoi

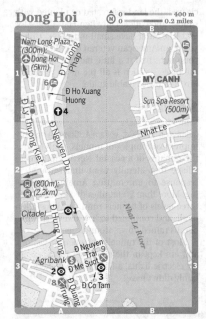

speaker and can help with bike rentals and transport. Rooms are clean and good value.

Sun Spa Resort RESORT HOTEL **$$$**
(☎052-384 2999; www.sunsparesortvietnam.com; My Canh; r & ste US$90-165, bungalow & villa from US$190; ❄@🛜🏊) Huge beachside resort in landscaped grounds complete with two pools, a spa and tennis courts. The rooms and villas are spacious and well presented, but perhaps don't really hit the five-star billing.

Tu Quy VIETNAMESE **$**
(17 Đ Co Tam; meals 20,000-40,000d; ⊙7am-8.30pm) This area is famous for its *banh khoai* (shrimp pancake) restaurants, of which Tu Quy is one of the best and has streetside tables with the river in sight.

QB Teen INTERNATIONAL **$**
(3 Đ Le Loi; meals 32,000-80,000d; ⊙7am-9pm; 🛜) Small place that serves pretty decent (for Dong Hoi) Western fare including pizza, pasta and omelettes as well as a few Vietnamese dishes. It's air-conditioned.

❶ Information

Staff at both the Nam Long and Sunshine hotels can organise motorbike (150,000d to 200,000d per day) and bicycle rentals (80,000d), provide maps and book bus tickets.

Agribank (2 Đ Me Suot; ⊙7.30am-4pm Mon-Fri, 7.30am-12.30pm Sat) Has an ATM and exchange services.

❶ Getting There & Away

AIR
The airport is 6km north of town. Vietnam Airlines operates daily flights to Hanoi and four connections per week to HCMC.

BUS
From the **bus station** (Đ Tran Hung Dao), travellers can catch services south to Danang (115,000d, 5½ hours, eight daily), via Hue (92,000d, four hours) and Dong Ha (54,000d, two hours), and north to Hanoi (174,000d, eight hours). It's easy to leave an open-tour bus in Dong Hoi, but for a pick-up, book via a travel agency or hotel.

To get to Laos, buses leave for the Lao towns of Vien Chan and Savannakhet (430,000d, 12 hours, both at 6.30am Monday to Saturday only) via the quiet Cha Lo–Na Phao border crossing where Lao visas are available.

Local buses (98,000d, four hours, five daily) also leave for the border at Lao Bao.

TRAIN
The **train station** (Ga Dong Hoi; Đ Thuan Ly) is 3km west of the centre. Trains leave for destinations including Hanoi (374,000d, 9½ hours to 11½ hours, five daily), Hue (118,000d, three to four hours, six daily) and Danang (155,000d, five hours, six daily). All prices quoted are for soft seats on express trains.

SOUTH-CENTRAL VIETNAM

Demilitarised Zone (DMZ)

♩ 053

Most of the bases and bunkers have long vanished, but this 5km strip of land on either side of the Ben Hai River is still known by its American War moniker: the DMZ. From 1954 to 1975 it acted as a buffer between the North and the South. Ironically, the DMZ became one of the most militarised areas in the world, forming what *Time* magazine called 'a running sore'.

The area just south of the DMZ was the scene of some of the bloodiest battles in America's first TV war, turning Quang Tri, The Rockpile, Khe Sanh, Lang Vay and Hamburger Hill into household names.

Fast forward several decades and there's not much left to see. Most sites have been cleared, the land reforested or planted with rubber and coffee. Only Ben Hai, Vinh Moc and Khe Sanh have small museums. Unless you're an American veteran or military buff, you might find it a little hard to appreciate the place – which is all the more reason to hire a knowledgeable guide.

⊙ Sights

Vinh Moc Tunnels HISTORICAL SITE
(admission 20,000d; ⊙ 7am-4.30pm) A highly impressive complex of tunnels, Vinh Moc is the remains of a coastal North Vietnamese village that literally went underground in response to unremitting American bombing. More than 90 families disappeared into three levels of tunnels running almost 2km in all, and continued to live and work while bombs rained down around them.

Most of the tunnels are open to visitors, and are kept in their original form (except for electric lights, a luxury the villagers certainly didn't have).

South-Central Vietnam

WATCH YOUR STEP

Millions of tonnes of ordnance were dropped on Vietnam during the American War – it's estimated that about a third did not explode. Death and injury still happen most days. At many places there's still a chance of encountering live mortar rounds, artillery projectiles and mines. Watch where you step and don't leave the marked paths. Never touch any leftover ordnance.

It's not just the DMZ that's affected. It's estimated that as much as 20% of Vietnam remains uncleared, with more than 3.5 million mines and 350,000 to 800,000 tonnes of unexploded ordnance (UXO). In the one-year period between 2012 and 2013 the NGO Mines Advisory Group estimated it cleared 185,639 sq metres of battle-affected areas, removed and destroyed 16,035 unexploded ordnance items and 2188 cluster bombs.

Between 1975 and 2007 unexploded ordnance resulted in 105,000 injuries and over 45,000 deaths. Every year hundreds die and are injured – a disproportionate number of them children or from the ethnic minority groups.

The People's Army is responsible for most ongoing mine clearance. It's joined by foreign NGOs such as the **Mines Advisory Group** (www.maginternational.org) and **Clear Path International** (www.clearpathinternational.org), whose efforts are well worth supporting.

Dong Ha has an excellent new Mine Action Visitor Centre. Drop by if you're in the area.

An English-speaking guide will accompany you around the complex, pointing out the 12 entrances until you emerge at a glorious beach, facing the South China Sea. The museum has photos and relics of tunnel life, including a map of the tunnel network.

The turn-off to Vinh Moc from Hwy 1 is 6.5km north of the Ben Hai River in the village of Ho Xa. Follow this road east for 13km.

Khe Sanh Combat Base   HISTORICAL SITE
(museum 20,000d; ⊙ museum 7am-5pm) The site of the most famous siege of the American War, the USA's Khe Sanh Combat Base was never overrun, but saw the bloodiest battle of the war. About 500 Americans, 10,000 North Vietnamese troops and uncounted civilian bystanders died around this remote highland base. It's eerily peaceful today, but in 1968 the hillsides trembled with the impact of 1000kg bombs, white phosphorus shells, napalm, mortars and endless artillery rounds, as desperate American forces sought to repel the NVA.

The 75-day siege of Khe Sanh began on 21 January 1968 with a small-scale assault on the base's perimeter. As the marines and South Vietnamese rangers braced for a fullscale ground attack, Khe Sanh became the focus of global media attention. It was the cover story for both *Newsweek* and *Life* magazines, and made the front pages of countless newspapers around the world. During the next two months the base was subjected to continuous ground attacks and artillery fire, and US aircraft dropped 100,000 tonnes of explosives in its vicinity. But the expected attempt to overrun the base never came.

On 7 April 1968, after heavy fighting, US troops reopened Hwy 9 and linked up with the marines, ending the siege.

It now seems clear that the siege was an enormous diversion to draw US attention away from the South Vietnamese population centres in preparation for the Tet Offensive, which began a week after the siege started.

Today the site is occupied by a small **museum**, which contains some fascinating old photographs, plus a few reconstructed bunkers and American aircraft. Most of the area is now planted with coffee, and vendors offer high-grade local Arabica beans for sale at the entrance.

Khe Sanh is 3km north of the small town of Huong Hoa.

Truong Son National Cemetery   CEMETERY
An evocative memorial to the legions of North Vietnamese soldiers who died along the Ho Chi Minh Trail, this cemetery is a sobering sight. More than 10,000 graves dot these hillsides, each marked by a simple white tombstone headed by the inscription *liet si* (martyr). Many graves lie empty, simply bearing names, representing a fraction of Vietnam's 300,000 soldiers missing in action.

Truong Son was used as a base by the May 1959 Army Corps from 1972 to 1975. The corps had the mission of constructing and maintaining the Ho Chi Minh Trail.

Around the DMZ

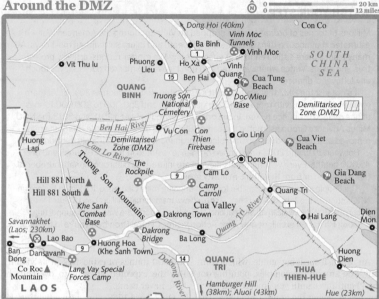

The cemetery is not on most tour itineraries, and its isolated location and simple design give it a powerful dimension. It's 27km northwest of Dong Ha; the turn-off from Hwy 1 is close to Doc Mieu.

Ben Hai River   RIVER
(museum 20,000d; ⏰museum 7am-4.30pm) Once the border between North and South Vietnam, Ben Hai River's southern bank now has a grandiose reunification monument, its stylised palm leaves oddly resembling missiles. Cua Tung Beach's fine golden sands are just east of here. Ben Hai's northern bank is dominated by a reconstructed flag tower and small museum full of war mementoes.

Ben Hai is 22km north of Dong Ha on Hwy 1.

Hamburger Hill   HISTORICAL SITE
FREE Hamburger Hill (Ap Bia) was the site of a tumultuous battle in May 1969 between US forces and the NVA over a 900m-high mountain – resulting in over 600 North Vietnamese and 72 American deaths. Today you need a special permit (costing US$25 and only obtained in the town of Aluoi) and a guide to get a glimpse of the remaining trenches and bunkers.

There's a rudimentary visitor centre (with a map and information in English) at the base of the hill, from where a 6km trail leads up the mountain. Bring water and be sure to stick to the main trail.

Hamburger Hill is 8km northwest of Aluoi, about 6km off Hwy 14. It's less than 2km from the Laos border. Security is tight around here and you're sure to get your permits inspected by border guards.

Con Thien Firebase   HISTORICAL SITE
Only one bunker remains of the US Marine Corps base that used to cover the three small hills here. In September 1967 Con Thien was besieged by the NVA, provoking a US response of 4000 bombing sorties. Today the region (though cleared of mines) is still studded with unexploded ordnance – stick to the paths.

Con Thien Firebase is 15km west of Hwy 1 and 8km south of Truong Son National Cemetery.

Camp Carroll   HISTORICAL SITE
Camp Carroll was named after a Marine Corps captain who was killed while trying to seize a nearby ridge. Its colossal cannons were used to shell targets as far away as Khe Sanh (though these days there isn't much to

see except a Vietnamese memorial marker). The turn-off to Camp Carroll is 10km west of Cam Lo; it's 3km from Hwy 9.

The Rockpile
HISTORICAL SITE

Visible from Hwy 9, this 230m-high karst outcrop once had a US Marine Corps look-out on top and a base for American long-range artillery nearby. You'll need a guide to point out the hill to you. The Rockpile is 29km west of Dong Ha on Hwy 9.

Dakrong Bridge
BRIDGE

Crossing the Dakrong River 13km east of the Khe Sanh bus station, this bridge was rebuilt in 2001 and bears a marker hailing its importance as a conduit for the Ho Chi Minh Trail.

❶ Getting There & Around

Virtually everyone explores the DMZ on a tour. Standard tours are cheap (US$10 to US$15 for a day trip) and can be arranged by any hotel or cafe in Hue or Dong Ha. No matter where you sign up you'll probably wind up as part of a large group. Most take in The Rockpile, Khe Sanh, Vinh Moc and Doc Mieu and leave Hue at 7am, returning by about 5pm. If you're travelling from Hue bear in mind the distances covered, around 300km, and that much more time is spent driving than sightseeing.

A more meaningful experience, particularly for American veterans, is to see the DMZ independently. Reckon on US$100 or so per day for a car and expert guide.

Dong Ha
☎ 053 / POP 88,800

Dong Ha is an important transport hub that sits at the intersection of Hwys 1 and 9. Its dusty, traffic-plagued main drag looks pretty dismal – this is because the town was completely flattened during the American War. However the town does have its attractive aspects, with a string of riverside seafood restaurants. Dong Ha makes a useful base for exploring the DMZ and is the gateway town to the Lao Bao border crossing.

◎ Sights

Mine Action Visitor Centre
MUSEUM

(☎ 093 521 1281; Đ Ly Thuong Kiet; ☺ 8am-5.30pm Mon-Fri, weekends by appointment) FREE The Quang Tri Province was the most heavily bombed part of Vietnam and it remains the most strewn with ordnance. This very worthwhile, well-organised new museum provides an excellent historical overview, with photographs that include the destruction of the citadel of Quang Tri in 1972 and people attempting to deactivate mines with bamboo sticks.

Information panels (in English and Vietnamese) detail the grim reality for locals: cluster bombs cause 46% of incidents, of which 80% are fatal. More than 7000 people have died in the province since the

CENTRAL VIETNAM DONG HA

GONE UNDERGROUND

In 1966 the USA began a massive aerial and artillery bombardment of North Vietnam. Just north of the Demilitarised Zone (DMZ), the villagers of Vinh Moc found themselves living in one of the most heavily bombed and shelled strips of land on the planet. Small family shelters could not withstand this onslaught and villagers either fled or began tunnelling by hand and with simple tools into the red-clay earth.

The Viet Cong (VC) found it useful to have a base here and encouraged the villagers to stay. After 18 months of tunnelling, an enormous complex was established, creating new homes on three levels from 12m to 23m below ground, plus meeting rooms and even a maternity unit (17 babies were born underground). Whole families lived here, their longest stay lasting 10 days and 10 nights. Later, the civilians and VC were joined by North Vietnamese soldiers, whose mission was to keep communication and supply lines to nearby Con Co Island open.

Other villages north of the DMZ also built tunnel systems, but none was as elaborate as Vinh Moc. The poorly constructed tunnels of Vinh Quang village (at the mouth of the Ben Hai River) collapsed after repeated bombing, killing everyone inside.

US warships stationed off the coast consistently bombarded the Vinh Moc tunnels (craters are still visible), and occasionally the tunnel mouths that faced the sea were struck by naval gunfire. The only ordnance that posed a real threat was the 'drilling bomb'. It scored a direct hit once but failed to explode, and no one was injured; the inhabitants adapted the bomb hole for use as an air shaft.

ℹ️ GETTING TO LAOS: DONG HA TO SAVANNAKHET

Getting to the border The Lao Bao/Dansavanh border crossing, on the Sepon River (Song Xe Pon), is one of the most popular and least problematic border crossings between Laos and Vietnam. Buses to Savannakhet in Laos run from Hue via Dong Ha and Lao Bao. From Hue, there's a 7am air-con bus (340,000d, 9½ hours), on odd days only, that stops in Dong Ha at the Sepon Travel office around 8.30am to pick up more passengers. It's also easy to cross the border on your own; Dong Ha is the gateway. Buses leave the town to Lao Bao (55,000d, two hours) roughly every 15 minutes. From here *xe om* charge 12,000d to the border. You can check schedules and book tickets at Tam's Cafe.

At the border The border posts (open 7am to 6pm) are a few hundred metres apart. Lao visas are available on arrival, but Vietnamese visas need to be arranged in advance. There are several serviceable hotels on the Vietnamese side. Try not to change currency in Lao Bao; money-changers offer terrible rates.

Moving on *Songthaew* head regularly to Sepon, from where you can get a bus or another *songthaew* to Savannakhet.

war ended. Minority people are particularly vulnerable as they seek scrap metal to sell.

Films (from 11 minutes to over an hour) are also available to view.

Call an hour ahead and Phu, the excellent English-speaking manager, will accompany you around the museum. He'll also open up on weekends on request.

Bao Tang Quang Tri   MUSEUM
(8 Đ Nguyen Hue; ⊙ 7.30-11am & 1.30-5pm Tue, Thu, Sat & Sun) **FREE** A modest museum that documents the history of the Quang Tri Province with a focus on its ethinic minorities.

🌐 Tours

Dong Ha has several excellent guides and agencies offering illuminating tours of the DMZ and beyond.

Annam Tour   MILITARY
(📞 0905 140 600; www.annamtour.com; 207B Đ Nguyen Du) Outstanding tailor-made tours, guided by military historian Mr Vu (who speaks excellent English) or his very able assistant Vinh, a war veteran. Using iPads to show photographs and maps, the sights and battlegrounds come to life. Trips cost around US$120 per day, and can be set up from Hue too.

Tam's Tours   MILITARY, FOOD
(📞 0905 425 912; http://tamscafe.jimdo.com; 79 Đ Hung Vuong) Excellent backpacker-priced tours taking in the DMZ sights using English-speaking war veterans cost US$22 to US$30 by motorbike (per person per day), or in a car it's US$65 to US$85. Tam also offers an excellent evening food tour (US$20) that includes five local specialities.

DMZ Tours   MILITARY, ADVENTURE
(📞 053-356 4056; www.dmztours.net; 260 Đ Le Duan) Itineraries for American veterans, quality DMZ tours and adventure trips including boat trips to Can Co Island. Prices start at US$118 (two people) for a day's touring around the main war sites in a car.

Sepon Travel   MILITARY, TRANSPORT
(📞 053-385 5289; www.sepontour.com; 189 Đ Le Duan) DMZ tours and can book buses to Savannakhet (Laos).

🛏️ Sleeping

DMZ Hotel   HOTEL $
(📞 053-356 0757; http://dmzhotel.jimdo.com; 50 Ly Thuong Kiet; s US$8, d US$10-13; ❄️@🛜) Excellent new backpackers' HQ with helpful English-speaking staff and well-priced rooms with cable TV and minibar. Breakfast is available and free pick-ups/drop-offs to the bus and train station are offered.

Violet Hotel   HOTEL $
(📞 053-358 2959; Đ Ba Trieu; s 200,000d, tw 250,000-330,000d; ❄️🛜) Represents outstanding value, with inviting modern rooms all with minibar, TV, fan and air-con; some also have rice-paddy views and a balcony. In a quiet location 1km from the centre.

Huu Nghi Hotel   HOTEL $
(📞 053-385 2361; www.huunghihotel.com.vn; 68 Đ Tran Hung Dao; s/d/tr 380,000/440,000/570,000d; ❄️🛜) Spacious, inviting rooms all with smart furnishings including wardrobe, reading light, bed with comfortable mattress, and flat-screen TV – some also have commanding river views. Breakfast is included.

Saigon Quang Binh   HOTEL $$
(☑ 053-382 2276; www.sgquangbinhtourist.com.
vn; 20 Quach Xuan Ky; r US$60-125; ❄☎) The
fanciest place in town. Though it has a great
riverside location and rooms are certainly
smart, service is a bit spotty considering the
official rates (check their website for promo-
tions). The rooftop bar-cafe is great for a
beer or coffee, though.

✕ Eating & Drinking

Dong Ha is famous for seafood. Head to the
strip of riverside restaurants on Đ Hoang
Dieu for wonderful *cua rang me* (crab in
tamarind sauce), *vem nuong* (grilled clams)
and steamed or roasted squid. There's an-
other groups of places by the Violet Hotel for
Vietnamese meat and seafood. Tam's Tours
also offers an excellent street and local food
walking tour.

★ **Tam's Cafe**   CAFE $
(http://tamscafe.jimdo.com; 79 Đ Hung Vuong;
meals US$2; ⊙7am-6pm; ☎) In new premises,
but the winning formula remains the same.
Tam's offers excellent Vietnamese food and
Western snacks such as pizza, as well as
smoothies and juices. It's run by the ever-
helpful Tam, a switched-on, fluent English
speaker who works around the clock to help
travellers, offering inexpensive tours and in-
dependent travel advice. The cafe employs
and supports deaf people.

❶ Information

For impartial travel and tourist information and
a useful city map, head to Tam's Cafe. There's
several ATMs in town including **Vietcombank** (Đ
Tran Hung Dao).

❶ Getting There & Away

BUS

Dong Ha bus station (Ben Xe Khach Dong Ha;
☑ 053-385 1488; 68 Đ Le Duan) is near the
intersection of Hwys 1 and 9. Buses to Dong
Hoi (58,000d, two hours), Hue (46,000d, 1½
hours), Danang (75,000d, 3½ hours), Khe Sanh
(30,000d, 1½ hours) and Lao Bao (49,000d, two
hours) depart regularly.

It is sometimes necessary to change buses in
Khe Sanh for Lao Bao. Buses are also advertised
to Savannakhet in Laos, but the station won't
book a ticket for foreigners; Sepon Travel and
Tam's Cafe will.

There are also three daily minibus connec-
tions (120,000d) from Tam's Cafe to Phong Nha
Farmstay and Son Trach village at noon, 1pm,

and 5pm; on the return leg it heads south via
Hue to Danang at 5am and 7.30am.

You can check all transport schedules at Tam's
Cafe.

CAR & MOTORCYCLE

A one-way car trip to the Lao Bao border will set
you back US$45. Motorbikes can be hired from
US$5 per day.

TRAIN

Dong Ha's **train station** (Ga Dong Ha; 2 Đ Le
Thanh Ton), 2km south of the Hwy 1 bridge, has
trains to destinations including Hanoi (sleeper
from 630,000d, 11 to 14 hours, five daily), Dong
Hoi (from 66,000d, 1½ to 2½ hours, six daily)
and Hue (from 52,000d, 1½ to 2½ hours, six
daily).

Quang Tri

☑ 053 / POP 28,600

Quang Tri once boasted an important cita-
del, but little of its old glory remains. In the
Easter Offensive of 1972, North Vietnamese
forces laid siege to and then captured the
town. This provoked carpet bombing and
artillery shelling by the USA and South Vi-
etnamese forces, which all but destroyed
Quang Tri.

Remnants of the ancient moat, ramparts
and gates of the citadel remain. It's off Đ
Tran Hung Dao, 1.6km north of Hwy 1.

Outside Quang Tri, along Hwy 1 towards
Hue, is the skeleton of Long Hung Church.
It bears countless bullet holes and mortar
damage from the 1972 bombardment.

The bus station (Đ Tran Hung Dao) is about
1km from Hwy 1, but buses can also be
flagged down on the highway.

Hue

☑ 054 / POP 361,000

Palaces and pagodas, tombs and temples,
culture and cuisine, history and heartbreak,
there's no shortage of poetic pairings to de-
scribe Hue (pronounced 'hway'). A Unesco
World Heritage site, this deeply evocative
capital of the Nguyen emperors still reso-
nates with the glories of imperial Vietnam,
even though many of its finest buildings
were destroyed during the American War.

Hue owes its charm partly to its location
on the Perfume River – picturesque on a
clear day, atmospheric even in less flattering
weather. There's always restoration work go-
ing on to recover Hue's royal splendour, but
today the city is very much a blend of new

Hue

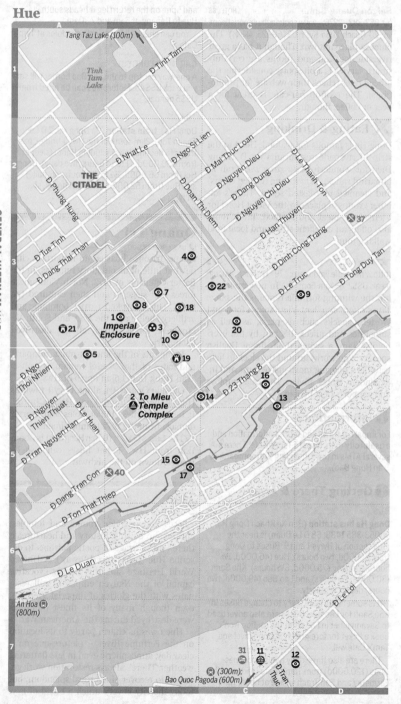

THE CITADEL

Tang Tau Lake (100m)

Tinh Tam Lake

Đ Tinh Tam

Đ Nhat Le

Đ Ngo Si Lien

Đ Mai Thuc Loan

Đ Nguyen Dieu

Đ Phung Hung

Đ Doan Thi Diem

Đ Dang Dung

Đ Nguyen Chi Dieu

Đ Le Thanh Ton

Đ Han Thuyen

Đ Tue Tinh

Đ Dang Thai Than

37

Đ Dinh Cong Trang

Đ Tong Duy Tan

Đ Le Truc

4

7

22

8

18

9

1

Imperial Enclosure

21

3

10

20

5

19

16

2 To Mieu Temple Complex

14

Đ 23 Thang 8

13

Đ Ngo Thoi Nhiem

Đ Nguyen Thien Thuat

Đ Le Huan

Đ Tran Nguyen Han

15

17

40

Đ Dang Tran Con

Đ Ton That Thiep

Đ Le Duan

Đ Le Loi

An Hoa (800m)

31

11

12

Đ Tran Thuc

(300m); Bao Quoc Pagoda (600m)

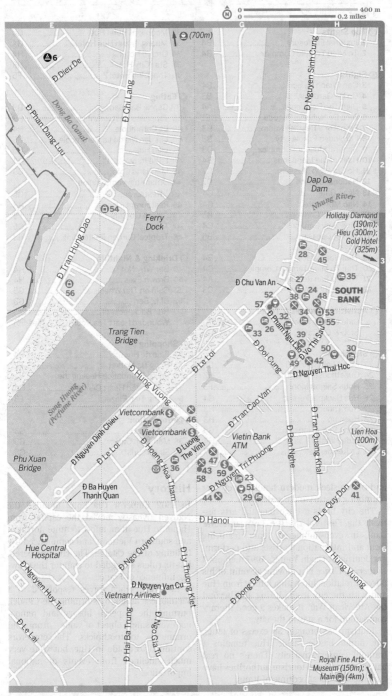

0   400 m
0   0.2 miles

CENTRAL VIETNAM HUE

Đ Dieu De

Đ Chi Lang

Dong Ba Canal

Đ Phan Dang Luu

Đ Tran Hung Dao

Ferry Dock

Trang Tien Bridge

Song Huong (Perfume River)

Phu Xuan Bridge

Đ Ba Huyen Thanh Quan

Hue Central Hospital

Đ Nguyen Huy Tu

Đ Le Lai

Đ Hai Ba Trung

Đ Nguyen Van Cu
Vietnam Airlines

Đ Ngo Quyen

Đ Ly Thuong Kiet

Đ Ngo Gia Tu

Đ Hanoi

Đ Hung Vuong

Đ Le Loi

Đ Nguyen Dinh Chieu

Đ Le Loi

Vietcombank
Vietcombank

Đ Hoang Hoa Tham

Đ Luong The Vinh

Vietin Bank ATM

Đ Doi Cung

Đ Tran Cao Van

Đ Nguyen Tri Phuong

Đ Ben Nghe

Đ Tran Quang Khai

Đ Le Quy Don

Đ Hung Vuong

Đ Dong Da

Đ Nguyen Sinh Cung

Dap Da Dam

Nhung River

Holiday Diamond (190m); Hieu (300m); Gold Hotel (325m)

SOUTH BANK

Đ Chu Van An

Đ Pham Ngu Lao

Đ Vo Thi Sau

Đ Nguyen Thai Hoc

Lien Hoa (100m)

Royal Fine Arts Museum (150m); Main (4km)

6
54
56
28
45
35
27
24
48
52
57
38
34
53
55
32
26
39
33
42
50
30
49
25
46
36
47
43
59
58
23
44
51
29
41

Hue

and old as sleek modern hotels tower over crumbling century-old Citadel walls.

The city hosts a huge biennial arts festival, the Festival of Hue (www.huefestival. com), in even-numbered years, featuring local and international artists and performers. Journalist Gavin Young's 1997 memoir *A Wavering Grace* is a moving account of his 30-year relationship with a family from Hue and with the city itself, during and beyond the American War. It makes a good literary companion for a stay in the city.

Tourism has brought an excess of touts, but, minor hassles aside, Hue remains a tranquil conservative city. There's no real bar scene and local tourism authorities have lamented the local bedtime of 10pm.

History

In 1802 Emperor Gia Long founded the Nguyen dynasty, moved the capital from Hanoi to Hue in an effort to unite northern and southern Vietnam, and commenced the building of the Citadel. The city prospered, but its rulers struggled to counter the growing influence of France.

In 1885, French forces responded to a Vietnamese attack by storming the Citadel, burning the imperial library and removing every single object of value – from gold ornaments to toothpicks. The emperors continued to reside in Hue, but were very much sidelined from events of national importance.

It was only in 1968 that attention shifted to Hue again, during the Tet Offensive. While the Americans concentrated on holding Khe Sanh, North Vietnamese and Viet Cong (VC) forces seized Hue, an audacious assault that commanded headlines across the globe.

During the 3½ weeks that the North controlled the Citadel, more than 2500 people were summarily shot, clubbed to death or buried alive. The North called them – ARVN soldiers, wealthy merchants, government workers, monks, priests and intellectuals – 'lackeys who owed blood debts'. The USA and South Vietnamese responded by levelling whole neighbourhoods, battering the Citadel and even using napalm on the imperial palace. Approximately 10,000 people died in Hue, including thousands of VC troops, 400 South Vietnamese soldiers and 150 US Marines – but most of those killed were civilians.

◎ Sights

Most of Hue's principal sights (and a sizeable chunk of its population) reside within the moats of its Citadel, including the Imperial Enclosure. Other museums and pagodas are dotted around the city. All the principal royal tombs are some distance south of Hue.

Inside the Citadel

Built between 1804 and 1833, the Citadel (Kinh Thanh) is still the heart of Hue. Heavily fortified, it consists of 2m-thick, 10km-long walls, a moat (30m across and 4m deep), and 10 gateways.

The Citadel has distinct sections. The Imperial Enclosure and Forbidden Purple City formed the epicentre of Vietnamese royal life. On the southwestern side were temple compounds. There were residences in the northwest, gardens in the northeast and in the north the Mang Ca Fortress (still a military base).

★ **Imperial Enclosure**   HISTORICAL SITE
(admission 105,000d; ⊙ 7am-5.30pm) The Imperial Enclosure is a citadel-within-a-citadel, housing the emperor's residence, temples and palaces and the main buildings of state within 6m-high, 2.5km-long walls. Today much of it is in ruins. What's left is only a fraction of the original – the enclosure was badly bombed during the French and American wars, and only 20 of its 148 buildings

survived. Restoration and reconstruction of damaged buildings is ongoing.

This is a fascinating site, worth exploring for half a day. However, as there's only very limited information available (some in English and French) and signage is very poor, it's difficult to know exactly where you are at times.

Expect a lot of broken masonry, rubble, cracked tiling and weeds as you work your way around. Nevertheless it's enjoyable as a leisurely stroll and some of the less-visited areas are highly atmospheric. There are little cafes and souvenir stands dotted around.

We've organised the sights inside the Imperial Enclosure as you'll encounter them inside the compound, beginning at the Ngo Mon Gate entrance and moving anticlockwise around the enclosure.

➡ **Ngo Mon Gate**
The principal entrance to the Imperial Enclosure is Ngo Mon Gate, which faces the Flag Tower. The central passageway with its yellow doors was reserved for the use of the emperor, as was the bridge across the lotus pond. Others had to use the gates to either side and the paths around the pond.

On top of the gate is Ngu Phung (Belvedere of the Five Phoenixes); on its upper level is a huge drum and bell. The emperor appeared here on important occasions, most notably for the promulgation of the lunar calendar. On 30 August 1945, the Nguyen dynasty ended here when Emperor Bao Dai abdicated to a delegation sent by Ho Chi Minh.

➡ **Thai Hoa Palace**
This palace (Palace of Supreme Harmony; 1803) is a spacious hall with an ornate timber roof supported by 80 carved and lacquered columns. It was used for the emperor's official receptions and important ceremonies. On state occasions the emperor sat on his elevated throne, facing visitors entering via the Ngo Mon Gate.

No photos are permitted, but be sure to see the impressive audio-visual display, which gives an excellent overview of the entire Citadel, its architecture and the historical context.

➡ **Halls of the Mandarins**
Located immediately behind Thai Hoa Palace on either side of a courtyard, these halls were used by mandarins as offices and to prepare for court ceremonies.

The hall to the left has been set up for cheesy tourist photos where you can pose in

Hue's Imperial Enclosure

EXPLORING THE SITE

An incongruous combination of meticulously restored palaces and pagodas, ruins and rubble, the Imperial Enclosure is approached from the south through the outer walls of the Citadel. It's best to tackle the site as a walking tour, winding your way around the structures in an anticlockwise direction.

You'll pass directly through the monumental **Ngo Mon Gateway** ❶ where the ticket office is located. This dramatic approach quickens the pulse and adds to the sense of occasion as you enter this citadel-within-a-citadel. Directly ahead is the **Thai Hoa Palace** ❷ where the emperor would greet offical visitors from his elevated throne. Continuing north you'll step across a small courtyard to the twin **Halls of the Mandarins** ❸, where mandarins once had their offices and prepared for ceremonial occasions.

To the northeast is the Royal Theatre, where traditional dance performances are held several times daily. Next you'll be able to get a glimpse of the Emperor's Reading Room built by Thieu Tri and used as a place of retreat. Just east of here are the lovely Co Ha Gardens. Wander their pathways, dotted with hundreds of bonsai trees and potted plants, which have been recently restored.

Guarding the far north of the complex is the Tu Vo Phuong Pavilion, from where you can follow a moat to the Truong San residence and then loop back south via the **Dien Tho Residence** ❹ and finally view the beautifully restored temple compound of To Mieu, perhaps the most rewarding part of the entire enclosure to visit, including its fabulous **Nine Dynastic Urns** ❺.

TOP TIPS

Allow half a day to explore the Citadel. Drink vendors are dotted around the site, but the best places to take a break are the delightful Co Ha Gardens, the Tu Vo Phuong Pavilion and the Dien Tho Residence (the latter two also serve food).

Dien Tho Residence
This pretty corner of the complex, with its low structures and pond, was the residence of many Queen Mothers. The earliest structures here date from 1804.

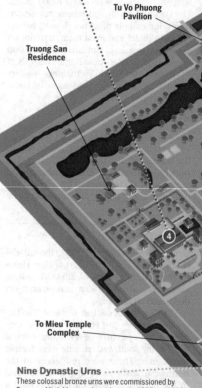

Tu Vo Phuong Pavilion

Truong San Residence

To Mieu Temple Complex

Nine Dynastic Urns
These colossal bronze urns were commissioned by Emperor Minh Mang and cast between 1835 and 1836. They're embellished with decorative elements including landscapes, rivers, flowers and animals.

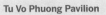

Tu Vo Phuong Pavilion

The two-storey Tu Vo Phuong Pavilion, elevated above a moat, was once a defense bastion for the northern part of the Imperial Enclosure. It combines both European and Vietnamese architectural styles (note the elaborate roof dragons).

Halls of the Mandarins

Unesco-sponsored conservation work is ongoing in the eastern hall here to preserve the elaborate ceiling and wall murals.

Emperor's Reading Room

Co Ha Gardens

Royal Theatre

③

②

①

⑤

Ngo Mon Gateway

A huge, grandiose structure that guards the main approach to the Imperial Enclosure, this gateway has a fortified lower level and a more architecturally elaborate upper part. It dates from 1833.

Thai Hoa Palace

Be sure to check out this palace's incredible ironwood columns, painted in 12 coats of brilliant scarlet and gold lacquer. The structure was saved from collapse by restoration work in the 1990s.

imperial costume on a throne. The opposite hall showcases some fascinating old photographs (including boy-king Vua Duya Tan's coronation), gilded Buddha statues and assorted imperial curios.

Behind the courtyard are the ruins of the **Can Chanh Palace**, where two wonderful long galleries, painted in gleaming scarlet lacquer have been reconstructed.

➡ Emperor's Reading Room

(Thai Binh Lau) The exquisite (though crumbling) little two-storey Emperor's Reading Room was the only part of the Forbidden Purple City to escape damage during the French reoccupation of Hue in 1947. It's currently being renovated and is not open to visitors, but it's worth checking out the Gaudi-esque roof mosaics.

➡ Royal Theatre

(Duyen Thi Duong; ☑ 351 4989; www.nhanhac.com. vn; tickets 70,000d; ☺ performances 9am, 10am, 2.30pm & 3.30pm) The Royal Theatre, begun in 1826 and later home to the National Conservatory of Music, has been rebuilt on its former foundations. Cultural performances here last 30 minutes.

Southeast of here almost nothing remains of the Thai To Mieu temple complex (p174; it's now a plant nursery) and former **University of Arts**.

➡ Co Ha Gardens

Occupying the northeast corner of the Imperial Enclosure, these delightful gardens were developed by the first four emperors of the Ngyguen dynasty but fell into disrepair. They've been beautifully re-created in the last few years, and are dotted with little gazebo-style pavilions (one a cafe) and ponds. This is one of the most peaceful spots in the entire Citadel.

➡ Forbidden Purple City

(Tu Cam Thanh) In the very centre of the Imperial Enclosure, there's almost nothing left of the once-magnificent Forbidden Purple City. This was a citadel-within-a-citadel-within-a-citadel and reserved solely for the personal use of the emperor – the only servants allowed into this compound were eunuchs who would pose no threat to the royal concubines.

The Forbidden Purple City was almost entirely destroyed in the wars, and its crumbling remains are now overgrown with weeds.

➡ Truong San Residence

In 1844 Emperor Thieu Tri described this as one of the most beautiful spots in Hue, but it was utterly devastated by war. Check out the imposing entrance gate complete with prancing dragons and phoenixes, and the oval moat. The exterior has been impressively restored, while the interior remains empty except for its elaborate columns and tiles.

➡ Dien Tho Residence

The stunning, partially ruined Dien Tho Residence (1804) once comprised the apartments and audience hall of the Queen Mothers of the Nguyen dynasty. The audience hall houses an exhibition of photos illustrating its former use, and there is a display of embroidered royal garments.

Just outside is an enchanting **pleasure pavilion**, a carved wooden building set above a lily pond. This has now been transformed into a delightful little cafe.

➡ Thai To Mieu Temple Complex

Taking up the southwest corner of the Imperial Enclosure, this highly impressive walled complex has been beautifully restored.

The imposing three-tiered **Hien Lam Pavilion** sits on the south side of the complex, it dates from 1824. On the other side of a courtyard is the solemn **To Mieu Temple**, housing shrines to each of the emperors, topped by their photos.

Between these two temples are **Nine Dynastic Urns** (dinh), cast between 1835 and 1836, each dedicated to one Nguyen sovereign.

About 2m in height and weighing 1900kg to 2600kg each, the urns symbolise the power and stability of the Nguyen throne. The central urn, also the largest and most ornate, is dedicated to dynasty founder Gia Long. Also in the courtyard are two dragons, trapped in what look like red phone boxes.

On the north side of the complex, a gate leads into a small walled enclosure that houses the **Hung To Mieu Temple**, a reconstruction of the 1804 original, built to honour Gia Long's parents.

Nine Holy Cannons   CANNON

Located just inside the Citadel ramparts, near the gates to either side of the Flag Tower, are the Nine Holy Cannons (1804), symbolic protectors of the palace and kingdom. Commissioned by Emperor Gia Long, they were never intended to be fired. Each brass cannon is 5m long and weighs about

A FIERY PROTEST

Behind the main sanctuary of the Thien Mu Pagoda is the Austin motorcar that transported the monk Thich Quang Duc to the site of his 1963 self-immolation. He publicly burned himself to death in Saigon to protest against the policies of South Vietnamese President Ngo Dinh Diem. A famous photograph of this act was printed on the front pages of newspapers around the world, and his death inspired a number of other self-immolations.

The response of the president's notorious sister-in-law, Tran Le Xuan (Madame Nhu), was to crassly proclaim the self-immolations a 'barbecue party', saying 'Let them burn and we shall clap our hands'. Her statements greatly aggravated the already substantial public disgust with Diem's regime. In November both President Diem and his brother Ngo Dinh Nhu (Madame Nhu's husband) were assassinated by Diem's military. Madame Nhu was overseas at the time.

Another self-immolation sparked fresh protest in 1993. A man arrived at the pagoda and, after leaving offerings, set himself alight chanting the word 'Buddha'. Although his motivation remains a mystery, this set off a chain of events whereby the pagoda's leading monks were arrested and linked with the independent United Buddhists of Vietnam, the banned alternative to the state-sanctioned Vietnam Buddhists. This led to an official complaint to the UN by the International Federation of Human Rights accusing the Vietnamese government of violating its own constitution, which protects freedom of religion.

10 tonnes. The **four cannons** near **Ngan Gate** represent the four seasons, while the **five cannons** next to **Quang Duc Gate** represent the five elements: metal, wood, water, fire and earth.

Outside the Citadel

Dieu De National Pagoda BUDDHIST TEMPLE
(Quoc Tu Dieu De; 102 Đ Bach Dang) FREE Overlooking Dong Ba Canal, this pagoda was built under Emperor Thieu Tri's rule (1841–47) and is famous for its four low towers, one to either side of the gate and two flanking the sanctuary.

Dieu De was a stronghold of Buddhist and student opposition to the South Vietnamese government and the American War and many arrests were made here when police stormed the building in 1966.

The pavilions on either side of the main sanctuary entrance contain the 18 La Ha, whose rank is just below that of Bodhisattva, and the eight Kim Cang, protectors of Buddha. In the back row of the main dais is Thich Ca Buddha, flanked by two assistants.

Royal Fine Arts Museum MUSEUM
(150 Đ Nguyen Hue; ⊙ 6.30am-5.30pm summer, 7am-5pm winter) FREE This recently renovated museum is located in the baroque-influenced An Dinh Palace, commissioned by Emperor Khai Dinh in 1918 and full of elaborate murals, floral motifs and *trompe lœil* details. Emperor Bao Dai lived here with his family after abdicating in 1945. Inside you'll find some outstanding ceramics, paintings, furniture, silverware, porcelain and royal clothing, though information is a little lacking.

Bao Quoc Pagoda BUDDHIST TEMPLE
(Ham Long Hill) FREE Founded in 1670, this hilltop pagoda is on the southern bank of the Perfume River and has a striking triple-gated entrance reached via a wide staircase. On the right is a centre for training monks, which has been functioning since 1940.

To get here, head south from Đ Le Loi on Đ Dien Bien Phu and take the first right after crossing the railway tracks.

General Museum Complex MUSEUMS
(Đ 23 Thang 8; ⊙ 7-11am & 1.30-4.30pm Tue-Sun) FREE Formerly a school for princes and the sons of high-ranking mandarins, this slightly rundown complex has a pagoda devoted to archaeology, a small Natural History Museum and a building with exhibitions about anticolonial resistance.

National School NOTABLE BUILDING
(Truong Quoc Hoc; 10 Đ Le Loi; ⊙ 11.30am-1pm & from 5pm) One of the most famous secondary schools in Vietnam, the National School was founded in 1896. Its former pupils include General Vo Nguyen Giap and Ho Chi Minh

(who attended for a year in 1908). You can visit the school during lunch break and after classes finish.

Ho Chi Minh Museum   MUSEUM
(7 Ð Le Loi; ⊙ 7-11am & 1.30-4pm Tue-Sun) FREE
The father of the modern Vietnamese nation spent 10 years in Hue, and you'll find some intriguing photographs as well as a collection of certificates and medals here. There's very little information in English though.

Tang Tau Lake   LAKE
(Ð Dien Tien Hoang) An island on Tang Tau Lake, which is northeast of Tinh Tam Lake, was once the site of a royal library. It is now occupied by the small **Ngoc Huong Pagoda**.

☞ Tours

Stop & Go Café   TOUR
(☑ 054-382 7051; www.stopandgo-hue.com; 3 Ð Hung Vuong) Personalised motorbike and car tours. A full-day DMZ car tour guided by a Vietnamese vet costs US$27 per person for four people, representing a good deal. Guided trips to Hoi An stopping at beaches are also recommended.

Cafe on Thu Wheels   TOUR
(☑ 054-383 2241; minhthuhue@yahoo.com; 10/2 Ð Nguyen Tri Phuong) Inexpensive cycle, motorcycle (from US$10 per person) and car tours (DMZ from US$40 per person) around Hue and beyond, run by Minh, who is a great character.

🛏 Sleeping

Hue offers great value for money: rates are well below those in the capital or HCMC. The main tourist enclave is centred on the lanes between Ð Le Loi and Ð Vo Thi Sau.

★ Huenino   GUEST HOUSE $
(☑ 054-625 2171; www.hueninohotel.com; 14 Ð Nguyen Cong Tru; r US$14-24; ⊖ ✳ @ �🕉) Family-owned, this warm, welcoming guesthouse has an artistic flavour with stylish furniture, artwork and smallish rooms with minibar, cable TV and good-quality beds. A generous breakfast is included.

★ Jade Hotel   GUEST HOUSE $
(☑ 054-393 8849; http://jadehotelhue.com; 17 Nguyen Thai Hoc; r US$15-25; ⊖ ✳ @ �🕉) You'll find simply excellent service standards at this fine place; staff are very sweet and welcoming indeed. Rooms enjoy soft comfy mattresses and there's a nice lobby-lounge for hanging out.

Star City Hotel   HOTEL $
(☑ 054-383 1358; http://starcityhotelhue.com; 2/36 Vo Thi Sau; r US$12; ✳ @ �🕉) Offering really cheap rates, this five-storey hotel has a lift, and clean, spacious rooms all with TV and air-con. It's set off the street so traffic noise isn't an issue.

Hue Backpackers   HOSTEL $
(☑ 054-382 6567; www.vietnambackpackerhostels. com; 10 Ð Pham Ngu Lao; dm US$8-12, r US$18; ✳ @ �🕉) Backpackers' mecca thanks to its central location, eager-to-please staff, good info and sociable bar-restaurant. Dorms (some with queen-sized beds) are well designed and have air-con and lockers.

Hung Vuong Inn   HOTEL $
(☑ 054-382 1068; truongdung2000@yahoo.com; 20 Ð Hung Vuong; r US$11-17; ✳ @ �🕉) Nine spacious rooms with cable TV and attractive bathrooms, and the location is convenient, although it's on a busy road. There's a restaurant that's very popular with travellers here too.

Hue Thuong   HOTEL $
(☑ 054-388 3793; www.huethuonghotel.com; 11 Ð Chu Van An; r US$15-22; ✳ @ �🕉) A great little minihotel, where the rooms, though smallish, have a real sparkle and are very well presented – all come with purple and white linen and attractive furniture.

Guesthouse Nhat Thanh   GUEST HOUSE $
(☑ 054-393 5589; nhatthanhguesthouse@gmail. com; 17 Ð Chu Van An; r US$14-16; ✳ �🕉) If you ignore the off-putting overdose of tour advertising in the lobby, this is not a bad choice. Rooms are spacious with good beds, minibar and TV.

Binh Minh Sunrise 1   HOTEL $
(☑ 054-382 5526; www.binhminhhue.com; 36 Ð Nguyen Tri Phuong; r US$15-35; ✳ @ �🕉) A six-storey hotel that offers a central location, pleasant staff and fair-sized rooms; a little dated in appearance but some have a balcony. Budget options exclude air-con and breakfast.

Moonlight Hotel Hue   HOTEL $$
(☑ 054-397 9797; www.moonlighthue.com; 20 Pham Ngu Lao; r US$44-65, ste US$70-140; ⊖ ✳ @ �🕉✳) A 'new generation' Hue hotel where the rooms boast a very high spec for the modest bucks charged, all with polished wooden floors, marble-clad bathrooms (with tubs) and lavish furnishings. Pay a bit more for a balcony with a Perfume

PERFUME RIVER BOAT TRIPS

Many sights around Hue, including Thien Mu Pagoda and several of the Royal Tombs, can be reached by boat via the Perfume River.

Most hotels and travellers' cafes offer shared tours hitting the main sights (from as little as US$4 to around US$18 per person). These tours usually run from 8am to 4pm. There are many different itineraries; some of the better ones start with a morning river cruise, stopping at pagodas and temples, then after lunch you transfer to a minibus to hit the main tombs and then return to Hue by road. On the cheaper options you'll often have to hire a motorbike to get from the moorings to the tombs, or walk (in the intense heat of the day).

If you ask at the moorings on the south side of the river you can theorectically negotiate your own route. Rates for chartering a boat start at US$7 or so for an hour's cruise up the river. However, be warned that boats are slow. Reckon on a full day to visit some of the more impressive, distant tombs. Be clear on your requirements, preferably in writing.

River view. Breakfast is great but the pool area is small and covered.

Orchid Hotel
HOTEL $$

(☎054-383 1177; www.orchidhotel.com.vn; 30A Đ Chu Van An; r US$30-75; ❋❋@🛜🛁) This is a very well-run modern hotel rightly renowned for its warm service; staff really make an effort here. The accommodation is excellent, all options have laminate flooring, bright scatter cushions and a DVD player, while some pricier rooms even have a jacuzzi with city views. Your complimentary breakfast is good (eggs are cooked to order) and children are well looked after.

Gold Hotel
HOTEL $$

(☎054-381 4815; www.goldhotelhue.com; 28 Đ Ba Trieu; r US$35-42, ste US$60-80; ❋@🛜🏊) Impressive new hotel a short walk or *cyclo* (pedicab) ride from the river. It has a main restaurant area and immaculately presented modern rooms with superb bathrooms (all have tubs). It's efficiently run and excellent value, though the pool area is a bit of an afterthought.

Holiday Diamond
HOTEL $$

(☎054-381 9845; http://hueholidaydiamondhotel. com; 6, 14 Nguyen Cong Tru; r US$24-30, f US$36; ❋@🛜) Book ahead as it extremely popular, and it's easy to understand why as the friendly, attentive and helpful staff really make the place. Rooms are fine value and breakfast is included.

Muong Thanh Hue Hotel
HOTEL $$

(☎054-393 6688; http://muongthanh.vn; 38 Đ Le Loi; r from US$64; ❋❋@🛜🏊) Formerly the Mercure, this hotel soars above the Perfume River in a prime location and has rooms with polished wood furnishings, hip bathrooms, balconies and all mod cons. The kidney-shaped pool is smallish though, and service could be a little sharper.

Thai Binh Hotel 2
HOTEL $$

(☎054-382 7561; www.thaibinhhotel-hue.com; 2 Đ Luong The Vinh; r US$20-35; ❋@🛜) One street away from the tourist thoroughfare, this powder-blue hotel is near to the action, yet quiet. Views from the higher floors are excellent, staff are pretty efficient and there's a restaurant (meals from US$3).

★Pilgrimage Village
RESORT HOTEL $$$

(☎054-388 5461; www.pilgrimagevillage.com; 130 Đ Minh Mang; r/bungalows from US$110/153; ❋❋@🛜🏊) Designed around a verdant valley that includes a 40m pool, lotus ponds and a state-of-the-art spa and yoga space, this feels more like a Zen ecoretreat than a hotel. Rooms are all supremely comfortable, but for the ultimate experience book one of the bungalows with private plunge pool. There's a fine restaurant, lovely breakfast room and bar. Located about 3km from the centre of Hue. Check their website for promotions that cut rates to below US$90, a real steal.

La Residence
HOTEL $$$

(☎054-383 7475; www.la-residence-hue.com; 5 Đ Le Loi; r from US$155; ❋❋@🛜🏊) Once the French governor's residence, this wonderful hotel resonates with art-deco class, with its original features and period detailing. A frangipani-lined path leads down to the 30m pool, from where you can gaze over the Perfume River. Rooms are sumptuously appointed, the restaurants are excellent, and service is polished and professional.

Hotel Saigon Morin
HOTEL $$$

(☑ 054-382 3526; www.morinhotel.com.vn; 30 Đ Le Loi; r/ste from US$118/236; ⊜✳@⊜☎☒) Built in 1901, this was the first hotel in central Vietnam and once the hub of French colonial life in Hue. The building is very classy, with accommodation set around two inner courtyards and a small pool. Rooms are grand and beautifully presented, with plush carpets and period detail that evoke a real 'wow' factor.

✕ Eating

We have the famed fussy eater Emperor Tu Duc to thank for the culinary variety of Hue, and an imperial cuisine banquet is usually a memorable experience.

Royal rice cakes, the most common of which are *banh khoai,* are worth seeking out. You'll find these along with other variations *(banh beo, banh loc, banh it* and *banh nam)* in street stalls and restaurants at Dong Ba Market and around town.

Vegetarian food has a long tradition in Hue. Stalls in Dong Ba Market serve lots of options on the first and 15th days of the lunar month.

Lien Hoa
VEGETARIAN $

(3 Đ Le Quy Don; meals 30,000-55,000d; ⊙ 11am-9.30pm; ✎) No nonsense, very local Viet vegie restaurant renowned for providing filling food at rock-bottom rates. Fresh *banh beo* (steamed rice pancakes), noodle dishes, crispy fried jackfruit and aubergine with ginger all deliver. The menu has very rough English translations to help you order (staff speak little or no English).

Take
JAPANESE $

(34 Đ Tran Cao Van; meals 60,000-140,000d; ⊙ 11.30am-9.30pm) An authentic Japanese restaurant with tasteful furnishings (including lanterns, calligraphy wall hangings and even fake cherry blossom) and a winsome menu that takes in sushi, tempura and yakitori dishes.

Restaurant Bloom
CAFE $

(14 Đ Nguyen Cong Tru; meals from 35,000-80,000d; ⊙ 7am-9.30pm; ☎) Ideal for pasta, a sandwich, baguette or homemade cake (baked on the premises), this likeable little cafe employs disadvantaged youths and graduates of the ACWP (Aid to Children Without Parents) training program. Food is MSG-free.

Mandarin Café
VIETNAMESE $

(☑ 054-382 1281; 24 Đ Tran Cao Van; mains from 26,000d; ☎✎) Owner-photographer Mr Cu, whose inspirational pictures adorn the walls, has been hosting backpackers here for years, and his relaxed restaurant has lots of vegetarian and breakfast choices. Also operates as a tour agency.

Japanese Restaurant
JAPANESE $

(☑ 054-382 5146; 12 Đ Chu Van An; dishes US$1.50-9; ⊙ 6-9pm) This simple little place offers all your usual Japanese favourites (including teriyaki and udon and soba noodles). The restaurant might be lacking a little in ambience, but it does employ former street children and supports a home for them.

Hieu
NOODLES $

(Đ Ba Trieu; bowl 40,000d; ⊙ 6am-10.30am) This breakfast street kitchen serves up *bun bo hue* (Hue-style rice noodle soup) which is accompanied by a caveman-sized hunk of pork or beef, shredded banana flower and chilli.

Stop & Go Café
INTERNATIONAL $

(3 Đ Hung Vuong; meals 20,000-60,000d; ⊙ 7am-10pm; ☎) Atmospheric little place with decent Vietnamese and backpacker fare: *banh beo,* beef noodle soup, tacos, pizza and pasta, and filling Western breakfasts. It's worth dropping by for the excellent travel information.

Caphé Bao Bao
VIETNAMESE $

(38 Đ Le Thanh Ton; meals 20,000-35,000d; ⊙ 10.30am-8pm) A simple courtyard place serving delicious and very cheap barbecued pork kebabs, served with noodles and vegetables.

Little Italy
ITALIAN $$

(☑ 054-382 6928; www.littleitalyhue.com; 2A Đ Vo Thi Sau; mains 45,000-115,000d; ⊙ 7am-10pm) Large trattoria with a decent line-up of Italian favourites (pasta, calzone, pizzas and seafood), a wide choice of beers and a palatable Sicilian house wine.

La Carambole
FRENCH $$

(☑ 054-381 0491; www.lacarambole.com; 19 Đ Pham Ngu Lao; meals 85,000-280,000d; ⊙ 7am-11pm; ☎) Run by an affable Frenchman and his Vietnamese partner, this restaurant offers reliable European and local cuisine, including imperial-style Hue specialities.

Omar Khayyam's Indian Restaurant INDIAN $$

(☑054-382 1616; www.omarkhayyamhue.com; 34 Đ Nguyen Tri Phuong; mains 48,000-170,000d; ☺noon-10pm; ☎) If you're after a spice fix, this Indian has curries, samosas and vegie dishes. They use imported Australian lamb for their full-flavour rogan josh, or order a thali (from 145,000d) for a real treat.

Tropical Garden Restaurant VIETNAMESE $$

(☑054-384 7143; 27 Đ Chu Van An; dishes 25,000-160,000d; ☎) This place has tables set under thatched shelters in a pretty, fecund tropical garden. The cuisine is good, featuring many central Vietnamese specialities, though prepare yourself for the live band (7pm to 9pm nightly) and its popularity with tour groups.

★Les Jardins de La Carambole FRENCH, VIETNAMESE $$$

(☑054-354 8815; www.lesjardinsdelacarambole.com; 32 Dang Tran Con; meals US$12-30; ☺7am-11pm; ☎) A memorable dining experience, this incredibly classy and refined French restaurant occupies a gorgeous colonial-style building in the Citadel quarter. The menu majors in Gallic classics, there's a lengthy wine list and informed service. It's just the place for romantic meal – arrive by *cyclo* and it's easy to roll back the years to Indochine times.

🍷 Drinking

★Brown Eyes BAR

(Đ Chu Van An; ☺5pm-late; ☎) The most popular late-night bar in town, with a good blend of locals and traveller-revellers and a party vibe. DJs drive the dance floor with r 'n' b, hip hop and house music anthems, and staff rally the troops with free shots. It's open 'till the last one passes out'.

DMZ Bar BAR

(www.dmz.com.vn; 60 Đ Le Loi; ☺7am-1am; ☎) Ever-popular riverside bar with a free pool table, cold Huda beer, cocktails (try a watermelon mojito) and a good craic most nights. Also serves Western and local food till midnight, smoothies and juices. Happy hour is 3pm till 8pm.

Café on Thu Wheels BAR

(10/2 Đ Nguyen Tri Phuong; ☺6.30am-11pm; ☎) Hole-in-the-wall bar par excellence. Graffiti-splattered walls, a sociable vibe and good info from the feisty owner, Thu, and her family.

They also offer good tours, serve cheap grub and have books and mags to browse.

Hue Backpackers BAR

(10 Đ Pham Ngu Lao; ☺6am-11pm; ☎) There's always a buzz about this backpackers' drinking den, which packs 'em in with its infused vodkas, cocktail list and happy hour (8pm to 9pm). A good bet for the footy, or big sporting events.

Wounded Heart Tea Room TEAROOM

(23 Đ Vo Thi Sau; tea 40,000d; ☺8am-6pm) Attached to a fair-trade shop, this little place specialises in Vietnamese tea (including jasmine, ginger and olong) but they'll also rustle up a coffee if you so desire. Delicious complimentary snacks are served with your drink.

Bar Why Not? BAR

(21 Đ Vo Thi Sau) This place has a more relaxed vibe than some other bars in town, a sensational list of cocktails and a popular street terrace.

🛍 Shopping

Hue produces the finest conical hats in Vietnam. The city's speciality is 'poem hats', which, when held up to the light, reveal shadowy scenes of daily life. It's also known for its rice paper and silk paintings.

Spiral Foundation Healing the Wounded Heart Center HANDICRAFTS

(☑054-383 3694; www.hwhshop.com; 23 Đ Vo Thi Sau; ☺8am-6pm) Generating cash from trash, this store stocks lovely handicrafts – such as quirky bags from plastic, and picture frames from recycled beer cans – made by artists with disabilities. Profits aid heart surgery for children in need.

Blue de Hue ANTIQUES

(43 Vo Thi Sau; ☺7.30am-6.30pm) Well-regarded antiques store selling stonework, ceramics, laquerware and wooden carvings.

Dong Ba Market MARKET

(Đ Tran Hung Dao; ☺6.30am-8pm) Just north of Trang Tien Bridge, this is Hue's largest market, selling anything and everything.

Trang Tien Plaza SHOPPING CENTRE

(6 Đ Tran Hung Dao; ☺8am-10pm) A small shopping centre between Trang Tien Bridge and Dong Ba Market with a Coopmart supermarket.

ⓘ Information

INTERNET ACCESS

Virtually every hotel and guesthouse in town has wi-fi, as do many cafes and restaurants. There are internet cafes on the tourist strips of Đ Hung Vuong and Đ Le Loi.

MEDICAL SERVICES

Hue Central Hospital (Benh Vien Trung Uong Hue; ☎ 054-382 2325; 16 Đ Le Loi; ⊙ 6am-10pm)

MONEY

Vietcombank (30 Đ Le Loi; ⊙ Mon-Sat 7.30am-3.30pm) Located at the Hotel Saigon Morin.

Vietin Bank ATM (12 Đ Hung Vuong)

POST

Post Office (8 Đ Hoang Hoa Tram; ⊙ 7am-5.30pm Mon-Sat)

TRAVEL AGENCIES

Most of the travel agencies and tour operators pool clients on their budget tours, so no matter who you book a (standard) DMZ tour with you're likely to end up on a large bus with other tourists.

Of course, more specialist, bespoke trips are available but cost far more.

DMZ Travel (☎ 054-224 1904; www.dmz.com.vn) All kinds of tours are offered: budget-priced boat trips along the Perfume River (150,000d), DMZ tours (350,000d) and Phong Nha including Paradise cave (580,000d). Bus tickets to Laos are also sold.

Mandarin Café (☎ 054-382 1281; www.mrcumandarin.com; 24 Đ Tran Cao Van) Mr Cu (who speaks English and French) offers great information, transport and tours to most places in the Hue region, and beyond.

Sinh Tourist (☎ 054-382 3309; www.thesinhtourist.vn; 7 Đ Nguyen Tri Phuong) Books open-tour buses and buses to Laos.

ⓘ Getting There & Away

AIR

Vietnam Airlines (☎ 054-382 4709; 23 Đ Nguyen Van Cu; ⊙ closed Sun) has two daily flights to both Hanoi and HCMC. VietJet (p481) also connects Hue daily with the capital and HCMC.

BUS

The main bus station, 4km southeast of the centre, has connections to Danang and south to HCMC. **An Hoa bus station** (Hwy 1), northwest of the Citadel, serves northern destinations, including Dong Ha (44,000d, two hours, every 30 minutes). One daily bus at 11.15am (look for 'Phuc Vu' in the windscreen) heads for Phong Nha Farmstay and Son Trach (150,000d, four hours).

There's also a useful minibus connection (500,000d, five hours) between Hue Backpackers and Phong Nha Farmstay/Son Trach village, leaving the hostel in Hue at 1pm and stopping at the Vinh Moc Tunnels and the Ben Hai River museum. Entrance tickets and a tour guide at the tunnels are included.

Hue is a regular stop on open-tour bus routes. Most drop off and pick up passengers at central hotels. Expect some hassle from persistent hotel touts when you arrive.

Mandarin, Sinh and Stop & Go Café can arrange bookings for buses to Savannakhet, Laos.

TRAIN

The **Hue train station** (☎ 054-382 2175; 2 Đ Phan Chu Trinh) is at the southwestern end of Đ Le Loi.

ⓘ Getting Around

Hue's recently upgraded Phu Bai Airport is 14km south of the city. Metered taxis meet all flights and cost about 190,000d to the centre, or use the minibus service for 50,000d. Vietnam Airlines also runs an airport shuttle, which can collect you from your hotel (tickets 60,000d).

TRANSPORT FROM HUE

DESTINATION	AIR	BUS	CAR/ MOTORBIKE	TRAIN
Danang	n/a	US$3.50, 3hr, frequent	2½-4hr	US$3.50-6, 2½-4hr, 7 daily
Dong Hoi	n/a	US$4-7, 4hr, 12 daily	3½hr	US$5-11, 3-5½hr, 7 daily
Hanoi	from US$30, 1hr, 3 daily	US$20-32, 13-16hr, 9 daily	16hr	US$24-42, 12-15½hr, 6 daily
HCMC	from US$34, 1¼hr, 4 daily	US$26-42, 19-24hr, 9 daily	22hr	US$32-55, 19½-23hr, 5 daily
Ninh Binh	n/a	US$14-22, 10½-12hr, 8 daily	11hr	US$19-35, 10-13hr, 5 daily
Vinh	n/a	US$9-17, 7½-9hr, 7 daily	7hr	US$23-38, 6½-10hr, 5 daily

Pedal power is a fun way to tour Hue and the nearby Royal Tombs. Many hotels rent out bicycles for US$1 to US$2 per day. Motorbikes are available from US$5 to US$10. A car with driver costs around US$40 to US$50 per day.

With so many tourists, *cyclo* drivers usually quote extortionate prices in Hue, and you'll do well to get a short ride for 25,000d. It's usually cheaper and quicker to get a metered taxi. A typical street scene is a foreigner walking down the street with two *cyclos* and a motorbike in hot pursuit – the drivers yelling, 'hello cyclo' and 'hello motorbike' and the foreigner yelling, 'no, thank you, no!'

For a taxi, try the reliable **Mai Linh** (054-389 8989).

Around Hue

South of Hue are the extravagant mausoleums of the rulers of the Nguyen dynasty (1802–1945), spread out along the banks of the Perfume River between 2km and 16km south of the city. There also some fine pagodas and other sights.

Almost all royal tombs were planned by the emperors during their lifetimes, and some were even used as residences while they were still alive.

Most of the mausoleums consist of five essential elements. The first is a stele pavilion dedicated to the accomplishments, exploits and virtues of the emperor. Next is a temple for the worship of the emperor and empress. The third is an enclosed sepulchre, and fourth an honour courtyard with stone elephants, horses, and civil and military mandarins. Finally, there's a lotus pond surrounded by frangipani and pine trees.

Most people visit them on an organised tour from Hue, either by boat or a combination of boat and bus, but it's perfectly possible to rent a *xe om* or your own bike and do a DIY tour.

⊙ Sights

Tomb of Tu Duc　　　　TOMB
(admission 80,000d) This tomb, constructed between 1864 and 1867, is the most popular, and certainly one of the most impressive of the royal mausoleums. Emperor Tu Duc designed it himself, for use both before and after his death. The enormous expense of the tomb and the forced labour used in its construction spawned a coup plot that was discovered and suppressed.

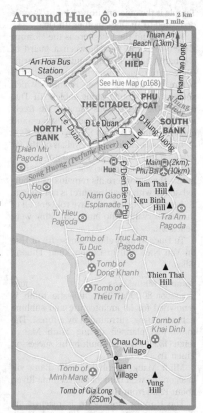

Around Hue

Tu Duc lived a life of imperial luxury and carnal excess (he had 104 wives and countless concubines), though no offspring.

From the entrance a path leads to the shore of **Luu Khiem Lake**. The tiny island to the right, **Tinh Khiem**, is where Tu Duc used to hunt small game. Across the water to the left is **Xung Khiem Pavilion**, where he would sit with his concubines, composing or reciting poetry.

Hoa Khiem Temple is where Tu Duc and his wife, Empress Hoang Le Thien Anh, were worshipped – today it just houses a jumble of dusty, unlabelled royal artefacts. The larger throne was for the empress; Tu Duc was only 153cm tall.

Minh Khiem Chamber, to the right behind Hoa Khiem Temple, was originally meant to be a theatre. Cheesy dress-up photo ops and cultural performances are available here today. Directly behind Hoa Khiem

Temple is the quieter Luong Khiem Temple dedicated to Tu Duc's mother, Tu Du.

Just around the lakeshore is the Honour Courtyard. You pass between a guard of elephants, horses and diminutive mandarins (they were even shorter than the emperor) before reaching the Stele Pavilion, which shelters a 20-tonne stone tablet. Tu Duc drafted the inscriptions himself. He freely admitted that he had made mistakes and chose to name his tomb Khiem ('modest').

The tomb, enclosed by a wall, is on the far side of a tiny lagoon. It's a drab grey monument and the emperor was never interred here – the site where his remains were buried (along with great treasure) is not known. To keep it a secret from grave robbers, all of the 200 servants who buried the king were beheaded.

Tu Duc's tomb is about 5km south of Hue on Van Nien Hill in Duong Xuan Thuong village.

Tomb of Minh Mang   TOMB
(admission 80,000d) This majestic tomb is renowned for its architecture and sublime natural setting, surrounded by a forest. The tomb was planned during Minh Mang's reign (1820–1840) but built by his successor, Thieu Tri.

Minh Mang's tomb is in An Bang village, on the west bank of the Perfume River, about 12km from Hue.

The Honour Courtyard is reached via three gates on the eastern side of the wall. Three granite staircases lead from the courtyard to the square Stele Pavilion (Dinh Vuong).

Sung An Temple, which is dedicated to Minh Mang and his empress, is reached via three terraces and the rebuilt Hien Duc Gate. On the other side of the temple, three stone bridges span Trung Minh Ho (Lake of Impeccable Clarity). The central bridge was for the emperor's use only. Minh Lau Pavilion (Pavilion of Light) stands on the top of three superimposed terraces that represent the 'three powers': the heavens, the earth and water. To the left is the Fresh Air Pavilion, to the right, the Angling Pavilion.

From a stone bridge across crescent-shaped Tan Nguyet Lake (Lake of the New Moon), a monumental staircase with dragon banisters leads to Minh Mang's sepulchre. The gate to the tomb is opened only once a year on the anniversary of the emperor's death.

Thien Mu Pagoda   BUDDHIST TEMPLE
FREE Built on a hill overlooking the Perfume River, 4km southwest of the Citadel, this pagoda is an icon of Vietnam and as potent a symbol of Hue as the Citadel. The 21m-high octagonal tower, Thap Phuoc Duyen, was constructed under the reign of Emperor Thieu Tri in 1844. Each of its seven storeys is dedicated to a *manushi-buddha* (a Buddha that appeared in human form).

Since the 1960s it has been a flashpoint of political demonstrations.

Thien Mu Pagoda was originally founded in 1601 by Nguyen Hoang, governor of Thuan Hoa province. Over the centuries its buildings have been destroyed and rebuilt several times.

To the right of the tower is a pavilion containing a stele dating from 1715. It's set on the back of a massive marble turtle, a symbol of longevity. To the left of the tower is another six-sided pavilion, this one sheltering an enormous bell (1710), which weighs 2052kg and is said to be audible 10km away.

The temple itself is a humble building in the inner courtyard, past the triple-gated entrance where three statues of Buddhist guardians stand at the alert. In the main sanctuary behind the bronze laughing Buddha are three statues: A Di Da, the Buddha of the Past; Thich Ca, the historical Buddha (Sakyamuni); and Di Lac Buddha, the Buddha of the Future.

The best time to visit is early in the morning, before the tour groups show up. For a scenic bicycle ride, head southwest (parallel to the Perfume River) on riverside Đ Tran Hung Dao, which turns into Đ Le Duan after Phu Xuan Bridge. Cross the railway tracks and keep going on Đ Kim Long. Thien Mu Pagoda can also be reached by boat.

Tomb of Khai Dinh   TOMB
(admission 80,000d) This hillside monument is a synthesis of Vietnamese and European elements. Most of the tomb's grandiose exterior is covered in blackened concrete, creating an unexpectedly Gothic air, while the interiors resemble an explosion of colourful mosaic.

Khai Dinh was the penultimate emperor of Vietnam, from 1916 to 1925, and widely seen as a puppet of the French. The construction of his flamboyant tomb took 11 years.

Steps lead to the Honour Courtyard where mandarin honour guards have a mixture of Vietnamese and European fea-

TOMBS & DUNES

From the centre of Hue it's only 15km north to the coast, the road shadowing the Perfume River before you hit the sands of **Thuan An Beach** where there's a large resort hotel. If you continue southeast from here there's a beautiful, quiet coastal road to follow with very light traffic (so it's ideal for bikers). The route actually traverses a narrow coastal island, with views of the Tam Giang-Cau Hai lagoon on the inland side and simply stunning sandy beaches and dunes on the other. This wonderful coastal strip is virtually undeveloped, but between September and March the water's often too rough for swimming.

From Thuan An the road winds past villages alternating with shrimp lagoons and vegetable gardens. Thousands and thousands of garishly colourful and opulent graves and family temples line the beach, most the final resting places of Viet Kieu (overseas Vietnamese) who wanted to be buried in their homeland. Little tracks cut through the tombs and sand dunes to the beach. Just pick a spot and the chances are you'll have a beach to yourself.

At glorious **Phu Thuan beach** (about 7km southeast of Thuan An) a spectacular new place, the **Beach Bar Hue** (☑ 090-899 3584; www.beachbarhue.com; Phu Thuan beach; dm/bungalow 250,000/600,000d, meals 100,000d) has excellent backpacker-geared dorms and bungalows and sits pretty on a sublime stretch of sand (with no hawkers...for now). There's a funky little bamboo-and-thatch bar for drinks and snacks. Next door a hip hotel, Villa Louise, was nearing completion when we passed by, which will have wonderful villas (around US$150 per night), 16 rooms (from US$60), two pools and a spa.

Around 8km past Beach Bar Hue, the remains of **Phu Dien**, a small Cham temple, lie in a hollow in the sand just off the beach. Protected by a glass greenhouse-style structure it's an unexpected find. You'll find a few seafood shacks here, too.

Continuing southeast a narrow but paved road weaves past fishing villages, shrimp farms and giant sand dunes and the settlement of Vinh Hung until you reach the mouth of another river estuary at Thuon Phu An, where there's a row of seafood restaurants. This spot is 40km from Thuan An. Cross the Tu Hien bridge here and you can continue around the eastern lip of the huge Cau Hai lagoon and link up with Hwy 1.

tures. Up three more flights of stairs is the stupendous main building, **Thien Dinh**. The walls and ceiling are decorated with murals of the Four Seasons, Eight Precious Objects and Eight Fairies. Under a graceless, gold-speckled concrete canopy is a gilt bronze statue of Khai Dinh. His remains are interred 18m below the statue.

The tomb of Khai Dinh is 10km from Hue in Chau Chu village.

Ho Quyen
ARENA

FREE Wildly overgrown but still evocative, Ho Quyen was built in 1830 for the royal pastime of watching elephants and tigers face off in combat. The tigers (and leopards) were usually relieved of their claws and teeth so that the elephants – a symbol of the emperor's power – triumphed every time. You can climb up grassy ramparts and look down on the old arena and imagine the scene – the last fight was held here in 1904.

The south-facing section was reserved for the royal family, while diametrically opposite are the tiger cages. Ho Quyen is about 3km outside Hue in Truong Da village. Follow Đ Bui Thi Xuan west from the train station, then look out for the blue sign near the market that indicates the turn-off on the left. Follow this lane for about 200m to a fork in the road and go right.

Tu Hieu Pagoda
BUDDHIST TEMPLE

FREE Nestled in a pine forest, this popular pagoda was built in 1843 and later co-opted by eunuchs from the Citadel (who have their own cemetery on the left-hand side). Tu Hieu is associated with Zen master Thich Nhat Hanh, who studied at the monastery here in the 1940s, but lived in exile for more than 40 years, and was only permitted to return to Vietnam in 2005.

Today 70 monks reside at Tu Hieu; they welcome visitors to the twin temples (one dedicated to Cong Duc, the other to Buddha). You can listen to their chanting (daily at 4.30am, 10am, noon, 4pm and 7pm). Tu Hieu Pagoda is about 5km from the centre of Hue, on the way to the tomb of Tu Duc.

Thanh Toan Bridge BRIDGE

A classic covered Japanese footbridge in picturesque countryside and without a souvenir shop in sight, this makes a lovely diversion from Hue. The bridge is in sleepy Thuy Thanh village, 7km east of Hue. Finding it is a bit tricky. Head north for a few hundred metres on Ð Ba Trieu until you see a sign to the Citadel Hotel. Turn right and follow the bumpy dirt road for another 6km past villages, rice paddies and several pagodas.

Nam Giao Esplanade HISTORICAL BUILDING

This three-tiered esplanade was once the most important religious site in Vietnam, the place where the Nguyen emperors made animal sacrifices and elaborate offerings to the deity Thuong De. Ceremonies (the last was held in 1946) involved a lavish procession and a three-day fast by the emperor at the nearby Fasting Palace.

The Fasting Palace, located at the furthest end of the park, has an informative display of photographs and English captions.

Since 2006 the ceremony has been re-enacted as part of the Festival of Hue. Nam Giao Esplanade is at the southern end of Ð Dien Bien Phu, about 2km from the railway tracks.

Tomb of Thieu Tri TOMB

(admission 80,000d) The only royal tomb not enclosed by a wall, the recently restored monument of Thieu Tri (built 1848) has a similar floor plan to his father Minh Mang's tomb, but is substantially smaller. The tomb is about 7km from Hue.

Tomb of Gia Long TOMB

(admission free) FREE Emperor Gia Long founded the Nguyen dynasty in 1802 and ruled until 1819. Both the emperor and his queen are buried here. The rarely visited tomb is presently in a state of ruin. It is around 14km south of Hue and 3km from the west bank of the Perfume River.

Bach Ma National Park

A French-era hill station, this **national park** (Vuon Quoc Gia Bach Ma; ☑054-387 1330; www.bachma.vnn.vn; adult/child/under 6yr 40,000/20,000d/free) reaches a peak of 1450m at Bach Ma mountain, only 18km from the coast. The cool climate attracted the French, who built over a hundred villas here. Not surprisingly the Viet Minh tried hard to spoil the holiday – the area saw some heavy fighting in the early 1950s and again during the American War.

The national park, extended in 2008, stretches from the coast to the Annamite mountain range at the Lao border. More than 1400 species of plants, including many rare ferns and orchids, have been discovered in Bach Ma, representing a fifth of the flora of Vietnam. There are 132 kinds of mammals, three of which were only discovered in the 1990s: the antelope-like saola, Truong Son muntjac and the giant muntjac. Nine species of primates are also present, including small numbers of the rare red-shanked Douc langur. It's hoped wild elephants will return from the Lao side of the border.

As most of the park's resident mammals are nocturnal, sightings demand a great deal of effort and patience. Bird-watching is fantastic, but you need to be up at dawn for the best chance of glimpsing some of the 358 species logged, including the fabulous crested argus pheasant.

The road to the summit has recently been upgraded. At the visitor centre by the park entrance you'll find a small exhibition on the park's flora and fauna, and hiking trail booklets.

Of the several hiking trails, the **Rhododendron Trail** (from Km 10 on the road) leads to the upper reaches of a spectacular waterfall; it's 689 steps down to its base for a dip. The **Five Lakes Trail** passes pools for swimming before you reach a (much smaller) waterfall. The short **Summit Hike** takes you to a viewpoint with magnificent views (on a clear day) over the forest, Cau Hai lagoon and coast.

You can book village and bird-watching tours and English- or French-speaking guides (250,000d per day). Unexploded ordnance is still in the area, so stick to the trails. Cars and motorbikes are not permitted inside the national park.

Bach Ma is the wettest place in Vietnam, with the heaviest of the rain falling in October and November (and bringing out the leeches). It's not out of the question to visit then, but check road conditions first. The best time to visit Bach Ma is from February to September, particularly between March and June.

🛏 Sleeping & Eating

National Park GUEST HOUSES $
(☑054-387 1330; bachmaeco@gmail.com; campsites per person 10,000d; r with fan/air-con

180,000/270,000d) The park authority has a small camping ground and two functional guesthouses near the entrance, with basic twin-bed rooms that have en-suite bathrooms. There's also a guesthouse near the summit. Note that karaoke can be a part of the nocturnal park life.

Give at least four hours' notice for meal requirements, as fresh food is brought up to the park on demand.

❶ Getting There & Around

Bach Ma is 28km west of Lang Co and 40km southeast of Hue. The turn-off is signposted in the town of Cau Hai on Hwy 1. You can also enter from the town of Phu Loc.

Bach Ma is not very well set up for independent travellers. It's well worth considering a tour here from Danang or Hue, or organising your own trip with a car and driver.

From the visitor centre it's a steep, serpentine 16km ascent; the road almost reaches the summit. Private transport is available from the visitor centre (but costs a hefty 1,000,000d return). Walking down from the summit takes about three to four hours; you'll need water and sunscreen.

Buses from Danang (46,000d, two hours) and Hue (24,000d, one hour) stop at Cau Hai, where *xe om* drivers can ferry you to the entrance. Cau Hai has a train station, but it's only served infrequently.

Lang Co Beach

🌐 054

Lang Co is an attractive island-like stretch of palm-shaded white sand, with a crystal-clear, turquoise lagoon on one side and 10km of beachfront on the other. As a beach resort it's more geared to Vietnamese day trippers than Western travellers, but if the weather's nice the ocean is certainly inviting (if you stay away from the central section, which could be cleaner).

High season is April to July. From late August till November rains are frequent, and from December to March it can get chilly.

▣ Sleeping

Most of the accommodation is north of the town along the highway.

Chi Na Guesthouse GUEST HOUSE $
(🌐054-387 4597; s/d 170,000/200,000d; ▣▣▣)
One of several clean, basic guesthouses north of the centre, but here the family speaks a little English. Rooms are ageing but serviceable.

Vedana Lagoon RESORT $$$
(🌐054-381 9397; www.vedanalagoon.com; Phu Loc; bungalows/villas from US$125/175; ▣▣▣▣▣▣)
Combining contemporary chic with natural materials, this remote but commodious spa hotel has gorgeous villas and bungalows that boast thatched roofs, modish furnishings and outdoor bathrooms. Some have private pools, others jut over the lagoon to maximise the views. The complex includes a wonderful wellness centre (for t'ai chi and yoga classes). Vedana is 15km north of Lang Co.

Minh Hang SEAFOOD $$
(meals 50,000-100,000d; ⊘7am-9pm) The best seafood restaurant on the north side of Lang Co, and has a lagoon (instead of highway and rumbling trucks) view. Try the lemon pepper squid or spicy clams with lemongrass.

❶ Getting There & Away

Lang Co is on the north side of the Hai Van Tunnel and Danang.

Lang Co's **train station** (🌐054-387 4423) is 3km from the beach, in the direction of the lagoon. Getting a *xe om* to the beach shouldn't be difficult. The train journey from here to Danang (41,000d, 1½ to two hours, five daily) is one of the most spectacular in Vietnam. Services also connect to Hue (53,000d, 1½ to two hours, four daily).

Hai Van Pass & Tunnel

The **Hai Van (Sea Cloud) Pass** crosses over a spur of the Truong Son mountain range that juts into the sea. About 30km north of Danang, the road climbs to an elevation of 496m, passing south of the Ai Van Son peak (1172m). It's an incredibly mountainous stretch of highway – you may have seen the spectacular views on BBC TV's *Top Gear* Vietnam special. The railway track, with its many tunnels, goes around the peninsula, following the beautiful and deserted shoreline.

In the 15th century this pass formed the boundary between Vietnam and the kingdom of Champa. Until the American War it was heavily forested. At the summit is a bullet-scarred French fort, later used as a bunker by the South Vietnamese and US armies.

If you cross in winter, the pass serves as something of a visible dividing line between the climates of the north and south, protecting Danang from the fierce 'Chinese winds' that sweep in from the northeast. From about

November to March the exposed Lang Co side of the pass can be wet and chilly, while just to the south it's often warm and dry.

The top of the pass is the only place you can pull over for a while. The view is well worth it, but you'll have to fight off a rather large crowd of very insistent vendors and dodgy money-changers.

In 2005, the 6280m-long Hai Van Tunnel opened, bypassing the pass and shaving an hour off the journey between Danang and Hue. Motorbikers and cyclists are not permitted to ride through the tunnel (but you can pay to have your bike transported through in a truck). Sure it saves time, but on a nice day it really is a shame to miss the views from the pass.

Despite the odd hair-raising encounter, the pass road is safer than it used to be. If you can take your eyes off the highway, keep them peeled for the small altars on the roadside – sobering reminders of those who have died in accidents on this winding route.

Ba Na Hill Station

✔ 0511 / ELEV 1485M

A hill resort inherited from the French, lush Ba Na (per person 10,000d, per motorbike/car 5000/10,000d) has refreshingly cool weather and gorgeous countryside views. Established in 1919, the resort area once held 200-odd villas, but only a few ruins remain.

Until WWII the French were carried up the last 20km of rough mountain road by sedan chair, but now a 5km (the world's longest) cable car system has really opened up access. The ride involves a rise of almost 1300m, a truly spectacular trip over dense jungle. However, be warned that a tourism boom has resulted in a lot of ugly construction (and a serious garbage problem) once you get to the hill top, including a castle-like theme park.

Take an extra layer or two whatever time of year you visit – when it's 36°C on the coast, it could be 15°C on the mountain. Cloud and mist also cling to the hill top, so if you can, try to visit on a clear day.

Mountain tracks lead to waterfalls and viewing points. Near the top is the Linh Ung Pagoda (2004) and a colossal 24m-high white seated Buddha that's visible for miles around.

There's an ATM at Ga Suoi Mo, the (lowest) cable-car station. Up on the hill you can change money at the hotels. As all hotels at the hill station are poor value for money, it's best to see Ba Na on a day trip.

❶ Getting There & Away

Ba Na is 42km west of Danang. By far the best way to get to the hill station is via the new cable-car link (return 400,000d), which is in two sections. There's a cafe at the central station, with poor, overpriced food. You might get stuck for a while waiting for the second leg of the ride. Note that the service can be suspended during heavy wind. Otherwise you can access Ba Na via a beautiful, very steep winding road that is tough unless you have a powerful motorbike. Locals offer rides for around 100,000d.

Danang

✔ 0511 / POP 977,000

Nowhere in Vietnam is changing as fast as Danang. For decades it had a reputation as a provincial backwater, but big changes are ongoing. Stroll along the Han riverfront and you'll find gleaming new modernist hotels, apartments and restaurants are emerging. Spectacular new bridges now span the Han river and in the north of the city the landmark new D-City is rising from the flatlands. Venture south and the entire China Beach strip has been set aside for five-star hotel developments. Oh, and for good measure, a revamped international airport opened in 2012.

That said, the city itself still has few conventional sightseeing spots, except for a very decent museum. So for most travellers, a day or two off the tourist trail enjoying the city's restaurants and nightlife is probably enough.

Danang also makes a great base for day trips. The city is part of a long thin peninsula, at the northern tip of which is Nui Son Tra (called Monkey Mountain by US soldiers). China Beach and the five Marble Mountains lie southwest of the city.

History

Known during French colonial rule as Tourane, Danang succeeded Hoi An as the most important port in central Vietnam during the 19th century, a position it retains to this day.

As American involvement in Vietnam escalated, Danang became the recipient of the first American combat troops in South Vietnam – 3500 Marines in March 1965. Memorably they stormed Nam O Beach in full battle gear, only to be greeted by a bevy of *ao dai*–wearing Vietnamese girls bearing cheerful flower garlands. A decade later, with the Americans and South Vietnamese in full retreat, the scene could not have been more different as desperate civilians fled the city. On 29 March 1975 two truckloads of communist guerrillas, more than half of them women, declared Danang liberated without firing a shot.

Today Danang has one of the most vibrant economies in Vietnam. Indeed it's regularly dubbed 'Silicon City' due to its booming web sector.

◉ Sights

★ Museum of Cham Sculpture   MUSEUM
(Bao Tang; Map p188; 1 Ð Trung Nu Vuong; admission 30,000d; ☉ 7am-5pm) This fine museum has the world's largest collection of Cham artefacts, housed in buildings that marry French-colonial architecture with Cham elements.

Founded in 1915 by the École Française d'Extrême Orient, it has more than 300 pieces on display including altars, lingas, garudas, apsaras, Ganeshas and images of Shiva, Brahma and Vishnu – all dating from the 5th to 15th centuries.

The treasures come from Dong Duong (Indrapura), Khuong My, My Son, Tra Kieu and other sites.

Note that the museum's organisation and English captions could be better, so it's worth hiring a well-informed guide (or pick up one of the guidebooks at the museum shop).

There are also exhibits focusing on Cham culture today, with a handful of contemporary artefacts and photos of the Kate Festival (the Cham New Year).

Cao Dai Temple   BUDDHIST TEMPLE
(Map p188; 63 Ð Hai Phong) **FREE** This is the largest Cao Dai temple in Central Vietnam, serving about 50,000 followers. A sign reading *van giao nhat ly* (all religions have the same reason) hangs from the ceiling in front of the main altar. Behind the gilded letters is a picture of the founders of five of the world's great religions: Mohammed, Laotse (wearing Eastern Orthodox–style robes), Jesus, a Southeast Asian–looking Buddha and Confucius (looking as Chinese as could be).

Behind the main altar sits an enormous globe with the Cao Dai 'divine eye' symbol on it. As with all Cao Dai temples, prayers are held four times a day, at 5.30am, 11.30am, 5.30pm and 11.30pm.

Ho Chi Minh Museum   MUSEUM
(Map p193; 3 Ð Nguyen Van Troi; ☉ 7-11am & 1.30-4.30pm) **FREE** Despite its huge grounds, this museum is typically unenlightening for a site venerating Ho Chi Minh. At the front is a display of the usual US, Soviet and Chinese weaponry. Hidden behind the Party buildings are a replica of Ho Chi Minh's house in Hanoi and a museum about him.

Danang Cathedral   CHURCH
(Map p188; Ð Tran Phu) **FREE** Known to locals as Con Ga Church (Rooster Church) because of the weathercock on top of the steeple, the candy-pink Danang Cathedral was built for the city's French residents in 1923. Today it serves a Catholic community of over 4000 – it's standing room only if you arrive late.

Phap Lam Pagoda   BUDDHIST TEMPLE
(Map p188; 574 Ð Ong Ich Khiem; ☉ 5-11.30am & 1-9pm) **FREE** Recently rebuilt, this pagoda has three giant Buddha statues in the courtyard, and an equally imposing large gold one in the temple.

⟲ Tours

Trong's Real Easy Riders   MOTORBIKE TOURS
(Map p188; ☑ 0903 597 971; www.easyridervn. com; 12/20 Nguyen Thi Minh Khai) A motorbike collective that operates out of Danang. A four-day trip to the central highlands costs US$280; day trips are also possible.

⊨ Sleeping

Danang has a fast-expanding selection of modern hotels along the riverside, though good budget hotels are hard to come by. For information on accommodation just across the river, see My Khe Beach (p195).

Zion Hotel   HOTEL $
(Map p188; ☑ 0511-382 8333; http://sion.com.vn; 121/7 Hoang Van Thu; s/d US$15/20-25; ✸ @ ✆) There's a scarlet theme running through this new excellent-value hotel from the lobby to the inviting, modern rooms. Boasts a convenient location and staff are eager to please.

Bao Ngoc Hotel   HOTEL $
(Map p188; ☑ 0511-381 7711; baongochotel@dng. vnn.vn; 48 Ð Phan Chu Trinh; r US$18-22; ✸ @ ✆) Spacious, carpeted and comfortable rooms full of solid, dark-wood furniture and some with sofas. The ageing five-storey building also retains a glint of colonial character, with its chocolate-brown French-style shutters.

Danang

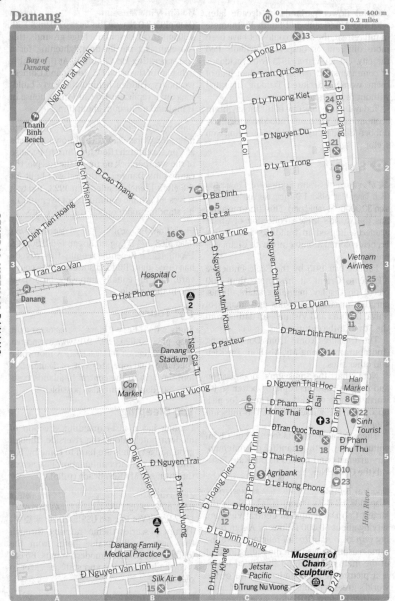

Hai Van Hotel HOTEL **$**

(Map p188; ☎0511-382 3750; kshaivan.dng@vnn.vn; 2 Đ Nguyen Thi Minh Khai; s/d US$14/20; ❄☎) It's never going to win a design award, but this old-fashioned place has functional spacious rooms that represent a reasonable deal.

New Moon Hotel HOTEL **$$**

(Map p188; ☎0511-382 8488; http://newmoon hotel.vn; 126 Đ Bach Dang; r 440,000-1,100,000d; ❄@☎) Modern minihotel with a selection of inviting rooms in different price categories, all with flat-screen TV, minibar, wi-fi

Danang

and en-suite marble bathrooms, while the river-view options enjoy incredible vistas.

Rainbow Hotel HOTEL $$
(Map p188; ☎0511-382 2216; www.rainbowhotel.com.vn; 220 Đ Bach Dang; r 630,000-1,100,000d; ❄@☎) This modern place enjoys a prime riverfront location, and yet rates are backstreet modest. Rooms have contemporary decor and flooring, artwork, modern furniture and all mod cons, but do vary quite a bit; book a river-view for inspirational vistas.

Sun River Hotel HOTEL $$
(Map p188; ☎0511-384 9188; www.sunriverhoteldn.com.vn; 132-134 Đ Bach Dang; r 860,000-1,800,000d; ❄@☎) A tempting option, this riverfront hotel offers immaculate rooms with really fancy bathrooms (some with space-age showers). Note the standard-class options do not have windows and only the VIPs have a river view.

Stargazer Hotel HOTEL $$
(Map p188; ☎0511-381 5599; www.stargazer.net; 77 Đ Tran Phu; r 350,000-600,000d; ❄@☎) A welcoming hotel with neat, if smallish, rooms with attractive wood furniture, large TVs and comfy beds with duvets. Number 301 has a balcony and river view.

Novotel Danang Premier Han River HOTEL $$$
(Map p188; ☎0511-392 9999; 36 Bach Dang; r/ste from US$95/164; ❄❄@☎❄) Towering riverside landmark, which opened in 2013, with hip, commodious rooms and unmatched views over the Han river towards the beach and ocean. Staff are welcoming and well trained, and facilities include a pool, spa and fitness centre. Those that enjoy the high life should check out the 35th-floor sky bar.

Brilliant Hotel HOTEL $$$
(Map p188; ☎0511-384 3863; www.brillianthotel.vn; 162 Bach Dang; r from US$78; ❄☎❄) New riverside hotel with a contemporary design theme throughout, from the swish lobby to the impressive rooms (all with river views and hip bathrooms). Service is good, and the complimentary breakfast quite a feast. However, the pool is tiny.

✗ Eating

Danang's restaurant scene is on the up and becoming more cosmopolitan by the day. Street food is great here, with copious *bun cha* (barbecued pork), *com* (rice) and *mi quang* (noodle soup) stalls.

To really explore the local food scene try **Danang Food Tour** (http://danangfoodtour.com; per person US$45-90) run by an expat foodie.

Quan Com Hue Ngon VIETNAMESE, BARBECUE $
(Map p188; 65 Tran Quoc Toan; meals 50,000-80,000d; ⊙3-9pm) Fab new barbecue place, all charcoal smoke and sizzling meats, where you grill your own. There's a street terrace, and the welcoming English-speaking owner will help with the menu.

Com Tay Cam Cung Dinh VIETNAMESE $
(Map p188; K254/2 Đ Hoang Dieu; dishes 15,000-40,000d; ⊙11am-8pm) This simple place is good for local dishes including *hoanh thanh* – a wonton-like combination of minced pork and shrimp. It's down a little alley.

Com Nieu
VIETNAMESE **$**

(Map p188; 25 Đ Yen Bai; dishes 18,000-130,000d; ⏰7.30am-9.30pm) A contemporary restaurant that offers a wide choice of tasty Vietnamese fare, including succulent seafood and the clay-pot rice signature dish.

Mr Duc's
VIETNAMESE, INTERNATIONAL **$**

(Map p188; 11 Tran Quoc Toan; meals 40,000-80,000d; ⏰11am-9.30pm) A clean, casual place rightly popular for its good-value dishes: beef steak and chips, rice with chicken and roti, noodles, and shrimp hot pots.

★Waterfront
INTERNATIONAL, BAR **$$**

(Map p188; ☏0511-384 3373; www.waterfrontdanang.com; 150-152 Đ Bach Dang; meals 95,000-360,000d; ⏰10am-11pm; 🛜) Riverfront lounge-cum-restaurant that gets everything right on every level. It works as a stylish bar for a chilled glass of NZ Sauvignon Blanc or an imported beer and also as a destination restaurant for a memorable meal (book the terrace deck for a stunning river vista). The menu is features imported meats, Asian seafood and also terrific 'gourmet' sandwiches.

Le Bambino
FRENCH, INTERNATIONAL **$$**

(Map p188; ☏0511-389 6386; www.lebambino.com; 122/11 Đ Quang Trung; meals 120,000-300,000d; ⏰11.30am-1.30pm & 4.30-10pm Mon-Sat, 4.30-10pm Sun; 🛜) Atmospheric place run by a couple (French husband, Vietnamese wife) who have crafted a great menu that takes in French classics, pub food, barbecued meat (try the ribs) and a few Vietnamese favourites. Eat inside or around the pool, and don't neglect the wine list or the cheese selections, both of which are superb.

Phi Lu Chinese Restaurant
CHINESE, VIETNAMESE **$$**

(Map p193; 1-3 Đ 2/9; meals 40,000-300,000d; ⏰11am-9.30pm; 🛜) This large formal place decked out in Chinese style, including red lanterns at night, always seems to be busy, a good sign. It's excellent for seafood, beef dishes and noodles, but beware the menu with its comical English translations.

Bread of Life
INTERNATIONAL **$$**

(Map p188; www.breadoflifedanang.com; 4 Đ Dong Da; meals 65,000-150,000d; ⏰8.30am-9.30pm; 🛜) Excellent American-style diner-cum-bakery with a good menu of burgers, Mexican food, sandwiches, pizza and pasta. A very good bet for brekkie; the bacon burrito really hits the spot. Run by deaf staff, proceeds go towards training activities for the deaf in Danang.

Madame Lan
VIETNAMESE **$$**

(Map p188; www.madamelan.com; 4 Bach Dang; meals 100,000-220,000d; ⏰10am-10pm; 🛜) Huge restaurant in a new French colonial-style development where you can eat in an open courtyard or in one of the river-facing dining rooms. The menu has lots of good choices including squid with chilli and salt, and green papaya salad with shrimp and garlic.

Red Sky
INTERNATIONAL **$$**

(Map p188; www.redskydanang.com; meals 70,000-260,000d; ⏰11am-2pm & 5-11pm Mon-Fri, 11am-11pm Sat & Sun; 🛜) This casual bar-restaurant scores highly for Western grub, including good-value steaks, generous salads (US$7), chicken wings and Italian food. Happy hour (5pm to 8pm) is very popular. Staff are attentive and welcoming and it's air-conditioned.

Vietnamese Home
VIETNAMESE, INTERNATIONAL **$$**

(Map p188; 34 Đ Bach Dang; meals 60,000-270,000d; ⏰7am-10pm; 🛜) Rustic-style restaurant with a huge bougainvillea-fringed courtyard and adjoining dining rooms. The menu is extremely comprehensive, including Western breakfasts, seafood, meat dishes, frog, snail, noodles and soup. There are cheap rice-based dishes for those on a budget.

🍷 Drinking

For a lounge-bar-style drink with a view, also check out Waterfront.

★Luna Pub
BAR

(Map p188; www.lunadautunno.vn; 9A Tran Phu; ⏰11.30am-late; 🛜) Half-bar, half-Italian restaurant, this hot new hang-out is a cool warehouse-sized space with an open frontage, a DJ booth in the cabin of a truck, cool music, an amazing drinks selection and some shisha smoking action. Also popular with the expat crowd for its authentic Italian food (pizza, pasta, salads and more).

Memory Lounge
LOUNGE, BAR

(Map p188; www.loungememory.com; 7 Đ Bach Dang; drinks from US$5; ⏰10am-midnight Mon-Sat; 🛜) This landmark bar-restaurant juts over the river right by the Song Han bridge. It works better as a bar, as the restaurant prices are stratospheric and the cooking rarely hits the heights. During the day, it's fine for a coffee, or later on a beer with a view. Note that Vietnamese bands and crooners are often part of the evening entertainment.

Tulip Brewery   BAR
(Map p193; 174 Đ 2/9; ⊘11am-11pm; 📶) Huge Czech-style brewery pub (with vats proudly on display) that draws the locals in their hundreds. Lager-style and dark beer on tap, plus a menu of Western (try the German sausages) and Vietnamese dishes. The bar is located quite a way south of the centre.

Tam's Pub & Surf Shop   BAR
(Map p193; 38 An Thuong 5; ⊘7am-11pm; 📶) A stone's throw from China Beach, this is a friendly, popular bar-restaurant with pub grub (think burgers or fish 'n' chips). You can rent boards (US$5 per day, deposit required) and get advice here.

Bamboo 2 Bar   BAR
(Map p188; 230 Đ Bach Dang; ⊘10am-midnight; 📶) Sociable, but rather predictable expat bar with clientele of boozy regulars, beers for 25,000d and a busy pool table. A good place to catch sports (Aussie Rules, Premier League football).

❶ Information

Virtually all hotels and cafes have wi-fi and you will find plenty of internet cafes in the central zone.

The website www.indanang.com is an excellent source of information, with lots of restaurant reviews and listings.

Agribank (Map p188; 202 Đ Nguyen Chi Thanh; ⊘7.30am-3.30pm Mon-Sat) ATM and exchange service.

Danang Family Medical Practice (Map p188; 📞0511-358 2700; www.vietnammedicalpractice.com; 50-52 Đ Nguyen Van Linh; ⊘7am-6pm) Set up like a minihospital with in-patient facilities, this is an excellent practice run by an Australian doctor.

Hospital C (Benh Vien C; Map p188; 📞0511-382 1483; 122 Đ Hai Phong; ⊘24hr) The most advanced of the four hospitals in town.

Main Post Office (Map p188; 64 Đ Bach Dang; ⊘7am-5.30pm) Near the Song Han Bridge.

Sinh Tourist (Map p188; 📞0511-384 3258; www.thesinhtourist.vn; 154 Đ Bach Dang) Books open-tour buses and tours, and offers currency exchange.

❶ Getting There & Away

AIR
Danang's renovated international airport has **Silk Air** (Map p188; 📞0511-356 2708; www.silkair. com; HAGL Plaza Hotel, 1 Đ Nguyen Van Linh) flights to Singapore and Siem Riep, Lao Airlines flights to Pakse, Savannakhet and Vientiane, and there are a few connections to China including a Dragon Air flight to Hong Kong. For domestic destinations, **Jetstar Pacific** (Map p188; 📞0511-358 3538; www.jetstar.com; 307 Đ Phan Chu Trinh) and **VietJet** (📞1900 1886; www. vietjetair.com) have daily flights from Danang to HCMC and Hanoi, while **Vietnam Airlines** (Map p188; 📞0511-382 1130; www.vietnamairlines. com; 35 Đ Tran Phu) operates direct flights to Hanoi, HCMC, Dalat, Nha Trang, Haiphong, Buon Ma Thuot, Pleiku and Vinh.

BUS
Danang's **intercity bus station** (Map p193; 📞0511-382 1265; Đ Dien Bien Phu) is 3km west of the city centre. A metered taxi to the riverside will cost around 60,000d.

Buses leave for all major centres, including Quy Nhon (122,000d, six hours, six daily).

For Laos, there are three weekly buses to Savannakhet at 8pm (340,000d, 14 hours) and a daily service to Pakse at 6.30am (330,000d, 13 hours). Buses to the Lao Bao border alone are 128,000d (six hours); you may have to change buses at Dong Ha.

TRANSPORT FROM DANANG

DESTINATION	AIR	BUS	CAR/MOTORBIKE	TRAIN
Dong Hoi	n/a	US$8–13, 6½hr, 7 daily	6–7hr	US$10–17, 5½–8½hr, 6 daily
Hanoi	from US$36, 1hr 10min, 9 daily	US$24–34, 16–19hr, 7 daily	19hr	US$28–45, 14½–18hr, 6 daily
HCMC	from US$33, 1hr 15min, 18 daily	US$24–39, 19–25hr, 9 daily	18hr	US$31–50, 17–22hr, 5 daily
Hue	n/a	US$3–4, 3hr, every 20min	2½–4hr	US$3.50–6, 2½–4hr, 6 daily
Nha Trang	from US$38, 30min, 2 daily	US$15–22, 10–13hr, 8 daily	13hr	US$18–29, 9–12hr, 5 daily

Yellow public buses to Hoi An (18,000d, one hour, every 30 minutes) travel along Đ Bach Dang. However, foreigners are routinely charged 50,000d on this route, and sometimes extra for luggage.

Sinh Tourist open-tour buses will pick up from the company office twice daily to both Hue (80,000d to 89,000d, 2½ hours) and Hoi An (70,000d, one hour).

CAR & MOTORCYCLE
A car to Hoi An costs around 330,000d via your hotel or a local travel agency, while xe om will do it for around 120,000d. Bargain hard if you want to stop at the Marble Mountains or China Beach en route.

TRAIN
Danang's **train station** (202 Đ Hai Phong) has services to all destinations on the north–south main line.

The train ride to Hue is one of the best in the country – it's worth taking as an excursion in itself.

❶ Getting Around

TO/FROM THE AIRPORT
Danang's airport is 2km west of the city centre.

CYCLO & XE OM
Danang has plenty of motorbike taxis and cyclo drivers; as usual, be prepared to bargain. Trips around town shouldn't cost more than 25,000d.

TAXI
If you need a metered taxi, use **Mai Linh** (☎ 0511-356 5656).

Around Danang
☑ 0511

Nui Son Tra (Monkey Mountain)
ELEV 850M
Jutting out into the sea like a giant pair of Mickey Mouse ears, the Son Tra peninsula is crowned by the mountain that the American soldiers called Monkey. Grandly overlooking Danang to the south and the Hai Van Pass to the north, it was a prized radar and communications base during the American War. Until recently it was a closed military area (and virtually untouched except for the port Cang Tien Sa), but new roads and beach resorts are opening up the peninsula.

The highlight of visiting Monkey Mountain is the view from the **summit**, which is stupendous on a clear day. All that remains of the American military presence are a couple of radar domes (still used by the Vietnamese military and a no-go for tourists) next to a helicopter pad, now a lookout point. The steep road to the summit is pretty deserted and road conditions can be iffy. If you're going on a motorbike, you'll need a powerful one to make it to the top. The turn-off to this road is about 3km before Tien Sa Port and marked by a blue sign that reads 'Son Tra Eco-Tourism'.

Most Vietnamese who come here head to one of the beach resorts along the peninsula's southwestern coast. The other big attraction on the peninsula is **Linh Ung** (Map p193), a colossal new Buddha statue positioned on a lotus-shaped platform that looks south to Danang city; there's a monastery here too. Eventually you should be able to complete a loop of the peninsula; when completed, the road will make an incredibly scenic drive.

On the other side of Nui Son Tra, next to the port, is sheltered **Tien Sa Beach**. A memorial near the port commemorates an unfortunate episode of colonial history. Spanish-led Filipino and French troops attacked Danang in August 1858, ostensibly to end Emperor Tu Duc's mistreatment of Catholics. The city quickly fell, but the invaders were hit by cholera, dysentery, scurvy, typhus and mysterious fevers. By the summer of 1859, the number of invaders who had died of illness was 20 times the number who had been killed in combat.

Many of the tombs of Spanish and French soldiers are below a **chapel** (Map p193) that's located behind Tien Sa Port.

🛌 Sleeping & Eating
There's some construction around the coastline, but Son Tra is pretty quiet on the whole and a delight to explore by motorbike. Luxury hotels are the name of the game here.

Son Tra Resort & Spa HOTEL $$$
(☎ 0511-392 4924; www.sontra.com.vn; Son Tra; villa US$220-250; ❄ 🛜 🏊 🚗) Looking directly over a sheltered white sand beach, these handsome villas are well maintained, spacious and attractive, all with kitchens, hardwood floors and sea views. They're ideal for families. Book online and deals as cheap as US$100 are possible.

InterContinental Danang Sun Peninsula Resort HOTEL $$$
(☎ 0511-393 8888; http://danang.intercontinental. com; Son Tra; r/ste from US$230/400; ❄ 🛜 🏊 🚗)

Around Danang

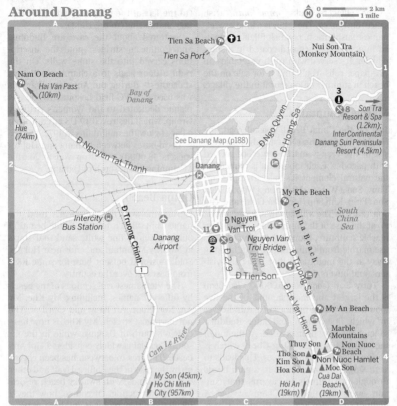

CENTRAL VIETNAM AROUND DANANG

Spilling down a hillside this huge resort hotel dominates this corner of Son Tra, with golf buggies whisking its pampered guests around the landscaped grounds. There's an impressive spa, fully loaded fitness centre and huge main pool.

Bay Ban　　　　　　　　　SEAFOOD **$$**
(Map p193; ☎0511-221 4237; Son Tra; meals 80,000-250,000d; ◷11am-9.30pm) Authentic seafood restaurant that's very popular with Vietnamese families on weekends and during holiday season, but usually quiet the rest of the time. Eat right over the water in one of the thatched shelters in the bay. There are all kinds of delicious fresh fish, spider crab, eel and shrimp dishes.

Nam O Beach

Nam O Beach, 15km northwest of the city, was where the first US combat troops landed in South Vietnam in 1965. Today Nam O

Beach has reverted to a more humble form. There are a few hotels located here, but the beach is not as attractive as those south of Danang.

The villagers make *nuoc mam* (fish sauce) and *goi ca*. The latter is a kind of Vietnamese sushi: fresh, raw fish fillets marinated in a special sauce and coated in a spicy powder. It's served with fresh vegetables on rice-paper rolls. You'll find it for sale on the beach in summer or look for it in the village.

Marble Mountains

Just off the China Beach coastal road, the **Marble Mountains** (Ngu Hanh Son) consist of five craggy marble outcrops topped with pagodas. Each mountain is named for the natural element it's said to represent: Thuy Son (Water), Moc Son (Wood), Hoa Son (Fire), Kim Son (Metal or Gold) and Tho Son (Earth). The villages that have sprung up at the base of the mountains specialise in marble sculpture, though they now astutely use marble from China rather than hacking away at the mountains that bring the visitors (and buyers) in.

Thuy Son (admission 15,000d; ☺7am-5pm) is the largest and most famous of the five mountains, with a number of natural caves in which first Hindu and later Buddhist sanctuaries have been created. At the top of the staircase is a gate, **Ong Chon**, which is pockmarked with bullet holes. This leads to **Linh Ong Pagoda**. Behind it, a path heads through two tunnels to caverns that contain several Buddhas and Cham carvings. A flight of steps also leads up to another cave, partially open to the sky, with two seated Buddhas in it.

Immediately to the left as you enter Ong Chon Gate is the main path to the rest of Thuy Son, beginning with **Xa Loi Pagoda**, a beautiful stone tower that overlooks the coast. Stairs off the main pathway lead to **Vong Hai Da**, a viewing point that would yield a brilliant panorama of China Beach if it weren't so untended. The stone-paved path continues to the right and into a minigorge. On the left is **Van Thong Cave**, opposite which is a cement Buddha.

Exit the gorge through a battle-scarred masonry gate. There's a rocky path to the right leading to **Linh Nham**, a tall chimney-shaped cave with a small altar inside. Nearby, another path leads to **Hoa Nghiem**, a shallow cave with a Buddha. Left of here is cathedral-like **Huyen Khong Cave**, lit by an opening to the sky. The entrance to this spectacular chamber is guarded by two administrative mandarins

(to the left of the doorway) and two military mandarins (to the right).

Scattered about the cave are Buddhist and Confucian shrines; note the inscriptions carved into the stone walls. On the right a door leads to a chamber with two stalactites – during the American War this was used as a VC field hospital. Inside is a plaque dedicated to the Women's Artillery Group, which destroyed 19 US aircraft from a base below the mountains in 1972.

Local buses between Danang and Hoi An (tickets 18,000d) can drop you at Marble Mountains, 10km south of Danang.

China Beach

During the war the Americans used the name China Beach to refer to the beautiful 30km sweep of fine white sand that starts at Monkey Mountain and ends near Hoi An. Soldiers would be sent here for some R&R from bases all over the country.

The Vietnamese call sections of the beach by different names, including My Khe, My An, Non Nuoc, An Bang and Cua Dai. The northernmost stretch, My Khe, is now basically a suburb of Danang, while in the far south Cua Dai is widely considered Hoi An's beach. The area in between has been carved up by the likes of the Raffles, Hyatt and other five-star brands, with swanky beach resorts under construction. Of course, how they'll fill all those ritzy rooms is another matter.

The best time for swimming at China Beach is from April to July, when the sea is at its calmest. At other times the water can get rough. Be warned that lifeguards only patrol some sections of the beach.

The surf can be very good from around mid-September to December.

◉ Sights & Activities

My Khe   BEACH
Just across the Song Han Bridge, My Khe is fast becoming Danang's easternmost suburb. In the early morning and evening the beach fills up with city folk doing t'ai chi. Tourists emerge during peak sun-tanning hours, while locals start showing up in the evening. Despite its popularity, the beach is still largely free from hawkers.

The water can have a dangerous undertow, especially in winter. However, it's protected by the bulk of Nui Son Tra and is safer than the rest of China Beach.

My An & Non Nuoc
BEACHES

Much of the central section of China Beach has been parceled off for luxury resort developments. The inland side of the coastal road has a scattering of budget hotels between exclusive golf courses designed by the likes of Greg Norman.

🛏 Sleeping & Eating

All of these places are just a short stroll from the sea. Locals head here for seafood and sea breezes (ocean winds, that is, not cocktails).

Eena Hotel
HOTEL $

(Map p193; ☑ 0511-222 5123; www.geocities.jp/een-ahotel; Khu An Cu 3, My Khe; s 150,000-400,000d, d & tw 350,000-800,000d; 🐾@🛜) This Japanese-owned minihotel is a great base with its immaculately clean, light, spacious, white rooms. There's a lift, fast wi-fi, friendly English-speaking staff and a good complimentary breakfast.

Bien Nho Hotel
HOTEL $

(Map p193; ☑ 0511-396 7401; biennhohoteldng@gmail.com; 4 Truong Sa, Hoa Hai, My An beach; r 300,000-400,000d; 🐾🛜) Great little minihotel, just across the road from the beach break on My An so a good option for surfers. Offers well-kept rooms and the jovial owner speaks some English.

An's Hotel
APARTMENTS $$

(Map p193; ☑ 0511-395 8831; nhjenny@yahoo.com; 5 Hoang Ke Viem; apt US$20-40; 🐾🛜) A two-minute walk from My Khe beach, these simple, serviced apartments have excellent discounts for longer stays. There's a cafe downstairs and the owners have lots of similar options close by.

Fusion Maia
HOTEL $$$

(Map p193; ☑ 0511-396 7999; http://maiadanang.fusion-resorts.com; Đ Truong Sa, Khue My Beach; ste/villas from US$400/600; 😊🐾@🛜🏊) Contemporary beachfront hotel with an outstanding spa (all guests get a minimum of two treatments per day). And what a wellness zone it is, with treatment rooms, saunas and steam rooms set around a courtyard-style garden. Suites and villas don't disappointment either: all boast minimalist decor, private pool and gadgets including music-loaded iPods. Free shuttle buses run to/from Hoi An.

ℹ Getting There & Around

The My Khe section of China Beach is just 3km or so east of central Danang and costs around 40,000d by taxi.

Hoi An

🕑 0510 / POP 134,000

Graceful, historic Hoi An is Vietnam's most atmospheric and delightful town. Once a major port, it boasts the grand architecture and beguiling riverside setting that befits its heritage, but the 21st-century curses of traffic and pollution are almost entirely absent. Whether you've as little as a day or as long as a month in the town, it'll be time well spent.

Hoi An owes its easygoing provincial demeanour and remarkably harmonious old-town character more to luck than planning. Had the Thu Bon River not silted up in the late 19th century – so ships could no longer access the town's docks – Hoi An would doubtless be very different today. For a century, the city's allure and importance dwindled until an abrupt rise in fortunes in the 1990s, when a tourism boom transformed the local economy. Today Hoi An is once again a cosmopolitan melting pot, one of the nation's most wealthy towns, a culinary mecca and one of Vietnam's most important tourism centres.

This revival of fortunes has preserved the face of the Old Town and its incredible legacy of tottering Japanese merchant houses, Chinese temples and ancient tea warehouses – though, of course, residents and rice fields have been gradually replaced by tourist businesses. Lounge bars, boutique hotels, travel agents and a glut of tailor shops are very much part of the scene here. And yet, down by the market and over on Cam Nam Island you'll find life has changed little. Travel a few kilometres further – you'll find some superb bicycle, motorbike and boat trips – and some of central Vietnam's most enticing, bucolic scenery and beaches are within easy reach.

History

The earliest evidence of human habitation here dates back 2200 years: excavated ceramic fragments are thought to belong to the late Iron Age Sa Huynh civilisation, which is related to the Dong Son culture of northern Vietnam. From the 2nd to the 10th centuries, this was a busy seaport of the Champa kingdom, and archaeologists have found the foundations of numerous Cham towers around Hoi An.

In 1307 the Cham king presented Quang Nam province as a gift when he married a Vietnamese princess. When his successor

Hoi An

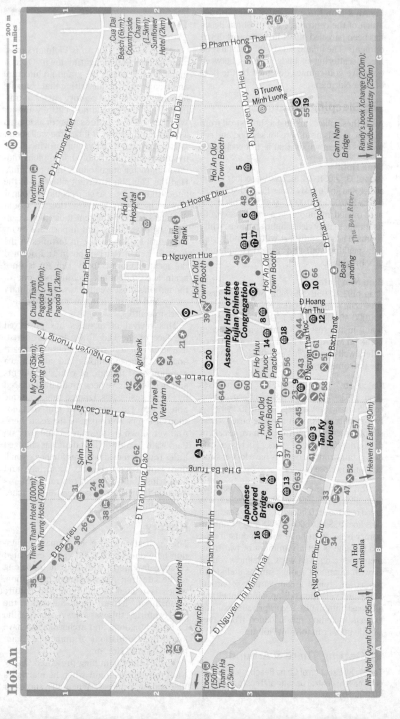

0 0   200 m
0 0   0.1 miles

Cua Dai Beach (6km); Countryside Charm (1.5km); Sunflower Hotel (2km)

Đ Pham Hong Thai

29

59   30

Đ Nguyen Duy Hieu

Đ Truong Minh Luong

55 19

Cam Nam Bridge

Randy's book Xchange (200m); Windbell Homestay (250m)

Northern (1.75km)

Đ Ly Thuong Kiet

Đ Cua Dai

Hoi An Old Town Booth

5

Đ Hoang Dieu

48

6

11 17

Thu Bon River

Chuc Thanh Pagoda (700m); Phuoc Lam Pagoda (1.2km)

Đ Thai Phien

Hoi An Hospital

Vietin Bank

Đ Nguyen Hue

49

Hoi An Old Town Booth

Assembly Hall of the Fujian Chinese Congregation

1

Hoi An Old Town Booth

Đ Phan Boi Chau

10 66

Boat Landing

My Son (35km); Danang (30km)

Đ Nguyen Truong To

Agribank

7

39

8

18

Đ Hoang Van Thu

12 44

Đ Nguyen Thai Hoc

61

Đ Bach Dang

21

53

42

54

20

46

Đ Le Loi

Dr Ho Huu Phuoc 14 Practice

43 56

51

58

Go Travel Vietnam

64

60

Hoi An Old Town Booth

65 9

26 22

50 45

Đ Tran Phu

3

Tan Ky House

41

57

15

Đ Tran Cao Van

Đ Tran Hung Dao

62

Đ Hai Ba Trung

25

13 63

37

33 47

52

Heaven & Earth (90m)

Sinh Tourist

31

24 28

38

Japanese Covered Bridge

4

2

40

34

Thien Thanh Hotel (100m); Nhi Trung Hotel (700m)

36 26

27

35

16

Đ Phan Chu Trinh

War Memorial

Church

Đ Ba Trieu

Đ Nguyen Thi Minh Khai

32

Local (150m); Thanh Ha (2.5km)

Nha Nghi Quynh Chan (95m)

An Hoi Peninsula

Hoi An

refused to recognise the deal, fighting broke out and chaos reigned for the next century. By the 15th century peace was restored, allowing commerce to resume. During the next four centuries Hoi An – also known as Faifoo to Western traders – held sway as one of Southeast Asia's major ports. Chinese, Japanese, Dutch, Portuguese, Spanish, Indian, Filipino, Indonesian, Thai, French, British and American ships came to call, and the town's warehouses teemed with treasures:

high-grade silk (for which the area is famous), fabrics, paper, porcelain, tea, sugar, molasses, areca nuts, pepper, Chinese medicines, elephant tusks, beeswax, mother-of-pearl, lacquer, sulphur and lead.

Chinese and Japanese traders in particular left their mark on Hoi An. Both groups came in the spring, driven south by monsoon winds. They would stay in Hoi An until the summer, when southerly winds would blow them home. During their four-month

WATERWORLD

Hoi An's riverside location makes it vulnerable to flooding during the rainy season (October and November). It's common for the waterfront to be hit by sporadic floods of about 1m and a typhoon can bring levels of 2m or more.

sojourn in Hoi An, they rented waterfront houses for use as warehouses and living quarters. Some began leaving full-time agents in Hoi An to take care of their off-season business affairs.

The Japanese ceased coming to Hoi An after 1637 (when the Japanese government forbade contact with the outside world), but the Chinese lingered. The town's Chinese assembly halls still play a special role for southern Vietnam's ethnic Chinese, some of whom come from all over the region to participate in congregation-wide celebrations.

This was also the first place in Vietnam to be exposed to Christianity. Among the 17th-century missionary visitors was Alexandre de Rhodes, who devised the Latin-based *quoc ngu* script for the Vietnamese language.

Although Hoi An was almost completely destroyed during the Tay Son Rebellion, it was rebuilt and continued to be an important port until the late 19th century, when the Thu Bon River silted up. Danang (Tourane) took over as the region's main port.

Under French rule Hoi An served as an administrative centre. It was virtually untouched in the American War, thanks to the cooperation of both sides. The town was declared a Unesco World Heritage site in 1999 and there are now very strict rules in place to safeguard the Old Town's unique heritage.

Today Hoi An's economy is booming. Tourist arrivals rose 22% between 2012 and 2013, and at times the Old Town can struggle to contain the sheer number of visitors. A glut of new accommodation options have opened around the town's periphery, as Hoi An expands to meet the seemingly insatiable demand from the ever-hungry tourism sector.

◉ Sights

By Unesco decree more than 800 historical buildings in Hoi An have been preserved, so much of the Old Town (www.hoianworldheritage.org.vn; tickets 120,000d) looks as it did several centuries ago.

The Chinese who settled in Hoi An identified themselves according to their province of origin. Each community built its own assembly hall, known as *hoi quan* in Vietnamese, for social gatherings, meetings and celebrations.

All the old houses except Diep Dong Nguyen and Quan Thang now offer short guided tours. They are efficient, but sometimes coming across as perfunctory. You'll be whisked to a heavy wooden chair while your guide recites a carefully scripted introduction to the house, and given a souvenir soft sell. You're free to wander around the house after the tour.

One downside to putting these old houses on show is that what were once living spaces now seem dead and museum-like, the family having sequestered itself away from visitors' eyes. Huge tour groups can completely spoil the intimacy of the experience too, as they jostle for photo opportunities.

All four museums are small. Displays are pretty basic and the information provided minimal.

Eighteen of these buildings are open to visitors and require an Old Town ticket for admission; the fee goes towards funding conservation work. Buying a ticket at any of the Old Town booths is easy enough; planning your visit around the byzantine admission options is another matter. Each ticket allows you to visit five different heritage attractions: museums, assembly halls, ancient houses and a traditional music show at the Handicraft Workshop. Tickets are valid for three days.

Despite the number of tourists who flood into Hoi An, it is still a conservative town. Visitors should dress modestly, especially since some of the old houses are still private homes.

★ **Japanese Covered Bridge**   BRIDGE
(Cau Nhat Ban) FREE This beautiful little bridge is emblematic of Hoi An. A bridge was first constructed here in the 1590s by the Japanese community in order to link them with the Chinese quarters across the stream.

The structure is very solidly constructed because of the threat of earthquakes. Over the centuries the ornamentation has remained relatively faithful to the original understated Japanese design. The French flattened out the roadway for their motor vehicles, but the original arched shape was restored in 1986.

The entrances to the bridge are guarded by weathered statues: a pair of monkeys on one side, a pair of dogs on the other. According to one story, many of Japan's emperors were born in the years of the dog and monkey. Another tale says that construction of the bridge started in the year of the monkey and was finished in the year of the dog. The stelae, listing all Vietnamese and Chinese contributors to a subsequent restoration of the bridge, are written in *chu nho* (Chinese characters) – the *nom* script had not yet become popular.

While access to the Japanese Bridge is free, you have to surrender a ticket to see a small, unimpressive temple built into the bridge's northern side.

★ Assembly Hall of the Fujian Chinese Congregation   TEMPLE
(Phuc Kien Hoi Quan; opposite 35 Đ Tran Phu; admission by Old Town ticket; ☉ 7am-5.30pm) Originally a traditional assembly hall, this structure was later transformed into a temple for the worship of Thien Hau, a deity from Fujian province. The gaudy, green-tiled triple gateway dates from 1975.

The mural on the right-hand wall depicts Thien Hau, her way lit by lantern light as she crosses a stormy sea to rescue a foundering ship. Opposite is a mural of the heads of the six Fujian families who fled from China to Hoi An in the 17th century.

The penultimate chamber contains a statue of Thien Hau. To either side of the entrance stand red-skinned Thuan Phong Nhi and green-skinned Thien Ly Nhan, deities who alert Thien Hau when sailors are in distress.

In the last chamber, the central altar contains seated figures of the heads of the six Fujian families. The smaller figures below them represent their successors as clan leaders. Behind the altar on the right are three fairies and smaller figures representing the 12 *ba mu* (midwives), each of whom teaches newborns a different skill necessary for the first year of life: smiling, sucking and so forth. Childless couples often come here to pray for offspring and leave fresh fruit as offerings.

★ Tan Ky House   HISTORICAL BUILDING
(101 Đ Nguyen Thai Hoc; admission by Old Town ticket; ☉ 8am-noon & 2-4.30pm) Built two centuries ago by an ethnically Vietnamese family, this gem of a house has been lovingly preserved through seven generations.

Look out for signs of Japanese and Chinese influences on the architecture. Japanese elements include the ceiling (in the sitting area), which is supported by three progressively shorter beams, one on top of the other. Under the crab-shell ceiling are carvings of crossed sabres wrapped in silk ribbon. The sabres symbolise force, the silk represents flexibility.

The interior is brightened by a beautiful detail: Chinese poems written in inlaid mother-of-pearl hang from some of the columns that hold up the roof. The Chinese characters on these 150-year-old panels are formed entirely of birds gracefully portrayed in various positions of flight.

The courtyard has several functions: to let in light, provide ventilation, bring a glimpse of nature into the home, and collect rainwater and provide drainage. The carved wooden balcony supports around the courtyard are decorated with grape leaves, which are a European import and further evidence of the unique blending of cultures in Hoi An.

The back of the house faces the river and was rented out to foreign merchants. Marks on one wall record recent flood heights, including the 1964 record when the water covered almost the entire ground level. There are two pulleys attached to a beam in the loft – in the past they were used for moving goods into storage, and today for raising furniture for safekeeping from the floods.

The exterior of the roof is made of tiles; inside, the ceiling consists of wood. This design keeps the house cool in summer and warm in winter.

Tran Family Chapel   HISTORICAL BUILDING
(21 Đ Le Loi; admission by Old Town ticket; ☉ 7.30am-noon & 2-5.30pm) Built for worshipping family ancestors, this chapel dates back to 1802. It was commissioned by Tran Tu, one of the clan who ascended to the rank of mandarin and served as an ambassador to China. His picture is to the right of the chapel.

The architecture of the building reflects the influence of Chinese (the 'turtle' style roof), Japanese (triple beam) and vernacular (look out for the bow-and-arrow detailing) styles.

The central door is reserved for the dead – it's opened at Tet and on 11 November, the death anniversary of the main ancestor. Traditionally, women entered from the left and men from the right, although these distinctions are no longer observed.

CENTRAL VIETNAM HOI AN

HOI AN HOUSES: A CLOSER LOOK

The historical buildings of Hoi An not only survived the 20th century's wars, they also retain features of traditional architecture rarely seen today. As they have been for centuries, some shopfronts are shuttered at night with horizontal planks inserted into grooves that cut into the columns that support the roof.

Some roofs are made up of thousands of brick-coloured *am* and *duong* (yin and yang) roof tiles – so called because of the way the alternating rows of concave and convex tiles fit snugly together. During the rainy season the lichens and moss that live on the tiles spring to life, turning entire rooftops bright green.

A number of Hoi An's houses have round pieces of wood with an *am-duong* symbol in the middle surrounded by a spiral design over the doorway. These *mat cua* (door eyes) are supposed to protect the residents from harm.

Hoi An's historic structures are gradually being sensitively restored. Strict rules govern the colour that houses can be painted and the signs that can be used.

It's not just individual buildings that have survived – it's whole streetscapes. This is particularly true around Đ Tran Phu and waterside promenade Đ Bach Dang. In the former French quarter to the east of Cam Nam Bridge there's a whole block of colonnaded houses, painted in the mustard yellow typical of French colonial buildings.

The wooden boxes on the altar contain the Tran ancestors' stone tablets, with chiselled Chinese characters setting out the dates of birth and death, along with some small personal effects. On the anniversary of each family member's death, their box is opened, incense is burned and food is offered.

After a short tour you'll be shown to the 'antique' room, where there are lots of coins for sale, and a side room full of souvenirs.

Quan Cong Temple   CONFUCIAN TEMPLE

(Chua Ong; 24 Đ Tran Phu; admission by Old Town ticket) Founded in 1653, this small temple is dedicated to Quan Cong, an esteemed Chinese general who is worshipped as a symbol of loyalty, sincerity, integrity and justice. His partially gilded statue, made of papier-mâché on a wooden frame, is on the central altar at the back of the sanctuary. When someone makes an offering to the portly looking Quan Cong, the caretaker solemnly strikes a bronze bowl that makes a bell-like sound.

On the left of Quan Cong is a statue of General Chau Xuong, one of his guardians, striking a tough-guy pose. On the right is the rather plump administrative mandarin Quan Binh. The life-sized white horse recalls a mount ridden by Quan Cong.

Check out the carp-shaped rain spouts on the roof surrounding the courtyard. The carp is a symbol of patience in Chinese mythology and is popular in Hoi An.

Shoes should be removed when mounting the platform in front of the statue of Quan Cong.

Phuoc Lam Pagoda   BUDDHIST TEMPLE

(Thon 2a, Cam Ha; ⊗8am-5pm) This pagoda (founded in the mid-17th century) is associated with An Thiem, a Vietnamese prodigy and monk from the age of eight. When he was 18, he volunteered for the army so his brothers could escape the draft; he eventually rose to the rank of general. Later he returned to the monkhood, but to atone for his sins of war he volunteered to clean the Hoi An market for 20 years, then joined this pagoda as its head monk.

To reach the pagoda, continue past Chuc Thanh Pagoda for 500m. The path passes an obelisk that was erected over the tomb of 13 ethnic Chinese who were decapitated by the Japanese during WWII for resistance activities.

Museum of Trading Ceramics   MUSEUM

(80 Đ Tran Phu; admission by Old Town ticket; ⊗7am-5.30pm) Occupies a simply restored wooden house and contains artefacts from all over Asia, with oddities from as far afield as Egypt. While this reveals that Hoi An had some rather impressive trading links, frankly it would take an expert eye to appreciate the display. However, the small exhibition on the restoration of Hoi An's old houses provides a useful crash course in Old Town architecture.

Chinese All-Community
Assembly Hall
HISTORICAL BUILDING

(Chua Ba; ☎ 0510-861 935; 64 Ð Tran Phu; ☺ 8am-5pm) **FREE** Founded in 1773, this assembly hall was used by Fujian, Cantonese, Hainan, Chaozhou and Hakka congregations in Hoi An. To the right of the entrance are portraits of Chinese resistance heroes in Vietnam who died during WWII. The well-restored main temple is a total assault on the senses with great smoking incense spirals, demonic-looking deities, dragons and lashings of red lacquer – it's dedicated to Thien Hau.

Assembly Hall of the Chaozhou
Chinese Congregation
HISTORICAL BUILDING

(Trieu Chau Hoi Quan; opposite 157 Ð Nguyen Duy Hieu; admission by Old Town ticket; ☺ 8am-5pm) Built in 1752, the highlight in this congregational hall is the gleaming woodcarvings on the beams, walls and altar – absolutely stunning in their intricacy. You could stand here for hours to unravel the stories, but if you're just popping by quickly, look for the carvings on the doors in front of the altar of two Chinese women wearing their hair in an unexpectedly Japanese style.

Chuc Thanh Pagoda
BUDDHIST TEMPLE

(Khu Vuc 7, Tan An; ☺ 8am-6pm) Founded in 1454 by a Buddhist monk from China, this is the oldest pagoda in Hoi An. Among the antique ritual objects still in use are several bells, a stone gong that is two centuries old and a carp-shaped wooden gong said to be even more venerable.

To get to Chuc Thanh Pagoda, go north all the way to the end of Ð Nguyen Truong To and turn left. Follow the lane for 500m.

Handicraft Workshop
WORKSHOP

(9 Ð Nguyen Thai Hoc; admission by Old Town ticket) Housed in the 200-year-old Chinese trading house, the Handicraft Workshop has artisans making silk lanterns and practising traditional embroidery in the back. In the front is your typical tourist-oriented cultural show (10.15am and 3.15pm) with traditional singers, dancers and musicians. It makes a sufficiently diverting break from sightseeing.

Tran Duong House
HISTORICAL BUILDING

(25 Ð Phan Boi Chau; admission 20,000d; ☺ 8am-5.30pm) There's a whole block of colonnaded French colonial buildings on Ð Phan Boi Chau between Nos 22 and 73, among them the 19th-century Tran Duong House. It's still a private home, so a family member will show you around. There's some antique French and Chinese furniture, including a sideboard buffet and a sitting room set with elaborate mother-of-pearl inlay. By contrast, the large plain wooden table in the front room is the family bed.

Hoi An Museum of
History & Culture
MUSEUM

(7 Ð Nguyen Hue; admission by Old Town ticket; ☺ 7am-5.30pm) Housed in the Quan Am Pagoda, this museum provides a sampling of pre-Cham, Cham and port-era artefacts, with some huge bells, historic photos, old scales and weights alongside plenty of ceramics.

Quan Thang House
HISTORICAL BUILDING

(77 Ð Tran Phu; admission by Old Town ticket; ☺ 7am-5pm) This house is three centuries old and was built by an ancestor who was a Chinese captain. As usual, the architecture includes Japanese and Chinese elements. There are some especially fine carvings of peacocks and flowers on the teak walls of the rooms around the courtyard, on the roof beams and under the crab-shell roof (in the salon beside the courtyard).

Assembly Hall of the
Cantonese Chinese
Congregation
HISTORICAL BUILDING

(Quang Trieu Hoi Quan; 176 Ð Tran Phu; admission by Old Town ticket; ☺ 8am-5pm) Founded in 1786, this assembly hall has a tall, airy entrance hall that opens onto a splendidly over-the-top mosaic statue of a dragon and a carp. The main altar is dedicated to Quan Cong. The garden behind has an even more incredible dragon statue.

Assembly Hall of the Hainan
Chinese Congregation
HISTORICAL BUILDING

(Hai Nam Hoi Quan; 10 Ð Tran Phu; ☺ 8am-5pm) **FREE** Built in 1851, this assembly hall is a memorial to 108 merchants from Hainan Island who were mistaken for pirates and killed in Quang Nam Province in 1851. The elaborate dais contains plaques to their memory. In front of the central altar is a fine gilded woodcarving of Chinese court life.

Phung Hung Old House
HISTORICAL BUILDING

(4 Ð Nguyen Thi Minh Khai; admission by Old Town ticket; ☺ 8am-7pm) Just a few steps down from the Japanese Covered Bridge, this old house has a wide, welcoming entrance hall decorated with exquisite lanterns, wall hangings and embroidery. There's also an impressive suspended altar.

Diep Dong Nguyen House   HISTORICAL BUILDING

(58 Đ Nguyen Thai Hoc; ☉8am-noon & 2-4.30pm)
FREE Built for a wealthy Chinese merchant
in the late 19th century, this old house looks
like an apothecary from another era. The
front room was once a dispensary for *thuoc
bac* (Chinese medicine); the medicines were
stored in the glass-enclosed cases lining the
walls.

Museum of Folklore in Hoi An   MUSEUM

(33 Đ Nguyen Thai Hoc/62 Đ Bach Dang; ☉7am-
5.30pm) Located in a 150-year-old Chinese
trading house. The exhibits give some idea
of local customs and culture, though it's aw-
fully dusty and decontextualised for a folk-
history museum. The view of the river from
upstairs is very picturesque.

Phac Hat Pagoda   BUDDHIST TEMPLE

(673 Đ Hai Ba Trung) **FREE** Phac Hat Pagoda
has a colourful facade of ceramics and murals and an elaborate roof with snake-like
dragons. There's a huge central courtyard
containing hundreds of potted plants and
bonsai trees.

Museum of Sa Huynh Culture & Museum of the Revolution   MUSEUM

(149 Đ Tran Phu; admission by Old Town ticket;
☉7am-5.30pm) On the lower floor you'll find
stone, bronze, gold, glass and agate jewellery,
assorted ceramic fragments and burial jars
dating from the early Dong Son civilisation
of Sa Huynh. The upper floor's revolution
museum was closed at the time of research.

Museum of Sa Huynh Culture & Museum of the Revolution   LANDMARK

FREE This square well's claim to fame is that
it's the source of water for making authentic
cao lau, a Hoi An speciality. The well is said
to date from Cham times and elderly people
make their daily pilgrimage to fill pails here.
To find it, turn down the alley opposite 35 Đ
Phan Chu Trinh and take the second laneway to the right.

🏃 Activities

Diving & Snorkelling

A trip to the Cham islands is a superb excursion, and Hoi An's two dive schools offer
some tempting packages, including overnight camping and diving trips. The diving
is not world class, but can be intriguing,
with good macro life.

Both dive schools charge almost exactly
the same rates: a PADI Discover Scuba dive
costs US$70, two fun dives are US$75 to

US$80, while Open Water courses start at
US$360. Snorkelling costs US$35 to US$42,
depending on the trip, including gear.

It's usually only possible to dive or snorkel
between February and September; the best
conditions and visibility are in June, July
and August.

Cham Island Diving Center   DIVING

(☎0510-391 0782; www.chamislanddiving.com; 88
Đ Nguyen Thai Hoc) Run by a friendly, experienced team, this dive shop's mantra is 'no
troubles, make bubbles'. They've a large boat
and also a speedboat for zippy transfers.
Their overnight snorkelling and camping
trip costs US$80.

Blue Coral Diving   DIVING

(☎0510-627 9297; www.divehoian.com; 77 Đ Nguy-
en Thai Hoc) A friendly, professional outfit with
an 18m dive boat and additional speedboat.
Chief instructor is Steve Reid from the UK.

Massage & Spa

There are scores of massage and treatment
centres in Hoi An. Most are of a very average quality indeed, run by locals with little
or no experience and minimal training. At
these places a basic massage costs around
US$12 an hour – there's a strip of them on
Đ Ba Trieu. At the other end of the scale
you'll find some seriously indulgent places
that offer a wonderful spa experience (with
prices to match); these are mostly based in
the luxury hotels.

★ Palmarosa   SPA

(☎0510-393 3999; www.palmarosaspa.vn; 90 Đ Ba
Trieu; 1hr massage from US$21; ☉10am-9pm) A
cut above the competition this highly professional spa offers a full range of massages (including Thai and Swedish), scrubs, facials as
well as hand and foot care. A mineral mud
wrap is US$17.

Countryside Charm   SPA

(Duyen Que; ☎0570-350 1584; http://spahoian.vn;
512 Đ Cua Dai; 1hr massage from US$16; ☉8am-
11pm) On the beach road, this centre has
fairly functional premises, but you'll find
staff are well trained and know their stuff. A
70-minute hot-stone massage is US$22.

Ba Le Beauty Salon   SPA

(☎0905 226 974; www.balewellbeautysalon.com;
45-11 Đ Tran Hung Dao; ☉9am-6.30pm) Ba Le is
run by a fluent English speaker, who has
trained in the UK, and offers inexpensive
threading, waxing, facials, manicure and
pedicures.

TOURS AROUND HOI AN

The evergreen, quintessentially Vietnamese countryside and rural lanes around Hoi An beg to be explored, and you'll find several excellent tour operators offering trips in the region. Motorbike and bicycle trips are wildly popular and there's no better way to appreciate the countryside than on two wheels. Jeep tours are another option.

The idyllic **Cham Islands** make another perfect day-trip destination during the March to September season. Both Hoi An dive schools run tours.

Hoi An Motorbike Adventures (☑ 0510-391 1930; www.motorbiketours-hoian.com; 111 Ba Trieu, Hoi An; tours US$40-1050) Specialises in tours on cult Minsk motorbikes. The guides really know the terrain and the trips make use of beautiful back roads and riverside tracks.

Phat Tire Ventures (☑ 0510-653 9839; www.ptv-vietnam.com; 62 Ba Trieu) Offers a terrific mountain bike trip to My Son ruins that takes in country lanes and temple visits.

Hoi An Free Tour (☑ 0510-097 958 7744; www.hoianfreetour.com) Ride on a bike around the fringes of Hoi An with students. You get to meet the locals and see village life, they get to practise their English.

Taste of Hoi An (☑ 0905 382 783; www.tasteofhoian.com) Walk the streets to meet the vendors, then munch your lunch an ancient (air-conditioned!) Hoi An townhouse.

Heaven & Earth (☑ 0510-386 4362; www.vietnam-bicycle.com; 57 Đ Ngo Quyen, An Hoi; tours US$15-19) Cycling tours are well thought out and not too strenuous; they explore the Song Thu river delta area.

Love of Life (☑ 0510-393 9399; www.hoian-bicycle.com; 95B Đ Phan Chu Trinh; tours US$19) Has good bicycle tours along quiet country lanes past vegetable gardens and fishing villages, and walking tours of Hoi An.

Vietnam Jeeps (☑ 0510-391 1930; www.vietnamjeeps.com; 111 Ba Trieu) Heading up into the hills of behind Hoi An, this group offers tours in original US jeeps to a Co Tu tribal village. There are hot springs and great hikes in the region.

Hoi An Eco Tour (☑ 0510-392 8900; www.hoianecotour.com.vn; Phuoc Hai village; tours US$38-72) Offers cultural activities along the river: you can fish, paddle a basket boat, ride a buffalo or learn about wet rice planting.

 Courses

Cooking

Hoi An has become a mecca for Vietnamese cooking courses, with almost every restaurant offering classes. These range from a simple set-up in someone's backyard to purpose-built schools.

The town does make an ideal place for budding chefs. There are many local specialities unique to the Hoi An region, but most are fiendishly tricky to prepare.

Courses often start with a visit to the market to learn about key Vietnamese ingredients.

Green Bamboo Cooking School COOKING (☑ 0905 815 600; www.greenbamboo-hoian.com; 21 Đ Truong Minh Hung, Cam An; per person US$35) Directed by Van, a charming local lady, accomplished chef and confident English speaker, these courses are more personalised than most. Groups are limited to a maximum of 10, and take place in Van's spacious kitchen. You choose what you want to cook from a menu with dishes including banana blossom salad with shrimp and pork and lots of vegetarian choices. It's 5km east of the centre, near Cu Dai beach.

Morning Glory Cooking School COOKING (☑ 0510-224 1555; www.restaurant-hoian.com; 106 Đ Nguyen Thai Hoc; half-day course US$27) This is the cooking course that put cooking courses on the map. It's directed by the acclaimed Trinh Diem Vy, owner of several restaurants in town, or one of her protégés. Classes concentrate on local recipes including *cao lau* and 'white rose'. You'll learn to cook in a very professionally organised, school-room-style environment. However, note that classes can have up to 30 people and some people feel the whole experience is perhaps just a little too slick and organised.

Red Bridge Cooking School COOKING

(📞0510-393 3222; www.visithoian.com/redbridge; Thon 4, Cam Thanh) At this school, going to class involves a relaxing 4km cruise down the river. There are half-day (US$29) and full-day (US$47) courses, both of which include market visits. The half-day class focuses on local specialities, with rice-paper making and food decoration tips thrown in for good measure. The full-day class, which has a maximum of eight people, is more detailed: you'll learn how to make a classlic *pho* (beef noodle soup). As an added sweetener, there's a 20m swimming pool at the school! It's 4km east of the centre on the banks of the Thu Bon river.

Yoga

Hoi An Yoga YOGA

(📞0168 8741 406; http://hoianyoga.com; 193 Ly Thai To) Professional hatha and yin yoga classes either on An Bang beach (meet at La Plage restaurant) or in a studio 2km north of Hoi An. Weekdays only; check the website for the latest schedule.

⭐ Festivals

Hoi An is a delightful place to be on the 14th day of each lunar month, when the town celebrates a **Full Moon Festival** (⏱5-11pm). Motorised vehicles are banned from the Old Town, street markets selling handicrafts, souvenirs and food open up, and all the lanterns come out! Traditional plays and musical events are also performed.

🛏 Sleeping

Hoi An has an excellent selection of good-value accommodation in all price categories. There are only a couple of hotels in the Old Town, but plenty of options close by. Many budget and midrange places are spread out to the northwest around Đ Hai Ba Trung and Đ Ba Trieu. The pretty An Hoi Peninsula is also very close to the Old Town.

There were no hostels in Hoi An at the time of research, but three places have dorms. Many luxury hotels are a few kilometres from town, on the beach, but all offer shuttle-bus transfers.

The best places book up fast, so plan as far ahead as you can and confirm shortly before you arrive.

Nhi Trung Hotel HOTEL $

(📞0510-386 3436; 700 Đ Hai Ba Trung; r US$17-27; 🟦@🟦) Around 1.5km north of the Old Town, this well-run hotel has spacious, light rooms, some with balconies, that represent excellent value. The free breakfast (pancakes, omelettes, fruit) is superb.

Sunflower Hotel HOTEL $

(📞0510-393 9838; http://sunflowerhotelhoian. com; 397 Cua Dai; dm US$7, r US$20-22; 🟦@🟦🟦) Popular place 2km east of the centre with a hostel vibe that draws lots of young backpackers. Dorms are decent and the buffet breakfast will set you up for the day.

Phuong Dong Hotel HOTEL $

(📞0510-391 6477; www.hoianphuongdonghotel. com; 42 Đ Ba Trieu; s/d/tr US$13/16/20; 🟦@🟦) It's nothing fancy, but a safe budget bet: plain, good-value rooms with comfortable mattresses, reading lights, fridge and air-con. The owners rent motorbikes at fair rates too.

Hoang Trinh Hotel HOTEL $

(📞0510-391 6579; www.hoianhoangtrinhhotel.com; 45 Đ Le Quy Don; s/d/tr US$20/25/30; 🟦@🟦) Well-run hotel with helpful, friendly staff where travellers are made to feel welcome. Rooms are quite 'old school' Vietnamese but spacious and clean. A generous breakfast and pick-up are included.

Hoa Binh Hotel HOTEL $

(📞0510-391 6838; www.hoianbinhhotel.com; 696 Đ Hai Ba Trung; dm US$9, r US$15-25; 🟦@🟦🟦) A good selection of modern rooms, all with minibar, cable TV and air-con, and a reasonable dorm. The inclusive breakfast is good, but the pool is covered by a roof.

Nha Nghi Quynh Chan GUEST HOUSE $

(📞0510-353 3977; 9 Đ Nguyen Phuc, An Hoi; r US$15-20; 🟦🟦) Owned by a friendly lady, these five modern, well-kept rooms (all with fridge and some with balcony) are located in a block opposite the Vung Hung Riverside Resort.

★ Ha An Hotel HISTORIC HOTEL $$

(📞0570-386 3126; www.haanhotel.com; 6-8 Đ Phan Boi Chau; r US$60-120; 🟦@🟦) Elegant and refined, the Ha An feels more like a colonial mansion than a hotel. All rooms have nice individual touches – a textile wall hanging or painting – and views over a gorgeous central garden. The helpful, well-trained staff make staying here a very special experience. It's about a 10-minute walk from the centre in the French Quarter.

Thien Nga Hotel HOTEL $$

(📞0510-391 6330; thienngahotel@gmail.com; 52 Đ Ba Trieu; r US$35; 🟦@🟦🟦) This place has a fine selection of rooms, most are spacious, light and airy and have a balcony and a minimalist feel (though the bathrooms are more prosaic). Book one at the rear if you can for garden views. Staff are smiley and accommodating, and breakfast is generous. The pool is covered by a roof though.

Vinh Hung 3 Hotel
HOTEL **$$**

(☑0510-391 6277; www.hoianvinhhung3hotel.com; 96 Đ Ba Trieu; r US$37-43; ✳@🛜🛜) A fine minihotel with modish rooms that have huge beds, dark-wood furniture, writing desks and satellite TV; some rooms also have balconies. All bathrooms are sleek and inviting, and breakfast is included. The rooftop pool area is perfect for catching some rays or cooling off.

Thien Thanh Hotel
HOTEL **$$**

(Blue Sky Hotel; ☑0510-391 6545; www.hoianthienthanhhotel.com; 16 Đ Ba Trieu; r US$40-60, ste US$68; ✳@🛜🛜) Staff are dressed in traditional *ao dai* at this atmospheric hotel and maintain good service standards. The hotel's spacious, inviting and well-equipped rooms enjoy a few Vietnamese decorative flourishes, DVD players and bath-tubs. At the rear the pool is a small indoor-outdoor affair, but the oasis-like rear garden is a real bonus.

Long Life Riverside
HOTEL **$$**

(☑0510-391 1696; www.longlifehotels.com; 61 Đ Nguyen Phuc Chu; r US$42-75 ste US$90; ✳@🛜🛜) Impressive hotel with a peaceful riverside setting in An Hoi Peninsula where there's virtually zero traffic noise to contend with. Rooms are spacious, all boasting tasteful modern furnishings, a computer and state-of-the-art bathrooms complete with jazzy jacuzzi-style bath-tubs. The pool area, in the centre of the hotel, is a bit of an afterthought however.

Orchid Garden Hotel
GUEST HOUSE **$$**

(☑0510-386 3720; www.hoianorchidgarden; 382 Đ Cua Dai; r US$40-60; ✳🛜🛜) Between town and beach about 2.5km east of the centre, this little guesthouse has spacious accommodation with hardwood and marble flooring. The inviting bungalows with kitchen are ideal for self-catering and guests get free bike use and breakfast.

Hoi An Garden Villas
HOTEL **$$**

(☑0510-393 9539; http://hoiangardenvillas.com; 145 Đ Tran Nhat Duat; r US$64-114; ✳🛜🛜) Enjoying a tranquil location on a quiet, suburban lane this eight-roomed hotel has attractive rooms all with huge beds, bath-tubs, a balco-

ny or terrace with pool views and fine-quality furnishings. It's about 2km east of the centre.

Windbell Homestay
HOMESTAY **$$**

(☑0510-393 0888; www.windbellhomestay.com.vn; Chau Trung, Cam Nam Island; r US$65, villas from US$110; ⊖✳@🛜🛜) A luxury homestay with lovely spacious rooms and villas that either have a pool or garden view and a huge flat-screen TV. The host family is a delight. Located in Cam Nam island, a 10-minute walk from the Old Town, which offers a more local experience.

★ Hoi An Chic Hotel
HOTEL **$$$**

(☑0510-392 6799; www.hoianchic.com; Đ Nguyen Trai; r US$96; ⊖✳@🛜🛜) Surrounded by rice fields, halfway between the town and the beach, Hoi An Chic enjoys a tranquil, near-rural location. A lot of thought has gone into the design, with hip, colourful furnishings, outdoor bathrooms and an elevated pool. Staff are very eager to please, and there's a free shuttle (in an original US jeep!) to town. It's 3km east of the centre.

Little Hoi An
HOTEL **$$$**

(☑0510-386 9999; http://littlehoian.com; Đ Nguyen Phuc Chu; r/ste from US$75/90; ✳🛜🛜) Boasting a superb position opposite the old town in tranquil An Hoi this new hotel has real polish and class. Rooms are very comfortable indeed, with furnishings that are very high grade, and sleek en-suite bathrooms. Staff are welcoming and there's a good restaurant and small spa. The pool is tiny and covered.

Vinh Hung 1 Hotel
HISTORICAL HOTEL **$$$**

(☑0510-386 1621; www.vinhhunghotels.com.vn; 143 Đ Tran Phu; r US$80-110; ⊖✳@🛜) For a unique Hoi An experience, this hotel (occupying a 200-year-old townhouse) is unmatched. The whole timber structure simply oozes history and mystique – you can almost hear echoes of the house's ancestors as they negotiate spice deals with visiting traders from Japan and Manchuria. Rooms at the rear are a little dark – if you can, book 208 (featured in Michael Caine's version of *The Quiet American*), which has a wonderful street-facing wooden balcony.

Anantara Hoi An Resort
RESORT **$$$**

(☑0510-391 4555; http://hoi-an.anantara.com; 1 Đ Pham Hong Thai; r/ste from US$120/145; ⊖✳@🛜🛜) There's a real attention to detail at this large colonial-style resort with beautifully furnished rooms that have a really contemporary look, and wonderful bathrooms. The expansive grounds are immaculately maintained and there's a classy bar, fine restaurant, cafe, spa and sublime riverside pool area. It's located in the French Quarter, a short walk from the heart of town.

✖ Eating

Hoi An is a premier-league dining destination. Central Vietnamese cuisine is arguably the nation's most complex and flavoursome, combining judicious use of fresh herbs (which are sourced from organic gardens close by) with extraneous influence due to centuries of links with China, Japan and Europe.

The beauty of Hoi An is that you can snag a spectacular (and spectacularly) cheap meal at the central market and in casual eateries – or you can splash out on a serious fine-dining experience.

Being such a cosmopolitan place, Hoi An is also blessed with myriad international dining choices too, including a Parisian-style bakery and a North Indian tandoori.

★ **Mermaid Restaurant**   VIETNAMESE $
(☎ 0510-386 1527; www.restaurant-hoian.com; 2 Đ Tran Phu; most dishes 38,000-95,000d; ⊙ 10.30am-10pm) For local specialities, you can't beat this modest little restaurant, owned by local legend Vy, who chose the location because it was close to the market, ensuring the freshest produce was directly at hand. Hoi An's

---

A HOI AN TASTER

Hoi An is a culinary hot bed and there are some unique dishes you should be sure to sample.

'White rose' or *banh vac* is an incredibly delicate, subtely-flavoured shrimp dumpling topped with crispy onions. *Banh bao* is another steamed dumpling, this time with minced pork or chicken, onions, eggs and mushrooms that's said to be derived from Chinese dim sum. *Cao lau* is an amazing dish – Japanese-style noodles seasoned with herbs, salad greens and bean sprouts and served with slices of roast pork. Other local specialities are fried *hoanh thanh* (wonton) and *banh xeo* (crispy savoury pancakes rolled with herbs in fresh rice paper). Most restaurants serve these items, but quality varies widely.

---

holy culinary trinity (*cao lau*, white rose and *banh xeo*) are all superb, as are the special fried wontons.

Bale Well   VIETNAMESE $
(45-51 Đ Tran Cao Van; meals 45,000-85,000d; ⊙ 11.30am-10pm) Down a little alley near the famous well, this local place is renowned for one dish: barbecued pork, served up satay-style, which you then combine with fresh greens and herbs to create your own fresh spring roll. Non-touristy, and has plenty of atmosphere in the evenings.

The Market   VIETNAMESE $
(http://msvy-tastevietnam.com/the-market; Đ Nguyen Hoang, An Hoi; dishes 55,000-90,000d; ⊙ 11am-9.30pm; 🖥) Offering a (sanitised) street food–style experience for those slightly wary, this huge new place has food stations cranking out Vietnamese favourites like cabbage leaf dumplings with fish and mushrooms. You sit on benches in a courtyard-like space; drinks include lassis, fruit crushes, smoothies and juices.

Little Menu   VIETNAMESE $
(www.thelittlemenu.com; 12 Đ Le Loi; dishes 50,000-135,000d; ⊙ 7am-9.30pm; 🖥) English-speaking owner Son is a fantastic host at this great little restaurant with an open kitchen and short menu – try the fish in banana leaf or duck spring rolls.

Phone Café   VIETNAMESE $
(80b Đ Bach Dang; dishes 22,000-62,000d; ⊙ 7am-9pm) This humble-looking place serves up the usual faves, plus some good clay-pot specialities.

★ **Morning Glory**
Street Food Restaurant   VIETNAMESE $$
(☎ 0510-224 1555; www.restaurant-hoian.com; 106 Đ Nguyen Thai Hoc; dishes 45,000-130,000d; ⊙ 8am-11pm; 🖥🍴) An outstanding restaurant in historic premises that concentrates on street food and traditionally prepared dishes (primarily from central Vietnam). Highlights include the pork-stuffed squid, and shrimp mousse on sugarcane skewers . There's an excellent vegetarian selection (try the smoked eggplant) including many wonderful salads. Prices are reasonable given the surrounds, ambience and flavours.

★ **Cargo Club**   INTERNATIONAL, VIETNAMESE $$
(☎ 0510-391 0489; www.restaurant-hoian.com; 107 Đ Nguyen Thai Hoc; dishes 35,000-105,000d; ⊙ 8am-11pm; 🖥) Remarkable cafe-

restaurant, serving mainly Western food, with a terrific riverside location (the upper terrace has stunning views). A full day here catching the vibe and munching your way around the menu would be a day well spent. The breakfasts are legendary (try the eggs benedict), the patisserie and cakes are to die for, and fine dining dishes seriously deliver, too.

Ganesh Indian Restaurant INDIAN $$

(☑0510-386 4538; www.ganeshindianrestaurant.com; 24 Đ Tran Hung Dao; meals 65,000-135,000d; ⊘noon-10.30pm; ☜🖉) A highly authentic, fine-value North Indian restaurant where the tandoor oven pumps out perfect naan bread and the chefs' fiery curries don't pull any punches. Unlike many curry houses, this one has atmosphere, and also plenty of vegetarian choices. Slurp a lassi or slug back a beer and you're set.

White Sail Cafe VIETNAMESE, SEAFOOD $$

(Canh Buom Trang; 134 Đ Tran Cao Van; meals 50,000-155,000d; ⊘7am-10pm; ☜) Enjoyable little restaurant serving authentic Vietnamese food including great squid (stuffed or salt 'n' pepper), smoked eggplant with tamarind and caramelised prawns. Prices are moderate, though the kitchen can struggle a bit at busy times.

White Sail Seafood SEAFOOD $$

(47/6 Trang Hung Dao; dishes 45,000-140,000d; ⊘11.30am-10pm) Very local, no-frills place in someone's scruffy backyard, where it's all about the freshness of the seafood. Little English is spoken, but the cooking is first-rate, with perfectly grilled fish, crab, giant prawns and fragrant steamboats. Not to be confused with the tourist-geared White Sail Cafe.

Ca Mai VIETNAMESE $$

(45 Đ Nguyen Thi; meals 90,000-170,000d; ⊘7am-10pm; ☜) Casual new cafe owned by Duc (of Mango Mango fame) which has something for everyone with Hoi An specialities and pan-Asian dishes including great tempura and Peking duck. The cocktails here are amazing too (happy hour is 5 pm to 7pm).

Miss Ly Cafeteria 22 VIETNAMESE $$

(☑0510-386 1603; 22 Đ Nguyen Hue; dishes 28,000-110,000d; ⊘9am-9pm; ☜) A refined little restaurant run by a Vietnamese–North American team with mellow music and antique wall prints. Dishes include tasty *cao lau*, and other Vietnamese favourites are well presented.

Hai Cafe INTERNATIONAL $$

(www.visithoian.com; 98 Đ Nguyen Thai Hoc; meals 75,000-140,000d; ⊘7am-11pm; ☜) Hai Cafe has a front porch for people-watching, a rear courtyard garden and an atmospheric dining room. It's good for a Western breakfasts and Vietnamese dishes, and has a popular evening barbecue.

Gourmet Garden INTERNATIONAL $$

(www.gourmetgarden-hoian.com; 55 Đ Le Loi; tapas 40,000-60,000d, mains 85,000-130,000d; ⊘7am-10pm; ☜) This restaurant occupies a beautifully restored town house and Mediterranean-style rear patio, and has an eclectic menu of Asian and Western dishes, including lots of Spanish tapas. Doubles as a wine bar.

Mango Mango FUSION $$$

(☑0510-391 0839; www.themangomango.com; 45 Đ Nguyen Phuc Chu; meals US$25-35; ⊘7am-10pm; ☜) Celebrity chef Duc Tran's most beautiful Hoi An restaurant enjoys a prime riverside plot and puts a global spin on Vietnamese cuisine, with fresh, unexpected combinations to the max. Perhaps at times the flavour matches are just a little too out there, but the cocktails are some of the best in town.

Green Mango VIETNAMESE, INTERNATIONAL $$$

(www.greenmango.vn; 54 Đ Nguyen Thai Hoc; meals 130,000-300,000d; ⊘11.30am-9.30pm; ☜) The setting, inside one of Hoi An's most impressive traditional wooden houses is beautiful, and the accomplished cooking (both Western and Eastern) matches the surrounds. There's also one of the only air-conditioned dining rooms in the Old Town upstairs.

🍷 Drinking

Hoi An is not a huge party town as the local authorities keep a fairly strict lid on late-night revelry. The Old Town is a great place to treat yourself to a cocktail or a civilised glass of wine.

Bar action tends to be just across the river in An Hoi. Happy hours keep costs down considerably. Most bars close by 1am in Hoi An, though Why Not? usually stays open till the wee hours. If you've the stamina for more action, catch one of the free minibus shuttles that leave Before & Now to the Zero SeaMile club on Cua Dai Beach.

★ Dive Bar BAR

(88 Đ Nguyen Thai Hoc; ⊘8am-midnight; ☜) The best bar in town, with a great vibe thanks to the welcoming service, contemporary

electronic tunes and sofas for lounging. There's also a cocktail garden and bar at the rear, pool table and pub grub.

White Marble
BAR

(www.visithoian.com; 99 Đ Le Loi; ⊙ 11am-11pm; 🕾) Wine-bar-cum-restaurant in historic premises with an unmatched selection of wines (many are available by the glass, from US$4) and refined ambience. Lunch and dinner set meals cost 200,000d.

Why Not?
BAR

(10B Đ Pham Hong Thai; ⊙ 5pm-late; 🕾) Great late-night bar 1km east of the centre, run by a friendly local character. Choose a tune from YouTube and it'll be beamed over the sound system. There's a popular pool table and usually a party vibe in the air. Yes, things can get very messy.

Q Bar
LOUNGE, BAR

(94 Đ Nguyen Thai Hoc; ⊙ noon-midnight; 🕾) Q Bar offers stunning lighting, lounge music and electronica, and the best (if pricey at around 100,000d) cocktails and mocktails in town. Draws a cool crowd and it's gay-friendly.

Before & Now
BAR

(www.beforennow.com; 51 Đ Le Loi; ⊙ 7am-midnight; 🕾) Popular but slightly bland travellers' bar, complete with pool table and clichéd paintings of the likes of Che, Marilyn and so on. Happy hour is from 6pm to 9pm.

3 Dragons
PUB

(51 Đ Phan Boi Chau; ⊙ 7.30am-midnight; 🕾) Half sports bar (where you can watch everything from Aussie Rules to Indian cricket) half restaurant (burgers, steaks and local food).

Sun Bar
BAR

(44 Đ Ngo Quyen, An Hoi; ⊙ 5pm-1am; 🕾) Backstreet backpackers' bar with a booming sound system (choose a tune from the playlist), dance floor and happy hour (8pm to 11pm).

Shopping

Hoi An has a history of flogging goods to international visitors, and today's residents haven't lost their commercial edge. It's common for travellers not planning to buy anything to leave Hoi An laden down with extra bags – which, by the way, you can buy here too.

Clothes are the biggest lure. Hoi An has long been known for fabric production, and the voracity of tourist demand has swiftly shoehorned enough tailor shops for a small province into the tiny Old Town. Shoes, also copied from Western designs, are also popular but quality is variable.

Hoi An has over a dozen art galleries too; check out the streets near the Japanese Covered Bridge, along Đ Nguyen Thi Minh Khai. Woodcarvings are a local speciality: Cam Nam village and Cam Kim island are the places to head for.

★ Metiseko
CLOTHING

(www.metiseko.com; 86 Đ Nguyen Thai Hoc; ⊙ 9am-9.30pm) Winners of a 2013 Sustainable Development award, this ecominded store stocks gorgeous clothing (including kids' wear), accessories, and homeware such as cushions using natural silk and organic cotton.

★ Reaching Out
SOUVENIRS, CLOTHING

(www.reachingoutvietnam.com; 103 Đ Nguyen Thai Hoc; ⊙ 8am-8pm) Excellent fair-trade gift shop that stocks good-quality silk scarfs, clothes, jewellery, hand-painted Vietnamese hats, handmade toys and teddy bears. The shop employs and supports artisans with disabilities.

Lotus Jewellery
ACCESSORIES

(www.lotusjewellery-hoian.com; 100 Đ Nguyen Thai Hoc; ⊙ 8am-8.30pm) Very affordable and attractive hand-crafted pieces loosely modelled on butterflies, dragonflies, Vietnamese sampans, conical hats and Chinese symbols.

Mosaique Decoration
HANDICRAFTS

(www.mosaiquedecoration.com; 6 Đ Ly Quoc; ⊙ 7.30am-8pm) Offers stylish modern lighting, silk, linen and hemp clothing, bamboo matting, hand-embroidered cushion covers, gifts and furniture.

Avana
CLOTHING

(www.hoiandesign.com; 57 Đ Le Loi; ⊙ 8am-8pm) Stylish boutique run by a European fashion designer that stocks fab off-the-peg dresses, blouses, shoes and accessories (including great hats and bags).

Tuoi Ngoc
HANDICRAFTS

(103 Đ Tran Phu; ⊙ 7am-8pm) This family-owned business has been making Chinese-style lanterns for generations and has a great selection for sale.

Randy's Book Xchange
BOOKS

(www.randysbookxchange.com; To 5 Khoi Xuyen Trung; ⊙ 9.30am-6pm Mon-Sat) Head to Cam Nam Island and take the first right to get to this bookshop. Set up like a personal library,

GETTING CLOTHES THAT MEASURE UP

Let's face it: the tailor scene in Hoi An is out of control. The estimated number of tailors working here ranges anywhere from 300 to 500. Hotels and tour guides all have their preferred partners – 'We give you good price', they promise before shuttling you off to their aunt/cousin/in-law/neighbour (from whom they'll probably earn a nice commission).

In such a demanding environment, what's an aspiring fashionista, or someone who just wants a new suit or dress, to do? The first rule of thumb is that while you should always bargain and be comfortable with the price, you also get what you pay for. A tailor who quotes you a price that is drastically lower than a competitor's is probably cutting corners (pun intended) without telling you. Better tailors and better fabrics cost more, as do tighter deadlines.

Hoi An's tailors are renowned as master copiers – show them a picture ripped out of a magazine, and they'll whip up a near-identical outfit in a day or two. If you don't know what you want, the helpful shop assistants will heave out tomes of catalogues for you to leaf through. *Ao dai* (the national dress of Vietnam), summer dresses, winter coats, wedding dresses and suits are perfectly within their repertoire.

It helps if you know your fabrics and preferences, right down to details such as thread colour, linings and buttons. When buying silk, make sure you're paying for the real thing. The only real test is with a cigarette or match (synthetic fibres melt, silk burns). Similarly, don't accept on face value that a fabric is 100% cotton or wool without giving it a good feel for the quality. Prices currently hover around US$14 to US$18 for a man's shirt, or US$30 for a cotton dress. If a suit costs less than US$100, make sure the fabric and workmanship is up to scratch.

Although many travellers try to squeeze in a clothing order within a 48-hour sojourn, that doesn't leave much time for fittings and alterations. Remember to check the seams of the finished garment; well-tailored garments have a second set of stitches (known in the trade as blanket stitching), which binds the edge, oversewing the fabric so fraying is impossible.

Shops can pack and ship orders to your home country. Although there are occasional reports of packages going astray or the wrong order arriving, the local post office's hit rate is better than most.

In such a crowded field, it's tough to sort the wheat from the chaff, particularly since all the shops outsource their orders to a growing legion of anonymous workers. It may be worth your while to scour the Old Town for a small operation that isn't tainted by being too popular. If you're pressed for time, these are places that we regularly hear good things about (in alphabetical order): **A Dong Silk** (☑ 0510-386 3170; www.adongsilk.com; 40 Đ Le Loi; ⊗ 8am-9.30pm); **Hoang Kim** (☑ 0510-386 2794; 57 Nguyen Thai Hoc; ⊗ 8am-9pm); **Kimmy** (☑ 0510-386 2063; www.kimmytailor.com; 70 Đ Tran Hung Dao; ⊗ 7.30am-9.30pm);and **Yaly** (☑ 0510-391 0474; www.yalycouture.com; 47 Đ Nguyen Thai Hoc; ⊗ 8am-9pm).

it has more than 5000 used books for sale or exchange and offers digital downloads too.

ℹ Information

DANGERS & ANNOYANCES

Hoi An is one of the safer towns in Vietnam, but there are infrequent stories of late-night bag-snatching (or very occasionally) assaults on women. If you're a lone female, try to make sure you walk home with somebody.

There's an ongoing scam involving very pushy ladies (some hang around the marketplace) offering manicures or threading beauty treatments for a dollar or so. When you've had the treatment done they demand far, far more and can get very aggressive.

Hoi An has more than its share of small-time hustlers trying to peddle tours, boat trips, motorbikes, souvenirs and the like, so prepare yourself for plenty of attention.

EMERGENCY

Hoi An Police Station (☑ 0510-386 1204; 84 Đ Hoang Dieu)

INTERNET ACCESS

Min's Computer (2 Truong Minh Luong; per hr 5000d; ⊗ 7.30am-9pm) Lots of terminals and you can also print, scan, burn and Skype here.

MEDICAL SERVICES

Dr Ho Huu Phuoc Practice (☑ 0510-386 1419; 74 Đ Le Loi; ☉ 11am-12.30pm & 5-9.30pm) A local doctor who speaks English.

Hoi An Hospital (☑ 0510-386 1364; 4 Đ Tran Hung Dao; ☉ 6am-10pm) If it's anything serious, make for Danang.

MONEY

Agribank (Đ Cua Dai; ☉ 8am-4.30pm Mon-Fri, 8.30am-1pm Sat) and **Vietin Bank** (☑ 0510-386 1340; 4 Đ Hoang Dieu; ☉ 8am-5pm Mon-Fri, 8.30am-1.30pm Sat) change cash and have ATMs.

POST

Main Post Office (6 Đ Tran Hung Dao; ☉ 7am-5pm)

TOURIST INFORMATION

There are no official tourist information centres in Hoi An – try one of the travel agencies or tour operators. Four **Hoi An Old Town Booths** (☑ 0510-386 2715; ☉ 7am-5pm) sell Old Town tickets: these are located at 30 Đ Tran Phu, 10 Đ Nguyen Hue, 5 Đ Hoang Dieu and 78 Đ Le Loi.

TRAVEL AGENCIES

Competition is pretty fierce, so it's worth checking out a few options and negotiating.

Rose Travel Service (☑ 0510-391 7567; www.rosetravelservice.com; 37-39 Đ Ly Thai To; ☉ 7.30am-5.30pm) Offers tours all over Vietnam, car rental, bus bookings, and boat, jeep and motorbike trips.

Sinh Tourist (☑ 0510-386 3948; www.thesinhtourist.vn; 587 Đ Hai Ba Trung; ☉ 7.30am-6pm) Books reputable open-tour buses.

USEFUL WEBSITES

The website www.livehoianmagazine.com is excellent for cultural content, features and reviews.

ℹ️ Getting There & Away

AIR

The closest airport is 45 minutes away in Danang.

BUS

Most north–south bus services do not stop at Hoi An, as Hwy 1 passes 10km west of the town, but you can head for the town of Vinh Dien and flag down a bus there.

Open-tour buses are usually more convenient. You'll find very regular connections to and from Hue (US$4.50, four hours) and Nha Trang (seated/sleeping US$14/17, 11 to 12 hours).

The **bus station** (96 Đ Hung Vuong), 1km west of the town centre, mainly covers local routes. Buses to Danang (18,000d, one hour), Quang Ngai and other points leave from the **northern bus station** (Đ Le Hong Phong). Foreigners are routinely overcharged, they'll usually be asked for 50,000d for the ride to Danang.

Go Travel Vietnam (☑ 0510-392 9115; info@go-travel-vietnam.com; 61 Phan Chau Trinh; ☉ 9am-9pm) offers shuttle bus transfers between Hoi An and Danang airport and train station five times per day (80,000d, one hour).

CAR & MOTORCYCLE

To get to Danang (30km), you can either head north out of town and join up with Hwy 1, or head east to Cua Dai Beach and follow the China Beach coastal road. Motorbikes charge about 140,000d for the trip to Danang. Taxis cost approximately 350,000d and are cheaper if you *don't* use the meter but negotiate a price first.

A trip in a car to Hue starts from US$85 (depending on how many stops you plan to make along the way), while a half-day trip around the surrounding area, including My Son, is around US$50.

ℹ️ Getting Around

Hoi An is best explored on foot; the Old Town is compact and highly walkable. To go further afield, rent a bicycle (20,000d per day). The route east to Cua Dai Beach is quite scenic, passing rice paddies and a river estuary.

A motorbike without/with a driver will cost around US$5/12 per day. Reckon on about 60,000d for a taxi to the beach.

BOAT

Boat trips on the Thu Bon River can be a fascinating experience. A simple rowboat (which comes complete with rower) should cost about 70,000d per hour, and one hour is probably long enough. Some My Son tours include a return journey by boat, so you can cruise into central Hoi An in style.

Motorboats can be hired to visit handicraft and fishing villages in the area; expect to pay 140,000d to 170,000d per hour. Boatmen wait on the riverbank between the Cam Nam and An Hoi bridges in central Hoi An.

TAXI

For a metered cab, try **Hoi An Taxi** (☑ 0510-391 9919) or **Mai Linh** (☑ 0510-392 5925).

STAY SAFE

Note that the ocean can get very rough along the stretch of coast east of Hoi An, particularly between the months of October and March. Many local people get into trouble in heavy seas, resulting in regular fatalities. Four lifeguards work here now and there's a watchtower, but it still pays to be cautious.

Around Hoi An

Thanh Ha

This small village has long been known for its pottery industry. Most villagers have gradually switched from making bricks and tiles to making pots and souvenirs for the tourist trade. The artisans employed in this hot, sweaty and painstaking work don't mind if you come for a gander and a chat, though they're happier if you buy something.

Thanh Ha is 3km west of Hoi An and can be easily reached on bicycle.

Cam Kim Island

The master woodcarvers, who in previous centuries produced the intricate detail that graced the homes of Hoi An's merchants and the town's public buildings, came from Kim Bong village on Cam Kim Island. Most of the woodcarvings on sale in Hoi An are produced here.

Boats to the island leave from the boat landing at Đ Bach Dang in Hoi An (20,000d, 30 minutes). The village and island, quite rural in character, are also fun to explore by bicycle.

Cua Dai Beach

Heading east of Hoi An, you cruise through paddy fields and follow the meandering riverbank for 5km or so before hitting glorious golden sandy beaches. This palm-fringed coastline heads north all the way up to Danang, and, if you choose your spot carefully, there are still some wonderful undeveloped stretches.

The nearest beach to Hoi An, Cua Dai is subject to intense development and is probably best avoided. This is also where gangs of hard-selling beach vendors target tourists – even with an iPod and an eye mask, their attentions are impossible to block out. There are some seafood restaurants here (and the Zero SeaMile club), but better places lurk close by. The 5km of coastline south to Cua Dai port (where boats leave for the Cham Islands) is being totally transformed, as a strip of five-star resorts emerges from the sand dunes. Coastal erosion is a huge problem, and several of these hotels have seen opening ceremonies postponed for years due to vanishing beaches and resulting construction woes.

The shore-side club **Zero SeaMile** (Cua Dai Beach; ☉9am-3am; 🛜) really looks the part, with a large covered dance floor, stylish decor and even a pool. However, it's really a tacky disco at heart and the food is poor. Free hourly buses connect the club with the Before & Now bar in Hoi An from midnight between April and September.

🛏 Sleeping

Victoria Hoi An Resort BEACH RESORT **$$$** (📞0510-392 7040; www.victoriahotels.asia; r/ste from US$158/247; 🌀❄@🛜⛱) This handsome beachside hotel adopts a French colonial meets traditional Hoi An design; check out the vintage Citroëns outside. Rooms are commodious, modern and immaculately presented, some with teak floors and jacuzzis, and all with balconies. There's a 30m oceanside pool and good in-house dining.

Hoi An Riverside Resort HOTEL **$$$** (📞0510-386 4800; www.hoianriverresort.com; 175 Đ Cua Dai; r from US$118; 🌀❄@🛜⛱) Offers classy rooms with hardwood floors and tasteful decor, many with balconies right over the river. It's a well-run establishment, about a kilometre from the beach, and has a good restaurant, and massage and fitness facilities. A free shuttle bus connects the hotel with Hoi An.

An Bang Beach

Just 3km north of Cua Dai, An Bang is fast emerging as one of Vietnam's most happening and enjoyable beaches. The approach track is scruffy, but after you've parked and hit the shore it's easy to see what all the fuss is about – you're greeted with a wonderful stretch of fine sand, a huge empty ocean and an enormous horizon, with only the distant Cham Islands interrupting the seaside symmetry.

More and more cool little beachfront bar-restaurants are opening here, and the scene looks set to take off. At the time of research visitors were not being hassled by beach vendors, but as An Bang's star rises, this situation will probably change. Luckily the coastline immediately to the north – a glorious broad beach lined with casuarina and pandan trees and dotted with the curious coracles of local fishermen – remains pristine.

Sleeping & Eating

An Bang is where the in-the-know foreigners gravitate. The area is much quieter in the winter months.

★ An Bang Seaside Village BUNGALOW, VILLA $$$
(☎0126 944 4567; www.anbangseasidevillage.com; An Bang Beach; villa US$53-138; ❄📶) One of *the* best beachside locations in Vietnam, these wonderful cottages and villas are superbly situated between the coastal trees on glorious An Bang beach, close to restaurants. Each of the the six units combines modern (polished concrete) and natural materials beautifully, and boast stylish furnishings and lots of space. They're serviced daily and breakfast is included.

Nam Hai HOTEL $$$
(☎0510-394 0000; www.thenamhai.com; Dien Duong village; villas/pool villas from US$525/845; ❄@📶) About 8km north of An Bang and 15km from Hoi An, this beachfront temple of indulgence has it all: three pools (one is heated), butler service, vast villas kitted out with contemporary gadgets and private plunge pools, excellent fitness facilities and a world-class spa (try the four-hand Jade massage). Of course, all this comes at an astonishing cost, but at least service is both thoughtful and excellent.

La Plage INTERNATIONAL $
(☎0510-392 8244; www.laplagehoian.com; snacks/meals 70,000/130,000d; ⏲8am-10pm; 📶) Simple-looking French-Vietnamese-owned bamboo-and-thatch beachfront place that offers delicious snacks and Gallic-style sandwiches *such as tartine du pêcheur* (open-sided sandwich with fish topping). Seafood options are always strong, as are breakfasts.

★ Le Banyan Bar EUROPEAN $$
(An Bang beach; meals 130,000-240,000d; ⏲10am-10pm; 📶) Excellent new beachfront hang-out, very popular with Hoi An's cool expat crowd, with tables overlooking the waves. The food is to savour, with lots of Med-inspired salads (try the crispy chicken or chorizo), pasta, bruschettas and mains that include a tuna tartare. There's a full bar with lots of choices of wine.

Soul Kitchen INTERNATIONAL $$
(☎090 644 0320; www.soulkitchen.sitew.com; meals 80,000-180,000d; ⏲10am-10pm Tue-Sun, 10am-6pm Mon; 📶) Shorefront restaurant with a grassy garden and thatched dining area where the menu changes daily, but might include tuna carpaccio, seafood salad or calamari. You'll find good wines, cocktails and mocktails too.

Luna D'Autunno ITALIAN $$
(www.lunadautunno.vn; meals US$8-12; ⏲11am-10pm; 📶) Fine beachside Italian with an authentic menu of antipasti, salads, pasta, meat dishes and the best pizza, from a wood-fired oven, in central Vietnam.

Cham Islands

☎0510 / POP 2800

A breathtaking cluster of granite islands, set in aquamarine seas, around 15km directly offshore from Hoi An, the **Cham Islands** make a wonderful excursion. Until very recently they were closed to visitors and under close military supervision, but it's now possible to visit as a day trip, dive or snorkel the reefs, or stay overnight.

In the last year or two the serenity of the islands has been compromised (on weekends and Vietnamese holidays) by boatloads of day tripping tourists from the mainland,

THE CO TU MINORITY

Living high in the mountains inland from Hoi An, the Co Tu people are one of the smallest, and most traditional, minority groups in Vietnam. Most men and women wear elaborate tribal clothing of intricately woven textiles, elaborate beads and the odd tusk or horn for good measure. Until quite recently, facial tattoos were common.

Their villages comprise of stilt houses set around a *guol*, a community building used for meetings, rituals and performances.

One Co Tu settlement, Bho Hoong, has developed a fine community tourism project, and **homestay** (www.bhohoongbungalows.com; 2-day tours from US$150), allowing visitors to stay in the village. Co Tu guides have been trained and income is ploughed back into the area. This is a sensitive project and travellers are asked to only arrive via officially sanctioned tours (by motorbike or jeep), booked via the website. The village is simply not set up for random visits.

so try to plan your visit accordingly if you can. It'll have to be between March to September, as the ocean is usually too rough at other times.

Only the main island, **Hon Lao**, is inhabited – the other seven Chams are tiny, rocky specks, covered in dense bush. Dip beneath the ocean and you'll find a rich underwater environment, with 135 species of soft and hard coral and varied macrolife. The islands are officially protected as a marine park. Fishing and the collection of birds' nests (for soup) are the two key industries here.

Bai Lang, Hon Lao's little port, is the main village (aside from two remote hamlets). A pretty, very relaxed place, its leeward location has long offered protection for mariners from the rough waters of the South China Sea. You'll find its lanes are a delight to explore – the laid-back ambience and slow pace of life here are a real tonic for road-weary travellers.

Tiny **Bai Huong**, a fishing village 5km southeast of Bai Lang, is an idyllic but isolated spot where an excellent new homestay initiative has been set up.

Sights & Activities

Unsurprisingly divers and snorkellers are some of the main visitors. While the diving isn't world class (visibility can be poor and overfishing is a problem), it is intriguing: five species of lobster, 84 species of mollusc and some 202 species of fish are endemic to the Chams. Dive trips and overnight stays can be arranged through dive centres in Hoi An, such as Cham Island Diving Center (p202); a full-day trip that includes snorkelling, a short hike, lunch and beach time costs US$42.

Ong Ngu   BUDDHIST TEMPLE
The only real sight in Bai Lang is a tiny, but very curious temple, whose modest appearance belies a fascinating history: it's dedicated to the whales (and whale sharks) that were once abundant around the Chams. Locals worshipped whales as oceanic deities who would offer them protection at sea. When a carcass washed ashore, they'd clean the bones and perform an elaborate ceremony at the temple before giving the bones a burial. Sadly, whales are very seldom seen around the Chams today.

Beach   BEACH
A dirt track heads southwest from Bai Lang for 2km past a couple of little coves to a fine, sheltered beach, where there's great swimming in azure waters, powdery sand, hammocks and thatched parasols that belong to the excellent Cham Restaurant. Unfortunately, during busy holiday times the beach here is packed with boats coming and going. Trails also sneak up into the forested hills behind Bai Lang.

Sleeping & Eating

For the time being the Chams only have simple guesthouses (in Bai Lang) or homestays (in Bai Huong).

★ Bai Huong homestays   HOMESTAY $
(📱0120 237 8530; www.homestaybaihuong.com; per person 100,000d, meals 30,000-70,000d) Live with the locals in Bai Huong village. Visitors are given a bed with a mozzie net, and bathrooms have sit-down toilets and cold-water showers. Delicious home-cooked meals are available. The homestay program works with nine families, generating income from community tourism. Facilities are basic, little or no English is spoken by locals and there's usually only electricity from 6pm to 10pm. Guests are often able to go fishing and trekking and can hire snorkelling gear. The project has helped fund education for Bai Huong's children, including scholarships and a local library.

Luu Ly   GUEST HOUSE $
(📱0510-393 0240; r with shared bathroom 220,000d) An excellent place with neat little rooms that have mozzie nets, TVs and fans (and a generator to power them during blackouts). Three meals a day cost around 200,000d.

Thu Trang   GUEST HOUSE $
(📱0510-393 0007; r with shared bathroom 220,000d) Right by the whale temple, it's tidy, clean and simple and meals are available (around 200,000d for breakfast, lunch and dinner).

Cham Restaurant   VIETNAMESE $
(📱0510-224 1108; meals 50,000-120,000d; ⏱10am-5pm) About 2km south of town, Cham Restaurant sits pretty on a stunning sandy beach and serves wonderful Vietnamese dishes, including lots of seafood. Call ahead to book your meal.

ⓘ Getting There & Around

Public boats to Cham Island dock at Bai Lang village. There's a scheduled daily connection from Đ Bach Dang in Hoi An (20,000d, two hours, 7am daily) that travels via the Cua Dai dock; foreigners are routinely charged more – as much as 100,000d. Note that boats do not sail during heavy seas.

Bring a copy of your passport and visa, as the boat captain needs to prepare a permit. Tour agencies charge US$25 to US$40 for island tours, but most day trips are very rushed and give you little time to enjoy the Chams.

You can walk from Bai Lang to the beach in 30 minutes, it's another 40 minutes to Bai Huong. Local boatmen and *xe om* offer connections between Bai Lang and Bai Huong; the local rate is about 20,000d but expect to pay more.

My Son

The site of Vietnam's most extensive Cham remains, **My Son** (admission 100,000d; ◎6.30am-4pm) enjoys an enchanting setting in a lush jungle valley, overlooked by Cat's Tooth Mountain (Hon Quap). The temples are in poor shape – only about 20 structures survive where at least 68 once stood – but the intimate nature of the site, surrounded by gurgling streams, is still enthralling.

My Son was once the most important intellectual and religious centre of the kingdom of Champa and may also have served as a burial place for Cham monarchs. It was rediscovered in the late 19th century by the French, who restored parts of the complex, but American bombing later devastated the temples. Today it is a Unesco World Heritage site.

The ruins get very busy, so go early or late if you can. By departing from Hoi An at 5am or 6am, you will arrive to wake up the gods (and the guards) for sunrise and could be leaving just as the tour groups hit the area.

Archaeologists have divided My Son's monuments into 10 main groups, uninspiringly named A, A', B, C, D, E, F, G, H and K. Each structure within that group is given a number.

Note that only a handful of the monuments are properly labelled and there are virtually no information panels on-site.

History

My Son (pronounced 'me sun') became a religious centre under King Bhadravarman in the late 4th century and was continuously occupied until the 13th century – the longest period of development of any monument in Southeast Asia. Most of the temples were dedicated to Cham kings associated with divinities, particularly Shiva, who was regarded as the founder and protector of Champa's dynasties.

Because some of the ornamentation work at My Son was never finished, archaeologists know that the Chams first built their structures and only then carved decorations into the brickwork.

During one period in their history, the summits of some of the towers were completely covered with a layer of gold. After the area fell into decline, many of the temples were stripped of their glory. The French moved some of the remaining sculptures and artefacts to the Museum of Cham Sculpture in Danang – fortuitously so, because the VC used My Son as a base during the American War and American bombing destroyed many of the most important monuments.

◎ Sights

Group B   HINDU TEMPLE

The main *kalan* (sanctuary), **B1**, was dedicated to Bhadresvara, which is a contraction of the name of King Bhadravarman, who built the first temple at My Son, combined with '-esvara', which means Shiva. The first building on this site was erected in the 4th century, destroyed in the 6th century and rebuilt in the 7th century. Only the 11th-century base, made of large sandstone blocks, remains.

The niches in the wall were used to hold lamps (Cham sanctuaries had no windows). The linga inside was discovered during excavations in 1985, 1m below its current position.

B5, built in the 10th century, was used for storing sacred books and objects used in ceremonies performed in B1. The boat-shaped roof (the 'bow' and 'stern' have fallen off) demonstrates the Malay-Polynesian architectural influence. Unlike the sanctuaries, this building has windows and the Cham masonry inside is original. Over the window on the outside wall facing B4 is a brick bas-relief of two elephants under a tree with two birds in it.

The ornamentation on the exterior walls of **B4** is an excellent example of a Cham decorative style, typical of the 9th century and said to resemble worms. The style is unlike anything found in other Southeast Asian cultures.

My Son

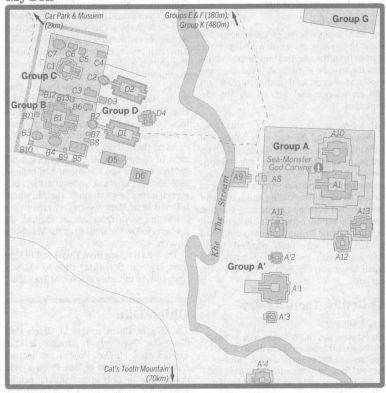

Car Park & Musuem (2km)

Groups E & F (180m); Group K (480m)

Group G

Group C

C7 C6 C5 C4
C1
C2
C3
D2
Group B
B12 B13
B11 B6 **Group D** D4
B1 B2
B3 B7 D1
B8
B10 B4 B9 B5 D5
D6

Group A
Sea-Monster God Carving
A10
A9 A8 A1
A11 A13
A12
A'2
Group A'
A'1
A'3
A'4

Khe The Stream

Cat's Tooth Mountain (70km)

B3 has an Indian-influenced pyramidal roof typical of Cham towers. Inside B6 is a bath-shaped basin for keeping sacred water that was poured over the linga in B1; this is the only known example of a Cham basin. **B2** is a gate.

Around the perimeter of Group B are small temples, **B7** to **B13**, dedicated to the gods of the directions of the compass *(dikpalaka)*.

Group A
HINDU TEMPLE

Group A was almost completely destroyed by US bombs. According to locals, the massive **A1**, considered My Son's most important monument, remained impervious to aerial bombing and was intentionally finished off by a helicopter-borne sapper team. All that remains is a pile of collapsed brick walls. After the destruction of A1, Philippe Stern, an expert on Cham art, wrote a letter of protest to US president Nixon, who ordered US forces to stop damaging Cham monuments.

A1 was the only Cham sanctuary with two doors. One faced east, in the direction of the Hindu gods; the other faced west towards Groups B, C and D and the spirits of the ancestor kings reputedly buried there. Inside A1 is a stone altar. Among the ruins, some of the brilliant brickwork (typical 10th-century style) is still visible. At the base of A1 on the side facing A10 (decorated in 9th-century style) is a **carving** of a small worshipping figure flanked by round columns, with a Javanese sea-monster god *(kala-makara)* above.

Group C
HINDU TEMPLE

The 8th-century **C1** was used to worship Shiva, portrayed here in human form. Inside is an altar where a statue of Shiva, now in the Museum of Cham Sculpture in Danang, used to stand. Note the motifs, characteristic of the 8th century, carved into the brickwork of the exterior walls. With the massive bomb crater in front of this group, it's amazing that anything's still standing.

My Son Museum
MUSEUM

(incl with entrance ticket; ◷ 6.30am-4pm) My Son's impressive museum contains many statues from the site and information about how the temples were constructed, the carvings and statues and architecture. Cham culture, religion and way of life are also explained.

Other Groups
HINDU TEMPLE

Buildings D1 and D2 were once meditation halls and now house small displays of Cham sculpture. Dating from the 8th century, Group A' is at present overgrown and inaccessible. Preservation work is ongoing at Group G, where scaffolding and roofs have been erected over the 12th-century temples. Group E was built between the 8th and 11th centuries, while Group F dates from the 8th century; both were badly bombed. If you follow the path towards K, a stand-alone small tower, you can loop back towards the car park.

❶ Getting There & Away

BUS & MINIBUS

Almost every hotel in Hoi An can arrange a day trip for you to My Son (US$4 to US$8). Most minibuses depart at 8am and return between 1pm and 2pm. If you go for the boat-ride option on the return leg, add an extra hour to the trip.

'Sunrise' trips do not mean you'll see the first ray of morning light hit the temples, but they will get you in early, beating the crowds.

CAR & MOTORCYCLE

My Son is about 55km from Hoi An. A hired car with driver costs around US$45. The site is adequately signposted so it's easy to find if you've got your own wheels.

Tra Kieu (Simhapura)

Formerly called Simhapura (Lion Citadel), Tra Kieu was the first capital of Champa and remained so from the 4th century to the 8th century. Today nothing remains of the ancient city except the rectangular ramparts. A large number of artefacts, including some of the finest carvings in the Museum of Cham Sculpture in Danang, were found here.

Atop Buu Chau Hill is the modern Mountain Church (Nha Tho Nui), built in 1970 to replace an earlier structure destroyed by an American bomb. It offers wonderful views. The church is about 200m from the morning market (Cho Tra Kieu).

The 19th-century Tra Kieu Church (Dia So Tra Kieu) is home to a museum (Van Hoa Cham) of Cham artefacts, collected by local people and then amassed by a priest. The artefacts are kept in a locked, dusty room on the 2nd floor of the building to the right of the church. According to local belief this church was the site of a miracle in 1885. Catholic villagers, under attack by anti-French forces, saw a vision of a lady in white, believed to be Mary, whom they credit with protecting them from intense shelling. To get here, follow the signs from the Mountain Church.

Tra Kieu is 6.5km from Hwy 1 and 19.5km from My Son. Some day trips to My Son from Hoi An include a stop-off at Tra Kieu.

Chien Dan

The elegant Cham towers at Chien Dan (Chien Dan Cham; Hwy 1; admission 12,000d; ◷ 8-11.30am & 1-5.30pm Mon-Fri) are located just outside the town of Tam Ky on a wide open field; the only other building nearby is a small museum. Dating from the 11th or 12th century, each *kalan* faces east. Many of the decorative friezes remain on the outside walls.

The middle tower was dedicated to Shiva; at the front left-hand edge of its base there are carvings of dancing girls and a fight scene. Look for the grinning faces high up between this and the left tower (honouring Brahma) and the two elephants at the rear. The right-hand tower is dedicated to Vishnu.

Although the towers escaped the bombing that ravaged My Son, scars from the American War are evident – witness the numerous bullet holes in the walls.

This rarely visited site is to the right of the road on your approach to Tam Ky, 47km south of Hoi An.

Southeast Coast

Best Places to Eat

➡ Lac Canh Restaurant (p241)

➡ Ganh Hao (p261)

➡ Nha Trang Xua (p241)

➡ Sandals (p253)

➡ Sailing Club (p241)

Best Places to Stay

➡ Mia Resort Nha Trang (p240)

➡ Some Days of Silence (p229)

➡ Jungle Beach (p229)

➡ Sunny Sea (p238)

➡ Six Senses Con Dao (p268)

Why Go?

Vietnam has an incredibly curvaceous coastline, and it is in this region that it is at its most alluring with vast tracts of coastline backed by towering sand dunes and cliffs. More and more of the voluptuous beaches along this stretch are being set aside for large tourism projects, but there are still untouched bays where you can play Robinson Crusoe for the day.

Nha Trang, Mui Ne and Con Dao attract the headlines here, but the beach breaks come thick and fast in this part of Vietnam. If your idea of paradise is reclining in front of turquoise waters, weighing up the merits of a massage or a mojito, then you have come to the right place. On hand to complement the sedentary delights are activities to set the pulse racing, including scuba diving, snorkelling, surfing, windsurfing and kitesurfing.

When to Go
Quang Ngai

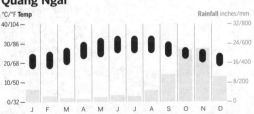

Jun Plan a midnight excursion to watch turtles nesting in the fabled Con Dao islands.

Oct See Cham people celebrate *kate*, or new year, at Po Klong Garai temple.

Dec Enjoy Christmas in Mui Ne with the best kitesurfing and windsurfing conditions.

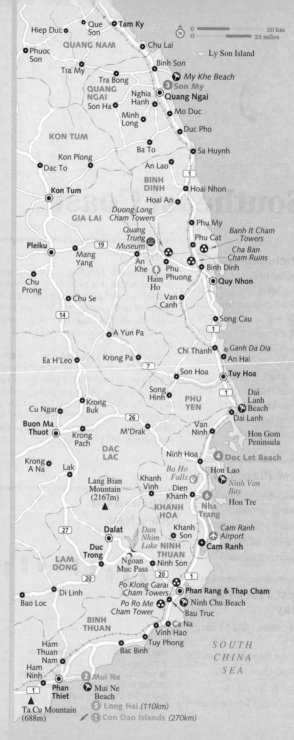

Southeast Coast Highlights

① Combine the beautiful beaches, snorkelling coral reefs and riding motorbikes along the empty coastal roads around the **Con Dao Islands** (p262).

② Kitesurf by day and chill at night in the beach-blessed resort of **Mui Ne** (p248).

③ Come face-to-face with the horrors of war at the poignant **Son My Memorial** (p220).

④ Search for and find the perfect beach in isolated **Doc Let** (p228).

⑤ Take a road trip between Phan Thiet and Long Hai via a spectacular lighthouse and the endless sands of **Ho Tram** (p257) and **Ho Coc** (p257).

⑥ Soak up the unique beach scene or explore offshore islands by boat in the bombastic town of **Nha Trang** (p230).

Quang Ngai

🎵 055 / POP 121,000

The eponymous capital of Quang Ngai province is something of an overgrown village with no obvious attractions, so most visitors only drop by for a spot of grazing at lunchtime. The few travellers who venture here come to pay their respects to the victims of the most famous atrocity of the American War. Perhaps it's the sombre mood induced by the memorial that has caused tourists to overlook one of Vietnam's less celebrated beaches, My Khe, just a couple of kilometres away.

Even before WWII, Quang Ngai was an important centre of resistance against the French. During the Franco–Viet Minh War, the area was a Viet Minh stronghold. In 1962 the South Vietnamese government introduced its ill-fated Strategic Hamlets Program. Villagers were forcibly removed from their homes and resettled in fortified hamlets, infuriating and alienating the local population and increasing popular support for the Viet Cong (VC). Some of the most bitter fighting of the American War took place here.

🛌 Sleeping

The beach at nearby My Khe is temptingly close and has a good accommodation option.

Hung Vuong Hotel   HOTEL $

(📞 055-381 8828; 33 Đ Hung Vuong; r 200,000-280,000d; 🅿 🛜) For a good-value budget bed, this is one of best cheapies in town, though the friendly family owners speak little English. The higher-priced rooms are almost quads.

Central Hotel   HOTEL $$

(📞 055-382 9999; www.centralhotel.com.vn; 1 Đ Le Loi ; r US$40-85; 🅿 @ 🛜 🏊) Four-star hotel where the standard rooms have shower only, but the VIP rooms have huge bath-tubs. Extra touches include a spa/massage centre, tennis court and a pool that is verging on Olympic sized.

Petro Song Tra Hotel   HOTEL $$

(📞 055-382 2665; www.petrosetco.com.vn; 2 Đ Quang Trung; r US$52-66; @ 🛜 🏊) This is the town's fancy dan residence, a riverside landmark complete with an opulent chandelier-heavy lobby and smart rooms, many with sweeping views.

🍴 Eating

Quang Ngai province is famous for *com ga*: boiled chicken over yellow rice (steamed with chicken broth) with mint, egg soup and pickled vegetables. You'll find *com ga* restaurants all over town. Locals tend to eat it with a spoon, so don't stress about struggling with the chopsticks.

SOUTHEAST COAST QUANG NGAI

THE LONG WALL OF VIETNAM

Stretching some 127km through the hinterlands of Quang Ngai and Binh Dinh provinces, the 'Long Wall of Vietnam' was only announced to the world in early 2011. Less the Great Wall of China and more Hadrian's Wall in the UK, this historic structure is now considered the longest monument in Southeast Asia. The wall runs roughly north to south, roughly paralleling the central Vietnamese coastline.

Back in 2005, Dr Andrew Hardy, head of the École Française d'Extrême Orient (EFEO) in Hanoi, discovered reference to the wall in an 1885 manuscript. Built in 1819, it was believed to have been a collaborative effort between lowland Viet people and highland Tre people to regulate trade and exact taxes. It was declared a National Heritage Site in March 2011 and there have been talks to develop tourism along the route, in consultation with English Heritage.

Sections of the wall are still in good condition, reaching up to 4 metres in height. However, there are currently no organised tours to the wall and no trained guides to introduce its history. The best chance of visiting the Long Wall of Vietnam is to talk to experienced Easy Riders in Hoi An, Nha Trang, Mui Ne or Dalat and ask them to incorporate it into an off-the-beaten-track itinerary. Parts of the wall are around 15km from the town of Quang Ngai. Some signs have been erected to help drivers locate some of most impressive parts. Two are in Ba Dong Commune (Ba To District) and another two are in Hanh Dung Commune (Nghia Hanh District).

Cay Gon
VIETNAMESE $

(13 Đ Quang Trung; dishes 20,000-30,000d, set menu 35,000d; ⊙7am-9pm) A simple, inexpensive place on busy Quang Trung that specialises in stews (including ribs, chicken, fish and pork) as well as seafood. It's half a block from the river.

Bac Son
VIETNAMESE $

(23 Đ Hung Vuong; mains 27,000-80,000d; ⊙7.30am-8.45pm) This ever-popular restaurant been in business since 1943, has good Vietnamese food, an English menu and a friendly owner.

Nhung 1
VIETNAMESE $

(474 Đ Quang Trung; meals 25,000-40,000d; ⊙7.30am-9pm) Nhung 1 is a bustling eatery on the main drag. Famous for *com ga*.

❶ Getting There & Away

AIR

The nearest airport is Chu Lai (VCL), 36km north of Quang Ngai; it's sometimes still called Tam Ky airport, its old name. **Vietnam Airlines** (www.vietnamairlines.com.vn) has flights from Chu Lai to Hanoi from 820,000d, and to HCMC from around 1,380,000d. A taxi here is around 380,000d.

BUS

Quang Ngai bus station (Đ Le Thanh Ton) is situated to the south of the centre, 50m east of Đ Quang Trung. Regular buses head to all the major stops on Hwy 1, including Danang (from 40,000d, two hours) and Quy Nhon (from 75,000d, 3½ hours). Open-tour buses can drop off here, but pick-ups are harder to arrange.

CAR & MOTORBIKE

By road from Quang Ngai, it's 100km to Hoi An, 174km to Quy Nhon and 412km to Nha Trang.

TRAIN

Trains stop at **Quang Ngai Train Station** (Ga Quang Nghia; ☑ 055 382 0280; 204 Đ Nguyen Chi Thanh), 1.5km west of the town centre. Destinations include Danang (81,000d, three hours), Quy Nhon (102,000d, five hours) and Nha Trang (258,000d, seven hours).

Around Quang Ngai

Son My (My Lai)

This tranquil rural spot was the setting for one of the most horrific crimes of the American War: a massacre committed by US troops that killed 504 villagers, many of them elderly people and children on 16 March 1968. The deeply poignant Son My Memorial (admission 10,000d; ⊙7am-4.30pm) was constructed as a monument to their memory.

The war crime was one of the pivotal moments of the conflict, shaping public perceptions in the USA and across the world. As *Life* magazine put it, 'the American people reacted to the massacre of My Lai with horror, shame and shock, but also with disbelief'.

Centred on a dramatic stone sculpture of an elderly woman holding up her fist in defiance, a dead child in her arms, the monument rises high above the landscape.

Surrounding the main sculpture, scenes have been re-created in peaceful gardens to reflect the aftermath of that fateful day. Burnt-out shells of homes stand in their original locations, each marked with a plaque listing the names and ages of the family that once resided there. The concrete connecting the ruins is coloured to represent a dirt path, and indented with the heavy bootprints of American soldiers and the bare footprints of fleeing villagers.

The massacre was painstakingly documented by a US military photographer, and these graphic images are now the showcase of a powerful museum on-site. Inevitably, the content is incredibly harrowing: villagers are shown cowering from troops, there are corpses of children and limbless victims. The display ends on a hopeful note, chronicling the efforts of the local people to rebuild their lives afterwards. A section honours the GIs who tried to stop the carnage, shielding a group of villagers from certain death, and those responsible for blowing the whistle.

The road to Son My passes through particularly beautiful countryside: rice paddies, cassava patches and vegetable gardens shaded by casuarinas and eucalyptus trees. However, if you look closely you can still make out the odd bomb crater, and the bare hilltops are testimony to the continuing environmental devastation caused by Agent Orange.

The best way to get to Son My is by motorbike (around 120,000d including waiting time) or regular taxi (about 330,000d return). From Quang Ngai head north on Đ Quang Trung (Hwy 1) and cross the long bridge over the Tra Khuc River. Take the first right (eastward, parallel to the river) where a triangular concrete stela indicates the way and follow the road for 12km.

My Khe Beach

A world away from the sombre atmosphere of the Son My Memorial, but only a couple of kilometres down the road, My Khe (not to be confused with the other My Khe Beach near Danang) is a superb beach, with fine white sand and clear water. It stretches for kilometres along a thin, casuarina-lined spit of sand, separated from the mainland by Song Kinh Giang, a body of water just inland from the beach.

If you follow the golden rule (avoid holidays and weekends) you've a good chance of having this pretty beach largely to yourself. The shoreline's profile is gently shelving so it's great for children and those not confident in deep water.

🛏 Sleeping & Eating

Accommodation options are very limited. Apart from My Khe Hotel there's only one other option (and it wasn't staffed when we dropped by). Dozens of ramshackle seafood shacks are spread along the beach here, although they can be a bit of a hard-sell. Fish and seafood are fresh and delicious, but settle on prices in advance.

My Khe Hotel HOTEL **$**
(☎ 055-384 3316; khudulichmykhe@gmail.com; My Khe; s/d/tr 320,000/360,000/480,000d; ❇ 🛜)

MY LAI MASSACRE

At about 7.30am on 16 March 1968, the US Army's Charlie Company landed by helicopter in the west of Son My, regarded as a Viet Cong stronghold. The area had been bombarded with artillery, and the landing zone was raked with rocket and machine-gun fire from helicopter gunships. They encountered no resistance during the 'combat-assault', nor did they come under fire at any time during the operation; but as soon as their sweep eastward began, so did the atrocities.

As the soldiers of the 1st Platoon moved through Xom Lang, they shot and bayoneted fleeing villagers, threw hand grenades into houses and bomb shelters, slaughtered livestock and burned dwellings. Somewhere between 75 and 150 unarmed villagers were rounded up and herded to a ditch, where they were executed by machine-gun fire.

In the next few hours, as command helicopters circled overhead and American Navy boats patrolled offshore, the 2nd Platoon, the 3rd Platoon and the company headquarters group also became involved in the attacks. At least half a dozen groups of civilians, including women and children, were assembled and executed. Villagers fleeing towards Quang Ngai were shot. As these massacres were taking place, at least four girls and women were raped or gang-raped by groups of soldiers.

According to the memorial here, a total of 504 Vietnamese were killed during the massacre; US Army sources determined the total number of dead at 347.

Troops who participated were ordered to keep their mouths shut, but several disobeyed orders and went public with the story after returning to the USA, including helicopter pilot Hugh Thompson Jr who managed to rescue several women and children on that fateful day. When it broke in the newspapers it had a devastating effect on the military's morale and fuelled further public protests against the war. It did little to persuade the world that the US Army was fighting on behalf of the Vietnamese people. Unlike WWII veterans, who returned home to parades and glory, soldiers coming home from Vietnam often found themselves ostracised and branded 'baby killers'.

A cover-up of the atrocities was undertaken at all levels of the US Army command, eventually leading to several investigations. Lieutenant William Calley, leader of the 1st Platoon, was court-martialled and found guilty of the murders of 22 unarmed civilians. He was sentenced to life imprisonment in 1971 and spent three years under house arrest at Fort Benning, Georgia, while appealing his conviction.

Calley was paroled in 1974 after the US Supreme Court refused to hear his case. The case still causes controversy – many claim that he was made a scapegoat because of his low rank, and that officers much higher up ordered the massacres. What is certain is that he didn't act alone.

For the full story of this event and its aftermath, pick up a copy of *Four Hours in My Lai* by Michael Bilton and Kevin Sim, a stunning piece of journalism.

An excellent new place just behind the beach with very smart rooms for the price, all with good quality furnishings, marble floors and flat-screen TVs. There's an attractive restaurant at the front.

Duc Chien SEAFOOD **$**
(My Khe beach; meals 40,000-100,000d; ⊗ 9am-8pm) Seafood place that specialises in delicious prawns in sweet chilli sauce, which you barbecue yourself. Order them with a green salad and a beer and you're set.

Quy Nhon

☑ 056 / POP 293,000

A large, prosperous coastal city, Quy Nhon (pronounced 'hwee ngon') is blessed with a terrific shoreline of sandy beaches. Its seaside appeal and tidy, litter-free streets make it the kind of place that affluent Vietnamese couples choose to retire to, spending their final days watching the ocean and walking the promenade. For foreign visitors its attractions are less obvious, though it's certainly a good spot to sample some fresh seafood.

Its sprawling layout and huge boulevards means it's something of a sweaty business getting around in the hot summer months (unless you have wheels).

During the American War there was considerable South Vietnamese, US, VC and South Korean military activity in the area. The mayor of Quy Nhon, hoping to cash in on the presence of US troops, turned his official residence into a large massage parlour.

⊙ Sights

★ Municipal Beach BEACH
The long sweep of Quy Nhon's beachfront extends from the port in the northeast to the hills in the south. It's a beautiful stretch of sand and has been given a major facelift in recent years, making it almost as nice as Nha Trang, but with a fraction of the visitors.

At the top end, the nicest section is near the Saigon Quy Nhon Hotel, where a grove of coconut trees lines the road. At dawn and in the evenings this area is packed with locals practising t'ai chi.

South along the shore, the waterfront opens up to a parklike promenade, punctuated by large hotels. Here the beach gets more beautiful and secluded, away from the

bustle of town. At night the bright lights of the squid boats give the illusion of a floating village far out to sea.

In the distance you can see a giant statue of Tran Hung Dao giving the Chinese the finger on the far headland. It is possible to climb the statue if the door is open and peek out through the eyes. Heading south, a striking socialist-realist war memorial dominates a small square.

Thap Doi Cham Towers HINDU TEMPLE
(admission 10,000d; ⊗ 8-11am & 1-6pm) This pair of Cham towers sits within the city limits in a pretty park. Steep steps lead up to the temples, which are open to the sky. Atypically for Cham architecture, they have curved pyramidal roofs rather than the usual terracing. The larger tower (20m tall) retains some of its ornate brickwork and remnants of the granite statuary that once graced its summit. The dismembered torsos of garuda (half-human, half-bird) can be seen at the corners of the roofs.

Take Ð Tran Hung Dao west away from the centre and look out for the towers on the right.

Binh Dinh Museum MUSEUM
(28 Ð Nguyen Hue; ⊗ 7-11am & 2-5pm Apr-Sep, 7.30-11am & 1.30-4.30pm Oct-Mar) **FREE** This small museum features exhibits on regional history. The entry hall focuses on local communism, including an interesting silk print (by Zuy Nhat, 1959) showing a fat French colonist sitting aloft mandarins, in turn supported by bureaucrats, and cruel bosses, with the struggling masses supporting the whole ensemble. The room to the left has a small natural history section and some Cham statues, while the rear room has the bulk of the impressive Cham collection.

The room to the right of the entrance is devoted to the American War, with local relics such as the 'Spittoon of Heroic Vietnamese Mother Huynh Thi Bon'.

Quy Hoa Beach & Leper Hospital BEACH
FREE Leprosy may not conjure up images of fun in the sun, but this really is a lovely spot. As leper hospitals go, this one is highly unusual, a sort of model village near the seafront, where treated patients live together with their families in small, well-kept houses.

Fronting the village is Quy Hoa Beach, a lovely stretch of sand and a popular weekend hang-out for the city's small expat community.

Quy Nhon

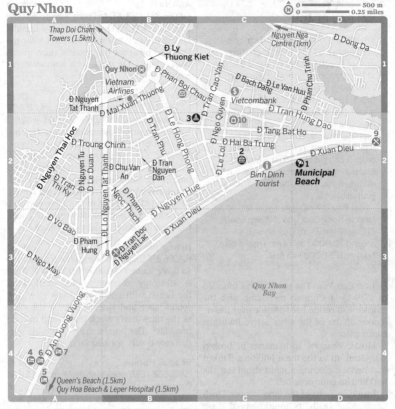

The hospital grounds are so well maintained that it looks a bit like a resort, complete with a guitar-shaped pavilion and numerous busts of distinguished and historically important doctors, both Vietnamese and foreign.

Depending on their abilities, the patients work in the rice fields, in fishing, and in repair-oriented businesses or small craft shops – one supported by Handicap International produces prosthetic limbs.

Just up from the beach, there's a dirt path to the hillside tomb of Han Mac Tu, a mystical poet who died in 1940.

If travelling by foot or bicycle, continue along the road past Queen's Beach until it descends to the hospital's entrance gates, about 1.5km south of Quy Nhon.

Long Khanh Pagoda
BUDDHIST TEMPLE

FREE It's hard to miss the 17m-high Buddha (built in 1972) heralding Quy Nhon's main pagoda, set back from the road by 143

Quy Nhon

WORTH A TRIP

BAI BAU BEACH

While the nearby Life Resort charges nonguests US$10 to lounge on their private beach (whether they've dined at the restaurant or not), if you head 2km south there's an even better beach (that costs a fraction of the price). **Bai Bau** (admission 10,000d) is a beautiful white-sand crescent no more than 150m wide, sheltered by rocky headlands, with mountains for a backdrop. It can get busy on the weekend and during Vietnamese holidays, but midweek you'll likely have the place to yourself.

Bai Bau is well signed, just off the road to Song Cau, about 20km south of Quy Nhon. From Quy Nhon it's around 70,000d by *xe om* (motorbike taxi) or 175,000d in a taxi.

Đ Tran Cao Van. The pagoda was founded in 1715 by a Chinese merchant, and the monks who reside here preside over the religious affairs of the city's active Buddhist community.

Mosaic dragons with manes of broken glass lead up to the main building, flanked by towers sheltering a giant drum (on the left) and an enormous bell.

Inside, in front of the large copper Thich Ca Buddha (with its multicoloured neon halo) is a drawing of multi-armed and multi-eyed Chuan De (the Goddess of Mercy); the numerous arms and eyes symbolise her ability to touch and see all.

Queen's Beach   BEACH
This stony little beach at the foot of Ganh Rang was once a favourite holiday spot of Queen Nam Phuong. There's a cafe and great views back over Quy Nhon. To get here, take Đ An Duong Vuong to the far south end of Quy Nhon's beachfront and continue as the road starts to climb. After it crosses a small bridge, pay the entrance fee (5000d). It's accessible by bicycle or *xe om* (motorbike taxi; 25,000d).

🛏 Sleeping

Quy Nhon offers great value for money, and most places are right on or just off the sparkling shoreline. The main strip for travellers is around Đ An Duong Vuong on the south side of town.

Anh Vy Hotel   HOTEL $
(☑ 056-384 7763; 8 Đ An Duong Vuong; r 160,000-250,000d; ❄ @ 🛜) Owned by a very friendly lady, and offering excellent travel information and bikes for hire. Boasts clean rooms with satellite TV; those with sea views cost a little more.

Hotel Au Co – Ben Bo Bien   HOTEL $
(☑ 056-374 7699; hotel_auco@yahoo.com; 8 & 24 Đ An Duong Vuong; r 160,000-300,000d; ❄ @ 🛜) Under the same ownership, these two hotels confusingly share the same name. Number 8 is slightly more atmospheric, with clean rooms (some with sea views and balconies). Number 24 is even more kitsch (some rooms even have fake plastic trees!). Bicycles (35,000d per day) and motorbikes (150,000d) are available for rent. Mr Thoai, the friendly owner, speaks good English.

Hoang Yen Hotel   HOTEL $$
(☑ 056-374 6900; www.hoangyenhotel.com.vn; 5 Đ An Duong Vuong; r 500,000-710,000d; ❄ @ 🛜 🏊) A 10-storey concrete hotel overlooking the beach with good-value rates given the rooms' spec and space. Secure a sea view, as the rates aren't much higher and include breakfast. The hotel's shady shoreside garden cafe is very popular for drinks.

Seagull Hotel   HOTEL $$
(☑ 056-384 6377; www.seagullhotel.com.vn; 5 Đ An Duong Vuong; r US$35-45; ❄ @ 🛜 🏊) This large oceanfront hotel has a three-star wing and more modern four-star accommodation. All rooms have generous balconies and it's located by a beautiful section of beach that's perfect for swimming.

Avani Quy Nhon
Resort & Spa   BOUTIQUE HOTEL $$$
(☑ 056-384 0132; www.avanihotels.com/quynhon; Bai Dai Beach; r US$118-136, ste US$168; ❄ @ 🛜 🏊) Stylish oceanfront resort, set on a lovely private beach 15km south of town, that exudes taste – there's a subtle Cham influence to the design. The spacious rooms, with stunning open-plan bathrooms, all face the waves. T'ai chi, yoga and snorkelling trips are offered and the spa is excellent.

🍴 Eating & Drinking

Quy Nhon also has lots of delicious street food all around the town centre.

Barbara's: The Kiwi Connection   CAFE $
(12 Đ An Duong Vuong; mains 35,000-80,000d; ⏰ 7am-10pm; 🛜) Barbara has moved on, and

the cafe has a new location but this place remains a popular meeting point thanks to the reliable travel information and Western treats: pizza, pasta, fish 'n' chips (50,000d), international breakfasts and Earl Grey tea. Accommodation is also available, but there's better value elsewhere.

Tinh Tam   VEGETARIAN $
(141 Đ Tran Cao Van; mains 10,000-20,000d; ⊗8am-8pm; ✐) Located next to Long Khanh Pagoda, this hole-in-the-wall serves vegetarian meals in basic surrounds. The mixed plate is filling and hearty.

★ C.ine   SEAFOOD $$
(✐056-651 2675; 94 Xuan Dieu; dishes 50,000-150,000d; ⊗11am-10pm) Likeable, very popular seafood restaurant with gingham tablecloths and views over the bay. Feast on delectable dishes including sweet soft-shell crab, hot and sour fish soup and green-mango prawn salad.

2000   SEAFOOD $$
(1 Đ Tran Doc; dishes 40,000-250,000d; ⊗10am-10pm) Super-fresh seafood – select yours from the bubbling tubs and tanks full of live crabs, shrimp and fish. There's also an upstairs dining area with a balcony. The seafood hot pots are legendary.

🛍 Shopping

Lon Market   MARKET
(Cho Lon, Đ Tang Bat Ho; 6am-4pm) Bustling central market where street sellers spill over into the surrounding roads. Great for photo opportunities.

Nguyen Nga Centre   HANDICRAFTS
(www.nguyennga.org; 91 Đ Dong Da; 7.30am-4pm Mon-Fri, 8am-1pm Sat) Sells lovely homemade weavings, handicrafts, clothing and jewellery, with the money going towards running a centre for disabled students.

ℹ Information

Barbara's: The Kiwi Connection (✐056-389 2921; www.barbaraquynhon.weebly.com; 12 Đ An Duong Vuong ; 🛜) Free tourist information including bus and train timetables and tickets, city and countryside tours, bike and motorbike hire, local maps and internet access.

Binh Dinh Tourist (✐056-389 2524; 10 Đ Nguyen Hue) Government-run tourist office.

Main Post Office (197 Đ Phan Boi Chau; ⊗6.30am-10pm)

Vietcombank (148 Đ Le Loi; ⊗7.30am-3pm Mon-Sat) With ATM.

ℹ Getting There & Away

AIR

Vietnam Airlines (✐056-382 5313; www.vietnamairlines.com; 1 Đ Nguyen Tat Thanh) links Quy Nhon with Ho Chi Minh City (HCMC) and Hanoi.

There's a minibus transfer (40,000d) for airline passengers between the Vietnam Airlines' office and Phu Cat airport, 32km north of the city.

BUS

Quy Nhon bus station (✐056-384 6246; Đ Tay Son) is on the south side of town, with very frequent buses to Quang Ngai (65,000d, 3½ hours, hourly), Nha Trang and towns in the central highlands including Pleiku (82,000d, four hours, six daily).

It's also possible to get a bus all the way to Pakse (from 388,000d, 20 hours, four per week) in Laos, crossing the border at Bo Y.

TRAIN

The nearest mainline station is Dieu Tri, 10km west of the city. Only very slow local trains stop at **Quy Nhon train station** (✐056-382 2036; Đ Le Hong Phong) which is at the end of a 10km spur off the main north–south track. Get to/from Dieu Tri by taxi (160,000d) or *xe om* for around 75,000d.

Destinations include Quang Ngai (118,000d, three hours) and all major towns on the main north-south line.

TRANSPORT FROM QUY NHON

DESTINATION	AIR	BUS	CAR/ MOTORBIKE	TRAIN (SOFT SEAT)
Danang	n/a	115,000d, 6hr,14 to 17 daily	7hr	5½hr, from 198,000d, 3 daily
HCMC	from 730,000d, 1hr, 1 daily	330,000d, 16hr, 10 daily	18hr	from 340,000d, 10hr, 3 daily,
Hanoi	from 1,300,000d, 1½hr, 6 weekly	from 520,000d, 23hr, 7 daily	around 26hr	from 750,000d, 17hr, 3 daily

Cha Ban Cham Area

The former Cham capital of Cha Ban (also known as Vijay and Quy Nhon) was located 26km north of Quy Nhon and 5km from Binh Dinh. While of archaeological importance, there's very little to see for the casual visitor. However, there are several interesting Cham structures dotted around the area.

Banh It Cham Towers

The most impressive of the area's Cham sites, this group of four towers sits atop a hill 20km to the north of Quy Nhon and is clearly visible from Hwy 1. The architecture of each tower is distinctly different, although all were built around the turn of the 12th century. The smaller, barrel-roofed tower has the most intricate carvings, although there's still a wonderfully toothy face looking down on it from the wall of the largest tower. A large Buddhist pagoda sits on the side of the hill under the lowest of the towers. There are great views of the surrounding countryside from the top of the hill.

The **towers** (Phuoc Hiep, Tuy Phuoc district; ⊘7-11am & 1.30-4.30pm) FREE are easily reached by taking Đ Tran Hung Dao out of Quy Nhon for about 30 minutes, when you'll see the towers in the distance to the right of the road. After the traffic lights joining the main highway, cross the bridge and turn right. Take the left turn heading up the hill to reach the entrance.

Duong Long Cham Towers

These **towers** (Binh Hoa, Tay Son district; ⊘7-11am & 1.30-4.30pm) FREE are harder to find, sitting in the countryside about 50km northwest of Quy Nhon. Dating from the late 12th century, the largest of the three brick towers (24m high) is embellished with granite ornamentation representing *naga* (a mythical serpent being with divine powers) and elephants (Duong Long means 'Towers of Ivory'). Over the doors are bas-reliefs of women, dancers, monsters and various animals. The corners of the structure are formed by enormous dragon heads.

It is best to visit the towers with a driver or a tour, as the site is reached by a succession of pretty country lanes through rice paddies and over rickety bridges.

Quang Trung Museum

Nguyen Hue, the second-oldest of the three brothers who led the Tay Son Rebellion, crowned himself Emperor Quang Trung in 1788. In 1789, Quang Trung led the campaign

---

THE LOST CITY OF CHAMPA

Cha Ban, which served as the capital of Champa from the year 1000 (after the loss of Indrapura/Dong Duong) until 1471, was attacked and plundered repeatedly by the Vietnamese, Khmers and Chinese.

In 1044 the Vietnamese prince Phat Ma occupied the city and carried off a great deal of booty along with the Cham king's wives, harem, female dancers, musicians and singers. Cha Ban was under the control of Jayavarman VII and the Khmer empire from 1190 to 1220. In 1377 the Vietnamese were defeated and their king was killed in an attempt to capture Cha Ban. The Vietnamese emperor Le Thanh Ton breached the eastern gate of the city in 1471 and captured the Cham king and 50 members of the royal family. During this, the last great battle fought by the Cham, 60,000 Cham were killed and 30,000 more were taken prisoner by the Vietnamese.

During the Tay Son Rebellion, Cha Ban served as the capital of central Vietnam, and was ruled by the eldest of the three Tay Son brothers. It was attacked in 1793 by the forces of Nguyen Anh (later Emperor Gia Long), but the assault failed. In 1799 they laid siege to the city again, under the command of General Vu Tinh, capturing it at last.

The Tay Son rebels soon reoccupied the port of Thi Nai (modern-day Quy Nhon) and then laid siege to Cha Ban themselves. The siege continued for over a year, and by June 1801, Vu Tinh's provisions were gone. Food was in short supply; all the horses and elephants had long since been eaten. Refusing to consider the ignominy of surrender, Vu Tinh had an octagonal wooden tower constructed. He filled it with gunpowder and, arrayed in his ceremonial robes, went inside and blew himself up. Upon hearing the news of the death of his dedicated general, Nguyen Anh wept.

that overwhelmingly defeated a Chinese invasion of 200,000 troops near Hanoi. This epic battle is still celebrated as one of the greatest triumphs in Vietnamese history.

During his reign, Quang Trung was something of a social reformer. He encouraged land reform, revised the system of taxation, improved the army and emphasised education, opening many schools and encouraging the development of Vietnamese poetry and literature. He died in 1792 at the age of 40. Communist literature portrays him as the leader of a peasant revolution whose progressive policies were crushed by the reactionary Nguyen dynasty, which came to power in 1802 and was overthrown by Ho Chi Minh in 1945.

The **Quang Trung Museum** (Phu Phong; admission 10,000d; ⊙8-11.30am & 1-4.30pm Mon-Fri) is built on the site of the brothers' house and encloses the original well and an ancient tamarind tree said to have been planted by the brothers. Displays include various statues, costumes, documents and artefacts from the 18th century, most of them labelled in English. Especially notable are the elephant-skin battle drums and gongs from the Bahnar tribe. The museum is also known for its demonstrations of *vo binh dinh*, a traditional martial art that is performed with a bamboo stick.

The museum is about 50km from Quy Nhon. Take Hwy 19 west for 40km towards Pleiku. The museum is about 5km north of the highway (the turn-off is signposted) in Phu Phong, Tay Son district.

Tuy Hoa

☑ 057 / POP 214,000

Currently being transformed by town planners into a vast, sprawling new city, Tuy Hoa is a somewhat soulless place characterised by the requisite vast plaza and multilaned boulevards. It's a possible overnight stop to break up a longer journey, especially for cyclists brave enough to tackle Hwy 1, but most visitors are just passing through.

The few sights the town has are all on hilltops visible from the main highway. There's a huge **seated Buddha** that greets you if you're approaching from the north. To the south of town the **Nhan Cham Tower** is an impressive sight, particularly when illuminated at night. The climb to the tower takes you through a small **botanic garden** and is rewarded with great views. On the same hill

HAM HO NATURE RESERVE

A beautiful nature reserve 55km from Quy Nhon, **Ham Ho** (☑ 057-388 0860; Tay Phu; admission 15,000d; ⊙7-11.30am & 1-4.30pm) can easily be combined with a trip to the Quang Trung Museum. Taking up a jungle-lined 3km stretch of clean, fish-filled river, the park is best enjoyed by kayak (70,000d). The further upriver you travel, the better the swimming spots. Accommodation (260,000d for a twin room) is available.

The road to Ham Ho is signposted to the south of Hwy 19 at Tay Son.

is a massive white **war memorial**, designed with sails that are vaguely reminiscent of the Sydney Opera House.

🛏 Sleeping & Eating

There are plenty of nondescript minihotels in addition to the following, and a glut of humble restaurants and street vendors along the main highway and Đ Tran Hung Dao.

The best dining is to be had on the beach, where a stretch of seafood shacks and *bia hoi* (draught beer) joints serve fresh seafood. Many charge by the kilogram, so be sure to agree on prices to avoid an expensive surprise.

Nhiet Doi Hotel   HOTEL $
(☑ 057-382 2424; www.nhietdoihotel.com; 216 Nguyen Hue; r 190,000-350,000d; ❄ 🛜) Modern minihotel with great-value rooms with attractive furnishings and comfortable beds. Staff speak little English but will help with motorbike rentals. Tasty meals (30,000d to 50,000d) are available.

Cendeluxe Hotel   HOTEL $$
(☑ 057-381 8818; www.cendeluxehotel.com; Đ Hai Duong; r/ste from US$55/121; ❄ @ 🛜 ⚊) This towering landmark dominates the city's skyline and claims most of the business trade as it's the most luxurious address in town. Rooms are very well equipped and spacious, and the pool area, spa, sky lounge and dining options are all excellent.

ⓘ Getting There & Away

AIR
Vietnam Airlines (☑ 057-382 6508; www.vietnamairlines.com; 353 Đ Tran Hung Dao) has five flights weekly to Hanoi (from 1,575,000d) and

EAST BY SOUTHEAST: VUNG RO BAY

Celebrated as Vietnam's most easterly point on the mainland, Vung Ro Bay is also famed for its beautiful and isolated bays, which hide some unspoilt beaches. It is also one of the deepest water ports in this part of Vietnam and hit the headlines back in February 1965 when a US helicopter detected the movement of a North Vietnamese supply ship in the area. Vung Ro was part of the alternative Ho Chi Minh Sea Trail and was being used to smuggle arms into South Vietnam for Viet Cong forces. The discovery of a sea supply route from north to south confirmed US suspicions and was used as justification to ramp up US involvement in the war. The small town of Vung Ro lies about 33km southeast of Tuy Hoa and can be reached by motorbike or car.

daily flights to HCMC (from 1,610,000d). The airport is 8km south of town.

BUS

From Tuy Hoa, there are very regular buses to Quy Nhon (46,000d, two hours) and Nha Trang (63,000d, three hours).

TRAIN

Tuy Hoa Train Station (☑ 057-382 3672; Đ Le Trung Kien) is on the road parallel to the highway, north of the main street. Destinations include Danang (eight hours) and Nha Trang (2½ hours).

Tuy Hoa to Nha Trang

♪ 058

The coastal drive between Tuy Hoa and Nha Trang on Hwy 1 provides tantalising glimpses of a number of remote and beautiful spots, while others are hidden away in the jungle along promontories or on secluded islands. Leave behind the guidebook for a day or two and go exploring. Money-changing facilities and ATMs are thin on the ground here, so plan ahead in Nha Trang, Tuy Hoa or Quy Nhon.

Dai Lanh Beach

Crescent-shaped Dai Lanh Beach has a split personality: a scruffy fishing village occupies the northern end, but yields to an attractive beach shaded by casuarina trees. The roar

of traffic from Hwy 1 does blight the setting, but when a new tunnel currently under construction is finished (scheduled for 2016), peace should return to Dai Lanh.

Accommodation options are grouped together in the fishing village. **Binh Lieu** (☑ 058-394 9138; Hwy 1; r 200,000-300,000d; ❄ 🛜) is the best of the minihotels, a new place with smart, well-equipped rooms; you pay more for a sea view (and will suffer less traffic noise). Fresh seafood features prominently at the beachside restaurants (mains from 50,000d to 150,000d).

Dai Lanh is 40km south of Tuy Hoa and 83km north of Nha Trang on Hwy 1.

Whale Island

About a kilometre south of Dai Lanh, a vast sand-dune causeway connects the mainland to Hon Gom, a mountainous peninsula almost 30km in length.

Boats for Whale Island leave from Hom Gom's main village, Dam Mon, set on a sheltered bay. Whale Island is a tiny speck on the map and home to the romantic and secluded **Whale Island Resort** (☑ 058-384 0501; www.whaleislandresort.com; s/d from US$33/45; 🛜), just a 15-minute boat ride from Dam Mon. It's fine place to get away from it all with good snorkelling and kayaking and a pretty beachside setting. Its rustic bamboo and timber (fan-cooled) bungalows are atmospheric, but the compulsory meals (US$28 per person per day) are expensive and meal times are set. Bus-boat transfers from Nha Trang cost US$20.

Rainbow Divers (contact their Nha Trang office, p236) has a permanent base on the island; two dives cost US$85. The scuba season is mid-January to mid-October. Whale sharks pass this way for a krill feed between April and July.

Doc Let Beach

One of Vietnam's best beaches, the chalk-white sands and shallow turquoise waters of Doc Let stretch for almost 18km, lining the shores of a huge bay.

The beach itself is divided into three sections. The northern part of the bay is where most of the tourism action is, with a cluster of beachfront hotels and cheaper guesthouses inland. Looming over the central section is the giant Hyundai shipyard and port, an important local employer but a real blot on the landscape. The isolated southern section is backed by a wooded promontory and is the place to really get away from it all.

There's little or no public transport, but with a rented bike it's easy to find your own piece of beachside paradise for the day.

🛏 Sleeping

Doc Let Resort   HOTEL $
(☑ 057-384 9152; bungalows 350,000-450,000d; ✳🕾) With a stunning beachfront location these aging but spacious bungalows are set in palm-shaded grounds and the restaurant serves up cheap grub. Lacks atmosphere, but worth considering.

★ Jungle Beach   BUNGALOWS $$
(☑ 057-366 2384; www.junglebeachvietnam.com; per person incl meals 500,000-750,000d; 🕾) Bagging an idyllic slab of beach heaven, this motley collection of basic rattan, bamboo-and-thatch huts and bungalows offers an end-of-the-road feel. There's a sociable vibe (meals are eaten together) and a delightful garden to enjoy. It *is* very isolated (but that's entirely the point) at the end of lonely road, 7km south of the shipyard.

★ Some Days of Silence   BOUTIQUE HOTEL $$$
(☑ 057-367 0952; www.somedaysresort.com; r US$110-120, bungalows US$170-180; ✳@🕾🏊) A simply stunning, artistically designed place that feels more an in-the-know retreat for beautiful people than a mere hotel. Elegant bungalows and rooms are lovingly decorated with works of art and feature four-poster beds, and bathrooms with pebble-detailing. There's a sublime tropical garden and white-sand beach, and the pagoda-style restaurant and adjoining terrace make a great setting for healthy, creative meals.

Paradise Resort   HOTEL $$$
(☑ 057-367 0480; www.vngold.com/doclet/paradise; per person incl meals US$45-50; ✳@🕾) This beachside place is a messy assortment of rooms (from many different eras), which are clean and presentable, if not easy on the eye. Aesthetics aside, the elderly French-Croat owner is a jolly soul who looks after his guests well, food is plentiful, beer cheap enough and the oceanic vistas are great.

ⓘ Getting There & Away

The turn-off for Doc Let is signposted just south of a toll road section on Hwy 1, around 4km past Ninh Hoa where there's a big sign for Hyundai Vinashin (shipyard). Continue 10km past photogenic salt fields, looking out for the signs to the resorts. Make a left turn through Doc Let village and then a right to the beach. Most of the hotels and resorts also offer some sort of transfer service for a fee.

There's a separate, direct (paved) road to Jungle Beach via the shipyard from the same Hwy 1 turn-off (look out for the signs to 'wild beach').

OFF THE BEATEN TRACK

GANH DA DIA

A smaller version of Ireland's Giant's Causeway, Ganh Da Dia is a spectacular outcrop of volcanic rock that juts into the ocean south of Quy Nhon. Half the fun is simply getting there, as the scenery in this coastal region is superb.

Ganh Da Dia is signposted from the small town of Chi Thanh, 68km south of Quy Nhon. Heading down Hwy 1, take the turning just past the river bridge on the northern side of town. The route to the coast meanders for 13km through a delightful pastural landscape of rice paddies and farming villages.

Consisting of hundreds of interlocked columns of volcanic rock, Ganh Da Dia was created millions of years ago as fluid molten basalt cooled. Some of the best sections are formed of incredibly regular pentagonal- and hexagonal-sided horizontal rocks. The Vietnamese call this place 'the cliff of stone plates', and it's regularly used by Buddhist monks for ceremonies.

You can bathe in the tiny rocky cove next to Ganh Da Dia, but the drop-dead gorgeous sandy beach on the south side of the bay, a five-minute walk away, is even more inviting. Fresh coconuts and snacks are sold by local villagers at the car park.

Continuing south (and avoiding Hwy 1) you can take a lovely coastal road to Tuy Hoa. Head inland (west) from Ganh Da Dia for 3.5km and then a side (paved) road heads south through sand dunes, past cacti and agave to the fishing village of An Hai, where a row of seafood restaurants faces the O Loan estuary and makes an ideal pit-stop.

From An Hai, it's 27km south to Tuy Hoa. The route has a few twists and turns, but the kilometre waymarks (which indicate the distance to Tuy Hoa) help guide you the right way.

Ninh Van Bay

Welcome to an alternate reality populated by European royalty, film stars and the otherwise rich and secretive. Sadly for the average punter, this place doesn't exist. Occupying a secluded bay with good snorkelling and kayaking abutting a dense jungle-covered peninsula, there are no roads to Six Senses Ninh Van Bay ([☑058-372 8222; www.sixsenses.com; villas US$690-1240; ⊖✳@🛜🏊]). The resort even has its own time zone – an hour ahead in an effort to encourage guests to enjoy the sunrise. The traditionally inspired architecture and the winding paths between buildings give the illusion of a jungle village – albeit one where every dwelling is an elegant two-storey villa, each with its own swimming pool. As you would expect for the price, the detail is superb and the setting is simply magical. Facilities include a wonderful Six Senses Spa and restaurants featuring Western and Asian cuisine.

Nha Trang

[☑] 058 / POP 375,000

Welcome to the beach capital of Vietnam. Loud and proud (say it!) the high-rise, high-energy resort of Nha Trang enjoys a stunning setting: ringed by a necklace of hills, with a sweeping crescent beach, the city's turquoise bay is dotted with tropical islands.

The beachfront has been given a huge makeover in recent years, with parks and sculpture gardens spread along the impressive shorefront, while the streets inland reveal a cosmopolitan array of dining options.

As the restaurants wind down, the nightlife cranks up – Nha Trang is a party town at heart, like any self-respecting resort should be. Forget the curfews of the capital; people play late in this town.

If cocktails and shooters aren't your flavour, there are some more sedate activities on offer. Try an old-school spa treatment with a visit to a mud bath or explore centuries-old Cham towers still standing in the centre of town.

This part of the country has its very own microclimate and the rains tend to come from October until December, a time best avoided if you are into lazing on the beach or diving in crystal-clear waters.

⊙ Sights

There are also several superb black-and-white photographic galleries in Nha Trang.

★ Nha Trang Beach   BEACH

(Map p232) Forming a magnificent sweeping arc, Nha Trang's 6km-long golden sand beach is the city's trump card. Various sections are designated for swimmers, where you won't be bothered by jetskis or boats. The turquoise water is fabulously inviting, and the promenade a delight to stroll.

Two popular lounging spots are the Sailing Club and Louisiane Brewhouse. If you head south of here, the beach gets quieter and it's possible to find a stretch of sand to yourself.

The best beach weather is generally before 1pm, as the afternoon sea breezes can whip up the sand.

During heavy rains, run-off from the rivers at each end of the beach flows into the bay, gradually turning it a murky brown. Most of the year, however, the sea is just like it appears in the brochures.

★ Po Nagar Cham Towers   BUDDHIST TEMPLE

(Thap Ba, Lady of the City; Map p231; admission 21,000d; ⊙6am-6pm) Built between the 7th and 12th centuries, these four Cham Towers are still actively used for worship by Cham, ethnic Chinese and Vietnamese Buddhists. Originally the complex had seven or eight towers, but only four towers remain, of which the 28m-high North Tower (Thap Chinh), which dates from AD 817, with its terraced pyramidal roof, vaulted interior masonry and vestibule, is the most magnificent.

The towers stand on a granite knoll 2km north of central Nha Trang on the banks of the Cai River. It's thought this site was first used for worship as early as the 2nd century AD. The original wooden structure was razed to the ground by attacking Javanese in AD 774, but was replaced by a stone-and-brick temple (the first of its kind) in 784.

The towers serve as the Holy See, honouring Yang Ino Po Nagar, the goddess of the Dua (Liu) clan, which ruled over the southern part of the Cham kingdom There are inscribed stone slabs scattered throughout the complex, most of which relate to history or religion and provide insight into the spiritual life and social structure of the Cham.

All of the temples face east, as did the original entrance to the complex, which is to the right as you ascend the hillock. In centuries past, worshippers passed through the pillared meditation hall, 10 pillars of which

Nha Trang

Nha Trang

can still be seen, before proceeding up the steep staircase to the towers.

In 918, King Indravarman III placed a gold *mukha-linga* (carved phallus with a human face painted on it) in the North Tower, but it was taken by Khmer raiders. This pattern of statues being destroyed or stolen and then replaced continued until 965, when King Jaya Indravarman IV replaced the gold *mukha-linga* with the stone figure, Uma (shakti, or female consort of Shiva), which remains to this day.

Above the entrance to the North Tower, two musicians, one of whose feet is on the head of the bull Nandin, flank a dancing four-armed Shiva. The sandstone doorposts are covered with inscriptions, as are parts of the walls of the vestibule. A gong and a drum stand under the pyramid-shaped ceiling of the antechamber. In the 28m-high pyramidal main chamber, there is a black-stone statue of the goddess Uma with 10 arms, two of which are hidden under her vest; she is seated and leaning back against a monstrous beast.

The Central Tower (Thap Nam) was built partly of recycled bricks in the 12th century on the site of a structure dating from the 7th century. It is less finely constructed than the other towers and has little ornamentation; the pyramidal roof lacks terracing or pilasters, although the interior altars were once covered with silver. There is a linga inside the main chamber.

The South Tower (Mieu Dong Nam), at one time dedicated to Sandhaka (Shiva),

still shelters a linga, while the richly ornamented Northwest Tower (Thap Tay Bac) was originally dedicated to Ganesh. To the rear of the complex is a less impressive museum with a few examples of Cham stonework.

To get here from central Nha Trang, take Đ Quang Trung (which becomes Đ 2 Thang 4) north across the Ha Ra and Xom Bong Bridges. Po Nagar can also be reached via the Tran Phu Bridge along the beachfront road.

This site has a continuing religious significance, so be sure to remove your shoes before entering.

Central Nha Trang

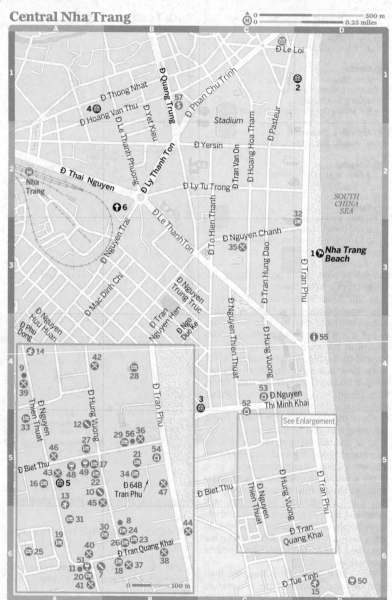

Long Son Pagoda

BUDDHIST TEMPLE

(Map p231; ⏱ 7.30-11.30am & 1.30-5.30pm) FREE
This striking pagoda was founded in the late
19th century. The entrance and roofs are
decorated with mosaic dragons constructed
of glass and ceramic tile, while the main

sanctuary is a hall adorned with modern in-
terpretations of traditional motifs.

Behind the pagoda is a huge white
Buddha (Map p231; Kim Than Phat To) seated on
a lotus blossom. Around the statue's base are
fire-ringed relief busts of Thich Quang Duc

Central Nha Trang

SOUTHEAST COAST NHA TRANG

and six other Buddhist monks who died in self-immolations in 1963.

The platform around the 14m-high Buddha has great views of Nha Trang and nearby rural areas. As you approach the pagoda from the street, the 152 stone steps up the hill to the Buddha begin to the right of the structure. Take some time to explore off to the left, where there's an entrance to another hall of the pagoda.

Beggars congregate within the complex, as do a number of scam artists. There's a persistent scam here, where visitors are approached by children (and occasionally older people) with pre-printed name badges claiming to work for the monks. After showing you around the pagoda, whether invited to or not, they will then demand money 'for the monks' or, if that fails, insist that you buy postcards for 200,000d. The best course of action is to firmly let them know you don't require their services when they first appear. If they persist, tell them you're not going to give them any money. If you do want to make a contribution towards the upkeep of the complex, leave it in the donation boxes as you would in any other pagoda.

The pagoda is located about 400m west of the train station, just off Đ 23 Thang 10.

Nha Trang Cathedral CHURCH

(Map p232; cnr Đ Nguyen Trai & Đ Thai Nguyen) **FREE** Built between 1928 and 1933 in French Gothic style, complete with stained-glass windows, Nha Trang Cathedral stands on a small hill overlooking the train station. It's a surprisingly elegant building given that it was constructed of simple cement blocks. Some particularly colourful Vietnamese touches include the red neon outlining the crucifix, the pink back-lighting on the tabernacle and the blue neon arch and white neon halo over the statue of St Mary.

In 1988 a Catholic cemetery not far from the church was disinterred to make room for a new railway building. The remains were brought to the cathedral and reburied in the cavities behind the wall of plaques that line the ramp up the hill.

Alexandre Yersin Museum MUSEUM

(Map p232; ✉ 058-382 2355; 10 Đ Tran Phu; admission 28,000d; ◷ 7.30-11am & 2-4.30pm Mon-Fri, 8-11am Sat) Highly popular in Vietnam, Dr Alexandre Yersin (1863–1943) founded Nha Trang's Pasteur Institute in 1895. He learned to speak Vietnamese fluently, introduced rubber and quinine-producing trees to Vietnam, and discovered the rat-borne microbe that causes bubonic plague.

You can see Yersin's library and office at this small, interesting museum; displays include laboratory equipment (such as astronomical instruments) and a fascinating 3-D photo viewer.

Tours are conducted in French, English and Vietnamese, and a short film on Yersin's life is shown.

Yersin travelled throughout the central highlands and recorded his observations. During this period he came upon the site of what is now Dalat and recommended that a hill station be established there.

Today, the Pasteur Institute in Nha Trang coordinates vaccination and hygiene programs for the country's southern coastal region. The institute produces vaccines and carries out medical research and testing to European standards. Physicians at the clinic here offer medical advice to around 70 patients a day.

Hon Chong Promontory LANDMARK

(Map p231; admission 11,000d) The narrow granite promontory of Hon Chong offers fine views of the mountainous coastline north of Nha Trang and the nearby islands.

The beach here has a more local flavour than Nha Trang Beach (but the accompanying refuse is unpleasant). Still, it's fun to watch local kids do Acapulco-style swan dives into the ocean.

There is a reconstructed traditional Ruong residence and a cafe; a taxi here from the city centre is around 30,000d.

About 300m south of Hon Chong (towards Nha Trang) and a few dozen metres from the beach is tiny Hon Do (Red Island), which has a Buddhist temple on top. To the northeast is Hon Rua (Tortoise Island), which really does resemble a tortoise. The two islands of Hon Yen (Bird's-Nest Island) are off in the distance to the east.

National Oceanographic Museum MUSEUM

(Map p231; ✉ 058-359 0037; 1 Cau Da; adult/child 30,000/12,000d; ◷ 6am-6pm) Housed in a grand French-colonial building in the port district of Cau Da at the far south end of Nha Trang, this poorly maintained museum has 60,000 or so jars of pickled marine specimens, stuffed birds and sea mammals, and displays of local boats and fishing artefacts. Unfortunately, there are also live seals kept here in small, dirty tanks.

VINPEARL LAND

Nha Trang's answer to Disneyland (well, sort of), the island resort of **Vinpearl Land** (✉ 058-359 0111; www.vinpearlland.com; Hon Tre Island; adult/child 500,000/350,000d; ◷ 8am-9pm) has funfair rides, a water park, arcade games, aquarium and plenty of other attractions. Compared to some adventure parks it feels a little dated, but it will keep children amused for a full day, including the world's longest over-the-sea cable car ride and one of the biggest wave pools in Southeast Asia. The leading attraction is undoubtedly the water park, with more than 20 serious slides for adrenalin-seekers.

Most visitors arrive by cable car or fast boat, both included in the ticket price. Both depart from the coast just south of Cau Da dock area.

Note that Vinpearl does feature dolphin shows, and animal 'performances' that feature monkeys dressed in costume.

Long Thanh Gallery
ART GALLERY

(Map p232; ☎058-382 4875; www.longthanhart.com; 126 Đ Hoang Van Thu; ☉8am-5.30pm Mon-Sat) FREE This gallery showcases the work of Vietnam's most prominent photographer. Long Thanh developed his first photo in 1964 and continues to shoot extraordinary black-and-white images of everyday Vietnamese moments and compelling portraits. The powerful images capture the heart and soul of Vietnam.

Do Dien Khanh Gallery
ART GALLERY

(Map p232; ☎058-351 2202; www.ddk-gallery.com; 126B Đ Hong Bat; ☉8am-6pm Mon-Fri) FREE Do Dien Khanh is a welcoming host and very talented photographer of Vietnamese landscapes and life – his portraits of surrounding Cham communities are hauntingly beautiful.

Mai Loc Gallery
ART GALLERY

(Map p232; www.mailocphotos.com; 99 Đ Nguyen Thien Thuat; ☉8-11am & 2.30-10.30pm) A private gallery that showcases the powerful, highly accomplished monochrome photography of Mai Loc, a native of Nha Trang. Ask him about his life story (he's an ex-gold miner, *cyclo* driver and tour guide).

🏃 Activities

The Nha Trang area is a key diving, surfing, wake-boarding, parascending, white-water rafting and mountain-biking centre. Boat trips around the bay and up the Cai river are also a great day out.

Islands

Island tours are a big part of the Nha Trang experience.

Hon Yen
ISLAND TOURS

(Bird's-Nest Island) Also known as Salangane Island, this is the two lump-shaped islands visible from Nha Trang Beach. These and other islands off Khanh Hoa province are the source of Vietnam's finest *salangane* (swiftlet) nests. There is a small, secluded beach here. The 17km trip out to the islands takes three to four hours by small boat from Nha Trang.

Hon Mieu
ISLAND TOURS

This is billed as an outdoor **aquarium** (Ho Ca Tri Nguyen; admission 50,000d) but it's actually a fish-breeding farm, where over 40 species of fish, crustacean and other marine creatures are raised. Surrounding the tanks are an incredibly kitsch concrete collection of giant shrimps, fang-bearing sharks and so on.

Hon Mieu is included in most island-hopping boat tours. DIY travellers can catch one of the regular ferries that travel here from Cau Da dock.

Hon Mun
SNORKELLING

(Ebony Island) Pretty Hon Mun island is well known as a snorkelling and dive site. The coral is in fair condition and visibility usually good, but it can get very crowded as it's on the main day-tripping agenda. Litter can also be a big issue.

Hon Mot
SNORKELLING

Sandwiched neatly between Ebony Island and Hon Tam, or Silkworm Island, is tiny Hon Mot, a popular place for snorkelling.

Hon Tre
THEME PARK

(Bamboo Island) This large island is totally dominated by the sprawling Vinpearl Land amusement park – you'll see the Hollywood-style sign from afar. You can access this island by cable car or boat.

Hon Lao
ISLAND TOURS

(Monkey Island) A tourist trap popular with local tourists, the 1000 or so resident monkeys on this island are accustomed to receiving food handouts (peanuts and potato chips are for sale). However, these are wild animals and should be treated as such. Bear in mind that monkey bites are a possible source of rabies.

Aside from being unwilling to participate in a cuddle, the monkeys are materialistic. They'll grab the sunglasses off your face or snatch a pen from your shirt pocket and run off.

A word of warning: there's also a bear-and-monkey show that you may want to avoid. Travellers have reported seeing the animals being abused.

Diving

Nha Trang is Vietnam's most popular scuba-diving centre, although not necessarily its best. Visibility averages 15m but can be as much as 30m, depending on the season. February to September is considered the best time to dive, while October to December is the worst time of year.

There are around 25 dive sites in the area. There are no wrecks to visit, but some sites have good drop-offs and there are a few small underwater caves to explore. Frankly, it's not world-class diving, but the waters support a good variety of soft and hard corals, and a reasonable number of small reef fish.

A full-day outing including boat transport, two dives and lunch typically costs between US$60 and US$85 with a professional dive school. Snorkellers can usually tag along for US$15 to US$20.

Most dive operators also offer a range of dive courses, including a 'discover diving' program for uncertified first-time divers to experience the underwater world with the supervision of a qualified dive master. PADI courses start at US$340, SSI are a little less.

There are a dozen or so dive operators with offices in the tourist centre of Nha Trang. We've heard reports about the odd dodgy set-up not following responsible diving practices and even using fake PADI/SSI accreditation. These tend to charge ridiculously cheap prices (as low as US$35 for two dives).

Stick to reputable operators such as the following recommended schools:

Mark Scott Dive Center DIVING
(Map p232; ☑ 0122 903 7795; www.divingvietnam. com; 24/4 Đ Hung Vuong) Owned by a larger-than-life Texan, an instructor since 1991, this new school has quickly established an excellent reputation. SSI courses are offered.

Sailing Club Divers DIVING
(Map p232; ☑ 058-352 2788; www.sailingclubdiv-ers.com; 72-74 Đ Tran Phu) Offers professional instruction, modern equipment and multilingual instructors. This is the underwater arm of the famous Sailing Club.

Angel Dive DIVING
(Map p232; ☑ 058-352 2461; www.angeldiveviet-nam.info; 1/33 Đ Tran Quang Khai) Reliable operator with English, French and German instruction, plus the choice of PADI or SSI certification. Snorkelling trips cost US$20 per person.

Rainbow Divers DIVING
(Map p232; ☑ 058-352 4351; www.divevietnam. com; 90A Đ Hung Vuong) Large, well-established PADI dive school, part of a nationwide chain. Here at HQ, there is also a popular restaurant and bar.

Adventure Sports

From mountain biking to white-water rafting, Nha Trang offers lots of activities to get the pulse racing.

Vietnam Active ADVENTURE SPORTS
(Map p232; ☑ 058-351 5821; www.vietnamac-tive.com; 47 B1 Nguyen Thien Thuat) This well-organised new outfit offers a diverse range of excellent activities including mountain-biking trips (from US$45 for four people) to scuba-diving courses. Exact prices depend upon numbers. Stretch those aching limbs afterwards at one of their Hatha or Ashtanga yoga classes.

Shamrock Adventures RAFTING, KAYAKING
(Map p232; ☑ 058-352 7548; www.shamrockad-ventures.vn; Đ Tran Quang Khai; trips per person incl lunch from US$40) Offers white-water rafting (though it's not that dramatic by international standards) which can be combined with some mountain biking as well as kayak and fishing trips.

River Trips

A impressive broad estuary, the Cai river just north of central Nha Trang is best explored as day trip by boat.

Nha Trang River Tour BOAT TRIP
(☑ 0914 047 406; www.nhatrangrivertour.com; 24 Luong Dinh Cua; from US$40 per person) Pham is a well-organised, interesting guide and his tours are a worthwhile alternative to the island cruises, concentrating on cultural sights and cottage industries (rice-paper making, mat weavers, embroidery) along the Cai river.

Spas & Thermal Baths

There is a burgeoning spa industry in Nha Trang. However, locals swear that the only way to get really clean is to get deep down and dirty in a natural mud bath, and there are now three places dotted around Nha Trang where you can get stuck in (the mud). Try to avoid weekends, when Vietnamese families descend en masse. The best places include the following:

★**I Resort** THERMAL BATHS
(☑ 058-383 8838; www.i-resort.vn; 19 Xuan Ngoc, Vinh Ngoc; ◷7am-8pm) Just the place to really indulge, this new upmarket thermal spa is the most attractive of the three mudfests around Nha Trang, with hot mineral mud baths (250,000d per person for four people), lovely bathing pools and even waterfalls. The rural setting is gorgeous, with distant mountain views, and there's a decent restaurant and spa/massage centre. Budget spending at least half a day here, it's well worth it. Call for a shuttle (20,000d one way) from your hotel.

It's 7km northwest of the centre, a taxi here is about 130,000d

Thap Ba Hot Spring Center THERMAL BATHS
(Map p231; ☑ 058-383 4939; www.thapbahot-spring.com.vn; 25 Ngoc Son; ◷7am-7.30pm)

TRIPPING THE BAY BY BOAT

The 71 offshore islands around Nha Trang are renowned for the remarkably clear water surrounding them. Trips to these islands have been a huge draw for years now, and virtually every hotel and travel company in town books island-hopping boat tours.

Back in the day (well the 1990s) party boat tours involved a bumpy ride out to sea on a leaky fishing boat, copious joints and rice wine shots in a 'floating bar' (a tube in the ocean). Unsurprisingly, local party officials deemed the ganja and drinking games a bit too counter-revolutionary for their tastes.

Today there's more of a choice – with everything from backpacker booze cruises to family-geared outings.

Frankly, most of these trips are extremely touristy, involving whistle-stop visits to the Tri Nguyen Aquarium (admission 50,000d), some snorkelling on a degraded reef and a bit of beach time (beach admissions 30,000d). The booze cruises feature (very) organised entertainment with a DJ on the deck (or a cheesy boy band) and lots of drinking games. If this sounds like your idea of hell, well, you've been warned. The boat trip over, the mayhem often rumbles on to various bars, helping cement Nha Trang's reputation as a party town.

Keep the following tips in mind:

➡ Choose the right tour. Some are geared towards Asian families, others are booze cruises aimed solely at the backpacker market.

➡ Remember sunscreen and drink plenty of water.

➡ Entrance charges to the aquarium and beach are not usually included.

➡ If you're more interested in snorkelling than drinking, the dive schools' trips will be more appropriate.

Some decent boat-trip operators include the following:

Funky Monkey (Map p232; ☑ 058-352 2426; www.funkymonkeytour.com.vn; 75A Đ Hung Vuong; cruise incl pick-up 100,000d) This backpacker fun–geared trip includes live entertainment from the Funky Monkey boy band, as well as the usual stops.

Nha Trang Tours (Map p232; ☑ 058-352 4471; www.nhatrangtour.com.vn; 1/24 Đ Tran Quang Khai) Budget party-themed booze cruises for US$8 or snorkelling trips for around US$15.

Khanh Hoa Tourist Information (☑ 058-352 8000; khtourism@dng.vnn.vn; Đ Tran Phu; cruise incl lunch 349,000d) For something a little different, consider a far-flung boat trip to beautiful Van Phong Bay. The two-hour trip there puts many off, but the remote, secluded bays certainly help compensate. Contact the tourist office for details and bookings.

This was the original hot thermal mud centre, and it remains decent value. For 250,000/500,000d you get a single/double wooden bathtub full of gooey mud, or it's 120,000d per person for a communal slop-up. There are also mineral water swimming pools, though the more expensive VIP packages are overpriced. Located 7km northwest of Nha Trang (130,000d in a taxi).

To get here by yourself, follow the signpost on the second road to the left past the Po Nagar Cham Towers and continue along the winding road for 2.5km.

100 Egg Mud Bath   THERMAL BATHS
(Tam Bun Tram Trung; ☑ 058-371 1733; www.tam-buntramtrung.vn; Nguyen Tat Thanh, Phuoc Trung;

☺ 8am-7pm) Enjoying a pretty valley location 6km southwest of Nha Trang, this place gets its names from the egg-shaped private pods (300,000d/180,000d per adult/child) where couples or kids can indulge in a little mud play. All kinds of mud plastering (250,000d), wraps and scrubs are offered. You'll also find pools and tubs (that can be filled with herbs and essential oils) scattered around this huge complex, which also has a restaurant.

From the Cau Binh Tan bridge on the southwest side of town head along Đ Nguyen Tat Thanh until you reach the highway at Phuoc Trung, it's just over the road from here and clearly signposted.

Vy Spa
SPA

(Map p232; ☑ 0128 275 8662; 78B Đ Tue Tinh; ⊙ 8am-9pm) This is a simple, fine-value place that's not really a 'spa' (more a converted store), but the massages and treatments are superb value and professional. Chose from Vietnamese, Thai or Swedish massages (all around 200,000d per hour) or try a facial (150,000d) or scrub.

Su Spa
SPA

(Map p232; ☑ 058-352 3242; www.suspa.vn; 93 Đ Nguyen Thien Thuat; ⊙ 8am-9.30pm) It's right in the heart of the city, but the relaxed atmosphere and attention should let you banish all those urban blues. One of the most expensive spas in town, it's stylishly designed and offers good scrubs, rubs, tubs and body massages (from US$24).

☞ Tours

Brewery Tour
BEER

(Map p232; ☑ 058-352 1948; www.louisianebrewhouse.com.vn; Louisiane Brewhouse, 29 Đ Tran Phu; tour 200,000d) Learn all about microbrewing and how malt and hops become ale and lager on the informative tours run by the Louisiane.

Lanterns Tours
CULTURE

(Map p232; www.lanternsvietnam.com; 34/6 Đ Nguyen Thien Thuat; tour US$25) Taking you to the non-touristy town of Ninh Hoa, this day trip run by the non-profit restaurant Lanterns includes visits to local markets, a ride in a bullock cart, lunch with a local family and return transport. A minimum of three people is required.

🛏 Sleeping

Nha Trang has hundreds of hotels, from dives to the divine, and most places are within a blocks or two of the beach. Top-end choices line Đ Tran Phu, the waterfront boulevard; budget places tend to be a little inland.

There is a cluster of cheapies on an alleyway at 64 Đ Tran Phu, very close to the beach. All offer similar air-conditioned rooms for around US$10 or so, cheaper if you go with the flow of a fan. Most budget places don't include breakfast.

You'll find a group of good new hotels close to where Đ Hung Vuong meets Đ Tran Quang Khai.

Discounts of 20% to 30% are common in midrange and top-end places when business is slow.

★ Sunny Sea
HOTEL $

(Map p232; ☑ 058-352 5244; http://sunnyhotel.com.vn; 64B/9 Đ Tran Phu; r US$10-15; ❋ @ ☎) An exceptional place owned by a welcoming local couple (a doctor and nurse) and Kim, the ever-helpful receptionist. Newly renovated, the rooms boast new mattresses, minibar, modern bathrooms and some have a balcony. The location is great, on a quiet lane just off the beach, and there's a lift.

Sao Mai Hotel
HOTEL $

(Map p232; ☑ 058-352 6412; www.saomainhatranghotel.com; 99 Đ Nguyen Thien Thuat; dm US$6, r US$12-25; ❋ @ ☎) Long-standing budget favourite that's moved a little upmarket but remains superb value, with friendly management and 32 immaculately clean, spacious rooms. The five-bed dorm has air-con, en-suite bathroom and lockers.

Mojzo Inn
HOSTEL $

(Map p232; ☑ 0988 879 069; 120/36 Đ Nguyen Thien Thuat; dm US$7, r US$16-19; ❋ @ ☎) The name is more cocktail list than hotel bed, but this funky new hostel gets most things right, with well-designed dorms and a lovely cushion-scattered lounge area.

Ngoc Thach
HOTEL $

(Map p232; ☑ 058-352 5988; ngocthachhotel@gmail.com; 6I Quan Tran, Đ Hung Vuong; r US$15-18; ❋ ☎) A great deal, the spacious, modern rooms (some with balcony) here are in excellent shape and have a real sparkle considering the modest tarrifs. There's a lift.

Perfume Grass Inn
HOTEL $

(Map p232; ☑ 058-352 4286; www.perfume-grass.com; 4A Đ Biet Thu; r US$14-35; ❋ @ ☎) This welcoming inn has plenty of character, particularly the pricier rooms with their wooden panelling and floors. Free breakfast, a slim garden and friendly English-speaking management add to the appeal.

Ha Tram Hotel
HOTEL $

(Map p232; ☑ 058-352 1819; http://hatramhotel.weebly.com; 64B/5 Đ Tran Phu; r US$8-14; ❋ @ ☎) One of the smarter hotels on budget alley; most rooms here are light and bright, well equipped and include smart bathrooms. The larger ones have two double beds.

Mai Huy Hotel   HOTEL **$**
(Map p232; ☑ 058-352 7553; maihuyhotel.com; 7H Quan Tran, Đ Hung Vuong; r with fan/air-con from US$8/14; ❄ @ ♠) Long-standing backpacking base where the family owners take good care of their guests. The rooms vary quite a bit; pay a little more and things smarten up considerably.

Rosy Hotel   HOTEL **$**
(Map p232; ☑ 058-352 2661; www.rosyhotelnha trang.com; 20 Quan Tran, Đ Hung Vuong; r 220,000-340,000d; ❄ @ ♠) A well-run modern mini-hotel on an alley off Đ Hung Vuong, the Rosy offers comfort and cleanliness for very modest rates; you pay a bit more for a breezy balcony.

Backpacker's House   HOSTEL **$**
(Map p232; ☑ 058-352 3884; www.backpackers house.net; 54G Đ Nguyen Thien Thuat; dm US$7-8, r US$12-24; ❄ @) For those about to party, this hostel could fit the bill as there's a sociable vibe (there's a bar-restaurant downstairs). Dorms are adequate, though the bathrooms could be cleaner; rooms are smart.

Hotel An Hoa   HOTEL **$**
(Map p232; ☑ 058-352 4029; www.anhoahotel. vn; 64B/6 Đ Tran Phu; r with fan/air-con US$10-12; ❄ @ ♠) A reliable option in budget alley, this friendly hostel has small rooms with no windows or air-con, or bigger and better rooms with larger bathrooms and a smarter trim.

Perfume Grass Inn 2   HOTEL **$**
(Map p232; ☑ 058-352 2588; www.perfume-grass.com; 64B/8 Tran Phu; s US$6-8, d US$10-12; ❄ @ ♠) Certainly worth considering if you're short on dong, this decent no-frills place has functional tiled rooms with low ceilings; you pay a little more for a balcony.

Le Duong   HOTEL **$$**
(Map p232; 5 & 6 Quan Tran, Đ Hung Vuong; r 450,000-700,000d; ❄ ♠) New in 2013, this inviting modern hotel has 50 beautifully presented, light, spacious rooms with pale furniture and white linen that represent excellent value. Prices are flexible to a degree, depending on demand.

Golden Summer Hotel   HOTEL **$$**
(Map p232; ☑ 058-352 6662; www.goldensummer hotel.com.vn; 22-23 Tran Quang Khai; r US$25-50; ❄ ♠) Modish new hotel, with a super-stylish lobby and inviting, modern rooms all with nice artistic touches such as statement photography on the walls. The location is excellent with myriad restaurants and the beach a short stroll away.

Summer Hotel   HOTEL **$$**
(Map p232; ☑ 058-352 2186; www.thesummer hotel.com.vn; 34C Đ Nguyen Thien Thuat; r US$32-106; ❄ @ ♠ ⛱) Smart three-star hotel with affordable prices, and rooms with high comfort levels and appealing trim. The pool is on the rooftop.

Nhi Phi Hotel   HOTEL **$$**
(Map p232; ☑ 058-352 4585; www.nhiphihotel.vn; 10A Đ Biet Thu; r US$45-75; ❄ @ ♠ ⛱) Imposing new Sinh Tourist–owned colossus in the heart of the uptown action with an amazing lobby atrium, small rooftop pool and well-furnished rooms (those above the 7th floor have fine city views).

Green Peace E Hotel   HOTEL **$$**
(Map p232; ☑ 058-352 2835; www.greenpeaceho tel.com.vn; 102 Đ Nguyen Thien Thuat; r 550,000-750,000d; ❄ @ ♠) The reception experience (complete with an overload of tour advertising and slightly uninterested staff) is off-putting, but persevere and you'll find the cream-and-white rooms are quite smart and contemporary, with flat-screen TVs and hip bathrooms.

Golden Rain Hotel   HOTEL **$$**
(Map p232; ☑ 058-352 7799; www.goldenrainhotel. com; 142 Đ Hung Vuong; r US$29-58; ❄ @ ♠ ⛱) Conveniently located and rooms are elegant enough; some include large windows. The rooftop pool and gym round things off nicely.

King Town Hotel   HOTEL **$$**
(Map p232; ☑ 058-352 5818; www.kingtownhotel. com.vn; 92 Đ Hung Vuong; r US$23-43; ❄ @ ♠ ⛱) On the popular Hung Vuong strip, King Town has a good range of rooms with silk trim and stylish bathrooms. Tucked away on the top floor is a rooftop swimming pool with city views.

La Suisse Hotel   HOTEL **$$**
(Map p232; ☑ 058-352 4353; www.lasuissehotel. com; 3/4 Đ Tran Quang Khai; r US$30-35; ❄ @ ♠) Switzerland is famous for its hoteliers and there is a touch of la Suisse about the efficient service here. Rooms are spacious, but the decor (think flowery bedspreads) is looking passé.

Ha Van Hotel   HOTEL **$$**
(Map p232; ☑ 058-352 5454; www.in2vietnam.com; 3/2 Đ Tran Quang Khai; r from US$28; ❄ @ ♠) The rooms here are comfortable and spacious

enough, but the tired carpets and dated furniture are in need of makeover. However, as staff are well trained and welcoming, travel info is good, and breakfast is included, it's still worth considering.

★ Mia Resort Nha Trang HOTEL $$$
(☎058-398 9666; www.mianhatrang.com; Bai Dong, Cam Hai Dong; r/villa US$210/270; ☀❋@☎☎) First impressions are electric at this exceptional hotel. Oceanic. The sense of occasion as you check in at Mia's al fresco reception is quite something, high above a horizon-filling expanse of big blue. You can relax now.

The sky-high standards continue effortlessly through the resort: simply superb accommodation units (each with sea view) all with outdoor bathrooms, a 40m pool, a stunning waveside restaurant. Oh, and the setting – nestled in a private cove beach – is breathtaking.

Evason Ana Mandara Resort & Spa RESORT HOTEL $$$
(Map p231; ☎058-352 2522; www.evasonresorts.com; Đ Tran Phu; villa US$279-537; ❋@☎☎) Exuding taste, this fine hotel consists of a charming cluster of spacious oceanside villas that have a colonial feel thanks to the classic furnishings and four-poster beds. The location, on prime beachfront plot in the south of the city, with two swimming pools (one 30m) is the best in town. Other perks include the Western and Vietnamese restaurants, Six Senses spa and well-stocked library.

Novotel Nha Trang HOTEL $$$
(Map p232; ☎058-625 6900; www.novotel.com/6033; 50 Đ Tran Phu; r/ste from US$125/249; ❋@☎☎) Stylish and very contemporary, this oceanfront hotel features split-level rooms with sunken bath-tubs – invest in a sea view on the upper floor to see Nha Trang in all its glory. Staff are very well trained and helpful. The gym is well equipped for a workout, though the pool is on the small side.

Sheraton Nha Trang Hotel & Spa HOTEL $$$
(Map p232; ☎058-388 0000; www.sheraton.com/nhatrang; 26-28 Đ Tran Phu; r from US$163, ste from US$291; ❋@☎☎) One of the tallest buildings in Nha Trang, the Sheraton dominates the oceanfront boulevard, and the views from its cocktail lounge are simply staggering. Rooms are spacious and modern with open-plan bathrooms, however wi-fi is not included in the rates. Check the web for specials as low as US$120 a night.

✖ Eating

As a resort town, Nha Trang caters to a decidedly international clientele and there's an array of cosmopolitan flavours to savour: from Cretan to Indian. Đ Tran Quang Khai and Đ Biet Thu are popular hunting grounds, but more authentic Vietnamese grub is found further afield. Seafood-lovers are in for a treat with fresh fish, crab, shrimp and an assortment of exotic shells on offer.

For a traditional local experience, try **Dam Market** (Map p231; Đ Trang Nu Vuong; ⊙6am-4pm), which has a colourful collection of stalls, including *com chay* (vegetarian) options, in the 'food court'.

Nha Hang Yen's VIETNAMESE $
(Map p232; 3/2A Tran Quang Khai; dishes 55,000-120,000d; ⊙7am-9.30pm; ☎) Stylish restaurant with a hospitable atmosphere and a winning line-up of flavoursome clay-pot, noodle and rice dishes. Lilting traditional music and waitresses in *ao dai* add to the vibe.

Omar's Tandoori Cafe INDIAN $
(Map p232; www.omarsindianrestaurant.com; 89B Đ Nguyen Thien Thuat; mains 55,000-136,000d; set meal 150,000d; ⊙noon-10pm; ☎) For a true taste of the subcontinent, look no further. Dishes include a superb rogan josh (120,000d), delicious butter chicken (79,000d) and authentic naan bread.

Hy Lap GREEK $
(Map p232; 1 Đ Tran Quang Khai; meals 30,000-75,000d; ⊙noon-10pm) Casual, inexpensive hole-in-the-wall Greek place run by an extremely welcoming Cretan couple. Only has six tables (all outside, so if it's raining...) but good for mousaka, souvlaki or a salad.

Au Lac VEGETARIAN $
(Map p232; 28C Đ Hoang Hoa Tham; meals 15,000-30,000d; ⊙11am-7pm; ✐) Long-running vegan/vegetarian near the corner of Đ Nguyen Chanh. A mixed plate is just about the best value meal you can find in Nha Trang.

Café des Amis CAFE $
(Map p232; 2D Đ Biet Thu; dishes 27,000-110,000d; ⊙7am-9.30pm; ☎) A backpacker favourite thanks to cheap eats and plentiful beer, this place has a strong selection of Vietnamese dishes, inexpensive seafood and a pick-and-mix of international dishes.

★**Lac Canh Restaurant** VIETNAMESE $$
(Map p231; 44 Đ Nguyen Binh Khiem; dishes 30,000-150,000d; ⊙11am-8.45pm) A totally local experience, this bustling, smoky, scruffy and highly enjoyable place is rammed most nights with groups firing up the table-top barbecues (beef is the speciality, but there are other meats and seafood, too). Note that there are a few interesting specialities not on the English menu including spicy stir-fried frog and noodles with crab eggs (65,000d). Closes quite early.

★**Nha Trang Xua** VIETNAMESE $$
(Thai Thong, Vinh Thai; dishes 52,000-210,000d; ⊙8am-9.30pm; 🛜) A classic Vietnamese restaurant set in a beautiful old house in the countryside surrounded by rice paddies and a lotus pond, around 7km west of town (100,000d in a taxi). Think a refined menu, beautiful presentation and atmospheric surrounds. Highlights include the Vietnamese salads, five-spice beef and seafood.

Oh! Sushi JAPANESE $$
(Map p232; ☑058-352 5729; www.ohsushibar. com; 17C Đ Hung Vuong ; meals 70,000-250,000d; ⊙11am-11pm) Intimate, highly authentic Japanese restaurant where you're greeted with a warm *'irashaimase'* (welcome) on arrival. Sit on a stool and watch the chefs slice 'n' dice, then feast on udon, soba or a bento-style set meal on one of the little tables (there are more upstairs).

Lanterns VIETNAMESE $$
(Map p232; www.lanternsvietnam.com; 34/6 Đ Nguyen Thien Thuat; dishes 48,000-158,000d; ⊙7.30am-9.30pm; 🛜🖉) Now in superb new premises with an expansive terrace, this restaurant supports local orphanages and provides scholarships programs. Flavours are predominantly Vietnamese, such as lemon and chilli pork and tofu curry, with set menus available (from 108,000d), plus a few international offerings. Cooking classes and tours are also offered.

Louisiane Brewhouse INTERNATIONAL $$
(Map p232; www.louisianebrewhouse.com.vn; 29 Đ Tran Phu; mains 62,000-360,000d; ⊙7am-1am; 🛜) It's not only the beer that draws a crowd here, as there is an eclectic menu with breakfast classics, superb salads, fish and seafood (red snapper is 140,000d) and Vietnamese, Japanese and Italian dishes. The beachside setting is superb with tables grouped around a pool and giant copper beer vats.

Lang Nuong Phu Dong Hai San SEAFOOD $$
(Map p231; Đ Tran Phu; dishes 30,000-165,000d; ⊙2pm-3am) The decor is basic (think plastic chairs and strip lights) but the seafood is fresh and delicious. Choose from scallops, crab, prawns and lobster, all at market prices.

The Refuge INTERNATIONAL $$
(Map p232; www.refuge-nhatrang.com; 1L Đ Hung Vuong; 7.30am-10pm; ⊙mains 60,000-165,000d; ❊🛜) A Swiss-owned log cabin–style restaurant with great crêpes, salads (try the goat's cheese), cheeses and grilled beef and lamb steaks (you choose your own sauce). Wine by the glass costs 40,000d to 65,000d. Unusually around here, the premises are air-conditioned, so it's a real retreat from the tropical heat.

Le Petit Bistro FRENCH $$
(Map p232; ☑058-352 7201; 26D Đ Tran Quang Khai; mains 50,000-250,000d; ⊙lunch & dinner; ❊🛜) Arguably the most popular of the French restaurants with the French crowd (always a good sign), this is the place for the *fromage* you have been pining for, some select cold cuts or duck specialities. The wine list is professional for those who like to quaff.

Veranda INTERNATIONAL $$
(Map p232; 66 Đ Tran Phu; mains 48,000-172,000d; set menu 255,000d; ⊙7am-10pm; ❊🛜) Stylish little promenade-facing restaurant with an international outlook to the menu: vegie curry (48,000d), egg noodles with calamari (62,000d) and beef tenderloin (160,000d). There's an air-conditioned dining room and a terrace.

Truc Linh 2 VIETNAMESE $$
(Map p232; ☑058-352 1089; 21 Đ Biet Thu; dishes 44,000-190,000d; ⊙6am-9.45pm) The Truc Linh empire includes several eateries in the heart of backpackersville. Number 2 has a pretty garden setting and serves dishes from seafood to barbecued meats.

★**Sailing Club** INTERNATIONAL $$$
(Map p232; ☑058-352 4628; www.sailingclub nhatrang.com; 72-74 Đ Tran Phu; meals 180,000-400,000d; 🛜) A beachfront institution. People-watch from elegant seating by day, sip on a cocktail at sundown, dine on gourmet food under the stars and then burn it all off on the dance floor. There are three separate menus (Vietnamese, Italian and Indian) plus a smattering of other

international dishes including wraps for 150,000d – mix 'n' match as you please.

Grill House
INTERNATIONAL $$$

(Map p232; www.grillhousenhatrang.com; 1/18 Đ Tran Quang Khai; mains 55,000-450,000d; ☉11am-10pm; ❄ ⓐ) This grill restaurant offers meat lovers the chance to sate their appetite. Try the mixed grill, a bust-your-gut burger or a giant T-bone. Seafood is also on offer. There's Chilean wine by the glass (50,000d) and the premises are air-conditioned.

 Drinking

Pay serious attention to your drink (see boxed text below) and possessions (consult Dangers and Annoyances, opposite) if you're in the party bars of Nha Trang.

Many thefts have been reported from the Why Not? bar on Đ Tran Quang Khai.

★ Guava
LOUNGE BAR

(Map p232; www.guava.vn; 17 Đ Biet Thu; ☉7am-1am; ⓐ) Groovy Guava is the only game in town for quality electronic music – DJs spin house and lounge here on weekends. There's always a friendly vibe, good service and a busy pool table. Choose from sunken sofas inside or a leafy garden patio at the rear. Pub grub here is filling and good value, try the Sunday 'hangover breakfast'.

Sailing Club
BAR, CLUB

(Map p232; www.sailingclubnhatrang.com; 72-74 Đ Tran Phu; ☉7am-2am) Sailing Club is the definitive Nha Trang night spot with a good mix of locals and foreigners. It's an upmarket venue, with expensive drinks, DJs and bands, and draws the city's beautiful crowd. On Thursdays, Fridays and Saturdays a bonfire is lit on the beach and the action moves to the sand (weather permitting!).

DRINK SPIKING

There have been a number of reports of laced cocktail buckets doing the rounds in popular night spots. This might mean staff using homemade moonshine instead of legal spirits or could mean the addition of drugs of some sort by other punters. While buckets are fun and communal, take care in Nha Trang and try and keep an eye on what goes into the bucket. You don't want your night to end in paranoia or robbery.

Oasis
BAR

(Map p232; 3 Đ Tran Quang Khai; ☉7am-2am; ⓐ) Buzzing bar on a corner plot with large garden terrace that's popular for bucket-downing and shisha-puffing. Happy hour runs right through from 4pm to midnight. It's a good choice for big sporting events.

Louisiane Brewhouse
BREWERY

(Map p232; ☎058-352 1948; 29 Đ Tran Phu; per glass 40,000d; ☉7am-midnight; ⓐ) Microbreweries don't get much more sophisticated than this. Louisiane's copper vats sure have a helluva view, gazing over an inviting swimming pool down to a private strip of sand. There are six brews to try, including a red ale and a dark lager, or for 110,000d you can sample the lot.

Crazy Kim Bar
BAR

(Map p232; http://crazykimvietnam.wordpress.com; 19 Đ Biet Thu; ☉8am-midnight; ⓐ) With more of a pub atmosphere, this place is home to the commendable 'Hands off the Kids!' campaign, working to prevent paedophilia – part of the profits go towards the cause. Crazy Kim's has regular themed party nights, devilish cocktail buckets, shooters, cheap beer (from 25,000d), good tunes and tasty grub.

Altitude
BAR

(Map p232; 26-28 Đ Tran Phu; ☉noon-midnight; ⓐ) Located on the 28th floor of the Sheraton Nha Trang, this bar has simply out-of-this-world views of the coast – you can pick out every footprint in the sand below (if you eyes are up to it!). The interior is non-smoking. Expect five-star prices; a beer is 93,000d (gulp).

Nghia Bia Hoi
BIA HOI

(Map p232; 7G/3 Đ Hung Vuong; ☉11am-10pm) Drawing a backpacker crowd, this is a popular *bia hoi* joint. They serve a light lager and a darker brown beer, as well as snacks.

Red Apple Club
BAR

(Map p232; 54H Đ Nguyen Thien Thuat; ☉7am-midnight; ⓐ) Yes it's a bit of a cliché, but this party-themed backpacker bar sure packs 'em in with cheap beer, flowing shots and regular promotions. Watch out for the beer funnel, as things can get very messy.

 Shopping

Nha Trang has some good arts and crafts shops in the blocks around the corner of Đ Tran Quang Khai and Đ Hung Vuong.

Fashion boutiques selling everything from slingbacks to sunglasses are concentrated along Đ Nguyen Thi Minh Khai.

Saga du Mekong
CLOTHING

(Map p232; www.sagadumekong.com; 1/21 Đ Nguyen Dinh Chieu; ⊙9am-6pm) This stylish fashion boutique specialises in linen, silk, bamboo and fine cotton clothing – perfect for the tropical climes. Stocks Western sizes and has its own factory for quality control.

Ni Na
ACCESSORIES

(Map p232; 82A Đ Nguyen Thi Minh Khai ; ⊙7.30am-6pm) The sign outside says 'shoes and handbags' and that's certainly true as you'll find lots of innovative, fashionable designs inside, including some fetching stacked footwear. Also stocks purses, belts and sunglasses.

XQ
HANDICRAFTS

(Map p232; www.xqhandembroidery.com; 64 Đ Tran Phu; ⊙8am-8pm) At this place, designed to look like a traditional rural village, you are invited to enjoy a complimentary glass of green tea as you wander around. You can watch the artisans at work in the embroidery workshop and gallery.

Cu Meo
CLOTHING, ACCESSORIES

(Map p232; 37 Đ Nguyen Thi Minh Khai; ⊙8am-6pm) This hip boutique is renowned for its modish ladies' shoe designs but also stocks lingerie, swimwear and dresses.

Bambou
CLOTHING

(Map p232; www.bamboucompany.com; 15 Đ Biet Thu; ⊙8am-7pm) Specialises in casual clothing for men, women and kids, with Vietnamese motifs, including beachwear. Natural materials including tencel and bamboo are used.

Information

DANGERS & ANNOYANCES
The vast vast majority of visitors experience no troubles at all in Nha Trang. While there's no need to be paranoid, you should take a little extra care here as the town certainly has its share of thieves.

There are many ways for you and your valuables to part company. Young travellers are most frequently targeted. We hear many stories about people getting pickpocketed in bars and clubs: packed dance floors are particularly popular hunting ground for thieves. Do you really need to carry a smart phone and credit card on your night out? It's safest to just to carry the cash you'll need for a good time.

We've also heard reports of thefts on the beach (bags are taken when you've dozed off).

Drive-by bag-snatching is an issue, which can be highly dangerous if you fall victim while on the back of a *xe om*. It's safer to wear bags close to your chest rather than as a backpack.

Keep phones and tablets out of sight, not on restaurant tables. If you're using a map app to find your way around, hold the phone or tablet with two hands.

Some female tourists have reported being photographed by young Vietnamese males when emerging from the water or just lying on the beach. These guys are quite blatant about it and are rather persistent.

At tourist sites unobservant foreigners may be overcharged – check the price on pre-printed tickets, and check your change.

INTERNET ACCESS
Virtually all hotels and most restaurants and cafes have wi-fi. Many places also have a PC or two.

MEDICAL SERVICES
Pasteur Institute (Map p232; ☏058-382 2355; 10 Đ Tran Phu; 7am-11am 1pm-4.30pm) Offers medical consultations and vaccinations. Located inside the Alexandre Yersin Museum.

MONEY
There are ATMs all over Nha Trang.
Vietcombank (Map p232; 17 Đ Quang Trung; ⊙7.30am-4pm Mon-Fri) Changes travellers cheques and has an ATM.

POST
Main Post Office (Map p232; 4 Đ Le Loi; ⊙6.30am-8pm)

TOURIST INFORMATION
Khanh Hoa Tourist Information (Map p232; ☏058-352 8000; khtourism@dng.vnn.vn; Đ Tran Phu) Government-run tourism office on the seafront with various tour programs, including boat trips.

TRAVEL AGENCIES
Sinh Tourist (Map p232; ☏058-352 2982; www.thesinhtourist.vn; 2A Đ Biet Thu) Inexpensive local tours, including a city tour for 200,000d (excluding entrance fees), as well as open-tour buses.
Highland Tours (Map p232; ☏058-352 4477; www.highlandtourstravel.com; 54G Đ Nguyen Thien Thuat) An extensive program of affordable tours in the Nha Trang area, to the central highlands and along the coast. A day trip along the Cai river costs from US$27.

ℹ Getting There & Away

AIR

Vietnam Airlines (☎ 058-352 6768; www. vietnamairlines.com) connects Nha Trang with Hanoi (three daily) and to HCMC and Danang daily. Vietjet Air (p481) usually have the cheapest fares if you book well ahead, flying to both Hanoi and HCMC daily. **Jetstar** (www.jetstar. com) offer five weekly connections with Hanoi.

BUS

Phia Nam Nha Trang bus station (Đ 23 Thang 10) is Nha Trang's main intercity bus terminal, 500m west of the train station. Very regular daily buses head north to Quy Nhon and Danang. Heading south, there are very frequent connections to Phan Rang (46,000d, two hours) and HCMC, including sleeper buses from 7pm. Buses also head west into the Central Highlands, to Dalat and Buon Ma Thuot (100,000d to 120,000d, five hours, seven daily).

Nha Trang is a major stopping point on all of the open-tour buses. These are the best option for accessing Mui Ne, which is not served by standard buses. These buses usually depart between 6am and 8am, before continuing on to HCMC. There are also regular open-tour buses to Dalat (five hours) and Hoi An (11 hours).

CAR & MOTORBIKE

One of the best trips to experience is the mountain pass from Nha Trang to Dalat, as seen on the BBC *Top Gear* special. It's a stunning journey by car or motorbike. Throw the mountain road back down from Dalat to Mui Ne into the mix and you have a great loop. There are quite a number of Easy Riders based in Nha Trang.

TRAIN

The **Nha Trang train station** (☎ 058-382 2113; Đ Thai Nguyen; ⊙ ticket office 7-11.30am, 1.30-6pm & 7-9pm) is west of the cathedral in the centre of town. It's on the main north-south line with good connections to destinations including Quy Nhon, Danang and HCMC.

ℹ Getting Around

TO/FROM THE AIRPORT

Cam Ranh international airport is 30km south of the city via a beautiful coastal road. A shuttle bus runs the route (60,000d), leaving from the site of the old airport (near 86 Đ Tran Phu) two hours before scheduled departure times, taking about 40 minutes.

Departing town, taxis are a more convenient option (to avoid waiting around). **Nha Trang Taxi** (☎ 058-382 6000), the official maroon-coloured cabs, cost 380,000d from the airport to downtown. It's cheaper in the other direction, 300,000d from town out to the airport. It's best to fix a price ahead rather than use taxi meters, which work out to be more expensive.

BICYCLE

Most of Nha Trang is pretty flat so it's easy to get around all the sights, including Thap Ba, by bicycle. Hotels have bikes to rent from 30,000d per day. Watch out for the one-way system around the train station, and the chaotic roundabouts.

TAXI & XE OM

It's safer to take a metered taxi with a reputable company such as **Mai Linh** (☎ 058-382 2266).

Nha Trang has an excessive number of *xe om* drivers. A motorcycle ride anywhere in the centre shouldn't cost more than 25,000d. Be careful at night, when some less reputable drivers moonlight as pimps and drug dealers.

Around Nha Trang

Thanh Citadel

This citadel dates from the 17th-century Trinh dynasty. It was rebuilt by Prince Nguyen Anh (later Emperor Gia Long) in 1793 during his successful offensive against the Tay Son Rebels. Only a few sections of the walls and gates remain. It's 11km west of Nha Trang near Dien Khanh town.

TRANSPORT FROM NHA TRANG

DESTINATION	AIR	BUS	CAR/MOTORBIKE	TRAIN
HCMC	from US$28, 1hr, 6 daily	US$10–14, 11hr, 13 daily	10hr	US$11–17, 7-9hr, 6 daily
Mui Ne	n/a	US$8, 6hr, open buses only	5hr	n/a
Dalat	n/a	US$7, 5hr, 17 daily	4hr	n/a
Quy Nhon	n/a	US$6.50, 5hr, hourly	4hr	US$5.50-8, 4hr, 5 daily
Danang	from US$55, 1hr, 1 daily	US$11-14, 12hr, 13-16 daily	11hr	US$16-26, 9-11hr, 5 daily

Ba Ho Falls

The three waterfalls and refreshing pools at **Ba Ho Falls** (Suoi Ba Ho) are in a forested area about 20km north of Nha Trang and about 2km west of Phu Huu village. Turn off Hwy 1 just north of Quyen Restaurant, and you'll find them a 20-minute walk from the parking area. It's fun clambering upstream through the pools, though they are slippy so take care. Entrance is 15,000d.

Cam Ranh Harbour

The gorgeous natural harbour of **Cam Ranh Bay** starts 25km south of Nha Trang and 56km north of Phan Rang. With the opening of the stunning airport road, beautiful **Bai Dai** (Long Beach), forming the northern head of the harbour, has become much more accessible.

Until very recently, the Vietnamese military controlled Cam Ranh Harbour's entire shoreline, and access was restricted to the odd fishing boat. However, times are a-changing and these days the entire strip south of the Mia Resort to the aiport has been earmarked for development. No less than 39 giant resort hotels have been approved for construction, including the likes of Hyatt and Marriott, and enormous advertising billboards now line the coastal road.

As of mid-2013 little or no construction had actually started, so it should be possible to find a virgin stretch of sand. Some of the best surf breaks in Vietnam are found along here.

At the northern tip of Bai Dai, **Shack Vietnam** (www.shackvietnam.com) offers board rental and surfing instruction (500,000d), as well as kayak hire. In addition, ice-cold beer, delicious fish tacos (40,000d each), burgers, burritos and fish 'n' chips are on the menu. Shack Vietnam is located in the middle of a strip of 20 or so locally owned seafood restaurants, all with near-identical menus.

A one-way journey in a taxi to the north end of Bai Dai costs around 230,000d, and reckon on 300,000d to hit the central stretch. There's no public transport along Bai Dai road. As traffic is very light, this is a region that's ideal to explore on a motorbike.

Phan Rang & Thap Cham

☑ 058 / POP 178,000

This really is a tale of two cities: Phan Rang hugging the shoulders of Hwy 1 and Thap Cham straddling Hwy 20 as it starts its long climb to Dalat. Anyone travelling Vietnam from north to south will notice a big change in the vegetation when approaching the joint capitals of Ninh Thuan province. The familiar lush green rice paddies are replaced with sandy soil supporting only scrubby plants. Local flora includes poinciana trees and prickly-pear cacti with vicious thorns. The area is famous for its production of table grapes, and many of the houses on the outskirts of town are decorated with vines on trellises.

The area's best-known sight is the group of Cham towers known as Po Klong Garai, from which Thap Cham (Cham Tower) derives its name. However, with the advent of a new mountain highway between Dalat and Nha Trang, this temple sees far fewer visitors than in the past. There are many more towers dotted about the countryside in this area and the province is home to tens of thousands of Cham people. The Cham, like other ethnic minorities in Vietnam, have suffered from discrimination and are usually poorer than their ethnic-Vietnamese neighbours. There are also several thousand Chinese in the area, many of whom come to worship at the 135-year-old **Quang Cong Pagoda** (Đ Thong Nhat), a colourful Chinese temple in the town centre.

With two major highways (1A and 20) intersecting in the town, this area makes a good pit stop on the coastal run. As the twin towns of Phan Rang and Thap Cham are both industrial and not particularly attractive, consider basing yourself at nearby Ninh Chu Beach, 6km to the east.

◉ Sights

Po Klong Garai Cham Towers   HINDU TEMPLE
(Thap Cham; admission 15,000d; ⊙7am-5pm) These four brick towers date from the end of the 13th century. Built as Hindu temples, they stand on a brick platform at the top of **Cho'k Hala**, an exposed granite hill covered with cacti. It can be furnace-hot here.

Over the entrance to the largest tower (the *kalan*, or sanctuary) is a beautiful carving of a dancing Shiva with six arms. Note the inscriptions in the ancient Cham language on the doorposts. These tell of past restoration efforts and offerings of sacrifices and slaves.

CHAM NEW YEAR

The Cham New Year (*kate*) is celebrated at Po Klong Garai in the seventh month of the Cham calendar (around October). The festival commemorates ancestors, Cham national heroes and deities such as the farmers' goddess Po Ino Nagar.

On the eve of the festival, a procession guarded by the mountain people of Tay Nguyen carries King Po Klong Garai's clothing to the accompaniment of traditional music. The procession lasts until midnight. The following morning the garments are carried to the tower, once again accompanied by music, along with banners, flags, singing and dancing. Notables, dignitaries and village elders follow behind. This colourful ceremony continues into the afternoon.

The celebrations then carry on for the rest of the month, as the Cham attend parties and visit friends and relatives. They also use this time to pray for good fortune.

Inside the *kalan*'s vestibule is a statue of the bull Nandin, vehicle of the Hindu god Shiva. Nandin is also a symbol of the agricultural productivity of the countryside. To ensure a good crop, farmers would place an offering of fresh greens, herbs and areca nuts in front of Nandin's muzzle. Under the main tower is a *mukha-linga* sitting under a wooden pyramid. Liquor is offered and incense burned here.

Inside the smaller tower opposite the entrance to the sanctuary, you can get a good look at some of the Cham's sophisticated building technology; the wooden columns that support the lightweight roof are visible. The structure attached to it was originally the main entrance to the complex.

Po Klong Garai is just north of Hwy 20, at a point 6km west of Phan Rang towards Dalat. The towers are on the opposite side of the tracks to Thap Cham train station. Some of the open-tour buses running the coastal route make a requisite pit stop here.

Po Ro Me Cham Tower HINDU TEMPLE

(admission free, donation welcome) Po Ro Me is one of the most atmospheric of Vietnam's Cham towers, thanks in part to its isolated setting on top of a craggy hill with sweeping views over the cactus-strewn landscape. The temple honours the last ruler of an independent Champa, King Po Ro Me (r 1629–51); his image and those of his family are found on the external decorations.

The temple is still in active use, with ceremonies taking place twice a year. The rest of the time it's locked up, but the caretakers at the foot of the hill will open the sanctuary for you. Consider leaving a small donation with them and don't forget to remove your shoes.

The occupants of the temple aren't used to having their rest disturbed, and it can be a little creepy when the bats start chattering and swooping overhead in the confined dark space. Through the gloom you'll be able to make out a blood-red and black centrepiece – a bas-relief representing the deified king in the form of Shiva. Behind the main deity and to the left is one of his queens, Thanh Chanh. Look out for the inscriptions on the doorposts and a stone statue of the bull Nandin.

Note the flame motif repeated around the arches. This is a symbol of purity, cleansing visitors of any residual bad karma.

The best way to reach the site is with your own motorbike or a *xe om*. The route is tricky. Take Hwy 1 south from Phan Rang for 9km. Turn right at the turn-off to Ho Tan Giang, a narrow sealed road just after the petrol station, and continue for a further 6km. Turn left in the middle of a dusty village at a paddock that doubles as a football field and follow the road as it meanders to the right until the tower comes into sight. A sign points the way cross-country for the last 500m.

Cham Cultural Centre MUSEUM

(Thap Cham; ⊙7am-5pm) **FREE** At the base of the Po Klong Garai towers, this large modern structure (built in attractive, vaguely Cham style) is dedicated to Cham culture. There's some superb photography of Cham people, village life and customs exhibited here, as well as paintings, pottery, traditional dress and agricultural tools.

It's a good reminder that while the Cham kingdom is long gone, the Cham people are an important minority in this region.

There are also numerous souvenir stalls.

Bau Truc Village

NEIGHBOURHOOD

This Cham village is known for its pottery and you'll see several family shops in front of the mud and bamboo houses. On the way to Po Ro Me turn right off Hwy 1 near the war memorial, into the commune with the banner 'Lang Nghe Gom Bau Truc'. Inside the village take the first left for some of the better pottery stores.

🛏 Sleeping & Eating

The twin towns are not relaxing places to stay due to traffic congestion and industry. Nearby Ninh Chu Beach, 6km east of Phan Rang, is far more inviting, with a much better choice of accommodation.

Com ga (chicken with rice) is a local speciality. There are *com ga* restaurants on Đ Tran Quang Dieu, the best is **Phuoc Thanh** (3 Đ Tran Quang Dieu; mains 25,000-50,000d), located just north of Đ 16 Thang 4, the road to Ninh Chu Beach.

Another local delicacy is roasted or baked *ky nhong* (gecko), served with fresh green mango. If you prefer self-catering and have quick reflexes, most hotel rooms in Vietnam have a ready supply.

Phan Rang is the grape capital of Vietnam. Stalls in the market sell fresh grapes, grape juice and dried grapes (too juicy to be called raisins).

Ho Phong Hotel HOTEL $

(☑ 058-392 0333; 363 Đ Ngo Gia Tu; r 275,000-550,000d; ❄@🛜) This fancy-pants hotel is highly visible by night when it's lit up like a Christmas tree. Inside things are more subdued, with attractive well-furnished rooms with power showers.

ⓘ Getting There & Away

BUS

Phan Rang bus station (opposite 64 Đ Thong Nhat) is on the northern outskirts of town. Regular buses head north to Nha Trang (47,000d, 2½ hours, every 45 minutes), northwest to Dalat (71,000d, four hours, hourly), and south to Ca Na (20,000d, one hour, every 45 minutes) and beyond.

CAR & MOTORBIKE

Phan Rang is 344km from HCMC, 147km from Phan Thiet, 104km from Nha Trang and 108km from Dalat.

TRAIN

The **Thap Cham train station** (☑ 068-388 8029; 7 Đ Phan Dinh Phung) is about 6km west of Hwy 1, within sight of Po Klong Garai Cham towers, but only slower trains stop here. Destinations include Nha Trang (around 2½ hours) and HCMC (around eight hours).

Ninh Chu Beach

☑ 068

Southeast of Phan Rang, the giant bite-shaped bay of Ninh Chu is popular with Vietnamese tourists on weekends and holidays, but relatively tranquil the rest of the time. Some litter blights the scene, but the 10km-long beach is attractive and makes a quieter alternative to Phan Rang as a base for visiting the Cham ruins. There are new resort hotels are springing up around the bay.

🛏 Sleeping & Eating

Hotel resorts are scattered along the shoreline. Budget accommodation is concentrated at the north end of the bay, where there's a fishing village and a row of beachfront seafood restaurants.

Nha Nghi Dieu Hien GUESTHOUSE $

(☑ 068-387 3399; ⏰ s/d 150,000/200,000d; ❄) A simple place run by a friendly (non-English speaking) couple with clean rooms, all with TV, fan and air-conditioning. It's 200m from the north end of the beach.

Anh Duong Hotel HOTEL $

(☑ 068-389 0009; r 245,000-500,000d; ❄🛜) Away from the shore, this roadside place offers inexpensive, good-value rooms with smart trim. It's a short walk to the beach.

Con Ga Vang Resort RESORT $$

(☑ 068-387 4899; www.congavangresort.com; r 400,000-900,000d, ste 1,300,000-2,200,000d; ❄@🛜🏊) The room prices here are pretty enticing when you factor in smart, spacious rooms, attractive coconut-fringed swimming pool and tennis courts. The hotel's beachfront **Huong Dua Restaurant** (mains 40,000-100,000d) has great value seafood, and service is good.

Bau Truc Resort BOUTIQUE HOTEL $$

(☑ 068-387 4223; www.bautrucresort.com; r US$45-140; ♨❄@🛜🏊) Formerly the Den Gion, this large hotel resort has a good range of well-appointed bungalows with contemporary bathrooms set in a lush garden by the beach. The pool is huge and breakfast is included, taken at the open-air restaurant (dinner mains 50,000d to 155,000d). Aim for a discount off the rack rates.

❶ Getting There & Away

Turn left (southeast) into Đ Ngo Gia Tu, the street immediately before the Cai River bridge in Phan Rang, and continue on, following the signs for 7km.

Unless you're driving yourself, it's easiest to take a xe om (around 30,000d) or a metered taxi (70,000d).

Ca Na

♪ 068

During the 16th century, princes of the Cham royal family would fish and hunt tigers, elephants and rhinoceros here. Today Ca Na is better known for its white-sand beaches, which are dotted with huge granite boulders. The best of the beach is just off Hwy 1, a kilometre north of the fishing village. It's a beautiful spot, but it's tough to ignore the constant honking and rumble of trucks.

The terrain is studded with magnificent prickly-pear cacti. Bright yellow Lac Son, a small pagoda on the hillside, makes for an interesting but steep climb.

If you stay here, be aware that there are no banks or ATMs and absolutely no one accepts credit cards.

Ca Na Hotel (☎ 068-376 0922; www.canahotel.com.vn; r 200,000-350,000d; ❄@☎) is a small hotel with eight bungalows and a further 12 rooms in the 'motel' building. Accommodation here is rarely patronised, though its huge roadside restaurant (meals 50,000d to 120,000d) is always busy.

❶ Getting There & Away

Ca Na is 114km north of Phan Thiet and 32km south of Phan Rang. Most long-haul buses cruising Hwy 1 will drop off or pick up people here. Local buses from Phan Rang (18,000d, one hour) head to Ca Na fishing village – ask to be let out on the highway and catch a xe om for the last kilometre.

Mui Ne

♪ 062 / POP 17,000

Once upon a time, Mui Ne was an isolated stretch of beach where pioneering travellers camped on the sand in the early 1990s, but it was too beautiful to be ignored. Times have changed and it is now a string of resorts,

expanding in number every year. However, the beach retains much of its charm and the resorts are, for the most part, mercifully low-rise, set amid pretty gardens by the sea. The original fishing village is still here, but tourists outnumber locals these days. Mui Ne is definitely moving upmarket, as more exclusive resorts open their doors, complemented by swish restaurants and swanky shops, but there is still a (kite)surfer vibe to the town.

Mui Ne is the adrenalin capital of southern Vietnam. There's no scuba diving or snorkelling to speak of, but when Nha Trang and Hoi An get the rains, Mui Ne gets the waves. Surf's up from August to December. For windsurfers, the gales blow as well, especially from late October to late April, when swells can stir things up big-time. Kitesurfing has really taken off and the infinite horizon is often obscured by dozens of kites flapping in the wind. If this all sounds too much like hard work you can simply lounge around on the beach, watching others take the strain.

Mui Ne sees only about half the rainfall of nearby Phan Thiet. The sand dunes help protect its unique microclimate, and even during the wet season (from June to September) rains tend to be fairly light and sporadic.

One major problem the area faces is the steady creep of coastal erosion. Many resorts north of Km 12 have almost completely lost their beaches and rely on sandbagging to keep the little they have left.

Road safety is another serious issue. There are no traffic-calming measures along the main coastal road, and speeding cars and trucks have little regard for pedestrians. Take care.

It's almost impossible to get lost in Mui Ne, as everything is spread out along a 10km stretch of highway. Most accommodation lines the beach side, while restaurants and shops flank the other.

◉ Sights

Sand Dunes   BEACH
Mui Ne is famous for its enormous red and white sand dunes. The white dunes are the more impressive, the near-constant oceanic winds sculpting the sands into wonderful Saharaesque formations. But as this is Vietnam (not deepest Mali) there's little chance of experiencing the silence of the desert.

Prepare yourself for the hard-sell as children press you to hire a plastic sledge to ride

Mui Ne Beach

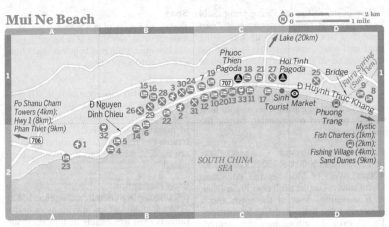

Mui Ne Beach

SOUTHEAST COAST MUI NE

the dunes. Unless you're supermodel-light, it can be tricky to travel for more than a few metres this way.

Quad bikes and dune buggies also destroy the peace. Bizarrely, ostrich riding (100,000d) is on offer here as an activity, but we don't recommend it. Expect some litter too; periodically there's a clean-up,

but the red dunes were badly littered on our last visit.

You'll need a jeep to explore the dunes properly, but be careful to agree on an itinerary for the tour, preferably in writing. We've heard complaints, particularly about 'sunset tours' that cut short with the sun high in the sky.

Also of interest is the Fairy Spring (Suoi Tien), which is really a stream that flows through a patch of dunes with interesting sand and rock formations. It's a beautiful trek wading up the stream from the sea to its source, though it might be wise to hire a local guide. You can do the trek barefoot, but if you're heading out into the big sand dunes, you'll need leather soles on your feet; sandals are even questionable during the midday sun.

Po Shanu Cham Towers HINDU TEMPLE
(Km 5; admission 5000d; ⊙ 7.30-11.30am & 1.30-4.30pm) West of Mui Ne, the Po Shanu Cham towers occupy a hill near Phan Thiet, with sweeping views of the town and a cemetery filled with candylike tombstones. Dating from the 9th century, this complex consists of the ruins of three towers, none of which are in very good shape. There's a small pagoda on the site, as well as a gallery and shop.

🏃 Activities

Golf

Tropical Minigolf Mui Ne MINIGOLF
(97 Đ Nguyen Dinh Chieu; one round 100,000d; ⊙ 10am-10.30pm) This attractive palm-shaded minigolf course is dotted with craggy rock formations to challenge your putting skills. Rates include a cold drink, or pay 120,000d at night and a cocktail is included.

Sealinks Golf & Country Club GOLF
(☑ 062-374 1777; www.sealinksvietnam.com; Km 8, Mui Ne; for 18 holes 1,350,000d) Fine 7671yd course with ocean views and a challenging layout that includes lots of water hazards. Play a discounted twilight round from 2.30pm. The complex includes a resort hotel and driving range.

Spas

There's an excess of spa/massage places, at least 25 or so, along the Mui Ne strip, most of a low quality offering body massages from as little at US$7 per hour.

Xanh Spa SPA
(☑ 062-384 7440; www.miamuine.com; 24 Đ Nguyen Dinh Chieu; 1hr massage from 645,000d) Gorgeous upmarket spa offering the full gamut of massages, facials, body treatments and wraps. Essential oils and natural products are used. A steam room has recently been added.

Song Huong Spa SPA
(241 Đ Nguyen Dinh Chieu; 1hr massage from US$10; ⊙ 8am-9pm) Budget spa offering an extensive range of massages, beauty treatments, steam bath and jacuzzi in clean, orderly surroundings. Staff are professional and welcoming. Located in the grounds of the Son Huong Hotel

Watersports

Consider investing in a short kitesurfing lesson before opting for a multiday course, as it's a tricky skill to master. Bear in mind it is an extreme sport and most places will not offer a refund on an immersion course for anyone who drops out.

Surfpoint Kiteboarding School KITESURFING, SURFING
(☑ 0167 342 2136; www.surfpoint-vietnam.com; 52A Đ Nguyen Dinh Chieu; 5hr course US$250 incl all gear; ⊙ 7am-6pm) With well-trained instructors and a friendly vibe, it's no surprise Surfpoint is one of the best regarded kite schools in town. A three-hour taster costs US$145. Surfing lessons on softboards are also offered (from US$50) when waves permit.

THE MUI NE STRIP

Heading east from Phan Thiet, development is sporadic until the Km 8 mark and the rather splendid looking University of Phan Thiet. After this, there are several resorts, restaurants and a golf course, as the main strip takes shape. From Km 10 to Km 12, Mui Ne has quite a Russian feel, with souvenir shops and spas galore emblazoned with Cyrillic script. Km 12 to Km 14 is where many of the popular midrange resorts and restaurants are found. From here there is a break in the resorts, with a strip of seafood stalls and some late-night beach clubs before another cluster of backpacker accommodation and restaurant-bars around the Km 16 strip. This is where the village of Ham Tien (the original settlement) starts before giving way to more backpacker accommodation around Km 18. Look out for superb views over the Mui Ne fishing fleet around Km 20 and you've arrived at the end of the strip.

Jibes KITESURFING
(☎068-384 7405; www.windsurf-vietnam.com; 84-90 Đ Nguyen Dinh Chieu; ⏰7.30am-6pm) Set up in 2000, this is the original kitesurfing school, offering lessons and renting state-of-the-art gear, including windsurfs, surfboards, kitesurfs and kayaks.

Sankara Kitesurfing Academy KITESURFING
(☎0914 910 607; http://muinekiteschool.com; 78 Đ Nguyen Dinh Chieu) This school is run by experienced kitesurfers and offers kitesurfing lessons and equipment rentals. Lessons start at US$99 for two hours, or US$270 for five hours.

Vietnam Kitesurfing Tours KITESURFING
(☎0909 469 803; www.vietnamkitesurfingtours.com; 68 Nguyen Dinh Chieu) Based in the Rach Dua Resort these guys promise that there's better kiting than Mui Ne, and they'll get you there. One place is in a military-controlled border zone, for which you'll need a permit.

Mystic Fish Charters SAILING
(☎0127 287 8801; www.mysticfishcharters.com; 108 Đ Huynh Thuc Khang) Hello sailor! Experience a sailing trip aboard a Corsair Marine Sprint catamaran. Trips start at US$300, but this can be split between eight.

Courses

Taste of Vietnam COOKING
(☎0916 655 241; www.c2skykitecenter.com/cooking-school; Sunshine Beach Resort, 82 Đ Nguyen Dinh Chieu; ⏰9am-12.30pm) Well-regarded Vietnamese cooking classes by the beach. Pay US$30 and a market visit is included. Make sure you have a light breakfast first as there's lots of grub to try!

Sleeping

Mui Ne has a great range of places to stay in all price categories. Most accommodation is either right on the coastal road or just off it, though some good new places have been built on the hills behind town. Wherever you are, you won't be far from the beach.

Coco Sand Hotel GUESTHOUSE $
(☎0127 364 3446; cocosandcatdua@yahoo.com.vn; 119 Đ Nguyen Dinh Chieu; r US$12-15; ❄📶) Down a lane on the inland side of the main drag, these simple, clean rooms are quite spacious and excellent value. The owners are all smiles and there's a little garden with hammocks.

Mui Ne Backpackers GUESTHOUSE $
(☎062-384 7047; www.muinebackpackers.com; 88 Đ Nguyen Dinh Chieu; dm US$6-10; r US$20-60; ❄@📶🏊) Popular with young travellers for its sociable vibe and shoreside location, the dorms (with en-suite bathrooms and good mattresses) are a good bet, though the rooms are little pricey and quite plain. Lots of tours offered; transport tickets can be arranged.

Song Huong Hotel HOTEL $
(☎062-384 7450; www.songhuonghotel.com; 241 Đ Nguyen Dinh Chieu; r US$12-20; ❄📶) Run by welcoming family owners this hotel is set well back from the road and boasts spacious, light airy rooms in a modern house. Breakfast is included.

Lu Hoang Guesthouse HOTEL $
(☎062-350 0060; 106 Đ Nguyen Dinh Chieu; r US$16-22; ❄@📶) This guesthouse has been lovingly decorated and several rooms include a sea view and breezy balconies, plus all have spotless bathrooms. The charming owners really make an effort here.

Duy An Guesthouse GUEST HOUSE $
(☎062-384 7799; 87A Đ Huynh Thuc Khang; s/d US$12/15; ❄@📶) Close to the western end of the strip, the Duy An has friendly owners who speak good English. Room options include quads and there are bikes for hire.

Sea Winds Resort GUEST HOUSE $
(☎062-384 7018; sea.winds.resort@gmail.com; 139 Đ Nguyen Dinh Chieu; r US$9-21; ❄@📶) Set back off the road, all the simple, fine-value rooms here have aspects over a lovely little garden and TV. Fan rooms are very spacious for this sort of money.

Hai Yen Guesthouse GUEST HOUSE $
(☎062-384 7243; www.haiyenguesthouse.com; 132 Đ Nguyen Dinh Chieu; r US$17-28; ❄@📶🏊) Boasts a good selection of rooms, including some with three beds, set behind the seafront swimming pool. Spend a little more to enjoy a sea views.

Mui Ne Lodge GUEST HOUSE $
(☎062-384 7327; www.muinelodge.com; 150 Đ Nguyen Dinh Chieu; r US$14-26; ❄@📶) The lodge offers 12 plain rooms with fan and flatscreen TV that represent decent value, and there's a bar area with a pool table.

Duyen Vu Guesthouse GUEST HOUSE $
(☎062-374 3404; 77A Đ Huynh Thuc Khang; r US$12; ❄@📶) Fronted by a large restaurant, there

are only a small number of bungalow-style rooms overlooking a sandy, shady garden.

Mui Ne Hills 1
BOUTIQUE HOTEL **$$**

(☑ 0908 052 350; www.muinehills.com; 69 Đ Nguyen Dinh Chieu; r US$40-55; ❄ @ ⊗ ☎) High above the coast, this fine villa-style hotel has wonderful vistas from its pool. Rooms are superb value, all with contemporary design touches and full facilities, but it's the personal touch from staff and owners that guests rightly rave about. Note that it's located, up a dusty, very steep lane.

Xin Chao
BOUTIQUE HOTEL **$$**

(☑ 062-374 3086; www.xinchaohotel.com; 129 Đ Nguyen Dinh Chieu; r US$20-50; ❄ @ ⊗ ☎) Impressive new hotel (owned by kitesurfers) set well back from the busy coastal road. A lot of thought has gone into the design, with rooms grouped around a pool at the rear. A small lounge area (with pool table) and roadside bar-restaurant add to its appeal.

Full Moon Beach Hotel
HOTEL **$$**

(☑ 062-384 7008; www.fullmoonbeach.com.vn; 84 Đ Nguyen Dinh Chieu; r from US$56; ❄ @ ⊗ ☎) An artistically-designed place where the committed owners have consistently upgraded the facilities to keep up with the competition. It features a bamboo-shaded pool, rooms with four-poster beds and terracotta tiling, and an oceanfront bar. Worth trying to negotiate a discount.

Mui Ne Hills 2
HOTEL **$$**

(☑ 0908 052 350; www.muinehills.com; 69 Đ Nguyen Dinh Chieu; r/ste from US$35/60; ❄ ⊗ ☎) The layout of this place isn't as good as its upmarket sister hotel, with rooms grouped around a walled compound; those on the ground floor feel a bit hemmed in. However, given the quality of the furnishings, pleasingly modern design and good breakfast it's still a good-value place to stay. Around 300m north of the main strip, via an incredibly steep access road.

Rang Garden Bungalow
HOTEL **$$**

(☑ 062-374 3638; 233A Đ Nguyen Dinh Chieu; r US$20-40; ❄ @ ⊗ ☎) Rooms are set in attractive villas around the generously proportioned swimming pool. The higher standard rooms enjoy great details and more space, and there's a small restaurant out front.

Bao Quynh Bungalow
HOTEL **$$**

(☑ 062-374 1007; www.baoquynh.com; 26 Đ Nguyen Dinh Chieu; r US$49-149; ❄ @ ⊗ ☎) This attractively designed resort has lovely grounds and offers decent rooms and spacious bungalows, though their decor would benefit from an upgrade and beds are very firm. Nevertheless, staff are welcoming and it's located on a decent stretch of beach.

Joe's Garden Resort
HOTEL **$$**

(☑ 062-384 7177; www.joescafegardenresort.com; 86 Đ Nguyen Dinh Chieu; r US$18-58; ❄ @ ⊗) These bamboo huts and rooms feature nice decorative touches. They're scattered around a leafy plot to the rear of Joe's Cafe, a busy bar-restaurant. Breakfast is included.

Hiep Hoa Beachside Bungalow
HOTEL **$$**

(☑ 062-384 7262; www.muinebeach.net/hiephoa; 80 Đ Nguyen Dinh Chieu; r with fan/air-con from US$20/30; ❄ @ ⊗ ☎) Yes, the decor's a bit dated at this family-run hotel, but comfort levels are higher than at the cheapest guesthouses. Rooms all have a porch and face a central garden.

★ Mia Resort
BOUTIQUE HOTEL **$$$**

(☑ 062-384 7440; www.miamuine.com; 24 Đ Nguyen Dinh Chieu; r US$90, bungalows US$130-190; ❄ @ ⊗ ☎) Everything is right at this stylish beachfront hotel, with gorgeous accommodation with designer furnishings dotted around a beautiful tropical garden. The pool area is particularly attractive, facing the ocean and bordered by the excellent Sandals Restaurant, and the friendly, efficient staff really give the hotel a little extra polish that is lacking in other places of similar price.

★ Cham Villas
BOUTIQUE HOTEL **$$$**

(☑ 062-374 1234; www.chamvillas.com; 32 Đ Nguyen Dinh Chieu; r US$150-185; ❄ @ ⊗ ☎) A really relaxing place to stay and unwind, this luxury hotel's lovely villas are spaced well apart around a stunning garden. The secluded, partly shaded pool area is particularly beautiful in the morning, with birdsong in the air and dappled light on the water. Book early during peak periods.

Allez Boo Resort
RESORT HOTEL **$$$**

(☑ 062-374 1081; www.allezbooresort.com; 8 Đ Nguyen Dinh Chieu; r US$80-410; ❄ @ ⊗ ☎) An outstanding place with a very classy ambience thanks to the French Colonial–style buildings. The grounds are huge, spilling down to the shore, where you'll find a pool and huge (shaded) jacuzzi.

Sunsea Resort
BOUTIQUE HOTEL **$$$**

(☑ 062-384 7700; www.sunsearesort-muine.com; 50 Đ Nguyen Dinh Chieu; r US$74-135; ✳@🛜🏊) One of the most attractive hotels in Mui Ne, the elegant accommodation blends natural materials (thatch, lacquerware and rosewood) with modern design. There is a second shady pool fronted by the cheaper rooms with garden view. The Sukothai Restaurant is well regarded for Thai cuisine.

Villa Aria Mui Ne
BOUTIQUE HOTEL **$$$**

(☑ 062-374 1660; www.villaariamuine.com; 60A Đ Nguyen Dinh Chieu; r US$110-180; ✳🛜🏊) Delightful new modish hotel with hip rooms set on both sides of a gorgeous garden, and an inviting pool on the ocean side. The restaurant is a wonderful place for breakfast, and it's located close to the centre of the action. Online discounts often drop rates to below US$100.

Anantara Mui Ne Resort & Spa
RESORT **$$$**

(☑ 062-374 1888; http://mui-ne.anantara.com; 12A Đ Nguyen Dinh Chieu; r/villa from US$108/220; ✳@🛜🏊) Formerly the L'Anmien, the accommodation here is very luxurious indeed, some villas have private pools and even the cheapest rooms are beautifully finished and have huge balconies.

Victoria Phan Thiet Beach Resort
RESORT **$$$**

(☑ 062-381 3000; www.victoriahotels-asia.com; Km 9; r US$170-460; ✳@🛜🏊) The original luxury resort in Mui Ne, the Victoria is still a good place to stay. The open-plan bungalows feature huge bathrooms with deep tubs and Balinese-style outdoor showers. There is a lengthy strip of beach and two pools.

Shades
APARTMENTS **$$$**

(☑ 062-374 3236; www.shadesmuine.com; 98A Đ Nguyen Dinh Chieu; apt US$80-170; ✳@🛜🏊) Ticking the right contemporary design boxes, Shades offers luxurious studio apartments, and studios with open-plan kitchens and modern trim, some with sea views. Breakfast is included.

🍴 Eating

Mui Ne has an incredible selection of restaurants, most geared to the cosmopolitan tastes of its visitors, with Russian, Italian, Thai and Indian cuisine all present. Indeed, at times is seems the only thing tricky to find is good authentic local food.

After years of rumours, virtually all of the once-famous but illegally built seafront shacks (collectively known the Bo Ke restaurants) were removed by police in 2013. If you really want to eat great seafood by the shore, nearby Phan Thiet has lots of great places.

Try the **goat restaurants** in Ham Tien around the Km 18 mark for a local experience. Choose from barbecued goat or goat hot pot, herbs and all.

As Mui Ne is an upmarket resort rather than a backpacker stronghold, it's one of the most expensive places to dine out in Vietnam.

★ Com Chay Phuoc
VEGETARIAN **$**

(15B Đ Huynh Thuc Khang; meals 20,000d; ⊙7am-9pm; ☑) An exceptional little roadside vegetarian place owned by Di, the ever-helpful English-speaking owner. There's no menu, but always four or five freshly cooked Vietnamese dishes (and sometimes traditional Indian music on the stereo). You eat on bamboo tables in very clean surrounds. It's right opposite the Eiffel Tower of the Little Paris resort, on the far east of the strip.

Phat Hamburgers
INTERNATIONAL **$**

(253 Đ Nguyen Dinh Chieu; burgers 55,000-95,000d; ⊙11am-9.30pm; 🛜) Roadside burger joint with variety of options, from gourmet to classic, served with great fries. Sip on a shake (try the chocolate and mint) while you feast on meat.

Lam Tong
VIETNAMESE, SEAFOOD **$**

(92 Đ Nguyen Dinh Chieu; dishes 28,000-115,000d; ⊙11.30am-9.30pm) You're eating under a corrugated roof, and staff can be brusque verging on rude, but this beachfront restaurant serves good seafood, Vietnamese classics, and some vegetarian dishes.

Peaceful Family Restaurant
VIETNAMESE **$**

(Yen Gia Quan; 53 Đ Nguyen Dinh Chieu; dishes 30,000-70,000d; ⊙7am-9.30pm) A long-running local restaurant, the family here serve up traditional Vietnamese cuisine under a breezy thatched roof. Prices are pretty reasonable and the service is always efficient and friendly.

★ Sandals
INTERNATIONAL **$$**

(24 Đ Nguyen Dinh Chieu; Mia Resort; meals 90,000-350,000d; ⊙7am-10pm; 🛜) This outstanding hotel restaurant is the most atmospheric place in town. It's particularly romantic at night, with tables set around the shoreside pool or in the elegant dining rooms. Waiting staff are knowledgeable, attentive and welcoming.The menu is superb with everything

from pasta dishes to Malay-style laksa executed and presented beautifully. Get stuck into the extensive wine list or enjoy a fresh juice with your meal.

Shree Ganesh
INDIAN $$

(57 Đ Nguyen Dinh Chieu; mains 52,000-160,000d; ☺11.30-10pm; 🖥📶) Excellent, authentic Indian restaurant with wide selection of dishes from the subcontinent, including plenty of choice for vegetarians (such as a generous thali). The garlic naan really is to savour.

Rung Forest
VIETNAMESE $$

(65A Đ Nguyen Dinh Chieu; dishes 70,000-200,000d; ☺5-10pm) An incredible building, with something of a forest screening tables from the road and lots of tribal art, masks and statues about this place. The menu includes good clay pots and hot pots, lots of seafood and some Western options.

Villa Aria Mui Ne
INTERNATIONAL $$

(mains 85,000-180,000d; ☺7am-9.30pm; 🖥) Beautifully designed hotel restaurant with tables set on a shoreside deck and a menu that includes salads (from 75,000d), soups, pasta and noodles. There's a good cocktail list.

Oliver's
ITALIAN $$

(📞062-374 3272; 229C Đ Nguyen Dinh Chieu; mains 50,000-165,000d; ☺10am-11pm; 🖥) Previously called La Taverna, this place is popular thanks to its thin-crust pizzas and home-made pastas. The extensive menu also includes Vietnamese faves, fresh seafood and Italian vino.

Snow
FUSION $$

(📞062-374 3123; 109 Đ Nguyen Dinh Chieu; mains 50,000-250,000d; ☺noon-10pm; ❄🖥) One of the few air-conditioned restaurants in Mui Ne, it's aptly named Snow. Choose from decent Japanese sushi and sashimi or sample Russian, international and Vietnamese cuisine. Rumbles on as a cocktail bar later in the evening.

DRUNK AND DISORDERLY

Perhaps due in some part to the insane drink promotions on offer in Mui Ne night spots, the odd fight breaks out each month. Keep your distance from trouble, especially if it involves local Vietnamese, as you don't know who they are, how many friends they have or what they might be carrying in their pockets.

Drinking

It wouldn't be a surf centre without a legion of beachside bars, and Mui Ne delivers.

Joe's Café
BAR

(www.joescafegardenresort.com; 86 Đ Nguyen Dinh Chieu; ☺7am-1am; 🖥) Mui Ne's premier live music (every night at 7.30pm) hangout with a sociable bar area, tables under trees, lots of drinks specials, an extensive food menu and pool table. Draws a slightly older crowd.

Fun Key
BAR

(124 Đ Nguyen Dinh Chieu; ☺10am-1am; 🖥) With a faintly boho ambience, this bar is popular with the backpacker crowd. Overlooks the ocean and has drink promotions to rev things up.

Dragon Beach
BAR, NIGHTCLUB

(120-121 Đ Nguyen Dinh Chieu ; ☺8am-2am) With a great shoreside location that catches the sea breeze, this place is the most happenning dance floor in town. Western and local DJs playing deep house, techno and drum 'n' bass. There's a chill-out deck with cushions to one side. Happy hour is 8pm to 10pm.

Wax
BAR

(68 Đ Nguyen Dinh Chieu; ☺noon-late; 🖥) A well-established beach bar, Wax has happy hour until midnight when they light up the beach bonfire. There are also fire shows around 11pm nightly. Drunken bopping and beachside flopping draw the crowds.

Sankara
BAR, NIGHTCLUB

(www.sankaravietnam.com; 78 Đ Nguyen Dinh Chieu; ☺11am-1am; 🖥) Superstylin' beach lounge, including chill-out pavilions and day beds, a swimming pool and a globalista menu. However, though it looks the part, Sankara can lack atmosphere, and prices reflect the chic.

DJ Station
BAR, NIGHTCLUB

(120C Đ Nguyen Dinh Chieu; ☺5pm-late; 🖥) One of the more popular bar-clubs in Mui Ne with a resident DJ, drink promotions and er...sexy dancers some nights. Popular with Russians on the lash. Happy hour is 7pm till 11pm.

Deja Vu
BAR

(21 Đ Nguyen Dinh Chieu; ☺noon-1am; 🖥) A hip lounge-bar at the Phan Thiet end of the strip, offering shishas, cocktails and an international menu.

ℹ️ Information

The website www.muinebeach.net is an excellent resource run by Adam Bray, an expert on the area, though the listings could be updated a bit more frequently.

Internet and wi-fi is available at pretty much all hotels and resorts, as well as at many restaurants and bars. There are several ATMs along the main Mui Ne strip.

Main Post Office (348 Đ Huynh Thuc Khang; ⊙7am-5pm) In Mui Ne village.

Sinh Tourist (www.thesinhtourist.vn; 144 Đ Nguyen Dinh Chieu) Operates out of Mui Ne Resort, booking open-tour buses, and trips around Mui Ne and offering credit-card cash advances.

ℹ️ Getting There & Away

Mui Ne offers both north and south links to Hwy 1. The northern link is a wonderfully scenic stretch, passing giant dunes, deserted beaches and a beautiful lake ringed with water lilies.

BUS

Open-tour buses are the most convenient option for Mui Ne, as most public buses only serve Phan Thiet. Several companies have daily services to/from HCMC (120,000d to 149,000d, six hours), Nha Trang (120,000d, five hours) and Dalat (110,000d, four hours).

Sleeper open-tour night buses usually cost more; Sinh Tourist's prices are HCMC (209,000d), Nha Trang (209,000d), Hoi An (378,000d) and Hue (477,000d).

Phuong Trang (www.futabuslines.com.vn; 97 Đ Nguyen Dinh Chieu) has four to five comfortable buses a day running between Mui Ne and HCMC (135,000d).

Local buses (9000d, 45 minutes, every 15 minutes) make trips between Phan Thiet bus station and Mui Ne, departing from the Coopmart, on the corner of Đ Nguyen Tat Thanh and Đ Tran Hung Dao.

CAR

It costs around US$110 to rent a car for the run to HCMC (five to six hours). There are numerous rental agencies dotted along the main strip. **Saigon 2 Mui Ne** (☑ 0126 552 0065; www.saigon-2muine.com) gets good reports for reliability, its website even has a forum where you can search for people to share a ride with.

If you've a little more time, consider hiring a car to take you along the scenic coastal road to Vung Tau, perhaps stopping at the Ke Ga lighthouse en route. A one-way trip (five to six hours for a leisurely drive) costs US$100. You can then take the hydrofoil from Vung Tau directly to the heart of HCMC. This is a far more relaxing way to travel to central HCMC as it avoid the chaos of Hwy 1.

MOTORBIKE

Easy Riders operate from Mui Ne, although there are not as many riders as in Dalat or Nha Trang. One of the best trips to experience by motorbike is actually the triangle between these three destinations, as the mountain roads from Mui Ne to Dalat and on to Nha Trang are some of the most dramatic in the south.

A *xe om* ride from Phan Thiet to Mui Ne will cost around 75,000d.

ℹ️ Getting Around

CAR & MOTORBIKE

Periodically the local police clamp down on tourists riding motorbikes in Mui Ne without the correct documentation and issue fines. However, dozens of visitors still rent scooters, which cost about 120,000d per day.

The area isn't highly populated and it's not on the main highway, but traffic still moves very fast along the main strip. Take care.

TAXI

Mui Ne is so spread out that it's difficult to wander about on foot if it is very hot. There are plenty of *xe om* drivers to take you up and down the strip; no trip should cost more than 20,000d to 40,000d, depending on how far you want to go.

Mai Linh (☑ 062-389 8989) operates metered taxis, although call ahead to book later in the evening or ask the restaurant or bar to assist.

Phan Thiet

☑ 062 / POP 179,000

Before the discovery of Mui Ne, Phan Thiet was an emerging resort town in its own right, but it has been eclipsed by the new kid on the block. The town is traditionally known for its *nuoc mam* (fish sauce), producing 16 to 17 million litres of the stinky stuff per annum. During the colonial period, the Europeans lived in their own segregated zone stretching along the northern bank of the Phan Thiet River, while the Vietnamese, Cham, Southern Chinese, Malays and Indonesians lived along the southern bank.

The river flowing through the centre of town creates a small fishing harbour, which is always chock-a-block with brightly painted boats. To get to Phan Thiet's beachfront, turn off Đ Tran Hung Dao (Hwy 1) into Đ Nguyen Tat Thanh – the road opposite the Victory Monument, an arrow-shaped concrete tower with a cluster of victorious patriots around the base.

LIZARD FISHING

When most people think of fishing in the mountains they conjure up images of hooking river trout or lake bass. But in the arid foothills of the south-central coast (notably around places such as Ca Na, Phan Rang, Phan Thiet and Mui Ne) there is a whole other kind of angling, and a walk in these hills can yield one of the strangest sights in Vietnam – lizard fishing.

These lizards, called *than lan nui,* are members of the gecko family and good for eating. The traditional way of catching the lizards is by setting a hook on a long bamboo fishing pole and dangling bait from the top of a boulder until the spunky little reptiles strike.

Lizards are served grilled, roasted or fried, and are often made into a pâté (complete with finely chopped bones) and eaten as a dip with rice-paper crackers.

Phan Thiet has some excellent **seafood restaurants** off its seafront promenade, including **Song Bien** (☎ 062-382 9868; 162 Le Loi; meals 70,000-200,000d; ⊗ 11am-9pm; ☎).

❶ Getting There & Away

Phan Thiet bus station (☎ 062-382 1361; Đ Tu Van Tu) is on the northern outskirts of town. The nearest train station to Phan Thiet is 12km west of town in dusty little Muong Man.

Ta Cu Mountain

📘 062

The highlight here is the **white reclining Buddha** (Tuong Phat Nam). At 49m long, it's the largest in Vietnam. The pagoda was constructed in 1861, but the Buddha was only added in 1972. It has become an important pilgrimage centre for Buddhists, who stay overnight in the pagoda's dormitory. Foreigners can't do this without police permission, but **Thien Thay Hotel** (☎ 062-386 7484; r 280,000d; ❄) offers basic rooms atop the mountain.

The mountain is just off Hwy 1, 28km south from Phan Thiet. From the highway it's a beautiful two-hour trek (15,000d), or a 10-minute cable-car ride (85,000d return) and a short, but steep, hike.

Phan Thiet to Long Hai

📘 064

A beautiful road parallels the coast between Phan Thiet and Long Hai, passing some memorable scenery, and traffic is light. There are pockets of tourism development, but for now most this coastline is a beguiling mix of giant sand dunes, fishing villages, wide ocean views and some near-deserted beaches. This region makes a great day trip from Vung Tau or Long Hai, or a rewarding scenic road to enjoy. The most impressive sight is the majestic Ke Ga lighthouse.

There's very limited public transport so a motorbike or car is the way to go. Savvy travellers are now using this road to avoid tackling the nightmarish Hwy 1, and then taking the hydrofoil from Vung Tau to HCMC.

Immediately south of Phan Thiet, the first section of the road is beautiful, with a casuarina-lined shoreline and the ocean to the east, while the inland scenery is dominated by rust-red sand dunes.

Ke Ga Lighthouse

Around 30km south of Phan Thiet, the spectacular **Ke Ga lighthouse** (admission 20,000d; ⊗ 7am-4.30pm) dates from the French era. Constructed in 1899, it sits on a rocky islet some 300m from the shore, towering almost 40m above the ocean. It's possible to swim (or even wade) across if the tide is low, but most visitors hire a boatman (250,000d return) to get across. A staircase winds up to the top, from where there are magnificent vistas over the ocean and inland hills.

Ke Ga to Ho Coc

From Ke Ga the coastal road pushes southwest, passing fields bursting with dragon fruit (the main crop), reaching **La Gi**, 22km down the road. There's no reason to hang around La Gi, an isolated market town, but it does have hourly bus connections (37,000d, two hours) to Long Hai.

Continuing southwest of La Gi, the coastal road keeps snaking along the shoreline, with towering sand dunes on the inland side. Chunks of the near-virgin coastline have been parceled off here and there, awaiting hotel resorts and mass tourism, but it's not hard to find a beach for a revitalising dip. The section around 7km north of Ho Coc is particularly scenic and worth investigating the lonely (for now) road hugging an undeveloped shore.

Ho Coc Beach

With golden sands, rolling inland dunes and clear waters, this beach makes a tempting place to stop. The giant **Saigon-Ho Coc Beach Resort** (☑064-387 8175; r 800,000-3,500,000d; ✻@⊚✖), very much geared at the local market, has grabbed a large chunk of the shoreline, but on weekdays it's still peaceful here and you should have the beach largely to yourself.

About 300m inland from the beach **Hotel Ven Ven** (☑064-379 1121; http://venvenhotel.com; r 600,000-1,000,000d; ✻@⊚) is very tasteful, with classy, well-appointed rooms in lush gardens. The restaurant here is good, if quite pricey, and strong on seafood (meals 60,000d upwards), including an excellent fish curry.

Ho Tram Beach

South of Ho Coc, the coastal road soon unexpectedly becomes a four-lane highway, which is designed to facilitate access to the gargantuan **Grand Ho Tram Strip**, a casino resort complex, plus restaurants and shops. A concrete blot on the landscape, this isolated Vegas-style development was originally constructed by the MGM group, but after an on-off saga lasting years they finally abandoned the project, and a local business took over and opened the resort in July 2013.

Casino aside, Ho Tram consists of nothing more than a tiny fishing village, scruffy open-air market and a fine beach (though the central section is strewn with rubbish) and a handful of places to stay.

🍴 Sleeping & Eating

Local villagers steam, fry and grill delicious fresh seafood right on the beach in Ho Tram. Make sure you try the delicious steamed clams or mussels served with a topping of peanuts, spring onion, lime and chilli; a portion of six costs around 30,000d.

Hoa Bien Motel   HOTEL $
(☑064-378 2279; http://nhanghihoabien.com; r 350,000-600,000d; ✻⊚) An excellent deal, the spacious rooms with modern facilities and bathrooms are well presented at this small hotel, 100m from the beach. The helpful owners speak some English.

**Ho Tram Beach
Resort & Spa**   BOUTIQUE HOTEL $$$
(☑064-378 1525; www.hotramresort.com; r/bungalow from US$80/130; ✻@⊚✖) This beautifully landscaped complex is dotted with attractive bungalows in Hoi An-meets-Bali style, each with high ceilings and stylish decor and outdoor bathrooms. There's also a spa, salt-water infinity pool and an open-plan restaurant that's open to nonguests for a memorable lunch stop.

Sanctuary   BOUTIQUE RESORT $$$
(☑064-78 1631; www.sanctuary.com.vn; villas US$565-999; ✻@⊚✖) Home to state-of-the-art contemporary villas, this is the ultimate getaway for those wanting to really indulge. Three-bedroom villas include open-plan kitchens, private pools and flat-screen TVs. No detail is missed but this sybaritic experience certainly does have a premium price.

Long Hai

☑064

If Vung Tau is all a bit bling for you, then consider Long Hai, a more local seaside retreat within a few hours' drive of HCMC. The fishing village of Long Hai, now only 15km northeast of Vung Tau thanks to a major bridge, has a pretty white-sand beach and the area benefits from a microclimate that brings less rain than other parts of the south. This is why Bao Dai, the last emperor of Vietnam, built a private residence here (now the Anoasis Beach Resort).

Long Hai can be a peaceful place to visit during the week, but it loses its local character on the weekends when Vietnamese tourists pack the sands. Most of the resort hotels are on the northeast of town, on the road that heads to Ho Tram.

⊙ Sights & Activities

The western end of Long Hai's beach is where fishing boats moor and is not so clean. However, the eastern end is pretty, with white sand and swaying palms. For an even prettier beach, keep heading east.

After the Tet holiday, Long Hai hosts an annual major **fishermen's pilgrimage festival**, where hundreds of boats come from afar to worship at **Mo Co Temple**.

🍴 Sleeping

Thuy Lan Guesthouse   GUEST HOUSE $
(☑064-366 3567; Rte 19; r 250,000-450,000d; ✻@⊚) About 150m from the beach this small guesthouse has light, airy rooms with modern bathrooms and firm beds, some with balconies. Some English spoken.

Anoasis Beach Resort
RESORT $$$

(☑ 064-386 8227; www.anoasisresort.com.vn; Provincial Rd 44; r from US$80-320; ❄ @ 🛜 ☎) Emperor Bao Dai's former residence has plenty of charm – the bungalows, cottages and villas, some with private pools, are set in stunning gardens fronting a private beach. Service standards are OK, though staff only speak limited English. There's a plush spa and tennis courts.

✗ Eating

There's a rustic cluster of thatch-roof beachside restaurants called **Can Tin 1** (mains around 30,000-100,000d; ⊙ 7am-9pm), **2**, **3** and **4** (all with the same opening hours and prices) near Military Guesthouse 298. These serve reliable Vietnamese cuisine, including fresh seafood dishes.

ⓘ Getting There & Away

Long Hai takes about three hours to reach by road from HCMC. It is more relaxing to arrive by a combination of hydrofoil and road via Vung Tau. The 15km road between Vung Tau and Long Hai will cost about 100,000d by *xe om* or about 220,000d by metered taxi.

From Mui Ne, follow the road less travelled along coastal Rte 55. It is very scenic, passing a series of stunning beaches and the Ke Ga lighthouse, and traffic is mercifully light for Vietnam.

Vung Tau

☑ 064 / POP 212,000

A popular weekend escape from HCMC, Vung Tau rocks at weekends when beach-starved locals and expats descend in numbers, but it is relatively quiet during the week. The city enjoys a spectacular location on a peninsula, with ocean on three sides, and the light and sea air makes it a refreshing break from sultry HCMC.

Oil is big business here, so the horizon is regularly dotted with oil tankers, and petro dollars dominate the economy, inflating prices considerably.

Vung Tau is a remarkably civilised-looking city of broad boulevards and imposing colonial-era buildings, but a slightly seedy bar scene also flourishes here, accommodating the tastes (and wallets) of retired Anzac servicemen, Russian expats and oil workers.

Historically few travellers bothered to visit the city, but new transport connections have put Vung Tau on the map. Hydrofoil links from central HCMC are now excellent, and

the new coastal road to Mui Ne via Ho Trang offers a tempting, off-the-beaten-track route.

◉ Sights

Welcome to Rio di Vietnam, where soaring forested peaks rise over a turquoise bay. There's even a giant Jesus, though few would compare Vung Tau's beaches to the Copacabana.

Worldwide Arms Museum
MUSEUM

(http://worldwidearmsmuseum.wordpress.com; 14 Đ Hai Dong; admission 100,000d; ⊙ 9am-5pm) An outstanding, and unexpected find in the backstreets of Vung Tau, this is a superb museum, even if you've little interest in warfare. There's a simply stunning collection of military uniforms and weaponry from all over the world: Samuri nobility, crusaders in chain mail, Roman legionaries, Royal horseguards, even African warriors in leopard skins alongside dozens of vintage pistols, muskets, swords and helmuts, all in modern displays with English translations.

There's also a private primate rescue centre with spacious enclosures for gibbons and monkeys rescued from traffickers. It is not a zoo, but the private passion of the museum owner who takes care of the mammals.

Giant Jesus
MONUMENT

(parking 2000d; ⊙ 7.30-11.30am & 1.30-5pm) FREE Atop Small Mountain with his arms outstretched to embrace the South China Sea, this 32m Giant Jesus is the biggest in the world, or so the locals claim – 6m taller than his illustrious Brazilian cousin. It is possible to ascend to the arms for a panoramic view.

Some 900-odd stairs wind their way up the mountain, a Vietnamese version of stairway to heaven, but it is possible to take a short-cut by motorbike up a bumpy mountain road if you can find a local who knows the way. It starts from Hem 220, off Đ Phan Chu Trinh.

Lighthouse
LIGHTHOUSE

(parking 2000d; ⊙ 7am-5pm) FREE Built by the French, this 1910 lighthouse boasts a spectacular 360-degree view of Vung Tau. From Cau Da Pier on Đ Ha Long, take a sharp right on the alley north of the Hai Au Hotel, then roll on up the hill. Although Jesus and the lighthouse look temptingly close, it is not possible to walk or drive directly between them, as there is a military base in the hills here.

Vung Tau

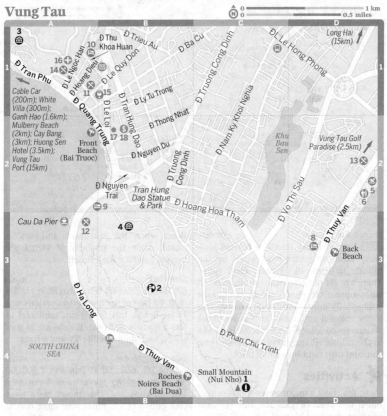

Vung Tau

◎ Sights
1 Giant Jesus	C4
2 Lighthouse	B3
3 White Villa	A1
4 Worldwide Arms Museum	B3

⊕ Activities, Courses & Tours
5 Seagull & Dolphin Pools	D2
6 Surf Station	D2

⊜ Sleeping
7 Lan Rung Resort & Spa	B4
8 Lua Hong Motel	D3
9 Lucy's Hotel	A2
10 Son Ha Hotel	A1

⊗ Eating
11 Bistrot 9	A1
12 David Italian Restaurant	A3
13 Imperial Plaza	D2
14 Tommy's 3	A1

◉ Drinking & Nightlife
Lucy's Sports Bar	(see 9)
15 Red Parrot	B1

ⓘ Information
16 International SOS	A1
17 OSC Vietnam Travel	B2
18 Vietcombank	B2

White Villa MUSEUM

(Bach Dinh, Villa Blanche; Đ Tran Phu; admission 15,000d; ⊙7am-4pm) The weekend retreat of French governor Paul Doumer (later French President) this gorgeous, grand colonial-era residence has extensive gardens and an oddly empty interior (besides the odd piece of furniture and some Ming pottery retrieved from shipwrecks off the coast). It sits about 30m above the road, up a winding lane.

Around Vung Tau

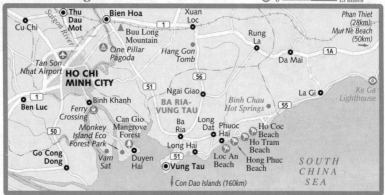

French Field Guns LANDMARK

FREE Further along Tran Phu beyond Mulberry Beach, a pretty road winds up the hillside to some old French Field Guns. There are six of these massive cannons, all with support trenches, demonstrating how strategically important Cap St Jacques was to the colonial authorities as it guarded the waterways to Saigon. Look out for Hem 444 in the fishing village, about 8km from Vung Tau, and turn right on a small track.

🏃 Activities

Vung Tau is not a major water-sports centre, but if the weather gods are smiling, some residents surf and kitesurf.

Vung Tau Golf Paradise GOLF

(☎064-385 9697; www.golfparadise.com.vn) On the eastern side of the Vung Tau peninsula this 27-hole course is quite a challenge, with mature trees lining the fairways.

Surf Station SURFING, WINDSURFING

(☎064-526 101; www.vungtausurf.com; 8 Đ Thuy Van) Based at the Vung Tau Beach Club, Surf Station offers board rental and kitesurfing and surfing classes.

Seagull & Dolphin Pools SWIMMING

(Đ Thuy Ban, Back Beach) These pools are almost opposite the Imperial Plaza. Both charge 50,000d for the day.

🛏 Sleeping

During weekends and holidays, Vung Tau's hundred or more hotels can be heavily booked, so it is sensible to make a reservation. Most foreigners prefer to stay on Front Beach where the restaurants and bars are found, while the majority of Vietnamese visitors head for Back Beach.

Son Ha Hotel HOTEL $

(☎064-385 2356; 17A Đ Thu Khoa Huan; r US$18; ❄@🛜) One of the few budget options near Front Beach, this family-run minihotel offers a homely welcome. Rooms are in good shape, including satellite TV and a fridge.

Lua Hong Motel HOTEL $

(☎064-381 8992; 137 Đ Thuy Van; r 300,000-380,000d; ❄@🛜) For a more Vietnamese take on Vung Tau. This 'motel' has a touch (but only a touch, mind you) more decorative flair than some of the neighbouring places, plus sea views.

Huong Sen Hotel HOTEL $$

(☎064-355 1711; 182 Đ Tran Phu; r US$29-49; ❄@🛜) Right at the end of Mulberry Beach, this is affiliated with the long-running Huong Sen in HCMC. Rates are very reasonable for the standards and it's a nice escape if you want to get away from the honky tonk part of town.

Lucy's Hotel HOTEL $$

(☎064-385 8896; www.lucyssportsbar.com; 138 Ha Long ; r 600,000d; ❄🛜) These comfortable rooms, above a popular bar, could be just the ticket if you're looking for a place to kip down just steps from the ferry terminal. All have a balcony overlooking the bay, modern bathrooms and staff are friendly.

Lan Rung Resort & Spa HOTEL $$

(☎064-352 6010; www.lanrungresort.com; 3-6 Đ Ha Long; 7 from US$71; ❄@🛜🏊) Lan Rung is also one of the few places with a beachside setting, albeit a rocky one. The rooms are attractive and include heavy wooden furniture and all the facilities you'd expect. There are seafood and Italian restaurants. Service is willing, but expect a few communication issues.

✗ Eating

There's great seafood, and lots of international flavours available in Vung Tau.

Bistrot 9   FRENCH, INTERNATIONAL **$**
(9 Đ Truong Vinh Ky; snacks/meals from 55,000/90,000d; ⊙7.30am-9.30pm; 🐾) An atmospheric bistro on a quiet side street that's perfect for breakfast or brunch, crêpe, panini or a full-on splurge (try the salmon carpaccio or pork with Dijon mustard). They also sell homemade gourmet chocolates and have the best wine selection in town.

Imperial Plaza   VIETNAMESE **$**
(159 Đ Thuy Van; meals from 50,000d; ⊙8am-9pm; ⊛) This shopping centre offers a selection of dining options including a small food court. Perfect (and air-conditioned) for those overheating with indecisiveness: choose from pizza through to *pho*.

★Ganh Hao   SEAFOOD **$$**
(☑064-355 0909; 3 Đ Tran Phu; mains 55,000-210,000d; ⊙11.30am-9pm; 🐾) Impressive sea-food restaurant, with tables positioned on terraces by the ocean, that's always packed with locals, so try to get here as early as possible. The menu is extensive, with delicious fish, lobster, crab, squid and prawn dishes, though wine is expensive. It's huge, and somehow, despite the crowds, it all ticks over efficiently.

Cay Bang   SEAFOOD **$$**
(☑064-383 8522; 69 Đ Tran Phu; mains 52,000-230,000d; ⊙11am-10pm) A seafood institution with a great location on the water, Cay Bang is set under the shadow of the Virgin Mary and Baby Jesus. At weekends, it draws a huge crowd of the Vung Tau faithful for the shellfish, hot pots and grilled fish.

Tommy's 3   INTERNATIONAL **$$**
(www.tommysvietnam.com; 3 Đ Ba Cu; mains 60,000-300,000d; ⊙7am-11pm; 🐾) Boasts a prime front terrace that draws a mixed crowd of locals, expats and tourists. The food is mainly Western and familiar, with big portions of steaks and burgers, plus local food including tasty noodle dishes.

David Italian Restaurant   ITALIAN **$$**
(130 Đ Ha Long; mains 60,000-200,000d; ⊙11am-10pm) Located on a prime strip overlooking the hydrofoil dock, this is an authentic Italian-run restaurant. The pasta is freshly prepared and the pizzas are the best in town.

SOUTHEAST COAST VUNG TAU

ANZAC SITES AROUND VUNG TAU

Nearly 60,000 Australian soldiers were involved in the American War throughout the 1960s and 1970s. The **Long Tan Memorial Cross** commemorates a particularly fierce battle that took place on 18 August 1966 between Australian troops and Viet Cong fighters. Originally erected by Australian survivors of the battle, the current cross is a replica installed by the Vietnamese in 2002. It's located about 18km from Ba Ria town or 55km from Vung Tau, near the town of Nui Dat. Permits are no longer necessary, and can be combined with the seldom-visited **Lon Phuoc tunnels**, an underground network that is a much smaller version of the more famous Cu Chi.

At Minh Dam, 5km from Long Hai, there are **caves** with historical connections to the Franco–Viet Minh and American Wars. Although the caves are little more than spaces between the boulders covering the cliff-face, VC soldiers bunked here off and on between 1948 and 1975; you can still see bullet holes in the rocks from the skirmishes that took place. Steps hewn into the rock-face lead up to the caves, with spectacular views over the coastal plains at the top.

Nearby there is a **mountain-top temple** with more great panoramic views of the coastline.

Tommy's (☑064-351 5181; www.tommysvietnam.com; 3 Đ Ba Cu) operate tours for returning vets that include Long Tan, Long Phuoc and Minh Dam. The cost including transport and guide is US$120 for up to three people.

Otherwise hook up with a *xe om* driver and expect to pay US$20 or so for a tour around these sights.

🍷 Drinking

Vung Tau nightlife is raucous by Vietnamese standards with lots of hostess bars and the occasional floor show.

Lucy's Sports Bar
SPORTS BAR

(www.lucyssportsbar.com; 138 Đ Ha Long; ⊘7am-midnight; 🤶) Non-sleazy, non-hostess bar with a busy pool table, great sea-facing terrace and sociable vibe. As the name indicates there's a viewing diet of sports events – from test cricket to Aussie Rules. Also serves pub grub.

Red Parrot
PUB

(6 Đ Le Quy Don; ⊘noon-midnight; 🤶) One of the late-night spots that picks up as the evening wears on, this is Vung Tau at its most decadent, complete with war veterans, oil workers, alcoholics and working girls. Check out the vintage Vespas.

ℹ️ Information

Consult www.vungtau-city.com for relatively up-to-date information on the city of Vung Tau.

International SOS (☑064-385 8776; www.internationalsos.com; 1 Đ Le Ngoc Han; ⊘24hr) A well-respected clinic with international standards and international prices.

Main Post Office (8 Đ Hoang Dieu; ⊘7am-5.30pm) Located at the ground level of the Petrovietnam Towers building.

OSC Vietnam Travel (☑064-385 2008; www.oscvietnamtravel.com.vn; 2 Đ Le Loi; ⊘7am-4.30pm) Government-run travel agency that offers transport booking and a host of local trips.

Vietcombank (27-29 Đ Tran Hung Dao; ⊘7.30am-3.30pm) Exchanges cash, travellers cheques and offers credit-card advances.

ℹ️ Getting There & Away

BUS

From Mien Dong bus station in HCMC, air-con minibuses (50,000d, 2½ hours, frequent) leave for Vung Tau between 6am and 7pm. From Vung Tau's **bus station** (192A Đ Nam Ky Khoi Nghia) to Mulberry Beach or Back Beach, a *xe om* will cost around 30,000d.

BOAT

It's much more enjoyable to catch a hydrofoil. There are three boat operators to HCMC (200,000d to 250,000d, 90 minutes), all using the same terminals. The best boats are run by **Vina Express** (☑HCMC 08-3825 3333, Vung Tau 064-385 6530) and **Petro Express** (☑HCMC 08-3821 0650, Vung Tau 064-3351 5151); those operated by Greenlines are in poor condition. Services leave every 30 minutes until 4.45pm and there are additional boats at weekends, when it's important to book ahead. In Vung Tau the boat leaves from Cau Da pier.

Two ferries connect Con Son Island with Vung Tau, with sailings approximately every second day. Boats do not leave when seas are rough (and conditions aboard the boats are pretty rough too). Tickets can be purchased from the office at 1007/36 Đ 30/4 which reads **BQL Cang Ben Dam Huyen Con Dao** (bunk bed 270,000d; ⊘7.30-11.30am & 1.30-4.30pm Mon-Fri). The ferry departs at 5pm from Vung Tau port, which lies about 15km west of the city, the journey takes 12 hours.

ℹ️ Getting Around

Vung Tau is easily traversed on two wheels or four. Guesthouses and restaurants can arrange bicycle hire (per day US$2) and motorbike hire (from US$6 to US$9 per day). Metered taxis will likely work out cheaper than trying to negotiate with ruthless *cyclo* or *xe om* drivers. **Mai Linh** (☑064-356 5656) is a reliable operator and has plenty of taxis cruising the streets.

Con Dao Islands

☑064 / POP 6000

Isolated from the mainland, the Con Dao Islands are one of the star attractions in Vietnam. Long the Devil's Island of Indochina, the preserve of political prisoners and undesirables, this place is now turning heads thanks to its striking natural beauty. Con Son, the largest of this chain of 15 islands and islets, is ringed with lovely beaches, coral reefs and scenic bays, and remains partially covered in thick forests. In addition to hiking, diving and exploring empty coastal roads and deserted beaches, there are some excellent wildlife-watching opportunities such as the black giant squirrel and the endemic bow-fingered gecko.

Although it seems something of an island paradise, Con Son was once hell on earth for the thousands of prisoners who languished in confinement here in no less than a dozen jails during French rule and the American-backed regime.

Roughly 80% of the land area in the island chain is part of Con Dao National Park, which protects Vietnam's most important sea-turtle nesting grounds. For the past decade, the World Wildlife Foundation (WWF) has been working with local park rangers on a long-term monitoring program. During nesting season (May to

Con Dao Islands

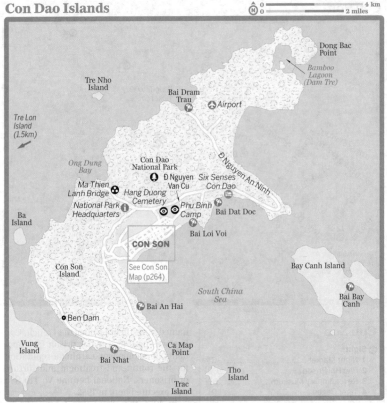

November) the park sets up ranger stations to rescue threatened nests and move them to the safe haven of hatcheries. Other interesting sea life around Con Dao includes the dugong, a rare marine mammal in the same family as the manatee.

Many visitors to Con Son are package-tour groups of former VC soldiers who were imprisoned on the island. The Vietnamese government subsidises these jaunts as a show of gratitude for their sacrifice.

The driest time to visit Con Dao is from November to February, although the seas are calmest from March to July. The rainy season lasts from June to September, but there are also northeast and southwest monsoons from September to November that can bring heavy winds. September and October are the hottest months, though even then the cool island breezes make Con Dao relatively comfortable when compared with HCMC or Vung Tau.

Change has been almost glacial, but with the arrival of the über-luxurious Six Senses Con Dao, the islands are now on the radar of the international jet-set. Travellers are discovering the islands as transport connections improve, but as flights are quite expensive (and the islands' cost of living is approximately double the mainland's), numbers are still small.

History

Occupied at various times by the Khmer, Malays and Vietnamese, Con Son Island also served as an early base for European commercial ventures in the region. The first recorded European arrival was a ship of Portuguese mariners in 1560. The British East India Company maintained a fortified trading post here from 1702 to 1705 – an experiment that ended when the English on the island were massacred in a revolt by the

Con Son

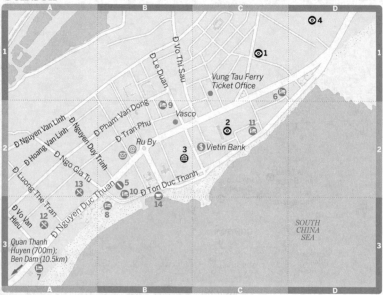

Makassar soldiers they had recruited on the Indonesian island of Sulawesi.

Con Son Island has a strong political and cultural history, and an all-star line-up of Vietnamese revolutionary heroes were incarcerated here. (Many streets are named after them.) Under the French, Con Son was used as a major prison for opponents of colonialism, earning a reputation for the routine mistreatment and torture of prisoners. National heroine Vo Thi Sau was executed here in 1952.

In 1954 the island was taken over by the South Vietnamese government, which continued to utilise its remoteness to hold opponents of the government (including students) in horrendous conditions.

During the American War, the South Vietnamese were joined here by US forces. The US built prisons here and maintained the notorious 'tiger cages' as late as 1970, when news of their existence was broken by a *Life* magazine report.

◎ Sights

◎ Con Son Town

There's nowhere quite like it in all Vietnam. This delightful pocket-sized island capital, with its litter-free streets, well-kept municipal buildings and air of calm and prosperity would, make a perfect location for a period film.

The main seafront promenade of Đ Ton Duc Thanh is a delight to stroll, lined with

French-era villas, some crumbling, others renovated into hotels. Nearby is the local market, busiest between 7am and 9am.

Of course, the town's genteel appearance and character is tempered considerably by the presence of several prisons, cemeteries and reminders of the islands' historic role as a penal colony. There are ghosts everywhere in Con Son.

All the following sights are in Con Son town, share the same opening hours and are covered by a single ticket costing 20,000d, which you can purchase in the museum.

Phu Hai Prison   HISTORICAL BUILDING
(⊘ 7-11.30am & 1-5pm) The largest of the 11 jails on the island, this prison dates from 1862. Thousands of prisoners were held here, with up to 200 prisoners crammed into each detention building. During the French era all prisoners were kept naked, chained together in rows, with one small box serving as a toilet for hundreds. One can only imagine the squalor and stench. Today, emaciated mannequins that are all too lifelike re-create the era.

It's a huge complex, where political and criminal classes were mixed together. 'Solitary' rooms where prisoners considered to be particulary dangerous contained as many as 63 inmates, herded together so tightly that there was no room to lie down. The prison church dates from the US era, but it was never used.

Tiger Cages   HISTORICAL BUILDING
The notorious cells dubbed tiger cages were built in 1940 by the French to incarcerate nearly 2000 political prisoners. There are 120 chambers with ceiling bars, where guards could poke at prisoners like tigers in a Victorian zoo. Prisoners were beaten with sticks from above, and sprinked with quick lime and water (which burnt their skin, and caused blindness).

The tiger cages were deliberately constructed away from the main prison, out of sight, and only accessed by an alleyway. They were unknown to the outside world until 1970, when a US congressional aide, Tom Harkin, visited Con Son and saw evidence of brutal torture of the prisoners he met there. Harkin had been tipped off about their existence by a former inmate and managed to break off the pre-arranged tour, and using a map given to him, discovered the tiger cages behind a vegetable garden, and photographed the cells and prisoners inside. The images were published by *Life* magazine in July 1970.

Hang Duong Cemetery   CEMETERY
Some 20,000 Vietnamese prisoners died on Con Son and 1994 of their graves can be seen at the peaceful Hang Duong Cemetery, located at the eastern edge of town. Sadly, only 700 of these graves bear the name of the victims.

Vietnam's most famous heroine, Vo Thi Sau (1933–52) was buried here, the first woman executed by a firing squad on Con Son, on 23 January 1952. For more Vo Thi Sau, see the boxed text below.

Today's pilgrims come to burn incense and leave offerings at her tomb, mirrors, combs and lipstick (symbolic because she died so young). You may even encounter fruit, and meals of sticky rice and pork.

In the distance behind the cemetery you'll see a huge monument symbolising three giant sticks of incense.

Phu Binh Camp   HISTORICAL BUILDING
(⊘ 7-11.30am & 1-5pm) On the edge of town, this prison was built in 1971 by the Americans, and had 384 chambers. The cells had corrugated-iron roofs, and were infernally

SOUTHEAST COAST CON DAO ISLANDS

THE TEENAGE MARTYR

If breeze is blowing from the north, you can probably smell the incense from a specific grave in Con Son's cemetary: the tomb of Vo Thi Sau, a national icon.

Vo Thi Sau, a teenage resistance fighter executed in Con Dao during the French occupation, was politically active from a very early age. She killed a French captain in a grenade attack at the age of 14, and was only captured years later following a second assassination attempt. Vo Thi Sau was taken to Con Dao and executed here, aged 19.

Visit the cemetery at midnight and you'll find crowds of people packed around her grave, saying prayers and making offerings. The Vietnamese believe that this is the most auspicious time to pay respects and venerate the spirit of this national heroine, who was killed in the early hours of 23 January 1952.

hot. The original structures remain in situ, but there's not that much left to see today. It was known as Camp 7 until 1973, when it closed following evidence of torture.

After the Paris Agreements in 1973, the name was changed to Phu Binh Camp.

Revolutionary Museum   MUSEUM

(⊙ 7-11am & 1.30-5pm) Located in the former French comandant's residence, this museum has exhibits on Vietnamese resistance against the French, communist opposition to the Republic of Vietnam, and the treatment of political prisoners. You'll also find a painting of Vo Thi Sau (facing death with her head held high), a diorama of the Con Daos and some stuffed wildlife: boas, lizards and monkeys.

An impressive-looking new Con Son Museum building (located at the eastern end of Đ Nguyen Hue) has been constructed. Exhibits from the Revolutionary Museum will be relocated here once it opens its doors.

⊙ Con Son Beaches

Con Dao has some excellent beaches. Enquire in hotels about snorkelling gear rental for about 100,000d per day or rent new gear through Dive! Dive! Dive! (p267) for US$10 per day.

Sandflies can be a big problem on Con Dao beaches, make sure you bring insect repellent.

Bai Dat Doc   BEACH

The best beach in the island, Bai Dat Doc is a simply beautiful cove, consisting of a kilometre-long crescent of pale sand, backed by green hills. It has a gently shelving profile and no pollution, so it's ideal for swimming. Though it's backed by the luxury bungalows of the Six Senses hotel, it's not a private beach and there are access points close to the road.

Very rarely dugongs have been seen frolicking in the water off the nearby cape.

Bai Dram Trau   BEACH

Reached via a dirt track 1km before the airport, Bai Dram Trau is a sublime but remote 700m half-moon crescent of soft sand, fringed by casuarina trees and bookended by forest-topped rocky promontories. It's best visited at low tide.

There's some snorkelling on reefs offshore and three very simple seafood shacks (all open noon till dusk only).

Bai Loi Voi   BEACH

On the north side of Con Son Town, Bai Loi Voi is a broad sand-and-shingle beach with lots of sea shells and casuarinas for shade. There's a good stretch of sandy beach right in the centre of Con Son, around the Con Dao Resort.

Bai An Hai   BEACH

Bai An Hai on the south side of town is appealing, but there are a good number of fishing boats moored nearby.

Tre Lon   ISLAND

Some of the more pristine beaches are on the smaller islands, such as the beautiful white-sand beach on Tre Lon, to the west of Con Son Island.

Bay Canh   ISLAND

Perhaps the best all-round island to visit is Bay Canh, to the east, which has lovely beaches, old-growth forest, mangroves, coral reefs and sea turtles (seasonal). There is a fantastic two-hour walk to a functioning French-era lighthouse on Bay Canh's eastern tip, although it involves a steep climb of 325m. Once at the summit, the panoramic views are breathtaking.

🏃 Activities

For more information on treks and boat trips around the Con Dao Islands, visit www.condaopark.com.vn, the official website for Con Dao National Park. It costs 20,000d to enter the park by day or 40,000d by night.

Overnight turtle-watching tours cost around 1,500,000 per person if booked via the national park office or Dive! Dive! Dive!. Note that nesting turtles are very rarely seen outside the main season (late June to early September).

Diving & Snorkelling

Experienced divers who know the waters of Vietnam have long talked up Con Dao as the most pristine marine environment in the country. The waters around the islands are officially protected, and there's abundant healthy coral (table, staghorn and brain are all in evidence). Marine life includes green and hawksbill turtles, rays, kingfish, lots of parrotfish and groupers and some sharks.

That said, things could be even better, as official protection is weak. Some boatmen still anchor directly on the reef, and illegal fishing affects fish numbers. Turtle eggs are also still occassionally traded under the counter, though penalties can be severe.

THE RETURN OF THE GREEN SEA TURTLE

Two decades ago the fate of the green sea turtle (Chelonia mydas) in Con Dao was in jeopardy. They were prized for their meat, and their shells had value as souvenirs. To make matters worse, the turtles' numbers were decimated by destructive fishing practices. And yet, today, following a decade of local and foreign initiatives, the turtle has made a remarkable comeback. One of Vietnam's most important sea-turtle nesting sites lies scattered around the shores of the Con Dao archipelago. The World Wildlife Foundation (WWF) has given substantial help, as have other international organisations, by setting up conservation stations on the islands of Bay Canh, Tre Lon, Tai and Cau. According to the WWF, since 1995 more than 800,000 hatchlings have been released into the sea. Up to 85% of sea-turtle eggs hatch successfully, which is the highest percentage in Vietnam. WWF has also launched a satellite tracking program (the first of its kind in Vietnam) to give conservation workers a better understanding of migration patterns, as well as key habitats used by the turtles for feeding and mating. Though the population is on the rise, many turtles still die after nesting, often by getting ensnared in fishing nets.

Visitors wishing to see the turtles in their natural habitat can arrange a trip to Bay Canh Island and spend the night at the conversation site. (Turtles only lay their eggs at night, each nest producing an average of 90 eggs.) The best time to see them is during the nesting season, which is from May to November. For information on trips, inquire at Con Dao National Park headquarters. Tours prices vary depending on numbers, but you need to budget around 1,500,000d per person plus extra for the guide, 40,000d for overnight park fees and 150,000d for basic accommodation. Dive! Dive! Dive! (p267) also offers boat trips to see the turtles, including an afternoon dive and a night dive, plus meals and overnight camping. Non-divers and snorkellers can join these trips for a reasonable price.

Diving is possible year-round, but for ideal conditions and good visibility, January to June is considered the best time, while November and December can see big storms. Prices are generally more expensive than at mainland destinations, but also more rewarding.

Wrecks, including a 65m freighter resting in 30m to 40m with abundant sealife, offer huge potential for more experienced divers.

Cheapo snorkelling trips are offered by some hotels but we've heard reports of boatmen spearfishing illegally on some of these trips. Dive! Dive! Dive!'s excursions do cost more, but are environmentally sound.

★ **Dive! Dive! Dive!** DIVING
(☎ 064-383 0701; www.dive-condao.com; Đ Nguyen Hue; ⊙ 8am-9pm) An experienced, conservation-minded American-run operation, offering both both PADI and SSI courses. Instructor Larry has years of experience diving the waters of Vietnam and offers daily dive (two dives are US$160) and snorkelling tours (US$40 including equipment). Dive! Dive! Dive! is licensed to operate in 31 dive sites around the islands. The seafront dive shop is a great source of general information on the Con Daos.

Trekking
There are lots of treks around Con Son Island, as much of the interior remains heavily forested. It is necessary to take a national park guide when venturing into the forest. Rates range from 180,000d to 300,000d depending on the duration of the trek.

It's a steep uphill climb to the old fruit plantations of **So Ray**, following a slippery but well-marked trail (lined with information panels about trees and wildlife) through dense rainforest. The plantation is home to a sociable troop of long-tailed macaques, with sweeping views over the main town to the other Con Dao islands beyond. The return hike takes about 90 minutes.

Bamboo Lagoon LAGOON
(Dam Tre) One of the more beautiful walks leads through thick forest and mangroves, past a hilltop stream to Bamboo Lagoon. There's good snorkelling in the bay here. This leisurely two-hour trek starts from near the airport runway, but you'll definitely need a local guide to do this.

Ong Dung Bay BEACH
A hike that you can do yourself is a 1km walk (about 30 minutes each way) through rainforest to Ong Dung Bay. The trail begins a

few kilometres north of town. The bay has only a rocky beach, although there is a good coral reef about 300m offshore.

Ma Thien Lanh Bridge

BRIDGE

Near the trailhead for Ong Dung Bay, you'll find the ruins of the Ma Thien Lanh Bridge, which was built by prisoners under the French occupation. The bay itself has only a rocky beach, although there is a good coral reef about 300m off shore.

🛏 Sleeping

Accommodation options have greatly improved in Con Dao over the last few years and there are now a dozen or more guesthouses and minihotels in Con Son town.

However, expect to pay about double the rate for the equivalent place on the mainland.

Nha Nghi Thanh Xuan

GUEST HOUSE $

(☑064-383 0261; 44 Đ Ton Duc Thang; r 350,000-450,000d; ☎) Painted in marine blue, this guesthouse has rooms with good mattresses and duvets, the upstairs rooms are light and airy. The owners speak little or no English.

Hai Nga Mini Hotel

HOTEL $

(☑064-363 0308; 7 Đ Tran Phu; r 400,000-600,000d; ❄@☎) A good option for sharers, some rooms here sleep up to five people, and all have air-con. Run by a friendly family who can speak some English and German.

Con Dao Sea Cabanas

HOTEL $$

(☑064-383 1555; www.condaoseacabanas.com/en; Đ Nguyen Duc Thuan; r 650,000-750,000d; ❄@☎) Well worth considering, these two rows of cute A-frame bungalows enjoy a nice position right by a stretch of beach. Frills (if not thrills) include satellite TV, two beds, a porch, minibar and showers with a view of the night sky. They're located very close to the town's new dock.

Con Dao Resort

HOTEL $$

(☑064-383 0939; www.condaoresort.com.vn; 8 Đ Nguyen Duc Thuan; r US$58-94; ❄@☎☀) Facing an inviting sandy beach, this slightly dated resort hotel, complete with extensive manicured gardens and a large swimming pool, certainly enjoys a great location. Rooms are spacious and comfortable enough, but showing their age.

ATC Con Dao Resort & Spa

HOTEL $$

(☑064-383 0111; www.atcvietnam.com; 8 Đ Ton Duc Thang; r US$65-90, ste from US$120; ❄@☎☀) This place's renovated accommodation is some of the most attractive in town, offering smart, inviting and comfortable rooms with terracotta tiling and great ocean-facing balconies. There are also older rooms and bungalows that need a refurb. The kidney-shaded swimming pool is lovely and breakfast is included.

★ Six Senses Con Dao

BOUTIQUE HOTEL $$$

(☑064-383 1222; www.sixsenses.com; Dat Doc Beach; villas from US$685; ❄@☎☀) Bagging an unmatched position on the island's best beach, this ultra-luxe hotel is in a class (and location) of its own. There are fifty or so ocean-facing timber-clad beach units fusing contemporary style with rustic chic, each with its own pool, giant bath-tub and Bose stereo. Brad and Angelina stayed here in 2011.

There are several places to eat, from a casual air-conditioned cafe where you can grab a panini to the magnificent restaurant by the sands. Diving, sailing trips and trekking can all be arranged. Located 4km west of Con Son town.

Saigon Con Dao Resort

HOTEL $$$

(☑064-383 0155; www.saigoncondao.com; 18 Đ Ton Duc Thang; r US$78-128, ste from US$172; ❄@☎☀) Originally set in a cluster of old French buildings on the waterfront, an impressive new wing was recently added with a swimming pool which is where most foreign visitors are hosted. The old wing is mostly reserved for visiting veterans and party loyalists on tours of the Con Dao prisons. Service is a bit spotty for the rates charged.

🍴 Eating & Drinking

The dining scene is fast improving in Con Son, with lots of options scattered around the town. Six Senses Con Dao is the place for a sumptuous treat with a virtuoso menu.

If you're on a tight budget, check out the small night market (p265) around the intersection of Đ Tran Huy Lieu and Đ Nguyen An Ninh for cheap eats.

Quan Thanh Huyen

VIETNAMESE $$

(Khu 3, Hoang Phi Yen; meals 70,000-160,000d; ☉noon-9pm) South of town by a water-lily-filled lake, this lovely little restaurant enjoys a great setting, with little gazebos next to the water and an orchestra of croaking frogs. Offers authentic local cuisine including hot pots and snakehead fish straight from the lake.

Thu Tam

VIETNAMESE $$

(Đ Nguyen Hue; mains 25,000-170,000d; ☉11.30am-9pm) On the Con Son strip, offering fresh seafood from bubbling tanks. Shells in many shapes and sizes, or go for a huge fish to feed a family.

Tri Ky VIETNAMESE **$$**

(7 Đ Nguyen Duc Thuan; mains 40,000-200,000d; ⊙lunch & dinner) It's not much to look at (think a huge covered terrace with plastic chairs and striplights) but is popular for its fresh seafood, particularly grilled squid, grouper and crab.

★**Con Son Cafe** CAFE, BAR

(Đ Ton Duc Thanh; ⊙7am-9.30pm) Formerly the customs house, this elegant French colonial structure has a lovely breezy, shady terrace from where you can gaze out over the bay's fishing boats. Serves tea, coffee, shakes, beers and cocktails. French composer Camille Saint-Saens, lived in this building, writing his opera *Brunhilda* in 1895.

❶ Information

Larry of Dive! Dive! Dive! (p267) is a great contact, and very knowledgeable about the islands. Though he's obviously keen to take you out diving or snorkelling, he'll give you a map and chat for free and can organise motorbikes for hire.

There are three ATMs in Con Dao.

Internet access is available at hotels in town, including free wi-fi for guests, plus there are often terminals in the lobby for wired access.

National Park Headquarters (☎064-383 0669; www.condaopark.com.vn; 29 Đ Vo Thi Sau; ⊙7-11.30am & 1.30-5pm daily) The national park headquarters is a good place to get information. Since the military controls access to parts of the national park, stop here first to learn more about possible island excursions and hikes, plus pick-up a useful free handout on walks around the island. Some hiking trails have interpretive signage in English and Vietnamese. The headquarters also has an exhibition hall with displays on the diversity of local forest and marine life, threats to the local environment, and local conservation activities.
Ru By (64 Đ Nguyen Hue; ⊙7am-9.30pm; 🛜) Cybercafe on the main drag.

Vietin Bank (Đ Le Duan; ⊙8am-2pm Mon-Fri, 8am-noon Sat) Doesn't change foreign currency.

❶ Getting There & Away

AIR

There are three daily flights between Con Son and HCMC jointly operated by **Vasco** (☎064-383 1831; www.vasco.com.vn; 44 Đ Nguyen Hue) and **Vietnam Airlines** (www.vietnamairlines. com). Tickets cost US$75 one way and are rarely discounted. Con Son is also connected to Can

Tho in the Mekong Delta via Vasco/Vietnam Airlines, one-way flights cost US$65.

The tiny airport is about 15km from the town centre. All of the big hotels on the island provide free transport both to and from the airport. Although it's advisable to book a hotel in advance, it is possible to show up and grab a seat on one of the hotel shuttle vans that meet the planes; drivers charge 50,000d and will usually drop you off at your hotel or in the town centre.

BOAT

There are two ferries connecting Con Son Island with Vung Tau, with sailings three to four times a week. Facilities are basic and the crossing can be very rough at certain times of years, leading to frequent cancellations. The ferries depart from Ben Dam port at 5pm, taking around 12 hours. Seats cost 145,000d but it is better to invest in a sleeper berth for 275,000d, with six bunks to a room.

Tickets can be purchased from a small office near the market in town. Look out for the sign at the kiosk on Đ Vo Thi Sau that reads **BQL Cang Ben Dam Huyen Con Dao** (⊙8-11.30am & 1-5pm). A *xe om* to Ben Dam will cost about 100,000d, a taxi about 300,000d.

❶ Getting Around

BOAT

Exploring the islands by boat can be arranged through the national park office. A 12-person boat costs around 2,000,000d to 5,000,000d per day depending on the destinations. Local fishermen also offer excursions, but be sure to bargain hard.

MOTORBIKE & BICYCLE

This is one of the best places in Vietnam to ride a bike, with little traffic, no pollution and good surfaced roads. There's only one main road, connecting the airport in the north to Ben Dam in the south via Con Son town.

Most hotels rent motorbikes for about US$7 to US$10 per day. Bicycles cost around US$2 per day. There are good coastal cycling routes, such as from Con Son town to Bai Nhat and onto the tiny settlement of Ben Dam. The ups and downs are pretty gentle and, thankfully, there is little motorised traffic. If motorbiking or cycling to Ben Dam, be very careful of the high winds around Mui Ca Map. Locals have been blown off their bikes during gales.

TAXI

Con Son island now has several **taxis** (☎064-361 6161). However, as metered rates are astronomically high (around 20,000d per km!) negotiate hard for a fixed-price rate to destinations outside Con Son town.

Southwest Highlands

Best Places to Eat

➡ V Cafe (p279)

➡ Thanh Tram (p287)

➡ Le Rabelais (p280)

➡ Trong Dong (p279)

Best Places to Stay

➡ Forest Floor Lodge (p284)

➡ Ana Mandara Villas Dalat (p278)

➡ Dreams 3 (p278)

➡ Family Hotel (p292)

Why Go?

There's a rugged charm to this distinctly rural region, with pine-studded hilltops soaring over intensively farmed fields and remote, bumpy roads meandering through coffee plantations. The scenery lacks the immediate appeal of Vietnam's far north, but the hill-tribe villages here are less-visited than the heavily touristed areas around Sapa.

Two national parks are of key interest. Cat Tien is a Unesco-listed biosphere with an impressive variety of flora and fauna. Yok Don is Vietnam's largest protected area and is home to elephants and prolific birdlife (including the giant ibis). Both parks give visitors the opportunity to explore Vietnam's all-too-rare wild side.

Dalat, a former French hill station that still boasts plenty of colonial charm, makes a great base. Fast establishing itself as Vietnam's highland adventure sports mecca, it offers myriad biking and hiking trips for daytime thrills and an array of atmospheric restaurants and bars for after-dark chills.

When to Go
Dalat

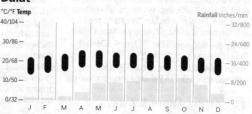

Mar Great for the annual Coffee Festival in Buon Ma Thuot or elephant races in nearby Don.

Oct Autumn in Dalat, the perfect time for exploring or adrenaline-pumping activities.

Dec Trek or cycle through Cat Tien National Park in cooler times, visiting the wild gibbons.

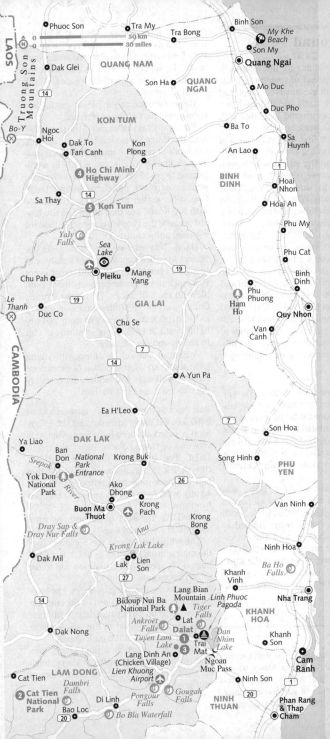

Southwest Highlands Highlights

1 Crank up the adrenalin with a hike, biking trip, horse ride or even a canyoning or climbing adventure in the hills around **Dalat** (p276).

2 Track down wild gibbons in the early morning, then seek out crocodiles by torchlight in the lush forests and lakes of **Cat Tien National Park** (p282).

3 Revel in the fresh air and French flair of **Dalat** (p272), Vietnam's mountain resort par excellence.

4 Fire up a motorbike and explore the twists and turns of the **Ho Chi Minh Highway** (p285).

5 Discover the hill-tribe customs and culture in remote village homestays around **Kon Tum** (p291).

Dalat & Around

☑ 063 / POP 227,000 / ELEV 1475M

Dalat is Vietnam's alter ego: the weather is spring-like cool instead of tropical hot, the town is dotted with elegant French-colonial villas rather than stark socialist architecture, and the farms around are thick with strawberries and flowers, not rice.

The French came first, fleeing the heat of Saigon. They left behind not only their holiday homes but also the vibe of a European town. The Vietnamese couldn't resist adding little touches to, shall we say, enhance Dalat's natural beauty. Whether it's the Eiffel Tower–shaped radio tower, the horse-drawn carriages or the zealously colourful heart-shaped cut-outs at the Valley of Love, this is a town that takes romance very seriously, although it teeters on the brink of kitsch.

Dalat is a big draw for domestic tourists. It's Le Petit Paris, the honeymoon capital and the City of Eternal Spring (daily temperatures hover between 15°C and 24°C) all rolled into one. For travellers, the moderate climate makes it a superb place for all kinds of adrenaline-fuelled activities – mountain biking, forest hiking, canyoning and climbing.

History

Home to hill tribes for centuries, 'Da Lat' means 'river of the Lat tribe' in their language. The city was established in 1912 and quickly became fashionable with Europeans. At one point during the French colonial period, some 20% of Dalat's population was foreign, and grand villas remain scattered around the city.

During the American War, Dalat was spared by the tacit agreement of all parties concerned. Indeed, it seems that while South Vietnamese soldiers were being trained at the city's military academy and affluent officials of the Saigon regime were relaxing in their villas, VC cadres were doing the same thing not far away (also in villas). On 3 April 1975, Dalat fell to the North without a fight.

◉ Sights

◉ Dalat

Hang Nga Crazy House   NOTABLE BUILDING
(☑ 063-382 2070; 3 Đ Huynh Thuc Khang; admission 40,000d; ☉ 7am-7pm) A free-wheeling architectural exploration of surrealism, Hang Nga Crazy House defies definition. Joyously designed, outrageously artistic, this private home is a monument to the creative potential of concrete, with sculptured rooms connected by super-slim bridges and an excess of cascading lava-flow-like shapes. Think Gaudi on acid.

Wander around as you please; getting lost is definitely part of the experience.

The brainchild of owner Mrs Dang Viet Nga, the Crazy House has been an imaginative work in progress since 1990. Hang Nga, as she's known locally, has a PhD in architecture from Moscow and has designed a number of other buildings around Dalat. One of her earlier masterpieces, the 'House with 100 Roofs', was torn down as a fire hazard because the People's Committee thought it looked antisocialist.

Hang Nga started the Crazy House project to entice people back to nature, and though it's becoming more outlandish every year, she's not likely to have any more trouble with the authorities. Her father, Truong Chinh, was Ho Chi Minh's successor, serving as Vietnam's second president from 1981 until his death in 1988. There's a shrine to him in the ground-floor lounge.

A note of caution for those with young kids: the Crazy House's maze of precarious tunnels, walkways and ladders are certainly not child safe. Be extra vigilant.

Bao Dai's Summer Palace   HISTORICAL BUILDING
(off Đ Trieu Viet Vuong; admission 15,000d; ☉ 7am-5pm) A faded art-deco-influenced villa, this was one of three palaces Bao Dai kept in Dalat. The building's design is striking, though it's in serious need of restoration and the once-modern interior is distinctly scruffy, with tatty net curtains and chipped furniture.

Bao Dai's imposing office, with its royal and military seals and flags is still impressive.

The white bust above the bookcase is of the man himself (he died in 1997); the flags, huge desk, spears and crossbows add to the sense of occasion.

Upstairs are the living quarters. The huge semicircular couch was used by the emperor and empress for family meetings, with their three daughters seated in the yellow chairs and their two sons in the pink chairs.

The palace is set in a pine grove, 2km southwest of the city centre. It's very much on the local tourist trail, so expect lots of tour groups.

Crémaillère
Railway Station HISTORICAL BUILDING
(Ga Da Lat; 1 Đ Quang Trung; ☺ 6.30am-5pm) **FREE**
Dalat's wonderful art deco train station is no longer connected to the Vietnamese rail network, though you can turn back the clock by riding one of the five scheduled trains that run to Trai Mat (return 124,000d, 30 minutes) daily between 7.45am and 4pm. Arrive early and note that the train won't leave without at least two passengers.

A crémaillère (cog railway) linked Dalat and Thap Cham from 1928 to 1964, but was closed due to VC attacks. There are old locomotives on display at the station, including a Japanese steam train, and the classy waiting room retains a colonial feel.

Lam Dong Museum MUSEUM
(✐ 063-382 0387; 4 Đ Hung Vuong; admission 10,000d; ☺ 7.30-11.30am & 1.30-4.30pm Mon-Sat) Housed in a modern pink building, this hillside museum displays ancient artefacts and pottery, as well as costumes and musical instruments of local ethnic minorities, and propaganda about the government support for their mountain neighbours. There are informative exhibits about Alexandre Yersin and the history of Dalat on the upper level.

Xuan Huong Lake LAKE
Created by a dam in 1919, this banana-shaped lake was named after an anti-authoritarian 17th-century Vietnamese poet. The lake can be circumnavigated along a scenic 7km sealed path that passes the flower gardens, golf club and the Dalat Palace hotel. Swan paddle boats are available for rent, a very popular pastime for visiting Vietnamese.

Du Sinh Church CHURCH
(Church; Đ Huyen Tran Cong Chua) **FREE** This hilltop church resembles a temple more than a traditional church; it was built in 1955 by Catholic refugees from the north. The four-post, Sino-Vietnamese steeple was constructed at the insistence of a Hue-born priest of royal lineage. Under the entrance archway there's a statue in classical Greek style flanked by two golden Chinese dragons.

To get here, follow Đ Tran Phu out of the centre until it becomes Đ Hoang Van Thu. Turn left onto Đ Huyen Tran Cong Chua towards the former Couvent des Oiseaux, now a teachers' training college, and the church is 500m southwest up the road.

THE PEOPLE OF THE MOUNTAIN

The uneasy relationship in the central highlands between the hill tribes and the Vietnamese majority dates back centuries, when Vietnamese expansion pushed the tribes up into the mountains. While French-colonial rule recognised the tribes as a separate community, South Vietnam later attempted to assimilate them through such means as abolishing tribal schools and courts, prohibiting the construction of stilt houses and appropriating their land.

In response the minority people formed nationalist guerrilla movements, the best-known of which was the Front Unifié de Lutte des Races Opprimées (FULRO) or the United Front for the Struggle of the Oppressed Races. In the 1960s the hill tribes were courted by the US as allies against North Vietnam, and were trained by the CIA and US Special Forces.

They paid dearly for this after the war, when government policies brought more ethnic Vietnamese into the highlands, along with clampdowns on education in native languages and religious freedom (many hill-tribe people belong to unauthorised churches). Many of these minority people have been relocated to modern villages, partly to discourage slash-and-burn agriculture. It also speeds up assimilation.

In 2001 and 2004 protests erupted, which the government quickly and, according to human-rights organisations, violently suppressed. International human-rights groups point to more deaths than the government admits to, and thousands of hill-tribe people fled to Cambodia or the US afterwards. Ask the ethnic Vietnamese and many will probably repeat the state's line that the protests were the work of outsiders. Talk to any organisation that works with the minority people and you'll hear a different story: one of continuing government surveillance, harassment and religious persecution.

Central Dalat

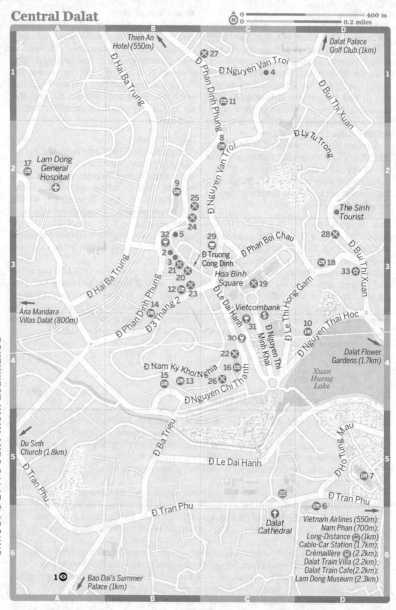

Map labels (from image):

0 — 400 m
0 — 0.2 miles

Thien An Hotel (550m)

Đ Hai Ba Trung

Đ Phan Dinh Phung

27

Đ Nguyen Van Troi

4

Dalat Palace Golf Club (1km)

Đ Bui Thi Xuan

11

Đ Ly Tu Trong

8

Lam Dong General Hospital

17

9

25

24

32 5

The Sinh Tourist

2

29

Đ Truong Cong Dinh

Đ Phan Boi Chau

28

3

21

20

Hoa Binh Square

18

33

23

12

Đ Le Dai Hanh

19

Đ Le Thi Hong Gam

14

Ana Mandara Villas Dalat (800m)

Đ Phan Dinh Phung

Đ 3 Thang 2

Đ Hai Ba Trung

Vietcombank

Đ Nguyen Thai Hoc

10

Dalat Flower Gardens (1.7km)

31

30

Đ Nguyen Thi Minh Khai

22

16

Đ Nam Ky Khoi Nghia

15 13 26

Xuan Huong Lake

Đ Nguyen Chi Thanh

Du Sinh Church (1.8km)

Đ Ba Trieu

Đ Le Dai Hanh

Đ Tran Phu

Đ Ho Tung Mau

7

Đ Tran Phu

Đ Tran Phu

6

Dalat Cathedral

Vietnam Airlines (550m);
Nam Phan (700m);
Long-Distance (1km);
Cable-Car Station (1.7km);
Crémaillère (2.2km);
Dalat Train Villa (2.2km);
Dalat Train Cafe (2.2km);
Lam Dong Museum (2.3km)

1

Bao Dai's Summer Palace (1km)

Dalat Flower Gardens
GARDEN
(Vuon Hoa Thanh Pho; ☏ 063-382 2151; Đ Tran Nhan Tong; admission 10,000d; ☺ 7.30am-4pm) These gardens were established in 1966 and throughout the grounds you'll find hydrangeas, fuchsias and orchids, the latter in shaded buildings to the left of the entrance. Like any good Vietnamese park, the gardens have been embellished with kitsch topiary.

Central Dalat

◎ Sights
1 Hang Nga Crazy House A6

✪ Activities, Courses & Tours
2 Groovy Gecko Adventure Tours B3
3 Highland Holiday Tours B3
4 Phat Tire Ventures C1
5 Pine Track Adventures B3

⊜ Sleeping
6 Dalat Hotel du Parc D5
7 Dalat Palace D5
8 Dreams 3 ....C2
9 Dreams Hotel B2
10 Empress Hotel D4
11 Green City C1
12 Hoan Hy Hotel B3
13 Hotel Chau Au – Europa B4
14 Hotel Phuong Hanh B3
15 Le Phuong Hotel B4
16 Ngoc Lan Hotel C4
17 Pink House Villa Hotel A2
18 Thi Thao Hotel D3

✸ Eating
Cafe de la Poste .... (see 6)
19 Central Market C3
20 Da Quy B3
21 Goc Ha Thanh B3
22 Lan Mot Nguoi C4
Le Rabelais .... (see 7)
23 Long Hoa B3
24 Momiji B3
25 Nhat Ly B2
26 Quan Oc Trang C4
27 Trong Dong C1
28 V Cafe D3

⊙ Drinking & Nightlife
29 Cafe Tung C3
30 Cafe-Bars C4
31 Envy Lounge Bar C4
32 The Hangout B3

✪ Entertainment
33 Escape Bar D3

◉ Around Dalat

Truc Lam Pagoda & Cable Car
BUDDHIST TEMPLE

(Ho Tuyen Lam) For a spiritual recharge, visit Truc Lam Pagoda, which enjoys a hilltop setting and has splendid gardens. It's an active monastery (ask about meditation sessions) and the grounds are expansive enough to escape the odd tour group. Be sure to arrive by cable car (adult one-way/ return 50,000/70,000d, child 30,000/40,000d; ⊙7.30-11.30am & 1.30-5pm). The terminus is 3km south of the centre), which soars over majestic pine forests.

From the monastery it's a 15-minute walk down to the shore of **Tuyen Lam Lake** (actually a reservoir), where there are cafes, and boats for hire. Both the pagoda and lake can also be reached by road via turn-offs from Hwy 20.

Bidoup Nui Ba National Park
NATURE RESERVE

(☑ 063-374 7449; www.bidoupnuiba.gov.vn) Occupying a densely forested highland plateau, this national park encompasses evergreen and coniferous woodlands, bamboo groves and grasslands at altitudes between 650m and 2288m. Hill-tribe guides are available to guide you along trails, and there's an impressive visitor centre, 32km north of Dalat, with interactive displays about the flora and fauna and K'Ho hill-tribe crafts and culture.

Bidoup Nui Ba has 96 endemic plants, including the Dalat pine, and nearly 300 species of orchids. Yellow-cheeked gibbons can be heard in the early morning if you're fortunate, while the national park is also home to black bears and the vampire flying frog (which was only discovered in 2010).

The pleasant 3.5km trail from the visitor centre to a waterfall only fringes the national park; to penetrate deep inside Bidoup Nui Ba consider one of three other options, which include ascents of Lang Biang and Bidoup mountains. The longer trails do not start from the visitor centre itself, but staff there can organise guides and logistics.

There are five comfortable bungalows, each with three en-suite rooms (300,000d) at the visitor centre, as well as a canteen (meals 30,000d to 70,000d).

Cuong Hoan Traditional Silk Centre
ART GALLERY

(☑ 063-852 338; ⊙7.30am-5pm) Here you can inspect the entire process of silk production, which involves sorting cocoons, unravelling the threads and then dyeing and weaving them into shimmering new fabric. You can even sample the cooked grub, which has a nutty flavour. There are some beautiful garments and lengths of cloth for sale. The centre is in Nam Ban Village, 30km west of Dalat.

Waterfalls
WATERFALL

There are a number of waterfalls around Dalat, though none are royally spectacular and the focus tends to be on commerce rather than nature. If you're exploring the countryside, others include **Ankroët Falls, Gougah Falls** (admission 7000d; ☺7am-4pm) and **Pongour Falls** (admission 10,000d; ☺7am-4pm).

➧ Elephant Falls

FREE These imposing curved falls are best seen from below, but be prepared to negotiate an uneven and sometimes hazardous path to get here. Nearby, **Linh An Pagoda** has several large Buddhas (including a particularly happy Buddha with neon haloes and a room built into his ample belly). The falls are near Nam Ban village, 30km west of Dalat.

You can easily combine these falls with a visit to Cuong Hoan Traditional Silk Centre.

➧ Datanla Falls

(admission 10,000d, bobsled ride adult one-way/return 30,000/40,000d) This is the closest waterfall to Dalat, so expect loud music and lots of tour groups. The cascade is quite modest, but the **bobsled ride** is certainly a blast. Datanla is 7km south of Dalat. Take Hwy 20 and turn right about 200m past the turn-off to Tuyen Lam Lake. It's well signposted.

Lat & Lang Dinh An Villages
VILLAGE

There are two minority villages a short drive from Dalat, both unremarkable despite their popularity. Less than 1km from the base of Lang Bian Mountain is Lat Village (pronounced 'lak'), a community of about 6000 people spread across nine hamlets. Lang Dinh An (Chicken Village) is home to about 600 of the Koho people; it's on Hwy 20, 17km from Dalat.

If you're interested in hill-tribe life, you're better off heading to Kon Tum or the far north of the country.

Only five of Lat Village's hamlets are actually Lat; residents of the other four are members of the Chill, Ma and Koho tribes. It's a sleepy little place with a few handicraft shops. Sometimes it hosts wine-drinking sessions or gong performances for tour groups.

Lang Dinh An has the distinction of having a giant concrete chicken caught mid-strut in the village centre, and offers the same woven objects and 'cultural' activities as Lat Village.

Activities

Dalat's cool climate and mountainous surrounds mean this is a great area for all kinds of outdoor activities. Adventure outfits are clustered along Đ Truong Cong Dinh, offering trekking, mountain biking, kayaking, canyoning, abseiling and rock climbing, as well as trips to the coast. Compare prices, but make sure that you're comfortable with all the equipment and safety procedures.

★ Phat Tire Ventures
ADVENTURE TOUR

(☑063-382 9422; www.ptv-vietnam.com; 109 Đ Nguyen Van Troi) A highly professional and experienced operator with mountain biking trips from US$49, trekking from US$31, kayaking from US$39, canyoning from US$45 and white-water rafting (US$72) in the rainy season. Combined bike-riding/rafting trips to Mui Ne (US$115) are definitely the best way to hit the coast.

Groovy Gecko Adventure Tours
ADVENTURE TOUR

(☑063-383 6521; www.groovygeckotours.net; 65 Đ Truong Cong Dinh) Experienced agency operated by a lively young team with prices starting at US$35 for rock climbing, canyoning or mountain biking, and two-day treks from US$59.

Pine Track Adventures
ADVENTURE TOUR

(☑063-383 1916; www.pinetrackadventures.com; 72B Đ Truong Cong Dinh) Run by an enthusiastic local team, this operator offers canyoning, trekking, biking and some excellent multi-sport packages. A six-day trip taking in Dalat and the ride down to Mui Ne is US$510.

Highland Holiday Tours
ADVENTURE TOUR

(☑063-351 1047; www.highlandholidaytours.com.vn; 47 Đ Troung Cong Dinh) New agency offering mountain biking and motorcycle tours, trekking and canyoning. Two-day bike trips to Nha Trang are US$170, or rides into Cat Tien cost US$180.

Dalat Palace Golf Club
GOLF

(☑063-382 1202; www.dalatpalacegolf.vn; Đ Tran Nhan Tong) This attractive 18-hole course near the lake was once used by Emperor Bao Dai himself. Rounds start at US$50. To get here, follow Đ Ba Huyen Thanh Quan north along Xuan Huong Lake and turn left onto Đ Tran Nhan Tong. The clubhouse is about 300m on the left.

EASY DOES IT

For many travellers, the highlight of their trip to the highlands is an off-the-beaten-track motorcycle tour with an Easy Rider. Besides the romance of cruising down endless highways, the Easy Riders' stock-in-trade is good company and insider knowledge, providing a brief but intimate window into highland life.

The flip side to the popularity of the Easy Riders is that now everyone claims to be one. In central Dalat, you can't walk down the street without being invited (sometimes harassed) for a tour. Some Easy Riders have banded together to protect 'their' brand, donning blue jackets and charging membership fees. Similarly, in Danang, Hoi An and Nha Trang, the Easy Rider moniker applies to other packs of motorcycle guides, with jackets of different colours.

Whether you're speaking to a jacket-wearing chap or an indie-spirited upstart, it's prudent to find out just what they can show you that you can't see on your own. Easy Rider excursions start at US$25 for a day ride close to Dalat, ramping up to US$50 to US$70 per day for extended trips across the highlands and to the coast, or even all the way north to Hanoi.

Not every jacketed Easy Rider is a good guide and many freelance riders are perfectly talented guides (perhaps because they don't have a 'brand' behind them). In the convoluted politics of the motorcycle-guide world, some freelancers now disdain the term Easy Rider and call themselves Free Riders or just plain motorcycle guides.

Before you commit to a long-haul trip, it's a good idea to test a rider out with a day trip. Is he a safe driver? How is his command of English? Can you spend the next 48 hours or more with him? Are your bags safely strapped on the bike? Is the seat padded and the helmet comfortable (and clean)? Most riders can produce a logbook of glowing testimonials from past clients; also, check internet forums for recommendations.

One more important element to consider is the route. The most beautiful roads in southern Vietnam are actually the new-ish coastal highways that link Dalat to Mui Ne and Nha Trang, plus the old road to the coast via Phan Rang, although this is currently in poor condition. The main roads through the central highlands, particularly the Buon Ma Thuot to Pleiku run, are not particularly scenic, so it may be wise to discuss a back-roads option. If breathtaking scenery is the order of the day, consider motorbiking the far north of Vietnam around the Northwest Loop, Sapa, Ha Giang and Cao Bang, or take a look at the area between the DMZ and Phong Nha-Ke Bang National Park.

🛏 Sleeping

Dalat has an incredible choice of budget places, and some fine upmarket colonial-style hotels. You won't need to worry about air conditioning as the climate is temperate.

★**Dreams Hotel**   GUEST HOUSE **$**
(☑063-383 3748; dreams@hcm.vnn.vn; 138-140 Đ Phan Dinh Phung; r US$20-25; ❂@☎) An incredibly hospitable guesthouse owned by a family that looks after its guests with affection and care. Boasts spotless rooms, a legendary breakfast spread, and hot tub and sauna.

Thien An Hotel   HOTEL **$**
(☑063-352 0607; thienanhotel@vnn.vn; 272A Đ Phan Dinh Phung; s US$18, d US$22-25; @☎) Superb, very welcoming family hotel providing spacious well-equipped rooms, glorious breakfasts (including Vegemite and Marmite), a cosy atmosphere and high levels of cleanliness. Free bicycles provided.

Le Phuong Hotel   HOTEL **$**
(☑063-382 3743; www.lephuonghotel.com; 80 Đ Nguyen Chi Thanh; s 300,000d, d 350,000-500,000d; ❄@☎) From the gleaming lobby to the stylish, spacious minimalist rooms, this family run hotel is a great deal. Cleanliness standards are high and it's conveniently located.

Green City   HOTEL **$**
(☑063-382 7999; www.dalatgreencityhotel.com; 172 Đ Phan Dinh Phung; s/d/tw US$17/19/21; @☎) New place switched on to travellers' needs with attractive, well-presented rooms, all with fine wooden beds, fresh linen, TV and minibar. Loafers will love the sofa-strewn lobby.

MADAGUI FOREST RESORT

Madagui Forest Resort (☎061-394 6999; www.madagui.com.vn; Km 152, Hwy 20; adult/child 30,000/20,000d, paintballing 58,000d, plus per shot 1500d) is a one-stop shop for adventures en route to or from Dalat. It's more geared at the local rather than foreign tourist market, but there are still lots of activities on offer that might appeal, including whitewater rafting, kayaking, mountain biking, horse riding, fishing and even crocodile feeding. **Paintballing** is a major draw here, although it is a fairly surreal experience. And no, Rambo costumes are not available. Accommodation is on offer (from 1,550,000d a night), but it's probably better experienced as a pit stop between Dalat and HCMC.

Hotel Chau Au – Europa   HOTEL $
(☎063-382 2870; europa@hcm.vnn.vn; 76 Đ Nguyen Chi Thanh; r 250,000-350,000d; ❄@☎) Run by Mr Duc, the delightful and helpful owner who speaks English and French, this place has excellent rooms, most with two double beds and some with fine city views.

Hoan Hy Hotel   HOTEL $
(☎063-351 1288; www.hoanhydalathotel.com; 14-16 Đ 3 Thang 2; r 350,000d; @☎) Near the epicentre of town, these smart rooms are fine value for money with midrange touches and tasteful decor. It's above a popular bakery, so you can enjoy fresh bread each morning.

Pink House Villa Hotel   HOTEL $
(☎063-381 5667; ahomeawayfromhome_dalat@yahoo.com; 7 Đ Hai Thuong; s/d/tr US$10/15/20; @☎) A well-run family owned place, where many rooms have great views. It's managed by the affable (if unfortunately named) Mr Rot, who can arrange motorbike tours in the countryside around Dalat.

Hotel Phuong Hanh   HOTEL $
(☎063-356 0528; 7/1 Đ Hai Thuong; r US$7-12; @☎) Worth considering if you're after a real cheapie. This is a well-maintained place with lots of rooms, most with two double beds, in decent condition for the price.

★Dreams 3   HOTEL $$
(☎063-383 3748, 063-382 5877; dreams@hcm. vnn.vn; 138-140 Đ Phan Dinh Phung; r US$30-35; ❂@☎) This commodious new venture owned by the amazing 'Dreams Team' offers incredibly tasteful accommodation. All rooms have high-quality mattresses and modish bathrooms, and some have a balcony. On the top floor there's a jacuzzi, steam room and sauna; a restaurant is planned. The only downer is the location on a traffic-heavy street.

Dalat Train Villa   APARTMENT $$
(☎063-381 6365; www.dalattrainvilla.com; 1 Đ Quang Trung; apt US$70; ❂☎) A stunning French-era villa that's been sensitively converted into four apartments, perfect for families or groups. Each unit has a lounge, small kitchen and large-screen TV. There's a converted train-carriage cafe on your doorstep for meals. About 2km east of the centre.

Dalat Hotel du Parc   HOTEL $$
(☎063-382 5777; www.hotelduparc.vn; 7 Đ Tran Phu; s & d US$50-70, ste US$110; ❄@☎) A respectfully refurbished 1932 building that offers colonial-era style at enticing prices. The old lobby lift sets the tone and the spacious rooms include classy furnishings and polished wooden floors. However, it's slightly lacking in facilities.

Empress Hotel   HOTEL $$
(☎063-383 3888; www.empresshotelvn.com; 5 Đ Nguyen Thai Hoc; r/ste from US$42/57; ❄@☎) In a prime location overlooking the Xuan Huong Lake, this is an intimate and atmospheric place to stay. The rooms are modern, spacious and tasteful, and many face onto the peaceful courtyard garden. Check the website for promotional discounts.

Thi Thao Hotel   HOTEL $$
(☎063-383 3333; www.thithaogardenia.com/en; 29 Đ Phan Boi Chau; r from US$28; ❂❄@☎) Also known as the Gardenia Hotel, and offering stylish, bright, modern rooms with flat-screen TVs and superb bathrooms. It's all very tasteful and good value.

★Ana Mandara
Villas Dalat   BOUTIQUE HOTEL $$$
(☎063-355 5888; www.anamandara-resort.com; Đ Le Lai; r US$82-102, ste from US$138; ❂❄@☎) Elegant property spread across 17 lovingly restored French colonial villas. Rooms are finished in period furnishings and each villa has a lounge with fireplace and the option of private dining. The spa is glorious. Located in the suburbs, quite a hike from the centre.

Ngoc Lan Hotel HOTEL $$$
(☑ 063-382 2136; www.ngoclanhotel.vn; 42 Đ Nguyen Chi Thanh; r/ste from US$84/142; ✳ @ 🛜) Luxury hotel where the rooms have clean white lines with stylish purple accents. The modern decor juxtaposes nicely with the colonial character of the building, including wooden floors and French windows. It's right in the heart of town, so expect some noise.

Dalat Palace COLONIAL HOTEL $$$
(☑ 063-382 5444; www.dalatpalace.vn; 12 Đ Tran Phu; s US$246-306, d US$260-320, ste US$446-510; ⊜ ✳ @ 🛜) With unimpeded views of Xuan Huong Lake, this grande dame of hotels has vintage Citroën cars in its sweeping driveway, and lashings of wood panelling and period class. The opulence of French-colonial life has been splendidly preserved: claw-foot tubs, fireplaces, chandeliers and paintings. However, it can be achingly empty at times, and consequently can lack ambience.

Online deals can reduce rates to as low as US$130.

✖ Eating

There's a wide selection of restaurants geared towards travellers along Đ Truong Cong Dinh. For cheap eats in the day, head to the upper level of the **Central Market** (Cho Da Lat). At night you'll find **food stalls** around the market along Đ Nguyen Thi Minh Khai.

★ Trong Dong VIETNAMESE $
(☑ 063-382 1889; 220 Đ Phan Dinh Phung; mains 40,000-80,000d; ⊗ 11.30am-9.30pm) Intimate restaurant run by a very hospitable team where the menu has been creatively designed – shrimp paste on a sugarcane stick and beef wrapped in *la lut* leaf excel.

★ Goc Ha Thanh VIETNAMESE $
(53 Đ Truong Cong Dinh; mains 35,000-119,000d; ⊗ 7am-10pm; 🛜) Casual new place with attractive bamboo furnishings owned by a welcoming Hanoi couple. Strong on dishes such as coconut curry, hotpots, clay pots, stir fries and noodles.

Lan Mot Nguoi VIETNAMESE $
(58 Đ Nguyen Chi Thanh; meals 32,000-68,000d; ⊗ 10am-10pm) Specialising in steaming hotpots, this modern place has a casual air and draws a faithful local clientele. Try the spicy seafood hotpot.

Da Quy VIETNAMESE, WESTERN $
(Wild Sunflower; 49 Đ Truong Cong Dinh; dishes 30,000-72,000d; ⊗ 8am-10pm) Run by Loc, a friendly English speaker, this place has a sophisticated ambience but unsophisticated prices. Try the traditional clay-pot dishes, a hotpot or something from the Western menu.

★ V Cafe INTERNATIONAL $$
(☑ 063-352 0215; www.vcafedalatvietnam.com; 1/1 Đ Bui Thi Xuan; meals 80,000-170,000d; ⊗ 7am-10.30pm; 🛜) Atmospheric bistro-style place that serves international cuisine, such as chicken curry Calcutta and Mexican-style quesadillas. The interior is decorated with stunning photography and there's live music most nights.

Nhat Ly VIETNAMESE $$
(88 Đ Phan Dinh Phung; dishes 35,000-130,000d; ⊗ 11am-9.30pm) This place serves hearty highland meals on tartan tablecloths including sumptuous hotpots, grilled meats and seafood – try the steamed crab in beer (1kg costs 280,000d). Draws plenty of locals; always a good sign.

Quan Oc Trang SEAFOOD $$
(58 Đ Nguyen Chi Thanh; dishes 35,000-80,000d; ⊗ 11.30am-9pm) Simple, local seafood place

DELECTABLE DALAT

Dalat is a vegetable lover's heaven; its climate is conducive to growing peas, carrots, radishes, tomatoes, cucumbers, avocados, capsicums, lettuce, beets, green beans, potatoes, garlic, spinach, squash and yams. Translation: you can get meals here that are unavailable elsewhere in the country.

The Dalat area is justly famous for strawberry jam, dried blackcurrants and candied plums, persimmons and peaches. Apricots are popular, often served in a heavily salted hot drink. Other local delicacies include avocado ice cream, sweet beans (*mut dao*) and strawberry, blackberry and artichoke extracts (for making drinks). Artichoke tea, another local speciality, is said to lower blood pressure and benefit the liver and kidneys.

Dalat wine is served all over Vietnam. The reds are pleasantly light, while the whites tend to be heavy on the oak.

NATIONAL HIGHWAY 20: ROADSIDE ATTRACTIONS

Open tour buses and private cars tackle the twists and turns from Ho Chi Minh City to Dalat, and there are several possible stops along the way.

Langa Lake

The HCMC–Dalat road (Hwy 20) spans this reservoir, which is traversed by a bridge. Lots of floating houses, where families harvest the fish underneath, can be seen here. It's a very scenic spot for photography, and most tourist vehicles on the HCMC–Dalat road make a short pit stop here.

Volcanic Craters

Near Dinh Quan on Hwy 20 there are three volcanoes, now extinct, but nonetheless very impressive. The craters date from the late Jurassic period, about 150 million years ago. You'll have to do a little walking to see the craters. One is on the left-hand side of the road, about 2km south of Dinh Quan, and another on the right-hand side about 8km beyond Dinh Quan, towards Dalat.

Underground Lava Tubes

A bit beyond the volcanic craters, towards Dalat, are underground lava tubes. These rare caves were formed as the surface lava cooled and solidified, while the hotter underground lava continued to flow, leaving a hollow space. Lava tubes differ sharply in appearance from limestone caves (the latter are formed by underground springs). While limestone caves have abundant stalactites and stalagmites, the walls of lava caves are smooth.

The easiest way to find the lava tubes is to first find the teak forest on Hwy 20 between the Km 120 and Km 124 markers. The children who live around the forest can point you to the entrance of the lava tubes. However, you are strongly advised not to go into the tubes alone; as with caving there is the risk of becoming lost or stuck. Local kids hang out on the roadside and will sometimes act as guides for a small fee of 40,000d or so. Take a torch (flashlight).

of the plastic stool and near-zero-English variety, with excellent shellfish, steaming bowls of lemongrass- and herb-scented mussels, sea snails and soft-shell crab.

Dalat Train Cafe CAFE **$$**
(www.dalattrainvilla.com; 1 Đ Quang Trung; snacks/meals from 50,000/90,000d; ⏰7am-10pm; 📶) Calling all trainspotters! Don't miss the opportunity to step inside this lovingly restored French-era railway carriage for a snack or meal in a unique setting. Try the blue-cheese burger or a salad. There's a full wine list. It's 100m from the train station.

Long Hoa INTERNATIONAL **$$**
(📞063-382 2934; 6 Đ 3 Thang 2; dishes 30,000-123,000d; ⏰11am-2.30pm & 5.30-9.30pm) A cosy bistro run by a Francophile owner. Westerners come here for the Vietnamese food; Vietnamese come here to try the steaks. Top off your meal with a glass of Dalat wine.

Momiji JAPANESE, CAFE **$$**
(98 Đ Truong Cong Dinh; meals 80,000-150,000d; ⏰7.30am-10pm) Part Japanese restaurant, serving good set meals, sushi and sake,

and part cafe, with homemade cakes (including carrot cupcakes), green tea and cappuccino.

⭐**Le Rabelais** FRENCH **$$$**
(📞063-382 5444; www.dalatresorts.com; 12 Đ Tran Phu; meals US$30-50; ⏰7am-10pm; 📶) For arguably the finest colonial setting in Vietnam, the signature restaurant at the Dalat Palace is *the* destination with the grandest of dining rooms and a spectacular terrace that looks down to the lakeshore. Set dinner menus (US$65 to US$85) offer the full treatment, but lunch is decent value at US$29, while high tea is US$16. It's frequently pretty empty though.

Cafe de la Poste FRENCH **$$$**
(📞063-382 5777; Đ Tran Phu; meals from US$10; ⏰7am-10pm; 📶) In a stunning French colonial building with a sweeping curved mahogany bar and huge mirrors, this place has lashings of style (although it can be short on patrons). The menu features salads, sandwiches, pastas and fresh bakery products, but the best value is the set lunch (370,000d).

🍷 Drinking & Entertainment

While Dalat has a lively night-market scene, sadly the same cannot be said for its night scene. Locals flock to the lively strip of **cafe-bars** (Đ Le Dai Hanh).

The Hangout
BAR

(71 Đ Truong Cong Dinh; ⊙11am-11pm; 🛜) Popular hangout for some of Dalat's Easy Riders, as well as visiting backpackers, with a relaxed vibe and a popular pool table. The owner, a fluent English speaker, is an excellent source of local information.

Envy Lounge Bar
LOUNGE

(Đ Le Dai Hanh; ⊙5pm-1am) With disco glitterballs, velour sofas and zany lighting, this bar is aimed directly at visiting Saigon hipsters. Expect expensive drinks and live cover bands.

★Escape Bar
LIVE MUSIC

(basement, Blue Moon Hotel, 4 Đ Phan Boi Chau; ⊙4pm-midnight; 🛜) Outstanding live-music bar, owned by blues guitarist Curtis who performs here virtually every night with a rotating band (from 9pm). Yes, covers of classics are played, but the improvisation is such that each tune takes on a life of its own. Sunday is a jam session. The bar's decor, all 1970s chic and 'groovy baby' furnishings, suits the sonics perfectly.

🛍 Shopping

There's a good selection of Vietnamese coffee in Dalat; check out the shops in and around the Central Market.

ℹ Information

Lam Dong General Hospital (☑063-382 1369; 4 Đ Pham Ngoc Thach; ⊙24hr)
Main Post Office (14 Đ Tran Phu; ⊙7am-6pm)
The Sinh Tourist (☑063-382 2663; www.thesinhtourist.vn; 22 Đ Bui Thi Xuan) Tours, including city sightseeing trips, and open-tour bus bookings.

Vietcombank (6 Đ Nguyen Thi Minh Khai; ⊙7.30am-3pm Mon-Fri, to 1pm Sat) Changes travellers cheques and foreign currencies.

ℹ Getting There & Away

AIR

Vietnam Airlines (☑063-383 3499; www.vietnamairlines.com; 2 Đ Ho Tung Mau) has daily services to HCMC, Danang and Hanoi. **Vietjet Air** (p481) also flies daily to Hanoi. **Lien Khuong Airport** is 30km south of the city.

BUS

Dalat's modern **long-distance bus station** (Đ 3 Thang 4) has timetables and booking offices; it's about 1.5km south of Xuan Huong Lake by road. From here there are express buses to HCMC, other cities in the highlands, Danang and Nha Trang. **Phuong Trang** (☑063-358 5858) operates smart double-decker buses, including several sleeper services, to HCMC (US$11, seven to eight hours, roughly hourly).

Dalat is a major stop for open-tour buses. The Sinh Tourist has daily buses to Mui Ne (129,000d, four hours), Nha Trang (129,000d, five hours) and HCMC (179,000d, eight hours).

CAR & MOTORCYCLE

From Nha Trang, a new-ish high road offers spectacular views – a dream for motorbikers and cyclists – hitting 1700m at Hon Giao mountain and following a breathtaking 33km pass.

Highway 27 to Buon Ma Thuot is scenic, but in poor condition with many potholes.

ℹ Getting Around

TO/FROM THE AIRPORT

The Vietnam Airlines shuttle bus between Lien Khuong Airport and Dalat (40,000d, 40 minutes) is timed around flights. It leaves from the airline's office at 40 Đ Ho Tung Mau two hours before each departure. Private taxis to/from the airport cost around 250,000d.

BICYCLE

The hilly terrain makes it hard work getting around Dalat. Several hotels rent out bicycles

TRANSPORT FROM DALAT

DESTINATION	BUS	AIR	CAR/MOTORBIKE
HCMC	US$9–11, 7-9hr, every 30min	from US$34, 1hr, four daily	9hr
Mui Ne	n/a	n/a	5hr
Nha Trang	US$6.50, 4–5hr, 17 daily	n/a	4hr
Buon Ma Thuot	US$6, 5hr, nine daily	n/a	4hr
Danang	US$15, 12hr, three daily	from US$49, 1hr, one daily	13hr
Hue	US18, 15hr, three daily	n/a	15hr

and some provide them free to guests. It's also well worth looking into cycling tours.

CAR

Daily rentals (with driver) start at US$40.

MOTORCYCLE

For short trips around town (10,000d to 20,000d), *xe om* drivers can be flagged down around the Central Market area. Self-drive motorbikes are 150,000d to 200,000d per day.

TAXI

Taxis are easy to find; try **Mai Linh** (☑ 063-352 1111).

Bao Loc

POP 166,000

Bao Loc is all about tea, silk and the cultivation of mulberry leaves (which make up the silkworms' diet). Roadside rest stops offer free samples of the local tea. It's a practical place to break the journey between HCMC (180km) and Dalat (118km); Easy Riders often stop here.

Nearby **Dambri Falls** (admission 10,000d) is one of the highest (90m), most magnificent and easily accessible waterfalls in Vietnam. To reach the falls, turn off the main highway north of Bao Loc and follow the road for 18km through tea and mulberry plantations. The high peak to your right is May Bay Mountain.

Ngoan Muc Pass

ELEV 980M

The spectacular Ngoan Muc Pass is 43km southeast of Dalat. On a clear day you can see the ocean, 55km away. As the highway winds down the mountain it passes under two gargantuan water pipes that link the lake with the hydroelectric power station at the base of the pass.

South of the road (to the right as you face the ocean) you can see the steep tracks of the crémaillère linking Thap Cham with Dalat. At the top of the pass there's a **waterfall** next to the highway, pine forests and an old train station.

Cat Tien National Park

☑ 061 / ELEV 700M

Cat Tien (☑ 061-366 9228; www.cattiennational park.vn; adult/child 50,000/20,000d; ⊘ 7am-10pm) ✎ comprises an amazingly biodiverse area of lowland tropical rainforest. The 72,000-hectare park is one of the outstanding natural treasures in Vietnam, and the hiking, mountain biking and bird-watching here are the best in the south of the country. Always call ahead for reservations as the park can accommodate only a limited number of visitors. However, a word of caution: visitors rarely see any of the larger mammals resident in the park, so don't come expecting to encounter tigers and elephants (or rhino, now thought to be extinct in Vietnam).

Cat Tien was hit hard by defoliants during the American War, but the large old-growth trees survived and the smaller plants have recovered. In 2001 Unesco added Cat Tien National Park to its list of biosphere reserves. As there are good overnight options, it's worth spending at least two full days here, if possible.

Fauna in the park includes 100 types of mammal including the bison-like guar, 79 types of reptile, 41 amphibian species, plus an incredible array of insects, including 400 or so butterfly species. Of the 350-plus birds, rare species include the orange-necked partridge and Siamese fireback.

THE LAST RHINO

Tragically, it's now believed that the Asian mainland's very last Javan rhinoceros was killed in Cat Tien in 2010 (almost certainly by poachers, as rangers found the animal's remains minus its horn). A small group of a dozen or so rhino survived in isolation in the Cat Tien area until the 1990s, their presence one of the reasons for the establishment of a national park. But by 2008 scientists analysing dung samples found that they all belonged to the same individual, who lived a lonely last few years.

Once found across Asia from Myanmar to southern China, only 50 or so wild Javan rhino remain, in an isolated corner of Java.

The International Union for Conservation of Nature considers that 'the cause of population decline is mainly attributable to the excessive demand for rhino horn and other products for Chinese and allied medicine systems'. See p464 for more information.

Sights & Activities

Cat Tien National Park can be explored on foot, by mountain bike, by 4WD and also by boat along the Dong Nai River. There are well-established **hiking trails** in the park, but these require the services of a guide (from 250,000d), as well as transportation to and from the start of the trail.

Wherever you decide to go, be sure to book a guide in advance and take plenty of insect repellent. Leaches are a big problem; you can rent 'leach socks' at the park HQ for a small fee.

Cat Tien also has a small **bear sanctuary** where animals rescued from bile farms can roam a forested enclosure complete with pools and climbing towers.

Crocodile Swamp   LAKE

(Bau Sau; admission 140,000d, guide fee 300,000d, boat trip 350,000d) A visit to the Crocodile Swamp is popular. It involves a 9km drive from the park headquarters and a 4km trek to the swamp; the walk takes about three hours return. Night treks are popular, as you've the chance of seeing crocs then, as well as other wildlife.

Dao Tien Endangered
Primate Species Centre   NATURE RESERVE

(www.go-east.org; adult/child incl boat ride 150,000d/50,000d; ⊙8am & 2pm) This centre, located on an island in the Dong Nai River, is a rehabilitation facility which hosts gibbons, black-shanked douc, silvered langur and pygmy loris that have been illegally trafficked. The eventual goal of the centre is to release the primates back into the forest. You can view primates in a semi-wild environment and hear their incredible calls.

A large reforestation project is now underway on the island, with hundreds of native fruit-tree saplings planted to provide the primates with foraging territory, and encourage them to learn the necessary skills to move around the forest canopy.

Tours

We've received mixed reviews about budget tours from HCMC. For a reputable customised birding, biking or hiking tour, contact Sinhbalo Adventures (p337).

Sleeping & Eating

The national park offers several accommodation options and there are also some good, new, privately run places just outside

WILD GIBBON TREK

Golden-cheeked gibbons have been reintroduced into Cat Tien and this experience offers a rare insight into the lives of these charismatic primates. The trek (US$60 per person, maximum four people) runs daily and involves a 4am start to get out to the gibbons in time for their dawn chorus. Relax in a hammock as the forest slowly comes alive with their songs before watching the family go about their everyday business.

In the afternoon the trip includes a fully guided tour of the Dao Tien primate centre. The project is a combined effort between **Go East** (www.go-east. org) and the national park authorities. All proceeds are ploughed back into the national park and assisting the rangers in their protection efforts. To avoid disappointment, book in advance through ecotourism@cattiennationalpark.vn, or call ahead (✆061-366 9228).

the park's entrance. Try to avoid weekends and holidays if possible, when locals descend in large numbers.

★ Ta Lai Long House   GUEST HOUSE $

(✆0938 887 105; www.vietadventure.vn/discov erydetail; dm 315,000d) Excellent, new, traditional-style lodge managed by Westerners and locals from the S'Tieng and Ma minorities. Accommodation is in a well-constructed timber long house, with good, screened bedding and modern facilities.

Green Hope Lodge   GUEST HOUSE $$

(✆061-366 9919; www.greenhopelodge.com; Nam Cat Tien; r US$45-60; ❄⊛) A short walk from the park entrance, this fine, friendly, new lodge has attractive modern rooms with screened, comfortable beds and en suites. The riverside location is close to the jungle (you may even hear gibbons call in the morning). Tasty local grub is available. It's efficiently managed by Vung, a fluent English speaker.

Cat Tien National Park   GUEST HOUSE $$

(✆061-366 9228; namcattien@yahoo.com.vn; small/big tents 220,000/350,000d, bungalows from 580,000d; ⊛) Rooms at the national park's HQ are fairly basic and overpriced but include a bathroom. Large tents (sleeping up to 12) operate on a communal basis.

★ **Forest Floor Lodge** ECOLODGE $$$
(☑061-366 9890; www.vietnamforesthotel.com; luxury tents from US$136, houses/studios from US$136/152; ❄@☎) This ecolodge sets the standard for atmospheric accommodation in Vietnam's national parks. There are several lovely safari tents overlooking the Dong Nai River, and a range of rooms set in reclaimed, traditional wooden houses. The lodge and restaurant are located across from the Dao Tien primate centre, so it's often possible to see and hear gibbons on the island.

The **Hornbill Bar-Restaurant** here serves a wide range of Vietnamese and international food and has a good selection of wines.

Park Restaurants CAFE, RESTAURANT $
(mains from 25,000d; ☉7am-9pm) There are two small restaurants near the park entrance, including a simple thatch-roof canteen and a fully blown restaurant. Hotpots here hit the spot perfectly.

ⓘ Getting There & Around

BICYCLE
Bicycle hire is available in the park, starting from just 20,000d per day.

THE NEW BATTLE FOR THE HIGHLANDS

In 2001 and 2004 protests erupted in Buon Ma Thuot, Pleiku and other parts of the highlands, objecting to the government's resettlement and land policies and alleged discrimination against hill tribes. There were more incidents in 2007 and while things have generally quietened down today, tensions remain over religious issues (most hill-tribe people are Protestant) and land rights.

A report commissioned by the United Nations High Commissioner for Refugees (UNHCR), entitled 'The Situation of Indigenous Groups in the Central Highlands' concluded that 'the obvious signs of more personal freedoms and economic reform can be seen in cities all over Vietnam. Yet what happens in the Central Highlands all too often remains behind closed doors, both for most outsiders and international observers, but also for many ordinary Vietnamese'.

BOAT
One approach to Cat Tien National Park is to take a boat across Langa Lake and then go by foot from there. Phat Tire Ventures (p276) is a reputable ecotour operator in Dalat that can offer this option.

BUS
All buses between Dalat and HCMC (every 30 minutes) pass the junction Vuon Quoc Gia Cat Tien on Hwy 20 for the park. The junction is around four hours' travel (100,000d) from both cities. From this junction, you can hire a motorbike (around 170,000d, but negotiate very hard) to cover the remaining 24km to the park. Lodges can also arrange a transfer from the main road.

Whichever way you come, you'll be dropped off at the park office, 100m before the boat that crosses the Dong Nai River to park headquarters. Buy your entrance ticket here, which includes the price of the boat crossing.

Lak Lake

The largest natural body of water in the central highlands, Lak Lake (Ho Lak) is surrounded by bucolic rural scenery, which sufficiently impressed Emperor Bao Dai enough to build yet another of his palaces overlooking the lake. There are two minority villages around the lake that often receive visitors.

On the south shores near the town of Lien Son lies **Jun village**, a fairly traditional M'nong settlement filled with rattan and wooden stilt houses. The villagers are surprisingly nonplussed about visitors, even though **DakLak Tourist** (☑0500-385 2246; www.daklaktourist.com.vn) has a small office and runs elephant rides (US$30 per hour). The second village of **M'lieng** is on the southwestern shore and can be reached by elephant or boat; enquire at DakLak Tourist.

🛏 Sleeping & Eating

Accommodation standards in the two established midrange places have declined in recent years. Mr Duc at **Cafe Duc Ma** (☑0500-358 6280; 268 Đ Nguyen Tat Thanh; per person US$5) in the village can organise a stay in one of several traditional stilt longhouses, along with activities such as gong concerts, elephant rides, and kayaking or walking tours.

★ **Sinthai Ho Lak** GUEST HOUSE $
(☑0905 424 239; Jun village; per person US$5) Very inviting, inexpensive new longhouse, with comfortable, screened beds in a well-

HO CHI MINH TRAIL

This legendary route was not one but many paths that formed the major supply link for the North Vietnamese and VC during the American War. Supplies and troops leaving from the port of Vinh headed inland along mountainous jungle paths, crossing in and out of Laos, and eventually arrived near Saigon. With all the secrecy, propaganda and confusion regarding the trail, it's hard to say how long it was in full; estimates range from over 5500km (said the US military) to more than 13,000km (boasted the North Vietnamese).

While elephants were initially used to cross the Truong Son Mountains into Laos, eventually it was sheer human power that shouldered supplies down the trail, sometimes supplemented by ponies, bicycles or trucks. Travelling from the 17th Parallel to the vicinity of Saigon took about six months in the mid-1960s; years later, with a more complex network of paths, the journey took only six weeks but it was still hard going.

Each person started out with a 36kg pack of supplies, as well as a few personal items (eg a tent, spare uniform and snake antivenom). What lay ahead was a rugged and mountainous route, plagued by flooding, disease and the constant threat of American bombing. At their peak, more than 500 American air strikes hit the trail every day and more ordnance was dropped on it than was used in all the theatres of war in WWII.

Despite these shock-and-awe tactics and the elaborate electronic sensors along the McNamara Line, the trail was never blocked. Most of it has returned to the jungle, but you can still follow sections of the trail today. Note that this is usually the more developed trail from the early 1970s, as the older trail was over the border in Laos. The **Ho Chi Minh Highway** is the easiest way to get a fix; it's a scenic mountain road running along the spine of the country. Starting near Hanoi, it passes through some popular tourist destinations and former battlefields, including the Phong Nha caves, Khe Sanh, Aluoi, Kon Tum and Buon Ma Thuot on its way to Saigon. The most spectacular sections include the roller-coaster ride through the Phong Nha-Ke Bang National Park, where looming karsts are cloaked in jungle.

Travel this route by car (or 4WD), motorbike or even bicycle if you are training for the King of the Mountains jersey; or arrange a tour through the Easy Riders in Dalat or one of the leading motorbike touring companies in Hanoi. **Explore Indochina** (www. exploreindochina.com) specialises in trail tours. **Hoi An Motorbike Adventures** (www. motorbiketours-hoian.com) offers shorter rides along sections between Hoi An and Phong Nha.

kept communal room (with en suite). The restaurant (meals from 45,000d) is excellent, with lake fish, duck and salads.

Bao Dai Villa　　　　　COLONIAL HOTEL $$
(☎0500-358 6184; www.daklaktourist.com.vn; r US$32-54; ❄) Pretend to live like a king at this isolated former royal residence on a hilltop overlooking the lake. It's actually not that palatial, but there are six enormous rooms. The small cafe here serves drinks and meals (from 40,000d).

ⓘ Getting There & Away

Nine daily buses connecting Dalat (90,000d, four hours) and Buon Ma Thuot (25,000d, one hour) pass the lake. It's also regularly visited on the Easy Rider trail. All the tour agencies in Buon Ma Thuot also offer tours.

Buon Ma Thuot

☏ 0500 / POP 326,000 / ELEV 451M

The Ede name translates as 'Thuot's father's village', but Buon Ma Thuot has outgrown its rustic origins without acquiring any real charm. An affluent, modern, but rather characterless city (pronounced 'boon me tote') it is inundated by traffic from three highways.

Its only saving grace is coffee: the region grows some of the best in Vietnam, plenty of which is sold and drunk in town. Buon Ma Thuot plays host to an annual Coffee Festival in March that sees gallons of the black nectar drunk and elephant races held in nearby Don village.

Most travellers stop in Buon Ma Thuot en route to the attractions around it: Yok Don National Park, a couple of striking waterfalls

Buon Ma Thuot

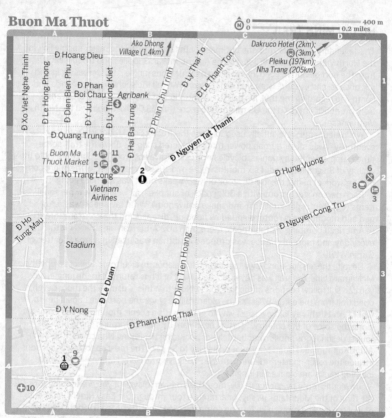

Buon Ma Thuot

and heaps of minority villages. The province is home to 44 ethnic groups, including some who have migrated here from the north. Among indigenous hill tribes, the dominant groups are the Ede, Jarai, M'nong and Lao.

◎ Sights & Activities

Ethnographic Museum   MUSEUM
(Đ Y Nong; admission 20,000d; ⊙8am-4pm) Built along the lines of a concrete wigwam, this is a rarity in Vietnam – a fine provincial museum with highly informative displays in English, French and Vietnamese (including vast information panels and audiovisuals). Some of the photography is outstanding. The content concentrates on Dak Lak province and its minority culture, environment and history.

Victory Monument   MONUMENT
Smack in the centre of town, this monument commemorates the events of 10 March 1975

when VC and North Vietnamese troops liberated the city. It's an interesting piece of socialist realist sculpture, consisting of a column supporting a central group of figures holding a flag, with a modernist arch forming a rainbow over a concrete replica tank.

Dak Lak Water Park
SWIMMING POOL

(Đ Nguyen Chi Thanh; adult/child 38,000/25,000d; ⏱8am-5.30pm) Strictly in the 'if you have time to kill' category, the waterslides at Dak Lak Water Park are a passable diversion on a hot afternoon. It's about 4km from town, just before the bus station.

🛏 Sleeping

Thanh Cong Hotel
HOTEL $

(☑0500-385 8243; thanhconghotel51@gmail.com; 51 Đ Ly Thuong Kiet; r 220,000-400,000d; ✴@🎧) One of the better places on backpacker-friendly Đ Ly Thuong Kiet. It's welcoming enough, with decent rooms (some with bath tubs), and all rates include breakfast.

Thanh Phat
GUEST HOUSE $

(☑0500-385 4857; 41 Đ Ly Thuong Kiet; s/d 170,000/250,000d; ✴🎧) Nothing fancy, but the owners are welcoming and the rooms – all with fan, air-con and hot-water bathrooms – are quite presentable for the (extremely low) rates.

★ Damsan Hotel
HOTEL $$

(☑0500-385 1234; www.damsanhotel.com.vn; 212-214 Đ Nguyen Cong Tru; r US$36-55, ste US$68; ✴@🎧🏊) An excellent place, which dates from the 1970s but remains in good shape. Rooms at the rear overlook a verdant valley dotted with bamboo, and the pool is huge (30m). It's on a side street, close to an array of cafes, bars and restaurants.

Dakruco Hotel
HOTEL $$$

(☑0500-397 0888; www.dakrucohotels.com; 30 Đ Nguyen Chi Thanh; r US$65-200; ✴@🎧🏊) Imposing four-star hotel about 2km east of the centre. Rooms are modern and inviting, though the chintzy, grandiose lobby is a little over the top. Facilities include a (mediocre) rooftop spa and tennis court.

🍴 Eating & Drinking

There's a limited choice of places in BMT. You'll find casual inexpensive restaurants dotted around the streets north of the Victory Monument. For a coffee or a beer, Đ Nguyen Cong Tru has scores of atmospheric places.

★ Thanh Tram
VIETNAMESE $

(22 Đ Ly Thuong Kiet; meals 30,000d; ⏱10.30am-9pm) There's only one dish here: delicious, roll-your-own, rice-paper rolls, with salad and herbs, fried pork and raw garlic, served with either a meaty broth or fish sauce and chilli.

Cafe Hoa Da Quy
CAFE $

(173 Đ Nguyen Cong Tru; meals 30,000d; ⏱9am-10pm; 🎧) Casual, open-sided, three-storey bar-restaurant with rattan seating and a rooftop bar. There are always five cheap dishes on the menu, including choices like pasta, and beef with noodles.

Black & White Restaurant
CAFE, BAR

(171 Đ Nguyen Cong Tru; ⏱7am-9.30pm; 🎧) Quite a find, this stylish place has a unique selling point – its awesome hi-fi – which is set up for customers to use. As the CD selection is pretty limited, BYO tunes and let the system rip. Coffees are around 20,000d and cocktails are also offered (but there aren't any meals served, despite the name).

Museum Cantin
CAFE

(Đ Y Nong; ⏱7am-6pm) To the side of the ethnographic museum, this likeable cafe with shady tables that overlook a banyan tree is a great place to escape the city traffic. It's a popular place for students and intellectuals to enjoy a coffee.

🛍 Shopping

Stock up on coffee here, as the price is lower and the quality higher than in HCMC or Hanoi. Browse the **coffee shop strip** on Đ Ly Thuong Kiet before you buy.

ℹ Information

Permits are required to visit minority villages in the area, except for Ako Dhong and Ban Don. Local travel agencies can make the arrangements.

Agribank (37 Đ Phan Boi Chau; ⏱7.30am-2.30pm Mon-Sat) Changes currency and travellers cheques.

Dak Lak General Hospital (☑0500-385 2665; 2 Đ Mai Hac De; ⏱24hr)

DakLak Tourist (☑0500-385 8243; www.daklaktourist.com.vn; 51 Đ Ly Thuong Kiet) On the ground floor of Thanh Cong Hotel; offers tours of villages, waterfalls, Lak Lake and Yok Don National Park.

Vietnam Highland Travel (☑0500-385 5009; highlandco@dng.vn.vn; Thanh Binh Hotel, 24 Đ Ly Thuong Kiet) Experienced guides, homestays and off-the-beaten-track trekking trips.

❶ Getting There & Around

AIR

There are daily **Vietnam Airlines** (📞 0500-395 4442; 17-19 Đ No Trang Long) flights serving HCMC (from 442,000d) and Hanoi (from 1,230,000d), and services four times a week to Danang (from 720,000d). Vietjet Air connects BMT to HCMC daily (from 320,000d). Jetstar flies to HCMC (from 467,000d) and Vinh (from 594,000d). The airport is 8km east of town; a taxi should cost about 120,000d.

BUS

Buon Ma Thuot is often called 'Dak Lak' (the province it is located in) on bus timetables. The city's **bus station** (71 Đ Nguyen Chi Thanh) is about 4km northeast of the centre with services to Dalat (120,000d, five hours, five daily), Nha Trang (115,000d, five hours, eight daily) and Pleiku (100,000d, four hours, every 30 minutes).

CAR & MOTORCYCLE

Highway 26 links the coast with Buon Ma Thuot, intersecting Hwy 1A at Ninh Hoa (157km), 34km north of Nha Trang. The road is surfaced and in good condition, although fairly steep in places. Highway 14 to Pleiku (199km) is in good shape, while Hwy 27 to Dalat is scenic but was in poor shape at the time of research.

TAXI

For reliable metered fares, use **Mai Linh** (📞 0500-381 9819).

AN ELEPHANT'S LIFE

Behind the apparently glorious status of the elephant in Vietnam is a tortured history spanning centuries. Prized by kings, these gentle and intelligent creatures were trapped around present-day Yok Don National Park by M'nong hunters. The animals were then tamed through savage beatings before being presented as royal gifts or put to work by the tribe.

And what work it was – elephants were (and still are) used as combination bulldozers, fork-lifts and semitrailers. Now they're more often seen in the lucrative tourist industry, lugging people through the forests or as part of minority festivals.

It's not necessarily a better life. Many elephants were trapped as babies so that they would be easier to train – neglecting the fact that they need their mother's milk up to the age of four in order to develop healthily. It's also easy to overestimate what adult elephants can tolerate. Elephant skin appears to be rough and impermeable, but it's as sensitive as human skin, vulnerable to sunburn, dirt and infections.

Another misconception is that elephants are strong, even indefatigable, but their spines were not designed to carry heavy burdens for extended periods of time. Above all, they need 250kg of food a day – an expensive undertaking, even for the most successful owner.

Before you decide on an elephant ride, take a closer look at the animal and its work environment:

➡ The elephant should have a shaded area to rest, with clean water and food. There should be enough slack in the chain so that it can move around. Given enough space, elephants don't defecate where they eat (who would want to?).

➡ The seat placed on the elephant should be made of light bamboo, not heavy wood, and there should be about seven layers of padding between the seat and the skin. There should be rubber hoses to line the binding ropes, or they will abrade the skin horribly.

➡ The elephant should work for only four or five hours a day, bearing up to only two adults at a time.

➡ The elephant caretaker should not have to use the bullhook or whip on the elephant with every command.

Though elephant trapping was banned in 1990, it was not strictly enforced. Without alternative employment, these elephants' fate seems grim: a lifetime of tourist rides, illicit employment in logging and construction, or, if the money runs out, abandonment or death.

Vietnam's native elephant species has been listed as endangered since 1976. The government annouced the creation of three conservation areas to help protect wild elephants (in Pu Mat, Cat Tien and Yok Don national parks) in 2013, but as there are only an estimated 100 or so wild elephants remaining in Vietnam, many see the action as too little, too late.

Compiled with assistance from Jin Pyn Lee

Around Buon Ma Thuot
☎ 0500

Yok Don National Park

Yok Don National Park (☎ 0500-378 3049; www.yokdonnationalpark.vn; admission free as part of package), the largest of Vietnam's nature reserves, has been gradually expanded and today encompasses 115,545 hectares of mainly dry deciduous forest. The park runs all the way up to the border with Cambodia, with the beautiful Srepok River flowing through it.

Unfortunately, deforestation is a big problem, particularly in the region closest to the entrance.

Yok Don is home to 67 mammal species including wild elephants, tigers, leopards and rare red wolves. However, these exotica are very rare (and virtually never encountered by visitors). More common wildlife includes muntjac deer, monkeys and snakes.

Within the park's boundaries are four **minority villages**, predominantly M'nong but also with Ede and Lao people. Three villages are accessible while the fourth is deep inside the park.

The delicate balance between ecological conservation and the preservation of local cultures is a challenge, considering the poverty of the region's people and their traditional means of survival, such as hunting.

To explore the national park, you'll have to either engage your own guide from Buon Ma Thuot or pick one up at the park entrance. Guides cost 170,000d for basic sightseeing or 280,000d per half day for trekking. Overnight trek prices start at 1,000,000d (including accommodation in a ranger station). There's also a 100,000d boat fee to cross the Srepok River.

Elephant rides (220,000d per hour per person) are available.

🛏 Sleeping & Eating

At the park entrance, 5km southeast of the main tourist centre Ban Don, **Yok Don Guesthouse** (☎ 0500-378 3049; r US$23; ❄) has rooms with hot water. Minority **stilt houses** (per person 160,000d) or **bungalow** (per person 320,000d) accommodation is also available. The bungalows are either beside the lake or out on nearby Aino Island,

reached via a rickety series of bamboo suspension bridges.

There's a **restaurant** (meals from 30,000d) in Ban Don, which sometimes hosts performances of gong music and dancing.

ℹ Information

Ban Don Tourist Centre (☎ 0500-378 3020; ttdl.buondon@gmail.com) is 5km beyond the turn-off into the national park. Be aware that it's a pretty touristy set-up and can get overrun with busloads of visitors. Gong performances and bucket-style drinking games are part of the evening entertainment.

ℹ Getting There & Around

Local buses head from Buon Ma Thuot bus station to Yok Don National Park (20,000d, roughly hourly).

Motorbike taxis in Buon Ma Thuot can take you to the park for around 220,000/350,000d one way/return.

Dray Sap & Dray Nur Falls

Located on the Krong Ana River, these stunning **waterfalls** (☎ 0500-321 3194; admission 20,000d) offer good riverside trekking opportunities. From the car park, the first one is the 100m-wide Dray Sap ('smoky falls' in Ede). For a better view, head down the path beside the river to a **suspension bridge** that crosses the river.

Across the bridge, follow the path through cornfields for another 250m. It leads to another bridge overlooking the 30m-wide Dray Nur waterfall. At the end of this bridge is a dirt path that brings you closer to Dray Nur.

However, bear in mind that due to the many dams located on the Srepok River, these falls have no water during dry season.

The falls are signposted from Hwy 14; the turn-off is about 15km southwest of Buon Ma Thuot. Drive for another 11km through a small industrial zone, then farmland, before you arrive at the entrance to the falls.

Pleiku
☎ 059 / POP 259,000 / ELEV 785M

The rather forgettable capital of Gia Lai province, Pleiku is better known as a strategic American and South Vietnamese base during the American War than for any postwar accomplishments. It makes an adequate pit stop, but there's little to detain a traveller

TO DIE JARAI

The Jarai minority of the Pleiku area honour their dead in graveyards set up like miniature villages. These graveyards are located to the west of the village, where the sun sets.

Each grave is marked with a shelter or bamboo stakes. Carved wooden figures are placed along the edge, often pictured in a squatting position with their hands over their faces in an expression of mourning. A jar is placed on the grave that represents the deceased person, and objects that the deceased might need in the next world are buried with them.

For seven years after the death, relatives bring food to the grave and pass death anniversaries at the gravesite, mourning and celebrating the deceased by feasting and drinking rice wine. After the seventh year, the spirit is believed to have moved on from the village and the grave is abandoned.

for more than a few hours. Torched by departing South Vietnamese soldiers in 1975, the city was rebuilt in the 1980s with help from the Soviet Union, which thoroughly explains its lack of appeal today.

In 2001 and 2004 Pleiku was the scene of hill-tribe protests against the government. The surrounding area is perfectly safe for travellers but remains sensitive politically, so you'll need a permit to explore the province.

◎ Sights

Ho Chi Minh Museum   MUSEUM
(1 Phan Dinh Phuong; ⊙8-11am & 1-4.30pm Mon-Fri) FREE The Ho Chi Minh Museum offers the usual paeans to Uncle Ho, with an emphasis on his affinity for hill-tribe people and their love for him. There are also displays about Bahnar hero Anh Hung Nup (1914–98), who led the hill tribes against the French and Americans. There's a **statue** (cnr Đ Le Loi & Đ Tran Hung Dao) of him nearby.

🛏 Sleeping & Eating

Duc Long Gia Lai Hotel   HOTEL $
(☏059-387 6303; thienhc@diglgroup.com; 95-97 Đ Hai Ba Trung; s/d 300,000/350,000d; ❋@⌘) Spacious, well-presented, pine-trimmed rooms (some with balconies and bath tubs)

and an elevator make this a popular choice. There are several other options close by if it's full.

HAGL Hotel Pleiku   HOTEL $$
(☏059-371 8459; www.haglhotelpleiku.vn; 1 Phu Dong; r US$48-62; ❋⌘) An opulent marble-rich lobby sets a luxurious tone and the spacious, very-well-equipped rooms won't disappoint either (those at the rear are quieter). The restaurant is surprisingly reasonably priced, but give the (disappointing) spa a miss. However, note that the parent company, the HAGL group, has been accused by Global Witness of breaching Cambodian laws related to forest clearing.

Com Ga Hainan   VIETNAMESE $
(73 Đ Hai Ba Trung; meals 30,000-50,000d; ⊙10am-8.30pm) A block from the Duc Long hotel, this busy, simple place serves delicious crispy chicken and rice with a side salad of lettuce, tomato and onion.

ℹ Information

A permit (US$10) and guide (US$20) are compulsory to visit villages in Gia Lai province. This puts many travellers off, who usually skip Pleiku and head north to Kon Tum. All tourist agencies in town can arrange the permit.

Gia Lai Tourist (☏059-387 4571; www.gialaitourist.com; 215 Đ Hung Vuong) A variety of well-priced tours lead by English- and French-speaking guides.

Vietin Bank (1 Đ Tran Hung Dao; ⊙7am-3.30pm Mon-Fri, 7am-noon Sat) Foreign exchange and credit-card advances.

ℹ Getting There & Around

AIR

Vietnam Airlines (☏059-382 4680; www.vietnamairlines.com; 18 Đ Le Lai) has two daily flights to Hanoi (from 783,000d), five daily to HCMC (from 930,000d) and one daily to Danang (from 417,000d). The airport is about 5km from the town and accessible by taxi (90,000d) or xe om (around 40,000d).

BUS

Pleiku's **bus station** (45 Đ Ly Nam De) is located about 2.5km southeast of town. Regular buses head to Buon Ma Thuot (100,000d, four hours, every 30 minutes), Kon Tum (20,000d, one hour, every 30 minutes) and Quy Nhon (75,000d, three hours, five daily). It's also possible to catch buses towards the border crossings for Cambodia and Laos.

Kon Tum

📀 060 / POP 52,300 / ELEV 525M

Kon Tum's relaxed ambience, river setting and relatively traffic-free streets make it a worthwhile stop for travellers intent on exploring the surrounding hill-tribe villages, of which there are 700 dotting the area. You'll also find a few intriguing sights in town, and the accommodation options are good. If you've the choice, Kon Tum is a far better base than Pleiku or Buon Ma Thuot for exploring this part of the highlands.

The region saw its share of combat during the American War. A major battle between the South and North Vietnamese took place in and around Kon Tum in the spring of 1972, when the area was devastated by hundreds of American B-52 raids.

More recently, in the 2004 protests against government policies in the highlands, hill tribes in Kon Tum province clashed with police and soldiers. On the surface things have cooled off, but relations between the hill tribes and the authorities remain fraught.

◉ Sights

Minority Villages   VILLAGE
There are several clusters of Bahnar villages on the periphery of Kon Tum. Village life here centres on the traditional *rong* house (*nha rong*), a tall thatched-roof community house built on stilts. The stilts were originally there to provide protection from elephants, tigers and other animals.

East of town **Kon Tum Konam** and **Kon Tum Kopong** each have *rong* houses. To the

south is the village **Kon Harachot** and there are others to the west.

Generally the local people welcome tourists and it's fine to wander around the village. But ask permission before pointing a camera into people's faces or homes. You also probably won't see people in traditional garb unless they're on their way to Mass in the Bahnar language, held on Sunday nights at the Immaculate Conception Cathedral.

Guided day trips to villages are available from about 400,000d for a guide/motorbike driver, depending on the places visited. Permits are no longer required, but be on the safe side by checking in with Kon Tum Tourist before venturing off.

If you have time to spend several days here, Kon Tum Tourist can arrange village homestays. Because the guides are careful not to intrude too frequently on any one village, visitors are always welcomed and traditions remain intact.

Immaculate Conception Cathedral CHURCH
(Đ Nguyen Hue) Built entirely from wood, this stunning cathedral from the French era has a dark frontage, sky-blue trim and wide terraces. Inside it's light, airy and elegant, with incredible interlocking beams. Seating on all four sides faces a central altar. The heart of the 160-year-old Kon Tum diocese, it primarily serves the ethnic minority community, and the altar is bedecked in traditional woven fabrics.

Seminary & Hill-Tribe Museum MUSEUM
(Đ Tran Hung Dao; ⊙8-11am & 2-4pm Mon-Sat)
FREE This lovely old Catholic seminary wouldn't look out of place in a provincial French town. Built in 1934, it has a chapel

---

ⓘ GETTING TO CAMBODIA: PLEIKU TO BAN LUNG

Getting to the border Remote and rarely used by foreigners, the Le Thanh/O Yadaw border crossing lies 90km from Pleiku and 64km from Ban Lung, Cambodia. From Pleiku there's a daily Noi Thinh bus at 7.30am (60,000d, two hours) from the main marketplace on Đ Tran Phu direct to the Cambodian border at Le Thanh. You can also get to Le Thanh by buses from the main bus terminal, travelling via Moc Den (40,000d, two hours, four daily), from where local buses (20,000d, 15km) head to the border. Get as early a start as you can.

At the border Cambodian visas are issued at the border. Vietnamese visas need to be organised in advance.

Moving on From O Yadaw, on the Cambodia side of the border, local buses (US$8) or motorbikes (around US$25) head to Ban Lung. There are far fewer transport options in the afternoon.

Kon Tum

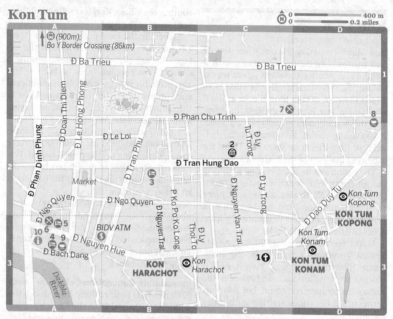

Kon Tum

⊙ Sights
1 Immaculate Conception
   Cathedral C3
2 Seminary & Hill-Tribe Museum C2

🛏 Sleeping
3 Family Hotel B2
4 Indochine Hotel A3
5 Viet Nga Hotel A3

⊗ Eating
6 Dakbla Restaurant A3
7 Quan 58 .... C1

🍷 Drinking & Nightlife
8 Eva Cafe D1
9 Indochine Coffee A3

ⓘ Information
   Highlands Eco Tours .... (see 5)
10 Kon Tum Tourist A3

with beautiful wood carvings and a 'traditional room' upstairs that functions as an unofficial museum of hill-tribe life and the Kon Tum diocese. You may have to ask one of the seminary residents to unlock the museum for you.

🛏 Sleeping

★ Family Hotel
HOTEL $

(☎ 060-386 2448; phongminhkt@yahoo.com; 55 & 61 Đ Tran Hung Dao; s/d US$15/18; ❉ @ 🛜) The sign behind reception says 'home sweet home' and that's a fitting summary of this excellent, family owned place. Bungalow-style rooms face a lovely garden at the rear.

Viet Nga Hotel
HOTEL $

(☎ 060-224 0247; 160 Đ Nguyen Hue; s with fan 150,000d; r with air-con 200,000-300,000d; ❉ @ 🛜) An excellent, family-run minihotel for dong-sensitive travellers. Rooms are very clean and have attractive furnishings, a fridge and TV. Staff speak a few words of English.

Indochine Hotel
HOTEL $$

(☎ 060-386 3335; www.indochinehotel.vn; 30 Đ Bach Dang; r 630,000-1,260,000d; ❉ @ 🛜) Right on the riverbank, this large concrete hotel's spacious rooms have great views and all the mod cons. Prices include a breakfast buffet.

🍴 Eating & Drinking

Dakbla Restaurant
VIETNAMESE, WESTERN $

(168 Đ Nguyen Hue; mains 40,000-100,000d; ⊙ 8am-10pm) Half-museum, half-restaurant, this atmospheric place has good Vietnamese

---

ℹ️ **GETTING TO LAOS: KON TUM TO ATTAPEU**

Getting to the border The Bo Y/Phou Keau border crossing lies 86km northwest of Kon Tum and 119km northeast of Attapeu (Laos). From Pleiku bus station, Mai Linh buses leave daily at 6.30am for Attapeu (250,000d, seven hours), continuing to Pakse (420,000d, 11½ hours). Kon Tum Tourist can arrange for you to join the bus when it passes through Kon Tum at around 8.15am.

Crossing the border independently can be a challenge. On the Vietnam side, the nearest major town is Ngoc Hoi, which can be reached by bus from Kon Tum (34,000d, 1½ hours). You'll have to catch a minibus from Ngoc Hoi to the border (12,000d, 30 minutes). On the Laos side, things are even quieter and you'll be at the mercy of passing traffic to hitch a ride onwards.

At the border Vietnamese visas aren't available at this border, but Lao visas are available for most nationalities (between US$30 and US$40).

Moving on Buses from Pleiku arrive in Attapeu around 1.30pm, where a free lunch is included as part of your fare if you're travelling with Mai Linh. You'll arrive in Pakse around 6pm.

---

and Western menus that include plenty of vegetarian choices. Its walls are festooned with tribal artefacts (masks, drums, gongs).

Quan 58   VIETNAMESE $
(58 Đ Phan Chu Trinh; hotpot 90,000d; ⊙11am-9pm) All goat, all the time. Try it steamed *(de hap)*, grilled *(de nuong)*, sautéed *(de xao lan)*, curried *(de cari)* or opt for the ever-popular hotpot *(lau de)*.

Eva Cafe   CAFE
(1 Đ Phan Chu Trinh; ⊙7am-9pm) Very quirky neighbourhood cafe with lots of seating in log-cabin-like and treehouse-style spaces with tribal masks overhead. A nice place to unwind with a beer or coffee, as local couples have established.

Indochine Coffee   CAFE, BAR
(30 Đ Bach Dang; ⊙7am-10pm) A highly unexpected find in deepest Kon Tum province, this modernist cafe – concrete flooring shaded by artistically arranged bamboo pillars and roofing – is where the hipsters hang. Join them for a tea, coffee or beer.

ℹ️ Information

BIDV ATM (1 Đ Tran Phu)
Highlands Eco Tours (☏060-391 2788; www.vietnamhighlands.com; 41 Đ Ho Tung Mau)

Independently run travel company specialising in minority village trips, homestays in off-the-beaten-track communities, trekking and battlefield visits. From US$35 per day.

Kon Tum General Hospital (☏060-386 2565; 224A Đ Ba Trieu; ⊙6am-9pm)
Kon Tum Tourist (☏060-386 1626; ktourist@dng.vnn.vn; 2 Đ Phan Dinh Phung) Staff here can arrange tours to Bahnar and Jarai villages, including homestays.

ℹ️ Getting There & Around

BUS

Kon Tum's **bus station** (279 Đ Phan Dinh Phung) has hustlers eager to sell you overpriced tickets, many working with bus conductors. There are very regular services to Pleiku (20,000d, one hour, every 30 minutes). For Danang (130,000d, seven hours, seven daily) try to catch one of the Mai Linh buses (at 7.30am and 3pm), which are well-maintained and don't overcharge foreigners.

XE OM

Kon Tum is easy to traverse on foot, but *xe om* (20,000d for a short ride) are in ready supply.

TAXI

If you need a taxi, try **Mai Linh** (☏060-395 5555).

Ho Chi Minh City

🔊 08 / POP 7.5 MILLION

Includes ➡

Best Places to Eat

➡ May (p326)

➡ Nha Hang Ngon (p323)

➡ Temple Club (p323)

➡ ...hum Vegetarian Cafe & Restaurant (p327)

➡ Baba's Kitchen (p327)

Best Places to Stay

➡ Madame Cuc 127 (p319)

➡ Giang Son (p319)

➡ Ma Maison Boutique Hotel (p323)

➡ Park Hyatt Saigon (p318)

➡ Blue River Hotel (p321)

Why Go?

Ho Chi Minh City (HCMC) is Vietnam at its most dizzying: a high-octane city of commerce and culture that has driven the whole country forward with its pulsating energy. A chaotic whirl, the city breathes life and vitality into all who settle here – visitors cannot help but be hauled along for the ride.

From the finest of hotels to the cheapest of guesthouses, the classiest of restaurants to the tastiest of street stalls, the choicest of boutiques to the scrum of the markets, HCMC is a city of contrasts. Wander through timeless alleys before catching up with the present in designer malls beneath sleek skyscrapers. The ghosts of the past live on in buildings that one generation ago witnessed a city in turmoil, but the real beauty of (erstwhile) Saigon's urban collage is the the seamless blending of these two worlds into one thrilling, seething mass, while a host of new and exhilarating tours get you way off the beaten track.

When to Go
Ho Chi Minh City

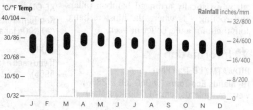

Feb Hardly any rain, the least humidity and a city filled with blooms for the Tet celebrations.

Mar Also has low rain and humidity, plus the annual *cyclo* challenge.

Dec December is a whisper cooler than normal for HCMC and comparatively dry.

History

Saigon was originally part of the kingdom of Cambodia and, until the late 17th century, was a small port town known as Prey Nokor. As Vietnamese settlers moved south it was absorbed by Vietnam and became the base for the Nguyen Lords, who were the rulers of southern Vietnam from the 16th to the 18th centuries.

During the Tay Son rebellion in the 18th century, a group of Chinese refugees established a settlement nearby, which became known by their Vietnamese neighbours as Cholon (big market). After seeing off the rebels, Nguyen Anh constructed a large citadel here (roughly where the American and French embassies now stand).

Both Saigon and Cholon were captured by the French in 1859 (who destroyed the citadel in the process) and Saigon became the capital of Cochinchina a few years later. It wasn't until 1931, after the neighbouring cities had sprawled into each other, that they were officially combined to form Saigon-Cholon (the name Cholon was dropped in 1956).

The city served as the capital of the Republic of Vietnam from 1956 until 1975, when it fell to advancing North Vietnamese forces and was renamed Ho Chi Minh City.

◉ Sights

With pockets of elegance and French colonial grandeur and a ceaseless hubbub on its chaotic streets, Ho Chi Minh City has rewarding sights for temple- and museum-goers, market-hounds, history junkies, architecture fans, park lovers or simply anyone itching to see Vietnam's most economically vibrant city in action. Three days should be sufficient to get a handle on the main sights, but Ho Chi Minh's easygoing, friendly and enterprising personality snares many a traveller into longer stays.

In reality, HCMC is not so much a city as a small province stretching from the South China Sea almost to the Cambodian border. Rural regions constitute about 90% of the land area where around 25% of the municipality's population live; the other 75% is crammed into the remaining 10% of land – the urban centre.

HCMC is divided into 19 urban districts (*quan,* derived from the French *quartier*) and five rural districts (*huyen,* derived from the Chinese *xian*). The majority of places and sights converge in District 1, the district still known as Saigon (although many residents still refer to the whole city as Saigon, just to confuse things), which includes the tireless backpacker district of Pham Ngu Lao (PNL) and the more upmarket area of Dong Khoi. The city's neoclassical and international-style buildings, along with its tree-lined streets set with shops, cafes and restaurants, give neighbourhoods such as District 3 an attractive, almost French atmosphere.

◉ Dong Khoi Area

This well-heeled area, immediately west of the Saigon River, packages the heart of

---

HO CHI MINH CITY IN...

One Day

Slurp up a steaming bowl of *pho* (rice-noodle soup) and then follow our **walking tour** (p327) head to the nearby **War Remnants Museum** (p303), tour the **Reunification Palace** (p304) and, if there's still time, the **HCMC Museum** (p298). In the evening, catch the sunset views from the **Alto Heli Bar** (p331), followed by a meal at **Nha Hang Ngon** (p323) or **Temple Club** (p323). Have a nightcap at **Vasco's** (p330) or one of the other bars in the courtyard of the former opium refinery.

Two Days

Spend the morning in **Cholon** (p307), wandering around the market and historic temples. Catch a taxi up to District 3 for a cheap traditional lunch at **Pho Hoa** (p326) or **Banh Xeo 46A** (p326) and then walk through Da Kao ward to the **Jade Emperor Pagoda** (p300) and **History Museum** (p303). It's your last night in HCMC, so make the most of it. Start your evening at another of the city's superb restaurants – perhaps **May** (p326), **Cuc Gach Quan** (p326) or **...hum Vegetarian Cafe & Restaurant** (p327) – and then catch a band at **Acoustic** (p332) or **Yoko** (p332). If you're ready for the evening to descend into a very Saigon state of messiness, continue on to **Cargo** (p332) or **Apocalypse Now** (p330).

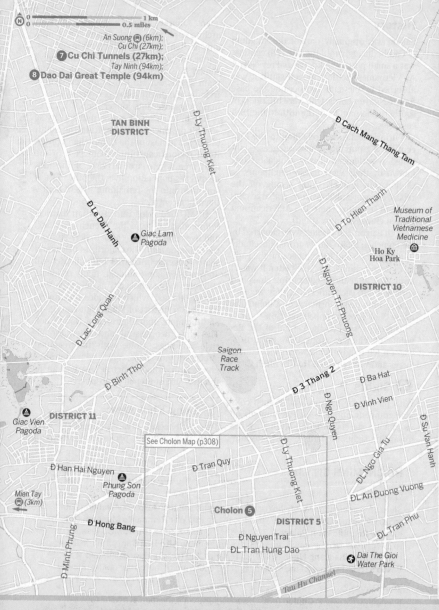

An Suong (6km);
Cu Chi (27km);
7 Cu Chi Tunnels (27km);
Tay Ninh (94km);
8 Dao Dai Great Temple (94km)

TAN BINH DISTRICT

Đ Ly Thuong Kiet

Đ Cach Mang Thang Tam

Đ To Hien Thanh

Museum of Traditional Vietnamese Medicine

Ho Ky Hoa Park

DISTRICT 10

Đ Le Dai Hanh

Giac Lam Pagoda

Đ Nguyen Tri Phuong

Đ Lac Long Quan

Saigon Race Track

Đ 3 Thang 2

Đ Ba Hat

Đ Vinh Vien

Đ Binh Thoi

Đ Ngo Quyen

Đ Su Van Hanh

Giac Vien Pagoda

DISTRICT 11

See Cholon Map (p308)

Đ Han Hai Nguyen

Đ Tran Quy

Đ Ly Thuong Kiet

ĐL Ngo Gia Tu

Mien Tay (3km)

Phung Son Pagoda

Cholon 5

DISTRICT 5

ĐL An Duong Vuong

Đ Minh Phung

Đ Hong Bang

Đ Nguyen Trai

ĐL Tran Hung Dao

ĐL Tran Phu

Dai The Gioi Water Park

Tau Hu Channel

Ho Chi Minh City Highlights

1 Soak up the city's electric energy and admire views of the neon city from a high-altitude perch in one of its **rooftop bars** (p330).

2 Witness the turbulence of conflict in the **War Remnants Museum** (p303).

3 Feast on an eye-opening selection of **local and international cuisine** at the

city's standout restaurants and street stalls (p323).

4 Smother yourself in clouds of incense within the mystical world of the **Jade Emperor Pagoda** (p300).

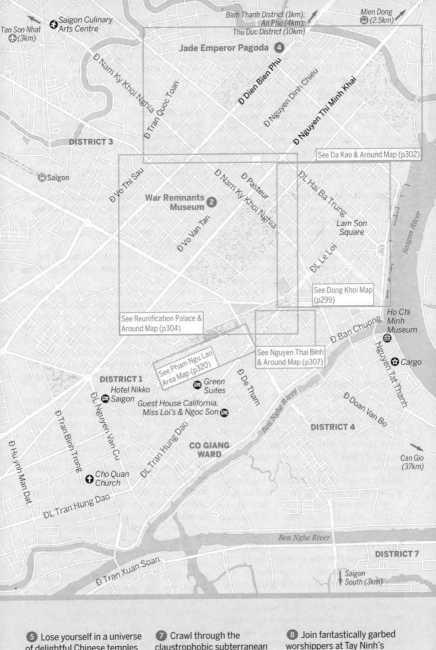

5 Lose yourself in a universe of delightful Chinese temples in **Cholon** (p307).

6 Tag along with one of the entertaining and imaginative **tours** (p316) of the city.

7 Crawl through the claustrophobic subterranean warrens and underground chambers of the Viet Cong in the **Cu Chi Tunnels** (p342).

8 Join fantastically garbed worshippers at Tay Ninh's astounding **Cao Dai Great Temple** (p313).

old Saigon into a swish enclave of designer stores and skyscrapers. Slicing from the river to august Notre Dame Cathedral via the Opera House (Municipal Theatre), ritzy Đ Dong Khoi is the main shopping strip and lends its name to the encircling civic centre and central business district. Yet it's the wide, tree-lined boulevards of Le Loi and Nguyen Hue, perpetually swarming with motorbikes, that leave more of an impression – not least if you've survived crossing them on foot. It's in these grand thoroughfares that French colonial elegance and urban modernity fashion an alluring concoction.

★ Notre Dame Cathedral
CATHEDRAL

(Map p299; Đ Han Thuyen; ⊙ Mass 9.30 Sun) Built between 1877 and 1883, Notre Dame Cathedral rises up romantically from the heart of HCMC's government quarter, facing Đ Dong Khoi. A brick, neo-Romanesque church with two 40m-high square towers tipped with iron spires, the Catholic cathedral is named after the Virgin Mary. The walls of the interior are inlaid with devotional tablets and some stained glass survives. English-speaking staff dispense tourist information from 9am to 11am Monday to Saturday. If the front gates are locked, try the door on the side of the building that faces Reunification Palace.

★ Central Post Office
HISTORIC BUILDING

(Map p299; 2 Cong Xa Paris) Right across the way from Notre Dame Cathedral, HCMC's striking French post office is a period classic, designed by Gustave Eiffel and built between 1886 and 1891. Painted on the walls of its grand concourse are fascinating historic maps of South Vietnam, Saigon and Cholon, while a mosaic of Ho Chi Minh takes pride of place at the end of its barrel-vaulted hall.

Note the magnificent tiled floor of the interior and the copious green-painted wrought iron.

Opera House
NOTABLE BUILDING

(Nha Hat Thanh Pho; Map p299; ☑ 08-3829 9976; Lam Son Sq) Gracing the intersection of Đ Dong Khoi and ĐL Le Loi, this grand colonial edifice with a sweeping staircase was built in 1897 and is one of the city's most recognisable buildings. Officially known as the Municipal Theatre, the Opera House captures the flamboyance of France's belle époque.

People's Committee Building
NOTABLE BUILDING

(Hôtel de Ville; Map p299; ĐL Nguyen Hue) HCMC's ornate People's Committee Building, one of the city's most prominent landmarks, is the home of the Ho Chi Minh City People's Committee. Built between 1901 and 1908, the former Hôtel de Ville decorates the northwestern end of ĐL Nguyen Hue and is one of the most photographed buildings in Vietnam but is not open to the public.

HCMC Museum
MUSEUM

(Bao Tang Thanh Pho Ho Chi Minh; Map p299; www.hcmc-museum.edu.vn; 65 Đ Ly Tu Trong; admission 15,000d; ⊙ 8am-5pm) A grand, neoclassical structure built in 1885 and once known as Gia Long Palace (and later the Revolutionary Museum), HCMC's city museum is a singularly beautiful and impressive building, telling the story of the city through archaeological artefacts, ceramics, old city maps and displays on the marriage traditions of its various ethnicities.

The struggle for independence is extensively covered, with most of the upper floor devoted to it.

Deep beneath the building is a network of reinforced concrete bunkers and fortified corridors. The system, branches of which stretch all the way to Reunification Palace, included living areas, a kitchen and a large meeting hall. In 1963 President Diem and his brother hid here before fleeing to Cha Tam Church (p312). The network is not open to the public because most of the tunnels are flooded.

In the gardens are various pieces of military hardware, including the American-built F-5E jet used by a renegade South Vietnamese pilot to bomb the Presidential Palace (now Reunification Palace) on 8 April 1975.

★ Bitexco Financial Tower
VIEWPOINT

(Map p299; http://saigonskydeck.com; 2 Đ Hai Trieu; adult/child 200,000/130,000d; ⊙ 9.30am-9.30pm) The 68-storey, 262m-high, Carlos Zapata–designed skyscraper dwarfs all around it. It's meant to be shaped like a lotus bulb, but a CD rack with a tambourine shoved into it also springs to mind. That tambourine is the 48th-floor Saigon Skydeck, with a helipad on its roof. The views are, of course, extraordinary but not weather-proof, so choose a clear day and aim for sunset (or upend a drink in the Alto Heli Bar instead).

Ton Duc Thang Museum
MUSEUM

(Bao Tang Ton Duc Thang; Map p299; ☑ 08-3829 7542; 5 Đ Ton Duc Thang; ⊙ 7.30-11.30am & 1.30-5pm Tue-Sun) FREE This small patriotic museum is dedicated to Ton Duc Thang, Ho Chi Minh's successor as president of Vietnam. Born in

Dong Khoi

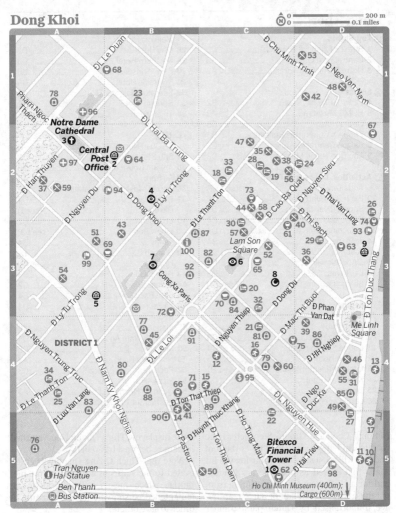

1888 in Long Xuyen in the Mekong Delta region, he died in office in 1980. Photos and exhibits celebrate his role in the Vietnamese Revolution, enhanced by some fascinating displays on French colonial brutality.

As so few people visit, it's one of the quietest parts of town.

Saigon Central Mosque
MOSQUE
(Map p299; 66 Đ Dong Du) Built by South Indian Muslims in 1935 on the site of an earlier mosque, lime green Saigon Central Mosque is an immaculately clean and well-tended island of calm in the bustling Dong Khoi area.

In front of the sparkling white and blue structure, with its four decorative minarets, is a pool for the ritual ablutions required by Islamic law before prayers.

Several Malaysian and Indian restaurants serving halal food are nearby, including an excellent but humble eatery directly behind the mosque. Take off your shoes before entering the building.

22 Ly Tu Trong
HISTORICAL SITE
(Map p299; 22 Đ Ly Tu Trong) The ground floor of this innocuous-looking building on Ly Tu Trong is currently occupied by the Vietnam

Dong Khoi

National Chemical Group. Step across the road to Chi Lang Park to look up at the roof and you will see a structure (housing the lift shaft) that served as a temporary landing pad for a US helicopter evacuating personnel the day before the fall of Saigon, an image immortalised by Dutch photographer Hubert Van Es.

The photograph is commonly misunderstood to depict US citizens leaving the roof of the US Embassy, but this building actually housed CIA staff.

Venerable Thich Quang Duc Memorial MONUMENT

(Map p304; cnr Đ Nguyen Dinh Chieu & Đ Cach Mang Thang Tam) This peaceful memorial park is dedicated to Thich Quang Duc, the Buddhist monk who self-immolated in protest at this intersection not far from the Presidential Palace (today's Reunification Palace) in 1963. The memorial was inaugurated in

2010, displaying Thich Quang Duc wreathed in flames, before a bas-relief.

Note that Thich Quang Duc has been elevated to the status of a Bo Tat on the memorial, which means a Boddhisattva (an enlightened person who forgoes Nirvana in order to save others).

◉ Da Kao & Around

This old District 1 ward, directly north of the city centre, is home to most of the consulates and some beautiful buildings dating from the French colonial period. Hidden within its historic streets (and those bordering it in the eastern corner of District 3) are some of HCMC's hippest new restaurants and bars, along with some of the city's best traditional eateries.

★ Jade Emperor Pagoda TAOIST TEMPLE

(Phuoc Hai Tu | Chua Ngoc Hoang; Map p302; 73 Đ Mai Thi Luu; ⊙7am-6pm, on 1st & 15th of lunar month 5am-7pm) Built in 1909 in honour of the supreme Taoist god (the Jade Emperor or King of Heaven, Ngoc Hoang), this is one of the most spectacularly atmospheric temples in HCMC, stuffed with statues of phantasmal divinities and grotesque heroes. The pungent smoke of *huong* (incense) fills the air, obscuring the exquisite woodcarvings.

Its roof encrusted with elaborate tilework, the temple's statues, depicting characters from both Buddhist and Taoist lore, are made from reinforced papier mâché. Inside the main building are two especially fierce and menacing Taoist figures. On the right (as you face the altar) is a 4m-high statue of the general who defeated the Green Dragon (depicted underfoot). On the left is the general who defeated the White Tiger, which is also being stepped on.

Worshippers mass before the ineffable Jade Emperor, who presides – draped in luxurious robes and shrouded in a dense fug of incense smoke – over the main sanctuary. He is flanked by his guardians, the Four Big Diamonds (Tu Dai Kim Cuong), so named because they are said to be as hard as diamonds.

Out the door on the left-hand side of the Jade Emperor's chamber is another room. The semienclosed area to the right (as you enter) is presided over by Thanh Hoang, the Chief of Hell; to the left is his red horse. Other figures here represent the gods who dispense punishments for evil acts and rewards for good deeds. The room also contains the famous Hall of the Ten Hells, carved wooden panels illustrating the varied torments awaiting evil people in each of the Ten Regions of Hell. Women queue up at the seated effigy of the City God, who wears a hat inscribed with Chinese characters that announce 'At one glance, money is given'. In a mesmerising ritual, worshippers first put money into a box, then rub a piece of

Da Kao & Around

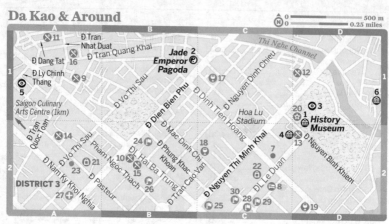

Da Kao & Around

red paper against his hand before circling it around a candle flame.

On the other side of the wall is a fascinating little room in which the ceramic figures of 12 women, overrun with children and wearing colourful clothes, sit in two rows of six. Each of the women exemplifies a human characteristic, either good or bad (as in the case of the woman drinking alcohol from a jug). Each figure represents a year in the 12-year Chinese astrological calendar. Presiding over the room is Kim Hoa Thanh Mau, the Chief of All Women. Upstairs is a hall

to Quan Am, the Goddess of Mercy, opposite a portrait of Dat Ma, the bearded Indian founder of Zen Buddhism.

The multifaith nature of the temple is echoed in the shrine's alternative name Phuoc Hai Tu (福海寺; Sea of Blessing Temple), the message of which is clearly Buddhist. Similarly, the Chinese characters (佛光普照: *Phat Quang Pho Chieu*) in the main temple hall mean 'The light of Buddha shines on all'.

Outside, a small pond seethes with turtles, some of which have auspicious inscriptions on their shells.

★ **History Museum**   MUSEUM
(Bao Tang Lich Su; Map p302; Đ Nguyen Binh Khiem; admission 15,000đ; ⊘ 8-11.30am & 1.30-5pm Tue-Sun) Built in 1929 by the Société des Études Indochinoises, this notable Sino-French museum houses a rewarding collection of artefacts illustrating the evolution of the cultures of Vietnam, from the Bronze Age Dong Son civilisation (which emerged in 2000 BC) and the Funan civilisation (1st to 6th centuries AD), to the Cham, Khmer and Vietnamese.

Highlights include valuable relics taken from Cambodia's Angkor Wat, a fine collection of Buddha statues, the perfectly preserved mummy of a local woman who died in 1869, excavated from Xom Cai in District 5, and some exquisite stylised mother-of-pearl Chinese characters inlaid into panels. Also housing a branch of the shop Nguyen Freres (p334), the museum is just inside the main gate to the city's botanic gardens and zoo.

Botanic Gardens   GARDEN
(Thao Cam Vien; Map p302; 2 Đ Nguyen Binh Khiem; admission 8,000đ; ⊘ 7am-7pm) One of the first projects undertaken by the French after establishing Cochinchina as a colony was founding these fantastic, lush gardens. Once one of the finest such gardens in Asia, they're very agreeable for strolling beneath giant tropical trees, including towering Tung and So Khi trees. Also equipped with a miserable zoo, the gardens are next to the History Museum.

Military Museum   MUSEUM
(Bao Tang Quan Doi; Map p302; 2 ĐL Le Duan; ⊘ 7.30-11am & 1.30-4.30pm Tue-Sat) **FREE** A short distance from the History Museum, this small collection is devoted to Ho Chi Minh's campaign to liberate the south. The exhibits inside are of minor interest but some US, Chinese and Soviet war material is on display outdoors, including a South Vietnamese Air Force Cessna A-37 and a US-built F-5E Tiger with the 20mm nose gun still loaded.

The tank on display is one of the tanks that broke into the grounds of Reunification Palace on 30 April 1975.

Pho Binh   HISTORICAL SITE
(Map p302; 7 Đ Ly Chinh Thang, District 3; noodle soup 30,000đ) A humble noodle-soup restaurant may seem an unusual attraction, but there's more to Pho Binh than meets the eye. This was the secret headquarters of the Viet Cong (Vietnamese Communists; VC) in Saigon and from here they planned their attacks on the US embassy and other Saigon targets during the Tet Offensive of 1968. One wonders how many US soldiers ate here, completely unaware.

The *pho* (noodle soup) makes it a worthwhile stop for lunch or breakfast.

⊙ Reunification Palace & Around

Straddling District 1 and District 3, this grid of busy streets encloses the inviting spaces of Tao Dan Park and the pristine grounds of Reunification Palace. It's here that you'll find some of HCMC's most popular sights and a smattering of terrific restaurants.

★ **War Remnants Museum**   MUSEUM
(Bao Tang Chung Tich Chien Tranh; Map p304; ⌨ 08-3930 5587; 28 Đ Vo Van Tan, cnr Đ Le Quy Don; admission 15,000đ; ⊘ 7.30am-noon & 1.30-5pm) Once known as the Museum of Chinese and American War Crimes, the War Remnants Museum is consistently popular with Western tourists. Few museums anywhere drive home so effectively the brutality of war and its many civilian victims. Many of the atrocities documented here were well publicised but rarely do Westerners get to hear the victims of US military action tell their own stories.

While the displays are one-sided, many of the most disturbing photographs illustrating US atrocities are from US sources, including those of the infamous My Lai Massacre.

US armoured vehicles, artillery pieces, bombs and infantry weapons are on display outside. One corner of the grounds is devoted to the notorious French and South Vietnamese prisons on Phu Quoc and Con Son Islands. Artefacts include that most iconic of French appliances, the guillotine, and the notoriously inhumane 'tiger cages' used to house VC prisoners.

The ground floor of the museum is devoted to a collection of posters and photographs showing support for the antiwar movement internationally. This somewhat upbeat display provides a counterbalance to the horrors upstairs.

Even those who supported the war are likely to be horrified by the photos of children affected by US bombing and napalming. You'll also have the rare chance to see some of the experimental weapons used in the war (which were at one time military secrets), such as the *flechette*, an artillery shell filled with thousands of tiny darts.

HO CHI MINH CITY SIGHTS

Reunification Palace & Around

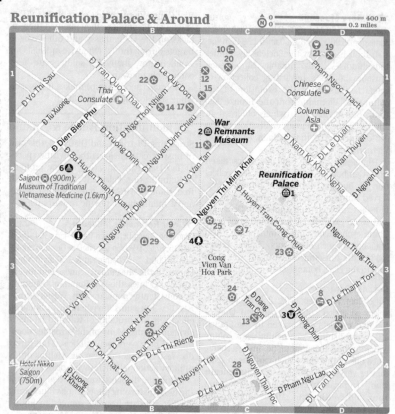

N
0 _____ 400 m
0 _____ 0.2 miles

Upstairs, look out for the **Requiem Exhibition**. Compiled by legendary war photographer Tim Page, this striking collection documents the work of photographers killed during the course of the conflict, on both sides, and includes works by Larry Burrows and Robert Capa.

The War Remnants Museum is in the former US Information Service building. Captions are in Vietnamese and English.

★**Reunification Palace**   HISTORICAL BUILDING
(Dinh Thong Nhat; Map p304; ☐ 08-3829 4117; Đ Nam Ky Khoi Nghia; adult/child 30,000/3000d; ◷7.30-11am & 1-4pm) Surrounded by Royal Palm trees, the dissonant 1960s architecture of this government building and the eerie mood that accompanies a walk through its deserted halls make it one of the most intriguing spectacles in HCMC. The building is deeply associated with the fall of Saigon in 1975, yet it's the overblown kitsch detailing and period motifs that steal the show.

The first Communist tanks to arrive in Saigon rumbled here on the morning of 30 April 1975 and it's as if time has stood still since then. After crashing through the wrought-iron gates – in a dramatic scene recorded by photojournalists and shown around the world – a soldier ran into the building and up the stairs to unfurl a VC flag from the balcony. In an ornate reception chamber, General Minh, who had become head of the South Vietnamese state only 43 hours before, waited with his improvised cabinet. 'I have been waiting since early this morning to transfer power to you', Minh said to the VC officer who entered the room. 'There is no question of your transferring power', replied the officer. 'You cannot give up what you do not have.'

In 1868 a residence was built on this site for the French governor-general of

Reunification Palace & Around

HO CHI MINH CITY SIGHTS

Cochinchina and gradually it expanded to become Norodom Palace. When the French departed, the palace became home to the South Vietnamese president Ngo Dinh Diem. So unpopular was Diem that his own air force bombed the palace in 1962 in an unsuccessful attempt to kill him. The president ordered a new residence to be built on the same site, this time with a sizeable bomb shelter in the basement. Work was completed in 1966, but Diem did not get to see his dream house as he was killed by his own troops in 1963.

The new building was named Independence Palace and was home to the successive South Vietnamese president, Nguyen Van Thieu, until his hasty departure in 1975. Designed by Paris-trained Vietnamese architect Ngo Viet Thu, it is an outstanding example of 1960s architecture, with an airy and open atmosphere.

The ground floor is arranged with meeting rooms, while upstairs is a grand set of reception rooms, used for welcoming foreign and national dignitaries. In the back of the structure are the president's living quarters; check out the model boats, horse tails and severed elephants' feet. The 2nd floor contributes a shagadelic card-playing room, complete with a cheesy round leather banquette, a barrel-shaped bar, hubcap light fixtures and groovy three-legged chairs set around a flared-legged card table. There's also a cinema and a rooftop nightclub, complete with helipad: James Bond/Austin Powers – eat your heart out.

Perhaps most fascinating of all is the basement with its telecommunications centre, war room and warren of tunnels, where hulking old fans chop the air and ancient radio transmitters sit impassively. Towards the end are rooms where videos appraise the palace and its history in Vietnamese, English, French, Chinese and Japanese. The national anthem is played at the end of the tape and you are expected to stand up – it would be rude not to.

Reunification Palace is open to visitors as long as official receptions or meetings aren't taking place. English- and French-speaking guides are on duty during opening hours.

Mariamman Hindu Temple   HINDU TEMPLE
(Chua Ba Mariamman; Map p304; 45 Đ Truong Dinh; ⊙7.30am-7.30pm) There may only be a small number of Hindus in HCMC, but this colourful slice of southern India is also considered sacred by many ethnic Vietnamese and Chinese. Indeed, it is reputed to have miraculous powers. The temple was built at the end of the 19th century and dedicated to the Hindu goddess Mariamman.

The lion to the left of the entrance used to be carried around the city in a street procession every autumn. In the shrine in the middle of the temple is Mariamman, flanked by her guardians Maduraiveeran (to her left) and Pechiamman (to her right). In front of the Mariamman figure are two linga (stylised phalluses that represent the Hindu god Shiva). Favourite offerings placed nearby include joss sticks, jasmine, lilies and gladioli.

Mariamman Hindu Temple is three blocks west of Ben Thanh Market. Remove your shoes before stepping onto the slightly raised platform and ignore pushy demands that you buy joss sticks and jasmine as you enter.

Tao Dan Park
PARK

(Map p304; Ð Nguyen Thi Minh Khai) One of the city's biggest and most attractive green spaces is 10-hectare Tao Dan Park, its bench-lined walks shaded with avenues of enormous tropical trees, including the ever-abundant flame tree and vast Sao Den and So Khi trees. It's fascinating to visit in the early morning and late afternoon when thousands of locals exercise.

Also noteworthy is the daily flocking here of the city's bird lovers (mainly elderly gentlemen), who arrive, cages in hand, at what is universally known as the bird cafe.

The park is split down the middle by Ð Truong Dinh. To the northeast of Ð Truong Dinh are a small contemporary sculpture garden and the old Cercle Sportif, an elite sporting club during the French colonial period and now the Workers' Club, with tennis courts, a colonnaded art deco swimming pool and a clubhouse.

Xa Loi Pagoda
BUDDHIST TEMPLE

(Chua Xa Loi; Map p304; 89 Ð Ba Huyen Thanh Quan; ⊙7-11am & 2-5pm) Famed as the repository of a sacred relic of the Buddha, this large 1956 building is most notable for its dramatic

---

LOCAL KNOWLEDGE

SOPHIE HUGHES: SAIGON ART DOYEN

Ho Chi Minh City (HCMC) resident Sophie Hughes (www.sophiesarttour.com) runs popular art tours around town five days a week.

What really fires you up about HCMC? The contrasts: the locals' friendly, laid-back attitude against the backdrop of a nonstop, frenzied metropolis. Look beyond the kitsch neon lights and shop signs and catch old Chinese shop houses, colonial French facades, the former residences of ambassadors, missionaries and merchants and the incredibly thin – and structurally remarkable – Vietnamese tube houses in alleyways all over HCMC. Most exciting of all is watching a new generation add another layer to their city through art, music and cafe culture.

Your favorite art gallery in town? San Art (p314): HCMC's most dynamic space for art. Comprising a gallery, open-access reading room and a full program of workshops, residencies, talks and screenings, this space is a true trailblazer. To top it off, the space is run by a fun, young and friendly team of people. All events are free and open to the public.

HCMC's best-kept architectural secret? The Fine Arts Museum (p307): built around a courtyard, this improbable mix of French and Chinese 1920s and '30s architectural styles is a treasure and a sanctuary from the incessant buzz of the streets. The museum houses an eclectic mix of propaganda art, combat art and early '90s abstract art.

Any standout bar that pulls an arty crowd? The Observatory (cnr Ð Le Lai & Ð Ton That Tung; 11am-late) is a cafe-restaurant-bar-gallery and multipurpose space set up by an artist and a DJ. In the heart of District 1, it's a versatile platform for art and hosts gigs, exhibitions, film screenings and discussion groups and is a go-to point for those who want to get a handle on HCMC's cultural scene.

Any graffiti/street art in town you recommend tracking down? Street art has been growing in HCMC over the last few years. Head to 15b Ð Vo Van Tan, District 1, for murals or to Saigon Outcast (www.saigonoutcast.com), an art hub where walls are adorned by the work of local artists. The space also runs music, film and art events – it's a little out of the city in D2. Check out Liar Ben's blog www.liarben.blogspot.com for up-to-date street art info.

history. In August 1963 truckloads of armed men under the command of Ngo Dinh Nhu, President Ngo Dinh Diem's brother, attacked the temple, which had become a centre of opposition to the Diem government.

The temple was ransacked and 400 monks and nuns, including the country's 80-year-old Buddhist patriarch, were arrested. This raid and others elsewhere helped solidify opposition among Buddhists to the regime, a crucial factor in the US decision to support the coup against Diem. The pagoda was also the site of several self-immolations by monks protesting against the Diem regime and the American War.

The etymology of the temple name points to its significance. The Chinese characters on the front of the temple – 'Sheli Si' (舍利寺; Sheli Temple), pronounced Xa Loi Chua in Vietnamese – mean 'Sarira Temple', from the Sanskrit word for 'Buddhist relic'.

Women enter the main hall of Xa Loi Pagoda, housing a giant golden Sakyamuni (the historical Buddha), by the staircase on the right as you come in the gate; men use the stairs on the left. The walls of the sanctuary are adorned with paintings depicting the Buddha's life. Behind the main hall, a further hall contains a painting of Bodhidharma, an Indian monk celebrated as the father of Zen Buddhism. Bodhidharma stayed at the Shaolin Temple in China, developing the exercises that would become **Shaolin Boxing**. He is depicted here carrying a shoe on a stick (the story goes that when Bodhidharma's coffin was opened after his death, it was empty apart from one shoe).

A monk preaches here every Sunday from 8am to 10am. On full- and new-moon days, special prayers are held from 7am to 9am and 7pm to 8pm.

Nguyen Thai Binh & Around

This District 1 ward is a busy workaday neighbourhood nestled between the central city, Ben Thanh Market, the Pham Ngu Lao backpacker strip and Ben Nghe channel.

★ Fine Arts Museum   ART GALLERY
(Bao Tang My Thuat; Map p307; 97A Ð Pho Duc Chinh; admission 10,000d; ☺9am-5pm Tue-Sun) With its airy corridors and breezy verandahs, this elegant 1929 colonial-era yellow-and-white building is stuffed with period details; it is exuberantly tiled throughout and home to some fine (albeit deteriorated) stained glass, as well as one of Saigon's old-

Nguyen Thai Binh & Around

est lifts. Hung from the walls is an impressive selection of art, including thoughtful pieces from the modern period.

As well as contemporary art, much of it (unsurprisingly) inspired by war, the museum displays historical pieces dating back to the 4th century. These include elegant Funan-era sculptures of Vishnu, the Buddha and other revered figures (carved in both wood and stone), and Cham art dating from the 7th to the 14th century.

More statuary is scattered around the grounds and in the central courtyard (accessed from the rear of the building). There's a selection of lovely prints for sale at the shop, costing from around 80,000d. Building No 2 alongside hosts lesser-known works and stages exhibitions.

The space on the pavement in front of the impressive old Railway Office, up the road between Ð Ham Nghi and ÐL Le Loi and facing the roundabout, was used for public executions in the early 1960s.

Cholon

Rummage through Cholon (District 5) and lift the lid on a treasure trove of historic temples and Chinese flavours. HCMC's Chinatown is less Chinese than it once was, largely due to the 1978–79 anticapitalist and anti-Chinese campaign, when many ethnic Chinese fled the country, taking with them their money and entrepreneurial skills. A lot of those refugees have since returned (with foreign passports) to explore investment possibilities. Full-form written Chinese characters (as

Cholon

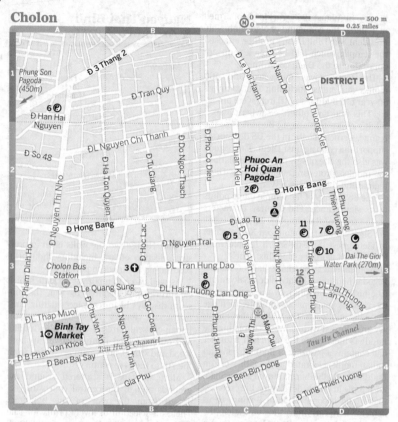

Cholon

opposed to the simplified system used in mainland China) decorate shopfronts and temples in abundance, adding to the sensation that you have strayed into a forgot-

ten corner of China. Cornering a Mandarin speaker isn't hard, although most Hoa-Kieu (Vietnamese-Chinese) residents chat in southern Chinese dialects.

Cholon means 'big market' and during the American War it was home to a thriving black market. Like much of HCMC, Cholon's historic shopfronts are swiftly disappearing under advertising hoardings or succumbing to developers' bulldozers, but some traditional architecture survives and an atmospheric strip of **traditional herb shops** (Map p308; Đ Hai Thuong Lan Ong) thrives between Đ Luong Nhu Hoc and Đ Trieu Quang Phuc, providing both a visual and an olfactory reminder of the old Chinese city.

A taxi from Pham Ngu Lao to Cholon costs around 100,000d or hop on bus 1 from Ben Thanh Market. For in-depth tours of Cholon, contact local expert and heritage buff, Tim Doling (p317).

★ **Binh Tay Market**   MARKET
(Cho Binh Tay; Map p308; www.chobinhtay.gov.vn;
57A ĐL Thap Muoi) Cholon's main market has
a great clock tower and a central courtyard
with gardens. Much of the business here is
wholesale but it's popular with tour groups.
The market was originally built by the
French in the 1880s; Guangdong-born philanthropist Quach Dam paid for its rebuild-
ing and was commemorated by a statue that
is now in the Fine Arts Museum.

Thien Hau Pagoda   TAOIST TEMPLE
(Ba Mieu, Pho Mieu, Chua Ba Thien Hau; Map p308;
710 Đ Nguyen Trai) This gorgeous 19th-century
temple is dedicated to the goddess Thien
Hau and always attracts a mix of worshippers and visitors, who mingle beneath the
large coils of incense suspended overhead.
It is believed that Thien Hau can travel over
the oceans on a mat and ride the clouds to
save people in trouble on the high seas.

There are intricate ceramic friezes above
the roof line of the interior courtyard, while
the protectors of the pagoda are said to be
two land turtles that live here. Near the large
braziers stand two miniature wooden structures in which a small figure of Thien Hau is
paraded around nearby streets on the 23rd
day of the third lunar month.

On the main dais are three figures of
Thien Hau, one behind the other, all flanked
by two servants or guardians. To the right is
a scale-model boat and on the far right is the
Goddess Long Mau, Protector of Mothers
and Newborns.

Khanh Van Nam Vien Pagoda   TAOIST TEMPLE
(Map p308; 269/2 Đ Nguyen Thi Nho) Built between 1939 and 1942, this temple is said to
be the only pure Taoist temple in Vietnam
and is unique for its colourful statues of Taoist disciples. Features to seek out include the
unique 150cm-high statue of Laotse – the supreme philosopher of Taoism and author of
the *Dao De Jing* (The Classic of the Way and
its Power) – located upstairs.

Laotse's mirror-edged halo is rather surreal, while off to his left are two stone plaques
with instructions for Taoist inhalation and
exhalation exercises. A schematic drawing
represents the human organs as a scene
from rural China. The diaphragm, agent of
inhalation, is at the bottom; the stomach is
represented by a peasant ploughing with a
water buffalo. The kidney is marked by four
yin and yang symbols, the liver is shown as
a grove of trees and the heart is represented

by a circle with a peasant standing in it,
above which is a constellation. The tall pagoda represents the throat and the broken
rainbow is the mouth. At the top are mountains and a seated figure that represent the
brain and imagination, respectively.

The temple operates a home for several
dozen elderly people. Next door is a free
medical clinic also run by the pagoda. Leave
a donation with the monks if you wish.

Quan Am Pagoda   BUDDHIST TEMPLE
(Chua Quan Am; Map p308; 12 Đ Lao Tu) One of
Cholon's most active and colourful temples,
this shrine was founded in the early 19th
century. It's named after the Goddess of
Mercy, whose full name is Quan The Am Bo
Tat, literally 'the Bodhisattva who listens to
the cries of the world' (觀世音菩萨 in Chinese characters), in reflection of her compassionate mission.

The goddess's name is usually shortened
to Quan Am (she is also worshipped in China, Korea and Japan) and her statue lies hidden behind a remarkably ornate exterior. In
Tibet, where she is also widely worshipped,
the goddess – who was once male – finds
earthly form in the Dalai Lama. Fantastic
ceramic scenes decorate the roof, depicting
figures from traditional Chinese plays and
stories. Other unique features of this temple are the gold-and-lacquer panels of the
entrance doors.

★ **Phuoc An Hoi Quan Pagoda** TAOIST TEMPLE
(Map p308; 184 Đ Hong Bang) Delightfully front-
ed by greenery and opening to an interior
blaze of red, gold, green and yellow, this
is one of the most beautifully ornamented
temples in town, dating from 1902. Of special interest are the elaborate brass ritual
ornaments and weapons and the fine woodcarvings on the altars, walls, columns, hanging lanterns and incense coils.

From the exterior, look out for the ceramic scenes, each containing innumerable
small figurines, that decorate the roof.

To the left of the entrance stands a life-
size figure of the sacred horse of Quan Cong.
Before departing on a journey, people make
offerings to the equine figure, before strok-
ing its mane and ringing the bell around its
neck. Behind the main altar, with its stone
and brass incense braziers, is a statue of
Quan Cong, to whom the temple is dedicated (the other name for the temple is the
Quan De Mieu); other shrines are dedicated
to Ong Bon and Nam Ba Ngu Hanh.

Tam Son Hoi Quan Pagoda TAOIST TEMPLE

(Chua Ba; Map p308; 118 Đ Trieu Quang Phuc) Retaining much of its original rich ornamentation, this 19th-century temple – a guildhall named after Sanshan (Three Mountains) in China's seaboard Fujian province – is dedicated to Me Sanh, the Goddess of Fertility, entreated by local women praying for children. Thien Hau – the Goddess of Seafarers – is also revered within the main shrine.

Among the striking figures is Quan Cong with his long black beard, to the right of the covered courtyard. Flanking him are two guardians, the Military Mandarin Chau Xuong on the left and the Administrative Mandarin Quan Binh on the right. Next to Chau Xuong is Quan Cong's sacred red horse.

Ong Bon Pagoda TAOIST TEMPLE

(Chua Ong Bon | Nhi Phu Mieu; Map p308; 264 ĐL Hai Thuong Lan Ong) This atmospheric temple is crammed with gilded carvings, smoking incense and the constant hubbub of kids from the large school next door. Built by Chinese immigrants from Fujian province, it's dedicated to Ong Bon, the guardian who presides over happiness and wealth and is seated in a gilded cabinet sparkling with LED lights, an intricately carved and gilded wooden altar before him.

Other shrines are dedicated to Thien Hau, Quan Am, the Jade Emperor and even the Monkey King. Along the walls of the chamber are murals of five tigers (to the left) and two dragons (to the right).

Nghia An Hoi Quan Pagoda TAOIST TEMPLE

(Map p308; 678 Đ Nguyen Trai) Noteworthy for its gilded woodwork, this temple has a large carved wooden boat hanging over its entrance and inside, to the left of the doorway, an enormous representation of Quan Cong's red horse with its groom. The temple is more accurately a guildhall (Hoi Quan), built in the early 19th century by Chinese from Yian (Nghia An) in China's Guangdong province.

Quan Cong – also called Quan De or Quan Vu, a deified Chinese general from the Three Kingdoms Period (184–280) – occupies a position in a glass case behind the main altar, with his assistants flanking him on both sides. Nghia An Hoi Quan lets its hair down on the 14th day of the first lunar month when various dances are staged in front of the temple.

Ha Chuong Hoi Quan Pagoda TAOIST TEMPLE

(Map p308; 802 Đ Nguyen Trai) This Fujian temple is dedicated to the Goddess of Seafarers,

City Walk
Old Saigon

START 23/9 PARK
END SHRI
LENGTH 4KM; 3 HOURS

Ho Chi Minh City may be rapidly modernising but this tour through District 1 strips back the layers of modern lacquer to reveal the fascinating historic city beneath.

Start at ❶ **23/9 Park**, which borders Đ Pham Ngu Lao and the city's unofficial backpacker district. The park owes its long, thin shape to a former tenure as the city's main railway terminus. Wander through the park to 1914 ❷ **Ben Thanh Market** (p333) – at its bustling best in the morning. The main entrance, with its belfry and clock, has become a symbol of HCMC.

Cross to the massive roundabout (carefully!) with an equestrian ❸ **statue of Tran Nguyen Han**, a trusted general of 15th-century leader Le Loi. On a pillar at its base is a small white bust of Quach Thi Trang, a 15-year-old girl who was killed near here during antigovernment protests in 1963.

Cross the road again, this time to the bus station. On Đ Pho Duc Chinh you'll see the lovely Sino-French ❹ **Fine Arts Museum** (p307), stuffed with period details (and art). Turn onto Đ Le Cong Kieu, a short street lined with ❺ **antique shops**. At the end turn (in quick succession) left, left again, then right onto Đ Ham Nghi. Before 1870 this wide boulevard was a canal with roads on either side.

Turn left onto Đ Ton That Dam and stroll through the colourful outdoor ❻ **street market**. Turn right onto Đ Huynh Thuc Khang and follow it to ĐL Nguyen Hue, another former canal – now a grand boulevard. Turn right, heading past the dramatic and contemporary form of the ❼ **Bitexco Financial Tower** (p298).

Turn left onto busy riverside Đ Ton Duc Thang. At the corner of Đ Dong Khoi is the grand 1925 ❽ **Majestic Hotel** (p319), requisitioned in WWII by the Japanese for use as their military barracks.

Continue along the river to the giant ❾ **statue of Tran Hung Dao**, defeater of the Mongols, lording it over a semicircular plaza with roads radiating out from it. Take the second one, Đ Ho Huan Nghiep,

turning right at the end onto Dong Khoi, formerly Rue Catinat and still the city's most famous street. At number 151 is the former **⑩ Brodard Café**, immortalised in Graham Greene's *The Quiet American*.

Further up Dong Khoi stands the **⑪ Caravelle Hotel** (p318). The curved corner section was the original 1959 hotel, which, during the American War, housed foreign news bureaux, the Australian and New Zealand embassies, and members of the press corps. In August 1964 a bomb exploded on the 5th floor. No one was killed but the hotel spent the rest of the war with its corner windows taped up in case of further bombings.

Across the road is the **⑫ Municipal Theatre** (p333), still referred to by its more romantic former name, the Opera House.

On the next corner is perhaps HCMC's most famous hotel, the **⑬ Continental**. Built in 1880, it was a favourite of the press corps during the French War. Graham Greene regularly stayed in room 214 and the hotel featured prominently in *The Quiet American*. Key scenes were set in the Continental Shelf, a cafe which once occupied the 1st-floor balcony.

Facing the Municipal Theatre, **⑭ Lam Son Park** often has interesting propaganda dis-

plays. Walk through it and turn right, where another little park features a prominent **⑮ statue of Ho Chi Minh** in front of the **⑯ People's Committee Building** (p298). At night, the exterior is usually covered with thousands of geckos.

Turn right, then left again, back onto Dong Khoi. Directly ahead is **⑰ Notre Dame Cathedral** (p298; built between 1877 and 1883), sitting behind a large white statue of (namesake) St Mary holding an orb. East of the cathedral is the magnificent French-style **⑱ Central Post Office** (p336).

Cross the square in front of the cathedral, turn right and head into 30/4 Park – a lovely formal space providing a grand approach to the **⑲ Reunification Palace** (p304). Stop to explore the palace or continue north along Pham Ngoc Thach to the large **⑳ Turtle Lake** (Ho Con Rua) roundabout, with its concrete walkways and unusual flowerlike sculpture.

Backtrack a block and turn left onto Đ Nguyen Thi Minh Khai, where you can finish with a drink at **㉑ Shri** (p330) on the 23rd floor of the Centec Tower, enjoying views to your starting point and far beyond.

Thien Hau (Thien Hau Thanh Mau), also known as Ma To. The four carved stone pillars, wrapped in painted dragons, were fashioned in China and delivered to Vietnam by boat.

Noteworthy murals can be seen either side of the main altar, while impressive ceramic relief scenes decorate the roof. To the right of Thien Hau is Chua Sinh Nuong Nuong, a Taoist fertility goddess; to the left of Thien Hau is the ever-popular Taoist God of Wealth. Blending Buddhism into the mix, a figure of Quan Am looks on mercifully, clothed in white and draped with a pearl necklace. Note the upright fan in the main hall, used for dispelling calamity.

The temple – actually a guildhall – becomes extremely active during the **Lantern Festival**, a Chinese holiday held on the 15th day of the first lunar month (the first full moon of the new lunar year).

Cha Tam Church CHURCH

(Map p308; 25 Đ Hoc Lac) Built around the turn of the 19th century, this decaying light-caramel painted church exudes a sleepy, tropical feel. A pew in the church is marked with a small plaque identifying the spot where President Ngo Dinh Diem was seized after taking refuge here with his brother Ngo Dinh Nhu on 2 November 1963, after fleeing the Presidential Palace.

When their efforts to contact loyal military officers (of whom there were almost none) failed, Diem and Nhu agreed to surrender unconditionally and revealed where they were hiding. The coup leaders sent an M-113 armoured personnel carrier to the church and the two were taken into custody. However, before the vehicle reached central Saigon the soldiers had killed Diem and Nhu by shooting them at point-blank range and then repeatedly stabbing their bodies.

When news of the deaths was broadcast on radio, Saigon exploded with jubilation. Portraits of the two were torn up and political prisoners, many of whom had been tortured, were set free. The city's nightclubs, which had closed because of the Ngos' conservative Catholic beliefs, were reopened. Three weeks later the US president, John F Kennedy, was assassinated. As his administration had supported the coup against Diem, some conspiracy theorists speculated that Diem's family orchestrated Kennedy's death in retaliation.

The mint green and white church interior is decorated with images of the Stations of the Cross, while holy water is dispensed from huge clam shells. The statue in the tower is of François Xavier Tam Assou (1855–1934), a Chinese-born vicar apostolic (delegate of the pope) of Saigon. Today, the church has a very active congregation of 3000 ethnic Vietnamese and 2000 ethnic Chinese. Masses are held daily.

Cholon Jamail Mosque MOSQUE

(Map p308; 641 Đ Nguyen Trai) The clean lines and minimal ornamentation of this mosque contrast starkly with nearby Chinese and Vietnamese Buddhist temples. Note the pool for ritual ablutions in the courtyard and the tiled mihrab (niche) in the wall of the prayer hall, indicating the direction of Mecca. This mosque was built by Tamil Muslims in 1935 but since 1975 it has served the Malaysian and Indonesian Muslim communities.

Cho Quan Church CHURCH

(133 Đ Tran Binh Trong; ☉ 4-7am & 3-6pm Mon-Sat, 4-9am & 1.30-6pm Sun) Originally built by the French and destroyed three times, this 19th-century house of worship is one of the city's largest churches, with good views from the belfry (a steep climb). The church is on the eastern fringe of District 5, between ĐL Tran Hung Dao and Đ Nguyen Trai.

◉ District 11

Immediately west of Cholon, the main enticements of District 11 are a couple of interesting old pagodas and a popular water park.

Giac Vien Pagoda BUDDHIST TEMPLE

(Đ Lac Long Quan, District 11; ☉ 7-11.30am & 1.30-7pm) In a land where so many ancient temples have been 'restored' in concrete and neon, it's a joy to discover one that looks its age. The temple was founded by Hai Tinh Giac Vien in the late 1700s and it is said that Emperor Gia Long, who died in 1819, used to worship here.

Architecturally similar to Giac Lam, it shares its atmosphere of scholarly serenity, although Giac Vien is less visited and more secluded, down an alley near Dam Sen Lake.

Hidden behind a warren of winding lanes, the approach to the pagoda has several impressive tombs on the right – a popular playground for local kids. The pagoda itself boasts some 100 lavish carvings of divine beings.

The main sanctuary is on the other side of the wall behind the Hai Tinh Giac Vien statue. The dais is set behind a fantastic

CAO DAISM

A thought-provoking fusion of East and West, Cao Daism (Dai Dao Tam Ky Pho Do) is a syncretic religion born in 20th-century Vietnam that embraces disparate elements of Buddhism, Confucianism, Taoism, native Vietnamese spiritualism, Christianity and Islam – with a dash of secular enlightenment thrown in for good measure. The term 'Cao Dai' (meaning 'high terrace'; 高台) is a euphemism for God; an estimated two to three million followers of Cao Daism exist worldwide.

Cao Daism was founded by the mystic Ngo Minh Chieu (also known as Ngo Van Chieu; born 1878), a civil servant who once served as district chief of Phu Quoc Island. Widely read in Eastern and Western religious works, he became active in seances and in 1919 began receiving revelations in which the tenets of Cao Daism were set forth.

Much of Cao Dai doctrine is drawn from Mahayana Buddhism, mixed with Taoist and Confucian elements (Vietnam's 'Triple Religion'). Cao Dai ethics are based on the Buddhist ideal of 'the good person' but incorporate traditional Vietnamese beliefs as well. The ultimate goal of the Cao Dai disciple is to escape the cycle of reincarnation. This can only be achieved by refraining from killing, lying, luxurious living, sensuality and stealing.

Read more on the official Cao Dai site: www.caodai.org.

brass incense basin with fierce dragon heads emerging from each side. The Guardian of the Pagoda is against the wall opposite the dais. Nearby rises a prayer tree similar to the one in Giac Lam Pagoda.

Phung Son Pagoda   BUDDHIST TEMPLE
(Phung Son Tu | Chua Go; 1408 ĐL 3 Thang 2, District 11) Built between 1802 and 1820 on the site of structures from the Funan period, dating back at least to the early centuries of Christianity, this Buddhist temple is extremely rich in gilded, painted and beautifully fashioned bronze, wood, ceramic and beaten-copper statuary. The **main dais**, with its many levels, is dominated by a large gilded A Di Da Buddha (the Buddha of Infinite Light; Amitābha).

Once upon a time, it was decided to move Phung Son Pagoda to a different site. The pagoda's ritual objects – bells, drums, statues – were loaded onto the back of a white elephant that slipped under the great weight, sending all the precious objects tumbling into a nearby pond. This event was interpreted as an omen that the pagoda should remain in its original location. Everything was recovered but the bell, which, until about a century ago, locals insist could be heard ringing whenever there was a full or new moon.

Prayers are held three times a day, from 4am to 5am, 4pm to 5pm and 6pm to 7pm. The main entrances are locked most of the time, but the side entrance (to the right as you approach the building) is open during prayer times.

Other Neighbourhoods

Giac Lam Pagoda   BUDDHIST TEMPLE
(Chua Giac Lam; 118 Đ Lac Long Quan, Tan Binh District; ⊙6am-noon & 2-8.30pm) Believed to be the oldest temple in HCMC (1744), Giac Lam is a fantastically atmospheric place set in peaceful, gardenlike grounds. The Chinese characters that constitute the temple's name (覚林寺) mean 'Feel the Woods Temple' and the looming Bodhi tree (a native fig tree, sacred to Buddhists) in the front garden was the gift of a Sri Lankan monk in 1953.

Next to the tree stands a gleaming white statue of compassionate Quan The Am Bo Tat on a lotus blossom, a symbol of purity.

Like many Vietnamese Buddhist temples, aspects of both Taoism and Confucianism can be found. For the sick and elderly, the pagoda is a minor pilgrimage site, as it contains a bronze bell that, when rung, is believed to answer the prayers posted by petitioners.

The main sanctuary lies in the next room, filled with countless gilded figures. On the dais in the centre of the back row sits the A Di Da Buddha, easily spotted by his colourful halo. The fat laughing fellow, seated with five children climbing all over him, is Ameda, the Buddha of Enlightenment, Compassion and Wisdom.

Prayers are held daily from 4am to 5am, 11am to noon, 4pm to 5pm and 7pm to 9pm.

About 3km from Cholon, Giac Lam Pagoda is best reached by taxi or *xe om* (motorbike taxi).

Le Van Duyet Temple — TEMPLE

(Đ Dinh Tien Hoang, Binh Thanh District) Dedicated to Marshal Le Van Duyet (1763–1831), this shrine is also his burial place, alongside that of his wife. The marshal was a South Vietnamese general and viceroy who helped put down the Tay Son Rebellion and reunify Vietnam; when the Nguyen dynasty came to power in 1802, he was elevated by Emperor Gia Long to the rank of marshal.

He fell out of favour with Gia Long's successor, Minh Mang, who tried him posthumously and desecrated his grave. Emperor Thieu Tri, who succeeded Minh Mang, restored the tomb, thus fulfilling a prophecy of its destruction and restoration. Le Van Duyet was considered a national hero in the South before 1975 but is disliked by the Communists because of his involvement in the expansion of French influence.

Among the items on display are a portrait of Le Van Duyet, some of his personal effects (including European-style crystal goblets), two wonderful life-size horse statues and a stuffed, mounted tiger.

During celebrations of Tet and on the 30th day of the seventh lunar month (the anniversary of Le Van Duyet's death), the tomb throngs with pilgrims. The caged birds for sale in and around the grounds are bought by pilgrims and freed to earn merit. The unfortunate creatures are often recaptured (and liberated again).

The temple is reached by heading north from Da Kao on Đ Dinh Tien Hoang.

Ho Chi Minh Museum — MUSEUM

(Bao Tang Ho Chi Minh; 1 Đ Nguyen Tat Thanh, District 4; admission 10,000d; ⊙ 7.30-11.30am & 1.30-5pm Tue-Sun) Nicknamed the 'Dragon House' (Nha Rong), this former customs house was built by the French authorities in 1863. The museum houses many of Ho Chi Minh's personal effects, including some of his clothing, his sandals and spectacles.

Otherwise, it covers the story of the man born Nguyen Tat Thanh – from his childhood to his political awakening, his role in booting out the French and leading North Vietnam, and his death in 1969 – mainly through photographs (captioned in Vietnamese and English).

The link between Ho Chi Minh and the museum building is tenuous: 21-year-old Ho, having signed on as a stoker and galley boy on a French freighter, left Vietnam from here in 1911 and began 30 years of exile in France, the Soviet Union, China and elsewhere.

On the waterfront, just across Ben Nghe Channel from District 1, the museum is easily reached on foot by heading south along the river on Đ Ton Duc Thang and crossing the bridge.

Museum of Traditional Vietnamese Medicine — MUSEUM

(www.fitomuseum.com.vn; 41 Đ Hoang Du Khuong; adult/child 50,000/25,000; ⊙ 8.30am-5.30pm Mon-Sat) A lovely piece of traditional architecture in itself, this absorbing and very well-stocked museum in District 10 affords fascinating insights into traditional Vietnamese medicine, itself heavily influenced by Chinese philosophy. Delve into the world of Vietnamese potions and remedies through the centuries and don't miss the Cham tower at the top, equipped with a fertility symbol.

San Art — GALLERY

(Map p302; www.san-art.org; 3 Me Linh, Binh Thanh District; ⊙ 10.30am-6.30pm Tue-Sat; 🖱) This inspiring, independent, nonprofit gallery was founded by artists, giving other local artists the opportunity to display and develop their intriguing work. There's an excellent open-resource library/reading room on the ground floor, with a great selection of contemporary-art books.

Saigon South — NEIGHBOURHOOD

Saigon's District 7 is a sleek, fashionable and well-designed retreat for the wealthy within the fringes of the city. Businesspeople, both expats and the local nouveau riche, have embraced this planned neighbourhood of wide streets, fancy shops and manicured parks. A centrepiece is the **Crescent** (Ho Ban Nguyet), a glitzy promenade along a scooped-out section of canal.

HCMC FOR CHILDREN

At first glance, Ho Chi Minh City's hectic streets might not look that kiddie-friendly, but there's the Saigon Skydeck (p298), water parks, swimming pools, water-puppet shows, plenty of leafy parks, family-friendly cafes and ice-cream shops. World Games on the Basement 2 level (unit B2-18) of the Vincom Center (p334) of Tower B is a fun, centrally located amusement arcade. Beyond the city is Dai Nam Theme Park (p342), the closest thing to Disneyland in Vietnam.

It's well worth visiting Saigon South for a stroll and a look around. If you're a fitness freak, it's one of the less petrol-fumed places for a jog. Plenty of big-name city restaurants and chains have colonised the area, so you won't go hungry. The Crescent is 7km south of Pham Ngu Lao; it should only take 15 minutes by cab (around 80,000d), outside of peak times.

🏃 Activities

River Cruises

There's always someone hanging around the vicinity of Bach Dang jetty (p337) looking to charter a boat to tour the Saigon River. Prices should be around US$10 per hour for a small boat or US$15 to US$30 for a larger, faster craft. It's best to set an itinerary and a time limit at the start and ask them to bring the boat to you, rather than you going to the boat.

Les Rives DINNER CRUISE
(Map p299; ☑0128 592 0018; www.lesrives experience.com; Bach Dang Pier; sunset cruise 7,380,000d, Mekong Delta adult/child 2,263,000/1,697,000d) Sunset boat tour (minimum two people) at 4pm along canals beyond the city edges, including light dinner and guide. Les Rives also offers a Mekong Delta cruise, departing at 7.30am and taking seven to nine hours. Les Rives can also convey you to the Cu Chi Tunnels (adult/child 1,697,000/1,132,000d) and Can Gio (adult/child 2,165,000/1,599,000d) by boat.

Bonsai River Cruise DINNER CRUISE
(Map p299; ☑08-3910 5095; www.bonsaicruise. com.vn; tickets US$36) Set on-board a striking wooden boat painted like a dragon, the Bonsai's dinner cruises feature live music. The price includes a welcome drink, canapés, buffet dinner, soft drink and, incongruously, a head and shoulder massage.

Tau Sai Gon DINNER CRUISE
(☑08-3823 0393; www.tausaigon.com) Saigon Tourist's large floating restaurant takes to the waters every evening, offering both an Asian and European menu. There's a fixed charge for the Sunday buffet lunch (per adult/child 150,000/100,000d; departing 11.30am, returning 1.30pm).

Indochina Junk DINNER CRUISE
(Map p299; ☑08-3824 8299; www.indochinajunk. com.vn) Another dinner cruise, this one with set menus (US$15 to US$35) in an atmospheric wooden junk.

Swimming Pools & Water Parks

Several inner-city hotels also offer access to their pools to nonguests for a fee, including the Legend, Park Hyatt, Majestic, Renaissance Riverside, Rex and May Hotel. For swimming trunks, shop around Ben Thanh Market or along Đ Truong Dinh by Tao Dan Park.

Dam Sen Water Park WATER PARK
(http://damsenwaterpark.com.vn; 3 Đ Hoa Binh, District 11; before 4pm adult/child 120,000/80,000d, after 4pm adult/child 100,000/70,000d; ⊙9am-6pm Mon-Sat, 8.30am-6pm Sun) Water slides, rivers with rapids (or slow currents) and rope swings.

Workers' Club SWIMMING
(Map p304; 55B Đ Nguyen Thi Minh Khai, District 3; admission 16,000d; ⊙6am-7pm) The swimming pool of the old Cercle Sportif still has its colonnades and some art deco charm.

Dai The Gioi Water Park WATER PARK
(Đ Ham Tu, Cholon; admission 35,000-65,000d; ⊙8am-9pm Mon-Fri, 10am-9pm Sat & Sun) Large pool and slides.

Massage & Spa

HCMC offers some truly fantastic hideaways for pampering – the perfect antidote to a frenetic day spent dodging motorbikes. Check out www.spasvietnam.com for extensive reviews and online bookings.

L'Apothiquaire SPA
(La Maison de L'Apothiquaire; ☑08-3932 5181; www.lapothiquaire.com; 64A Đ Truong Dinh, District 3; ⊙8.30am-9pm) Long considered the city's most elegant spa, L'Apothiquaire is housed in a beautiful white mansion tucked down a quiet alley, with a pool and sauna. Guests enjoy body wraps, massages, facials, foot treatments and herbal baths, and L'Apothiquaire makes its own line of lotions and cosmetics. Offshoot branches Artisan Beauté (Map p299; ☑08-3822 2158; 100 Đ Mac Thi Buoi, District 1; ⊙9am-8.30pm) and Saigon South (☑08-5413 6638; 103 Đ Ton Dat Thien, District 7; ⊙9.30-8am) are smaller and concentrate on beauty treatments.

Aqua Day Spa SPA
(Sheraton Saigon; Map p299; ☑08-3827 2828; www.aquadayspasaigon.com; 88 Đ Dong Khoi; 45min massage 1,100,000d; ⊙10am-11pm) One of HCMC's smartest hotel spas, this beautiful space offers a range of treatments, including warm-stone massage, foot pampering and facials.

Vietnamese Traditional Massage Institute
MASSAGE

(Map p320; ☑ 08-3839 6697; 185 Đ Cong Quynh, District 1; per hour in fan/air-con room 50,000/60,000d, per hour sauna 40,000d; ⊙ 8.30am-8pm) Not the classiest act in town, but it offers inexpensive, no-nonsense massages performed by well-trained blind masseurs from the HCMC Association for the Blind.

Just Men
SPA

(Map p299; ☑ 08-3914 1407; 40 Đ Ton That Thiep, District 1; massage from US$8; ⊙ 9am-8pm) Offering haircuts, shaves and excellent facials, or manicures and pedicures while nattering with all the other blokes.

Jasmine
SPA

(Map p299; ☑ 08-3827 2737; www.jasminespa. vn; 45 Đ Ton That Thiep, District 1; 1hr massage 506,000d; ⊙ 9am-8pm) Just Men's unisex sister.

Glow
SPA

(Map p299; ☑ 08-3823 8368; www.glowsaigon. com; 129A ĐL Nguyen Hue, District 1; 1hr massage 540,000d; ⊙ 11am-9pm) Offers an array of aromatherapy facials, hair treatments and therapeutic massage.

Other Activities

Vietnam Golf & Country Club
GOLF

(Cau Lac Bo Golf Quoc Te Viet Nam; ☑ 08-6280 0101; www.vietnamgolfcc.com; Long Thanh My Village, District 9; 18 holes weekday/weekend US$109/143) Playing golf has become a mark of status in Vietnam and this club, about 20km east of central HCMC, caters to the city's would-be high flyers.

🏫 Courses

Saigon Cooking Class
COOKING

(Map p299; ☑ 08-3825 8485; www.saigoncookingclass.com; 74/7 ĐL Hai Ba Trung, District 1; per adult/child under 12 US$39/25; ⊙ 10am & 2pm Tue-Sun) Watch and learn from the chefs at Hoa Tuc as they prepare three mains (including *pho bo* – beef noodle soup – and some of their signature dishes) and one dessert. A market visit is optional (per adult/child under 12 US$45/28, including a three-hour class).

Vietnam Cookery Centre
COOKING

(☑ 08-3512 7246; www.vietnamcookery.com; 362/8 Đ Ung Van Khiem, Binh Thanh District) Offers introductory classes, market visits and VIP premium classes.

Cyclo Resto
COOKING

(Map p304; ☑ 6680 4235; www.cycloresto.com.vn; 3-3a Đ Dang Tran Con; US$23) Fun and informative three-hour cooking class including a trip to **Thai Binh Market** (Map p320) by cyclo.

Saigon Culinary Arts Centre
COOKING

(☑ 097 7565 969; sgncookeryart@vnn.vn; 42/3 Đ Nguyen Van Troi) Market visits and much-recommended cooking classes.

University of Social Sciences & Humanities
LANGUAGE

(Dai Hoc Khoa Hoc Xa Hoi Va Nhan Van; Map p302; ☑ 08-3822 5009; www.vns.edu.vn; 12 Đ Dinh Tien Hoang) If you're planning a longer stay in HCMC, the university's group classes are a reasonably priced way to learn the language.

🚌 Tours

Before you sign up for a standard, middle-of-the-road, travel-agent tour of the city (the cheapest of which are available from agencies in the Pham Ngu Lao area) consider these far more enterprising, imaginative and fun tours that have recently unfolded in HCMC, covering everything from street food to Chinatown, the art scene, the back alleys and night tours of town. Motorbike/scooter tours often arrange pick-up from your hotel.

Hiring a *cyclo* for a half-day or full day of sightseeing is an interesting option, but be sure to agree on the price before setting out (most drivers charge around US$2 per hour).

XO Tours
TOUR

(☑ 09 3308 3727; www.xotours.vn; tours from US£38) Wearing *ao-dai* (traditional dress), these girls run scooter/motorbike foodie, sights and Saigon by night tours: super hospitable and fantastic fun.

Saigon Street Eats
TOUR

(☑ 0908 449 408; http://saigonstreeteats.com; from US$50) Highly entertaining three- to four-hour scooter foodie tours around the streets and backstreets of town with Barbara and her husband, Vu. Select your tour according to taste: morning *pho* tours, lunchtime veggie or evening seafood tours and prepare for some fun surprises. It's a hoot.

Back of the Bike Tours
TOUR

(☑ 0935 046 910; www.backofthebiketours.com) Hop on the back of a motorbike and dine like a local on the wildly popular four-hour Street Food tours, or lasso in the sights of Saigon. Excellent guides.

Vietnam Vespa Adventure TOUR
(Map p320; ☑0122 299 3585; www.vietnam-vespaadventure.com; 169A Đ De Tham) Zooming out of **Cafe Zoom** (Map p320; 169A Đ De Tham; mains 30,000-70,000d; ⊙breakfast, lunch & dinner), Vietnam Vespa Adventure offers entertaining guided city tours on vintage scooters as well as multiday trips around southern Vietnam. Embracing food, drink and music, the Saigon after Dark tour is excellent.

Sophie's Art Tour TOUR
(☑0121 830 3742; www.sophiesarttour.com) Highly engaging and informative four-hour tour from expert Sophie Hughes, who has her finger on the pulse of the HCMC art scene (see p306). Tours visit the Fine Arts Museum, private collections and contemporary-art spaces, explaining the influence of recent Vietnamese history on artistic style and technique.

Tim Doling TOUR
(☑0128 579 4800; www.historicvietnam.com; tim.doling@hcm.fpt.vn; tours 1,000,000d) Your Saigon and Cholon (Chinatown) heritage buff, with tours blending walking with minibus travel, bringing the city to life with insightful anecdotes and erudite observations.

Saigon Unseen TOUR
(☑090 831 7084; http://saigonunseen.com; US$45-105) Morning motorbike tours around local markets and off-the-beaten path parts of HCMC, plus an early-bird five-hour photography tour for excellent camera visuals of the city's lanes and backstreets.

✨ Festivals & Events

Tet NATIONAL HOLIDAY
(⊙First day of first lunar month) The whole city parties and then empties out for family breaks. Đ Nguyen Hue is closed off for a huge flower exhibition, blooms fill Tao Dan Park and everyone exchanges lucky money.

Saigon Cyclo Challenge CHARITY RACE
(⊙mid-Mar) Professional and amateur *cyclo* drivers find out who's fastest; money raised is donated to local charities.

🛏 Sleeping

District 1 is the obvious lodging choice in HCMC given its proximity to almost everything of interest, its relative closeness to the airport and its tempting array of establishments across all price ranges. Within District 1, you can either head east

towards Đ Dong Khoi for smarter options close to the city's best restaurants and bars, west towards Đ Pham Ngu Lao for budget accommodation and cheap tours, or somewhere in between – geographically and pricewise.

At the lower end, a few dollars can be the difference between a dank, stuffy, windowless shoebox and a pleasant, well-appointed room with air-conditioning, ventilation and free wi-fi. Needless to say, cheaper places exist but you get what you pay for. For rock-bottom prices, a swift door-to-door around Pham Ngu Lao will turn up dives for US$10 or even less.

Upgrading to a midrange property can seem rather pointless when excellent, comfortable, almost-hip rooms with all the bells and whistles are available for US$20 around Pham Ngu Lao. More discerning budget travellers can book ahead for similar places at slightly lower rates in the surrounding wards, such as the Co Giang and Nguyen Thai Binh wards.

At the top end, some of the city's best hotels occupy period, character-filled buildings where standards are international, as are the prices. The very best hotels, however, tend to be new builds, such as the Park Hyatt Saigon.

If you book ahead, many hotels will fetch you from the airport for between US$5 and US$10.

🛏 Dong Khoi Area

Home to most of HCMC's top-notch hotels, the Dong Khoi area is also sprinkled with some attractive midrange options.

Spring Hotel HOTEL $$
(Map p299; ☑08-3829 7362; www.springhotelvietnam.com; 44-46 Đ Le Thanh Ton; s US$35-45, d US$40-50, ste US$75-100; ❄@🛜) An old favourite, this welcoming hotel is handy for dozens of restaurants and bars on the popular Le Thanh Ton and Hai Ba Trung strips. Rooms are a little dated but bas-reliefs and moulded cornices add a touch of class.

Asian Ruby HOTEL $$
(Map p299; ☑08-3827 2837; www.asianrubyhotel.com; 26 Đ Thi Sach; d US$70-90; ❄🛜) This comfortable, spick-and-span midrange hotel is a gem, with a top location and polite staff, although for space it's worth outlaying an extra US$20 to upgrade to a deluxe room. Ask for a room facing out, not into the adjacent block.

King Star Hotel
HOTEL $$

(Map p299; ✆08-3822 6424; www.kingstarhotel.com; 8A ĐL Thai Van Lung; r US$50-90; ❄@🛜) Completely refurbished a few years ago, this spruce hotel verges on the boutique-business look. The decoration is contemporary and all rooms have flat-screen TVs and snazzy showers, but the cheapest have no window.

A & Em Hotel
HOTEL $$

(Map p299; ✆08-3825 8529; www.a-emhotels.com; 60 Đ Le Thanh Ton; r US$40-85) For a taste of overblown style, Asian bling and pseudo-luxury which includes putti-adorned phones, baroque-style furniture and ostentatious cornicework, tall and slender A & EM hotel has smallish but clean rooms. Cheaper rooms come without window or wardrobe. Many branches around town.

May Hotel
HOTEL $$

(Map p299; ✆08-3823 4501; www.mayhotel.com.vn; 28-30 Đ Thi Sach; d $80-90; ❄@🛜) The brown-grey marble theme on the floors is weary but rooms, all with bath-tub and flat-screen TV, are clean and inviting. Staff are dignified, but it's the top-floor pool (rare at this price) with its fine views that steals the show. Non-guests can take a dip for US$5 – a steal.

Thien Xuan
HOTEL $$

(Map p299; ✆08-3824 5680; www.thienxuanhotel.com.vn; 108 Đ Le Thanh Ton; r US$39-51; ❄@🛜) Mere metres away from Ben Thanh Market, this is another friendly midtier option. Windowless rooms are cheaper and quieter.

★ Park Hyatt Saigon
HOTEL $$$

(Map p299; ✆08-3824 1234; www.saigon.park.hyatt.com; 2 Lam Son Sq; r from US$300; ❄@🛜🏊) Sumptuously decorated with traditional Vietnamese-style furniture and objets d'art, this is the jewel in Saigon's hotel crown, matching a prime location opposite the Opera House with exemplary service, fastidiously attired staff, lavishly appointed rooms, an inviting pool, the acclaimed Xuan Spa and highly regarded (yet affordable) restaurants, including Opera (Italian) and Square One (Vietnamese and international). Even the 9th-floor smoking rooms are entirely odour free.

Intercontinental Asiana Saigon
HOTEL $$$

(Map p299; ✆08-3520 9999; www.intercontinental.com; cnr ĐL Hai Ba Trung & ĐL Le Duan; r from US$189; ❄@🛜🏊) Modern and tasteful without falling into generic blandness, the Intercontintental is a welcome addition to Saigon's ever-expanding range of luxury establishments. Rooms have separate shower cubicles and free-standing baths, and many enjoy supreme views. A neighbouring tower of apartment-style residences caters to longer stayers.

Caravelle Hotel
HOTEL $$$

(Map p299; ✆08-3823 4999; www.caravellehotel.com; 19 Lam Son Sq; r from US$310; ❄@🛜🏊) 🌿 One of the first luxury hotels to reopen its doors in postwar Saigon, the five-star Caravelle is a classic operation. Rooms in the modern 24-floor block are quietly elegant, with two bigger rooms on each floor (ask); the priciest rooms and suites are in the historic 'signature' wing. The rooftop Saigon Saigon Bar is a spectacular spot for a cocktail.

Lotte Legend Hotel Saigon
HOTEL $$$

(Map p299; ✆08-3823 3333; www.legendsaigon.com; 2A-4A Đ Ton Duc Thang; s US$160-390, d US$175-415; ❄@🛜🏊) Look beyond the overblown lobby to attractive green and cream shaded corridors and lovingly presented, light, bright rooms with a slight deco feel. Standard rooms are actually more tastefully decorated than the executive standard rooms, while river-view standard rooms are the same price as city view. Visible from the lobby is Saigon's most beautiful resort-style pool.

Liberty Central
HOTEL $$$

(Map p299; ✆08-3823 9269; www.libertycentralhotel.com; 177 Đ Le Thanh Ton; s US$155-200, d US$170-215; ❄@🛜🏊) Swathed in creamy marble, this chic, modern and efficient hotel has rooms furnished to a high standard and a rooftop pool offering thrilling city views. With a busy location near Ben Thanh Market, street noise is unavoidable.

Catina Saigon Hotel
HOTEL $$$

(Map p299; ✆08-3829 6296; www.hotelcatina.com.vn; 109 Đ Dong Khoi; d US$165-215; ❄@🛜) Accessed through a jewellery shop, this smart five-floor, 43-room boutique hotel at the heart of town is a good choice, with attractive discounts. Rooms are spacious, but superior and deluxe options are windowless (or have a fake window), so consider opting for premium deluxe.

Northern Hotel
HOTEL $$$

(Map p299; ✆08-3825 1751; www.northernhotel.com.vn; 11A Đ Thi Sach; rm $80-110; ❄@🛜) The glam 99-room Northern is a swish choice, with polite service and well-presented accommodation. Bathrooms are a cut above average, plus there's a rooftop bar and gym. Upgrade for a corner deluxe room for wraparound windows.

Majestic Hotel
HOTEL $$$

(Map p299; ☑08-3829 5517; www.majesticsaigon.com.vn; 1 Đ Dong Khoi; s/d from 4,599,000/5,019,000đ; ❉@ﬗ❊) Dollar for dollar it may not have the best rooms in town, but the colonial atmosphere of this venerable 1925 riverside hotel makes it a romantic option. Take a dip in the courtyard pool on a hot afternoon or sip a cocktail on the rooftop bar on a breezy evening. Breakfast and fruit basket included.

Duxton Hotel
HOTEL $$$

(Map p299; ☑08-3822 2999; www.duxtonhotels.com; 63 Đ Nguyen Hue; r from US$110; ❉ﬗ❊) A grand entry (complete with an oversized birdbath of a fountain) welcomes guests to this smart business hotel. It's well located for city explorations on foot.

Sheraton Saigon
HOTEL $$$

(Map p299; ☑08-3827 2828; www.sheraton.com/saigon; 88 Đ Dong Khoi; r from US$200; ⊖❉@❊) The Sheraton lives up to expectations with luxurious rooms, an excellent spa and an elegant pool.

Riverside Hotel
HOTEL $$$

(Map p299; ☑08-3822 4038; www.riversidehotel-sg.com; 18 Đ Ton Duc Thang; s $US59-150, d US$69-169; ❉@ﬗ) Its grand 1920s bones might hark back to better days, but the Riverside still delivers excellent value for money for a prime location.

Da Kao & Around

Sofitel Saigon Plaza
HOTEL $$$

(Map p302; www.sofitel.com; 17 ĐL Le Duan; d US$170) A faded, lacklustre '90s feel clings to the lobby, but rooms are spiffing at this cordial hotel and staff are particularly helpful and obliging.

Reunification Palace & Around

Saigon Star Hotel
HOTEL $$

(Map p304; ☑08-3930 6290; www.saigonstarhotel.com.vn; 204 Đ Nguyen Thi Minh Khai; s/d US$55/65; ❉ﬗ) The LED karaoke sign is off-putting but the recently recarpeted rooms at this decent hotel are fresh-looking and attractive, especially those with views over Tao Dan Park. Cheaper rooms are also pleasant, but come with shower rather than bath.

Sherwood Residence
APARTMENTS $$$

(Map p304; ☑08-3823 2288; www.sherwoodresidence.com; 127 Đ Pasteur; apt from US$125; ❉ﬗ❊) The epaulettes on the uniformed doormen provide a hint of what's to come in the grand (bordering on camp) lobby, with its painted and gilded ceiling inset, giant chandelier and lush circular carpet. The two- to three-bedroom apartments are much more restrained and available for monthly rental (around US$2000). In the complex you'll find a gym, sauna, kid's play area, small supermarket and wonderful indoor pool.

Lavender Hotel
HOTEL $$$

(Map p304; ☑2222 8888; http://lavenderhotel.com.vn; 208 Đ Le Thanh Ton; r from US$75, ste US$140; ❉ﬗ) Eschewing the nanna-ish connotations of its name, Lavender drapes itself stylishly in creamy marble and muted tones. The location, right by Ben Thanh Market, is excellent if potentially noisy.

Pham Ngu Lao Area

Pham Ngu Lao is HCMC's budget zone and it's easy to hunt for a hotel or guesthouse on foot. Four streets (Đ Pham Ngu Lao, Đ De Tham, Đ Bui Vien and Đ Do Quang Dau) along with a warren of intersecting alleys form the heart of this backpacker ghetto, with more than 100 accommodation choices. Don't let that backpacker tag put you off. Even midrange travellers can find excellent deals here, often at budget prices. Basic breakfasts are usually included.

Among the options are countless family-run guesthouses (US$10 to US$35) and mini-hotels (US$25 to US$55), and even the odd dorm. We have highlighted some of the better places but there are dozens more, with new places opening all the time.

★ Madame Cuc 127
GUEST HOUSE $

(Map p320; ☑08-3836 8761; www.madamcuchotels.com; 127 Đ Cong Quynh; s US$20, d US$25-30; ❉@ﬗ) The original and by far the best of the three hotels run by the welcoming Madame Cuc and her friendly and fantastic staff. Rooms are clean and spacious.

Giang Son
GUEST HOUSE $

(Map p320; ☑08-3837 7547; www.guesthouse.com.vn; 283/14 Đ Pham Ngu Lao; r US$16-28; ❉@ﬗ) Tall and thin, with three rooms on each floor, a roof terrace and charming service, Giang Son's sole downer is that there's no lift. Consider upgrading to a room with window.

Hong Han Hotel
GUEST HOUSE **$**

(Map p320; ☑ 08-3836 1927; www.honghan.net-firms.com; 238 Đ Bui Vien; r US$20-25; ❄ @ 🤶) Another corker guesthouse (seven floors, no lift), Hong Han has front rooms with ace views and smaller, quieter and cheaper rear rooms plus free breakfast served on the 1st-floor terrace.

Bich Duyen Hotel
GUEST HOUSE **$**

(Map p320; ☑ 08-3837 4588; bichduyenhotel@yahoo.com; 283/4 Đ Pham Ngu Lao; r US$17-30; ❄ @ 🤶) On the same slender lane as Giang Son, this spruce 15-room place follows a similar template. The US$25 rooms are worth the extra money for a window. No lift.

Giang Son 2
GUEST HOUSE **$**

(Map p320; ☑ 08-3920 9838; www.guesthouse.com.vn; 283/24 Pham Ngu Lao; rm US$18-25) Son of Giang Son some may say, with a more contemporary finish. Two double rooms come with balcony and staff are excellent. No lift.

PP Backpackers
HOSTEL **$**

(Map p320; ☑ 1262 501 823; Đ 283/41 Pham Ngu Lao; dm US$6, d US$16-18; ❄ @ 🤶) Very helpful, friendly and efficient staff at this cheap and welcoming hostel where you can nab a bargain dorm bed or fork out a bit more for an affordable double room.

Diep Anh
GUEST HOUSE **$**

(Map p320; ☑ 08-3836 7920; dieptheanh@hcm.vnn.vn; 241/31 Đ Pham Ngu Lao; r US$20; ❄ @ 🤶) A step above most PNL guesthouses, figuratively and literally (think thousand-yard stairs), Diep Anh's tall and narrow shape makes for light and airy upper rooms. The gracious staff ensure they're kept in good nick.

Long Guesthouse
GUEST HOUSE **$**

(Map p320; ☑ 08-3836 0184; 373/10 Pham Ngu Lao; dm/d US$8/18; 🤶) This popular, simple but clean 12-room guesthouse tucked away down an alley near Thai Binh Market is run by a pleasant and helpful family. Five- and six-bed dorm beds available.

Madame Cuc 64
GUEST HOUSE **$**

(Map p320; www.madamcuchotels.com; 64 Đ Bui Vien; s US$16-20, d US$25) A very reliable choice from Madame Cuc, with trademark helpful staff and decent, bright rooms (the cheapest with no window), but the Bui Vien positioning can be noisier than her other hotels.

Pham Ngu Lao Area

Pham Ngu Lao Area

⊙ **Sights**
1 Thai Binh Market A6

⊙ **Activities, Courses & Tours**
2 Vietnam Vespa Adventure.................. B2
3 Vietnamese Traditional Massage
   Institute A6

⊜ **Sleeping**
4 An An 2 Hotel B2
5 An An Hotel B2
6 Beautiful Saigon B2
7 Beautiful Saigon 2 .... B2
8 Beautiful Saigon 3 .... B2
9 Bich Duyen Hotel A4
10 Blue River Hotel A4
11 Cat Huy Hotel....................................... A5
12 Diep Anh A3
13 Elegant Inn B6
14 Elios Hotel A3
15 Giang Son A4
16 Giang Son 2 .... A4
17 Hong Han Hotel B5
18 Long Guesthouse A6
19 Madame Cuc 127 .... B6
20 Madame Cuc 184 .... A6
21 Madame Cuc 64 .... B2
22 Ngoc Minh Hotel A4
23 Nhat Thao.. B2
24 PP Backpackers.................................... A4
25 Spring House Hotel A3

⊗ **Eating**
26 Asian Kitchen A2

27 Baba's Kitchen B3
Café Zoom .... (see 2)
28 Chi's Cafe B2
29 Coriander B5
30 Crumbs B6
31 Dinh Y A6
32 Five Oysters... B5
33 Margherita & An Lac Chay A1
34 Mumtaz B5
35 Pho Hung B7
36 Pho Quynh A4
37 Sozo B3
38 Stella B3
39 Zen A2

⊙ **Drinking & Nightlife**
40 Allez Boo A2
41 Bobby Brewers B2
42 Go2.. B2
43 God Mother Bar B6
44 Le Pub A2
45 Long Phi B5
46 Spotted Cow B3

⊙ **Entertainment**
47 Galaxy B7
48 Universal Bar B2

⊙ **Shopping**
49 Blue Dragon B2
50 Gingko B4
51 Hanoi Gallery B3
52 SahaBook... A2

Nhat Thao GUEST HOUSE $
(Map p320; ☑ 08-3836 8117; Nhatthaohotel@yahoo.com; 35/4 Đ Bui Vien; r US$20-22; ❄ ☎) Small but clean rooms are offered in this family-run place, set behind a small courtyard. It's worth paying the extra US$2 for a window.

Elegant Inn GUEST HOUSE $
(Map p320; ☑ 6921 2860; www.eleganthotel.vn; 140 Đ Cong Quynh; r from US$40; ❄ @ ☎) Overseen by very helpful staff, this popular place has spick-and-span and reasonably sizeable rooms; tasty breakfasts included. As it's off the Bui Vien nightlife drag, it's a bit quieter.

Madame Cuc 184 HOTEL $
(Map p320; ☑ 08-3836 1679; www.madamcuchotels.com; 184 Đ Cong Quynh; s/tw/d US$16/20/25) Tucked away down an alley off Đ Cong Quynh, this clean and well-managed choice carries Madame Cuc's trademark motifs: friendly, welcoming staff, complimentary tea and coffee, free breakfast and good rooms. No lift.

Spring House Hotel HOTEL $
(Map p320; ☑ 3837 8312; www.springhousehotel.com.vn; 221 Đ Pham Ngu Lao; r US$18-40; ❄ @ ☎) Furnished in bamboo and rattan, this is a cosy hotel in the middle of the Pham Ngu Lao strip. Rooms come in many shapes and sizes.

Blue River Hotel HOSTEL $$
(Map p320; ☑ 08-3837 6483; blueriver1126@yahoo.com; 283/2C Đ Pham Ngu Lao; US$25-40; ❄ @ ☎) This welcoming and well-run 10-room place offers clean, spacious rooms, each with neat furnishings and a safe. A kitchen for guests' use is available, as is a piano (and more brand-new rooms across the way).

Cat Huy Hotel HOTEL $$
(Map p320; ☑ 08-3920 8716; www.cathuyhotel.com; 353/28 Pham Ngu Lao; r US$28-34; ❄ ☎) Stuffed away down an alley in Pham Ngu Lao, this lovely 10-room hotel offers modern, swish and chic accommodation. The

cheapest rooms are windowless, others have balconies. Airport pick-up is US$15. No lift.

Ngoc Minh Hotel HOSTEL $$

(Map p320; ☑08-3837 6407; www.ngocminh-hotel.net; 283/11 Đ Pham Ngu Lao; r US$20-35; ✳@🛜) This bright and friendly guest-house has 19 clean and well-presented rooms with all mod cons, a rooftop terrace decorated with blooming orchids and a lift. It's just east and across the road from the Blue River Hotel.

An An 2 Hotel HOSTEL $$

(Map p320; ☑08-3838 5665; southernhotel@hcm.vnn.vn; 216 Đ De Tham; s US$25-60, d US$28-65) The spotlessly clean, comfortable, compact and stylish rooms here are a good-value step into the midrange bracket. The lift-equipped hotel is in the very centre of the Pham Ngu Lao backpacking area, with panoramic views.

An An Hotel HOTEL $$

(Map p320; ☑08-3837 8087; www.anan.vn; 40 Đ Bui Vien; d US$36-55; ✳@🛜) Unassuming, unpretentious and affable, this skinny but smart midrange mini-hotel has well-proportioned, attractive rooms with showers fitted over bath-tubs. Unexpected extras include safety deposit boxes and in-room computers. The hotel has a lift.

Elios Hotel HOTEL $$

(Map p320; ☑08-3838 5584; www.elioshotel.vn; 233 Đ Pham Ngu Lao; s US$54-110, d US$62-118; ✳@🛜) The swish entrance, with its aquariums and elegant design, to this three-star hotel is proof of the ongoing gentrification of the PNL area. The dark-wood rooms are clean and modern, with safes and writing desks. For huge views, head to the rooftop Blue Sky Restaurant.

Beautiful Saigon 2 HOTEL $$

(Map p320; ☑08-3920 8929; www.beautifulsaigon2hotel.com; 40/19 Đ Bui Vien; s US$26-37, d $US29-42; ✳@🛜) Unlike its sister which sits around the corner on busy Bui Vien, this eight-room mini-hotel lurks down a back lane. The ground floor is taken up by a restaurant, giving it more of a guesthouse feel. Rooms have computers and deluxe versions have balconies; no lift.

Beautiful Saigon 3 HOTEL $$

(Map p320; ☑08-3920 4874; www.beautifulsaigon3hotel.com; 40/27 Bui Vien; s US$30-40, d US$36-49; 🛜) From the *ao dai*-clad girl at reception to the marble sheen and swishly presented

rooms, there's more than just a veneer of class at Saigon 3, and the alley location is off the noisy main drag. Rooms have computers and safe boxes, but the cheapest come without window. The hotel has a lift.

Beautiful Saigon HOTEL $$

(Map p320; ☑08-3836 4852; www.beautifulsaigonhotel.com; 62 Đ Bui Vien; s US$26-52, d $US30-57; ✳@🛜) Another tall and skinny mini-hotel, this one has a modern reception staffed by staff wearing red *ao dai*. A lift ascends to the tidy rooms, the cheaper of which are small and windowless.

Green Suites HOTEL $$

(☑08-3836 5400; www.greensuiteshotel.com; 102/1 Đ Cong Quynh; s US$24-45, d $US28-34, tr US$48; ✳@🛜) Down a quiet alley off Đ Cong Quynh, immediately south of Đ Bui Vien, this trim, comfy and spacious hotel exudes a pea green theme, although the tiled rooms are clean and, defiantly, not very green at all.

🛏 Nguyen Thai Binh & Around

Blue River Hotel 2 GUEST HOUSE $

(Map p307; ☑08-3915 2852; www.blueriverhotel.com; 54/13 Đ Ky Con; r US$18-25; ✳@🛜) Fronted by bamboo fronds, with a piano in the hall and within reach of both Dong Khoi and Pham Ngu Lao but far enough away to flee the tourist buzz, this friendly and quiet guesthouse is excellent. It's down a quiet cul-de-sac, offering a window into local urban life. Cheaper rooms have no window.

🛏 Co Giang

For a quieter and slightly cheaper alternative to Pham Ngu Lao, there's a string of excellent guesthouses in Co Giang ward (District 1) in a quiet alley connecting Đ Co Giang and Đ Co Bac. To reach the alley, head southwest on ĐL Tran Hung Dao, turn left at Đ Nguyen Kac Nhu and then first right onto Đ Co Bac. The guesthouses are down the first alley to the left.

All of the guesthouses down this lane are popular with long-timers (expat English teachers and the like), so you'll need to book well ahead to nab a place. Preference goes to longer-term bookings.

Ngoc Son GUEST HOUSE $

(☑08-3836 4717; ngocsonguesthouse@yahoo.com; 178/32 Đ Co Giang; s/d US$12/17; ✳🛜) Fresh as a daisy, this small guesthouse has a family lounge with feature wallpaper downstairs and good-value rooms above. The art and books in the bedrooms are a nice touch.

Guest House California
GUEST HOUSE $

(☑ 08-3837 8885; guesthousecaliforniasaigon@yahoo.com; 171A Đ Co Bac; r US$15-18; ✱ @ 🛜) No mirrors on the ceiling or pink champagne on ice but friendly and clean California has a guest kitchen, free laundry, a penchant for garden gnomes, a roof garden and further rooms across the way.

Miss Loi's
GUEST HOUSE $

(☑ 08-3837 9589; missloi@hcm.fpt.vn; 178/20 Đ Co Giang; s/d US$14/16; ✱ @ 🛜) The original Co Giang guesthouse, with a homely atmosphere and helpful staff. Miss Loi is an attentive host and rates include a light breakfast; rooms all have fridge and window.

🏠 Other Neighbourhoods

Thien Thao
HOTEL $$

(☑ 08-3929 1440; www.thienthaohotel.com; 89 Đ Cao Thang, District 3; r US$32-60; ✱ @ 🛜) All you'd want from a midrange hotel, Thien Thao has affable staff and clean, comfortable, smallish rooms kitted out with bathrobes, safes and proper shower stalls. From the Pham Ngu Lao area, take Đ Bui Thi Xuan, which becomes Đ Cao Thang.

⭐Ma Maison Boutique Hotel
HOTEL $$$

(☑ 08-3846 0263; www.mamaison.vn; 656/52 Cach Mang Thang Tam, District 3; s US$50-75, d US$75-120; ✱ 🛜) Down a peaceful lane off a busy arterial route, friendly Ma Maison is halfway between the airport and the city centre, and partly in the French countryside, decorwise. Wooden shutters soften the exterior of the modern, medium-rise block, while in the rooms, painted French provincial-style furniture and first-rate bathrooms add a touch of panache.

⭐Hotel Nikko Saigon
HOTEL $$$

(☑ 08-3925 7777; www.hotelnikkosaigon.com.vn; 235 Đ Nguyen Van Cu, District 1; d from US$125; ✱ @ 🛜 🏊) The location is a bit out of the way for sightseers, but this is one of HCMC's most supreme hotels, with roomy minimalist accommodation, faultless service and an obsessive attention to detail.

✗ Eating

Hanoi may consider itself more cultured, but HCMC is Vietnam's culinary capital. Delicious regional fare is complemented by a well-developed choice of international restaurants, with Indian, Japanese, Thai, Italian and East–West fusions well represented. Unsurprisingly, given its heritage, HCMC has a fine selection of French restaurants, from the casual bistro to haute cuisine.

Good foodie neighbourhoods include the Dong Khoi area, with a high concentration of top-quality restaurants, as well as the bordering sections of District 3. Some of Pham Ngu Lao's eateries, attempting to satisfy every possible culinary whim, are good value but generally less impressive, although others are standout. There are also a few escapes further afield for those willing to explore.

Markets have a good selection of stalls whipping up tasty treats. Ben Thanh's night market is particularly good.

Banh mi – cheap filled baguettes with a French look and very Vietnamese taste – are sold by street vendors. The fresh baguettes are stuffed with something resembling pâté (don't ask), pickled gherkins and various other fillings.

The largest concentration of vegetarian restaurants is around the Pham Ngu Lao area and you'll usually find one within a chopstick's throw of Buddhist temples.

✗ Dong Khoi Area

⭐Nha Hang Ngon
VIETNAMESE $

(Map p299; ☑ 08-3827 7131; 160 Đ Pasteur; mains 35,000-205,000d; ⊙ 7am-10pm; 🛜) Thronging with locals and foreigners, this is one of HCMC's most popular spots, with a large range of the very best street food. Food stalls, all offering a different dish, are set up in a leafy garden. Each stall specialises in a traditional dish, ensuring an authentic taste.

⭐Temple Club
VIETNAMESE $

(Map p299; ☑ 08-3829 9244; 29 Đ Ton That Thiep; mains 59,000-98,000d; ⊙ 11.30am-10.30pm; 🛜 ✗) This classy establishment, housed on the 2nd floor of a beautiful colonial-era villa decorated with spiritual motifs and elegant Chinese characters, offers a huge selection of delectable Vietnamese dishes, including vegetarian specialities, alongside a spectrum of spirited cocktails.

Huong Lai
VIETNAMESE $

(Map p299; 38 Đ Ly Tu Trong; mains 49,000-150,000d) A must for finely presented, traditional Vietnamese food, the airy and high-ceilinged loft of an old French-era shophouse is the setting for dining with a difference.

Staff are from disadvantaged families or are former street children and receive on-the-job training, education and a place to stay.

3T Quan Nuong
VIETNAMESE $

(Map p299; ☑ 08-3821 1631; 29 Ð Ton That Thiep; mains 85,000-280,000d; ⊙ 4-11pm) This breezy al-fresco Vietnamese barbecue restaurant on Temple Club rooftop is in many a Saigon diners' diary: choose your meat, fish, seafood and veggies and flame them up right there on the table.

Hoa Tuc
VIETNAMESE $

(Map p299; ☑ 08-3825 1676; 74/7 ÐL Hai Ba Trung; mains 50,000-190,000d; ⊙ 10.30am-10.30pm; ☎) In the trendy courtyard of the former opium refinery, Hoa Tuc offers atmosphere and style to match the excellence of its food. Signature dishes include mustard leaves rolled with crispy vegetables and shrimp, and spicy beef salad with kumquat, baby white eggplant and lemongrass. Home chefs can pick up tricks at an in-house cooking class.

Au Parc
CAFE $

(Map p299; www.auparcsaigon.com; 23 Ð Han Thuyen; mains 160,000-260,000d; ⊙ 7am-11pm; ☎) The laptop and tablet crowd flocks to this slender two-floor cafe for its Mediterranean and Middle Eastern–inflected selection of salads, quiches, baguettes, focaccia, pasta, mezze and light grills, from breakfast and brunch to dinner. Many ingredients are homemade and the smoothies, juices and views of the park are all sublime. There's a lounge upstairs.

5Ku Station
VIETNAMESE $

(Map p299; 29 Ð Thai Van Lung; meals from around 50,000d; ⊙ 5pm-late) Hopping with evening diners, this chain of makeshift-looking alfresco barbecue restaurants is fun, boisterous, outgoing and tasty. Grab yourself a wooden box seat, a cold beer and chow down on BBQ and hotpot alongside a mix of locals, travellers and expats. Branches move about so check on the latest address. At the time of writing there was another branch just around the corner on Ð Le Thanh Ton.

Tandoor
INDIAN $

(Map p299; ☑ 08-3930 4839; www.tandoorvietnam.com; 74/6 Ð Hai Ba Trung; mains 55,000-120,000d; ⊙ 11am-2.30pm & 5-11pm; ☎☑) Always full of Indian diners, this shiny, long-running restaurant sprawls up over several floors. The lengthy menu has vegetarian and

South Indian sections, but the focus here is mainly on authentic North Indian dishes.

Kem Bach Dang
ICE CREAM $

(Map p299; 26-28 Le Loi, cnr Ð Pasteur; ice creams from 50,000d; ⊙ 8am-11pm) Cool down with a freshly made coconut ice cream (served in a coconut) or a cooling banana split at this long-standing local ice-cream parlour on the corner of roaring Le Loi.

Fanny
ICE CREAM $

(Map p299; 29-31 Ð Ton That Thiep; per scoop 26,000-34,000d; ⊙ 8am-11pm; ☎) On the ground floor of the lavish French villa housing Temple Club, Fanny concocts excellent Franco-Vietnamese ice cream in a healthy range of home-grown flavours, including durian (an acquired taste), star anise and green tea.

Ganesh
INDIAN $

(Map p299; www.ganeshindianrestaurant.com; 15B4 Ð Le Thanh Ton; mains 52,000-99,000d; ☑) Offers an authentic range of north and south Indian meals, including tandoori dishes, thali plates and plentiful vegetarian selections, in pleasant surrounds.

Restaurant 13
VIETNAMESE $

(Map p299; ☑ 08-3823 9314; 15 Ð Ngo Duc Ke; mains 42,000-240,000d) Few marks for looks perhaps, but this is one of a handful of numbered eateries in this area that serve winning, no-nonsense Vietnamese favourites.

Xu
VIETNAMESE $$

(Map p299; ☑ 08-3824 8468; www.xusaigon.com; 1st fl, 75 ÐL Hai Ba Trung; 3-course set lunch Mon-Fri 290,000d, mains from 100,000d; ⊙ 11am-2.30pm & 6-11pm; ☎) This super-stylish restaurant-lounge serves up a menu of Vietnamese-inspired fusion dishes. It's pricey, but well worth the flutter for top service, a classy wine list and a happening lounge-bar. For a gastronomic adventure, embark on the tasting menu (850,000d).

Square One
VIETNAMESE $$

(Map p299; ☑ 08-3824 1234; www.saigon.park. hyattrestaurants.com/squareOne; Park Hyatt Saigon, 2 Lam Son Sq; mains from 210,000d; ⊙ noon-2.30pm & 5.30-10.30pm; ☎▥) With five open kitchens on the mezzanine level of the Park Hyatt, Square One concocts a faultless formula of style, ambience, good looks, fine food (Vietnamese and Western), crisply fresh ingredients and tip-top service. The Saturday brunch includes a popular free-flow wine and bubbly menu.

Warda

MIDDLE EASTERN **$$**

(Map p299; ☑ 08-3823 3822; 71/7 Đ Mac Thi Buoi; 140,000-258,000d; ⊙ 8am-midnight; ☎) Suitably located in a medina-like alley off Mac Thi Buoi, this chic place concocts sensuous flavours from Morocco to Persia. Lamb and prune tagine, sizzling kebabs, mezze – it's all here, including the inevitable shishas for an after-dinner puff.

Pacharan

SPANISH **$$**

(Map p299; www.pacharansaigon.com; 97 Đ Hai Ba Trung; tapas 80,000-160,000d; mains from 80,000d; ⊙ 10am-late; ☎) Spread over three floors, Pacharan's bites include succulent chorizo, marinated anchovies and chilli *gambas* (prawns), plus more substantial mains such as an authentic paella (for two). The rooftop terrace is great for sampling Spanish wine, there's a cosy bar downstairs and live music.

Bernie's Irish Bar & Restaurant

INTERNATIONAL **$$**

(Map p299; www.berniesirishpub.com; 19 Đ Thai Van Lung; mains 90,000-230,000d; ⊙ 7am-midnight; ☎) Load up on cold beer, Guinness, whisky, sports TV and quality expat comfort food. The menu ranges from Aussie steaks and burgers (with beetroot, naturally) to pizza, pasta, sandwiches, salads and excellent MSG-free Vietnamese dishes.

Annam Gourmet Market

COFFEESHOP **$$**

(Map p299; www.annam-gourmet.com; 16 Đ Hai Ba Trung; sandwiches from 70,000d, mains from 130,000d; ⊙ 8am-9pm Mon-Sat, 9am-8pm Sun) A quiet, relaxing and neat place for breakfast, brunch, a salad, bruschetta or baguette sandwich, this coffee shop on the upper floor of a delicatessen is stylish, with lime green sofas, a curved glass window and snappily dressed snackers and diners.

Elbow Room

AMERICAN **$$**

(Map p299; www.elbowroom.com.vn; 52 Đ Pasteur; mains 100,000-350,000d; ⊙ 8am-10pm Mon-Sat, to 5pm Sun; ☎) If you're a lumberjack, you'll be OK at this upmarket American-style cafe-bistro where there's a big breakfast with your name on it (pancakes, bacon, eggs, ham, fries, toast). Otherwise there's a hefty menu of burgers, burritos, hot dogs, pizza, pasta, sandwiches and, in a concession to the coronary-disease-adverse, wraps.

Ty Coz

FRENCH **$$**

(Map p299; ☑ 08-3822 2457; www.tycozsaigon.com; 178/4 Đ Pasteur; mains 190,000-300,000d; ⊙ 11am-1.30pm & 6-9.30pm Tue-Sat, 11am-2pm & 6-9pm Sun; ☎) The brothers who run this homely establishment are enthusiasm personified – eager to talk about the classic French dishes on their ever-changing whiteboard menu. When the weather's fine, the rooftop tables facing the cathedral book up quickly.

Skewers

MEDITERRANEAN **$$**

(Map p299; ☑ 08-3822 4798; www.skewers-restaurant.com; 9A Đ Thai Van Lung; mains 250,000-400,000d; ⊙ lunch Mon-Sat, dinner daily; ☎) With a winning line in perfectly done skewered meats, the Mediterranean menu here takes in all stops from the Maghreb to Marseilles. It's strong on atmosphere with an open-plan kitchen and draws a crowd, so book ahead.

Jaspas Wine & Grill

INTERNATIONAL **$$**

(Map p299; http://jaspas.com.vn; 74/7 ĐL Hai Ba Trung; 2/3-course lunch 200,000/300,000d, mains from 160,000) Light, uncomplicated, busy and popular Jaspas serves up Asian and Western favourites in a relaxed setting with an alfresco aspect. The grilled sea bass on mashed potato is awesome and, for indulgence, the Mars Bar cheesecake is the way to go.

Pizza 4P's

ITALIAN **$$**

(Map p299; http://pizza4ps.com/; 8/15 Đ Le Thanh Ton; mains from 140,000d; ⊙ 7am-11pm) This crisp, modern, chilled-out and unusual Italian-Japanese fusion restaurant, on several levels, has a pizza oven at its hub and a delicious bar to boot. Service is unflappable and prices are as tempting as the food. It's tucked away on the left fork of an alley off Đ Le Thanh Ton.

Le Jardin

FRENCH **$$**

(Map p299; ☑ 08-3825 8465; 31 Đ Thai Van Lung; mains 100,000-160,000d; ⊙ Mon-Sat; ☎) This place is consistently popular with French expats seeking an escape from the busier boulevards. It has a wholesome bistro-style menu with a shaded terrace cafe in the outdoor garden of the French cultural centre, Idecaf.

Maxim's Nam An

VIETNAMESE **$$**

(Map p299; ☑ 08-3829 6676; 15 Đ Dong Khoi; mains 160,000-350,000d) Something of a Saigon legend, this supper club is distinguished more for its over-the-top jazz-club ambience and live music than for the food, which is fine if not jaw-dropping. If you're after a memorable experience, you could do a lot worse.

La Fourchette
FRENCH $$

(Map p299; ☑ 08-3829 8143; 9 Đ Ngo Duc Ke; mains 160,000-180,000d; 🛜) Much-loved little restaurant in a central location serving, in proper French style, only a handful of choices each night.

Mogambo
AMERICAN $$

(Map p299; ☑ 08-3825 1311; 50 Đ Pasteur; mains 120,000-200,000d; ⊘ 9am-11pm; 🛜) Some residents swear this place has the best burgers in town. A good menu of Tex-Mex and Americana.

Black Cat
BURGERS $$

(Map p299; www.blackcatsaigon.com; 13 Đ Phan Van Dat; mains from 105,000d; ⊘ 7am-11pm) It's rather sombre inside and staff can seem pedestrian, but two-floor Black Cat's juicy burgers are worth miaowing about and the lip-smacking juices, smoothies and rich milkshakes (concocted with New Zealand ice cream) will have you purring.

★Cirrus
INTERNATIONAL $$$

(Map p299; www.cirrussaigon.com; 51st fl, Bitexco Financial Tower, 2 Đ Hai Trieu; 3-course dinner 980,000d; 🛜) Elevate yourself away from the hectic whirl at street level high up on the 51st floor of HCMC's tallest tower for a sure-fire combination of supreme food, tantalising views, impeccable service and stylish ambience.

El Gaucho
ARGENTINIAN $$$

(Map p299; ☑ 08-3825 1879; www.elgaucho.asia; 5 Đ Nguyen Sieu; mains 190,000-3,050,000d; ⊘ 5-11pm) Nirvana for the serious meat lover, El Gaucho matches hearty serves of fall-apart lamb shanks, tender skewers and juicy steaks to a fine-dining environment. They even make their own chorizo and *salchicha* (spicy sausage).

Mandarine
VIETNAMESE $$$

(Map p299; ☑ 08-3822 9783; www.orientalsaigon. com.vn; 11A Đ Ngo Van Nam; set menu per person US$38-120) Make no mistake: Mandarine is aimed firmly at wealthy tourists. Traditional architecture and nightly musical performances create a magical setting, while the set menus offer a tempting array of dishes from all regions of the country.

🍴 Da Kao & Around

★Cuc Gach Quan
VIETNAMESE $

(Map p302; ☑ 08-3848 0144; http://en.cucgach quan.com; 10 Đ Dang Tat; mains 50,000-200,000d; ⊘ 9am-midnight) It comes as little surprise that the owner is an architect when you step into this cleverly renovated old villa. The decor is rustic and elegant at the same time, which is also true of the food, which excels. Despite its tucked-away location in the northernmost reaches of District 1, this is no secret hideaway: book ahead.

Pho Hoa
VIETNAMESE $

(Map p302; 260C Đ Pasteur; mains 45,000-50,000d; ⊘ 6am-midnight) This long-running establishment is more upmarket than most but is definitely the real deal – as evidenced by its popularity with regular local patrons. Tables come preladen with herbs, chilli and lime, as well as *gio chao quay* (fried Chinese bread), *banh xu xe* (glutinous coconut cakes with mung-bean paste) and *cha lua* (porkpaste sausages wrapped in banana leaves).

Banh Xeo 46A
VIETNAMESE $

(Map p302; ☑ 08-3824 1110; 46A Đ Dinh Cong Trang; mains 25,000-50,000d; ⊘ 10am-9pm) Locals will always hit the restaurants that specialise in a single dish and this renowned spot serves some of the best *banh xeo* in town. These Vietnamese rice-flour pancakes stuffed with bean sprouts, prawns and pork (vegetarian versions available) are the stuff of legend.

Tib
VIETNAMESE $

(Map p302; ☑ 3829 7242; www.tibrestaurant.com. vn; 187 Đ Hai Ba Trung; mains 70,000-285,000d; 🛜) Visiting presidents and prime ministers have slunk down this lantern- and fairylight-festooned alley and into this atmospheric old house to sample Tib's imperial Hue cuisine. Although you could probably find similar food for less money elsewhere, the setting is wonderful. Tib Express (Map p304; www.tibrestaurant.com.vn; 162 Đ Nguyen Dinh Chieu; mains 28,000-50,000; ☑) and Tib Vegetarian (Map p302; www.tibrestaurant.com. vn; 11 Đ Tran Nhat Duat; mains 30,000-40,000; ☑) offer a cheaper, more relaxed take on the same.

★May
VIETNAMESE $$

(Map p302; http://may-cloud.com; 3/5 Hoang Sa; mains 55,000-220,000d; ⊘ 10.30am-11.30pm) Tucked away down a small alley in an old French villa and overseen by endlessly obliging staff, sublime May is a sensory and culinary sensation, with diners testifying to some of the best Vietnamese food in town, if not the entire country. MSG-free.

★**Ocean Palace**   CHINESE **$$**
(Map p302; ☑08-3911 8822; 2 ĐL Le Duan; 🖘) With full-on, bright, upscale Chinese opulence, it's not the place for a romantic tête-à-tête, but the cuisine at Ocean Palace – near the Botanical Gardens – is divine (and not as pricey as you may think) and service is attentive. The dim sum is a crowd-puller, but the menu throughout is a winner.

Camargue   MEDITERRANEAN **$$**
(Map p302; ☑08-3520 4888; www.vascosgroup. com; 1st fl, 74/7D Đ Hai Ba Trung; mains from 185,000d; ⊘6-10.30pm; 🖘) After relocating to a more central address, long-standing Camargue remains a romantic, elegant and successful choice; round things off with a drink at Vasco's next door.

✖ Reunification Palace & Around

Quan An Ngon   VIETNAMESE **$**
(Map p299; 138 Đ Nam Ky Khoi Nghia; mains from 35,000; ⊘6.30am-11pm) Always heaving with locals and foreigners alike, this is one of the most popular places in town for the taste of street food in stylish surroundings, set in a leafy garden ringed by food stalls and hung with lanterns. Each cook serves up a specialised traditional dish, ensuring an authentic taste, and they are all magnificent. Follow your nose and browse the stalls.

Cyclo Resto Company   VIETNAMESE **$**
(Map p304; www.cycloresto.com.vn; 3-3A Đ Dang Tran Con; five courses US$6; ⊘9am-9pm) The makeshift feel at this super-duper upstairs place detracts nothing from some of the best-value food in town, cooked to absolute perfection. For US$6 you get five fabulous Vietnemese dishes; the popular cooking course is US$23.

Beefsteak Nam Son   VIETNAMESE **$**
(Map p304; 157 Đ Nam Ky Khoi Nghia; mains from 50,000d; ⊘6am-10pm; 🖘) For first-rate, affordable steak in a simple setting, this is a superb choice. Local steak, other beef dishes (such as the spicy beef soup *bun bo Hue*), imported Canadian fillets and even cholesterol-friendly ostrich are on the well-priced menu.

Khoi Thom   MEXICAN **$**
(Map p304; www.khoithom.com; 29 Ngo Thoi Nhiem; set lunch 79,000d; ⊘11am-late) With its breezy alfreso seating area and top-notch menu, this vibrantly coloured and bubbly Vietnamese-Mexican restaurant hits all the right notes, including the splendid tequila cocktails and slammers (delivered by Tequila Girls) and live music on Fridays.

Pho 2000   VIETNAMESE **$**
(Map p304; ☑08-3822 2788; 1-3 Đ Phan Chu Trinh; mains 42,000-58,000d; ⊘6am-2am) Near Ben Thanh Market, Pho 2000 is where former US president Bill Clinton stopped by for a bowl.

★**...hum Vegetarian Cafe & Restaurant**   VEGETARIAN **$$**
(Map p304; ☑08-3930 3819; www.hum-vegetarian. vn; 32 Đ Vo Van Tan; mains 65,000-150,000d; ⊘7am-10pm) Even if you're not a vegetarian, this serene and elegant restaurant requires your attention. Everything – from the charming service to the delightful Vietnamese dishes and peaceful outside tables – makes dining here an occasion to savour.

Shri   JAPANESE FUSION **$$**
(Map p304; ☑08-3827 9631; 23rd fl, Centec Tower, 72-74 Đ Nguyen Thi Minh Khai; mains 200,000-400,000d; ⊘11am-midnight; 🖘) Perched up a tower block, romantic Shri looks out onto some of the choicest views in town. Book ahead for a terrace table or settle for the dark, industrial-chic, dining room. Two menus run side by side: a selection of Japanese-influenced Western mains and a more traditional (and considerably cheaper) Japanese section featuring sushi, sashimi, udon and ramen.

Marina   VIETNAMESE, SEAFOOD **$$**
(Map p304; ☑08-3930 2379; www.ngocsuong. com.vn; 172 Đ Nguyen Dinh Chieu; mains 50,000-500,000d) Ask a sample of well-to-do Saigonese where to go for seafood and the chances are they will recommend this place or its sister restaurant **Ngoc Suong** (Map p304; 17 Đ Le Quy Don), just around the corner. They're both geared to local tastes (bright lights, TVs playing sports, and bad piped music) but the food is delicious, particularly the soft-shell crabs.

✖ Pham Ngu Lao Area

★**Baba's Kitchen**   INDIAN **$**
(Map p320; ☑08-3838 6661; www.babaskitchen. in; 164 Đ Bui Vien; mains 50,000-210,000d; ⊘11am-11pm) Worth going out of your way to secure a table, two-storey Baba's has set Bui Vien alight with its fine flavours, aromas and spices of India. There's ample vegetarian choice and the atmosphere is as inviting as the cuisine is delectable. If you like your food

eye-poppingly spicy, the vindaloo dishes can assist, although the waiter may politely caution you that they are 'rather hot'.

Mumtaz
INDIAN $

(Map p320; ☑ 08-3837 1767; www.mumtazrest. com; 226 Đ Bui Vien; mains 45,000-90,000d; ☺ 11am-11pm; ✐) Excellent service, pleasant surrounds and succulent food are the hallmarks of this popular restaurant. The wide-ranging menu includes vegetarian options, tandoori dishes and the greatest hits of both north and south Indian cuisine. At 110,000d, the lunch buffet and thali plates are great value for big appetites.

Coriander
THAI $

(Map p320; 16 Đ Bui Vien; mains 40,000-180,000d; ☺ 11am-2pm & 5-11pm) The blonde-wood furniture and cheap bamboo wallpaper do recently relocated Coriander few favours, but the menu is stuffed with authentic Siamese delights. The lovely fried *doufu* (tofu) is almost a meal in itself, while the green curry is zesty and the claypot seafood fried rice is excellent.

Five Oysters
VIETNAMESE $

(Map p320; 234 Bui Vien; mains from 35,000d; ☺ 9.30am-11pm) With a strong seafood slant and friendly service, light and bright Five Oysters in backpackerland is frequently packed with travellers feasting on oysters (25,000d), grilled octopus, seafood soup, snail pie, *pho*, fried noodles, grilled mackerel with chilli oil and more.

Dinh Y
VEGETARIAN $

(Map p320; 171B Đ Cong Quynh; mains from 25,000d; ☺ 6am-9pm; ✐) Run by a friendly Cao Dai family, this humble eatery is in a very 'local' part of PNL near Thai Binh Market. The food is delicious and cheap and there's an English menu.

Margherita & An Lac Chay
INTERNATIONAL, VEGETARIAN $

(Map p320; 175/1 Đ Pham Ngu Lao; mains 25,000-77,000d; ☺ 8am-10pm; ✐) Another golden oldie, Margherita cooks up Vietnamese, Italian and Mexican food at a steal. Head up the stairs at the rear of the dining room to An Lac Chay, a purely vegetarian restaurant – with an entirely separate kitchen – offering an eclectic range of tasty choices, from Vietnamese sour soup through to four-cheese pizzas and Mexican dishes.

Mon Hue
VIETNAMESE $

(Map p304; ☑ 08-6240 5323; 98 Đ Nguyen Trai; mains 29,000-150,000d; ☺ 6am-11pm) Hue's famous cuisine comes to HCMC's hungry hordes through this chain of eight restaurants. This handy branch offers a good introduction for travellers who don't make it to the old capital.

Sozo
CAFE $

(Map p320; www.sozocentre.com; 176 Đ Bui Vien; cookies 25,000d; ☺ 7am-10.30pm; ☎) This charming cafe in the Pham Ngu Lao backpacker ghetto has excellent smoothies, doughy cinnamon rolls, homemade cookies, other sweet treats, bags of style, and trains and employs disadvantaged Vietnamese.

Pho Quynh
VIETNAMESE $

(Map p320; 323 Đ Pham Ngu Lao; pho 50,000d; ☺ 24hr) Occupying a bustling corner on Pham Ngu Lao, this place is regularly packed out. As well as regular *pho*, it specialises in *pho bo kho,* a stewlike broth.

Asian Kitchen
PAN-ASIAN $

(Map p320; ☑ 08-3836 7397; 185/22 Đ Pham Ngu Lao; mains 15,000-60,000d; ☺ 7am-midnight; ☎✐) A reliable PNL cheapie, the menu here includes Japanese, Vietnamese, Chinese and Indian.

Pho Hung
VIETNAMESE $

(Map p320; 241 Đ Nguyen Trai; mains 35,000-70,000d; ☺ 6am-3am) Popular *pho* place near backpackersville, open to the wee hours. No English spoken.

Stella
ITALIAN, CAFE $

(Map p320; ☑ 08-3836 9220; www.stellacaffe.com; 119 Đ Bui Vien; mains 25,000-119,000d; ☺ 7am-11.30pm; ☎) A class above some of the budget places here, this predominantly Italian cafe has salads, pasta, gnocchi and pizzas. The coffee is also pretty good.

Zen
VEGETARIAN $

(Map p320; ☑ 08-3837 3713; 185/30 Đ Pham Ngu Lao; mains 30,000-120,000d; ✐) The food at this long-running place is consistently good and cheap. From braised mushrooms in claypot to fried tofu with chilli and lemongrass, the menu is packed with taste and goodness.

Chi's Cafe
INTERNATIONAL, CAFE $

(Map p320; 40/27 Đ Bui Vien; mains from 40,000d; ☺ 7.15am-10.30pm; ☎✐) Hung with eye-catching oils, this relaxing spot is one of the better budget cafes in the area with big breakfasts, Western favourites and some local dishes.

Crumbs
BAKERY

(Map p320; 117 Cong Quynh; pies from 45,000d; ⊘ 7.30am-9.30pm) Style isn't this Pham Ngu Lao bakery's trump card, but there's loads of elbow room on the open-air terrace, the meat pies are rich and filling, and the scones, tarts, bread and cakes are all fresh and tasty.

✕ Nguyen Thai Binh & Around

Tiem Com Ga Hai Nam
CHINESE $

(Map p307; http://comgahainam.vn; 67 Đ Le Thi Hong Gam; mains from 33,000d; ⊘ 10am-10pm) Look beyond the stackable chairs, plastic bowls and discoloured toothpick dispensers at this utilitarian-looking Chinese-Singapore eatery, to some fantastic and good-value food. Try the speciality Hainanese chicken with rice or the delectable shrimp sour soup.

Tin Nghia
VEGETARIAN $

(Map p307; 9 ĐL Tran Hung Dao; mains 22,000-35,000d; ⊘ 7.30am-1pm & 4.30-8pm, closed 2nd & 16th of lunar month) This titchy Cao Dai vegetarian restaurant turns out delicious traditional treats without resorting to fake meat.

✕ An Phu (District 2)

The An Phu neighbourhood of District 2, east of the Saigon River, is popular with expat diners. You'll need to catch a taxi (130,000d to 150,000d from Pham Ngu Lao); make sure your driver knows how to get there before you set off.

Deck
FUSION $$

(⊘ 08-3744 6632; www.thedecksaigon.com; 33 Đ Nguyen U Di; mains 105,000-425,000d; ⊘ 8am-midnight; ☏) Housed in an architecturally impressive pavilion set between an elegant garden and the river, this is the kind of place where you could happily linger all afternoon, knocking off a few bottles of wine and several dim sum plates along the way. Mains combine European cooking styles with the flavours of Asia.

Mekong Merchant
CAFE, BISTRO $$

(⊘ 08-3744 6788; 23 Đ Thao Dien; breakfast 40,000-200,000d, mains 95,000-170,000d; ⊘ 8am-10pm; ☏) Thatched-roof buildings clustered around a courtyard provide an atmospheric setting for this informal but upmarket cafe-bistro-bar. It's worth the trip for the best eggs benedict and pizza in HCMC, although the speciality is Phu Quoc seafood – delivered directly and chalked up on the blackboard menu daily.

Trois Gourmands
FRENCH $$$

(⊘ 08-3744 4585; http://3gourmandsaigon.com; 18 Đ Tong Huu Dinh; mains from 400,000d; ⊘ lunch & dinner Tue-Sun) An elegant villa-with-swimming-pool setting is the venue for this impressive restaurant, overseen by the warm and welcoming former sommelier and Frenchman Gils Brault. Champions of fine food served through indulgent set menus, Trois Gourmands is worth the trek: cheese-lovers can come for the selection alone, made in-house, while the wine choice is naturally strong. If you find yourself immovable after your feast, there's always onsite accommodation (US$40).

✕ Other Neighbourhoods

★ Scott & Binh's
INTERNATIONAL $$

(⊘ 0948 901 465; http://bizuhotel.com/scottbinhs; 15-17 Đ Cao Trieu Phat; mains from 115,000d; ⊘ 4-11pm Tue-Fri, 11am-3pm & 4-11pm Sat, 11am-3pm & 4-9pm Sun; ☏) A drag to reach in District 7 is the only fly in this restaurant's appetising ointment – a modest price to pay for some of the best food in HCMC, overseen by Scott who acts as attentive host to newcomers, repeat diners and all breezing by. The comfort-food choices are extensive and unfailingly excellent, from ravishing burgers to Jamaican jerk swordish and smoked seafood pesto.

🍷 Drinking & Nightlife

Happening HCMC is concentrated around the Dong Khoi area, with everything from dives to designer bars. However, places in this area generally close around 1am as they are under the watchful gaze of local authorities. Pham Ngu Lao rumbles on into the wee hours.

HCMC's hippest club night is the semiregular **Everyone's a DJ** (www.everyonesadjvietnam.wordpress.com) loft party, held at various venues, including Cargo (p332). Other purveyors of fine events worth looking out for include dOSe and **The Beats Saigon** (www.thebeats-saigon.com).

Most of the following dance clubs don't really warm up until after 10pm; ask around popular bars about the latest greatest places. Not quite a club but more than a bar, Lush is a reliable option.

🍷 Dong Khoi Area

Many of Dong Khoi's coolest bars double as restaurants or are flung out at the top of hotels.

★ **2 Lam Son**   COCKTAIL BAR

(Map p299; www.saigon.park.hyatt.com; 2 Lam Son Sq, enter ĐL Hai Ba Trung; ⊙5pm-late) A chic blend of wood, glass and steel, the Park Hyatt's ground floor cocktail bar is a super-stylish meeting ground for Saigon's makers and shakers, with an intimate lounge level slung out above.

★ **Vesper**   BAR

(Map p299; Ground fl, Landmark Building, 5B Đ Ton Duc Thang; ⊙10am-late Mon-Sat) From the sinuous curve of the hardwood bar to the smoothly arranged bottles on the shelves, soft chill-out rhythms, funky caramel leather furniture and fine tapas menu, Vesper is a cool spot by the river. There's a roadside terrace, but traffic noise is epic.

Fuse   NIGHTCLUB

(Map p299; 3A Đ Ton Duc Thang; ⊙7pm-late) Small club, loud techno.

Apocalypse Now   NIGHTCLUB

(Map p299; ☑3824 1463; 2C Đ Thi Sach; ⊙7pm-2am) Others have come and gone, but 'Apo' has been around since the early days and remains one of the must-visit clubs. A sprawling place with a big dance floor and an outdoor courtyard for cooling off, it's quite a circus, with a cast comprising travellers, expats, Vietnamese movers and shakers, plus the odd hooker (some odder than others). The music is thumping and it's apocalyptically rowdy. The 150,000d weekend charge gets you a free drink.

Vasco's   BAR, NIGHTCLUB

(Map p299; www.vascosgroup.com; 74/7D ĐL Hai Ba Trung; ⊙4pm-late; 🖝) One of the hippest hang-outs in town: downstairs is a breezy spot for cocktails and pizza, while the upstairs nightclub-like space regularly hosts DJs and live bands.

Temple Club Bar & Lounge   BAR

(Map p299; 29 Đ Ton That Thiep; ⊙11.30am-midnight) For the ultimate colonial chill-out, sip a G&T in this elegant shrine to Indochine. Frequently deserted, the lounge is one of the quietest, most tranquilising and civilised corners of HCMC.

DRINKS WITH A VIEW

There's something madly exciting about gazing over the neon city at night, preferably with a cocktail in hand. It's well worth the extra dong to enjoy the frenetic pace of life on the streets from the lofty vantage point of a rooftop bar. Among our favourite spots are the following:

Rooftop Garden Bar (Map p299; www.rexhotelvietnam.com; 141 ĐL Nguyen Hue; ⊙24hr) Once a car dealership and garage, the Rex Hotel's relatively diminutive height works to this bar's advantage, leaving you close enough to soak up the energy of the street. The decor is several shades of camp: life-size elephants, birdcage lanterns, topiary draped in fairy lights and, to cap it all off, a giant, rotating, golden crown. There's also live music most nights.

Alto Heli Bar (p331) Secure a window seat and catch the sun going down from this snappy 52nd-floor vantage point over town.

Level 23 Nightspot (Map p299; www.sheraton.com/saigon; 23rd fl, Sheraton Hotel, 88 Đ Dong Khoi; ⊙6pm-midnight Tue-Sun) This rooftop space is great for evening views of Ho Chi Minh City and the glittering streams of traffic heading down ĐL Le Loi. Last stop 23rd floor, with live music and food.

Shri (Map p304; ☑08-3827 9631; 23rd fl, Centec Tower, 72-74 Đ Nguyen Thi Minh Khai; ⊙10am-midnight Mon-Sat, from 5pm Sun) On the Centec Tower's 23rd floor, Shri's stylish terrace has a separate area for non-diners reached by stepping stones over a tiny stream.

Saigon Saigon (Map p299; www.caravellehotel.com; 19 Lam Son Sq; ⊙11am-2am; 🖝) One of the city's first high-rise bars, the Caravelle Hotel's rooftop – on the top floor of the Orginal Wing – combines live music, great views, some alfresco tables and a pretty hefty drinks tab.

M Bar (Map p299; www.majesticsaigon.com.vn; 1 Đ Dong Khoi; ⊙4pm-1am) On the 8th floor of the Majestic Hotel, this is a great spot for a sundowner, with panoramic views of the river and a certain colonial-era cachet.

Alto Heli Bar
BAR

(Map p299; 52nd fl, Bitexco Financial Tower, 2 Đ Hai Trieu; ⊙11.30am-2am) For high-altitude cocktails, a supremely chilled-out ambience, tapas bites and weekend international DJs, Alto – alongside the helipad on the 52nd floor of the Bitexco Financial Tower – has considerable cachet.

Alibi
COCKTAIL BAR

(Map p299; www.alibi.vn; 5A Đ Nguyen Sieu; ⊙10am-late; 🛜) A happening New York–looking bar, with black-and-white photographs on the wall and a long central table, Alibi turns out creative cocktails and, upstairs, excellent fusion food.

Lush
BAR, NIGHTCLUB

(Map p302; www.lush.vn; 2 Đ Ly Tu Trong; ⊙7.30pm-late) Once you're done chatting in the garden bars, move to the central bar for serious people-watching and ass-shaking. The decor is very manga, with cool graphics plastering the walls. DJs spin most nights, with Fridays devoted to hip hop.

La Fenetre Soleil
CAFE, BAR

(Map p299; 1st fl, 44 Đ Ly Tu Trong; coffee from 40,000d; ⊙9am-midnight; 🛜) Making the most of the bones of a French colonial building, this shabby-chic upstairs hang-out has exposed brickwork and beams, chandeliers, frilly mirrors, overhead fans chopping a breeze and a Japanese-Vietnamese menu. Live music draws crowds in the evening, with jazz on Thursdays.

L'Usine
CAFE

(Map p299; www.lusinespace.com; 151/1 Đ Dong Khoi; sandwiches from 95,000d; ⊙9am-10pm; 🛜) A very cool, tucked-away cafe in a colonial building, with huge plate-glass windows, high ceiling, marble-topped tables, photos of old Saigon, lashings of elegant charm, and baguette sandwiches and other wholesome fare on an appetising menu. A designer gift-cum-clothing store is attached; head through the Art Arcade, turn right along the enclosed lane between the buildings and zip upstairs.

Refinery
BAR

(Map p299; www.therefinerysaigon.com; 74/7C ĐL Hai Ba Trung; ⊙11am-late; 🛜) With a black-and-red tiled floor and relaxed vibe in the old French opium refinery, this bistro bar has winning cocktails, appetising snacks and alfresco tables.

Wine Bar 38
WINE BAR

(Map p299; 38 Đ Dong Khoi; ⊙11am-midnight) Slick and smart, this contemporary two-floor wine bar with snappy leather furniture offers a magnificent choice of wines complemented by an outstanding menu.

Vino
WINE BAR

(Map p299; ☑08-3299 1315; www.vinovietnam. com; 74/17 ĐL Hai Ba Trung; ⊙10am-10pm; 🛜) Opening onto the opium refinery courtyard, Vino is an inviting shop window for a leading wine importer so it always has an array of tipples to choose from.

Casbah
BAR

(Map p299; 57 Đ Nguyen Du; ⊙8am-late; 🛜) A cobalt blue oasis with bead curtains up the scuffed stairs off an alley near the central post office, this is an exotic Arab-style choice for a coffee or a cocktail.

Phatty's
SPORTS BAR

(Map p299; www.phattysbar.com; 46-48 Đ Ton That Thiep; ⊙8am-late; 🛜) Its convivial atmosphere, good grub and big-screen sports make Phatty's a solid crowd-puller for after-work expats.

Drunken Duck
SPORTS BAR

(Map p299; 58 Đ Ton That Thiep; ⊙4pm-late; 🛜) The lethal shooters served here probably got the duck inebriated in the first place.

🍷 Da Kao & Around

★ Decibel
BAR

(Map p302; 79/2/5 Đ Phan Kê Bính; ⊙7.30am-midnight Mon-Sat) This small, two-floor restaurant-cafe-bar is a super-relaxed choice for a coffee or cocktail, with a fine cultural vibe, film night and art events.

Hoa Vien
MICROBREWERY

(Map p302; www.hoavien.vn; 18 bis/28 Nguyen Thi Minh Khai; ⊙8am-midnight; 🛜) An unexpected find in the backstreets of HCMC, this Czech restaurant brews up fresh pilsner daily.

🍷 Reunification Palace & Around

Cloud 9
BAR

(Map p304; 6th fl, 2 bis Cong Truong Quoc Te; ⊙5.30pm-midnight) Fashionable young things flock to the rooftop bar, while dance music pounds in the room below.

Hard Rock Cafe
BAR

(Map p299; www.hardrock.com; 39 Đ Le Duan; ⊙11am-midnight; 🛜) Live bands or DJs every Friday and Saturday night.

Pham Ngu Lao Area

Le Pub
PUB

(Map p320; ☑08-3837 7679; www.lepub.org; 175/22 Đ Pham Ngu Lao; ⊙9am-2am; 🛜) The name says it all – British pub meets French cafe-bar – and the pomegranate-coloured result, ranging over three floors, is a hit. An extensive beer list, nightly promotions, cocktail jugs and pub grub draw in the crowds.

Go2
BAR

(Map p320; 187 Đ De Tham; ⊙24hr; 🛜) There's no better street theatre than watching the crazy Bui Vien goings-on from the outside seats of this all-night venue. The music's usually excellent and there's a trashy club upstairs if you feel the need to boogie, and a rooftop bar if you want to cool off. Food's served into the wee hours or you can suck on a shisha pipe until you're sleepy.

Allez Boo
BAR

(Map p320; 195 Đ Pham Ngu Lao; ⊙7am-late) Hard to miss, Allez Boo unashamedly flaunts its tropical kookiness on a prominent street corner: think bamboo-lined walls, a rattan-shaded bar and shisha pipes. A ceaseless influx of backpackers and the late-night action upstairs ensures its popularity.

Spotted Cow
SPORTS BAR

(Map p320; 111 Đ Bui Vien; ⊙11am-midnight) Fun, Aussie-run, bovine-themed sports bar on Bui Vien with lots of drink specials.

Long Phi
BAR

(Map p320; 207 Đ Bui Vien; ⊙10am-5am Tue-Sun) One of the PNL originals, this French-run bar has loooooong hours and occasionally hosts live bands.

Bobby Brewers
CAFE

(Map p320; ☑08-3920 4090; www.bobbybrewers.com; 45 Đ Bui Vien; ⊙7am-10pm; 🛜) This Bui Vien outpost of a local chain ranges over three floors, offering juices, sandwiches, pastas and salads, plus movies upstairs (check website, phone for a schedule or grab a flier).

☆ Entertainment

Pick up *The Word HCMC, Asialife HCMC* or *The Guide* to find out what's on during your stay in HCMC, or log onto www.anyarena. com or www.thewordhcmc.com. Monthly listings include club nights, live music, art shows and theatre performances.

Live Music

HCMC has an enthusiastic live-music scene, with all styles of bands hitting the city's stages. Bernie's Bar & Grill has live bands every weekend and Pacharan on Wednesday and Friday nights. Most nights you'll find a Cuban band turning up the heat at Saigon Saigon Bar while Vasco's regularly hosts international artists.

★ Acoustic
LIVE MUSIC

(Map p304; ☑08-3930 2239; 6E1 Đ Ngo Thoi Nhiem; ⊙7pm-midnight; 🛜) Don't be misled by the name: most of the musicians are fully plugged and dangerous when they take to the intimate stage of the city's leading live-music venue. And judging by the numbers that pack in, the crowd just can't get enough. It's at the end of the alley, by the upended VW Beetle.

★ Cargo
LIVE MUSIC

(Đ 7 Nguyen Tat Thanh; ⊙3pm-midnight Wed-Sun) Hugely popular spacious warehouse venue for up-and-coming local acts, regional bands and DJ events backed up by a great sound system; it's across the river in District 4.

Yoko
LIVE MUSIC

(Map p304; ☑08-3933 0577; 22A Đ Nguyen Thi Dieu; ⊙8am-late; 🛜) Soulful portraits of John Lennon, Jim Morrison and James Brown look on at this cool shrine to live music. The environment: exposed t-beam joists and concrete floor; the music: anything from funk-rock to metal, kicking off around 9.30pm nightly.

Seventeen Saloon
LIVE MUSIC

(Map p307; www.17saloon.vn; 103A Pham Ngu Lao; ⊙7pm-2am) Love-it-or-loathe-it *yeeha*-style Wild West–themed Pham Ngu Lao bar has staff kitted out in boots, denim and cowboy hats with roof-raising rock classics from the resident Filipino band.

Universal Bar
LIVE MUSIC

(Map p320; 90 Bui Vien; ⊙to 2am) This rock-steady bar sees some great acts for the roof-lifting live music that takes to the floor nightly at 9.30pm. Seats are out front for people-watching along Bui Vien and multiple sports TVs provide further entertainment within.

Municipal Theatre
LIVE MUSIC, OPERA

(Map p299; ☑3829 9976; Lam Son Sq) The French-era Opera House is home to the HCMC Ballet and **Ballet & Symphony Orchestra** (www.hbso.org.vn) and hosts performances by visiting artists.

Conservatory of Music
LIVE MUSIC

(Nhac Vien Thanh Pho Ho Chi Minh; Map p304; ☑3824 3774; 112 Đ Nguyen Du) Performances of both traditional Vietnamese and Western classical music are held here.

MZ Bar
LIVE MUSIC

(Map p304; ☑3925 5258; www.m-zing.com; 56a Đ Bui Thi Xuan; ☺6pm-late) A live cover band blasts out danceable classics.

Water Puppets

Although it originates in the north, the art of water puppetry migrated south to HCMC to satiate tourist demands.

Golden Dragon Water Puppet Theatre
THEATRE

(Map p304; ☑3930 2196; www.goldendragon-waterpuppet.com; 55B Đ Nguyen Thi Minh Khai; US$7.50) The main water-puppet venue, with shows starting at 5pm, 6.30pm and 7.45pm and lasting about 50 minutes.

Saigon Water Puppet Theatre
THEATRE

(Map p302; History Museum, Đ Nguyen Binh Khiem; entry 40,000d) Within the History Museum, this small theatre has performances at 9am, 10am, 11am, 2pm, 3pm and 4pm, lasting about 20 minutes.

Cinemas

Tickets are around 60,000d to 70,000d; expect to pay around 120,000d for 3D films.

Lotte Cinema Diamond
CINEMA

(Map p299; http://lottecinemavn.com; 13th fl, Diamond Department Store, 34 Đ Le Duan) Three screens with films in their original language with Vietnamese subtitles.

Galaxy
CINEMA

(www.galaxycine.vn; tickets 60,000-160,000d) Hollywood blockbusters and local hits. There are branches at 116 Đ Nguyen Du (Map p304; 116 Đ Nguyen Du) and 230 Đ Nguyen Trai (Map p320; ☑08 3920 6688; 230 Đ Nguyen Trai)

🔒 Shopping

Junk is energetically peddled to tourists on the city's teeming streets, but plenty of great finds can be uncovered in bustling markets, antique stores, silk boutiques and

---

GAY & LESBIAN HCMC

There are few openly gay venues in town, but most of HCMC's popular bars and clubs are generally gay friendly. Apocalypse Now (p330) sometimes attracts a small gay contingent among an otherwise straight crowd, as does Le Pub (opposite) in Pham Ngu Lao. In the same area, **God Mother Bar** (Map p320; www.godmothersaigon.com; 129 Đ Cong Quynh) is a gay-friendly venue. The most happening night out is the monthly **Bitch Party** (www.bitchpartysaigon.com; admission incl 1st drink 100,000d), which moves around. **Centro Cafe** (Map p299; ☑08-3827 5946; 11-13 Lam Son Sq; ☎) attracts a gay crowd on Saturday nights.

---

speciality stores selling ceramics, ethnic fabrics, lacquered bamboo and custom-made clothing.

There are plenty of places where you can find chic apparel or custom-made *ao dai,* the couture symbol of Vietnam. This gorgeous outfit of silk tunic and trousers is tailored at shops in and around Ben Thanh Market and at the top end of Đ Pasteur. Male *ao dai* are also available, in a looser fit that comes with a silk-covered head wrap to match.

🔒 Dong Khoi Area

Any shopping journey should start along gallery- and boutique-lined Đ Dong Khoi and its intersecting streets, where high-quality handicrafts and gifts can also be found.

Ben Thanh Market
MARKET

(Cho Ben Thanh; Map p299; ĐL Le Loi, ĐL Ham Nghi, ĐL Tran Hung Dao & Đ Le Lai) The most central of all the markets, teeming Ben Thanh and its surrounding streets comprise one of the city's liveliest areas. Everything that's commonly eaten, worn or used by the Saigonese is piled high: vegetables, dried fruit, meats, spices, scorpions in alcohol, sweets, tobacco, clothing, one-day suits, wristwatches, blingtastic jewellery, hardware and more spill forth from a profusion of stalls. Souvenir items can be found in equal abundance. Vendors are determined and prices usually higher than elsewhere, so bargain vigorously (although some stalls have 'Fixed Price' signs).

Mekong Quilts HANDICRAFTS
(Map p299; ☎08-2210 3110; www.mekong-quilts.
org; 1st fl, 68 Đ Le Loi, District 1; ◷9am-7pm)
For beautiful handmade silk quilts, sewn by
the rural poor in support of a sustainable
income.

Dogma SOUVENIRS
(Map p299; www.dogmavietnam.com; 1st fl, 43
Đ Ton That Thiep; ◷9am-10pm) This colour-
fully kitsch store specialises in reproduction
propaganda posters, emblazoning their revolutionary motifs on coffee mugs, coasters,
jigsaws and T-shirts.

Mai Lam CLOTHING
(Map p299; www.mailam.com.vn; 132-134 Đ Dong
Khoi; ◷9am-9pm) Vibrant, colourful, creative
and highly inspiring, Mai Lam's carries
beautiful (but pricey) hand-stitched men's
and women's clothing and accessories.

L'Usine CLOTHING
(Map p299; 151/1 Đ Dong Khoi; ◷9am-10pm) Mar-
rying shopping and dining, this smooth upstairs outlet, next to the restaurant-cafe of
the same name, has an eye-catching line in
stylish threads and colourful bags.

Nguyen Freres ANTIQUES, HANDICRAFTS
(Map p299; 2 Đ Dong Khoi) Great for browsing,
with a spellbinding selection of ceramics,
chopsticks, Buddha heads, bags, scarves, textiles and more.

Annam Gourmet Market FOOD & DRINK
(Map p299; www.annam-gourmet.com; 16 Đ Hai Ba
Trung; ◷8am-9pm Mon-Sat & 9am-8pm Sun) This
large, fabulously stocked deli sells imported
cheeses, wines, chocolates and other delicacies over two floors, with a fine restaurant
crammed into the corner of the 1st level.

Mystere HANDICRAFTS
(Map p299; 141 Đ Dong Khoi; ◷9am-10pm) Attractive lacquerware, fabrics and jewellery
sourced from ethnic minority peoples and
hill tribes.

Khai Silk CLOTHING
(Map p299; ☎08-3829 1146; www.khaisilkcorp.com;
107 Đ Dong Khoi; ◷9.30am-8pm) This is one of
several branches in HCMC of the nationwide
silk empire. Expensive but high quality.

Song Handmade CLOTHING
(Map p299; http://maisonsong.com; 63 Đ Pasteur)
A central boutique specialising in sophisticated linens and cottons for men and
women.

Vincom Center MALL
(Map p299; 70-72 Le Than Ton & 45A Ly Tu Trong;
◷9am-10pm; 🛜) The Vincom Center is divided into two towers, with upscale shopping,
luxury brands (Dior, Hermès, Omega etc)
and a popular food court in the basement
of Tower B.

Sapa HANDICRAFTS, ACCESSORIES
(Map p299; 7 Đ Ton That Thiep; ◷8am-9pm) This
small store incorporates ethnic fabrics and
designs with modern styling; it also has
gifts, jewellery, lampshades and handbags
for sale.

Art Arcade ART
(Map p299; 151 Đ Dong Khoi) A passageway leading off Dong Khoi, lined with art vendors.

Nhu Y Oriental Lacquer Wares HANDICRAFTS
(Map p299; www.nhuylacquer.com; 22 Đ Ho Huan
Nghiep; ◷9am-9.30pm) Gorgeous collection
of eye-catching handmade boxes, Chinese
lacquered couplets, inscribed pictures and
more.

Fahasa Bookshop BOOKSTORE
(Map p299; 40 ĐL Nguyen Hue; ◷8am-10pm)
Government-run bookshops with dictionar-
ies, maps and general books in English and
French. Also has a location on **ĐL Le Loi**
(Map p299; 60-62 ĐL Le Loi; ◷8am-10pm).

Tax Trade Centre SHOPPING CENTRE
(Thuong Xa Tax; Map p299; cnr Đ Nguyen Hue &
Đ Le Loi; ◷9am-9.30pm) Mainly small stallholders, with lots of handicrafts on the top
floor.

**Diamond Department
Store** SHOPPING CENTRE
(Map p299; 34 Đ Le Duan; ◷10am-9.30pm) Four
floors of sleek, Western-style shopping
topped by a very American level of 10-pin
bowling, arcade games and junk food.

Saigon Centre SHOPPING CENTRE
(Map p299; 65 ĐL Le Loi) A tower block with
flashy international stores and cafes on its
lower floors.

Parkson Plaza CLOTHING
(Map p299; 41-45 Đ Le Thanh Ton) Clothing and
cosmetics.

Chi Chi CLOTHING
(Map p299; 144/1 Đ Pasteur; ◷8am-8.30pm)
Offers custom tailoring, with silk *ao dai*
starting at $78.

Da Kao & Around

Thu Quan Sinh Vien   BOOKSTORE
(Map p302; 2A ĐL Le Duan; ⊙8am-10pm; 🛜) Full
of university students making the most
of the free wi-fi in the appealing cafe, this
upmarket store stocks imported books and
magazines in English, French and Chinese.

Orange   CLOTHING, ACCESSORIES
(Map p302; 238B Đ Pasteur; ⊙9am-10pm) Funky
T-shirts and bags.

Reunification Palace & Around

Vinh Loi Gallery   ART
(Map p304; www.galleryvinhloi.com; 41 Đ Ba Huyen
Thanh Quan; ⊙9am-6pm) This excellent gallery
displays some tantalising artwork, including
pieces by Hanoi artist Bui Xuan Phai.

Gaya   HOMEWARES, CLOTHING
(Map p304; www.gayavietnam.com; 1 Đ Nguyen Van
Trang) Designer homeware and clothing bou-
tique that includes the collection of leading
Cambodian-French designer Romyda Keth.

Pham Ngu Lao Area

For cheap reproductions of famous paintings, visit the art shops along Đ Bui Vien.

Hanoi Gallery   PROPAGANDA POSTERS
(Map p320; 79 Đ Bui Vien; ⊙9am-10pm) Fans of
socialist realism should visit this very cool
little store selling both original (or so we're
told) propaganda posters (US$600) and A3
prints (US$8).

Gingko   CLOTHING
(Map p320; www.ginkgo-vietnam.com; 7 Đ Do
Quang Dau; ⊙8am-10pm) With three branches in the PNL area, this fun store sells lines
of exuberant, brightly coloured T-shirts
and hoodies, some decorated with Chinese
characters.

SahaBook   BOOKSTORE
(Map p320; www.sahabook.com; 175/24 Đ Pham
Ngu Lao; ⊙9am-5.30pm Mon-Fri) Specialises in
guidebooks and travel literature, with authentic Lonely Planet guidebooks with read-
able maps – unlike the knock-offs you'll see
on the street.

Blue Dragon   HANDICRAFTS
(Map p320; 1B Đ Bui Vien; ⊙8.30am-10.30pm)
Popular souvenir store that's full of ideas,
from cinnamon-bark boxes to ethnic bags,
jewellery, horn bracelets and clothing.

Nguyen Thai Binh & Around

Antique-hunters can head to Đ Le Cong Kieu,
directly across the road from the Fine Arts
Museum. There's no guarantee objects for
sale are actually old, so purchase with care.

Dan Sinh Market   MARKET
(Map p307; 104 Đ Yersin; ⊙7am-6pm) Also
known as the War Surplus Market, this
is the place for authentic combat boots or
rusty (perhaps less authentic) dog tags,
among the hardware stalls. There are also
handy gas masks, field stretchers, rain gear,
mosquito nets, canteens, duffel bags, pon-
chos, boots and flak jackets.

Other Neighbourhoods

Mai Handicrafts   HANDICRAFTS
(✎08-3844 0988; www.maihandicrafts.com; 298
Đ Nguyen Trong Tuyen, Tan Binh District; ⊙10am-
7pm Mon-Sat) ✐ A fair-trade shop dealing in
ceramics, ethnic fabrics and other gift items
that, in turn, support disadvantaged families
and street children. To get here, head northwest on ĐL Hai Ba Trung, which becomes Đ
Phan Dinh Phung and turn left on Đ Nguyen
Trong Tuyen.

❶ Information

DANGERS & ANNOYANCES

Be careful at all times but especially in the Dong
Khoi area and along the Saigon riverfront – motorbike 'cowboys' specialise in bag-, camera-,
laptop- and tablet-snatching. It's always best to
leave your passport in your hotel room.

MEDIA

Hotels, bars and restaurants around HCMC
carry free city-centric magazines, such as the
excellent monthly magazine the **Word HCMC**
(www.wordhcmc.com), **Asialife HCMC** (www.
asialifehcmc.com) and *The Guide,* a monthly
magazine published by the *Vietnam Economic
Times* (VET).

MEDICAL SERVICES

FV Hospital (Franco-Vietnamese Hospital;
✎08-5411 3333; www.fvhospital.com; 6
Đ Nguyen Luong Bang, District 7; ⊙24hr)
French-, Vietnamese- and English-speaking
physicians; superb care and equipment.
HCMC Family Medical Practice (Map p299;
✎24hr emergency 08-3822 7848; www.
vietnammedicalpractice.com; rear, Diamond

ℹ️ GETTING TO CAMBODIA: HCMC TO PHNOM PENH

Getting to the border The busy Moc Bai–Bavet border crossing is the fastest land route between HCMC and Phnom Penh. Pham Ngu Lao Traveller cafes sell through bus tickets (US$10 to US$15) to Phnom Penh; buses leave from Pham Ngu Lao between 6am and 3pm. Reliable bus companies include **Mekong Express** (www.catmekongexpress.com), **Sapaco** (www.sapacotourist.vn) and the cheaper **Kumho Samco** (www.kumhosamco.com.vn). Allow six hours for the entire trip, including time spent on border formalities.

At the border Cambodian visas (US$20) are issued at the border (you'll need a passport-sized photo). Moc Bai is two hours from HCMC by bus and is a major duty-free shopping zone for the Vietnamese, with several hypermarkets. It's a short walk from Moc Bai to Bavet (the Cambodian border), itself a mini-Macau complete with half-a-dozen or more casinos.

Moving on Most travellers have a through bus ticket from HCMC to Phnom Penh, a further four-hour bus ride away.

Department Store, 34 ĐL Le Duan; ⊘24hr) Well-run practice with branches in Hanoi and Danang.

International Medical Centre (Map p299; ☑08-3827 2366, 24hr emergency 08-3865 4025; www.cmi-vietnam.com; 1 Đ Han Thuyen; ⊘24hr) A nonprofit organisation with English-speaking French doctors.

International SOS (Map p302; ☑08-3829 8424; www.internationalsos.com; 167A Đ Nam Ky Khoi Nghia; ⊘24hr) Has an international team of doctors who speak English, French, Japanese and Vietnamese.

Columbia Asia (Map p304; ☑3823 8888; www.columbiaasia.com/saigon; 8 Alexandre de Rhodes; ⊘Emergency hours 8am-9pm)

MONEY

There are several exchange counters in the arrivals hall at Tan Son Nhat Airport just after clearing customs; most offer the official rates. Turn right after leaving the terminal for ATMs.

ATMs are widespread in town, although most will only dispense a maximum of 2,000,000d per day. Some ANZ ATMs in the inner city will allow withdrawals up to 4,000,000d; **Citibank** (Map p299; 115 Đ Nguyen Hue), in the foyer of the Sun Wah Tower, dispenses 8,000,000d, but only for Citibank cards (2,000,000d for other cards). Visa or MasterCard cash advances for larger amounts of dong, as well as US dollars, can be handled at bank counters during banking hours.

POST

Central Post Office (Map p299; 2 Cong Xa Paris; ⊘7am-9.30pm) Right across from Notre Dame Cathedral is the city's magnificent central post office (p298).

Federal Express (Map p299; ☑08-3829 0995; www.fedex.com; 146 Đ Pasteur; ⊘8am-6pm Mon-Fri, to 2pm Sat) Private postal carrier.

TRAVEL AGENCIES

HCMC's official government-run travel agency is **Saigon Tourist** (Map p299; ☑08-3824 4554; www.saigontourist.net; 45 Đ Le Thanh Ton; ⊘8-11.30am & 1-5.30pm). The agency owns, or is a joint-venture partner in, more than 70 hotels, numerous restaurants, a car-rental agency, golf clubs and assorted tourist traps.

There's a plethora of other travel agencies in town, virtually all of them joint ventures between government agencies and private companies. These places can provide cars, book air tickets and extend visas. Competition is keen and you can often undercut Saigon Tourist's tariffs by a reasonable margin if you shop around. Many agencies have multilingual guides.

Most tour guides and drivers are not paid that well, so if you're happy with their service, tipping is common. Many travellers on bus tours to Cu Chi or the Mekong Delta, for example, collect a kitty (say US$1 or US$2 per person) and give it to the guide and driver at the end of their trip.

Plenty of cheap tours – of varying quality – are sold around Pham Ngu Lao.

Another option is a customised private tour with your own car, driver and guide, which allows maximum flexibility and, split between a few people, can be surprisingly affordable.

Asiana Travel Mate (Map p320; ☑08-3838 6678; www.asianatravelmate.com; 113C Đ Bui Vien) Top-end tour agency.

Buffalo Tours (Map p302; ☑08-3827 9170; www.buffalotours.com; 157 Đ Pasteur; ⊘8.30am-5pm Mon-Fri, to 2.30pm Sat) Top-end tour agency.

Cafe Kim Tourist (Map p320; ☑08-3836 5489; www.thekimtourist.com; 270 Đ De Tham; ⊘7am-9pm)

Exotissimo (☑08-3519 4111; www.exotissimo.com; 41 Thao Dien, District 2; ⊘9am-6pm Mon-Sat)

Handspan Adventure Travel (☑08-3925 7605; www.handspan.com; 10th fl, Central Park Bldg, 208 Nguyen Trai) Excellent, high-quality tours from this HCMC branch of the Hanoi-based agency.

Innoviet (Map p320; ☑08-6291 5408; www.innoviet.com; 158 Ð Bui Vien; ⊗8am-9pm) Budget tour agency.

Sinh Tourist (Map p320; ☑08-3838 9593; www.thesinhtourist.vn; 246 Ð De Tham; ⊗6.30am-10.30pm) Budget tour agency.

Sinhbalo Adventures (Map p320; ☑08-3837 6766; www.sinhbalo.com; 283/20 Ð Pham Ngu Lao) For customised tours, this is a great choice. Sinhbalo specialises in cycling trips, but also arranges innovative special-interest journeys to the Mekong Delta, central highlands and further afield. Their most popular package trips include a two-day Mekong tour and three-day Mekong cycling tour.

ⓘ Getting There & Away

AIR

Ho Chi Minh City is served by Tan Son Nhat International Airport. The following airlines all fly domestically from HCMC:

Jetstar Pacific Airlines (☑1900 1550; www.jetstar.com) Flies to/from Hanoi, Hai Phong, Vinh, Hue and Danang.

VietJet (☑1900-1886; www.vietjetair.com) Flies to/from Hanoi, Danang, Haiphong, Quy Nhon, Nha Trang, Hue, Dalat, Buon Ma Thuot, Pleiku, Con Dao Islands and Phu Quoc Island.

Vietnam Air Service Company (VASCO; www.vasco.com.vn) Flies to/from Tuy Hoa, Chu Lai, Con Dao Islands and Ca Mau.

Vietnam Airlines (☑08-3832 0320; www.vietnamairlines.com) Flies to/from Hanoi, Hai Phong, Vinh, Dong Hoi, Hue, Danang, Quy Nhon, Nha Trang, Dalat, Buon Ma Thuot, Pleiku, Rach Gia and Phu Quoc Island.

BOAT

Hydrofoils (adult/child 200,000-250,000d/100,000-120,000d, 1¼ hours) depart for Vung Tau almost hourly from **Bach Dang jetty** (Map p299; Ð Ton Duc Thang). Following are the main companies:

Greenlines (☑08-3821 5609; www.greenlines.com.vn)

Petro Express (☑08-3821 0650)

Vina Express (☑08-3825 3333; www.vinaexpress.com.vn)

BUS

Intercity buses operate from three large stations on the city outskirts, all well served by local bus services from Ben Thanh Market. HCMC is one place where the open-tour buses really come into their own, as they depart and arrive in the very convenient Pham Ngu Lao area, saving the extra local bus journey or taxi fare.

Mien Tay bus station (Ben Xe Mien Tay; ☑08-3825 5955; Ð Kinh Duong Vuong) serves all areas south of HCMC, essentially the Mekong Delta. This huge station is about 10km west of HCMC in An Lac, a part of Binh Chanh district (Huyen Binh Chanh). A taxi here from Pham Ngu Lao costs around 150,000d. Buses and mini-buses from Mien Tay serve most towns in the Mekong Delta using air-con express buses and premium minibuses.

Buses to locations north of HCMC leave from the huge and busy **Mien Dong bus station** (Ben Xe Mien Dong; ☑08-3829 4056) in Binh Thanh district, about 5km from central HCMC on Hwy 13 (Quoc Lo 13; the continuation of Ð Xo Viet Nghe Tinh). The station is just under 2km north of the intersection of Ð Xo Viet Nghe Tinh and Ð Dien Bien Phu. Note that express buses depart from the east side, and local buses connect with the west side of the complex.

Buses to Tay Ninh, Cu Chi and points north-west of HCMC depart from **An Suong bus station** (Ben Xe An Suong) in District 12, but it's not really worth using them as the Cu Chi tunnels are off the main highway and a nightmare to navigate. Plus, tourist buses are extremely competitively priced and leave from District 1.

Plenty of international bus services connect HCMC and Cambodia, most with departures from the Pham Ngu Lao area. **Sapaco** (Map p320; ☑08-3920 3623; www.sapacotourist.vn; 309 Pham Ngu Lao) has nine direct daily services to Phnom Penh (230,000d; six hours; departing between 6am and 3pm), as well as one to Siem Reap (430,000d; 12 hours; 6am).

CAR & MOTORBIKE

Enquire at almost any hotel, tourist cafe or travel agency to arrange car rental. Just remember

TRANSPORT FROM HCMC

DESTINATION	AIR	BUS	TRAIN
Dalat	50min; from $39	7hr; $8–15	n/a
Nha Trang	55min; from $44	12hr; $10–20	6½hr; $17–31
Hue	80min; from $37	29hr; $26–37	18hr; $26–64
Hanoi	2hr; from $70	41hr; $35–49	30hr; $49–93

that your rental will include a driver as it's illegal for foreigners to drive in Vietnam without a Vietnamese licence. The agencies in the Pham Ngu Lao area generally offer the lowest prices. **Budget Car Rental** (☑ 08-3930 1118; www.budget.com.vn) offers new cars with English-speaking drivers at reasonable rates.

Motorbikes are available in the Pham Ngu Lao area for around US$10 to US$12 per day, although this is one city where it helps to have experience. Check the quality of the helmet provided.

TRAIN

Trains from **Saigon train station** (Ga Sai Gon; ☑ 3823 0105; 1 Đ Nguyen Thong , District 3; ☉ ticket office 7.15-11am & 1-3pm) head north to various destinations.

In Pham Ngu Lao, purchase tickets from **Hoa Xa Agency** (Map p320; ☑ 08-3836 7640; 275C Đ Pham Ngu Lao; ☉ 7.30am-6pm) or from most travel agents for a small fee.

ℹ Getting Around

TO/FROM THE AIRPORT

Tan Son Nhat Airport is 7km northwest of central HCMC. Choose Mai Linh or Vinasun taxis (and especially avoid similar-sounding imitations, usually more battered) in the rank; Mai Linh has a counter in arrivals. Sasco Taxi has the concession for the domestic terminal. From the arrivals taxi rank, a taxi should cost around 180,000d to Dong Khoi, plus a 15,000d vehicle access ticket to airport. You can pay in US dollars if you want.

Metered cabs will cost around 150,000d to District 1, so if you're travelling light you can head upstairs to the arrivals area or into the carpark of the domestic terminal to try to catch a rival cab after it has dropped someone off.

To get to the airport from town, ask your hotel to call a trustworthy taxi for you. Some cafes in the Pham Ngu Lao area offer runs to the airport – some have sign-up sheets where you can book share-taxis for around US$4 per person.

Most economical is the air-con bus (route 152; 5000d, plus a variable fee for luggage) to/from the international airport terminal. Buses leave approximately every 15 minutes and make regular stops along Đ De Tham (Pham Ngu Lao area) and international hotels along Đ Dong Khoi, such as the Caravelle and the Majestic. Buses are labelled in English, but you might also look for the words 'Xe Buyt San Bay'. This service only operates between 6am and 6pm.

Consider a motorbike taxi only if you're travelling light. Drivers can't access the airport, so you will need to walk outside and negotiate: 60,000d to the city centre is the going rate.

BICYCLE

A bicycle can be a useful (if sometimes scary) way to get around the city. Bikes can be rented from several outlets, including hotels, cafes and travel agencies.

Bicycle parking lots are usually just roped-off sections of pavement. For about 2000d you can leave your bicycle, bearing in mind that theft is a big problem. Your bicycle will have a number written on the seat in chalk or stapled to the handlebars and you'll be given a reclaim chit. Don't lose it. If you come back and your bicycle is gone, the parking lot is supposedly required to replace it.

BUS

Local buses are cheap and plentiful, serving more than 130 routes around greater HCMC. A useful, free Ho Chi Minh Bus Route Diagram (map to you and me) is available at the **Ben Thanh bus station** (Map p299; ĐL Tran Hung Dao).

Useful lines from Ben Thanh include the 152 (5000d) to Tan Son Nhat Airport, 149 to Saigon train station, 1 to Binh Tay Market in Cholon, 102

ℹ XE OM OR TAXI?

You'd expect to pay extra for the relative comfort and safety of an air-con taxi as opposed to a white-knuckle motorbike ride, and in theory that's the case. However, rampant overcharging by xe om (motorbike taxi) drivers in the tourist areas can make any difference negligible. Until you're familiar with the distances and fares involved, catching a metered taxi can help avoid being ripped off. Plus, if there's more than one of you, taxis are likely to be cheaper. However, weaving through the traffic on the back of a motorbike is often faster, especially in rush hour.

Just as there are unscrupulous xe om drivers, so too are there dodgy taxis with meters that spin around faster than Kylie in her gold hotpants. Whenever possible, only catch cabs from reputable companies, such as Vinasun and Mai Linh. But beware: both companies have spawned a raft of impersonators using similar logos, slightly altered names (Vinasum, Vina, Vinamet, Ma Lin, M.Group) and badly tampered meters.

If catching a xe om, agree on a price in advance. A trip from Pham Ngu Lao to Dong Khoi shouldn't cost more than 20,000d. One common trick is for drivers to offer to take you for 15,000d but then insist that they really said 50,000d.

to Mien Tay bus station and 26 to Mien Dong bus station. All buses have air-con and the average ticket price is just 3000d. Buy your ticket on board from the attendant.

CAR & MOTORBIKE

Travel agencies, hotels and tourist cafes all rent cars (with drivers) and motorbikes. Many expats swear that motorbike rental is the fastest and easiest way to get around the city – or to the hospital, if you don't know what you're doing. Note that your travel insurance may not offer cover, so check beforehand as things could get expensive and troublesome in the event of an accident. Even if you're an experienced biker, make sure you've spent some time observing traffic patterns before venturing forth. A 100cc motorbike can be rented for US$7 to US$10 per day, including some sort of helmet, and your passport may be kept as collateral. Before renting one, make sure it's in good working order.

Saigon Scooter Centre (☎ 08-3848 7816; www.saigonscootercentre.com; 25/7 Ð Cuu Long, Tan Binh district; ☺ noon-5pm Tue-Fri, 10am-4pm Sat) is a reliable source for restored classic Vespa scooters, new scooters and trail bikes. Daily rates start from US$10, with a minimum rental period of four days. For an extra fee it is possible to arrange a one-way service, with a pick-up of the bikes anywhere between HCMC and Hanoi.

CYCLO

A vanishing icon of Ho Chi Minh City, the *cyclo* remains a slow-moving feature along certain streets, particularly along Ð Pham Ngu Lao and around Ð Dong Khoi. Some Vietnamese may still enjoy them, but their use has long been overtaken by motorbike and taxi, and tourists remain the shrinking bedrock of this poorly paid trade. In HCMC, a few of the older riders are former South Vietnamese army soldiers and quite a few know at least basic English, while others are quite fluent. Some drivers weave stories of war, 're-education', persecution and poverty into the pedal-powered experience (and will often gladly regale you with tales over a bowl of *pho* or a beer at the end of the day).

In an effort to control HCMC's traffic problems, there are dozens of streets on which *cyclos* are prohibited. As a result, your driver must often take a circuitous route to avoid these trouble spots (and possible fines levied by the police) and may not be able to drop you at the exact address. Try to have some sympathy as it is not the driver's fault.

Overcharging tourists is *de rigueur*, so hammer out a price beforehand and have the exact change ready (get familiar with the currency – cyclo drivers may exploit ignorance). If more than one person is travelling, make sure you negotiate the price for both and not a per-passenger fee. It sometimes pays to sketch out numbers and

> ### ① GOING UNDERGROUND: THE HCMC METRO
>
> HCMC sorely needs a metro system to help marshal the transport chaos above ground. First proposed in 2001, the system will run to an estimated five or six lines, with the (part-underground, part-elevated) first line – linking Ben Thanh Market with Suoi Tien in the east – currently slated for a 2018 launch.

pictures with pen and paper so all parties agree. Unfortunately, 'misunderstandings' do happen. Unless the *cyclo* driver has pedalled you to all the districts of HCMC, US$25 is not the going rate. That said, don't just assume the driver is trying to cheat you.

Short hops around the city centre will cost around 20,000d to 25,000d; District 1 to central Cholon costs about 40,000d. You can rent a *cyclo* from around 50,000d per hour – a fine idea if you will be doing a lot of touring. Most *cyclo* drivers around the Pham Ngu Lao area can cook up a sample tour program. If hopping aboard a tour, aim for morning or late afternoon to avoid the hottest part of the day.

Enjoy *cyclos* while you can as the municipal government plans to phase them out, and it won't be too long before the *cyclo* disappears entirely from the city's streets. In the cause of charity, the annual Saigon Cyclo Challenge pits teams of high-paced riders against each other in a fun spectacle.

MOTORBIKE TAXI

For traffic-dodging speed and convenience, the *xe om* (sometimes called a *Honda om*), or motorbike taxi, is the way to go for many. *Xe om* drivers usually hang out on their parked bikes on street corners, touting for passengers. You'll rarely have to walk more than 10 steps before being offered a ride. The accepted rate is 20,000d for short rides (Pham Ngu Lao to Dong Khoi area for instance) or you can charter one for around US$3/15 per hour/day.

TAXI

Metered taxis cruise the streets, but it is worth calling ahead if you are off the beaten path. The flagfall is around 15,000d for the first kilometre; expct to pay around 20,000d (US$1) from Dong Khoi to Pham Ngu Lao. Be wary of dodgy taxi meters, rigged to jump quickly.

The following are HCMC's most highly regarded taxi companies:
Mai Linh Taxi (☎ 08-3838 3838)
Vinasun Taxi (☎ 08-3827 2727)

AROUND HO CHI MINH CITY

Rewarding escapes, such as wilderness areas and fascinating historical and cultural sights, are a short journey from town.

Cu Chi

If the tenacious spirit of the Vietnamese can be symbolised by a place, then few sites could make a stronger case than Cu Chi. This district of greater HCMC now has a population of about 350,000, but during the American War it had about 80,000 residents. At first glance there is scant evidence today of the vicious fighting, bombing and destruction that convulsed Cu Chi during the war. To see what went on, you have to dig deeper – underground.

The tunnel network of Cu Chi became legendary during the 1960s for its role in facilitating VC control of a large rural area only 30km to 40km from HCMC. At its peak the tunnel system stretched from the South Vietnamese capital to the Cambodian border; in the district of Cu Chi alone more than 250km of tunnels honeycomb the ground. The network, parts of which were several storeys deep, included countless trapdoors, constructed living areas, storage facilities, weapon factories, field hospitals, command centres and kitchens.

The tunnels facilitated communication and coordination between the VC-controlled enclaves, isolated from each other by South Vietnamese and American land and air operations. They also allowed the VC to mount surprise attacks wherever the tunnels went – even within the perimeters of the US military base at Dong Du – and to disappear suddenly without a trace via hidden trapdoors. After ground operations against the tunnels claimed large numbers of US casualties and proved ineffective, the Americans resorted to massive firepower, eventually turning Cu Chi's 420 sq km into what BBC journalists Tom Mangold and John Penycate, authors of *The Tunnels of Cu Chi*, have called 'the most bombed, shelled, gassed, defoliated and generally devastated area in the history of warfare'.

Cu Chi has become a place of pilgrimage for Vietnamese school children and Communist Party cadres.

History

The tunnels of Cu Chi were built over a period of 25 years, beginning sometime in the late 1940s. They were the improvised response of a poorly equipped peasant army to its enemy's high-tech ordnance, helicopters, artillery, bombers and chemical weapons.

The Viet Minh built the first tunnels in the red earth (soft during the rainy season, rock-hard during dry months) of Cu Chi during the war against the French. The excavations were used mostly for communication between villages and to evade French army sweeps of the area.

When the VC's National Liberation Front (NLF) insurgency began in earnest in around 1960, the old Viet Minh tunnels were repaired and new extensions were excavated. Within a few years the tunnel system assumed enormous strategic importance, and most of Cu Chi district and the nearby area came under VC control. In addition, Cu Chi was used as a base for infiltrating intelligence agents and sabotage teams into Saigon. The audacious attacks in the South Vietnamese capital during the 1968 Tet Offensive were planned and launched from Cu Chi.

In early 1963 the Diem government implemented the Strategic Hamlets Program, under which fortified encampments, surrounded by many rows of sharp bamboo spikes, were built to house people who had been 'relocated' from Communist-controlled areas. The first strategic hamlet was in Ben Cat district, next to Cu Chi. However, the VC were able to tunnel into the hamlets and control them from within, so that by the end of 1963 the first showpiece hamlet had been overrun.

Over the years the VC developed simple but effective techniques to make their tunnels difficult to detect or disable. Wooden trapdoors were camouflaged with earth and branches; some were booby-trapped. Hidden underwater entrances from rivers were constructed. To cook they used 'Dien Bien Phu kitchens', which exhausted the smoke through vents many metres away from the cooking site. Trapdoors were installed throughout the network to prevent tear gas, smoke or water from moving from one part of the system to another. Some sections were even equipped with electric lighting.

The series of setbacks and defeats suffered by the South Vietnamese forces in the Cu Chi area rendered a complete VC victory by the end of 1965 a distinct possibility. In the early

Around Ho Chi Minh City

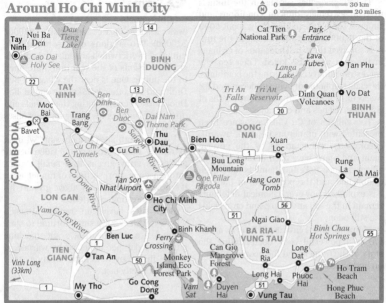

months of that year, the guerrillas boldly held a victory parade in the middle of Cu Chi town. VC strength in and around Cu Chi was one of the reasons the Johnson administration decided to involve US troops in the war.

To deal with the threat posed by VC control of an area so near the South Vietnamese capital, one of the USA's first actions was to establish a large base camp in Cu Chi district. Unknowingly, they built it right on top of an existing tunnel network. It took months for the 25th Division to figure out why they kept getting shot at in their tents at night.

The US and Australian troops tried a variety of methods to 'pacify' the area around Cu Chi, which came to be known as the Iron Triangle. They launched large-scale ground operations involving tens of thousands of troops but failed to locate the tunnels. To deny the VC cover and supplies, rice paddies were defoliated, huge swaths of jungle bulldozed, and villages evacuated and razed. The Americans also sprayed chemical defoliants on the area aerially and a few months later ignited the tinder-dry vegetation with gasoline and napalm. But the intense heat interacted with the wet tropical air in such a way as to create cloudbursts that extinguished the fires. The VC remained safe in their tunnels.

Unable to win this battle with chemicals, the US army began sending men down into the tunnels. These 'tunnel rats', who were often involved in underground fire fights, sustained appallingly high casualty rates.

When the Americans began using German shepherd dogs, trained to use their keen sense of smell to locate trapdoors and guerrillas, the VC began washing with American soap, which gave off a scent the canines identified as friendly. Captured US uniforms were put out to confuse the dogs further. Most importantly, the dogs were not able to spot booby traps. So many dogs were killed or maimed that their horrified handlers then refused to send them into the tunnels.

The USA declared Cu Chi a free-strike zone: little authorisation was needed to shoot at anything in the area, random artillery was fired into the area at night and pilots were told to drop unused bombs and napalm there before returning to base. But the VC stayed put. Finally, in the late 1960s, American B-52s carpet-bombed the whole area, destroying most of the tunnels along with everything else around. The gesture was almost symbolic by then because the USA was already on its way out of the war. The tunnels had served their purpose.

The VC guerrillas serving in the tunnels lived in extremely difficult conditions and suffered serious casualties. Only about 6000 of the 16,000 cadres who fought in the tunnels survived the war. Thousands of civilians in the area were also killed. Their tenacity was extraordinary considering the bombings, the claustrophobia of living underground for weeks or months at a time and the deaths of countless friends and comrades.

The villages of Cu Chi have since been presented with numerous honorific awards, decorations and citations by the government and many have been declared 'heroic villages'. Since 1975 new hamlets have been established and the population of the area has exploded; however, chemical defoliants remain in the soil and water, and crop yields are still poor.

Mangold and Penycate's *Tunnels of Cu Chi* is a powerful book documenting the story of the tunnels and the people involved on both sides.

◉ Sights

Cu Chi Tunnels HISTORICAL SITE

(www.cuchitunnel.org.vn; adult/child 80,000/ 20,000d) Two sections of this remarkable tunnel network (which are enlarged and up-graded versions of the real thing) are open to the public. One is near the village of Ben Dinh and the other is 15km beyond at Ben Duoc. Most tourists visiting the tunnels end up at Ben Dinh, as it's easier for tour buses to reach.

Visits to both sites usually start with an extremely dated propaganda video before guides in army greens lead small groups through some short sections of tunnel. Even if you wimp out and stay above ground, it's still an interesting experience.

Both sites have gun ranges attached where you shell out a small fortune to shell up and fire genuine AK47s and machine guns. You pay per bullet so be warned: if you're firing an automatic weapon, they come out pretty fast.

DAI NAM THEME PARK

Equal parts Disneyland, Buddhist fantasia, historical homage and national propaganda piece, **Dai Nam Theme Park** (Lac Canh Dai Nam Van Hien; ☑ 0650 351 2660; www.laccanh-dainamvanhien.vn; adult/child 100,000/50,000d, zoo adult/child 80,000/50,000d; ◔ 8am-6pm) is a fantastically cheesy experience. About 30km from HCMC on Hwy 13, it's split into four constituent parts sheltered behind giant walls (guarded by life-size model soldiers).

The **amusement park** (◔ 8am-6pm) has a serious rollercoaster with corkscrews and loops, a log flume, an indoor snow world and plenty of rides for smaller kids. Most hilarious is the Ngu Lan (Five Unicorns) Palace, a Buddhist take on Disney's 'It's a small world', where inflatable boats glide through tableaux representing life, death, reincarnation, a descent into hell (a splatterfest of body parts, torture and sadistic demons) and an eventual arrival in nirvana; it's definitely not suitable for small children. Its counterpart, the Ngu Phung (Five Phoenixes) Palace 'makes tourists feel like being lost in the heaven'. Each ride is charged separately (20,000d to 80,000d).

Dai Nam's 12.5-hectare **zoo** (adult/child 80,000/50,000d) is the only one in the greater HCMC area we'd recommend visiting. The menagerie include tigers, lions, white rhinos and bears. The neighbouring **beach** (adult/child 100,000/60,000d) has large fresh and saltwater pools and is a good place for cooling off the kids.

Best of all, for Disneyland kitsch on a monumental scale, is the **temple complex**. Set behind a vast plaza, there are artificial lakes, mountains, walking paths, towers and pagodas. In the mammoth temple every god, goddess and personage of importance in Vietnamese history gets a look in, with Ho Chi Minh taking pride of place.

Local bus 18 runs from Ben Thanh bus station to Dai Nam daily. There's plenty of car parking on site.

For lacquerware, it's well worth stopping off at **Tuong Binh Hiep** en route. This village has been known for producing quality lacquered goods since the early 18th century and you'll pick up items here for a fraction of the price you'll spend in HCMC. Tuong Binh Hiep is 5km south of the theme park; if you're coming from HCMC, turn left immediately after the second set of toll booths onto Đ Le Chi Dan. Various workshops are scattered along this road.

➡ Ben Dinh

The most visited of the tunnel sites, this small, renovated section is near the village of Ben Dinh, about 50km from HCMC. In one of the classrooms at the visitors centre a large map shows the extent of the network while another shows cross-section diagrams of the tunnels.

The section of the tunnel system presently open to visitors is a few hundred metres south of the visitors centre. It snakes up and down through various chambers along its 50m length. The tunnels are about 1.2m high and 80cm across, and are unlit. Some travellers find them too claustrophobic for comfort. A knocked-out M-41 tank and a bomb crater are near the exit, which is in a reforested eucalyptus grove.

Be warned that this site tends to get crowded and you can feel like you're on a tourist conveyor belt most days.

➡ Ben Duoc

Like Ben Dinh, the tunnels here have been enlarged to accommodate tourists, although they're still a tight squeeze. Inside the underground chambers are bunkers, a hospital and a command centre that played a role in the 1968 Tet Offensive. The set pieces include tables, chairs, beds, lights, and dummies outfitted in guerrilla gear.

What Ben Duoc has that Ben Dinh doesn't is the massive **Ben Duoc temple**, built in 1993 in memory of the Vietnamese killed at Cu Chi. It's flanked by a nine-storey tower with a flower garden in front. You'll only be permitted to enter if you're dressed appropriately – although temple wear (long trousers etc) may not be conducive to clambering through earthen tunnels.

Cu Chi War History Museum   MUSEUM

(Nha Truyen Thong Huyen Cu Chi; P) FREE The small Cu Chi War History Museum is not actually at the tunnel sites but just off the main highway in the central part of Cu Chi town. Like most similar museums, its displays consist mainly of photographs (some quite graphic) and large chunks of rusting military hardware. The subject is covered much more comprehensively in the War Remnants Museum in HCMC and you'll see many of the same photos at the tunnels themselves.

Cu Chi Wildlife Rescue Station   WILDLIFE

(www.wildlifeatrisk.org; adult/child US$5/free; ⊘ 7.30-11.30am & 1-4.30pm) Just a few kilometres down the road from the tunnels of Ben Dinh, this small centre is dedicated to the protection of wildlife that has been confiscated from owners or illegal traders. Animals here include bears, otters and gibbons. There is an informative display on the rather depressing state of wildlife in Vietnam, including the 'room of death' featuring a host of traps and baits. It's tough to navigate these back roads solo, so talk to a travel agent about incorporating it into a Cu Chi Tunnels trip.

❶ Getting There & Around

Cu Chi district covers a large area, parts of which are as close as 30km to central HCMC. The Cu Chi War History Museum is closest to the city, while the Ben Dinh and Ben Duoc tunnels are about 50km and 65km, respectively, from central HCMC.

CAR

To visit the rescue centre as well as the tunnels, consider hiring a car and driver, a relatively cheap option if shared between a few people. It is hard to find, so make sure your driver knows where to go.

PUBLIC TRANSPORT

Requiring several changes of bus, it is very difficult to visit by public transport. Tay Ninh buses pass though Cu Chi, but getting from the town of Cu Chi to the tunnels by public transport is tough.

TOURS

By far the easiest way to get to the tunnels is by guided tour and, as the competition is stiff, prices are exceptionally reasonable. For something different, hop on a boat to the Cu Chi tunnels with Les Rives (p315); boats depart twice daily, at 7am and 1.15pm, and include hotel pick-up, meals, refreshments, guide and admission fees. The entire trip takes five hours. **Exotissimo** (⊘ 08-3827 2911; www.exotissimo.com; 64 Đ Dong Du; per 1/2/3/4 people 3,110,000/3,90 0,000/4,600,000/6,200,000d; ⊘ 9am-6pm Mon-Sat) offers a cycling trip or you can join a fun motorbike tour with **Saigon Riders** (⊘ 0913 767 113; www.saigonriders.vn), which costs US$69 per person (minimum two people).

Tay Ninh

POP 127,000

Tay Ninh town, the capital of Tay Ninh province, serves as the headquarters of one of Vietnam's most intriguing indigenous religions, Cao Daism. The Cao Dai Great Temple at the sect's Holy See is one of Asia's most unusual and astonishing structures. Built between 1933 and 1955, the temple is a rococo extravaganza blending the dissonant architectural motifs of a French church, a Chinese temple and an Islamic mosque.

Tay Ninh province, northwest of HCMC, is bordered by Cambodia on three sides. The area's dominant geographic feature is Nui Ba Den (Black Lady Mountain), which towers above the surrounding plains. Tay Ninh province's eastern border is formed by the Saigon River. The Vam Co River flows from Cambodia through the western part of the province.

Because of the once-vaunted political and military power of the Cao Dai, this region was the scene of prolonged and heavy fighting during the Franco-Viet Minh War. Tay Ninh province served as a major terminus of the Ho Chi Minh Trail during the American War, and in 1969 the Viet Cong captured Tay Ninh town and held it for several days.

During the period of conflict between Cambodia and Vietnam in the late 1970s, the Khmer Rouge launched a number of cross-border raids into Tay Ninh province and committed atrocities against civilians. Several cemeteries around Tay Ninh are stark reminders of these events.

⊙ Sights

Cao Dai Holy See   TEMPLE

Home to the **Cao Dai Great Temple** (Thanh That Cao Dai), the Cao Dai Holy See, founded in 1926, is 4km east of Tay Ninh, in the village of Long Hoa. As well as the Great Temple, the complex houses administrative offices, residences for officials and adepts, and a hospital of traditional Vietnamese herbal medicine that attracts people from all over the south for its treatments. After reunification the government took parts of the complex for its own use (and perhaps to keep an eye on the sect).

Prayers are conducted four times daily in the Great Temple (suspended during Tet). It's worth visiting during prayer sessions (the one at noon is most popular with tour groups from HCMC) but don't disturb the worshippers. Only a few hundred adherents, dressed in splendid garments, participate in weekday prayers but during festivals several thousand may attend.

The Cao Dai clergy have no objection to visitors photographing temple objects, but do not photograph people without their permission, which is seldom granted. However, it is possible to photograph the prayer sessions from the upstairs balcony, an apparent concession to the troops of tourists who come here daily.

It's important that guests wear modest and respectful attire inside the temple, which means no shorts or sleeveless T-shirts.

Set above the front portico of the Great Temple is the **divine eye**. Lay women enter the Great Temple through a door at the base of the tower on the left. Once inside they walk around the outside of the colonnaded hall in a clockwise direction. Men enter on the right and walk around the hall in an anticlockwise direction. Hats must be removed upon entering the building. The area in the centre of the sanctuary is reserved for Cao Dai priests.

A **mural** in the front entry hall depicts the three signatories of the 'Third Alliance between God and Man': the Chinese statesman and revolutionary leader Dr Sun Yat-sen (Sun Zhongshan; 1866–1925) holds an ink stone, while the Vietnamese poet Nguyen Binh Khiem (1492–1587) and French poet and author Victor Hugo (1802–85) write 'God and humanity' and 'Love and justice' in Chinese and French (Nguyen Binh Khiem writes with a brush, Victor Hugo uses a quill pen). Nearby signs in English, French and German each give a slightly different version of the fundamentals of Cao Daism.

The main hall is divided into nine sections by shallow steps, representing the nine steps to heaven, with each level marked by a pair of columns. Worshippers attain each new level depending on their years as Cao Dai adherents. At the far end of the sanctuary, eight plaster columns entwined with multicoloured dragons support a dome representing the heavens. Under the dome is a giant star-speckled blue globe with the 'divine eye' on it.

The largest of the seven chairs in front of the globe is reserved for the Cao Dai pope, a position that has remained vacant since 1933. The next three chairs are for the three men responsible for the religion's law books. The remaining chairs are for the leaders of the three branches of Cao Daism, represented by the colours yellow, blue and red.

On both sides of the area between the columns are two pulpits similar in design to the *minbar* in mosques. During festivals the pulpits are used by officials to address the assembled worshippers. The upstairs balconies are used if the crowd overflows.

Up near the altar are barely discernible portraits of six figures important to Cao

Daism: Sakyamuni (Siddhartha Gautama, the founder of Buddhism), Ly Thai Bach (Li Taibai, a fairy from Chinese mythology), Khuong Tu Nha (Jiang Taigong, a Chinese saint), Laotse (the founder of Taoism), Quan Cong (Guangong, Chinese God of War) and Quan Am (Guanyin, the Goddess of Mercy).

Nui Ba Den
TEMPLE, MOUNTAIN

(Black Lady Mountain; adult/child 10,000/5000d chairlift one way/return adult 50,000/90,000d, child 30,000/50,000d) Fifteen kilometres northeast of Tay Ninh, Nui Ba Den rises 850m above the rice paddies, corn, cassava (manioc) and rubber plantations of the surrounding countryside. Over the centuries it has served as a shrine for various peoples of the area, including the Khmer, Cham, Vietnamese and Chinese, and there are several interesting **cave temples** here.

The summits of Nui Ba Den are much cooler than the rest of Tay Ninh province, most of which is only a few dozen metres above sea level.

Nui Ba Den was used as a staging area by both the Viet Minh and the VC, and was the scene of fierce fighting during the French and American Wars, when it was defoliated and heavily bombed by US aircraft.

Several stories surround the name 'Black Lady Mountain'. One is derived from the legend of Huong, a young woman who married her true love despite the advances of a wealthy Mandarin. While her husband was away doing military service, she would visit a magical statue of Buddha at the mountain's summit. One day Huong was attacked by kidnappers but, preferring death to dishonour, she threw herself off a cliff. She then reappeared in the visions of a monk who lived on the mountain, and he told her story.

The hike from the base of the mountain to the main temple complex and back takes about 1½ hours. Although steep in parts, it's not a difficult walk – plenty of older pilgrims in sandals make the journey to worship at the temple. Around the temple complex are a few stands selling snacks and drinks.

If you need more exercise, a walk to the summit and back takes about six hours. The fastest, easiest way is via the chairlift that shuttles the pilgrims up and down the hill. For a more exhilarating descent, try the 'slideway', a sort of winding track that drops 1700m around the mountain and is the closest thing to the luge in Vietnam.

Because of crowds, visiting on Sunday or during a holiday or festival is a bad idea.

Nui Ba Den appears prominently in a memoir published by former American soldier Larry Heinemann, *Black Virgin Mountain: A Return to Vietnam.*

ⓘ Getting There & Away

Tay Ninh is on Hwy 22 (Quoc Lo 22), 96km from HCMC. The road passes through **Trang Bang**, the place where the famous photograph of a severely burnt young girl, Kim Phuc, screaming and running, was taken during a napalm attack in the American War. Read more about her story in *The Girl in the Picture* (1999) by Denise Chong.

BUS & TOURS

Buses from HCMC to Tay Ninh leave from the An Suong bus station (minibus 50,000d), but by far the easiest way to get here is by one of the Tay Ninh/Cu Chi tours leaving from District 1. You could consider leaving one of the cheaper tours (US$7) at the Holy See. A taxi from here to Nui Ba Dem costs around 100,000d, while a xe om should be around 40,000d. It would then cost a similar amount to return to the bus station in Tay Ninh town.

One Pillar Pagoda

Officially known as Nam Thien Nhat Tru, most people call this Buddhist temple the **One Pillar Pagoda of Thu Duc** (Chua Mot Cot Thu Duc; 1/91 Đ Nguyen Du, Thu Duc district). Modelled on Hanoi's One Pillar Pagoda, the structure is similar but not identical, consisting of a small, one-room temple hall rising on a pillar above a pond, containing a multiarmed image of Quan Am, Goddess of Mercy. At the rear of the compound are tombs holding urns containing bones of monks and other Buddhist faithful.

Hanoi's original pagoda was built in the 11th century but rebuilt after destruction by the French in 1954. When Vietnam was partitioned during the same year, many Buddhist monks and Catholic priests fled south to avoid possible persecution. One monk from Hanoi, Thich Tri Dung, petitioned the South Vietnamese government for permission to construct a replica of Hanoi's famous One Pillar Pagoda. However, it was denied by President Ngo Dinh Diem, a Catholic with little tolerance for Buddhist clergy. Nevertheless, Thich and his supporters raised the funds and built the pagoda in 1958, in defiance of the president's orders.

At one point the Diem government ordered the monks to tear down the temple but they refused, despite being threatened with imprisonment. Faced with significant opposition, the government's dispute with the monks reached a standoff. However, the president's attempts to harass and intimidate the monks in a country that was 90% Buddhist did not go down well and ultimately contributed to Diem's assassination by his own troops in 1963.

The pagoda is 15km northeast of central HCMC. Traveller cafes and travel agencies in HCMC should be able to put together a customised tour to the pagoda or to arrange a car and driver for you.

Can Gio

Notable for its extensive mangrove forest, Can Gio is a low, palm-fringed island sitting at the mouth of the Saigon River, some 25km southeast of HCMC. It was formed from silt washing downstream from the river, so don't expect any white-sand beaches. A few hopeful resorts have sprung up along the murky 10km shoreline and more are planned, although it's hard to imagine them appealing to international visitors.

Of more interest is the forest. This listed Unesco Biosphere Reserve contains a high degree of biodiversity, with more than 200 species of fauna and 150 species of flora. If you're looking for a relatively traffic-free route to explore by motorbike, it's a great day trip.

◉ Sights

Monkey Island
Eco Forest Park
NATURE RESERVE
(www.cangioresort.com.vn; admission 30,000d) As with many 'ecotourism' activities in Vietnam, Saigon Tourist has got in on the act and turned the experience into a bit of an event. While this is the most interesting and accessible part of the forest to visit, it's hard to stomach the cruel conditions in which the stars of their animal circus (including bears and monkeys) are kept.

The island is also home to a monkey sanctuary, which houses at least a hundred wild but unafraid simians. Take care: like monkeys everywhere, the line between cheeky charmer, thieving pest and dangerous beast is very fine. Keep a firm hold on your possessions.

The motorboat ride (about 150,000d) through the waterways of the VC's Rung Sac base is the highlight of a visit. At the reconstructed base, dummies portray VC cadres

sawing open unexploded American bombs in order to salvage the explosives and wrestling with crocodiles, which were once common here but are now confined to crocodile farms like the one by the entrance. A small museum has wildlife displays, along with exhibits relating to local war history and archaeological finds.

Coming from HCMC, Monkey Island is to the right of the main road, about 34km past the ferry.

Vam Sat
NATURE RESERVE
This section of the forest is noted for crab-angling, a crocodile farm and Dam Doi (Bat Swamp), an area where fruit bats nest. Boats to Vam Sat (around 150,000d) depart from under Dan Xay Bridge, which is on the main road, 22km south of the ferry and 12km north of Monkey Island.

Duyen Hai
TOWN
Facing Vung Tau at the southeastern tip of Can Gio district, this small town has a Cao Dai temple and a large market, which is made very conspicuous by some rather powerful odours. Seafood and salt are the local specialities; the vegetables, rice and fruit are all imported by boat from around HCMC. Adjacent to the local shrimp hatchery is a vast cemetery and war memorial (Nghia Trang Liet Si Rung Sac), 2km from Can Gio Market.

ⓘ Getting There & Away

CAR & MOTORBIKE
Can Gio is about 60km southeast of central HCMC, and the fastest way to make the journey is by car or motorbike (about two hours). There's a ferry crossing (motorbike/car 2000/10,000d) 15km from HCMC at Binh Khanh (Cat Lai), a former US naval base. Once you get past the ferry, there is little traffic and the sides of the road are lined with mangrove forests. The motorbike ride is an excellent day out in itself.

TOURS
There are day trips from HCMC offered by Cafe Kim Tourist (US$25) and Saigon Tourist (from US$56). A boat trip to Can Gio is also offered by Les Rives (p315), which departs at 7.30am and takes a total of seven to nine hours. The trip includes hotel pick-up, meals, refreshments, guide and admission fees. Saigon Riders (p343) operates a fun motorbike trip to Can Gio, costing US$109 per person (all-inclusive, minimum two people), kicking off at 8am.

Mekong Delta

Off the Beaten Track

➡ Phu Quoc National Park (p375)
➡ Bang Lang (p365)
➡ Xeo Quyt Forest (p396)

Best Places to Stay

➡ Nam Bo Boutique Hotel (p363)
➡ La Veranda (p378)
➡ Xoai Hotel (p360)
➡ Bamboo Cottages (p380)
➡ Victoria Chau Doc Hotel (p390)

Why Go?

The 'rice bowl' of Vietnam, the Mekong Delta is a landscape carpeted in a dizzying variety of greens and slashed with mighty waterways. It's a water world where boats, houses, restaurants and even markets float upon the innumerable rivers, canals and streams that flow through the region like arteries. At times you can quite simply lose sight of land.

The area is both riparian and deeply rural, but it's also one of Vietnam's most densely populated regions, with nearly every hectare intensively farmed. Visitors can dwell on southern charm in little-visited riverside cities, sample fruits traded in the colourful floating markets, or feast on home-cooked delicacies before overnighting as a homestay guest. Mangrove forests, sacred Khmer pagodas and off-the-beaten-track attractions round out the picture.

Those seeking tropical hideaways can come ashore on Phu Quoc, a divine forested island fringed with white-sand beaches and crisscrossed with empty dirt roads that simply beg for motorbike exploration.

When to Go
My Tho

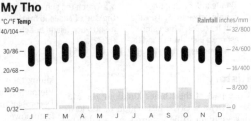

Nov The dry season starts, with Khmer longboat festivals in Tra Vinh and Soc Trang.

Jan While they shiver up north, Phu Quoc's beaches stay temperate and dry.

Mar A March visit avoids the Tet madness, and the summer heat and rain.

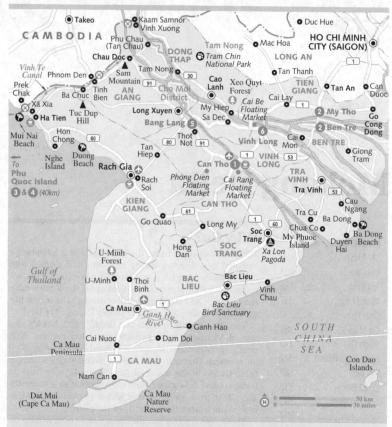

Mekong Delta Highlights

1 Join in the throngs amid the bustling commerce of the floating markets on a boat trip from **Can Tho** (p360).

2 Meander along the **canals** between My Tho and Ben Tre (p350), then step ashore a lush river island to feast on fresh fish.

3 Kick up red dirt on a motorbike ride to the far-flung corners of **Phu Quoc Island** (p372).

4 Watch the sun set across the Gulf of Thailand from a Phu Quoc Island **beach** (p372).

5 Witness a forest of trees entirely full of storks at breathtaking **Bang Lang** (p365).

6 Get a taste of rural river life at one of the many **homestays** (p359) around Vinh Long.

History

Once part of the Khmer kingdom, the Mekong Delta was the last region of modern-day Vietnam to be annexed and settled by the Vietnamese. Cambodians, mindful that they controlled the area until the 18th century, still call the delta Kampuchea Krom, or 'Lower Cambodia'.

The Khmer Rouge attempted to reclaim the area by raiding Vietnamese villages and killing their inhabitants. This provoked the Vietnamese army to invade Cambodia on 25 December 1978 and oust the Khmer Rouge from power.

Most of today's inhabitants of the Mekong Delta are ethnic Vietnamese, but significant populations of ethnic Chinese and Khmer, as well as a smaller Cham community, also exist.

When the government introduced collective farming to the delta in 1975, production fell significantly and food shortages hit Saigon, although farmers in the delta easily grew enough to feed themselves. The Saigonese would head down to the delta to buy sacks of black-market rice, but to prevent profiteering the police set up checkpoints and confiscated rice from anyone carrying more than 10kg. All this ended in 1986 and farmers in this region have since transformed Vietnam into one of the world's largest rice exporters.

❶ Getting There & Around

Most travellers visit the Mekong Delta on cheap and convenient organised tours. Those travelling on their own will have greater access to little-visited areas off the beaten track.

With the opening of several border crossings between Vietnam and Cambodia, including the river border at Vinh Xuong (near Chau Doc) and the land border at Xa Xia (near Ha Tien), many travellers are choosing these delta routes ahead of the original land crossing at Moc Bai–Bavet. Cambodian visas are available on arrival at all border crossings.

AIR

Flights head from Hanoi to Can Tho and from Ho Chi Minh City (HCMC) to Rach Gia and Ca Mau. Phu Quoc Island's new international airport welcomes flights from Hanoi, HCMC, Can Tho and Rach Gia.

BOAT

Some delta towns have ferry connections between them – a fascinating way to travel. The journey between Ca Mau and Rach Gia is particularly scenic. Boats to Phu Quoc Island leave from Rach Gia and Ha Tien.

BUS

It's surprisingly easy to travel the delta using public transport, and bus connections are excellent. Each urban centre has a bus station for both buses and minibuses – although it's usually located on the edge of town, requiring a short *xe om* (motorbike taxi) or taxi ride to your hotel. Minibuses tend to be faster, moderately more comfortable and not much more expensive.

Coming from HCMC, delta buses leave from Mien Tay bus station, 10km west of the centre. To avoid the slight inconvenience of reaching Mien Tay, consider booking one of the cheap day tours to My Tho departing from Đ Pham Ngu Lao and abandoning the tour after the boat trip.

CAR, MOTORCYCLE & BICYCLE

The most flexible transport option is by private car, bicycle or rented motorbike. Two-wheeling around the delta is good fun, especially along the maze of country roads and on Phu Quoc. Be prepared for toll roads and ferry crossings – although these are gradually being replaced with new bridges. Ferries are cheap and frequent.

TOURS

Dozens of tours head from HCMC to the Mekong Delta, either as day trips or longer jaunts. This is a great option if you're short on time, but it means abdicating control over your itinerary and choice of hotels.

The cheapest tours are sold around the Pham Ngu Lao area. Shop around before you book, but remember that you usually get what you pay for. This is not to say pricey tours are necessarily better, but sometimes 'rock-bottom' means a brief glance at the region from a packed bus full of other tourists. Rewarding motorbike and scooter tours of the Delta are run by Vietnam Vespa Adventure (p317) and Saigon Riders (p344).

LE VAN SINH: TOURISM TRAILBLAZER & CYCLING ENTHUSIAST

Few people have had more of an impact on Vietnam tourism than Le Van Sinh, owner of Sinhbalo Adventures.

What makes the Mekong Delta special? I have always been interested in waterways, as it is such a great way to relax – in a hammock, cruising along the river. The system of canals and floating markets here is incredible and so different that all tourists should see it.

Why cycle? Bicycles are the best way to enjoy the scenery and get off the beaten track. Cycling in the far north or even the central Highlands requires some experience and endurance, but for the pancake-flat Mekong, everyone can manage a few days exploring on two wheels. It doesn't matter whether you're a serious cyclist or a city slicker; there are so many routes in the Mekong to enjoy and explore.

Best routes? My favourite back roads include the small trail under the shade of coconut palms that runs from Ben Tre through Mo Cay and the pretty town of Tra Vinh to Can Tho. Most tourists only experience Hwy 1A on the way to Can Tho, but this is another world.

My Tho

☑ 073 / POP 180,000

Gateway to the Mekong Delta, My Tho is the capital of Tien Giang province and an important market town – although for the famous floating markets, you'll need to continue on to Can Tho.

My Tho's proximity to HCMC means it's a popular day-trip destination for a taste of river life – a flotilla of boats tour the local islands and their cottage industries daily. The riverfront makes for a pleasant stroll and the town is easily explored on foot.

My Tho was founded in the 1680s by Chinese refugees fleeing Taiwan after the fall of the Southern Ming dynasty. The economy is based on tourism, fishing and the cultivation of rice, coconuts, bananas, mangoes, longans and citrus fruit.

👁 Sights

Vinh Trang Pagoda   BUDDHIST TEMPLE
(60A Đ Nguyen Trung Truc; ⏱ 9-11.30am & 1.30-5pm) **FREE** Giant Buddha statues tower over the beautiful grounds of this peaceful temple around 1km east of the city centre, where the monks maintain an ornate sanctuary, decorated with carved and gilded wood. They also provide a home for children with disabilities, orphans and other kids in need; donations are always welcome.

To get here, head north on Le Loi, turn right onto Nguyen Trai and take the bridge across the river. After 400m turn left onto Nguyen Trung Truc. The entrance to the sanctuary is about 200m from the turn-off, on the right-hand side of the building as you approach it from the ornate gate.

My Tho Market   MARKET
(Cho My Tho; Đ Trung Trac) Spilling out onto the street facing Bao Dinh Channel, this market offers a typically Vietnamese array of dried fish, exotic fruits, doomed animals and strange smells.

Cao Dai Temple   BUDDHIST TEMPLE
(85 Đ Ly Thuong Kiet; ⏱ dawn-dusk) A colourful little temple with its all-seeing divine eye.

🖝 Tours

In a prominent building on the riverfront, the **My Tho Tourist Boat Station** (8 Đ 30 Thang 4) is home to several tour companies offering cruises to the neighbouring islands and through the maze of small canals. Depending on what you book, destinations

usually include a coconut-candy workshop, a honey farm (try the banana wine) and an orchid garden. A 2½-hour boat tour costs around 350,000d for one person or 450,000d for two. If you're a day-tripper, it's easiest to book your package (including connecting transport) through a HCMC-based tour operator. Prices are significantly better if you can join a group, although you may be able to negotiate a more flexible itinerary if you go it alone. Operators based at My Tho's Boat Station include the following:

Tien Giang Tourist (Cong Ty Du Lich Tien Giang; ☑ 073-387 3184; www.tiengiangtourist. com; 8 Đ 30 Thang 4)

Vietnamese Japanese Tourist (☑ 073-397 5559; www.dulichvietnhat.com; 8 Đ 30 Thang 4)

🛏 Sleeping

Song Tien Annex   HOTEL $
(☑ 073-387 7883; www.tiengiangtourist.com; 33 Đ Thien Ho Duong; r 450,000-500,000d; ❀ 🛜) Rooms at this becalming, clean and tidy hotel have hardwood floors, natty extras such as bathrobes and hair dryers, lovely bathrooms with free-standing claw-footed bathtubs and modern furniture.

Chuong Duong Hotel   HOTEL $$
(☑ 073-387 0875; 10 Đ 30 Thang 4; r 500,000-700,000d; ❀ 🛜) All rooms have a river view and come with the obvious amenities at this smart hotel. The restaurant here is worth a visit for its range of dishes, plus there's a lively coffee shop.

Song Tien   HOTEL $$
(☑ 073-387 2009; www.tiengiangtourist.com; 101 Đ Trung Trac; r 450,000-850,000d; ❀ 🛜) This friendly, smart and well-looked-after hotel has decent-enough rooms with satellite TV and minibars. Check the rooms: cheaper ones are windowless and there are occasional traces of mould.

🍴 Eating & Drinking

My Tho is known for a special vermicelli soup, *hu tieu My Tho,* which is richly garnished with fresh and dried seafood, pork, chicken, offal and fresh herbs. It is served either with broth or dry and can also be made vegetarian.

Although *hu tieu* can be found at almost any eatery in town, there's a handful of speciality restaurants. Carnivores should try **Hu Tieu 44** (44 Đ Nam Ky Khoi Nghia; soups

My Tho

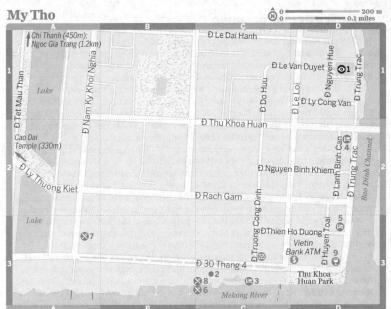

N 0 ——— 200 m
0 ——— 0.1 miles

20,000d), while vegetarians can indulge at **Hu Tieu Chay 24** (24 Đ Nam Ky Khoi Nghia; mains 10,000-14,000d).

Ngoc Gia Trang VIETNAMESE $
(☎073-387 2742; 196 Đ Ap Bac; mains 45,000-150,000d; ⊗8am-9pm) This friendly spot is down a lane off the main road into My Tho from HCMC, with tables set alongside ponds amid lots of greenery, and excellent, beautifully presented seafood.

Chi Thanh CHINESE, VIETNAMESE $
(☎073-387 3756; 279 Đ Tet Mau Than; mains 35,000-80,000d) This small but extremely popular restaurant does a steady trade in tasty Chinese and Vietnamese fare (beef, chicken, pork, squid, crab, noodles, hotpots). There's an English menu.

Night Market VIETNAMESE $
(Đ 30 Thang 4; ⊗5pm-late) Plonked right in front of the floating restaurant, this popular place packs in diners come evening, with a host of lively hotpot and fish stalls.

Floating Restaurant VIETNAMESE $
(Đ 30 Thang 4; mains from 30,000d; ⊗8am-9.30pm) By the Tourist Boat Station, this is a good choice for a breezy meal on the Mekong.

Lac Hong BAR, CAFE
(☎073-397 6459; 3 Đ Trung Trac; ⊗6-11pm; ⓢ) Set in a gorgeous old colonial-era trading house on the riverfront with lounge chairs and, upstairs, breezes and river views. Live music on Thursdays.

THE RIVER OF NINE DRAGONS

The Mekong River is one of the world's great rivers and its delta is one of the world's largest. It originates high in the Tibetan Plateau, flowing 4500km through China, between Myanmar (Burma) and Laos, through Laos, along the Laos–Thailand border, and through Cambodia and Vietnam on its way to the South China Sea. At Phnom Penh (Cambodia), the Mekong River splits into two main branches: the Hau Giang (Lower River, also called the Bassac River), which flows via Chau Doc, Long Xuyen and Can Tho to the sea; and the Tien Giang (Upper River), which splits into several branches at Vinh Long and empties into the sea at five points. The numerous branches explain the Vietnamese name for the river: Song Cuu Long (River of Nine Dragons).

The Mekong's flow begins to rise around the end of May and reaches its highest point in September. A tributary of the river that empties into the Mekong at Phnom Penh drains Cambodia's Tonlé Sap Lake. When the Mekong is at flood stage, this tributary reverses its direction and flows into Tonlé Sap, acting as one of the world's largest natural flood barriers. Unfortunately, deforestation in Cambodia is disturbing this delicate balancing act, resulting in more flooding in Vietnam's portion of the Mekong River basin.

In recent years seasonal flooding has claimed the lives of hundreds and forced tens of thousands of residents to evacuate from their homes. Floods cause millions of dollars' worth of damage and have a catastrophic effect on regional rice and coffee crops.

Living on a flood plain presents some technical challenges. Lacking any high ground to escape flooding, many delta residents build their houses on bamboo stilts to avoid the rising waters. Many roads are submerged or turn to muck during floods; all-weather roads have to be built on raised embankments, but this is expensive. The traditional solution has been to build canals and travel by boat. There are thousands of canals in the Mekong Delta – keeping them properly dredged and navigable is a constant but essential chore.

A further challenge is keeping the canals clean. The normal practice of dumping all garbage and sewage directly into the waterways behind the houses that line them is taking its toll. Many of the more populated areas in the Mekong Delta are showing signs of unpleasant waste build-up. The World Wildlife Fund (WWF) is one organisation that's working with local and provincial governments to help preserve the environment.

In 2013, Laos declared its intention to build the 260-megawatt Don Sahong Dam on the Mekong, without consulting downstream neighbours, while its construction of the 1260-megawatt Xayaburi Dam continues in the north of the country. Dams on the Chinese stretch of the river have already been blamed for reduced water levels, and environmental groups have petitioned the Laos government to put plans on hold after concerns that the target of 11 dams will disrupt the breeding cycles of dozens of fish species. There are also fears that the reduced flows will cause more salt water to enter the Vietnamese section (a process exacerbated by global warming), which could have a catastrophic effect on rice production.

ⓘ Getting There & Around

New bridges and freeways have considerably shortened travel distances to My Tho. It takes only about an hour to 90 minutes (traffic depending) from central HCMC (70km), while Ben Tre town is a mere 17km away via the new bridge.

The **My Tho bus station** (Ben Xe Tien Giang, 42 Đ Ap Bac) is 3km west of the town centre on Đ Ap Bac, the main road to HCMC. Buses head to HCMC's Mien Tay bus station (35,000d), Can Tho (50,000d), Cao Lanh (32,000d) and Ca Mau (123,000d).

Around My Tho

Phoenix Island

Until his imprisonment for anti-government activities and the consequent dispersion of his flock, the Coconut Monk (Dao Dua) led a small community on Phoenix Island (Con Phung), a few kilometres from My Tho. The Coconut Monk left his family to pursue a monastic life and for three years he sat on a stone slab under a flagpole and meditated day and night.

In its heyday the island was dominated by a somewhat trippy open-air sanctuary (admission 5000d; ☺8-11.30am & 1.30-6pm). The dragon-emblazoned columns and quirky tower, with its huge metal globe, must have once been brightly painted, but these days the whole place has become faded, rickety and silent. Nevertheless, it is seriously kitsch, with a model of the Apollo rocket set among the Buddhist statues. With some imagination you can almost picture how it all must have appeared as the Coconut Monk presided over his congregation, flanked by enormous elephant tusks and seated on a richly ornamented throne.

Plaques on the 3.5m-high porcelain jar (created in 1972) on the island tell all about the Coconut Monk. He founded a religion, Tinh Do Cu Si, a fusion of Buddhism and Christianity. Representations of Jesus and the Buddha appeared together, as did the Virgin Mary and eminent Buddhist women, together with the cross and Buddhist symbols. Today only the symbols remain, as the Tinh Do Cu Si community has dissolved from the island.

Private boat operators can include the island as part of an organised tour. It's possible to spend the night at the simple Con Phung Hotel (☏075-382 2198; www.conphungtourist.com; r from 200,000d; ❄). The VIP quarters have river views, but all rooms include TV, fridge and hot water. The restaurant serves a range of delta-flavour dishes (mains from 40,000d).

Other Islands

Famed for its longan orchards, Dragon Island (Con Tan Long) makes for a pleasant stop and stroll, just a five-minute boat trip from My Tho. Some of the residents of the island are shipwrights, and the lush palm-fringed shores are lined with wooden fishing boats. The island has some small restaurants and cafes.

Tortoise Island (Con Qui) and Unicorn Island (Thoi Son) are popular stops for the coconut candy and banana wine workshops.

Tan Thach Village

Across the river in Ben Tre province, this former ferry stop has faded into obscurity with the opening of the new bridge. The only reasons to visit are to chill out in its rustic guesthouse or to visit its riverside restaurant – a popular stop on the river tours.

🍽 Sleeping & Eating

Thao Nhi Guesthouse　　GUEST HOUSE $
(☏075-386 0009; thaonhitours@yahoo.com; Hamlet 1, Tan Thach Village; r US$6-15; ❄) A traditional homestay-type experience amid abundant greenery with basic rooms and bungalows with fans. There are hearty meals, free bike rental and the owner's son speaks excellent English and offers tours.

Hao Ai　　VIETNAMESE $
(Hamlet 2, Tan Thach Village; mains 50,000-80,000d) Set in landscaped gardens complete with chickens and buffaloes, this attractive island restaurant does a roaring trade with tour groups exploring the delta. Lunch only.

❶ Getting There & Around

Part of Chau Thanh District, Tan Thach is 6km north of the Ben Tre bus station (30,000d by *xe om*); take Hwy 60 back towards My Tho, veer right at the big intersection marked Chau Thanh and follow it to the end. The guesthouse and restaurant are both down the last narrow road to the right; Thao Nhi is signposted to the right after 300m, where it's a further 50m down a small lane.

Ben Tre
☏075 / POP 143,000

As tourism took off in the Mekong Delta, the picturesque little province of Ben Tre was always ferry beyond the tourist traffic of My Tho and consequently developed at a more languid pace, although the opening of the Rach Mieu Bridge from My Tho funneled more visitors into the area. The town's sleepy waterfront, lined with ageing villas, is easy to explore on foot, as is the rustic settlement across the bridge to the south of the centre. This is also a good place to arrange boat trips in the area, particularly for those wanting to escape the tour bus bustle.

Ben Tre is famous for its *keo dua* (coconut candy). Many local women work in small factories making these sweets, spending their days boiling cauldrons of the sticky coconut goo before rolling it out and slicing sections off into squares.

◉ Sights

Ben Tre Museum　　MUSEUM
(Bao Tang Ben Tre; Ð Hung Vuong; ☺8-11am & 1-5pm) **FREE** In an ageing but atmospheric old yellow villa, this museum displays the usual assortment of rusty weapons, American War photos and artefacts yielded from archaeological digs.

Ben Tre

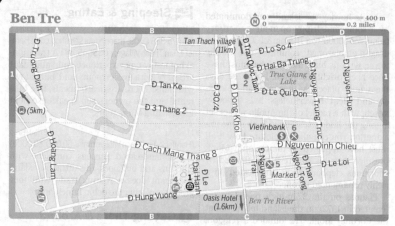

MEKONG DELTA BEN TRE

Ben Tre

⊙ Sights
1 Ben Tre Museum B2

⊙ Activities, Courses & Tours
2 Ben Tre Tourist C1

⊜ Sleeping
3 Ham Luong A2
4 Hung Vuong B2

⊗ Eating
5 Food Stalls C2
6 Nam Son C2

☞ Tours

Ben Tre Tourist   CYCLING, BOAT TOUR
(📞075-382 9618; www.bentretourist.vn; 65 Đ Dong
Khoi; ⊙7-11am & 1-5pm) Bike, motorboat and
speedboat rental; also arranges excursions
and tours.

🛏 Sleeping

Hung Vuong   HOTEL $
(📞075-382 2408; 166 Đ Hung Vuong; d/tw/ste
350,000/370,000/530,000d; ❄🐭) Good-value
Hung Vuong has an attractive riverfront
location, plus large clean rooms with tiled
floors, polished wooden furnishings and decent bathrooms.

Oasis Hotel   HOTEL $$
(http://bentrehoteloasis.com; 151C My An C, My
Thanh An; d US$27-35, f US$42; ❄@🛜🐭)
There's always a warm welcome at this pop-
ular, bright yellow and small hotel, run by an

affable and very helpful couple. It's south of
the river and best reached by taxi.

Ham Luong   HOTEL $$
(📞075-356 0560; www.hamluongtourist.com.
vn; 200 Đ Hung Vuong; d US$23-29, ste US$43;
❄@🛜🐭) The large, modern, riverfront
Ham Luong has huge, starkly decorated corridors, but the rooms are nicely furnished
and there's a swimming pool and gym.

🍴 Eating & Drinking

For ultra-cheap eats, head to the market,
where plenty of **food stalls** (dishes around
15,000d) await. Ham Luong's rooftop cafe is
good for a drink or an ice cream.

Nam Son   VIETNAMESE $
(📞075-382 2873; 40 Đ Phan Ngoc Tong; mains
20,000-60,000d) Centrally located, this place
attracts a lively local crowd thanks to its
popular grilled chicken, best washed down
with draught beer.

ⓘ Getting There & Away

Buses stop at the big **bus station** (Ben Xe Ben
Tre, Hwy 60), 5km northwest of the town centre (30,000d by *xe om*). Destinations include
HCMC (67,000d), Can Tho (55,000d), Ca Mau
(103,000d) and Ha Tien (134,000d). The last
buses to HCMC depart between 4pm and 5pm.

ⓘ Getting Around

Slow boats can be rented at the public pier
near the market. Figure on roughly 70,000d to
90,000d per hour, with a minimum of two hours
cruising the local canals.

Tra Vinh

📍 074 / POP 131,000

The boulevards of Tra Vinh, one of the prettiest towns in the Mekong Delta, are still lined with shady trees, harking back to an earlier era. With more than 140 Khmer pagodas dotting the province, Tra Vinh is a quiet place for exploring the Mekong's little-touted Cambodian connection. The town itself sees minimal tourist traffic, owing to an isolated location on a peninsula.

About 300,000 ethnic Khmer live in Tra Vinh province. They may seem an invisible minority as they all speak fluent Vietnamese and there's nothing outwardly distinguishing about their clothing or lifestyle. Dig a bit deeper and discover that Khmer culture is alive and well in these parts of Vietnam. Many of its numerous pagodas have schools to teach the Khmer language and many Tra Vinh locals can read and write Khmer at least as well as Vietnamese. Vietnam's Khmer minority are almost all followers of Theravada Buddhism. Between the ages of 15 and 20, most boys set aside a few months to live as monks (they decide themselves on the length of service). Khmer monks are allowed to eat meat, but cannot kill animals.

There is also a small but active Chinese community in Tra Vinh, one of the few such communities that remain in the Mekong Delta region.

◉ Sights

Ba Om Pond & Ang Pagoda   BUDDHIST TEMPLE
(Square Lake) Known as Ao Ba Om, this large, square pond surrounded by tall trees is a pleasing place for a stroll. It's a spiritual site for the Khmers and a picnic and drinking spot for local Vietnamese. It would have once served as a bathing pond for the 10th-century Angkor-era temple that was situated here.

Built on the temple ruins, Ang Pagoda (Chua Ang in Vietnamese; Angkor Rek Borei in Khmer) is a beautiful and venerable Khmer-style pagoda, fusing classic Khmer architecture with French colonial influences.

MEKONG DELTA TRA VINH

A NIGHT ON THE MEKONG

Spending the night onboard a boat on the Mekong River is a good way to explore more of the waterways that make up this incredible region and helps bring you closer to life on the river.

In addition to the options listed below, there are various companies offering luxury cruises between My Tho (including transfers from Ho Chi Minh City) and Siem Reap. **Pandaw Cruises** (www.pandaw.com; 7 nights US$1132-2713) is favoured by high-end tour companies. **Compagnie Fluviale du Mekong** (www.cf-mekong.com; 5 nights from US$2415) is smaller and is well regarded for its personal service and excellent food. Taking the competition to a new level of lush are **AmaWaterways** (www.amawaterways. com; 6 nights US$1599-2599) and **Heritage Line** (www.heritage-line.com; 7 nights US$3384-8129). The longer cruises mean a lot of time looking at very similar scenery, so it's arguably better just to opt for a shorter sector such as My Tho to Phnom Penh.

The more interesting options for overnighting on the Mekong include the following:

Bassac (📞 0710-382 9540; www.transmekong.com; overnight US$232) Offers a range of beautiful wooden boats for small groups. The standard itinerary is an overnight between Cai Be and Can Tho, but custom routes are possible.

Exotissimo (📞 08-3827 2911; www.exotissimo.com; overnight 4,123,000-12,659,000d) Up-market tour operator Exotissimo offers a variety of single- or multi-day tours of the delta by boat.

Le Cochinchine (📞 08-3993 4552; www.lecochinchine.com; price on application) Offers cruises on a luxurious converted rice barge and a traditional sampan that are akin to floating hotels. The main routes are Cai Be to Can Tho (overnight) or Cai Be to Sa Dec, Vinh Long and Can Tho (two nights). Private trips are available.

Mekong Eyes (📞 0710-246 0786; www.mekongeyes.com; price on application) A stunningly converted traditional rice barge, the name plays on the ever-present eyes painted on fishing boats throughout Vietnam. This stylish boat travels between Can Tho and Cai Be, but is also available for charter.

Tra Vinh

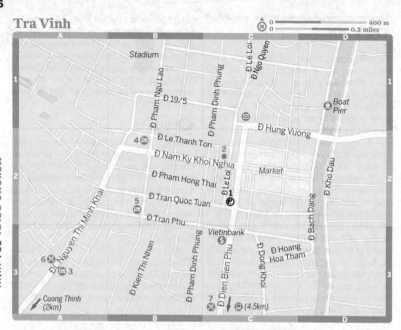

Tra Vinh

The interior features brightly painted scenes from the Buddha's life.

Opposite the pagoda entrance is the nicely presented **Khmer Minority People's Museum** (Bao Tang Van Hoa Dan Tac; ⊙ 7-11am & 1-5pm) `FREE`, which displays photos, costumes and other artefacts of traditional Khmer culture.

Ba Om Pond is 5km southwest of Tra Vinh, along the highway towards Vinh Long.

Ong Pagoda TAOIST TEMPLE
(Chua Ong & Chua Tau; 44 Đ Dien Bien Phu) The very ornate, brightly painted Ong Pagoda is a fully fledged Chinese pagoda and a very ac-

tive place of worship. The red-faced god on the altar is deified general Quan Cong who is believed to offer protection against war and is based on a historical figure, a 3rd century soldier.

The Ong Pagoda was founded in 1556 by the Fujian Chinese Congregation, but has been rebuilt a number of times. Recent visitors from Taiwan and Hong Kong have contributed money for the pagoda's restoration, which explains why it is in such fine shape.

Hang Pagoda BUDDHIST TEMPLE
(Chua Hang, Kampongnigrodha; Đ Dien Bien Phu) This modern Khmer pagoda is also known as the stork pagoda after the great white birds that nest in the tall trees here. It's a beautiful, peaceful complex and the birds are an interesting sight in themselves. The best time to see them is around dusk. The pagoda is located 6km south of town, about 300m past the bus station.

⌲ Tours

Tra Vinh Tourist BOAT TOUR
(☑ 074-385 8556; 64 Đ Le Loi; ⊙ 7.30-11am & 1.30-5pm) Arranges trips to various sites around the province, including boat cruises to local islands.

🛏 Sleeping

Tra Vinh Palace 2
HOTEL $

(☑074-386 3999; 48 Đ Pham Ngu Lao; d/tw/tr 180,000/220,000/250,000d; ❄@🛜) This friendly minihotel has sparkling rooms with tiled floors and either a bath-tub or a shub (shower tub). Double rooms are internal and windowless, so consider upgrading to a triple.

Hoan My
HOTEL $

(☑074-386 2211; 105A ĐL Nguyen Thi Minh Khai; r 200,000-360,000d; ❄🛜) With natty exposed brickwork, polished wooden floors and a lift, this hotel's trump card is its pricier rooms with oodles of space and balcony.

Tra Vinh Palace
HOTEL $

(☑074-386 4999; www.travinh.lofteight.com; 3 Đ Le Thanh Ton; r 250,000-350,000d; ❄🛜) Dominating the corner of a sleepy backstreet, this four-storey hotel is all pink columns, decorative plasterwork, terracotta tiling and balconies. The spacious rooms have high ceilings and mother-of-pearl-inlaid furniture.

🍴 Eating

Cuu Long Restaurant
VIETNAMESE $

(999 ĐL Nguyen Thi Minh Khai; mains from 70,000d) Behind the stolid facade of the government-run Cuu Long Hotel, this restaurant has an extensive English-language menu, including delicious salads and soups, and, for the more adventurous, snake and snails.

Cuong Thinh
VIETNAMESE $

(18A ĐL Nguyen Thi Minh Khai; mains 30,000-200,000d) Huge open-plan Cuong Thinh, 2km south of town on the road to Vinh Long, is popular for its traditional mains, local and regional favourites and palm-lined ambience.

Vi Huong
VIETNAMESE $

(37A Đ Dien Bien Phu; mains 15,000-45,000d) Cheap, cheerful hole-in-the-wall with wholesome traditional dishes like sour soup, fish in claypot and pork with rice.

❶ Getting There & Away

Tra Vinh is 65km from Vinh Long and 185km from HCMC. From Ben Tre it's easily reached by yet another new bridge and then a car ferry across the Co Chien River (per car 35,000d); work has already commenced on a bridge to replace this ferry.

The bus station (Ben Xe Khach Tra Vinh) is about 5km south of the town centre on Hwy 54, which is the continuation of the main street, Đ Dien Bien Phu. Buses head to HCMC (85,000d), Cao Lanh (49,000d) and Ha Tien (125,000d).

Vinh Long

☑070 / POP 130,000

The capital of Vinh Long province and plonked about midway between My Tho and Can Tho, Vinh Long may not be the largest town in the Mekong, but as a major transit hub it can be noisy and chaotic nonetheless. Flee the mayhem by heading to the riverfront, where plenty of cafes and restaurants afford respite. Despite a lack of in-town attractions, Vinh Long is the gateway to island life and some worthwhile sites, including Cai Be floating market, abundant orchards and rural homestays.

◉ Sights

Mekong River Islands
ISLAND

What makes a trip to Vinh Long worthwhile is not the town but the beautiful islands dotting the river. The islands are dedicated to agriculture, especially the growing of tropical fruits, which are shipped to markets in HCMC. This low-lying region is as much water as land and houses are generally built on stilts.

Some of the more popular islands to visit include Binh Hoa Phuoc and An Binh, but there are many others. You can take the public ferry to one of the islands and then walk or cycle around on your own. However, this isn't as interesting as a boat tour, since you won't cruise the narrow canals. You should be able to arrange a two- to three-hour

---

WORTH A TRIP

MEKONG RIVERSIDE RESORT & SPA

With a magnificent sense of seclusion, the four-star Mekong Riverside Resort & Spa (☑073-392 4466; www.mekongriversideresort.vn; Hoa Qui Ward, Hoa Khanh subdistrict, Cai Be district; lake/river view d US$85/110; ❄🛜⛲) has lovely thatched bungalows and stunning views across the vast river waters. Seize a fishing rod and angle for fish from your balcony or just sit back and watch the river boats cruise the Mekong at night. With free canoes, bird-watching tower and swimming pool, the resort offers the chance to fully experience the astonishing riverine world of the Mekong Delta. The resort can arrange transport.

Vinh Long

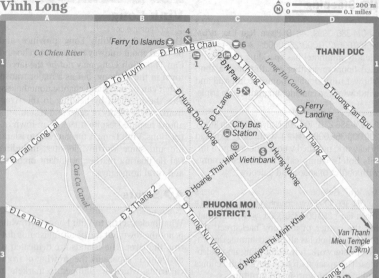

Vinh Long

cruise with one of the operators along the wharf for less than 300,000d.

Cai Be Floating Market MARKET
(☉ 5am-5pm) This bustling river market is worth including on a boat tour from Vinh Long, but aim for an early morning visit. Wholesalers on big boats moor here, each specialising in just a few types of fruit or vegetable, hanging samples of their goods from tall wooden poles. A notable sight is the huge and photogenic Catholic cathedral on the riverside.

It takes about an hour to reach the market from Vinh Long, but most people make detours on the way there or back to see the canals or visit orchards. For those travelling on an organised tour of the delta, it is customary to board a boat here, explore the islands and moor in Vinh Long before continuing to Can Tho.

Van Thanh Mieu Temple TEMPLE
(Phan Thanh Gian Temple; Đ Tran Phu; ☉ 5-11am & 1-7pm) Confucian temples such as this are rare in southern Vietnam. The front hall honours local hero Phan Thanh Gian, who led an uprising against the French colonists in 1930. When it became obvious that his revolt was doomed, Phan killed himself rather than be captured by the colonial army. The rear hall, built in 1866, has a portrait of Confucius above the altar.

Sitting in pleasant grounds across from the river, Van Thanh Mieu Temple is southeast of town; designed in Confucian style, it looks like it was lifted straight out of China. Don't confuse it with the smaller Quoc Cong Pagoda, which you'll pass on the way.

👉 Tours

Cuu Long Tourist BOAT TOUR
(☎ 070-382 3616; www.cuulongtourist.com; 2 Đ Phan B Chau; ☉ 7am-5pm) Offers a variety of boat tours ranging from three hours to three

days. Destinations include small canals, fruit orchards, brick kilns, a conical palm hat workshop and the Cai Be floating market.

🛏 Sleeping

You'll find much better accommodation in Ben Tre, Tra Vinh and Can Tho, and much more atmospheric accommodation in one of the local homestays. If you really must stay in Vinh Long town, the following are the best options.

Van Tram Guesthouse GUEST HOUSE $
(☑070-382 3820; 4 Đ 1 Thang 5; r 300,000-400,000d; ✿) A small, tall and slim place with just five rooms, the bonus here is the location near the river. Rooms (one with balcony) are a good size, but shower rooms are tiny.

Cuu Long Hotel HOTEL $$
(☑070-382 3656; www.cuulongtourist.com; 2 Đ Phan B Chau; s from 440,000d, d from 560,000d; ✿🖥) This clean but characterless government-run hotel sees midrange tour groups checking in as the boats leave from directly across the road. Rooms are spacious and have baths, and either balconies or river views.

🍴 Eating & Drinking

Dong Khanh VIETNAMESE $
(49 Đ 2 Thang 9; mains from 30,000d; ⊙6am-6pm) Popular and spacious Dong Khanh (the name means 'celebrate together') offers a varied menu, including hotpots, pork noodles, roast chicken and Cantonese rice. English-language menu.

Vinh Long Market VIETNAMESE $
(Đ 3 Thang 2) Great spot for local fruit and inexpensive street snacks.

Phuong Thuy VIETNAMESE $
(Đ Phan B Chau; mains from 30,000d; ⊙6am-10pm) Decent choice by the riverside, but it can fill up with tour groups.

Hoa Nang Cafe CAFE, BAR
(Đ 1 Thang 5; iced coffee 7000d; ⊙7am-11pm) Perched on the riverbank, this is a good

---

'HOMESTAYS' AROUND VINH LONG

For many travellers, the chance to experience river life and to share a home-cooked meal with a local family is a highlight of a Mekong visit. Perhaps 'homestay' is the wrong word: in most cases you won't actually be staying in the family home but in specially constructed accommodation more akin to a rudimentary hostel.

Some homestays have large communal rooms with bunks, while others offer basic bungalows with shared facilities and some even have rooms with en suites. Dinner and breakfast is usually included. In some places you'll share a meal with the family, while in bigger places the experience is more like a restaurant. The only constant that you can be guaranteed is a verdant, rustic setting and a taste of rural life.

Although many tourists book through group tours in Ho Chi Minh City, there's no reason you can't do it yourself – just take the ferry from Vinh Long and then a xe om (motorbike taxi) to your preferred choice. Note that some hosts are unlikely to speak much English, but welcome foreign guests just the same.

Ba Linh (☑070-385 8683, mobile 0939 138 142; balinhhomestay@gmail.com; 95 An Thanh, An Binh; r 350,000d) Run by friendly Mr Truong, this traditional-looking and popular place has six simple, high-roofed, partitioned rooms in a line, all with fan. Breakfast and dinner is included in the price.

Ngoc Sang (☑070-385 8694; 95/8 Binh Luong, An Binh Village; per person US$15) Readers love this friendly, canal-facing homestay. The food is good, free bikes are available and you can even help out in the family's orchard, if you feel so inclined.

Ut Trinh (☑070-395 4255, mobile 0919 002 505; vinhlongmekongtravel@yahoo.com; Hoa Qui, Hoa Ninh, An Binh; r US$15-25) Cordial owner Trinh speaks excellent English at this very pleasant, fresh and clean homestay with excellent rooms in two buildings on a veggie/fruit farm.

Nam Thanh (☑070-385 8883; namthanhhomestayvn@gmail.com; 172/9 Binh Luong, An Binh; from US$12) Four hundred metres from the jetty (the owner can pick you up), this friendly 26-bed camp-style homestay offers fold-up single beds in a communal space and sturdier doubles in rattan and bamboo quarters.

place to enjoy an iced coffee or scented tea in the morning or to quaff your first beer back on dry land after a river trip.

ℹ️ Getting There & Away

BOAT

Cargo boats sometimes take passengers from Vinh Long all the way to Chau Doc (near the Cambodian border); enquire locally, near the ferry landing.

BUS

Vinh Long's **city bus station** (Ben Xe Thanh Pho Vinh Long; Đ 3 Thang 2), conveniently located in the middle of town, has buses to HCMC (90,000d) and Sa Dec (9000d). For other services you're best to go to the **provincial bus station** (Hwy 1A), 3km south of town on the way to Can Tho. Buses to Can Tho (40,000d), HCMC (100,000d) and other destinations leave from here. A motorbike taxi will cost around 300,000d from the centre of town to the provincial bus station.

CAR & MOTORBIKE

Vinh Long is just off Hwy 1A, 33km from Can Tho, 66km from My Tho and 136km from HCMC.

Can Tho

📋 071 / POP 1.2 MILLION

The epicentre of the Mekong Delta, Can Tho is the largest city in the region and feels like a metropolis after a few days exploring the backwaters. As the political, economic, cultural and transportation centre of the Mekong Delta, it's a buzzing town with a lively waterfront lined with sculpted gardens and an appealing blend of narrow backstreets and wide boulevards. It is also the perfect base for nearby floating markets, the major draw for tourists who come here to boat along the many canals and rivers leading out of town.

◉ Sights

Ong Temple   TEMPLE
(32 D Hai Ba Trung; ⊙6am-8pm) FREE In a fantastic location facing the Can Tho River and decorated with huge incense coils, this Chinese temple is set inside the Guangzhou Assembly Hall (Đ Hai Ba Trung) and is the most interesting religious site in town. It was originally built in the late 19th century to worship Kuang Kung, a deity symbolising loyalty, justice, reason, intelligence, honour and courage, among other merits.

Approaching the engraved screen, the right side is dedicated to the Goddess of Fortune and the left side is reserved for the worship of General Ma Tien. In the centre of the temple is Kuang Kung flanked by the God of Earth and the God of Finance.

Can Tho Museum   MUSEUM
(1 ĐL Hoa Binh; ⊙8-11am & 2-5pm Tue-Thu, 8-11am & 6.30-9pm Sat & Sun) FREE The large, well-presented Can Tho Museum brings local history to life with manikins and life-size reproductions of buildings, including a Chinese pagoda and a house interior. Displays (with ample English translations) focus on the Khmer and Chinese communities, plant and fish specimens, rice production and, inevitably, the American War.

Munirensay Pagoda   BUDDHIST TEMPLE
(36 ĐL Hoa Binh; ⊙8am-5pm) FREE This pagoda was originally built in 1946 to serve Can Tho's Khmer community. The ornamentation is typical of Khmer Theravada Buddhist pagodas, with none of the multiple Bodhisattvas and Taoist spirits common in Vietnamese Mahayana pagodas.

☞ Tours

The undisputed highlight of any visit to Can Tho is taking a boat ride through the canals to a floating market. The cost is around US$5 per hour for a small boat, which can carry two or three passengers. For boat operators (mostly women), just wander along the riverside near the giant statue of Ho Chi Minh. You can also book through Can Tho Tourist, but this leaves little room for negotiation.

Larger motorboats can go further afield and it's worth hiring one to make a tour of the Mekong River itself. Check the going rates at Can Tho Tourist, then see what's on offer at the pier by the Ninh Kieu hotel. Prices range from 200,000d for a three-hour tour to 350,000d for a five-hour tour. Negotiation is the name of the game.

🛏️ Sleeping

Can Tho boasts the best range of accommodation in the Mekong Delta, so lie back and enjoy.

⭐ Xoai Hotel   HOTEL $
(📋0907 652 927; http://hotelxoai.com; 93 Đ Mau Than; s US$10, d US$14-26, tw US$19; ✳️@🛜) Fantastic value at this friendly, efficient hotel with bright, mango-coloured (the hotel

Can Tho

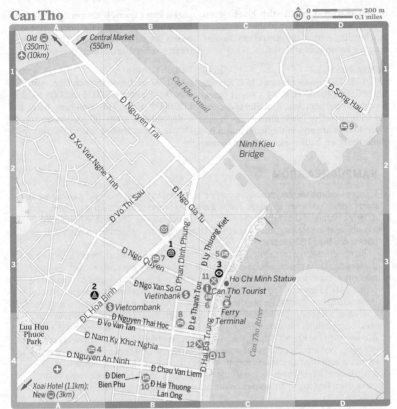

0 _____ 200 m
0 _____ 0.1 miles

name means 'Mango Hotel'), airy rooms. Helpful staff speak excellent English and there's a roof terrace with hammocks.

Kim Lan Hotel HOTEL **$**
(☎071-381 7049; www.kimlancantho.com.vn; 138A Đ Nguyen An Ninh; r US$20-48; ✴@🛜) 🅿 This very clean minihotel has chic rooms with contemporary furnishings and artworks on the wall. Even the small, windowless US$20 standard rooms are perfectly adequate, and deluxe rooms are lovely.

Xuan Mai Minihotel HOTEL **$**
(☎071-382 3578; tcdac@yahoo.com; 17 Đ Dien Bien Phu; r US$12; ✴🛜) Located down a small lane, this place is popular with budget tour groups thanks to spacious, clean and surprisingly quiet rooms with TVs, fridges and hot showers.

Phuong Nam HOTEL **$**
(☎071-376 3959; 118/9/39 Đ Tran Van Kheo; r US$20; ✴@🛜) On the same road as the

central market, this smartish hotel (seven storeys, with lift) is closer to the bus station in a bustling part of the central city. Rooms have big bathrooms and wi-fi.

★ **Kim Tho Hotel** HOTEL $$
(☎071-381 7517; www.kimtho.com; 1A Đ Ngo Gia Tu; r 950,000-1,400,000d; ❄ 📶) A smart hotel, verging on the boutique, Kim Tho is decked out with attractive fabric furnishings in the foyer. Rooms are stylish throughout and include designer bathrooms. Cheaper rooms are on lower floors, but superior rooms have hardwood flooring and the pricier river-view rooms are still a great deal. There is also a rooftop coffee bar on the 12th floor.

Saigon Cantho HOTEL $$
(☎071-382 5831; www.saigoncantho.com.vn; 55 Đ Phan Dinh Phung; s 476,000-1,190,000d, 562,000-1,190,000d; ❄ @) This well-kept hotel has a dependable range of good-value rooms. Deluxe rooms are like suites and come with

KAMPUCHEA KROM

Visitors to some Mekong provinces may be surprised to find Khmer towns whose inhabitants speak a different language, follow a different brand of Buddhism and have a vastly different history and culture to their Vietnamese neighbours. Though the Khmer are a minority in the Mekong, they were the first inhabitants here, with an ancestry dating back more than 2000 years.

Kampuchea Krom (meaning 'Lower Cambodia') is the unofficial Khmer name for the Mekong Delta region, whose indigenous inhabitants are the Khmer Krom, an ethnic minority living in southern Vietnam. The Khmer Krom trace their origins back to the 1st century AD, to the founding of Funan, a maritime empire that stretched from the Malay Peninsula to the Mekong. Archaeologists believe Funan was a sophisticated society that built canals, traded in precious metals and had a high level of political organisation as well as agricultural know-how. Following the Funan came the Chenla empire (630–802 AD) and then the Khmer empire, the mightiest in Southeast Asia, which saw the creation of Angkor Wat among other great achievements. By the 17th century, however, the empire was in ruins, under pressure from the expansionist Thais and Vietnamese. This was a time of rising power for the Vietnamese empire, which began expanding south, conquering first the Cham empire before setting their sights on Khmer lands in the Mekong Delta.

According to some historians, there were around 40,000 Khmer families living around Prey Nokor when the Vietnamese arrived in the 1600s, following the granting of settlement rights by King Chey Chettha in 1623. Prey Nokor was an important port for the Cambodian kingdom and was renamed Saigon in 1698. Waves of Vietnamese settlers populated the city as other colonists continued south. Prior to their arrival there were 700 Khmer temples scattered around south Vietnam. Over the next century the Khmer Krom fought and won some minor victories in the region, expelling the intruders, only to lose their gains in new rounds of attacks.

When the French subjugated Indochina in the 19th century, the hope of an independent Kampuchea Krom would be forever destroyed. Although the ethnic Khmer were a majority in southern Vietnam at that time, the French didn't incorporate the colony with Cambodia but made it a separate protectorate called Cochinchina. On 4 June 1949, the French formally annexed Kampuchea Krom, a day of sorrow for many Cambodians, although the writing had been on the wall centuries earlier as the area was colonised.

Since independence in 1954, the Vietnamese government has adopted a policy of integration and forced assimilation (the Khmer Krom must take Vietnamese family names and learn the Vietnamese language, among other things). According to the Khmer Kampuchea-Krom Federation (KKF; www.khmerkrom.org), the Khmer Krom continue to suffer persecution. They report difficult access to Vietnamese health services, religious discrimination (Khmer Krom are Theravada Buddhists, unlike Vietnam's Mahayana Buddhists) and racial discrimination.

The Khmer are the poorest segment of the population. Even their numbers remain a contentious topic: Vietnam reports one million Khmer Krom, while KKF claims there are seven million Khmer living in southern Vietnam.

flat-screen TVs and fruit baskets; all rooms have safety deposit boxes.

Ninh Kieu 2   HOTEL $$

(☑071-625 2377; www.ninhkieuhotel.com; 3 ĐL Hoa Binh; r 777,000-1,097,000d; ❀ ⬤) This large hotel has clean, comfortable rooms with handsome furnishings. The windowless, cheaper rooms are pleasantly furnished with a minute corner bath. Superior rooms may have windows facing the interior coutryard, so check first. The lobby is a study in Vietnamese glam, with big chandeliers, marble tiles and a neon sign over reception.

★Nam Bo Boutique Hotel   BOUTIQUE HOTEL $$$

(☑071-381 9139; www.nambocantho.com; 1 Đ Ngo Quyen; r from US$140) Presiding over a mere seven suites in a colonial-era building, this lovely riverfront hotel revels in traditional presentation and contemporary elegance, although service can be rather flat. Excellent restaurants on the top floor, and at ground level.

★Victoria Can Tho Resort   RESORT $$$

(☑071-381 0111; www.victoriahotels.asia; Cai Khe Ward; r US$91-230, ste US$277-310; ❀ @ ⬤ ⬤) With particularly gracious service, this hotel defines style and sophistication in the Mekong Delta. Designed with a French colonial look, the rooms – along stunning corridors – are set around an inviting pool that looks out over the river. Facilities include an excellent restaurant, an open-air bar and a riverside spa. There are plenty of activities on offer, including cycling tours, cooking classes and cruises on the *Lady Hau*, a converted rice barge.

🍴 Eating & Drinking

For tasty cheap eats, try the **central market food stalls** (Đ Tran Quang Khai). They're in their own covered area, two scant blocks north of the main market building. Another favourite, 'Hotpot Alley' is the place for fish and duck hotpots, with restaurants stuffed into an alley (Hem 1) between Đ Mau Than and Đ Ly Tu Trung east of Xoai Hotel.

Sao Hom   VIETNAMESE, INTERNATIONAL $

(50 Đ Hai Ba Trung; mains 45,000-160,000d; ⊙8am-11pm) Set in the (now upmarket) former market and overseen by staff in *ao dai* (the national dress of Vietnam), Sao Hom has an atmospheric, breezy riverside setting, and is a great spot for lunch or a morning coffee.

Mekong   VIETNAMESE, INTERNATIONAL $

(38 Đ Hai Ba Trung; mains from 25,000d; ⊙7am-8pm) Looking onto busy Hai Ba Trung, this travellers' favourite has a good blend of local and international food at reasonable prices. Try the lovely sour soup with fish (40,000d); good veggie selection.

Nam Bo   VIETNAMESE, INTERNATIONAL $

(☑071-382 3908; http://nambocantho.com; Nam Bo Boutique Hotel, 1 Đ Ngo Quyen; mains from 45,000d, set meals 210,000d; ⊙8am-11pm) With a charming, romantic Mediterranean feel, this restaurant on the ground floor of the Nam Bo hotel is more affordable than the restaurant on the top floor, but it doesn't have the views.

New Delhi Indian Food   INDIAN $

(128 Đ Hai Ba Trung; mains from 40,000d; ⊙10am-11pm) A deficiency in charm at this stark, soulless Indian restaurant (don't bring a date) is balanced out by a surfeit of fine flavours in its scrummy vindaloos, kormas, samosas and naans.

Phuong Nam   VIETNAMESE $

(48 Đ Hai Ba Trung; mains from 40,000d; ⊙10am-10pm) With check tablecloths and a Mediterranean feel, this place has an upstairs terrace for people-watching, although downstairs is slightly more upmarket. Snake is the speciality but vegetarian options get a look-in.

L'Escale   VIETNAMESE, INTERNATIONAL $$$

(☑071-381 9139; Nam Bo Boutique Hotel, 1 Đ Ngo Quyen; mains 70,000-410,000d; ⊙6am-10.30pm) With tantalising river views from the top of the Nam Bo hotel, this romantic choice impresses with its menu and strong wine list.

🛍 Shopping

Old Market   MARKET

(50 Đ Hai Ba Trung) Roofed with terracotta tiles edged with ceramic decorations, this atmospheric French-era market building is the centrepiece of the city's attractive riverfront tourist district. The blood, guts and chaos of the original market have moved north to the central market (and to some of the neighbouring streets), leaving upmarket tourist-orientated stalls selling lacquerware, clothes, pillowslips, postcards and the like.

Central Market   MARKET

(Đ Tran Van Kheo) Can Tho's local market sprawls over four buildings and several blocks abutting the Cai Khe Canal, which many local farmers and wholesalers still use to transport their goods. The main market building focuses on produce: a colourful, smelly mess of meat, fish, fruit and vegetables. Across the road is the cloth market.

Food stalls take up the following block and behind that is another large building full of bags, belts and jewellery.

ℹ️ Information

Can Tho Tourist (☎071-382 1852; www.canthotourist.com.vn; 50 Đ Hai Ba Trung) Helpful staff speak both English and French here and decent city maps are available, as well as general information on attractions in the area. There is also a booking desk for Vietnam Airlines and Jetstar.

Hospital (Benh Vien; ☎071-382 0071; 4 Đ Chau Van Liem)

Main Post Office (2 ĐL Hoa Binh) Postal services and internet access.

ℹ️ Getting There & Away

AIR

Can Tho opened a new international airport in early 2011, but at the time of writing the only services were **Vietnam Airlines** (www.vietnamairlines.com) and **VASCO** (www.vasco.com.vn) flights to Phu Quoc Island, the Con Dao Islands, Hanoi and HCMC (with flights to Danang on the cards). The airport is 10km northwest of the city centre, accessed from Đ Le Hong Phong, the continuation of Đ Nguyen Trai. A taxi into town will cost around 180,000d.

BUS

Can Tho has two bus stations. The **old bus station** (Ben Xe Khach Can Tho; cnr Đ Nguyen Trai & Đ Hung Vuong) is centrally located on the northern edge of the city centre, with regular buses to HCMC's Mien Tay bus station (100,000d to 110,000d), Cao Lanh (60,000d), Ben Tre (70,000d), My Tho (70,000d), Ca Mau (90,000d), Chau Doc (60,000d) and Long Xuyen (40,000d). The **new bus station** is in the southwest, with buses to HCMC (110,000d), Ca Mau (110,000d) and Dalat (320,000d).

BOAT

There are several boat services to other cities in the Mekong Delta, including hydrofoils to Ca Mau (150,000d, three to four hours), passing through Phung Hiep.

ℹ️ Getting Around

The *xe loi* is the main form of transport around Can Tho; these makeshift vehicles are unique to the Mekong Delta. Essentially a two-wheeled wagon attached to the rear of a motorbike, they resemble a motorised *cyclo*, but with four wheels touching the ground rather than two. Fares around town should be about 10,000d per person (they can carry two, or sometimes more). From the old bus station to the riverside is a 30,000d ride.

Around Can Tho

Arguably the biggest drawcard of the delta is its colourful **floating markets**, which hug the banks of wide stretches of river. Most market folk set out early to avoid the daytime heat, so try to visit between 6am and 8am and beat the tourist tide. The real tides, however, are also a factor, as bigger boats must often wait until the water is high enough for them to navigate.

Improved roads and public transport mean that some of the smaller, rural floating markets are disappearing, but many of the larger markets near urban areas are still going strong.

Rural areas of Can Tho province, renowned for their durian, mangosteen and orange orchards, can be easily reached from Can Tho by boat or bicycle.

⊙ Sights & Activities

Cai Rang Floating Market   MARKET

Just 6km from Can Tho in the direction of Soc Trang is Cai Rang, the biggest floating market in the Mekong Delta. There is a bridge here that serves as a great vantage point for photography. The market is best before 9am, although some vendors hang out until noon.

It is quite an experience to see this in full swing, but it's well worth getting up extra early to beat the tour-group crowds or you may end up seeing almost as many foreigners as market traders.

Cai Rang can be seen from the road, but getting here is far more interesting by boat (US$6). From the market area in Can Tho it takes about an hour by river, or you can drive to the Cau Dau Sau boat landing (by the Dau Sau Bridge), from where it takes only about 10 minutes to reach the market.

Phong Dien Floating Market   MARKET

Perhaps the Mekong Delta's best floating market, Phong Dien has fewer motorised craft and more stand-up rowing boats. Less crowded than Cai Rang, there are also far fewer tourists. It's at its bustling best between 6am and 8am. The market is 20km southwest of Can Tho; most get here by road.

A boat trip here will require a 3.30am start (return 600,000d), but you need to arrange it the day before. It is theoretically possible to do a whirlwind boat trip, visiting the small canals on the way and finishing back at the Cai Rang floating market. This journey should take approximately five hours return from Can Tho.

For trips on smaller boats (US$4 per hour), operators can be found along Đ Hai Ba Trung by the river, but inspect boats first; the faster alternative is to take a *xe om* or taxi and then hire a boat at the other end.

Bang Lang
BIRD-WATCHING

(admission 20,000d; ☺5am-6pm) On the road between Can Tho and Long Xuyen, Bang Lang (also called Vuon Co) is a magnificent 1.3-hectare bird sanctuary with astonishing views of thousands of resident storks. There is a tall viewing platform to see the storks filling the branches; it's an absolutely incredible sight (the best times of day are around dawn and dusk).

Bang Lang is in the Thot Not district, about 15km southeast of Long Xuyen. Look for a sign in the hamlet of Thoi An saying 'Ap Von Hoa'. Coming from Can Tho the sign is on the west side of the road, immediately after a small bridge. It is a couple of kilometres off the main highway – reachable on foot within 30 minutes, or you can hire a motorbike taxi for about 20,000d.

Soc Trang
☑ 079 / POP 174,000

It's not the most charming of Mekong towns, but Soc Trang is an important centre for the Khmer people, who constitute 28% of the province's population. It's a useful base for exploring Khmer temples in the area, although you can probably skip these if Cambodia is on your radar.

◎ Sights

Bat Pagoda
BUDDHIST TEMPLE

The Bat Pagoda (Chua Doi) is a large, peaceful, Khmer monastery compound with a resident colony of fruit bats. Literally hundreds of these creatures hang from the trees: the largest weigh about 1kg, with a wingspan of about 1.5m. They are not toilet trained, so watch out when standing under a tree, or bring an umbrella.

WORTH A TRIP

XA LON PAGODA

Originally built in wood in the 18th century, this magnificent Khmer pagoda was completely rebuilt in 1923 but proved to be too small. From 1969 to 1985, the present-day large pagoda was slowly built as funds trickled in from donations. The ceramic tiles on the exterior of the pagoda are particularly impressive.

The monks lead an austere life, eating breakfast at 6am and seeking alms until 11am, when they hold an hour of worship. They eat again just before noon, study in the afternoon and eat no dinner. The pagoda also operates a school for the study of Buddhism and Sanskrit.

It's located 12km from Soc Trang, towards Bac Lieu, on Hwy 1A.

Optimum times to visit are early morning and at least an hour before sunset, when the bats are most active. Around dusk hundreds of bats swoop out of the trees to forage in orchards all over the Mekong Delta, much to the consternation of farmers, who are known to trap the bats and eat them. Inside the compound the creatures are protected: the bats seem to know this and stick around.

The monks don't ask for money, although donations won't hurt. The pagoda is decorated with gilt Buddhas and murals paid for by overseas Vietnamese contributors. In one room there's a life-size statue of the monk who was the former head of the complex.

The Bat Pagoda is 2km south of Soc Trang, a 20,000d *xe om* ride away (or you can easily walk). Head south on Đ Le Hong Phong and after about a kilometre veer right onto Đ Van Ngoc Chinh.

Clay Pagoda
BUDDHIST TEMPLE

(163 Đ Ton Duc Thang) Buu Son Tu (Precious Mountain Temple) was founded over 200 years ago by a Chinese family named Ngo. Unassuming from the outside, this temple is highly unusual in that nearly every object inside is made entirely of clay. Consequently, it is better known as Chua Dat Set, or Clay Pagoda.

The hundreds of statues and sculptures that adorn the interior were hand-sculpted by the monk Ngo Kim Tong. From the age of 20 until his death at 62, this ingenious artisan dedicated his life to decorating the pagoda. Though the decor borders on kitsch, the pagoda is an active place of worship, and totally different from the Khmer and Vietnamese pagodas elsewhere in Soc Trang.

Entering the pagoda, visitors are greeted by one of Ngo's largest creations – a six-tusked clay elephant, which is said to have appeared in a dream of Buddha's mother. Behind this is the central altar, fashioned from more than five tonnes of clay. In the altar are a thousand Buddhas seated on lotus petals. Other highlights include a 13-storey Chinese-style tower over 4m tall. The tower features 208 cubby holes, each with a mini-Buddha figure inside, and is decorated with 156 dragons.

Needless to say, the clay objects in the pagoda are fragile, so explore with care. Donations are welcome.

Kh'leang Pagoda
BUDDHIST TEMPLE

(Chua Kh'leang; 68 Đ Ton Duc Thang) Except for the rather garish paint job, this pagoda could have been transported straight from Cambodia. Originally built from bamboo in 1533, it had a complete concrete rebuild in 1905. Several monks reside in the pagoda, which also serves as a base for over 150 novices who come from around the Mekong Delta to study at Soc Trang's College of Buddhist Education across the street.

There are seven religious festivals held here every year, drawing people from outlying areas of the province.

Khmer Museum
MUSEUM

(079-382 2983; 23 Đ Nguyen Chi Thanh; 7.30-11am & 1.30-5pm Mon-Fri) FREE Dedicated to the history and culture of Vietnam's Khmer minority, this small museum doubles as a sort of cultural centre. Traditional dance and music shows are periodically staged here for larger groups. Displays are limited to photos and a few traditional costumes and other artefacts.

The museum, opposite Kh'leang Pagoda, may appear closed; if so, rouse someone to let you in.

✸ Festivals & Events

Once a year, the Khmer community turns out for the Oc Bom Boc Festival (known as Bon Om Touk or the Water Festival in Cambodia), with longboat races on the Soc Trang River. Races are held according to the lunar calendar on the 15th day of the 10th moon, which roughly means November. The races start at noon, but things get jumping in Soc Trang the evening before. The event attracts visitors from all over Vietnam and even Cambodia, so hotel space is at a premium.

🛏 Sleeping & Eating

Soc Trang has several hotels but it's hard to be particularly enthusiastic about any of them, and you're better off continuing on to Can Tho. Few restaurants in Soc Trang have English menus, and prices are often omitted from the Vietnamese ones.

Que Huong Hotel
HOTEL $

(079-361 6122; 128 Đ Nguyen Trung Truc; r 270,000d, ste 450,000-600,000d; ❄ 🔊) Rooms here are in better shape than the no-nonsense exterior might first suggest. The suites include a sunken bath and a full-size bar, although drinks are not included. Wi-fi in lobby only.

Quan Hung
VIETNAMESE $

(24/5 Đ Hung Vuong; mains 40,000-130,000d) Down a lane off the main road into town, this large, open-sided restaurant is perpetually popular, serving up delicious grilled meat and fish. If there are a few of you, try a hotpot.

ℹ Getting There & Away

Buses run between Soc Trang and most Mekong cities. The bus station is on Hwy 1A, near the corner of Đ Hung Vuong, the main road into town. The 90-minute ride to Can Tho costs 60,000d; to Bac Lieu, 65,000d; and to Ha Tien, 130,000d.

Bac Lieu & Around

0781 / POP 136,000

Few people stop in Bac Lieu, but bird-watchers pass through en route to the excellent sanctuary near town. The town has a few elegant but forlorn French colonial buildings lining the waterfront, but little else of interest.

The grandest of these buildings is the Cong Tu Hotel (0781-395 3304; 13 Đ Dien Bien Phu; r 300,000-500,000d; ❄), built in 1919 as a private mansion with materials imported from France. The family's oldest son was a notorious playboy (cong tu) whose fabled exploits included burning money to boil an egg in an effort to impress a woman. After squandering the family fortune, the house was sold and converted into a hotel where you can still stay. Alternatively, inexpensive guesthouses line the road into town from Soc Trang (rooms cost around US$10).

Sights

Bac Lieu Bird Sanctuary NATURE RESERVE
(Vuon Chim Bac Lieu; ☎0781-383 5991; admission 15,000d; ⏱7.30am-5pm) This bird sanctuary, 6km southwest of town, is notable for its 50-odd species of bird, including a large population of graceful white herons. Bird populations peak in the rainy season – approximately May to October. The birds nest until about January, then fly off in search of greener pastures. There are basically no birds here from February until the rainy season begins again.

The trek is through dense (and often muddy) jungle: bring plenty of repellent, good shoes, water and binoculars. Pay the admission fee when you reach the entrance; an observation tower is located within the sanctuary. You can (and should) hire a guide here, as you may get lost without one. The guides aren't supposed to receive money, so tip them discreetly; most guides do not speak English. Transport and guides can also be arranged through the Bac Lieu Tourist office (at a mark-up).

Eating & Drinking

Pho Ngheu Thanh Huong VIETNAMESE $
(43 Tran Quynh; mains 25,000-47,000d) While you could probably buy similar *pho* (noodle soups) and *banh mi* (filled baguettes) from a street stall, this smart eatery offers a fairy-lit rooftop from which to watch the traffic zoom by.

Kitty CAFE, BAR
(cnr Đ Tran Phu & Ba Trieu; ⏱10am-11pm) This 1st-floor cafe overlooking one of the many busy roundabouts on Đ Tran Phu is black and white and chrome all over, with chic chairs and a wall of TV screens. A good spot for Vietnamese coffee and cake, or something a little harder.

Information

Bac Lieu Tourist (☎0781-382 4273; www.baclieutourist.com; 2 Đ Hoang Van Thu; ⏱7-11am & 1-5pm) Helpful tourist office with basic town maps and information about trips to the bird sanctuary.

Post Office (20 Đ Tran Phu) Off the main roundabout.

Getting There & Around

The **bus station** (Ben Xe Tinh Bac Lieu) is on the main road into town, 1km north of the centre. From here you can catch regular buses to Ho Chi Minh City (130,000d), Soc Trang (65,000d), Ha Tien (130,000d), Ca Mau (30,000d) and Can Tho (65,000d).

Ca Mau

☎0780 / POP 205,000

On the swampy shores of the Ganh Hao River, Ca Mau is the capital and sole city in Ca Mau province, which covers the southern tip of the Mekong Delta. It's a remote and inhospitable area that wasn't cultivated until the late 17th century. Owing to the boggy terrain, the province has the lowest population density in southern Vietnam. It incorporates the country's largest swamp and is known for its voracious mosquitoes.

Given that, it's perhaps surprising that Ca Mau city is such a pleasant place. With wide boulevards, parks and busy shopping streets, the town has developed rapidly in recent years but sees few tourists. The main attractions are the nearby swamps and forests, explorable by boat.

Sights

Ca Mau Market MARKET
(Đ Le Loi) Traditionally Ca Mau life was lived facing the water, and while the floating market has disappeared in recent years, the main market still sprawls along the streets to the west of Phung Hiep Canal, south of Đ Phan Ngoc Hien.

Cao Dai Temple TEMPLE
(Đ Phan Ngoc Hien) Like all Cao Dai places of worship, this temple (built in 1966) is a riot of colour and ornamentation.

Sleeping

Quoc Te Hotel HOTEL $
(International Hotel; ☎0780-366 6666; www.hotel-quocte.com; 179 Đ Phan Ngoc Hien; r from 280,000d; ❄📶🏊) Breakfast and airport pick-ups are included in the price at this business hotel with swimming pool, massage service and a lift. It falls short of international standards, but rooms are smart enough.

Thanh Son Hotel GUEST HOUSE $
(☎0780-355 0992; 23 Đ Phan Ngoc Hien; r 80,000-230,000d; ❄) This light and bright five-storey minihotel has clean rooms with tiled

Ca Mau

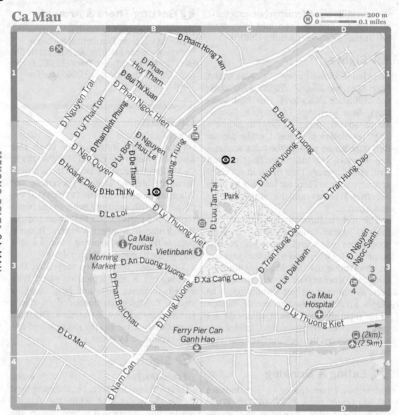

MEKONG DELTA CA MAU

Ca Mau

floors. Extras include TV and hot water, plus bathtubs in the more expensive rooms. Little English is spoken.

Anh Nguyet Hotel　　　　　　HOTEL **$$**
(☎0780-356 7666; www.anhnguyethotel.com; 207 Đ Phan Ngoc Hien; r US$29-49; ❈🛜) Romantically translating as the Moonlight Hotel, this

place attempts a glitzy look. Rooms are perfectly fine, although walls are thin and the carpets rather cheap.

✕ Eating

Ca Mau's speciality is shrimp, which is raised in ponds and mangrove forests. The best food is to be found at the cluster of small, cheap roadside restaurants and *banh mi* stalls in the streets around the market, particularly at the end of Đ Nguyen Huu Le. In the evening, the eastern end of Đ Pham Ngoc Hien becomes a big outdoor cafe.

Pho Xua　　　　　VIETNAMESE, SEAFOOD **$$**
(126 Đ Phan Ngoc Hien; mains 50,000-300,000d; ⊘7am-10pm) An atmospheric place set amid landscaped gardens draped in fairy lights, with a menu heavy on shrimp and other seafood dishes.

ℹ Information

Ca Mau Hospital (Benh Vien Ca Mau; ☎0780-383 1015; Đ Ly Thuong Kiet)

Ca Mau Tourist (☎0780-381 7057; www.camautravel.vn; 1B Đ An Duong Vuong; ☺9am-5pm)

ℹ Getting There & Around

AIR

Vietnam Air Service Company (VASCO; www.vasco.com.vn), a subsidiary of Vietnam Airlines, has two daily flights to and from HCMC (from 750,000d, one hour). The airport is 3km east of the centre, on Hwy 1A.

BOAT

At least three hydrofoils a day travel between Ca Mau and Rach Gia (125,000d, three hours) from **Ferry Pier Can Ganh Hao**, where you can also catch a speedboat south to Nam Can (60,000d, one hour). Boats to Can Tho (150,000d, three to four hours), with a stop in Phung Hiep, depart from **Cong Ca Mau pier** (Đ Quang Trung), 3km east of town.

BUS

Buses from HCMC to Ca Mau leave from Mien Tay bus station; express buses (130,000d) take around seven hours. Several daily express buses leave for HCMC between 5am and 10.30am. Daily buses also leave for Rach Gia (50,000d), Ha Tien (89,000d), Bac Lieu (50,000d), Can Tho (65,000d), Cao Lanh (83,000d), My Tho (100,000d) and Ben Tre (103,000d). The Ca Mau bus station is around 2.5km from the centre of town; head along Hwy 1A towards Bac Lieu.

CAR & MOTORBIKE

Hwy 1A now continues to Nam Can (50km), the southernmost town in Vietnam. Ca Mau is 176km from Can Tho (around three hours) and 329km from HCMC (approximately seven hours).

Around Ca Mau

U-Minh Forest

The town of Ca Mau borders the **U-Minh Forest** (admission 10,000d; ☺6am-5pm, closed Mar-May), a vast mangrove forest covering 1000 sq km of Ca Mau and Kien Giang provinces. Local people use certain species of mangrove as a source of timber, charcoal, thatch and tannin. When the mangroves flower, bees feed on the blossoms, providing both honey and wax.

As well as being an important habitat for waterfowl, the U-Minh Forest – the largest mangrove forest in the world beyond the Amazon basin – was a favourite hideout for the VC during the American War. The Americans responded with chemical defoliation, which caused enormous damage to the forests. The heavy rainfall slowly washed the dioxin out to sea and the forest is returning. Many eucalyptus trees have also been planted here because they have proved to be relatively dioxin-resistant.

Unfortunately the mangrove forests are being further damaged by clearing for shrimp-farming ponds, charcoal production and woodchipping, although the government has tried to limit these activities. In 2002 an area of 80 sq km was preserved as U Minh Thuong (Upper U-Minh) National Park.

The forest is known for its birdlife, and twitchers will enjoy a boat trip around Ca Mau, although the feathered flocks aren't nearly as ubiquitous as the swarms of mosquitoes. Thirty-minute boat trips around the forest cost 100,000d.

Ca Mau Tourist can arrange a boat tour for around US$140, but try to find better deals with locals down at the ferry pier where you can get a speedboat to Thu Bay (two hours), followed by a motorbike to U-Minh Forest for 70,000d.

Ca Mau Nature Reserve

Sometimes referred to as Ngoc Hien Bird Sanctuary, these 130 hectares form one of the least developed and most protected parts of the Mekong Delta region. Shrimp farming is prohibited here. Access is by boat.

ℹ TRAVEL BY HYDROFOIL

If you're tossing up between taking a hydrofoil or a bus, take the hydrofoil every time. They're less crowded and generally more comfortable, and the journey is also more interesting. The boats are low and long, meaning views are just above the waterline. The trip between Ca Mau and Rach Gia is particularly good, as it switches from a green, undeveloped section dotted with rattan houses near Ca Mau to a heavily built-up and industrial stretch approaching Rach Gia.

Rach Gia

☑ 077 / POP 206,000

A thriving port on the Gulf of Thailand and something of a southern boom town benefiting from a serious injection of Viet Kieu money, Rach Gia is home to significant numbers of both ethnic Chinese and ethnic Khmers. Most travellers zip straight through for boats to Phu Quoc Island, but the lively waterfront and bustling backstreets are worth exploration.

With its easy access to the sea and the proximity of Cambodia and Thailand, fishing, agriculture and smuggling are profitable trades in this province. The area was once famous for supplying the large feathers used to make ceremonial fans for the Imperial Court.

◉ Sights

Nguyen Trung Truc Temple   BUDDHIST TEMPLE

(18 Đ Nguyen Cong Tru) This temple is dedicated to Nguyen Trung Truc, a leader of the resistance campaign of the 1860s against the newly arrived French. The first temple structure was a simple building with a thatched roof; over the years it has been enlarged and rebuilt several times. In the centre of the main hall is a portrait of Nguyen Trung Truc on an altar.

Among other exploits, Nguyen Trung Truc led the raid that resulted in the burning of the French warship *Esperance*. Despite repeated attempts to capture him, Nguyen Trung Truc continued to fight until 1868, when the French took his mother and a number of civilians hostage and threatened to kill them if he did not surrender. Nguyen Trung Truc turned himself in and was executed by the French in the marketplace of Rach Gia on 27 October 1868.

Phat Lon Pagoda   BUDDHIST TEMPLE

(Chua Phat Lon; 151 Đ Quang Trung) This large Cambodian Theravada Buddhist pagoda, whose name means Big Buddha, was founded in the 19th century. Though all of the monks who live here are ethnic Khmers, ethnic Vietnamese also frequent the pagoda. Inside the sanctuary (*vihara*), figures of the Thich Ca Buddha (Sakyamuni, the Historical Buddha) wear pointed hats. Prayers are held here daily from 4am to 6am and 5pm to 7pm.

Kien Giang Museum   MUSEUM

(21 Đ Nguyen Van Troi; ⊗ 7.30-11am Mon-Fri & 1.30-5pm Mon-Wed) FREE Housed in an ornate gem of a French colonial-era building (once a private house), the collection here includes lots of war photos and some Oc-Eo artefacts and pottery.

🛏 Sleeping

There are clusters of hotels near the bus station on Đ Le Thanh Ton and near the boat pier on Đ Tu Do.

Kim Co Hotel   HOTEL $

(☑ 077-387 9610; www.kimcohotel.com; 141 Đ Nguyen Hung Son; r 350,000-400,000d; ❄️ 🛜) Centrally located, trim and tidy Kim Co is a masterclass in pastel shade. Bright and cheerful rooms have clean bathrooms, but most face the corridor, so pull the shades for privacy.

Hong Yen   HOTEL $

(☑ 077-387 9095; 259 Đ Mac Cuu; r 150,000-250,000d; ❄️ @ 🛜) Stretching over four pink floors, Hong Yen is a likeable minihotel with sizeable, clean rooms and friendly owners. There's a lift and some of the rooms have balconies.

🍴 Eating

Rach Gia is known for its seafood, dried cuttlefish, dried fish slices (*ca thieu*), fish sauce and black pepper.

Hai Au   VIETNAMESE, INTERNATIONAL $

(2 Đ Nguyen Trung Truc; mains 60,000-120,000d; ⊗ 6am-10pm; 🛜) A fancy restaurant by local standards, this cavernous eatery with chandeliers has a great location by the Cai Lon River. Seafood is popular, including crayfish and crab, and Western-style dishes also feature.

Quan F28   VIETNAMESE, SEAFOOD $

(28 Đ Le Thanh Thon; mains 25,000-60,000d) Convenient for the bus station hotels, this is lively by night and does inexpensive molluscs – shrimp, snails, blood cockles and the like.

ℹ Information

Benh Vien Hospital (☑ 077-394 9494; 80 Đ Nguyen Trung Truc) One of the better medical facilities in the Mekong Delta; privately operated.

Kien Giang Tourist (Du Lich Lu Hanh Kien Giang; ☑ 077-386 2081; ctycpdulichkg@vnn. vn; 5 Đ Le Loi; ⊗ 7am-5pm) Provincial tourism authority.

Rach Gia

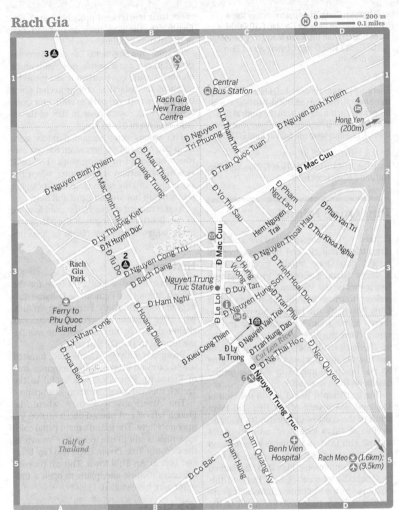

MEKONG DELTA RACH GIA

Main Post Office (☎ 077-387 3008; 2 Đ Mau Than) Has the usual attached internet services.

ℹ Getting There & Away

AIR

Vietnam Airlines has daily flights to and from HCMC (from 1,100,000d) and Phu Quoc Island (from 800,000d). The airport is 10km southeast of the centre, along Hwy 80 in the direction of Long Xuyen; a taxi into town will cost around 80,000d.

BOAT

Boats to Phu Quoc Island leave from the centrally located ferry terminal at the western end

Rach Gia

⦿ Sights

1 Kien Giang Museum	C4
2 Nguyen Trung Truc Temple	B3
3 Phat Lon Pagoda	A1

🛏 Sleeping

4 Hong Yen	D1
5 Kim Co Hotel	C3

🍴 Eating

6 Hai Au	C4
7 Quan F28	B1

of Đ Nguyen Cong Tru. Approximately three hydrofoils leave daily for Ca Mau (110,000d, three hours) from the **Rach Meo ferry terminal** (☑ 077-381 1306; Đ Ngo Quyen), about 2km south of town.

BUS

There are regular services to Ca Mau (50,000d, three hours), Ha Tien (38,000d, two hours) and other cities in the region from the **central bus station** (260A Đ Nguyen Binh Khiem) north of town. A taxi into town will cost around 20,000d.

CAR & MOTORBIKE

Rach Gia is 90km from Ha Tien, 120km from Can Tho and 270km from HCMC.

Phu Quoc Island

☑ 077 / POP 85,000

Fringed with white-sand beaches and with large tracts still cloaked in dense, tropical jungle, Phu Quoc rapidly morphed from a sleepy island backwater to a must-visit beach escape for Western expats and sun-seeking tourists. Beyond the resorts lining Long Beach, it's still largely undeveloped, so there's ample room for exploration and escaping. Dive the reefs, kayak in the bays, eat up the back-road miles on a motorbike, or just live the life of a lotus eater by lounging on the beach, indulging in a massage and dining on fresh seafood.

The tear-shaped island lies in the Gulf of Thailand, 45km west of Ha Tien and 15km south of the coast of Cambodia. It's no lightweight: at 48km long (with an area of 574 sq km), Phu Quoc is Vietnam's largest island (about the same size as Singapore). It's also politically contentious: Phu Quoc is claimed by Cambodia who call it Koh Tral and this explains why the Vietnamese have built a substantial military base covering much of the northern end of the island. It was only granted to Vietnam by the French in 1949, as part of the formal annexation of the Mekong Delta.

Phu Quoc is not really part of the Mekong Delta and doesn't share the delta's extraordinary ability to produce rice. The most valuable crop is black pepper, but the islanders here have traditionally earned their living from the sea. Phu Quoc is also famed across Vietnam for its production of high-quality fish sauce (nuoc mam).

The island is also well-known for its hunting dogs, which have ridgebacks, curly tails and blue tongues. Muscular and energetic, they are said to be able to pick up their master's scent from over 1km away (the nuoc

mam their masters eat probably helps). Unfortunately, the dogs have decimated much of the island's wildlife.

Despite development (a new international airport, a golf course, new roads and a planned 'casino eco-tourism resort project'), much of this island is still protected since becoming a national park in 2001. Phu Quoc National Park covers close to 70% of the island, an area of 314 sq km.

Phu Quoc's rainy season darkens skies from late May to October, when the sea gets rough and a lot of diving stops. The peak season for tourism is midwinter, when the sky is blue and the sea is calm, but it can get pretty damn hot around April and May.

At the time of research, the road leading to Sao Beach in the south of the island was being widened and resurfaced to help improve access.

History

Phu Quoc Island served as a base for the French missionary Pigneau de Behaine during the 1760s and 1780s. Prince Nguyen Anh, who later became Emperor Gia Long, was sheltered here by Behaine when he was being hunted by the Tay Son rebels.

Being a relatively remote and forested island (and an economically marginal area of Vietnam), Phu Quoc was useful to the French colonial administration as a prison.

The Americans took over where the French left off and housed about 40,000 VC prisoners here. The island's main penal colony, which is still in use today, was known as the Coconut Tree Prison (Nha Lao Cay Dua) and is near An Thoi town. Though it's considered a historic site, plans to open a museum here have stalled.

◉ Sights

Duong Dong   TOWN

The island's main town and chief fishing port on the central west coast is a tangle of hotels, restaurants, bars and shops. Scenic Long Beach ranges to the south, where most of the beach hotels, resorts and bars cluster. The old bridge in town is a great vantage point to photograph the island's fishing fleet crammed into the narrow channel.

The town itself is not that exciting, though the filthy, bustling market (Map p376) is interesting. In contrast, the excellent night market (p380) is scrupulously clean and filled with delicious food stalls.

Cau Castle
TAOIST TEMPLE

(Dinh Cau; Map p376; Đ Bach Dang, Duong Dong) **FREE** Less of a castle, more of a combination temple and lighthouse, Dinh Cau was built in 1937 to honour Thien Hau, the Goddess of the Sea, who provides protection for sailors and fishermen. The 'castle' is worth a quick look and gives you a good view of the harbour entrance.

Around sunset, locals stroll along the promenade leading from the castle to Đ Tran Hung Dao.

Fish Sauce Factory
FACTORY

(Map p376; Duong Dong; ⊙ 8-11am & 1-5pm) **FREE** The distillery of Nuoc Mam Hung Thanh is the largest of Phu Quoc's fish-sauce makers, a short walk from the market in Duong Dong. At first glance, the giant wooden vats may make you think you've arrived for a wine tasting, but one sniff of the festering *nuoc mam* essence jolts you back to reality.

Most of the sauce produced is exported to the mainland for domestic consumption, though an impressive amount finds its way abroad to kitchens in Japan, North America and Europe. There's no admission charge to visit, although you'd be best off taking a guide along unless you speak Vietnamese. Keep in mind that although *nuoc mam* makes a wonderful gift for your distant relatives, you may not be able to take it out of the country. Vietnam Airlines, among other carriers, has banned it from its planes.

Long Beach
BEACH

(Bai Truong; Map p376) Long Beach is draped invitingly along the west coast from Duong Dong almost to An Thoi port. Development concentrates in the north near Duong Dong, where the recliners and rattan umbrellas of the various resorts rule; like all beaches in Vietnam, these are the only stretches that are kept clean. With its west-facing aspect, sunsets can be stupendous.

There should be no problem for beachcombers to stretch out their towels on the sand, but you may get moved on quickly if you get too close to the paying guests.

Long Beach is easily accessible from Duong Dong on foot, but a motorbike or bicycle is necessary to reach some of the remote stretches flung out towards the southern end of the island. There are several small lanes heading from the main Đ Tran Hung Dao drag down to Long Beach that shelter some of the nicest places to stay and eat. There are a few bamboo huts where you can buy drinks, but bring water if planning a long hike along the beach. Beachside massages are popular, but be clear about what you're paying for: a neck rub can quickly turn into a foot massage, manicure and leg-hair threading – often all simultaneously.

Coi Nguon Museum
MUSEUM

(Map p374; www.coinguonphuquoc.com; 149 Tran Hung Dao; admission 20,000d; ⊙ 7am-5pm) With displays on Vietnamese medicines, Stone Age tools, local ceramics and a small room devoted to the island prison, this five-floor privately owned museum is an informative introduction to Phu Quoc history and culture.

Sao Beach
BEACH

(Bai Sao; Map p374) With white sand like powdered ivory, the delightful curve of beautiful Sao Beach bends out alongside a sea of mineral-water clarity just a few kilometres from An Thoi, the main shipping port at the southern tip of the island. There are a couple of beachfront restaurants, where you can settle into a deckchair or partake in water sports. If heading down to Sao Beach by motorbike, fill up with petrol before the trip as there are very few fuel stations on the way back.

Jet skis (450,000d for 10 minutes) can be hired on the beach.

Khem Beach
BEACH

(Bai Khem; Map p374) Undeveloped Khem Beach is one of the most beautiful beaches on the island, but is also one of the few remaining areas that's under military control. Consequently, it's generally closed to the public.

Vong Beach
BEACH

(Bai Vong; Map p374) The attractive Vong Beach is where the fast boats from the mainland dock. Other beaches in the vicinity are strewn with rubbish.

> ### ℹ️ ITINERARY PLANNING
>
> A popular round trip between HCMC and Phu Quoc is to travel overland through the Mekong Delta, take a ferry to the island from Rach Gia or Ha Tien and, tanned and rested, take the short one-hour flight back to HCMC. With the Vietnam–Cambodia border at Xa Xia–Prek Chak, it's also convenient to visit Phu Quoc as part of a loop through the Mekong Delta and the south coast of Cambodia.

Phu Quoc Island

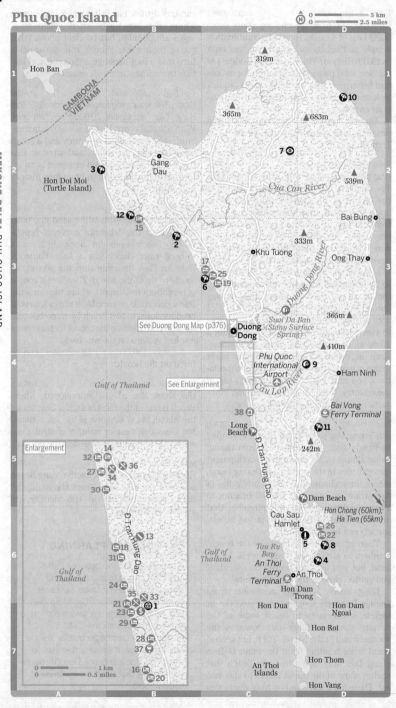

0 — 5 km
0 — 2.5 miles

Hon Ban

CAMBODIA
VIETNAM

319m

365m

683m

10

7

Gang
Dau

Hon Doi Moi
(Turtle Island)

3

Cua Can River

539m

Bai Bung

12

15

2

17

25

6

19

Khu Tuong

333m

Ong Thay

365m

Duong Dong River

Suoi Da Ban
(Stony Surface
Spring)

See Duong Dong Map (p376)

Duong
Dong

410m

Phu Quoc
International
Airport

9

Ham Ninh

See Enlargement

Cau Lop River

Gulf of Thailand

Bai Vong
Ferry Terminal

38

Long
Beach

11

242m

Dam Beach

Cau Sau
Hamlet

Hon Chong (60km);
Ha Tien (65km)

26

22

5

8

Tau Ru
Bay

An Thoi
Ferry
Terminal

An Thoi

4

Hon Dam
Trong

Hon Dua

Hon Dam
Ngoai

Hon Roi

Hon Thom

An Thoi
Islands

Hon Vang

Enlargement

14

32

36

27

34

30

D Tran Hung Dao

13

18

31

Gulf of
Thailand

24

35

33

21

1

23

29

28

37

0 — 1 km
0 — 0.5 miles

16

20

Phu Quoc Island

Cua Can Beach BEACH
(Bai Cua Can; Map p374) The most accessible of the northern beaches, Cua Can is about 11km from Duong Dong. It remains mercifully quiet during the week, but can get busy at weekends. A ride through the villages around Cua Can is interesting, with the road crossing the river several times on rickety wooden bridges.

Ong Lang Beach BEACH
(Bai Ong Lan; Map p374) Ong Lang Beach has a series of sandy bays sheltered by rocky headlands. Several midrange resorts in this area service those wanting to get away from it all.

Vung Bau, Dai & Thom Beaches BEACH
(Bai Vung Bau, Bai Dai, Bai Thom) Still retaining their isolated, tropical charm, these northern beaches are rarely peopled, let alone crowded. A newer road follows the coast along **Vung Bau** (Bai Vung Bau; Map p374) and **Dai** (Bai Dai; Map p374) beaches, cutting down on motorbike time and red dust in your face. The road from Dai to **Thom** (Bai Thom; Map p374) via Ganh Dau is very beautiful, pass-ing through dense forest with tantalising glimpses of the coast below.

Phu Quoc National Park NATURE RESERVE
(Map p374) About 90% of Phu Quoc is forested and the trees and adjoining marine environment enjoy official protection. Indeed, this is the last large stand of forest in the south, and in 2010 the park was declared a Unesco Biosphere Reserve.

The forest is most dense in the northern half of the island. The area is a forest reserve (Khu Rung Nguyen Sinh) and you'll need a motorbike or mountain bike to get through it. There are a few primitive dirt roads, but no real hiking trails.

Suoi Tranh & Suoi Da Ban WATERFALL
(admission 3000d, motorbike 1000d) Compared with the waterlogged Mekong Delta, Phu Quoc has very little surface moisture, but there are several springs originating in the hills. The most accessible of these is **Suoi Tranh** (Map p374); look for the entrance sign and concrete tree from the Duong Dong–Vong Beach road. From the ticket

MEKONG DELTA PHU QUOC ISLAND

Duong Dong

counter it's a 10-minute walk through the forest to the falls.

Suoi Da Ban (admission 3000d, motorbike 1000d) is a white-water creek tumbling across some attractive large granite boulders. There are deep pools and it's nice enough for a dip. Bring plenty of mosquito repellent.

For both of these falls, the best months to visit are between May and September – by the end of the dry season there's little more than a trickle.

Nha Tu Phu Quoc MONUMENT
(Map p374; ⊙7.30-11am & 1.30-4pm) FREE
Worth a visit when visiting Sao Beach in the south of the island, Phu Quoc's notorious old prison, built by the French in the late 1940s, contains a small museum that narrates the gruesome history of the jail. A war memorial stands south of the prison on the far side of the road.

An Thoi Islands ISLAND
(Quan Dao An Thoi) Just off the southern tip of Phu Quoc, these 15 islands and islets can be visited by chartered boat. It's a fine area for sightseeing, fishing, swimming and snorkelling. Hon Thom (Pineapple Island) is about 3km in length and is the largest island in the group.

Other islands here include Hon Dua (Coconut Island), Hon Roi (Lamp Island), Hon Vang (Echo Island), Hon May Rut (Cold Cloud Island), the Hon Dams (Shadow Islands), Chan Qui (Yellow Tortoise) and Hon Mong Tay (Short Gun Island). As yet, there is no real development on the islands, but expect some movement in future.

Most boats depart from An Thoi on Phu Quoc, but you can make arrangements through hotels and resorts on Long Beach. Also enquire at the dive operators, as they have boats heading down there regularly for diving. Boat trips are seasonal and generally do not run during the rainy season.

🏃 Activities
Diving & Snorkelling
Although Nha Trang is arguably the best all-round dive destination in Vietnam,

there's plenty of underwater action around Phu Quoc, but only during the dry months (from November to May). Two fun dives cost from US$40 to US$80 depending on the location and operator; four-day PADI Open Water courses hover between US$320 and US$360; snorkelling trips are US$20 to US$30.

Rainbow Divers DIVING, SNORKELLING
(Map p376; ☑ 0913 400 964; www.divevietnam. com; 11 Đ Tran Hung Dao; ⊙ 9am-6pm) This reputable PADI outfit was the first to set up shop on the island and offers a wide range of diving and snorkelling trips. As well as the walk-in office, it's well represented at resorts on Long Beach.

Flipper Diving Club DIVING
(Map p376; www.flipperdiving.com; 60 Đ Tran Hung Dao; ⊙ 9am-9pm) Centrally located (by the Coco Bar), multilingual PADI dive centre for everything from novice dive trips to full instructor courses.

Searama DIVING, SNORKELLING
(Map p374; ☑ 0126 479 1922; www.searama.com; 98B Đ Tran Hung Dao) French- and English-speaking operators; tends to be a bit cheaper than the competition.

Vietnam Explorer DIVING
(Map p376; ☑ 077-384 6372; 36 Đ Tran Hung Dao) Well-known outfit, also operating out of Nha Trang.

Kayaking

There are several places to rent kayaks along Sao Beach, and its protected, fairly calm waters make for a smooth ride. In addition to locals who hire out boats, you can ask at the beachside restaurants. The going rate is about 60,000d per hour.

☞ Tours

Your best bet for booking tours is through your hotel or resort, as there's no government-run tourist office in Duong Dong. Squid fishing at night is popular, and you'll spot the lights of boats (to lure the cephalopods to the surface) on the evening horizon.

Specialised companies and individuals offering boat excursions and fishing trips include the following:

Anh Tu's Tours BOAT TOUR
(☑ 077-399 6009; anhtupq@yahoo.com) Snorkelling, squid fishing, island tours, plus motorbike rental.

**Jerry's Jungle &
Beach Tours** BOAT TOUR, HIKING
(☑ 0938 226 021; jerrysjungletours@gmail.com; day trips from US$25) Archipelago explorations by boat, snorkelling, fishing, day and multi-day trips to islands, motorbike tours, bouldering, bird-watching, hiking and cultural tours around Phu Quoc.

John's Tours BOAT TOUR
(Map p376; ☑ 0919 107 086; www.johnsislandtours. com; 4 Đ Tran Hung Dao) Well represented at hotels and resorts; cruises include snorkelling, island-hopping and squid-fishing trips.

🛏 Sleeping

Accommodation prices on Phu Quoc yo-yo depending on the season and visitor numbers. Variations are more extreme than anywhere else in Vietnam, but tend to affect budget and midrange places more than the high-end resorts. Some places will treble their prices for the peak season of December and January, when bookings are crucial. Across all of the budget categories, you'll get less for your money than you'd expect for the price.

🛏 Duong Dong

Most travellers prefer to stay at the beach, but Duong Dong has some guesthouses if the beach is bursting at the seams. Prices are more reasonable here.

Sea Breeze HOTEL $
(Gio Bien; Map p376; ☑ 077-399 4920; www.sea-breezephuquoc.com; 62A Đ Tran Hung Dao; r with fan from US$15, r with air-con US$25-40; ❄ 🕸) A curvaceous hotel with clean, modern and attractive rooms. Accommodation road-side is noisier and rooms can get very bright in the morning – fine for early risers, not for late sleepers.

Hiep Phong Hotel GUEST HOUSE $
(Map p376; ☑ 077-384 6057; nguyet_1305@yahoo. com; 17 Đ Nguyen Trai; r US$15-20; ❄ @ 🕸) A very friendly family-run minihotel in the middle of town. The rooms include satellite TV, fridge and hot water – something you won't find on the beach at this price.

My Linh Hotel GUEST HOUSE $
(Map p376; ☑ 077-384 8674; 9 Đ Nguyen Trai; r US$10-15; ❄) Just a few doors down from Hiep Phong, this minihotel offers a similar sort of deal, with solid wooden beds and some balconies. English-speaking staff.

Long Beach

There are now several dozen resorts stretched in a continuous line along the sands of Long Beach. Some hotels provide free transport to and from the airport; enquire when making a booking. Most can be accessed off Đ Tran Hung Dao.

Mushrooms
GUEST HOUSE $

(Map p374; ☑ 0126 471 4249; 170 Đ Tran Hung Dao; dm US$6, d US$10-15) This spruce, clean and colourful outfit on the far side of the road has spic-and-span six- and four-bed dorms, and a couple of decent doubles, one sans shower.

Lien Hiep Thanh Hotel
RESORT HOTEL $

(Map p374; ☑ 077-384 7583; lienhiepthanh2007@ yahoo.com.vn; 118/12 Đ Tran Hung Dao; r with fan US$15-20, r with air-con US$30-60; ❉☎) This friendly place has simple rooms and bungalows amid trees and a great strip of beach. Beachfront rooms include air-con and hot water, and there's a small restaurant.

A74 Hotel
HOTEL $

(Map p374; ☑ 077-398 2772; www.a74hotel.com; 74 Đ Tran Hung Dao; r US$10-25; ❉) On the main drag near Long Beach, this friendly overspill option has basic and rather musty rooms, some with sea views.

Moon Resort
RESORT HOTEL $

(Map p374; ☑ 077-399 4520; www.moonresort.vn; 82 Đ Tran Hung Dao; bungalows with fan $15-25, with air-con US$25-49; ❉@☎) These rustic, woven rattan bungalows, set in a scrappy garden, are excellent value and right on the beach.

★Mai House
RESORT HOTEL $$

(Map p374; ☑ 077-384 7003; maihouseresort@ya-hoo.com; 118 Đ Tran Hung Dao; r with fan US$75, r with air-con US$95-240; ❉@☎) Dappled with palm shade, Mai House offers one of the most exquisite settings on Long Beach, nailing the whole tropical-paradise vibe with its well-tended gardens, open-sided restaurant and loungers shaded by rattan umbrellas. Scattered on the lawns, the bungalows are lovely and clean, although the back ones are much more tightly spaced than the front couple of rows. The food is excellent and the beach is gorgeous.

Sea Star Resort
RESORT HOTEL $$

(Map p374; ☑ 077-398 2161; www.seastarresort. com; r US$36-46, bungalows US$60-85; ❉@☎) A fun and friendly place to stay, this exten-sive compound includes 37 rooms and bun-galows, many fronting on to a manicured stretch of sand with sea-view balconies. Cheapest rooms are conjoined in a block and prices drop by about 20% in the low season.

Beach Club
RESORT HOTEL $$

(Map p374; ☑ 077-398 0998; www.beachclubviet-nam.com; Ap Cua Lap, Xa Duong To; r US$30-40; ☎) Run by an English-Vietnamese couple, this is a great escape from the main-drag bustle, with tightly grouped and well-kept rooms and bungalows on a small plot, plus a breezy beachside restaurant.

Paris Beach
RESORT HOTEL $$

(Map p374; ☑ 077-399 4548; www.phuquocparis-beach.com; Cau Ba Phong, Cua Lap, Duong To; r US$32-150; ❉@☎☀) With some lovely rooms facing the sea, this French-Vietnamese run resort hotel is next to Beach Club. It has a brand-new swimming pool and clean and spacious bungalows, with a tiled terrace where delicious food is served by the congenial hosts.

Thanh Kieu Beach Resort
RESORT HOTEL $$

(Map p374; ☑ 077-384 8394; www.thanhkieuresort. com; 100C/14 Đ Tran Hung Dao; r US$39-49; @☎) On a lovely beachfront, the attractive brick bungalows are set in a leafy garden dotted with swaying palms and clumps of bamboo. Rooms are well furnished and the popular Rainbow Bar is located here on the beach.

Phuong Binh House
RESORT HOTEL $$

(Map p374; http://phuongbinhhouse.com; 118 Đ Tran Hung Dao; r US$30-65; ❉☎) With clean but rather characterless cookie-cutter seaside accommodation, this small 17-room, friendly place is buried away at the end of the road to the beach.

Nhat Lan
GUEST HOUSE $$

(Map p374; ☑ 077-384 7663; nhanghinhatlan@ya-hoo.com; 118/13 Đ Tran Hung Dao; bungalows with fan/air-con US$25/60; ☎) The last in a string of affordable beachfront guesthouses, this place has rooms in a shady garden and six new, swish, glass-fronted beach-side bungalows.

★La Veranda
RESORT HOTEL $$$

(Map p374; ☑ 077-398 2988; www.laverandare-sort.com; 118/9 Đ Tran Hung Dao; r US$275-375; ❉@❉☀) With grounds shaded by palms, this is the most elegant place to stay on the island, designed in colonial style and small enough to remain intimate, with just 44 rooms. It has a stunning cobalt-blue pool with a kiddies' area, a stylish spa and all rooms feature large beds and designer bathrooms. The beach is great and for food you can choose between a cafe on the lawn and the Pepper Tree Restaurant (p381) upstairs, while drinks at Le Bar round off the day stylishly.

Famiana Resort & Spa
RESORT HOTEL $$$

(Map p374; ☎077-399 3026; www.famiana-resort.com; Đ Tran Hung Dao; r US$215-995; ✲@🖥🏊) This sedate 60-room resort has lovely accommodation, including stunning seafront villas with mezzanine floors, an inviting pool and a spotless stretch of beach.

Cassia Cottage
RESORT HOTEL $$$

(Map p374; ☎077-384 8395; www.cassiacottage.com; 100C Đ Tran Hung Dao; r US$120-190; ✲🖥🏊) Set in a flourishing garden, this seductive boutique-style resort on Long Beach has a sleepy beachside repose, rooms with handsome furnishings, two pools and a pretty garden restaurant with tables overlooking the sea.

Eden Resort
RESORT $$$

(Map p374; ☎077-398 5598; www.edenresort.com.vn; Cua Lap, Duong To; r US$195-425; ✲🖥🏊) From the elegant rattan furniture and well-tended greenery and landscaped setting, to the spotless bungalows and idyllic, deluxe sea-view rooms, this place is a good choice. Delightful pool and excellent service.

Saigon-Phu Quoc Resort
RESORT HOTEL $$$

(Map p376; ☎077-384 6999; www.sgphuquocresort.com; 1 Đ Tran Hung Dao; r US$159-480; ✲@🖥🏊) This smart resort features 98 rooms in villas or bungalows, most with views over the beach. The sprawling complex includes a disco, karaoke rooms, a spa, minigolf, tennis courts and pétanque courts. Check the website for seasonal deals.

Thien Hai Son Resort
RESORT HOTEL $$$

(Map p374; ☎077-398 3044; www.phuquocthienhaison.com; 68 Đ Tran Hung Dao; r US$90-99, bungalows US$132-161; ✲🖥🏊) There's a mixture of hotel blocks and bungalows in this sprawling lemon-and-lime beachfront complex.

🛏 Sao Beach

Lang Toi
GUEST HOUSE $$

(Map p374; ☎077-397 2123; Sao Beach; r US$35-45; 🖥) Also known as Gecko Jack's, this simple place on Sao Beach has four fan rooms, each with spacious bathrooms. Two rooms

come with sea view and verandah, two with a garden setting. Book ahead.

Mango Garden
B&B $$

(Map p374; ☎077-629 1339; mangogarden.inn@gmail.com; r US$35-50; ☉Oct-Mar; ✲🖥🏊) Best suited to those with their own (two) wheels, this isolated and hard-to-find B&B is reached by a bumpy dirt road (turn left just before Sao Beach and try to find the signs) away from the beach. Run by a Vietnamese-Canadian, the Western-style, generator-powered B&B is surrounded by gorgeous flower and mango gardens, enclosed by a high fence.

There's motorbike rental, 24-hour solar-powered hot water, fishing and snorkelling trips. Book well ahead.

🛏 Ong Lang Beach

Although it's rockier than Long Beach, Ong Lang, 7km north of Duong Dong, has the advantage of being substantially less crowded and, hence, feels much more like a tropical-island escape. Because of its relative isolation, expect to spend most of your time in and around your resort – although most places can arrange bike or motorbike hire to get you out and about. Definitely book ahead if planning to stay around here.

Mango Bay
RESORT HOTEL $$

(Map p374; ☎077-398 1693; www.mangobayphuquoc.com; r US$60-100, bungalows US$80-185, house US$235-395; @🖥) 🌿 Set around a small cove accessed from a dusty road through a mango orchard, this ecofriendly resort uses solar panels and organic and recycled building materials, and has its own butterfly garden. Strung out along the beach, accommodation ranges from rooms through bungalows with delightful open-air bathrooms, to a private house. All in all it's a romantic, if simple, getaway for those who want some privacy. Two buses head into town daily.

Freedomland
HOMESTAY $$

(Map p374; ☎077-399 4891; www.freedomlandphuquoc.com; 2 Ap Ong Lang, Xa Cua Duong; bungalows US$30-60; ☉Oct-Jun; @🖥) With an emphasis on community and socialising – fun communal dinners are a mainstay – Freedomland has 11 basic bungalows (mosquito nets, fans, no hot water) scattered around a shady plot. Guests who can't be bothered with the five-minute walk to the beach slump into the hammocks strung between the trees. It's a popular choice, particularly with solo budget travellers; it's best to call first. Shut in the rainy season.

Bo Resort RESORT HOTEL $$
(Map p374; ☑077-398 6142; www.boresort.com; bungalows US$38-117; @) With variously sized bungalows scattered higgledy-piggledy over a jungle-clad hill stretching down to a rocky beach, this French-run resort offers intimacy and seclusion, plus excellent food.

★**Chen Sea Resort & Spa** RESORT HOTEL $$$
(Map p374; ☑077-399 5895; www.centarahotel-sresorts.com; bungalow US$234-473; ❋@☎⚛) Competing for the title of the most upmarket resort on the island, tranquil and chilled-out 36-room Chen Sea has lovely villas with sunken baths and deep verandahs, designed to resemble terracotta-roofed houses. Almost indistinguishable from the sea, the large azure rectangle of the infinity pool faces the resort's beautiful sandy beach. The isolation is mitigated by plenty of activities on hand: borrow a bike, kayak or catamaran – or settle into the spa or the open-sided restaurant.

Vung Bau Beach

★**Bamboo Cottages & Restaurant** RESORT HOTEL $$
(Map p374; ☑077-281 0345; www.bamboophuquoc.com; r US$50-95; ❋@) Run by a friendly family with a coterie of cheeky dogs, Bamboo Cottages has Vung Bau Beach largely to itself. The focal point is a big, open-sided restaurant and bar, with the beach at its doorstep. Set around the lawns, the attractive, lemon-coloured villas have private, open-roofed bathrooms with solar-powered hot water. The family supports an education scholarship for local kids in need.

✗ Eating

Many of the recommended resorts have excellent restaurants, often beachside or with a sunset view. Guests staying at more remote resorts such as those at Ong Lang Beach tend to eat in, as it's a long way into town.

Some of the standouts include Bo Resort, Mai House and Pepper Tree Restaurant, each of which offers a combination of Vietnamese and French fare. For something a bit more local, try the seafood restaurants in the fishing village of Ham Ninh; there are several along the pier at the end of the main road, including Kim Cuong I (☑077-384 9978; mains 30,000-300,000d).

✗ Duong Dong

★**Dinh Cao Night Market** VIETNAMESE $
(Map p376; Đ Vo Thi Sau; ⊙5pm-midnight) Hands down the most atmospheric, affordable and excellent place to dine on the island, Duong Dong's night market has around a dozen stalls serving a delicious range of Vietnamese seafood, grills and vegetarian options. Look for a local crowd, as they are a discerning bunch, or try the excellent Thanh Xuan (Map p376; mains 45,000-100,000d), which offers freshly barbecued fish and seafood.

★**Buddy Ice Cream** ICE CREAM $
(Map p376; www.visitphuquoc.info; 26 Đ Nguyen Trai; mains 25,000-130,000d; ⊙8am-10pm; ☎) With the coolest music in town, this cafe is excellent for sides of free internet and tourist info with its New Zealand ice-cream combos, toasted sandwiches, fish 'n' chips, thirst-busting fruit juices, shakes, smoothies, all-day breakfasts, comfy sofas and book exchange.

✗ Long Beach

★**The Spice House at Cassia Cottage** VIETNAMESE $
(Map p374; www.cassiacottage.com; 100C Đ Tran Hung Dao; mains from 74,000d; ⊙7-10am & 11am-10pm) Nab a beachside high-table, order a papaya salad, grilled garlic, a cinnamon-infused okra or a delectable fish curry and time dinner to catch the sunset at this excellent restaurant.

Alanis Deli CAFE $
(Map p374; 98 Đ Tran Hung Dao; pancakes from 75,000d; ⊙8am-10pm) Fab caramel pancakes and coffees plus ace breakfasts and friendly service.

Oasis VIETNAMESE, WESTERN $
(Map p374; 118/5 Đ Tran Hung Dao; mains from 55,000d; ⊙7am-10pm, bar till later; ☎) On the lane leading to La Veranda and Rory's Beach Bar, Oasis feeds ravenous travellers with a menu embracing shepherd's pie, shrimp spring rolls, apple pie and winning all-day breakfasts.

Mondo TAPAS $
(Map p374; 82 Đ Tran Hung Dao; tapas 35,000-105,000d; ⊙7am-10pm Tue-Sun) Serving traditional Spanish tapas and other regional treats (pumpernickel bread, blue cheese and ham pasta) plus all-day Western-style breakfasts,

Mondo is a dependable Long Beach slot, with imported beers (Chimay, Duvel).

Le Cap Breton
FRENCH $

(Map p374; 143 Đ Tran Hung Dao; crêpes from 45,000d) This open, breezy place with dark wooden furniture has a tasty menu of Brittany crêpes and galettes (made with flour from France), backed up by Vietnamese/French and international dishes.

Pepper's Pizza & Grill
ITALIAN, GERMAN $

(Map p374; ☑ 077-384 8773; 89 Đ Tran Hung Dao; mains 65,000-190,000d; ⊙ 10am-11pm) Pepper's does fine pizzas and they'll even deliver to your resort. The rest of the menu is a mixture of Italian, German and Asian dishes, including steaks, ribs and the like.

Restaurant Chez Carole
VIETNAMESE, FRENCH $

(Map p374; 88 Đ Tran Hung Dao; mains 50,000-200,000d; ⊙ 10am-midnight) This place is French in accent, but the menu includes a whole lot of fresh Vietnamese seafood, such as the signature shrimps in cognac or pastis.

Itaca Resto Lounge
FUSION $$

(Map p374; www.itacalounge.com; 125 Đ Tran Hung Dao; mains 200,000-300,000d; ⊙ 4pm-1am) Shut at the time of research for a low-season spruce up, we didn't have the chance to eat at this much-applauded restaurant with a winning Mediterranean-Asian fusion menu (with tapas), much-enjoyed alfresco arrangement and friendly, welcoming hosts. It's not on the beach, so don't go for sea views, but the ambience is still charming.

Pepper Tree Restaurant
INTERNATIONAL $$

(Map p374; www.laverandaresort.com; La Veranda, 118/9 Đ Tran Hung Dao; mains US$6-20; ⊙ 6.30am-11pm) The Pepper Tree at La Veranda resort offers divine French cuisine, elegant Vietnamese dishes and delectable views of the surf and sunset.

✖ Ong Lang Beach

Sakura
VIETNAMESE $

(Map p374; mains from 45,000d; ⊙ 10am-10pm) This simple wood restaurant is run by the fluent English-speaking Kiem. Food is very tasty, but bring a fly swat and repellent.

🍸 Drinking & Nightlife

The following are all either on Long Beach or in Duong Dong. A handful of girlie bars take the action through to around 4am.

★ Le Bar
BAR

(Map p374; 118/9 Đ Tran Hung Dao; ⊙ 6am-11pm; 🛜) With its gorgeous tiled floor, art deco furniture and colonial charms, this highly elegant and well-poised upstairs lounge-bar at La Veranda is a superb spot for a terrace sundowner.

★ Rory's Beach Bar
BAR

(Map p374; 118/10 Đ Tran Hung Dao; ⊙ 9am-late) Phu Quoc's liveliest and most fun beach bar draws a steady torrent of travellers and island residents down the path to its seaside perch.

Drunkn Monkey
BAR

(Map p374; 82 Đ Tran Hung Dao; ⊙ 3pm-late) Friendly owner Steph has put much work into this solid choice on the main road, with amiable staff, big-projector sports TV, pool table, foot-tapping tunes and seats slung out the front.

Coco Bar
BAR

(Map p376; 60 Đ Tran Hung Dao; ⊙ 10am-late) With chairs and music spilling onto the pavement by the Flipper dive centre, Coco is a great place for a roadside bevvie and chat with the mix of travelling folk, Gallic wayfarers, local drinkers and passing pool sharks.

Safari Bar
BAR

(Map p374; Đ Tran Hung Dao) The welcoming English owner of this otherwise rather uneventful bar is a useful source of local info on all things Phu Quoc. The eats also get good press.

🛍 Shopping

Your best bets for souvenirs are the night market in Duong Dong and the pearl farm near the centre of Long Beach.

Phu Quoc Pearls
SOUVENIRS

(Map p374; www.treasuresfromthedeep.com; ⊙ 8am-5pm) For black, yellow, white, pink or any other colour of pearl, Phu Quoc Pearls – on an isolated stretch of Long Beach – is a requisite stop. A charming woman will prise open a live oyster with a blade to reveal the enclosed gem before directing you to the showroom. Admire your bounty with a drink in the attached cafe-bar.

Avid pearl hunters can find cheaper wares at kiosks in the village of Ham Ninh, but you have a guarantee of authenticity here.

MEKONG DELTA PHU QUOC ISLAND

Green Boutique ACCESSORIES
(Map p376; Đ Tran Hung Dao; ☺9am-noon & 3-9pm) Homemade skin and beauty products produced by the Vietnamese owner, Ut.

ℹ Information

There are ATMs in Duong Dong and in many resorts on Long Beach. A handy one is positioned at the top of the lane at 118 Đ Tran Hung Dao, not far from Oasis.

Post Office (Map p376; Đ 30 Thang 4) The post office is in downtown Duong Dong.

ℹ Getting There & Away

AIR

Demand can be high in peak season, so book ahead. A new international airport opened at the end of 2012.

Vietjet Air (☎1900 1886; www.vietjetair.com) Operates flights to/from Ho Chi Minh City (two daily).

Vietnam Airlines (Map p376; ☎077-399 6677; www.vietnamairlines.com; 122 Đ Nguyen Trung Truc) Flies to/from Rach Gia (from 500,000d, daily), Can Tho (from 500,000d, daily) and HCMC (from 450,000d, 10 daily).

BOAT

Fast boats connect Phu Quoc to both Ha Tien (1½ hours) and Rach Gia (2½ hours). Phu Quoc travel agents have the most up-to-date schedules and can book tickets. The ferry port on Phu Quoc is at Bai Vong on the east coast.

Also from Ha Tien, a massive 400-passenger car ferry (departing 8.20am from Ha Tien and 2pm from Phu Quoc; per passenger/motorbike/car 165,000d/100,000d/US$50) departs every day.

Savanna Express (☎077-369 2888; www.savannaexpress.com; adult/child 330,000/250,000d) Departs Rach Gia at 8.05am and Phu Quoc at 1.05pm; 2½ hours.

Superdong (☎Phu Quoc 077-398 0111, Rach Gia 077-387 7742; www.superdong.com.vn; to Rach Gia adult/child 320,000/250,000d, to Ha Tien adult/child 215,000-230,000/160,000d) Departs Rach Gia and Phu Quoc at 8am, 9am, 12.40pm and 1pm. Departs Ha Tien at 8am and 1pm and leaves Phu Quoc at 8.30am and 1.30pm.

ℹ Getting Around

TO/FROM THE AIRPORT

The island's brand-new Phu Quoc International Airport is 10km out of town. A taxi will cost around US$8 to Long Beach.

BICYCLE

If you can ride a bicycle in the tropical heat over these dusty, bumpy roads, all power to you. Bicycle rentals are available through most hotels from US$3 per day.

BUS

There is a skeletal bus service between An Thoi and Duong Dong. Buses run perhaps once every hour or two. A bus (20,000d) waits for the ferry at Bai Vong to take passengers to Duong Dong. Several hotels operate shuttles or will offer free transfers for guests.

MOTORBIKE

You won't have to look for the motorbike taxis – they'll find you. Some polite bargaining may be necessary. For short runs, 20,000d should be sufficient. Otherwise, figure on around 50,000d for about 5km. From Duong Dong to Bai Vong will cost you about 70,000d or so.

Motorbikes can be hired from most hotels and bungalows for around US$7 (semi-automatic) to US$10 (automatic) per day. The cheaper bikes tend to be pretty old and in poor condition, so inspect them thoroughly before setting out. Most places prefer not to rent out overnight, so make sure you are clear on the arrangements before taking the bike.

TAXI

There are several metered taxi companies operating on the island, with flagfall starting at 12,000d. **Mai Linh** (☎077-397 9797) is reliable and drivers always use the meter. It costs about 250,000d from Duong Dong to the dock at Vong Beach and around 45,000d from Duong Dong to Rory's Beach Bar.

Ha Tien

☎077 / POP 93,000

Ha Tien may be part of the Mekong Delta but lying on the Gulf of Thailand it feels a world away from the rice fields and rivers that typify the region. There are dramatic limestone formations peppering the area, which are home to a network of caves, some of which have been turned into temples. Plantations of pepper trees cling to the hillsides. On a clear day, Phu Quoc Island is visible to the west.

The town itself has a languid charm, with crumbling colonial villas and a colourful riverside market. Visitor numbers have recently soared thanks to the opening of the nearby border with Cambodia at Xa Xia–Prek Chak and the creation of a special economic zone – allowing visa-free travel in the town and its immediate surrounds.

Ha Tien

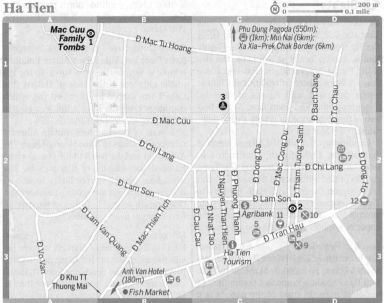

Oh yes, Ha Tien is on the map. And it's occupying a bigger portion of it thanks to major expansion plans that will see the city spread southwest along the coast. Already a precinct of markets and hotels has sprung up on land reclaimed from the river between the end of Phuong Thanh and the still-quite-new bridge (which superseded Ha Tien's atmospheric old pontoon bridge). With development concentrated in this neighbourhood, the charming colonial shopfronts around the old market have thankfully been left to decay in peace.

History

Ha Tien was a province of Cambodia until 1708. In the face of attacks by the Thai, the Khmer-appointed governor, a Chinese immigrant named Mac Cuu, turned to the Vietnamese for protection and assistance. Mac Cuu thereafter governed this area as a fiefdom under the protection of the Nguyen Lords. He was succeeded as ruler by his son, Mac Thien Tu. During the 18th century the area was invaded and pillaged several times by the Thai. Rach Gia and the southern tip of the Mekong Delta came under direct Nguyen rule in 1798.

During the Khmer Rouge regime, Cambodian forces repeatedly attacked Vietnamese

territory and massacred thousands of civilians here. The entire populations of Ha Tien and nearby villages (in fact, tens of thousands of people) fled their homes. Also during this period, areas north of Ha Tien along the Cambodian border were sown with mines and booby traps, some of which have yet to be cleared.

◉ Sights

★ Mac Cuu Family Tombs TOMB

(Lang Mac Cuu, Nui Binh San; Đ Mac Cuu) FREE
Not far from town are the Mac Cuu Family
Tombs, known locally as Nui Lang, the Hill
of the Tombs. Several dozen relatives of Mac
Cuu are buried here in traditional Chinese
tombs decorated with figures of dragons,
phoenixes, lions and guardians. At the bottom of the complex is an ornate shrine dedicated to the Mac family.

Heading up the hill, the largest tomb is
that of Mac Cuu himself, constructed in
1809 on the orders of Emperor Gia Long
and decorated with carved figures of Thanh
Long (Green Dragon) and Bach Ho (White
Tiger), protectors of Taoist temples. The
tomb of Mac Cuu's first wife is flanked by the
imperial symbols of dragons and phoenixes.

Tam Bao Pagoda BUDDHIST TEMPLE

(Sac Tu Tam Bao Tu; 328 Đ Phuong Thanh; ⊙ prayers
8-9am & 2-3pm) Founded by Mac Cuu in 1730,
Tam Bao Pagoda is home to a community of
Buddhist nuns. In front of the pagoda is a
statue of Quan The Am Bo Tat (Goddess of
Mercy) standing on a lotus blossom. Within
the sanctuary, the largest statue on the dais
represents A Di Da (Buddha of the Past),
made of painted brass.

Outside in the tranquil grounds are the
tombs of 16 monks. Near the pagoda is a
section of the city wall dating from the early
18th century.

Phu Dung Pagoda BUDDHIST TEMPLE

(Phu Cu Am Tu; Đ Phu Dung; ⊙ prayers 4-5am
& 7-8pm) This pagoda was founded in the
mid-18th century by Mac Thien Tich's wife,
Nguyen Thi Xuan. Her tomb and that of one
of her female servants are on the hillside
behind the pagoda. Nearby are the tombs
of four monks. Inside the main hall of the
pagoda, the most notable statue on the central dais is a bronze Thich Ca Buddha from
China.

Behind this hall is a small temple, Dien
Ngoc Hoang, dedicated to the Taoist Jade
Emperor. Head up the steep blue stairs to
the shrine. The figures inside are of Ngoc
Hoang (Jade Emperor) flanked by Nam Tao,
the Taoist God of the Southern Polar Star
and the God of Happiness (on the right);
and Bac Dao, the Taoist God of the Northern
Polar Star and the God of Longevity (on the
left). The statues are made of papier mâché
moulded over bamboo frames.

To get here, continue north past the Mac
Cuu Tombs and take the first right onto Đ
Phu Dung.

Thach Dong Cave Pagoda BUDDHIST TEMPLE

(Chua Thanh Van) This subterranean Buddhist
temple is 4km northeast of town. To the left
of the entrance is the Stele of Hatred (Bia
Cam Thu), shaped like a raised fist, which
commemorates the Khmer Rouge massacre
of 130 people here on 14 March 1978.

Several of the chambers contain funerary
tablets and altars to Ngoc Hoang, Quan The
Am Bo Tat and the two Buddhist monks who
founded the temples of this pagoda. The
wind here creates extraordinary sounds as
it funnels through the grotto's passageways.
Openings in several branches of the cave afford views of nearby Cambodia.

Markets MARKET

Ha Tien has a series of markets in large pavilions east of the bridge along the To Chau
River. Many of the goods are from Thailand
and Cambodia, and prices are lower than in
HCMC. Cigarette smuggling is particularly
big business. The **fish market** is a pretty
interesting sight, especially early in the
morning when the catch is being unloaded.

An open-sided market in the colonial
quarter (between Đ Tuan Phu Dat and Đ
Tham Tuong Sanh) opens at 3pm as a **night
market**, with a scattering of clothing and
food stalls.

Ngoc Tien Monastery BUDDHIST TEMPLE

(Tinh Xa Ngoc Tien) From Ha Tien's riverfront, this Buddhist monastery is a striking
sight – sprawling up the hill on the other
side of the river. The buildings themselves
are unremarkable but it's worth making
the steep climb up here for the sweeping
views of the town and countryside. It's easy
enough to follow your nose to the narrow
road at its base.

The monastery is reached via a tiny lane at
number 48; look for the yellow sign topped
with a swastika (symbolising eternity).

Dong Ho INLET

The name translates as East Lake, but
Dong Ho is not a lake but an inlet of the
sea. Dong Ho is said to be most beautiful
on nights when there is a full or almost-full
moon. According to legend, on such nights
fairies dance here. Linguists may be interested to learn that Dong Ho in Mandarin
is Dong Hu.

The 'lake' is just east of Ha Tien, and is bounded to the east by a chain of granite hills known as the Ngu Ho (Five Tigers) and to the west by the To Chan hills.

🛏 Sleeping

While there are loads of minihotels in town, the standard isn't particularly high – but then neither are the prices. Being local-style establishments, you're unlikely to get a top sheet or duvet cover on your bed.

Hai Phuong HOTEL $
(☑ 077-385 2240; So 52, Đ Dong Thuy Tram; r 200,000-700,000d; ✳🛜) Friendly and family-run, this smart six-level hotel is in good nick and some rooms have excellent river views from their balconies.

Anh Van Hotel HOTEL $
(☑ 077-395 9222; So 2, Đ Mach Thien Tich; d/tw/f 200,000/400,000/500,000d; ✳🛜) Set in the new part of town near the bridge, this large hotel has windowless and small cheaper rooms – it's worth paying extra for those with river views and smarter bathrooms.

Hai Yen Hotel HOTEL $
(☑ 077-385 1580; 15 Đ To Chau; r 250,000-400,000d; ✳) Quite elegantly presented at an empty Ha Tien intersection, this old-timer has a variety of decent accommodation from simple doubles to spacious rooms with balcony and river views.

Du Hung Hotel HOTEL $
(☑ 077-395 1555; duhung@hcm.vnn.vn; 27A Đ Tran Hau; r 250,000d; ✳) Right in the middle of the main drag, this minihotel offers good-value rooms and a lift. Opt for one of the corner rooms, with views of the river and coast.

Ha Tien Hotel HOTEL $$
(☑ 077-395 2093; 36 Đ Tran Hau; s 390,000-690,000d, d 440,000-790,000d, tr 590,000d; ✳🛜) A rambling place exuding a faded sense of midrange grandeur, this clean and central hotel has polite staff and spacious rooms, some with terrace.

River Hotel HOTEL $$$
(☑ 077-395 5888; www.riverhotelvn.com; Binh San Ward, Đ Tran Ha; d 1,890,000-2,100,000d; ✳🛜) With contemporary, spacious and stylish rooms, a towering and sinuous outline and ample river views, this new hotel enjoys an optimum position on the waterfront. A so-phisticated addition to town, it's become a beacon for Ha Tien's promenading socialites.

✗ Eating & Drinking

Ha Tien's speciality is an unusual variety of coconut – containing no milk, but with delicate and delicious flesh – that can only be found in Cambodia and this part of Vietnam. Restaurants all around the Ha Tien area serve up the coconut flesh in a glass with ice and sugar.

There are excellent food stalls in the night market.

Xuan Thanh VIETNAMESE $
(20 Đ Tran Hau; mains 35,000-200,000d; ⊘6am-9pm) You know you've hit the coast when shrimp is the cheapest dish on the menu, which also runs to seafood and grills. Try the delicately flavoured steamed fish with ginger and onion.

Floating Restaurant WESTERN, VIETNAMESE $
(Tran Hau Park; mains from 60,000d; ⊘6am-10pm) If you can stomach the super-kitsch music (Sergio Leone/Casablanca fusion on a loop) this restaurant has a certain river-borne charm for an evening drink or dinner.

★Oasis BAR
(☑ 077-370 1553; www.oasisbarhatien.com; 42 Đ Tuan Phu Dat; mains from 20,000d; ⊘9am-9pm; 🛜) Run by Ha Tien's only resident Western expat and his Vietnamese wife, this friendly little bar is not just a great spot for a cold beer or plunger coffee, it's also great for impartial travel information and for leafing through copies of the *Evening Standard,* the *Observer* and the *Daily Mail.* The menu runs to all-day, real-deal, full-English breakfasts, caramelised onion soup, mango shakes and more.

Thuy Tien CAFE
(☑ 077-385 1828; Đ Dong Ho; ⊘6am-10pm) Dotted with fairy lights and glowing with Chinese lanterns at night, this floating cafe is a breezy choice for a sundowner beer overlooking Dong Ho.

ℹ Information

Ha Tien Tourism (☑ 077-395 9598; 1 Đ Phuong Thanh) Handles transport bookings, including boats to Phu Quoc and buses to Cambodia. Also arranges Cambodian visas (US$25).

Post Office (☑ 077-385 2190; 3 Đ To Chau; ⊘7am-5pm) Also offers internet access.

ⓘ GETTING TO CAMBODIA: HA TIEN TO KEP

Getting to the border The Xa Xia–Prek Chak border crossing connects Ha Tien with Kep and Kampot on Cambodia's south coast, making a trip to Cambodia from Phu Quoc via Ha Tien, or vice versa, that much easier. Direct minibuses leave Ha Tien for Cambodia at around 1pm, heading to Kep (US$12, one hour, 47km), Kampot (US$15, 1½ hours, 75km), Sihanoukville (US$20, four hours, 150km) and Phnom Penh (US$18, four hours, 180km). Bookings can be made through Ha Tien Tourism (which also operates through the Oasis bar), which can arrange the Cambodian visa too. It's far better to change money in Ha Tien than at the border.

At the border Casinos have sprung up on the Cambodian side, making the zone popular for gamblers on both sides of the border.

Moving on As it costs only slightly more than taking local transport and is far comfier, most travellers opt for a through minibus ticket.

ⓘ Getting There & Away

BOAT

Ferries stop across the river from the town. See the Phu Quoc Getting There & Away section for details of the daily ferry services.

BUS

Ha Tien bus station (Ben Xe Ha Tien; Hwy 80) is on the main road to Mui Nai Beach and the Cambodian border, about 1km north from the centre; a motorbike into town will cost 20,000d. Buses from here head to Chau Doc (70,000d), Long Xuyen (70,000d), Rach Gia (50,000d), Ca Mau (140,000d), Soc Trang (130,000d), Can Tho (110,000-130,000d), Tra Vinh (125,000d), Ben Tre (145,000d) and Ho Chi Minh City (140,0000-180,000d, about 10 hours).

CAR & MOTORBIKE

Ha Tien is 90km from Rach Gia, 95km from Chau Doc, 206km from Can Tho and 338km from HCMC. The Ha Tien–Chau Doc road is narrow and bumpy but interesting, following a canal along the border. As you approach Ha Tien, the land turns into a mangrove forest that is infertile and almost uninhabited. The drive takes about three hours, and it's possible to visit Ba Chuc and Tuc Dup en route. If you don't plan to drive yourself, *xe om* drivers typically charge about US$20 to US$30 for this route, or you can arrange a car through travel agencies or hotels in town.

Around Ha Tien

Mui Nai

The beaches in this part of Vietnam face the Gulf of Thailand. The water is incredibly warm and becalmed; great for bathing and diving but hopeless for surfing. The best of them, Mui Nai (Stag's Head Peninsula; admission person/car 2500/10,000d), supposedly resembling the head of a stag with its mouth pointing upward, is 8km west of Ha Tien. The bay spills over with stalls selling loud-coloured water rings, swimsuits and beach balls, beneath a canopy of lofty palms. On top is a lighthouse and there are beaches on both sides of the peninsula, lined with simple restaurants and guesthouses.

There's no public transport to the beach. A *xe om* here should set you back around 40,000d.

Hon Giang & Nghe Islands

There are many islands along this coast and some locals make a living gathering swiftlet nests (the most important ingredient of that famous Chinese delicacy, bird's-nest soup) from their rocky cliffs. About 15km from Ha Tien and accessible by small boat, Hon Giang Island has a lovely, secluded beach.

Nghe Island, near Hon Chong, is a favourite pilgrimage spot for Buddhists. The island contains a cave pagoda (Chua Hang) next to a large statue of Quan The Am Bo Tat, which faces out to sea. Boats moored near Hon Chong's cave pagoda will transport you here for around US$150.

Hon Chong

You'll pass Khmer pagodas, Cao Dai temples, grandiose churches and karst outcrops en route to Hon Chong, home to photogenic stone grottoes and the nicest stretch of sand on the delta's mainland. Unfortunately, a permanent cloud of discharge from a cement factory can blight the otherwise scenic views. Beyond the beach, the main draw is an atmospheric Buddhist cave shrine.

After passing through the scrappy village, the road rounds a headland and follows Duong Beach (Bai Duong) for 3km. An entrance fee is charged only at the far end of the beach (per person/car 5000/10,000d), where there are food stalls, karaoke bars, and pigs and chickens wandering around. From the beach you can see rocky remnants of Father and Son Isle (Hon Phu Tu), several hundred metres offshore. It was said to be shaped like a father embracing his son, but the father was washed away in 2006. Boats can be hired at the shore to row out for a closer look at the orphan remains.

You need to walk through the market to reach the cave pagoda (Chua Hang), which is set against the base of a stony headland. The entry to the cave containing Hai Son Tu (Sea Mountain Temple) is inside the pagoda. Visitors light incense and offer prayers here before entering the cool grotto itself, whose entrance is located behind the altar. Inside are statues of Sakyamuni, Quan The Am Bo Tat and small cabinets enclosing green glass Buddhas. Mind your head on the low-hanging rock roof of the cave leading to the beach. The pagoda is swamped with pilgrims 15 days before and one month after Tet, while another deluge of worshippers arrives in March and April.

🛏 Sleeping & Eating

Green Hill Guesthouse   GUEST HOUSE $
(☏ 077-385 4369; r 500,000d; ❄) In an imposing villa on the northern headland of Duong Beach, this well-maintained and friendly, family-run place has spacious rooms, including the room of choice on the top floor.

Hontrem Resort   RESORT HOTEL $$
(☏ 077-385 4331; ctycpdulichkg@vnn.vn; r US$60; ❄🛜) The smartest place in Hon Chong by a stretch, Hontrem is draped over a hillock towards the end of the main strip. The hexagonal bungalows are attractively set overlooking the sea and include a large bed with light linen and generous baths. They even feature safes for valuables. The gardens are well kept and there's a reputable restaurant overlooking the beach. Breakfast included.

Tan Phat   RESTAURANT $
(mains 30,000-150,000d; ⊙7am-10pm; ❄) On Hon Chong's main road, a kilometre or so before Duong Beach, this seafood restaurant looks like a tumbledown shack from the outside, but serves excellent food and lovely sea views.

ℹ Getting There & Away

Hon Chong is 32km from Ha Tien towards Rach Gia. The access road branches off the Rach Gia–Ha Tien highway at the small town of Ba Hon. Buses can drop you off at Ba Hon, from where you can hire a motorbike to continue the journey on to Hon Chong (around 70,000d to 80,000d). A motorbike from Ha Tien will cost around 200,000d return.

Tuc Dup Hill

Because of its network of connecting caves, Tuc Dup Hill (216m) served as a strategic base of operations during the American War. *Tuc dup* is Khmer for 'water runs at night' and it is also known locally as 'Two Million Dollar Hill', in reference to the amount of money the Americans sank into securing it.

This is a place of historical interest but there isn't much to see. You'll pass near it if you're taking the back road through Ba Chuc to Chau Doc.

Ba Chuc

Ba Chuc's Bone Pagoda stands as a ghastly reminder of the horrors perpetrated by the Khmer Rouge. Between 1975 and 1978 Khmer Rouge soldiers regularly crossed the border into Vietnam and slaughtered innocent civilians. Over the border, things were even worse, where nearly two million Cambodians were killed during the period of Pol Pot's Democratic Kampuchea regime.

Between 12 April and 30 April 1978, the Khmer Rouge killed 3157 people at Ba Chuc. Only two people are known to have survived. Many of the victims were tortured to death. The Vietnamese government might have had other motives for invading Cambodia at the end of 1978, but certainly outrage at the Ba Chuc massacre was a major justification.

Undergoing reconstruction at the time of research, the Bone Pagoda has a common tomb housing the skulls and bones of more than 1100 victims. At the time of writing, the skulls were displayed in a small building nearby, divided by age group (including the minute skulls of toddlers and babies). There is still some blood on the walls above the floor of the Phi Lai Tu temple across the way.

Ba Chuc is located close to the Cambodian border; to reach it, follow the road that runs along the canal from Ha Tien to Chau Doc. Turn off this main road onto Hwy 3T and follow it for 4km.

Chau Doc

☑ 076 / POP 112,000

Draped along the banks of the Hau Giang River (Bassac River), Chau Doc sees plenty of travellers washing through on the river route between Cambodia and Vietnam. A likeable little town with significant Chinese, Cham and Khmer communities, Chau Doc's cultural diversity – apparent in the mosques, temples, churches and nearby pilgrimage sites – makes it fascinating to explore even if you're not Cambodia-bound. Taking a boat trip to the Cham communities across the river is another highlight, while the bustling market and intriguing waterfront provide fine backdrops to a few days of relaxation.

⊙ Sights

30 Thang 4 Park   PARK

(Đ Le Loi) Stretching from the market to the Victoria Chau Doc Hotel, this formal park is the city's main promenading spot and a superlative spot for river gazing. Sculptures and a fountain are framed by manicured lawns and paths, and if you're interested in getting river-borne, women may approach you here offering rides in small boats.

Chau Phu Temple   BUDDHIST TEMPLE

(Dinh Than Chau Phu; cnr Đ Nguyen Van Thoai & Đ Gia Long) In 1926 this temple was built to worship the Nguyen dynasty official Thoai

Ngoc Hau, buried at Sam Mountain. The structure is decorated with both Vietnamese and Chinese motifs; inside are funeral tablets bearing the names of the deceased as well as biographical information about them. There's also a shrine to Ho Chi Minh.

Mosques   MOSQUES

Domed, arched **Chau Giang Mosque**, in the hamlet of Chau Giang, serves the local Cham Muslims. To get there, take the car ferry from Chau Giang ferry landing across the Hau Giang River. From the ferry landing, walk inland from the river for 30m, turn left and walk 50m.

The **Mubarak Mosque**, where children study the Quran in Arabic script, is also on the river bank opposite Chau Doc. Visitors are permitted, but you should avoid entering during the calls to prayer (five times daily) unless you are a Muslim.

There are other small mosques in the Chau Doc area. They are accessible by boat but you'll need a local guide to find them all.

Floating Houses   NOTABLE BUILDINGS

These houses, whose floats consist of empty metal drums, are both a place to live and a livelihood for their residents. Under each house, fish are raised in suspended metal nets. The fish flourish in their natural river habitat, the family can feed them whatever

---

FISH FARMING & BIOFUEL

Fish farming constitutes around 20% of Vietnam's total seafood output and is widely practised in An Giang province, in the region near the Cambodian border. The highest concentration of 'floating houses' with fish cages can be observed on the banks of the Hau Giang River (Bassac River) in Chau Doc.

The fish farmed are two members of the Asian catfish family, basa (*Pangasius bocourti*) and tra (*Pangasius hypophthalmus*). About 1.1 million tonnes are produced by this method annually and much of it is exported, primarily to European and American markets (as well as Australia and Japan), in the form of frozen white fish fillets.

The two-step production cycle starts with capturing fish eggs from the wild, usually sourced in the Tonlé Sap Lake in Cambodia, followed by raising the fish to a marketable size – usually about 1kg.

One of the more interesting developments affecting fish farming is the move to convert fish fat, a by-product of processing, into biofuel. One kilogram of fish fat can yield 1L of biodiesel fuel, according to specialists. It is claimed that the biofuel will be more efficient than diesel, is nontoxic and will generate far fewer fumes.

Due to concerns about detrimental environmental effects from fish farming (particularly related to waste management and the use of antibiotics and other chemicals), the World Wildlife Fund (WWF) placed farmed Vietnamese *pangasius* on a red list for environmentally conscious European consumers to avoid. It was subsequently removed in 2011 and the WWF has devised a set of standards and an accreditation agency to certify sustainable Vietnamese producers.

Chau Doc

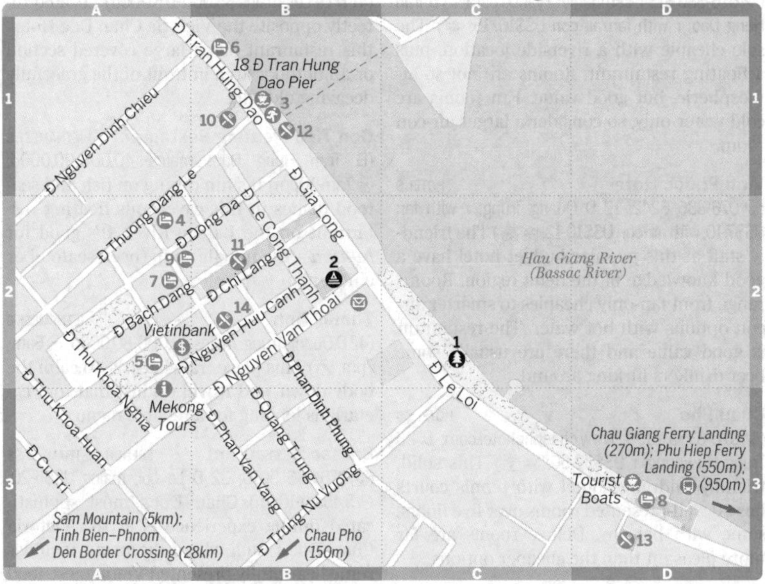

scraps are handy and catching the fish requires less exertion than fishing.

You can find these houses floating around Chau Doc and get a close-up look by hiring a boat (but please be respectful of their occupants' privacy).

Sleeping

★ Trung Nguyen Hotel HOTEL $

(☎076-386 6158; trunghotel@yahoo.com; 86 Đ Bach Dang; s/d/tw US$14/16/20; ❄@📶) One of the better budget places, with more midrange trim. Rooms are more decorative than the competition, with balconies overlooking the market. It's a busy corner site, so pack earplugs.

Song Sao Hotel HOTEL $

(☎076-356 1777; songsaohotel@yahoo.com; 12-13 Đ Nguyen Huu Canh; r 230,000-290,000d; ❄@📶) Overlooking the local pagoda, this friendly central hotel matches a smartly presented lobby to decent rooms with wood furnishings. Some rooms have a balcony, others have no view.

Hai Chau HOTEL $

(☎076-626 0066; www.haichauhotel.com; 61 Đ Thuong Dang Le; r US$18-28; ❄📶) Another decent, central choice, Hai Chau has 16 rooms spread over four floors above a restaurant, with a lift. Well-kept rooms are smartly fitted out with dark wooden furniture; some have a balcony.

Chau Doc

Sights

1 30 Thang 4 Park ... C2
2 Chau Phu Temple ... B2

Activities, Courses & Tours

3 Hang Chau ... B1

Sleeping

4 Hai Chau ... A2
5 Song Sao Hotel ... A2
6 Thuan Loi Hotel ... B1
7 Trung Nguyen Hotel ... A2
8 Victoria Chau Doc Hotel ... D3
9 Vinh Phuoc Hotel ... A2

Eating

Bassac Restaurant ... (see 8)
10 Bay Bong ... B1
11 Chau Doc Covered Market ... B2
12 Con Tien Floating Restaurant ... B1
13 Mekong ... D3
14 Thanh Tinh ... B2

Drinking & Nightlife

Bamboo Bar ... (see 8)
Tan Chau Salon Bar ... (see 8)

Thuan Loi Hotel
HOTEL $

(☑ 076-386 6134; ksthuanloi@yahoo.com; 18 Đ Tran Hung Dao; r with fan/air-con US$10/15; ✴) The sole cheapie with a riverside location, plus a floating restaurant. Rooms are not so atmospheric, but good value. Fan rooms are cold water only, so consider a larger air-con room.

Vinh Phuoc Hotel
HOTEL $

(☑ 076-386 6242; 12 Đ Quang Trung; r with fan US$7-10, with air-con US$10-12; ✴ @) The friendly staff at this popular budget hotel have a good knowledge of the delta region. Rooms range from fan-only cheapies to smarter air-con options with hot water. The restaurant is good value and there are usually some beer drinkers lurking around.

Chau Pho
HOTEL $$

(☑ 076-6356 4139; www.chauphohotel.com; Đ 88 Trung Nu Vuong; r US$32-50; ✴ ☎) This solid, friendly midrange hotel with tennis courts has 50 well-presented rooms over five floors, some with balcony. Deluxe rooms are far more pleasant than the cheaper options.

★ Victoria Chau Doc Hotel
HOTEL $$$

(☑ 076-386 5010; www.victoriahotels.asia; 32 Đ Le Loi; r from US$110, ste from US$175; ✴ @ ☎ ✉) Stylish for Chau Doc, the Victoria delivers classic colonial charm, overseen by *ao-dai*-clad staff. With a striking location on the riverfront, the grand rooms here have dark-wood floors and furniture, and inviting bathtubs. The swimming pool overlooks the busy river action and there's a small spa upstairs. A range of tours is available to guests.

✗ Eating

The **Chau Doc Covered Market** (Đ Bach Dang; ⊙ 7am-9pm) has tasty Vietnamese food (10,000d to 20,000d). At night, you can also try a variety of cool *che* (dessert soups) at *che* stalls on Đ Bach Dang, next to the pagoda. There are also lots of other inexpensive stalls with large whiteboard menus displaying their wares.

Bay Bong
VIETNAMESE $

(22 Đ Thuong Dang Le; mains 40,000-80,000d; ⊙ 9am-8pm) Visually it's a letdown – metal tables and chairs, white tiles – but the food is something, with tasty fish-and-vegetable hotpot, stir-fried rice with seafood, beef noodle soup and so forth.

Mekong
VIETNAMESE $

(41 Đ Le Loi; mains 35,000-175,000d) Located directly opposite the Victoria Chau Doc Hotel, this restaurant has a large covered section or an outdoor area in front of the gracefully decaying old villa.

Con Tien Floating Restaurant
VIETNAMESE $

(Đ Tran Hung Dao; mains 40,000-90,000d; ⊙ 7am-10pm) It's fun dining on fish and seafood dishes in this cavernous floating restaurant on the Bassac River. It's good for *hu tieu* – the noodle soup (beef, seafood or chicken).

Thanh Tinh
VIETNAMESE $

(42 Đ Quang Trung; mains 30,000-80,000d; ⊙ 6am-7pm; ✐) This place translates as 'to calm the body down' and it will do just that for vegetarians looking for a reliable menu.

Bassac Restaurant
FRENCH, VIETNAMESE $$

(☑ 076-386 5010; 32 Đ Le Loi; mains US$5-20; ⊙ 5.45am-10pm) Chau Doc's most sophisticated dining experience is at the Victoria Chau Doc Hotel, where the menu includes some beautifully presented Vietnamese food and a mouthwatering selection of inventive French dishes.

◗ Drinking & Nightlife

Chau Doc is pretty sleepy. For a stylish tipple, try the poolside **Bamboo Bar** (www.victoriahotels.asia; Victoria Chau Doc Hotel, 32 Đ Le Loi) or **Tan Chau Salon Bar** (www.victoriahotels.asia; Victoria Chau Doc Hotel, 32 Đ Le Loi; ⊙ 6am-11pm) at the Victoria Chau Doc Hotel. Another atmospheric but considerably cheaper spot for a casual drink is the Con Tien Floating Restaurant.

❶ Information

Mekong Tours (☑ 076-356 2828; www.mekongvietnam.com; 14 Đ Nguyen Huu Canh; ⊙ 8am-8pm) Local travel agency for booking boat or bus transport to Phnom Penh, boat trips on the Mekong and cars with drivers.

Post Office (☑ 076-386 9200; 2 Đ Le Loi)

❶ Getting There & Away

BUS

The buses from HCMC to Chau Doc leave from the Mien Tay bus station. Express buses can make the run in six hours and cost around 130,000d. **Chau Doc bus station** (Ben Xe Chau

Doc) is on the eastern edge of town, where Đ Le Loi becomes Hwy 91. Other destinations include Ha Tien (70,000d) and My Tho (51,000d).

CAR & MOTORBIKE

By road, Chau Doc is approximately 95km from Ha Tien, 117km from Can Tho, 181km from My Tho and 245km from HCMC.

ℹ Getting Around

Boats to Chau Giang district (across the Hau Giang River) leave from two docks: vehicle ferries depart from **Chau Giang ferry landing** (Ben Pha Chau Giang), opposite 419 Đ Le Loi; smaller, more frequent boats leave from **Phu Hiep ferry landing** (Ben Pha FB Phu Hiep), a little further southeast.

Private boats (80,000d for two hours), which are rowed standing up, can be hired from either of the ferry landing spots or from 30 Thang 4 Park, and are highly recommended for seeing the floating houses and visiting nearby Cham minority villages and mosques. Motorboats (per hour 100,000d) can be hired in the same area.

Around Chau Doc

Sam Mountain

A sacred place for Buddhists, Sam Mountain (Nui Sam, 284m) and its environs are crammed with dozens of pagodas and temples. A strong Chinese influence makes it particularly popular with ethnic Chinese, but Buddhists of all ethnicities visit here. The views from the top are excellent (weather permitting), ranging deep into Cambodia. There's a military outpost on the summit, a legacy of the days when the Khmer Rouge made cross-border raids and massacred Vietnamese civilians.

Along with the shrines and tombs, the steep path to the top is lined with the unholy clamour of commerce and there are plenty of cafes and stalls in which to stop for a drink or a snack. Walking down is easier than walking up (a 45-minute climb), so if you want to cheat, have a motorbike drop you at the summit (about 20,000d from the base of

MEKONG DELTA AROUND CHAU DOC

ℹ GETTING TO CAMBODIA: CHAU DOC TO PHNOM PENH

Vinh Xuong–Kaam Samnor Border Crossing

Getting to the border One of the most enjoyable ways to enter Cambodia is via the Vinh Xuong–Kaam Samnor border crossing located just northwest of Chau Doc along the Mekong River. Several companies in Chau Doc sell boat journeys from Chau Doc to Phnom Penh via the Vinh Xuong border. Hang Chau (☑Chau Doc 076-356 2771, Phnom Penh 855-12-883 542; www.hangchautourist.com.vn; per person US$24) boats depart Chau Doc at 7.30am from a pier at 18 Đ Tran Hung Dao, arriving at 12.30pm. From Phnom Penh they depart at noon. The more upmarket Blue Cruiser (☑HCMC 08-3926 0253, Phnom Penh 855-236-333 666; www.bluecruiser.com) leaves the Victoria Hotel pier at 7am, costing US$55 (US$44 in the reverse direction, leaving Phnom Penh at 1.30pm). It takes about five hours, including the border check. Also departing from this pier at 7am (and from Phnom Penh at 1.30pm) are Victoria Speedboats, exclusive to Victoria Hotel guests (US$97, five hours).

At the border If coming from Cambodia, arrange a visa in advance. If leaving Vietnam, Cambodian visas are available at the crossing, but minor overcharging is common (plan on paying around US$24).

Tinh Bien–Phnom Den Border Crossing

Getting to the border Eclipsed by the newer crossing of Xa Xia near Ha Tien, the Tinh Bien–Phnom Den border crossing is less convenient for Phnom Penh–bound travellers, but may be of interest for those who savour the challenge of obscure border crossings. Buses from Chau Doc to Phnom Penh (US$15 to US$21, five hours) depart at 7.30am and can be booked through Mekong Tours in Chau Doc. The roads leading to the border are terrible.

At the border Cambodian visas can be obtained here, although it's not uncommon to be charged US$25, several dollars more than the official rate.

Moving on Most travellers opt for a through bus ticket from Chau Doc.

the mountain). The road to the top is a pretty ride on the east side of the mountain. Veer left at the base of the mountain and turn right after about 1km where the road begins its climb. The mountain is open 24/7, with lights on the road for nocturnal climbs.

◉ Sights

Tay An Pagoda
BUDDHIST TEMPLE

(Chua Tay An; ⊙ 4am-10pm) Although founded in 1847 on the site of an earlier bamboo shrine, Tay An's current structure dates from 1958. Aspects of its eclectic architecture, particularly its domed tower, reflect Hindu and Islamic influences.

With a main gate of traditional Vietnamese design, on its roofline romp figures of lions and two dragons fighting for possession of pearls, chrysanthemums, apricot trees and lotus blossoms.

The temple itself is guarded by statues of a black elephant with two tusks and a white elephant with six tusks. Inside are arrayed fine carvings of hundreds of religious figures, most made of wood and some blinged up with disco-light halos. Statues include Sakyamuni, the 18 *a-la-han* (arhat) and the 12 *muoi hai ba mu* (midwives). The temple's name – Tay An – means 'Western Peace'.

If you're coming from Chau Doc on Hwy 91, Tay An Pagoda is located straight ahead at the foot of the mountain.

Temple of Lady Xu
BUDDHIST TEMPLE

(Mieu Ba Chua Xu; ⊙ 24hr) Founded in the 1820s to house a statue that's become the subject of a popular cult, this large temple faces Sam Mountain, on the same road as Tay An Pagoda. Originally a simple affair of bamboo and leaves, the temple has been rebuilt many times, most recently between 1972 and 1976, blending mid-20th-century design with Vietnamese Buddhist decorative motifs.

The statue itself is possibly a relic of the Oc-Eo culture, dating from the 6th century, and is also possibly that of a man – but don't suggest that to one of the faithful.

According to one of several legends, the statue of Lady Xu used to stand at the summit of Sam Mountain. In the early 19th century Siamese troops invaded the area and decided to take it back to Thailand. But as they carried the statue down the hill, it became heavier and heavier, and they were forced to abandon it by the side of the path.

One day some villagers who were cutting wood came upon the statue and decided to bring it back to their village in order to build

a temple for it; but it weighed too much for them to budge it. Suddenly, a girl appeared who, possessed by a spirit, declared herself to be Lady Xu. She announced to them that nine virgins were to be brought and that they would be able to transport the statue down the mountainside. The virgins were then summoned and carried the statue down the slope, but when they reached the plain, it became too heavy and they had to set it down. The people concluded that the site where the virgins halted had been selected by Lady Xu for the temple construction and it's here that the Temple of Lady Xu stands to this day.

Offerings of roast whole pigs are frequently presented to the statue, which is dressed in glittering robes and adorned with an astonishing headdress. Once a month a creation of vegetables representing a dragon, tortoise, phoenix and *qilin* is also proffered to the effigy. The Chinese characters in the portal where worshippers pray are 主处聖母, which mean 'the main place of the sacred mother'. A further couplet reads 爲国爲民, which means 'for the country and for the people'. The temple's most important festival is held from the 23rd to the 26th day of the fourth lunar month, usually late May or early June. During this time, pilgrims flock here, sleeping on mats in the large rooms of the two-storey resthouse next to the temple.

Tomb of Thoai Ngoc Hau
TOMB

(Lang Thoai Ngoc Hau; ⊙ 5am-10.30pm) A high-ranking official, Thoai Ngoc Hau (1761–1829) served the Nguyen Lords and, later, the Nguyen dynasty. In early 1829, Thoai Ngoc Hau ordered that a tomb be constructed for himself at the foot of Sam Mountain. The site he chose is nearly opposite the Temple of Lady Xu.

The steps are made of red 'beehive' stone *(da ong)* brought from the southeastern part of Vietnam. In the middle of the platform is the tomb of Thoai Ngoc Hau and those of his wives, Chau Thi Te and Truong Thi Miet. There's a shrine at the rear and several dozen other tombs in the vicinity where his officials are buried.

Cavern Pagoda
BUDDHIST TEMPLE

(Chua Hang; ⊙ 4am-9pm) Also known as Phuoc Dien Tu, this temple is halfway up the western (far) side of Sam Mountain, with amazing views of the rice fields. The lower part of the pagoda includes monks' quarters and two hexagonal tombs in which the founder of the pagoda, a female tailor named Le Thi

Tho, and a former head monk, Thich Hue Thien, are buried.

The upper section has two parts: the main sanctuary, in which there are statues of A Di Da (Buddha of the Past) and Thich Ca Buddha (Sakyamuni, the Historical Buddha); and an astounding complex of caverns and grottoes containing a host of deities, including a 1000-arm and 1000-eye Quan Am. There's also a mirror room of Buddhas and an effigy of Bodhidharma, the founder of Zen Buddhism.

According to legend, Le Thi Tho came from Tay An Pagoda to this site half a century ago to lead a quiet, meditative life. When she arrived, she found two enormous snakes, one white and the other dark green. Le Thi Tho soon converted the snakes, which thereafter led pious lives. Upon her death, the snakes disappeared.

🛏 Sleeping & Eating

There is a bustling community at the base of Sam Mountain, with hotels (both aimed at visiting Buddhists and businesspeople), guesthouses and restaurants lining the street.

❶ Getting There & Away

Most people get here by rented motorbike or on the back of a *xe om* (about 40,000d one-way). There are also local buses heading this way from Chau Doc (5000d).

Phu Chau (Tan Chau) District

Traditional silk-making has made Phu Chau (Tan Chau) district – where the market has a selection of competitively priced Thai and Cambodian goods – famous throughout southern Vietnam.

To get to Phu Chau district from Chau Doc, take a boat across the Hau Giang River from the Phu Hiep ferry landing, then catch a ride on the back of a *xe om* (about 60,000d) for the 18km trip.

Long Xuyen

☑ 076 / POP 300,000

Beyond a few minor sights and a lively market, the capital of An Giang province offers little to detain travellers. It's a relatively affluent city, making its money from agriculture (particularly cashew nuts) and fish processing.

Long Xuyen was once a stronghold of the Hoa Hao sect. Founded in 1939, the sect em-

Long Xuyen

◉ **Sights**
1 Long Xuyen Catholic Church A2

🛏 **Sleeping**
2 Dong Xuyen Hotel..................................B2
3 Long Xuyen Hotel A2

🍴 **Eating**
4 Hai Thue...B3
5 Hong Phat...B3

phasises simplicity in worship and does not believe in temples or intermediaries between humans and the Supreme Being. Until 1956 the Hoa Hao had an army and constituted a major military force in this region.

The town's other claim to fame is being the birthplace of Vietnam's second president, Ton Duc Thang.

History

During the 1st to 6th centuries AD, when southern Vietnam and southern Cambodia were under the rule of the Indian-influenced Cambodian kingdom of Funan, Oc-Eo (the scant remains of which lie 37km southwest of Long Xuyen) was a major trading city. Much of what is known about the Funan empire, which reached its height during the 5th century AD, comes from contemporary Chinese sources and the excavations at Oc-Eo and Angkor Borei in neighbouring Cambodia. The excavations have uncovered evidence of contact between Oc-Eo and what is now Thailand, Malaysia and Indonesia, as well as Persia and the Roman Empire.

An elaborate system of canals around Oc-Eo was once used for both irrigation and transportation, prompting Chinese travellers of the time to write about 'sailing across Funan' on their way to the Malay Peninsula. Most of the buildings of Oc-Eo were built on piles and pieces of these structures indicate the high degree of refinement achieved by Funanese civilisation. Artefacts found at Oc-Eo are on display at the History Museum and Fine Arts Museum in HCMC and at the History Museum in Hanoi.

⊙ Sights

Blue Sky Crocodile Land CROCODILE FARM
(Ca Sau Long Xuyen; ☑076-383 1298; 44/1A Đ Tran Hung Dao; admission 10,000d; ☺7am-6pm) For a close-up view of the reptile that once ruled the Mekong, head to this farm that's home to thousands of crocodiles ranging in size from 10cm to 4m. The meat and skin of these animals is largely exported, though some Vietnamese drop in to buy fresh or frozen crocodile meat or to eat at the on-site restaurant. A little shop sells crocodile-skin wallets and bags. The farm lies 8km south of town on the road to Can Tho.

Long Xuyen Catholic Church CHURCH
(Đ Tran Hung Dao) One of the largest churches in the Mekong Delta and dominating town, this impressive modern cathedral is topped by a 50m-high bell tower and can seat 1000 worshippers. Constructed between 1966 and 1973 – you can tell – the interior is cavernous and well-ventilated, with a sculptural centrepiece of a giant crucifix resting on a globe supported by two hands.

Cho Moi DISTRICT
Across the river from Long Xuyen, Cho Moi district is known for its groves of fruit such as bananas, durians, guava, jackfruit, longans, mangoes, mangosteens and plums. Take a boat from the passenger ferry terminal.

⊨ Sleeping

Dong Xuyen Hotel HOTEL $
(☑076-394 2260; www.angiangtourimex.com. vn; 9A Đ Luong Van Cu; r 400,000-770,000d, ste 800,000d; ❋⊛) The smartest place in town, Dong Xuyen has pleasantly furnished and well-equipped rooms. Staff are friendly and helpful and speak good English.

Long Xuyen Hotel HOTEL $
(☑076-384 1927; www.angiangtourimex.com.vn; 19 Đ Nguyen Van Cung; r 300,000-420,000d; ❋⊛) An overhaul is badly needed, but prices are reasonable and there's a good restaurant at this affordable hotel. Rooms have some charm and include satellite TV, hot water and shared balconies.

✕ Eating

Hong Phat VIETNAMESE $
(242/4 Đ Luong Van Cu; mains 30,000-80,000d; ☺9am-9pm) English menus, grilled meats, plenty of seafood, friendly staff and air-con make this a reliable and smart choice.

Hai Thue VIETNAMESE $
(☑076-384 5573; 245/3 Đ Luong Van Cu; mains 15,000-40,000d) A good stop for cheap, authentic Vietnamese food.

❶ Getting There & Away

BOAT
To get to the Long Xuyen ferry dock from Đ Pham Hong Thai, you'll need to cross Duy Tan Bridge and turn right. Passenger ferries leave from here to Sa Dec and other Delta destinations.

BUS
Buses from HCMC to Long Xuyen leave from the Mien Tay bus station (from 85,000d). **Long Xuyen bus station** (Ben Xe Khach Long Xuyen; ☑076-385 2125; opposite 96/3B Đ Tran Hung Dao) is a roadside terminus about 1.5km down Đ Phan Cu Luong, off Đ Tran Hung Dao, at the southern end of town. Buses from Long Xuyen head to Can Tho (62km), Chau Doc (55km), Ha Tien (130km) and Rach Gia (75km).

CAR & MOTORCYCLE
To get to Cao Lanh or Sa Dec you'll need to take the car ferry from An Hoa ferry terminal.

Cao Lanh
☑067 / POP 150,000
A newish town carved from the jungles and swamps of the Mekong Delta region, Cao Lanh is big for business, but draws few tourists. Its main appeal is as a base to explore Rung Tram (Tram Forest) and Tram Chim National Park, both reachable by boat.

Cao Lanh

◎ Sights

Dong Thap Museum   MUSEUM
(226 Đ Nguyen Thai Hoc; ◷ 7-11.30am & 1.30-5pm)
FREE The Dong Thap Museum is among
the Mekong's best museums, despite having no English captions. The ground floor
displays an anthropological history of Dong
Thap province, with exhibits of tools, sculpture, models of traditional houses and a few
stuffed animals and pickled fish. Upstairs is
devoted to war history and Ho Chi Minh.

War Martyrs Monument   MONUMENT
On the eastern edge of town off Hwy 30, the
War Memorial (Dai Liet Si) is Cao Lanh's
most prominent landmark, a sculpture featuring a large white concrete statue of a
decorated soldier holding flowers in front of
a stylised star. The rear of the statue is illustrated with storks, a symbol of the Mekong.

Within the grounds are the graves of 3112
VC who died fighting in the American War.

Tomb of Nguyen Sinh Sac   PARK
(Lang Cu Nguyen Sinh Sac; off Đ Pham Huu Lau; car
parking 6000d) The tomb of Ho Chi Minh's
father, Nguyen Sinh Sac (1862-1929), is the
centrepiece of a pretty 9.6-hectare park and
model heritage village. The tomb itself is lo-

Cao Lanh

◎ Sights
1 Dong Thap Museum	A3
2 Tomb of Nguyen Sinh Sac	A3
3 War Martyrs Monument	D1

⬤ Sleeping
4 Hoa Anh	C2
5 Nha Khach Dong Thap	B1
6 Song Tra Hotel	C2
7 Xuan Mai Hotel	B2

⊗ Eating
8 A Chau	B1
9 Ngoc Lan	C1

cated under a shell-shaped shrine set behind
a star-shaped lotus pond.

Although various plaques (in Vietnamese)
and tourist pamphlets extol Nguyen Sinh
Sac as a great revolutionary, scarce evidence
confirms that he was involved in the anticolonial struggle against the French. Next to
the shrine is a small museum devoted to Ho
Chi Minh consisting mainly of photographs
with Vietnamese captions.

The complex is located at the southwest
approach to town; turn right after Hoa Long
Pagoda and follow the fence around until
you get to the entrance.

🛏 Sleeping

Hoa Anh   HOTEL $
(☑ 067-224 0567; hoaanhhotel@yahoo.com.vn; 40 Đ Ly Tu Trong; r from 210,000d; ✸ 🗢) For 210,000d you'll get a tidy, smallish double with a small bathroom at this fresh-faced hotel near the bus station. The two-bed rooms are spacious, while the pricier rooms would fit a family.

Xuan Mai Hotel   HOTEL $
(☑ 067-385 2852; 33 Đ Le Qui Don; r 200,000-300,000d; ✸ 🗢) A cavernous restaurant, massage parlour and hotel rolled into one, this represents good value, with spacious but rather tacky rooms. Located behind the post office; rates include breakfast. No lift.

Nha Khach Dong Thap   HOTEL $
(☑ 067-387 2670; 48 Đ Ly Thuong Kiet; r 350,000-1,000,000d; ✸ 🗢) A Communist Party special, with large, airy, OK rooms, a reception dripping in marble, and corridors wide enough to take a jeep. However, little English is spoken and it has an institutionalised feel.

Song Tra Hotel   HOTEL $$
(☑ 067-385 2624; 178 Đ Nguyen Hue; r US$19-35, ste US$50; ✸) The exterior is clunky but rooms are in reasonable shape, with big windows, satellite TV, a minibar and hot water. Staff are friendlier than you'll find in most other state-run places.

🍴 Eating

Cao Lanh is famous for *chuot dong* (rice-field rats) so come with room in your stomach to sample the local delicacy. At the very least, it'll make a great story back home.

Ngoc Lan   VIETNAMESE $
(210 Đ Nguyen Hue; dishes from 35,000d; ⊙ 8am-9pm) The 'Magnolia' is a bright and inviting choice, with fresh and tasty pot-cooked pork (35,000d) and mixed-vegetable soup (80,000d). It's illuminated with a red-and-green LED sign at night.

A Chau   VIETNAMESE $
(☑ 067-385 2202; 42 Đ Ly Thuong Kiet; mains 20,000-70,000d) Shut for a refurb at the time of writing, this eatery usually has tasty *banh xeo* (fried pancakes, which you roll up and dip in fish sauce) as a speciality.

ℹ Information

Dong Thap Tourist (☑ 067-387 3026; www. dongthaptourist.com; 2 Đ Doc Binh Kieu; ⊙ 7-11.30am & 1.30-5pm) A particularly friendly, helpful outfit that can arrange boat and other tours of the surrounding area. It also has a branch (☑ 067-391 8487) at My Hiep village.

Post Office (85 Đ Nguyen Hue) Internet access available.

ℹ Getting There & Around

Cao Lanh Bus Station (Ben Xe Cao Lanh; 71/1 Đ Ly Thuong Kiet) is conveniently located right in the centre of town, with services to HCMC (65,000d), Sa Dec (15,000d), Vinh Long (17,000d), My Tho (30,000d), Tra Vinh (49,000d), Can Tho (45,000d), Soc Trang (55,000d), Vung Tau (112,000d) and Ca Mau (85,000d).

Sights around Cao Lanh are best visited by river. Although you could possibly arrange something privately with boat owners, you'll find it easier – though slightly more expensive – to deal with Dong Thap Tourist. Plan on about US$30 for a half-day boat tour.

Around Cao Lanh

◉ Sights & Activities

Xeo Quyt Forest   NATURE RESERVE
(Xeo Quyt, Xeo Quit; admission 5000d; ⊙ 7am-5pm) Southeast of Cao Lanh and accessible by boat tour is the magnificent 52-hectare Xeo Quyt Forest (also called Rung Tram) near My Hiep village. One vast swamp beneath a beautiful thick canopy of tall trees and vines, it's one of the last natural forests left in the Mekong Delta.

During the rainy season a marvellous 20-minute canoe tour (15,000d) takes you past old bunkers and former mine fields along narrow canals filled with ever-present dragonflies and choked with water hyacinths *(luc binh)*. It's an exquisite experience but splash on the repellent and try to get out by 4.30pm when the mozzies begin swarming. During the dry season you can explore this area on foot.

During the American War the VC had a base here, where top-brass VC lived in underground bunkers. Only about 10 VC were here at any given time; they were all generals who directed the war from here, just 2km from a US military base. The Americans never realised that the VC generals were living right under their noses. Naturally, they were suspicious about that patch of forest and periodically dropped some bombs on it to reassure themselves, but the VC remained safe in their underground bunkers.

From My Hiep, you can hire a boat (around US$20, seating up to 10 people) that takes around 40 minutes to make the 2km journey to Xeo Quyt. Dong Thap Tourist includes a guided trip in several of its tour programs.

Tram Chim National Park   NATURE RESERVE
(⊙7am-4pm) Tram Chim National Park is due north of Cao Lanh in Tam Nong district and notable for its eastern sarus cranes (*Grus antigone sharpii*). More than 220 species of bird have been identified within the reserve, but ornithologists will be most interested in these rare red-headed cranes, which grow to an impressive 1.8m high.

Seeing these birds, however, requires a considerable commitment (time, effort and money), so it's strictly for enthusiasts.

Birds nest here from about December to May; from June to November they migrate to northwest Cambodia, so schedule your visit to coordinate with the birds' travel itinerary if you want to see them. The birds are early risers, so morning visits are advised. During the day, they're engaged in the important business of eating.

Tam Nong is a sleepy town 45km from Cao Lanh. The one-way drive takes an hour by car. From Tam Nong it takes another hour by small boat (around 2,700,000d) to reach the area where the cranes live and another hour to return. Add to this whatever time you spend (perhaps an hour) bird-watching (bring your own binoculars), and then the requisite two hours to return to Cao Lanh, depending on your mode of transport. There are a few rudimentary guesthouses in Tam Nong if you decide to stay late or hit the park early. Tam Nong shuts down early so if you want to eat dinner here, make arrangements before 5pm.

Sa Dec

☑ 067 / POP 108,000
The drowsy former capital of Dong Thap province, Sa Dec is a comparatively peaceful city of tree-lined streets and fading colonial villas, ringed with orchards and flower markets. It trumpets a minor claim to fame as the setting for *The Lover,* a semi-autobiographical novel by Marguerite Duras, made into a film by Jean-Jacques Annaud.

⊙ Sights

Huynh Thuy Le Old House   HISTORICAL BUILDING
(Nha Co Huynh Thuy Le; ☑ 0939 533 523; 225A Đ Nguyen Hue; admission 10,000d) This wonder-

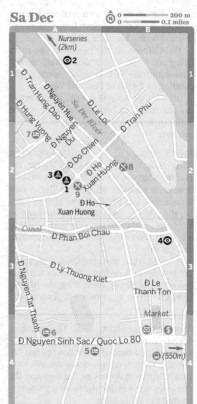

Sa Dec

⊙ Sights
1 Buu Quang Pagoda	A2
2 Cao Dai Temple	A1
3 Huong Pagoda	A2
4 Huynh Thuy Le Old House	B3

🛏 Sleeping
5 Bong Hong Hotel	A4
6 Phuong Nam	A4
7 Sa Dec Hotel	A2

✕ Eating
8 Night Market	B2
9 Quan Com Thuy	A2

fully atmospheric 1895 house on the riverfront was once the residence of Huynh Thuy Le, the 27-year-old son of a rich Chinese family who Marguerite Duras had an affair with in 1929 when she was only 15 – immortalising the romance in *The Lover.* The house is a Sino-French design with intricate interior woodwork, mother-of-pearl inlaid doors and original floor tiles, made in France.

The Chinese on the plaque in the main hall reads '中西共仰', which literally means 'China and the West admire together', celebrating its fusion of East and West.

It's possible to stay overnight in one of the charming but basic rooms here; shared bathrooms are located at the rear of the property.

Huong Pagoda
BUDDHIST TEMPLE

(Chua Huong; Đ Hung Vuong) Chua Huong, the Perfume Pagoda, was built in a classic Chinese style in 1838. Marguerite Duras fans should seek out the shrine of Huynh Thuy Le, the real-life inspiration for the lover in her book – although you may find it hard to tell from the photos of the septuagenarian and his wife.

A bright white statue of Quan The Am Bo Tat stands on a pedestal between this and the adjacent Buu Quang Pagoda (Đ Hung Vuong), which is somewhat less glamorous.

Nurseries
NURSERY

(Vuon Hoa; ⊙ 7am-5pm) FREE The nurseries operate year-round, though they are practically stripped bare of their flowers just before the Tet festival. Domestic tourists from HCMC arrive in droves on Sundays and the nurseries are a major sightseeing attraction around the Tet holiday.

Marigolds are sold in abundance to temples and the nurseries are inundated with water during the flood season, when gardeners get around by boat. There are many small operators lining the river and canals here, each with a different speciality. It's interesting to swing by in the morning and watch the plants being loaded on to boats. A motorbike from town will cost around 20,000d.

Cao Dai Temple
TEMPLE

(102 Đ Le Loi; ⊙ 6am-9pm) On the far side of the Sa Dec River, the drum tower of this Cao Dai temple is well worth a climb for glorious riverine views of town.

🛏 Sleeping & Eating

Phuong Nam
HOTEL $

(☏ 067-386 7867; hotelphuongnam@yahoo.com; 384A Đ Nguyen Sinh Sac; s 200,000-220,000d, d 270,000-350,000d; ❄ 🛜) This minihotel on

the highway has rooms ranging from small cheapies with tiny bathrooms and balcony, to large rooms with wooden floors. Twitchy wi-fi.

Bong Hong Hotel
HOTEL $

(☏ 067-386 8288; bonghonghotel@yahoo.com. vn; 251A Đ Nguyen Sinh Sac; r with fan 320,000d, r with air-con 420,000-550,000d, ste 840,000d; ❄ @ 🛜) The upper rooms with balconies are the most appealing at this hulking, cheerless hotel with musty fan rooms. Breakfast is included and there are tennis courts under palm trees next door.

Sa Dec Hotel
HOTEL $

(☏ 067-386 1430; sadechotel@yahoo.com.vn; 499 Đ Hung Vuong; r with fan 200,000d, r with air-con 260,000-300,000d, ste 400,000-500,000d; ❄ @ 🛜) Fan rooms with balcony are a bargain at this chipped and scuffed government-owned pad with once-groovy 1970s styling and funky spiral staircase.

Nha Co Huynh Thuy Le
GUEST HOUSE $$

(☏ 067-377 3937; thanhctydl@yahoo.com.vn; 225A Đ Nguyen Hue; s/d 650,000/900,000d) With top marks for charm, this glorious chunk of heritage on the riverfront revels in a fusion of Chinese and West. Fan rooms are basic and there are only four in all. Shared bathrooms are located at the back of the property. No TV or phones in rooms, but staff say wi-fi 'is coming'.

Night Market
VIETNAMESE $

(Đ Nguyen Hue; ⊙ 5pm-late) The hopping riverside night market has a lively string of hotpot restaurants come evening. Expect to pay around 20,000d for grilled chicken, 40,000d for grilled squid and 10,000d for a beer.

Quan Com Thuy
VIETNAMESE $

(☏ 067-386 1644; 439 Đ Hung Vuong; mains 50,000-100,000d; ⊙ 9am-9pm) This reputable meat-and-rice joint offers aluminium furniture, bright lights and a dependable menu.

ℹ Getting There & Away

Sa Dec is midway between Vinh Long, Chau Doc and Long Xuyen – although getting to the latter two requires a ferry crossing. Sa Dec Bus Station (Ben Xe Sa Dec) is on Hwy 80, immediately southeast of the centre. Services head to Vinh Long (13,000d), Cao Lanh (15,000d) and HCMC (65,000d to 95,000d).

Siem Reap & the Temples of Angkor

Best Temples for Sunrise or Sunset

➡ Angkor Wat (p408)
➡ Bayon (p409)
➡ Phnom Bakheng (p413)

Best Temples for Film Buffs

➡ Angkor Wat (p408)
➡ Bayon (p409)
➡ Beng Mealea (p414)
➡ Ta Prohm (p413)

Why Go?

Where to begin with Angkor? There is no greater concentration of architectural riches anywhere on earth. Choose from the world's largest religious building, Angkor Wat, one of the world's weirdest, Bayon, or the riotous jungle of Ta Prohm. All are global icons and have helped put Cambodia on the map as the temple capital of Asia. Today, the monuments are a point of pilgrimage for all Khmers, and no traveller to the region will want to miss their extravagant beauty.

Siem Reap was always destined for great things and offers everything from backpacker party pads to hip hotels, world-class wining and dining and sumptuous spas.

Despite the headline act that is Angkor and the sophistication of Siem Reap, Cambodia's greatest treasure is its people. The Khmers have been to hell and back, but they have prevailed with a smile and no visitor comes away from this kingdom without a measure of admiration and affection for its inhabitants.

When to Go
Siem Reap

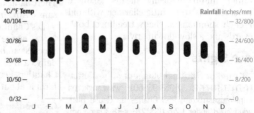

Dec–Jan Humidity is low, there are cool breezes and little rain. Peak season for visitors.

Feb–Jun Temperatures rise and in May or June the monsoon brings rain and humidity.

Jun–Oct The wet season: Angkor is surrounded by lush foliage and the moats are full of water.

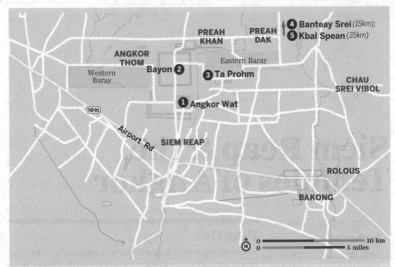

Siem Reap & the Temples of Angkor Highlights

1 See the sun rise over one of the world's most iconic buildings, the one and only **Angkor Wat** (p408).

2 Contemplate the serenity and splendour of the **Bayon** (p409), its 216 enigmatic faces staring out into the jungle.

3 Witness nature running riot at the mysterious ruin of **Ta Prohm** (p413), the *Tomb Raider* temple.

4 Stare in wonder at the delicate carvings adorning **Banteay Srei** (p414), the finest seen at Angkor.

5 Trek deep into the jungle to discover the River of a Thousand Lingas at **Kbal Spean** (p414).

SIEM REAP

063 / POP 119,500

Life-support system for the temples of Angkor, Siem Reap (pronounced see-em ree-ep) is the epicentre of the new Cambodia, a pulsating place that's one of the most popular destinations on the planet right now. At its heart though, Siem Reap – whose name rather undiplomatically means 'Siamese Defeated' – is still a little charmer, with old French shophouses, shady tree-lined boulevards and a slow-flowing river.

◎ Sights

★**Angkor National Museum**   MUSEUM
(សារមន្ទីរអង្គរ; ☎063-966601; www.angkornationalmuseum.com; 968 Charles de Gaulle Blvd; adult/child under 1.2m US$12/6; ◎8.30am-6pm, to 6.30pm 1 Oct-30 Apr) A worthwhile introduction to the glories of the Khmer empire, this state-of-the-art museum helps define Angkor's historic, religious and cultural significance. Displays include 1500 exquisite stone carvings and artefacts.

Les Chantiers Écoles   ARTISANAL SCHOOL
(កសិដ្ឋានស្ត្រៃ; www.artisansdangkor.com; ◎7.30am-5.30pm, silk farm 7am-5pm) FREE Les Chantiers Écoles is a school specialising in teaching wood- and stone-carving techniques, traditional silk painting, lacquerware and more to impoverished youngsters. Free guided tours are available daily to learn more about traditional techniques. There is also a beautiful shop called Artisans d'Angkor.

Les Chantiers Écoles also maintains a **silk farm**, where all stages of the production process can be seen. Free tours are available daily; a free shuttle bus departs from Les Chantiers Écoles at 9.30am and 1.30pm. The farm is about 16km west of Siem Reap.

Cambodian Cultural Village   CULTURAL VILLAGE
(☎063-963836; www.cambodianculturalvillage.com; Airport Rd; adult/child under 1.1m US$9/free; ◎8am-7pm) It may be kitsch, it may be kooky, but it's very popular with Cambodians and provides a diversion for families with children. This place tries to represent all of Cambodia in a whirlwind tour

of re-created houses and villages. There are dance shows and performances throughout the day, but it still doesn't attract many foreign visitors.

Activities

There is an incredible array of activities on offer in Siem Reap.

Angkor Golf Resort   GOLF
(063-761139; www.angkor-golf.com; green fees US$115) This world-class course was designed by celebrated British golfer Nick Faldo. Fees rise to US$175 with clubs, caddies, carts and all.

Angkor Palm   COOKING COURSE
(Pithnou St; per person US$12) Informal cooking classes held from 8am to 5pm.

Bodia Spa   SPA
(063-761593; www.bodia-spa.com; Pithnou St; 10am–midnight) Sophisticated spa near the Psar Chaa area offering a full range of scrubs, rubs and natural remedies, including its own line of herbal products.

Off Track   BICYCLE TOUR
(093-903024; www.kko-cambodia.org; tour US$35-40) Good-cause cycling tours around the paths of Angkor or into the countryside beyond the Western Baray. Proceeds go towards the Khmer for Khmer Organisation, which supports education and vocational training.

Quad Adventure Cambodia   QUAD BIKING
(092-787216; www.quad-adventure-cambodia. com; sunset ride US$30, full day US$170) All-terrain rides around Siem Reap take in rice fields at sunset, pretty temples and back roads through traditional villages where children wave and shout.

Sleeping

Siem Reap offers everything from US$3 shacks with shared toilets to five-star luxury palaces.

★ Ivy Guesthouse 2   GUEST HOUSE $
(012-800860; www.ivy-guesthouse.com; r US$6-15;) An inviting guesthouse with a chill-out area and bar, the Ivy is a lively place to stay. The restaurant is as good as it gets among the guesthouses in town, with a huge vegetarian selection.

Shadow of Angkor Guesthouse   GUEST HOUSE $
(063-964774; www.shadowofangkor.com; 353 Pokambor Ave; r US$15-25;) In a grand old French-era building overlooking the river, this friendly, 15-room place offers affordable air-con rooms in a superb setting. The newer annex across the river includes a swimming pool.

Downtown Siem Reap Hostel   HOSTEL $
(012 675881; www.downtownsiemreaphostel. hostel.com; Wat Damnak area; dm US$4-6, r US$13-17;) Also known as Bamboo Garden, this hostel has enticing rates given there is a small pool in the garden. Outside visitors can use the pool with a US$6 spend on food and drink.

Seven Candles Guesthouse   GUEST HOUSE $
(963380; www.sevencandlesguesthouse.com; 307 Wat Bo Rd; r US$10-20;) A good-cause guesthouse: its profits help a local foundation that seeks to promote education to rural communities. Rooms include hot water, TV and fridge.

★ HanumanAlaya   BOUTIQUE HOTEL $$
(063-760582; www.hanumanalaya.com; r US$60-100;) A blissful boutique

SIEM REAP & THE TEMPLES OF ANGKOR SIEM REAP

CAMBODIA ONLINE

Andy's Cambodia (www.blog.andybrouwer.co.uk) A great gateway to all things Cambodian, it includes regular Cambodian travel articles.

ConCERT (www.concertcambodia.org) Siem Reap–based organisation 'connecting communities, environment and responsible tourism'.

Lonely Planet (www.lonelyplanet.com/cambodia) Information on travelling to and within Cambodia, the Thorn Tree Travel Forum and up-to-date travel news.

Phnom Penh Post (www.phnompenhpost.com) The online version of Cambodia's newspaper.

Sam Vesna Center (www.samveasna.org) The best source of information on sustainable visits to Cambodia's world-class bird sanctuaries.

Siem Reap

0   500 m
0   0.25 miles

0   100 m

Angkor National Museum

HanumanAlaya (1km)

31

Street 7   22   36
26
The Lane   29
Sivatha St   32
28
19   23   4   18
Pub St   3
'Alley West' 'The Alley'   37   27
38   Street 9   15
12
Pokambor Ave

Pithnou St

Charles de Gaulle Blvd

24

Wat Bo Rd

Airport Rd

Royal Gardens

Cambodian Cultural Village (3.3km);
(8.3km)   Royal Residence

NH6

(3km)

25   Taphul St   16
Oum Khun St   St 3
Sivatha St
Oum Chhay St   Pokambor Ave   St 20
13   St 14   11   5
Siem Reap River Rd   St 21
Tep Vong St   10
17

Pithnou St   9
35
33   Wat Preah Prohm Roth   Wat Bo
My Home Tropical Villa (600m)   14   St 24
21   30
Sok San St

2
34   Pokambor Ave
Siem Reap River
Wat Dam Nak   Wat Bo Rd

See Enlargement

Psar Krohm St   7 Makara St
Tonlé Sap Rd   Kanell (200m)
8
7

20

6

Siem Reap

retreat, HanumanAlaya is set around a lush garden and pretty swimming pool. Rooms are decorated with antiques and handicrafts but include modern touches such as cable TV, minibar and safe.

Soria Moria Hotel BOUTIQUE HOTEL **$$**
(☎063-964768; www.thesoriamoria.com; Wat Bo Rd; r US$39-63; ❋@🕸🌐) 🏃 A hotel with a heart, promoting local causes to help the community, this boutique place has attractive rooms with smart bathroom fittings. Fusion restaurant downstairs, sky hot tub upstairs and a new pool.

Steung Siem Reap Hotel HOTEL **$$**
(☎063-965167; www.steungsiemreaphotel.com; near Psar Chaa; r from US$63; ❋@🕸🌐) In keeping with the French-colonial air around Psar Chaa, this hotel has high ceilings, louvre shutters and wrought-iron balconies. Three-star rooms feature smart wooden trim. The location is hard to beat.

Golden Banana BOUTIQUE HOTEL **$$**
(☎063-761259; 063-766655; www.golden-banana.com; B&B r US$22-31, boutique r US$55-136; ❋@🕸🌐) Prepare for some confusion, as this is Siem Reap's Banana Republic. There are now four Golden Bananas occupying

this crossroad near Wat Damnak, including the original B&B and a high-rise hotel, plus two boutique hotels under different ownership. All are gay-friendly.

★**La Résidence d'Angkor** BOUTIQUE RESORT **$$$**
(☎063-963390; www.residencedangkor.com; Stung Siem Reap St; r from US$280; ❋@🕸🌐) The 54 wood-appointed rooms, among the most tasteful and inviting in town, come with verandas and huge jacuzzi-sized tubs. The gorgeous swimming pool is perfect for laps. Check out the sumptuous Kong Kea Spa.

Shinta Mani BOUTIQUE RESORT **$$$**
(☎063-761998; www.shintamani.com; Oum Khun St; r US$83-230; ❋@🕸🌐) 🏃 Contemporary chic designed by renowned architect Bill Bensley, Shinta Mani Resort offers an inviting central pool, while Shinta Mani Club offers more exclusive rooms. Shinta Mani has won several international awards for responsible tourism practices.

Eating

Worthy restaurants are sprinkled all around town but Siem Reap's culinary heart is the Psar Chaa area, whose focal point, the Alley, is literally lined with mellow eateries offering great atmosphere.

There are some good restaurants that support worthy causes or help train Cambodia's future hospitality staff with a subsidised ticket into the tourism industry.

For self-caterers, markets have fruit and vegies. **Angkor Market** (Sivatha St) can supply international treats such as olives and cheeses.

★ **Marum**   RESTAURANT $

(www.marum-restaurant.org; Wat Polanka area; mains US$3.25-6.75; ◷11am-10pm Mon-Sat; 🛜)
🌿 Set in a delightful wooden house with a spacious garden, menu highlights include red-tree ant fritters and ginger basil meatballs. Part of the Tree Alliance group of training restaurants, this experience is a must.

VIETNAM–CAMBODIA RELATIONS

Entering Cambodia from Vietnam is a leap from a powerhouse economy into one of Southeast Asia's poorest nations. Though chaotic, Ho Chi Minh City (HCMC) and Hanoi feel downright urban and orderly compared to less-developed Siem Reap.

As any proud Cambodian might tell you, Vietnam wasn't always economically superior. Cambodia's Khmer empire once controlled much of mainland Southeast Asia, including the ports of Saigon. By the 1800s, however, Vietnam's political dominance was established and Cambodia came under its influence.

The French later occupied both countries but favoured Vietnamese workers and bureaucrats. Though the colonialists were driven out in 1954, the 20th century's latter half brought more war – this time proxy conflicts fed by China, the US and the Soviet Union. During the American War – in a period when Cambodia was backed by the US – American planes heavily bombed its countryside to wipe out communist guerrillas. This didn't work. A sect of hardline China-backed communists, the Khmer Rouge, overran the weak US-allied government in 1975 to found a Communist regime that went on to become one of the most notorious dictatorships of the 20th century.

By 1975 both Vietnam and Cambodia had birthed communist independence movements. But despite their ideological kinship, the ancient feud didn't die, and in the late 1970s Cambodia's Khmer Rouge under Pol Pot attempted to retake land lost to Vietnam centuries before, beginning with Phu Quoc Island and later mounting a series of short-lived invasions in Vietnam's Dong Thap province. The Vietnamese responded by invading and occupying Cambodia for a decade and installing supplicant Cambodian leaders. Many of the same individuals remain in power in Cambodia today.

Leaders in both countries now speak of brotherhood between the nations, but you may hear regular Cambodians on the street speaking of Vietnam as the bully next door, and Vietnamese colloquially speaking of Cambodia as a 'little brother'. Despite this sibling rivalry, Cambodia and Vietnam share plenty of cultural common ground. Gesturing with feet, for example, is taboo. Elders are revered. Both cultures prefer to tiptoe around social confrontation, and angry outbursts are regarded as a lapse into insanity.

Differences in the home, however, are more pronounced. Swayed by Confucianism, many Vietnamese worship long-dead ancestors. Cambodians usually honour only their immediate family. Vietnam's 'two-child' laws have also kept families smaller than those in Cambodia, where more children mean more hands to support the family.

In contrast to the go-getter vibe in HCMC and Hanoi, Siem Reap still oozes laid-back warmth, but Cambodia is slowly becoming more like its rival. Visitors expecting a crumbling backwater will be taken aback by Siem Reap's deluxe new resorts and chic lounges. Though you'll still hear roosters crowing, you might also find a KFC up the block.

On the street, the ever-growing tourism wave is exposing all walks of Cambodian life to outsiders. Though Cambodians openly grumble about Vietnam, the kingdom is following in its footsteps: shaking off a tragic past, welcoming global trade and sprouting office towers from a sea of tin-roof shacks. Vietnam may think of Cambodia as a 'little brother', but it must concede its sibling is growing by the day.

By Patrick Winn – Southeast Asia Correspondent, Global Post

Haven
FUSION $

(☎078-342404; www.haven-cambodia.com; Sok San St; mains US$3-7; ⊙11am-10pm; 🛜) 🍴 Dine here for the best of East meets West. The fish fillet with green mango is particularly zesty. Proceeds help young adult orphans make the step from institution to employment.

Blossom Cafe
CAFE $

(www.blossomcakes.org; St 6; cupcakes US$1.50; ⊙10am-5pm Mon-Sat; 🛜) 🍴 Cupcakes are elevated to an art form here, with an incredible rotating 48 flavours. Creative coffees, teas and juices are available. Profits assist Cambodian women in vocational training.

Blue Pumpkin
INTERNATIONAL $

(http://tbpumpkin.com; Pithnou St; mains US$2-6; ⊙6am-10pm; ❄🛜) Downstairs it could be any old cafe, albeit with a delightful selection of cakes, breads and homemade ice cream. Upstairs is another world of white minimalism, with day beds to lounge on. It has light bites, great sandwiches, filling specials and divine shakes.

Sugar Palm
CAMBODIAN $$

(www.sugarpalmrestaurant.com; Taphul St; mains US$5-9; ⊙11.30am-3pm & 5.30-10pm Mon-Sat; 🛜) Set in a beautiful wooden house, this is the place to sample traditional flavours infused with herbs and spices. Owner Kethana showed celebrity chef Gordon Ramsay how to prepare *amoc*.

Le Tigre de Papier
INTERNATIONAL $$

(www.letigredepapier.com; Pub St; mains US$2-9; ⊙24hr; 🛜) One of the best all-rounders in Siem Reap, the popular Tigre serves up authentic Khmer food, great Italian dishes and a selection of favourites from most other corners of the globe.

Cambodian BBQ
BARBECUE $$

(www.angkorw.com; The Alley; mains US$5-9; ⊙11am-11pm; 🛜) Crocodile, snake, ostrich and kangaroo meat add an exotic twist to the traditional *phnom pleung* (hill of fire) grills. It has spawned a dozen or more copycats in the surrounding streets, many of which offer discount specials.

Chamkar
VEGETARIAN $$

(www.chamkar-vegetarian.com; The Alley; mains US$4-8; ⊙11am-11pm, closed lunch Sun; 🛜) The name translates as 'farm' and the menu here includes some impressive Asian flavours, such as stuffed pumpkin or vegetable kebabs in black pepper sauce.

CAMBODIA FAST FACTS

Area 181,035 sq km

Border Crossings with Vietnam Eight

Capital Phnom Penh

Country Code ☑855

Head of State King Sihamoni

Population 15 million

Money US$1 = 4000r (riel)

National Holiday Chaul Chnam or Khmer New Year, mid-April

Phrases *sua s'dei* (hello), *lia suhn hao-y* (goodbye), *aw kohn* (thank you)

Le Malraux
FRENCH, ASIAN $$

(www.le-malraux-siem-reap.com; Sivatha St; mains US$5-15; ⊙7am-midnight) A good spot for gastronomers, this classy art-deco cafe-restaurant offers fine French food. Try the combination salmon tartar and carpaccio to start, followed by a quality cut from the selection of steaks.

★Cuisine Wat Damnak
CAMBODIAN $$$

(www.cuisinewatdamnak.com; Sivatha Blvd; 5-course menu US$22, 6-course menu US$26; ⊙dinner) Set in a traditional wooden house, this is the highly regarded restaurant from Siem Reap celeb chef Johannes Rivieres. Seasonal set menus focus on market-fresh ingredients and change weekly.

🍷 Drinking

Siem Reap is now firmly on Southeast Asia's nightlife map, with many of the most interesting places situated in the vicinity of Psar Chaa, on or near Pub St.

Miss Wong
COCKTAIL LOUNGE

(The Lane; ⊙5pm-late; 🛜) Miss Wong carries you back to the chic of 1920s Shanghai. The cocktails are a draw here, making it a cool place to while away an evening. Gay-friendly and extremely popular with the well-heeled expat crowd.

Asana
BAR

(www.asana-cambodia.com; The Lane; ⊙11am-late; 🛜) Also known as the wooden house, this traditional Cambodian countryside dwelling, dropped into the backstreets of Siem Reap, makes for an atmospheric place to imbibe.

Warehouse
BAR

(Pithnou St; ⊘10.30am-3am; 🛜) This lively bar opposite Psar Chaa has long been popular with resident expats and travellers in Siem Reap. Top tunes, table football, a pool table and devilish drinks keep them coming until the early hours.

Laundry Bar
BAR, NIGHTCLUB

(⊘4pm-late; 🛜) One of the most alluring bars in town thanks to low lighting and discerning decor, this is the place to come for electronica and ambient sounds. It heaves on weekends or when guest DJs crank up the volume. Happy hour until 9pm.

Mezze Bar
BAR

(mezzebarsiemreap.com; St 11; ⊘6pm-late; 🛜) One of the hippest bars in Siem Reap, Mezze is located above the madness that surrounds Pub St. Ascend the stairs to a contemporary lounge bar complete with original art and regular DJs.

☆ Entertainment

Classical dance shows take place all over town, but there are only a few worth considering.

Apsara Theatre
DANCE

(☎063-963561; www.angkorvillage.com/theatre.php; admission US$25) The setting is a striking wooden pavilion finished in the style of a wat, but the set menu is less inspiring. There are two shows per night and it's packed to the rafters with tour groups.

Temple Club
DANCE

(Pub St) Free traditional dance show upstairs from 7.30pm, providing punters order some food and drink from the very reasonably priced menu.

🛍 Shopping

Siem Reap has an excellent selection of Cambodian-made handicrafts. Psar Chaa is well stocked with anything you may want to buy in Cambodia, and lots you don't. There are bargains to be had if you haggle patiently and humorously. Angkor Night Market (www.angkornightmarket.com; ⊘4pm-midnight) is packed with silks, handicrafts and souvenirs. Up-and-coming Alley West is also a great strip to browse.

A number of shops support Cambodia's disabled and disenfranchised.

Artisans d'Angkor
HANDICRAFTS

(www.artisansdangkor.com; ⊘7.30am-6.30pm) One of the best places in Cambodia for quality souvenirs and gifts, with everything from silk clothing to elegant reproductions of Angkorian-era statuary.

Rajana
HANDICRAFTS

(☎063-964744; www.rajanacrafts.org; Sivatha St; ⊘9am-9pm Mon-Sat) This quirky little boutique offers original wooden and metalware objects, some hewn from the shells of de-commissioned weapons. Rajana promotes fair trade.

Samatoa
CLOTHING

(☎012 285930; www.samatoa.com; Pithnou St; ⊘8am-11pm) If you find yourself in need of a party frock, this designer dress shop offers original threads in silk, with the option of a tailored fit in 48 hours. Samatoa promotes fair trade.

Senteurs d'Angkor
HANDICRAFTS

(☎063-964860; Pithnou St; ⊘8.30am-9.30pm) Opposite Psar Chaa, this shop has an eclectic collection of silk and carvings, as well as a superb range of traditional beauty products and spices, all sourced locally.

DON'T MISS

ROLL UP, ROLL UP, THE CIRCUS HAS COME TO TOWN

Cambodia's answer to Cirque du Soleil, Phare (The Cambodian Circus; ☎015 499480; www.pharecambodiancircus.org; behind Angkor National Museum; adult/child US$15/8; premium seats US$35/18; ⊘7.30pm daily) is so much more than a conventional circus, with an emphasis on performance art. Cambodia's leading circus, theatre and performing arts organisation Phare Ponleu Selpak opened its big top for nightly shows in 2013 and several past stars have gone on to perform in international shows around the world. An inspiring night out for adults and children alike, Phare reinvests all proceeds into Phare Ponleu Selpak activities. Animal lovers will be pleased to note there are no animals used in any performance.

Smateria ACCESSORIES
(www.smateria.com; Alley West; ⏱10am-10pm)
Recycling rocks here, with funky bags made
from construction nets, plastic bags, motorbike seat covers and more. Fair-trade
enterprise employing Cambodians with disabilities.

❶ Information

Pick up the free *Siem Reap Angkor Visitors
Guide* (www.canbypublications.com) or the
two handy booklets produced by **Pocket Guide
Cambodia**(www.cambodiapocketguide.com), or
look them up online.

There are ATMs at the airport and in banks and
minimarts all over central Siem Reap, especially
along Sivatha Blvd. The greatest concentration of internet shops is along Sivatha Blvd and
around Psar Chaa.

Royal Angkor International Hospital (☎063-
761888; www.royalangkorhospital.com; Airport
Rd) A new international facility; affiliated with
the Bangkok Hospital, so very expensive.

Tourist Police (☎097-778 0013) At the main
Angkor ticket checkpoint.

❶ Getting There & Away

There are two main options for travelling between
Vietnam and Cambodia. Air travel is more con-
venient, with daily flight connections between
Ho Chi Minh City (HCMC), Hanoi and Siem Reap.
Road travel is a more daunting prospect as it takes
an entire day to travel direct between HCMC and
Siem Reap, including a change of bus in Phnom
Penh. However, it is easy enough to break the
journey in the lively Cambodian capital.

AIR

Siem Reap International Airport (REP; ☎063
761 261; www.cambodia-airports.com) is 7km
west of the centre. Vietnam Airlines offers
regular daily connections between Siem Reap
and HCMC (one way from US$135, five daily)
or Hanoi (from US$195, four daily). Silk Air also
offers two flights a week connecting Siem Reap
and Danang (from US$245).

BUS

Most travellers use international buses between
HCMC and Phnom Penh, crossing at the Moc
Bai (Vietnam)–Bavet (Cambodia) border. Buses
take about six hours or so, including border-
crossing formalities. Tickets usually cost US$10
to US$12. Regular services run throughout the
day between 6am and about 2pm in both directions. Buses leave from the Pham Ngu Lao area
of Ho Chi Minh City. In Phnom Penh, they arrive
and depart from various bus offices around the
city, including the following popular operators:

❶ VISAS FOR CAMBODIA

For most nationalities, one-month
tourist visas (US$20) are available on
arrival at Siem Reap and Phnom Penh
airports and all land border crossings.
One passport-sized photo is required.
One-month tourist e-visas (US$20
plus a US$5 processing fee), which
take three business days to issue and
are valid for entry to Cambodia at the
airports and the Bavet–Moc Bai border
crossing with Vietnam, are available at
www.mfaic.gov.kh.

Anyone planning a side trip to the
temples of Angkor and then returning
to Vietnam will need a multiple-entry
Vietnam visa or will need to arrange
another visa while in Cambodia.

Capitol Tour (☎023-217627; 14 St 182; US$23)
Mekong Express (☎023-427518; www.cat
mekongexpress.com; 2020 NH5)
Sapaco (☎023-210300; www.sapacotourist.
com; Sihanouk Blvd)

In theory it is possible to connect the same
day with a change of bus in Phnom Penh, but
this is easier travelling from Ho Chi Minh City to
Siem Reap as opposed to the other direction, as
Phnom Penh to Siem Reap services operate later
in the afternoon.

Tickets between Siem Reap and Phnom Penh
(six hours) cost US$5 to US$13, depending on
the level of service (air-con, leg room, a toilet, a
host). There are also some night buses between
Phnom Penh and Siem Reap, which could be useful for those in a hurry.

In Siem Reap, all buses depart from the bus
station, which is 3km east of town and about
1km south of NH6. Tickets are available at
guesthouses, hotels, bus offices, travel agencies
and ticket kiosks. Some bus companies send a
minibus around to pick up passengers at their
place of lodging. Be prepared for a rugby scrum
of eager *moto* (motorbike taxi) drivers when you
get off the bus in Siem Reap.

❶ Getting Around

From the airport, an official *moto*/taxi/van costs
US$2/7/8; *remork-motos* (tuk-tuk; US$5) are
available outside the terminal. From the bus
station, a *moto/remork* to the city centre should
cost about US$1/3.

Short *moto* trips around the centre of town cost
2000r or 3000r (US$1 at night). A *remork* should
be about double that, more with lots of people.

TEMPLES OF ANGKOR

Angkor is, quite literally, heaven on earth. It is the earthly representation of Mt Meru, the Mt Olympus of the Hindu faith and the abode of ancient gods. Angkor is the perfect fusion of creative ambition and spiritual devotion. The Cambodian 'god-kings' of old each strove to better their ancestors in size, scale and symmetry, culminating in the world's largest religious building, Angkor Wat.

The hundreds of temples surviving today are but the sacred skeleton of the vast political, religious and social centre of the ancient Khmer empire. Angkor was a city that, at its zenith, boasted a population of one million when London was an insignificant town of 50,000. The houses, public buildings and palaces of Angkor were constructed of wood – now long decayed – because the right to dwell in structures of brick or stone was reserved for the gods.

Angkor is one of the most impressive ancient sites on earth, the eighth wonder of the world, with the epic proportions of the Great Wall of China, the detail and intricacy of the Taj Mahal, and the symbolism and symmetry of the pyramids, all rolled into one.

Angkor Wat

The traveller's first glimpse of Angkor Wat (admission to all of Angkor: 1 day/3 days/1 week US$20/40/60), the ultimate expression of Khmer genius, is simply staggering, matched by only a few select spots on earth such as Peru's Machu Picchu or Jordan's Petra.

Soaring skyward and surrounded by a moat that would make its European castle counterparts blush, Angkor Wat is one of the most inspired and spectacular monuments ever conceived by the human mind. It is a sumptuous blend of form and function, a spellbinding shrine to Vishnu, its captivating image replicated in the reflective pools below, a feast for unbelieving eyes.

Like the other temple-mountains of Angkor, Angkor Wat replicates the spatial universe in miniature. The central tower is Mt Meru, with its surrounding smaller peaks, bounded in turn by continents (the lower courtyards) and the oceans (the moat). The seven-headed *naga* (mythical serpent)

serves as a symbolic rainbow bridge for humans to reach the abode of the gods.

Angkor Wat is surrounded by a moat, 190m wide, which forms a giant rectangle measuring 1.5km by 1.3km. Stretching around the outside of the central temple complex is an 800m-long series of astonishing bas-reliefs, designed to be viewed in an anticlockwise direction. Rising 31m above the third level (and 55m above the ground) is the central tower, which gives the whole ensemble its sublime unity.

Angkor Wat was built by Suryavarman II (r 1112–52), who unified Cambodia and extended Khmer influence across much of mainland Southeast Asia. He also set himself apart religiously from earlier kings by his devotion to the Hindu deity Vishnu, to whom he consecrated the temple – built, coincidentally, around the same time as European Gothic cathedrals such as Notre Dame and Chartres.

The upper level of Angkor Wat is once again open to modern pilgrims, but visits are strictly timed to 20 minutes.

Angkor Thom

It's hard to imagine any building bigger or more beautiful than Angkor Wat, but at Angkor Thom the sum of the parts add up to a greater whole. It is the gates that grab you first, flanked by a monumental representation of the Churning of the Ocean of Milk, 54 demons and 54 gods engaged in an epic tug of war on the causeway. Each gate (North, South, East, West and Victory) towers above the visitor, the magnanimous faces of the Bodhisattva Avalokiteshvara staring out over the kingdom. Imagine being a peasant in the 13th century approaching the forbidding capital for the first time? It would have been an awe-inspiring yet unsettling experience to enter such a gateway and come face to face with the divine power of the god-kings.

The last great capital of the Khmer empire, Angkor Thom – set over 10 sq km – took monumental to a whole new level. Built in part as a reaction to the surprise sacking of Angkor by the Chams, Jayavarman VII (r 1181–1219) decided that his empire would never again be vulnerable at home. Beyond the formidable walls is a massive moat that would have stopped all but the hardiest invaders in their tracks.

Temples of Angkor

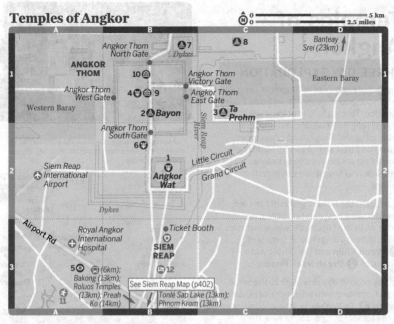

Temples of Angkor

◉ Sights

★ Bayon   BUDDHIST TEMPLE

Unique, even among its cherished contemporaries, Bayon epitomises the creative genius and inflated ego of Cambodia's legendary king, Jayavarman VII. It's a place of stooped corridors, precipitous flights of stairs and, best of all, a collection of 54 Gothic towers decorated with 216 coldly smiling, enormous faces of Avalokiteshvara that bear more than a passing resemblance to the great king himself.

These huge heads glare down from every angle, exuding power and control with a hint of humanity – this was precisely the blend required to hold sway over such a vast empire, ensuring the disparate and far-flung population yielded to his magnanimous will. As you walk around, a dozen or more of the heads are visible at any one time – full-face or in profile, almost level with your eyes or staring down from on high.

Bayon is now known to have been built by Jayavarman VII, though for many years its origins were unknown. Shrouded in dense jungle, it also took researchers some time to realise that it stands in the exact centre of the city of Angkor Thom. There is still much mystery associated with Bayon – such as its exact function and symbolism – and this seems only appropriate for a monument whose signature is an enigmatic smiling face.

Temples of Angkor

THREE-DAY EXPLORATION

The temple complex at Angkor is simply enormous and the superlatives don't do it justice. This is the site of the world's largest religious building, a multitude of temples and a vast, long-abandoned walled city that was arguably Southeast Asia's first metropolis, long before Bangkok and Singapore got in on the action.

Starting at the Roluos group of temples, one of the earliest capitals of Angkor, move on to the big circuit, which includes the Buddhist-Hindu fusion temple of **1 Preah Khan** and the ornate water temple of **2 Preah Neak Poan**.

On the second day downsize to the small circuit, starting with an atmospheric dawn visit to **3 Ta Prohm**, before continuing to the temple pyramid of Ta Keo, the Buddhist monastery of Banteay Kdei and the immense royal bathing pond of **4 Sra Srang**.

Next venture further afield to Banteay Srei temple, the jewel in the crown of Angkorian art, and Beng Mealea, a remote jungle temple.

Saving the biggest and best until last, experience sunrise at **5 Angkor Wat** and stick around for breakfast in the temple to discover its amazing architecture without the crowds. In the afternoon, explore **6 Angkor Thom**, an immense complex that is home to the enigmatic **7 Bayon**.

Three days around Angkor? That's just for starters.

TOP TIPS

» **Dodging the Crowds** Early morning at Ta Prohm, post sunrise at Angkor Wat and lunchtime at Banteay Srei does the trick.

» **Extended Explorations** Three-day passes can now be used on non-consecutive days over the period of a week but be sure to request this.

Bayon
The surreal state temple of legendary king Jayavarman VII, where 216 faces bear down on pilgrims, asserting religious and regal authority.

Terrace of the Leper King
Preah Palilay
Phimeanakas Temple
Tep Pranam
West Gate Angkor Thom
Baphuon Temple
Terrace of the Terrace of Elephants
7
South Gate Angkor Thom
Phnom Bakheng
Baksei Chamrong
5

Angkor Wat
The world's largest religious building. Experience sunrise at the holiest of holies, then explore the beautiful bas-reliefs – devotion etched in stone.

Angkor Thom
The last great capital of the Khmer empire conceals a wealth of temples and its epic proportions would have inspired and terrified in equal measure.

Preah Khan
A fusion temple dedicated to Buddha, Brahma, Shiva and Vishnu; the immense corridors are like an unending hall of mirrors.

Preah Neak Poan
If Vegas ever adopts the Angkor theme, this will be the swimming pool; a petite tower set in a lake, surrounded by four smaller ponds.

North Gate, Angkor Thom

Preah Pithu

Thommanon Temple

Prasat Suor Prat

Victory Gate Angkor Thom

East Gate Angkor Thom

Chau Say Tevoda

Ta Keo Temple

Ta Nei Temple

Banteay Srei

Banteay Kdei Temple

Roluos, Beng Mealea

Prasat Kravan

Bat Chum Temple

Ta Prohm
Nicknamed the *Tomb Raider* temple; *Indiana Jones* would be equally apt. Nature has run riot, leaving iconic tree roots strangling the surviving stones.

Sra Srang
Once the royal bathing pond, this is the ablutions pool to beat all ablutions pools and makes a good stop for sunset.

The eastward orientation of Bayon leads most people to visit early in the morning, preferably just after sunrise, when the sun inches upwards, lighting face after face. Bayon, however, looks equally good in the late afternoon, and if you stay for the sunset you get the same effect as at sunrise, in reverse. A Japanese team is restoring several outer areas of the temple.

Baphuon — HINDU TEMPLE

About 200m northwest of Bayon, the Baphuon is a pyramidal representation of mythical Mt Meru, which marked the centre of the city that existed before the construction of Angkor Thom. Restoration efforts were disrupted by the Cambodian civil war and all records were destroyed during the Khmer Rouge years, leaving French experts with the world's largest jigsaw puzzle. On the western side, the retaining wall of the second level was fashioned – apparently in the 15th or 16th century – into a reclining Buddha 60m in length.

Terrace of Elephants — HISTORICAL BUILDING

The 350m-long Terrace of Elephants – decorated with parading elephants towards both ends – served as a giant viewing stand for public ceremonies and as a base for the king's grand audience hall. As you stand here, try to imagine the pomp and grandeur

EXPLORING THE TEMPLES

Itinerary

If you have one day, hit Ta Prohm at dawn and explore the atmospheric jungle temple while it's still quiet. From there continue to Angkor Wat around 8am and enjoy the post-sunrise quiet to explore this mighty temple. In the afternoon, explore the temples within the walled city of Angkor Thom and the beauty of the Bayon in the late-afternoon light.

If you have three days, follow up the first action-packed day by beating the tourists to beautiful Banteay Srei, with a quick stop at Preah Khan along the way. Then make your way to the River of a Thousand Lingas at Kbal Spean. On the third day, head out to the Roluos area and then on to the massive jungle temple of Beng Mealea.

For those with a week, continue the three-day itinerary with a visit to the remote temple of Koh Ker. For a change of pace, take a boat to the watery village of Kompong Pluk.

Tickets & Guides

The ticket booth (1-day/3-day/1-week tourist pass US$20/40/60, children under 12 free; ☉5am-5.30pm) is on the road from Siem Reap to Angkor. Tickets issued after 5pm (for sunset viewing) are valid the next day. Tickets are not valid for Phnom Kulen or Beng Mealea. Get caught ticketless in a temple and you'll be fined US$100. The Khmer Angkor Tour Guide Association (☏063-964347; www.khmerangkortourguide.com) can arrange certified tour guides in 10 languages (US$25 to US$50 a day).

Eating

All the major temples have some sort of nourishment near the entrance. The most extensive selection of restaurants is opposite the entrance to Angkor Wat. Some excellent local Khmer restaurants line the northern shore of Sra Srang.

Transport

Bicycles are a great way to get to and around the temples, which are linked by flat roads in good shape. Various guesthouses and hotels rent out White Bicycles (www.thewhite bicycles.org; per day US$2) and proceeds go to local development projects.

Motos are a popular form of transport around the temples (around US$10 per day, more for distant sites). Drivers accost visitors from the moment they set foot in Siem Reap, but they're often knowledgeable and friendly.

Remorks (around US$15 a day, more for distant sites) take a little longer than motos but offer protection from the rain and sun. Even more protection is offered by cars (about US$30 a day, more for distant sites), though these tend to isolate you from the sights, sounds and smells.

Hiring a car to more remote sites will cost about US$50 to Kbal Spean and Banteay Srei, and about US$70 to Beng Mealea.

of the Khmer empire at its height, with infantry, cavalry, horse-drawn chariots and, of course, elephants parading across the Central Square in a colourful procession, pennants and standards aloft.

Terrace of the Leper King   HISTORICAL BUILDING
Just north of the Terrace of Elephants, the Terrace of the Leper King is a 7m-high platform. On top of the platform stands a nude, though sexless, statue, another of Angkor's mysteries. Legend has it that at least two of the Angkor kings had leprosy. It's more likely that it is Yama, the god of death, and that the Terrace of the Leper King housed the royal crematorium.

Around Angkor Thom

◉ Sights

★ Ta Prohm   BUDDHIST TEMPLE
The ultimate Indiana Jones fantasy, Ta Prohm is cloaked in dappled shadow, its crumbling towers and walls locked in the slow, muscular embrace of vast root systems. If Angkor Wat, the Bayon and other temples are testimony to the genius of the ancient Khmers, Ta Prohm reminds us equally of the awesome fecundity and power of the jungle. There is a poetic cycle to this venerable ruin, with humanity first conquering nature to rapidly create, and nature once again conquering humanity to slowly destroy.

Built from 1186 and originally known as Rajavihara (Monastery of the King), Ta Prohm was a Buddhist temple dedicated to the mother of Jayavarman VII. Ta Prohm is a temple of towers, close courtyards and narrow corridors. Ancient trees tower overhead, their leaves filtering the sunlight and casting a greenish pall over the whole scene. It is the closest most of us will get to feeling the magic of the explorers of old.

Phnom Bakheng   HINDU TEMPLE
Around 400m south of Angkor Thom, this hill's main draw is the sunset view of Angkor Wat, though this has turned into something of a circus, with hundreds of visitors jockeying for space. The temple, built by Yasovarman I (r 889–910), has five tiers with seven levels.

Preah Khan   BUDDHIST TEMPLE
(Sacred Sword) The temple of Preah Khan (Sacred Sword) is one of the largest complexes at Angkor, a maze of vaulted corridors, fine

---

FLIGHT OF THE GIBBON ANGKOR

New in 2013, Angkor is the ultimate backdrop for a zip-line experience in Asia. **Flight of the Gibbon Angkor** (☑ 0969999101; www.treetopasia.com; near Ta Nei Temple, Angkor; per person US$129; ☺ 7am-5pm) is inside the Angkor protected area and the course includes 10 zip lines, 21 treetop platforms, four skybridges and an abseil finish. A conservation element is included in the project with a pair of gibbons released in the surrounding forest. The price includes a transfer to/from any Siem Reap hotel, plus a lunch before or after the trip near Sra Srang.

---

carvings and lichen-clad stonework. Constructed by Jayavarman VII, it covers a very large area, but the temple itself is within a rectangular wall of around 700m by 800m. Preah Khan is a genuine fusion temple, the eastern entrance dedicated to Mahayana Buddhism, with equal-sized doors, and the other cardinal directions dedicated to Shiva, Vishnu and Brahma, with successively smaller doors, emphasising the unequal nature of Hinduism.

Preah Neak Poan   BUDDHIST TEMPLE
(Temple of the Intertwined Nagas) Another late-12th-century work of – no surprises here – Jayavarman VII, this petite temple just east of Preah Khan has a large square pool surrounded by four smaller square pools, with a circular 'island' in the middle. Water once flowed from the central pond into the four peripheral pools via four ornamental spouts, in the form of an elephant's head, a horse's head, a lion's head and a human head.

Roluos Group   HINDU TEMPLE
The monuments of Roluos, which served as the capital for Indravarman I (r 877–89), are among the earliest large permanent temples built by the Khmers and mark the dawn of Khmer classical art. **Preah Ko**, dedicated to Shiva, has elaborate inscriptions in Sanskrit on the doorposts of each tower and some of the best surviving examples of Angkorian plasterwork. The city's central temple, **Bakong**, with its five-tier central pyramid of sandstone, is a representation of Mt Meru. Roluos is 13km southeast of Siem Reap along NH6.

HEARTBEAT OF CAMBODIA

The largest freshwater lake in Southeast Asia, Tonlé Sap is an incredible natural phenomenon that provides fish and irrigation water for half of Cambodia's population.

The lake is linked to the Mekong at Phnom Penh by a 100km-long channel, the Tonlé Sap River. From mid-May to early October (the wet season), rains raise the level of the Mekong, backing up the Tonlé Sap River and causing it to flow northwest into the Tonlé Sap Lake. During this period, the lake swells from 2500 sq km to 13,000 sq km or more, its maximum depth increasing from about 2.2m to more than 10m. Around the start of October, as the water level of the Mekong begins to fall, the Tonlé Sap River reverses its flow, draining the waters of the lake back into the Mekong.

This extraordinary process makes the Tonlé Sap one of the world's richest sources of freshwater fish and an ideal habitat for water birds.

★ Banteay Srei   HINDU TEMPLE

Considered by many to be the jewel in the crown of Angkorian art, Banteay Srei – a Hindu temple dedicated to Shiva – is cut from stone of a pinkish hue and includes some of the finest stone carving anywhere on earth. Begun in AD 967, it is one of the few temples around Angkor not to be commissioned by a king, but by a Brahman, perhaps a tutor to Jayavarman V.

Banteay Srei, 21km northeast of Bayon and about 32km from Siem Reap, can be visited along with Kbal Spean and the Cambodia Landmine Museum.

Kbal Spean   RELIGIOUS, SPIRITUAL

Kbal Spean is a spectacularly carved riverbed, set deep in the jungle about 50km northeast of Angkor. More commonly referred to in English as the 'River of a Thousand Lingas', it's a 2km uphill walk to the carvings. From there you can work your way back down to the waterfall to cool off. Carry plenty of water.

At the nearby Angkor Centre for Conservation of Biodiversity, trafficked animals are nursed back to health. Free tours generally begin at 1pm Monday to Saturday.

Phnom Kulen   SACRED MOUNTAIN

The most sacred mountain in Cambodia, Phnom Kulen (487m) is where Jayavarman II proclaimed himself a devaraja (god-king) in AD 802, giving birth to Cambodia. A popular place of pilgrimage during weekends and festivals, the views it affords are absolutely tremendous.

Phnom Kulen is 50km from Siem Reap and 15km from Banteay Srei. The road toll is US$20 per foreign visitor, none of which goes towards preserving the site.

Beng Mealea   BUDDHIST TEMPLE

(admission US$5) Built by Suryavarman II to the same floor plan as Angkor Wat, Beng Mealea (admission US$5) is the Titanic of temples, utterly subsumed by jungle. Nature has well and truly run riot here. Jumbled stones lie like forgotten jewels swathed in lichen, and the galleries are strangled by ivy and vines.

Beng Mealea is about 65km northeast of Siem Reap on a sealed toll road.

Koh Ker   HINDU TEMPLE

(admission US$10) Abandoned to the forests of the north, Koh Ker, capital of the Angkorian empire from AD 928 to AD 944, is now within day-trip distance of Siem Reap. Most visitors start at Prasat Krahom, where impressive stone carvings grace lintels, doorposts and slender window columns. The principal monument is Mayan-looking Prasat Thom, a 55m-wide, 40m-high sandstone-faced pyramid whose seven tiers offer spectacular views across the forest. However, access to the top of Prasat Thom is currently prohibited for safety reasons.

Koh Ker is 127km northeast of Siem Reap (car hire is around US$90, 2½ hours).

Understand Vietnam

Vietnam Today

Vietnam's had a good couple of decades; a period of rising, sustained growth has benefited most. The standard of living has risen markedly, as cities have been transformed, education and health care have improved and the tourism sector continues to thrive. Yet a growing disconnection between a heavy-handed state and its people is evident, with widespread resentment regarding rampant corruption and evidence of growing, if limited, political dissent.

Best in Print

The Quiet American (Graham Greene) Classic novel set in the 1950s as the French empire is collapsing.

The Sorrow of War (Bao Ninh) The North Vietnamese perspective, retold in novel form via flashbacks.

Vietnam: Rising Dragon (Bill Hayton) A candid assessment of the nation that's one of the most up-to-date sources available.

Catfish & Mandala (Andrew X Pham) Beautifully written biographical tale of a Vietnamese-American who returns to his homeland.

Best on Film

Apocalypse Now (1979) The American War depicted as an epic 'heart of darkness' adventure.

The Deer Hunter (1978) Examines the emotional breakdown suffered by small-town servicemen.

Platoon (1986) Based on the first-hand experiences of the director, it follows idealistic volunteer Charlie Sheen to 'Nam.

Cyclo (Xich Lo; 1995) Visually stunning masterpiece that cuts to the core of Ho Chi Minh City's underworld.

The Quiet American (2002) Starring Michael Caine, it's atmospherically set in Saigon during the French colonial period, with rebellion in the air.

A Death in the Family

It seemed the entire nation paused for a little self analysis on 13 October 2013. The collective grief was palpable, as a united country buried its legendary war hero, General Vo Nguyen Giap, commander-in-chief of campaigns against the French, Japanese and Americans. He was 102. Charismatic, honest and brave, this wiry, determined, clean-living man – a freedom fighter with a popular touch – had devoted his life to his country.

For many Vietnamese the contrast between leaders like Giap and today's political and business elite was acute. Giap lived a simple life, dedicated to achieving the independence of his people, whereas many members of the latter are tainted by allegations of corruption, nepotism and paranoia. Most Vietnamese people have to pay backhanders for everything from getting an internet connection to securing a hospital appointment, while corrupt politicians demand millions of dollars to facilitate infrastructure projects. And when complaints are raised? Well, dissent is quickly silenced.

The Political & Economic

Vietnam's political system could not be simpler: the Communist Party is the sole source of power. Officially, according to the Vietnamese constitution, the National Assembly (or parliament) is the country's supreme authority, but in practice it's a tool of the Party and carefully controlled elections ensure 90% of delegates are Communist Party members.

Officially, communism is still king, but there can be few party hacks who really believe Vietnam is a Marxist utopia. Market-oriented socialism is the mantra. Capitalism thrives like never before, the dynamic private sector driving the economy. On the street, everyone seems to be out to make a fast buck.

The reality is that the state still controls around two-fifths of the economy. More than 100 of the 200 biggest companies in Vietnam are state-owned and the key sectors of oil production, shipbuilding, cement, coal and rubber are government controlled. Many of these state-controlled businesses are in deep trouble and haemorrhage money.

Corruption scandals are frequent: since 2011, nine Vinashin shipbuilding execs have been jailed following the company's near-collapse under US$4.5 billion of debt, while Vietnam Electricity's head honcho was sacked after losses of over US$1 billion were reported.

Vietnam's parliament voted to go ahead with constitutional amendments in late 2013. Of course, semantics can be misleading, and for the ruling party there's no question of a change in political direction.

Dissent & the Net

Dubbed the 'bamboo firewall', the entire nation's internet operates behind a state-controlled security system that blocks anything – including Facebook or Yahoo Messenger – that might potentially lead to trouble.

In September 2013 the Vietnamese government introduced new rules restricting all use of websites and online social media to the exchange of 'personal information' only. Political dissent is a complete no-no and arrests and trials are common.

Bloggers are particularly vulnerable, with 46 sentenced to prison for 'anti-state propaganda' in 2013, including Le Quoc Quan, a democracy activist and prominent Catholic. All newspapers and television channels are state run.

North & South

The Vietnamese economy has been buoyant for 20 years, but some areas are more buoyant than others. In 2013, Ho Chi Minh City's economy was growing at almost double the national rate (8.1% compared to 4.3%). It's the south that's benefited most from inward investment as Viet Kieu (overseas Vietnamese, the vast majority of whom are southerners) have returned and invested in the region.

The government is aware of these divisions and tries to balance the offices of state, so if the prime minister is from the south, the head of the Communist Party is from the north.

When it comes to the older generation, the south has never forgiven the north for bulldozing their war cemeteries, imposing communism and blackballing whole families. The north has never forgiven the south for siding with the Americans against their own people. Luckily for Vietnam, the new generation seems to have less interest in the country's harrowing history.

POPULATION: **92.6 MILLION**

LIFE EXPECTANCY: **MEN 70 YEARS, WOMEN 75 YEARS**

GDP GROWTH: **5%**

INFLATION: **9.1%**

ADULT LITERACY RATE: **93%**

if Vietnam were 100 people

86 would be Kinh
3 would be Thai & Muong
2 would be Khmer Krom
2 would be Tay
1 would be Hoa
6 would be Other

belief systems
(% of population)

80 None
10 Buddhist
6 Catholic
2 Hoa Hao
1 Cao Dai
1 Other

population per sq km

VIETNAM   UK   USA

♦ ≈ 30 people

Best Fruit

Mangosteen *(mang cut)* Subtle, fragrant and delicately flavoured.

Rambutan *(chom chom)* Looks like a sore testicle, but inside it's sweet and juicy.

Papaya *(du du)* Delicious unripe in salads, or refreshing when ripe.

Longan *(nhan)* Light-brown skin and a lychee-like flavour.

Best Experiences

Saddle up and see the nation on two wheels.

Squat down and get stuck into street food.

Meet the minorities in a mountain village.

Play *tram phan tram* (100% or bottoms-up) in a backstreet bar.

Best Drinks

Bia hoi The world's cheapest draught beer just keeps on flowing.

Ca phe Caffeine cravers unite: Vietnam's drip-fed coffee has a real kick.

Son Tinh liquor Special rice wine available in myriad flavours.

Fresh coconuts Available everywhere by the coast.

Vietnam's Place in the World

Today relations with the USA are politically cordial and economically vibrant (bilateral trade was worth US$24.9 billion in 2012). United States and Vietnamese militaries hold annual Defense Policy Dialogue talks. Vietnam's suppression of political dissent and issues of freedom of speech and religion remain areas of contention though. For the Vietnamese, the legacy of Agent Orange and dioxin poisoning remains unresolved – the USA has never paid compensation to the up to four million victims of dioxin poisoning resulting from aerial bombing during the American War.

The situation with Vietnam's traditional historic enemy China is far more complicated, and occasionally fraught. On the plus side trade is booming (though more one way than the Vietnamese would like) and borders are hyperbusy. Chinese is the second most popular foreign language studied in Vietnam. However, the Spratly Islands, rich in oil deposits, remain a potential flashpoint, with both nations claiming sovereignty. There have been regular protests in Hanoi against the Chinese occupation of the islands.

Vietnam counterbalances its power politics with China and the USA with active membership of the Association of Southeast Asian Nations (ASEAN). It enjoys cordial relations with most Southeast Asian countries, but there are ongoing tensions with Laos over the construction of dams on the Mekong River.

State of the Nation

Overall, most Vietnamese are pretty happy with their lot – for now. The last couple of decades have transformed the nation as blue-chip finance has flooded into a red-flag Communist society and comrades have become entrepreneurs. The country is stable. However, this status quo is very much dependent on the economy and with declining rates of growth, the situation is less rosy than it was a few years ago.

History

The Vietnamese trace their roots back to the Red River Delta where farmers first cultivated rice. Millennia of struggle against the Chinese then followed. Vietnam only became a united state in the 19th century, but quickly faced the ignominy of French colonialism and then the devastation of the American intervention. The Vietnamese nation has survived tempestuous, troubled times, but its strength of character has served it well. Today, the signs are it's continuing to grow with some promise.

To get an idea of Vietnam's turbulent history all you have to do is stroll through any town in the country and take at look at the street names. Then try it again somewhere else. You'll soon get déjà vu. The same names occur again and again, reflecting the national heroes who, over the last 2000 years, have repelled a succession of foreign invaders. If the street borders a river it'll be called Bach Dang (after the battles of 938 and 1288); a principal boulevard will be Le Loi (the emperor who defeated the Chinese in 1427).

The Vietnamese, in the backyard of a giant neighbour, have first and foremost had to deal with China. They've been resisting Chinese domination from as far back as the 2nd century BC and had to endure a 1000-year occupation. The struggle to nationhood has been immense.

Sure, the American War in Vietnam captured the attention of the West, but for the Vietnamese the Americans were simply the last in a long line of visitors who had come and gone. As far as Ho Chi Minh was concerned, no matter what was required or how long it took, they too would be vanquished.

In centuries past the Khmers, the Mongols and Chams were all defeated. There was a humbling period of colonialism under the French. As recently as 1979, just after the cataclysmic horrors of the American War, with the country on its knees, they took on an invading Chinese army – and sent them home in a matter of weeks.

Inevitably all these invaders have left their mark. The Chinese brought Buddhism, Taoism and the principles of Confucianism: community above individual, a respect for education and family. The French introduced

Archaeologists conducting excavations at Oc-Eo discovered a Roman medallion dating from AD 152, bearing the likeness of Antoninus Pius.

TIMELINE

2789 BC	2000 BC	300BC
The Van Lang kingdom, considered the first independent Vietnamese state, is founded by the Hung Vuong kings. It's referred to by both the Chin and Tang Chinese dynasties.	The Bronze Age Dong Son culture emerges in the Red River Delta around Hanoi, renowned for its rice cultivation and the production of bronzeware, including drums and gongs.	Vietnamese people of the northern region were culturally divided between Au Viet (highland Vietnamese) and Lac Viet (Vietnamese of the plains) who settled the Red River basin.

railways, and bequeathed some grand architecture and fabulous cuisine. And though the Americans left a devastated nation, Vietnamese pride remained intact.

In recent years progress has been remarkable, as Vietnam has become a key member of ASEAN and its economy has boomed – though systemic corruption, creaking infrastructure and an anti-democratic ruling party remain. But the country is united and prospering, its borders secure, and the Vietnamese people can look forward to a lasting period of stability and progress.

The Early Days

Humans first inhabited northern Vietnam about 500,000 years ago, though it took until 7000 BC for these hunter gatherers to practise rudimentary agriculture. The sophisticated Dong Son culture, famous for its bronze moko drums, emerged sometime around the 3rd century BC. The Dong Son period also saw huge advances in rice cultivation and the emergence of the Red River Delta as a major agricultural centre.

From the 1st to 6th centuries AD, southern Vietnam was part of the Indianised Cambodian kingdom of Funan – famous for its refined art and architecture. Based around the walled city of Angkor Borei it was probably a grouping of feudal states rather than a unified empire. The people of Funan constructed an elaborate system of canals both for transportation and the irrigation of rice. Funan's principal port city was Oc-Eo in the Mekong Delta, and archaeological excavations here suggest there was contact with China, Indonesia, Persia and even the Mediterranean. Later on, the Chenla empire replaced the Funan kingdom, spreading along the Mekong River.

The Hindu kingdom of Champa emerged around present-day Danang in the late 2nd century AD. Like Funan, it adopted Sanskrit as a sacred language and borrowed heavily from Indian art and culture. By the 8th century, Champa had expanded southward to include what is now Nha Trang and Phan Rang. The Cham were a feisty bunch who conducted raids along the entire coast of Indochina, and thus found themselves in a perpetual state of war with the Vietnamese to the north and the Khmers to the south. Ultimately this cost them their kingdom, as they found themselves squeezed between these two great powers.

The people of the Bronze Age Dong Son period were major traders in the region, and bronze drums from northern Vietnam have been found as far afield as the island of Alor, in eastern Indonesia.

One Thousand Years of Chinese Occupation

The Chinese conquered the Red River Delta in the 2nd century BC. Over the following centuries, large numbers of Chinese settlers, officials and scholars moved south seeking to impress a centralised-state system on the Vietnamese.

250 BC	225–248BC	111 BC	AD 40
Van Lang is conquered by a Chinese warlord and a new kingdom known as Au Lac is established at Co Loa, close to the modern-day capital of Hanoi.	Female warrior, Trieu Thi Trinh, described as a giant who rode war elephants to battle, confronts the Chinese for decades until defeat and her suicide in 248.	The Han emperors of China annex the Red River Delta region of Vietnam, heralding 1000 years of Chinese rule. Confucianism prevails as the governing philosophy.	The Trung Sisters (Hai Ba Trung) lead a rebellion against the Chinese occupiers, raising an army that sends the Chinese governor fleeing. They proclaim themselves queens of an independent Vietnam.

In the most famous act of resistance, in AD 40, the Trung Sisters (Hai Ba Trung) rallied the people, raised an army and led a revolt against the Chinese. The Chinese counter-attacked, but, rather than surrender, the Trung Sisters threw themselves into the Hat Giang River. There were numerous small-scale rebellions against Chinese rule – which was characterised by tyranny, forced labour and insatiable demands for tribute – from the 3rd to 6th centuries, but all were defeated.

However, the early Vietnamese learned much from the Chinese, including the advancement of dykes and irrigation works – reinforcing the role of rice as the 'staff of life'. As food became more plentiful the population expanded, forcing the Vietnamese to seek new lands. The Truong Son Mountains prevented westward expansion, as the climate was harsh and terrain unsuited to rice cultivation, so instead the Vietnamese moved south along the coast.

During this era, Vietnam was a key port of call on the sea route between China and India. The Chinese introduced Confucianism, Taoism and Mahayana Buddhism to Vietnam, while the Indian influence brought Theravada Buddhism and Hinduism (to Champa and Funan). Monks carried with them the scientific and medical knowledge of these two great civilisations and Vietnam was soon producing its own doctors, botanists and scholars.

For a closer look at China's 1000-year occupation of Vietnam, which was instrumental in shaping the country's outlook and attitude today, try *The Birth of Vietnam* by Keith Weller Taylor.

Liberation from China

In the early 10th century, the Tang dynasty collapsed, provoking the Vietnamese to launch a revolt against Chinese rule. In AD 938, popular patriot Ngo Quyen defeated Chinese forces by luring the Chinese fleet up the Bach Dang River in a feigned retreat, only to counter-attack and impale their ships on sharpened stakes hidden beneath the waters. This ended 1000 years of Chinese rule (though it was not to be the last time the Vietnamese would tussle with their mighty northern neighbour).

From the 11th to 13th centuries, Vietnamese independence was consolidated under the emperors of the Ly dynasty, founded by Ly Thai To. This was a period of progress that saw the introduction of an elaborate dyke system for flood control and cultivation, and the establishment of the country's first university. During the Ly dynasty, the Chinese, the Khmer and the Cham launched attacks on Vietnam, but all were repelled. Meanwhile, the Vietnamese continued their expansion southwards and slowly but surely began to consolidate control of the Cham kingdom.

Ho Chi Minh City (HCMC) began life as humble Prey Nokor in the 16th century, a backwater of a Khmer village in what was then the eastern edge of Cambodia.

Bach Dang Again

Mongol warrior Kublai Khan completed his conquest of China in the mid-13th century. For his next trick, he planned to attack Champa and demanded the right to cross Vietnamese territory. The Vietnamese

446	602	938	1010
Relations between the kingdom of Champa and the Chinese deteriorate. China invades Champa, sacks the capital of Simhapura and plunders a 50-tonne golden Buddha statue.	Rebellions by leaders including Ly Bon and Trieu Quang Phuc against Chinese rule ultimately fail as the Sui dynasty reconquers Vietnam, with its capital Dai La Thanh (Hanoi).	The Chinese are kicked out of Vietnam after 1000 years of occupation, as Ngo Quyen leads his people to victory in the battle of the Bach Dang River.	Thang Long (City of the Soaring Dragon), known today as Hanoi, is founded by Emperor Ly Thai To and becomes the new capital of Vietnam.

INDEPENDENT, CIVILISED & HEROIC

Following the successful 15th-century Le Loi rebellion against Chinese rule, poet Nguyen Trai issued a stirring nationalist declaration that is still quoted in Vietnamese school books and used by politicians today. The Great Proclamation (Binh Ngo Dai Cao) articulates the country's fierce spirit of independence: 'Our people long ago established Vietnam as an independent nation with its own civilisation. We have our own mountains and our own rivers, our own customs and traditions, and these are different from those of the foreign country to the north...We have sometimes been weak and sometimes been powerful, but at no time have we suffered from a lack of heroes.'

refused, but the Mongol hordes – all 500,000 of them – pushed ahead. They met their match in the revered general Tran Hung Dao. He defeated them at Bach Dang River, utilising acute military acumen by repeating the same tactics (and location) as Ngo Quyen in one of the most celebrated scalpings in Vietnamese history.

China Bites Back

The Chinese took control of Vietnam again in the early 15th century, taking the national archives and some of the country's intellectuals back to Nanjing – a loss that was to have a lasting impact on Vietnamese civilisation. Heavy taxation and slave labour were also typical of the era. The poet Nguyen Trai (1380–1442) wrote of this period: 'Were the water of the Eastern Sea to be exhausted, the stain of their ignominy could not be washed away; all the bamboo of the Southern Mountains would not suffice to provide the paper for recording all their crimes'.

One of the most prominent early missionaries was French Jesuit Alexandre de Rhodes (1591–1660), widely lauded for his work in devising *quoc ngu*, the Latin-based phonetic alphabet in which Vietnamese is written today.

Enter Le Loi

In 1418 wealthy philanthropist Le Loi sparked the Lam Son Uprising by refusing to serve as an official for the Chinese Ming dynasty. By 1425, local rebellions had erupted in several regions and Le Loi travelled the countryside to rally the people, and eventually defeat the Chinese.

Le Loi and his successors launched a campaign to take over Cham lands to the south, which culminated in the occupation of its capital Vijaya, near present-day Quy Nhon in 1471. This was the end of Champa as a military power and the Cham people began to migrate southwards as Vietnamese settlers moved into their territory.

The Coming of the Europeans

The first Portuguese sailors came ashore at Danang in 1516 and were soon followed by a party of Dominican missionaries. During the following decades the Portuguese began to trade with Vietnam,

1010–1225	1076	1288	14th century
Under the 200-year Ly dynasty Vietnam maintains many institutions and traditions of the Chinese era including Confucianism and its civil service structure. Wet rice cultivation remains vital.	The Vietnamese military, led by General Ly Thuong, attack the Sung Chinese and win a decisive battle near the present-day city of Nanning, and later defeat Cham forces.	The Mongols invade Dai Viet but General Tran Hung Dao repeats history by spearing the Mongol fleet on sharpened stakes on the Bach Dang River.	Cham forces led by king Che Bong Nga kill Viet Emperor Tran Due Tong and lay siege to his capital Thang Long in 1377 and 1383.

setting up a commercial colony alongside those of the Japanese and Chinese at Faifo (present-day Hoi An). With the exception of the Philippines, which was ruled by the Spanish for 400 years, the arrival of the Catholic Church has had a greater impact on Vietnam than on any country in Asia.

Lording It over the People

In a dress rehearsal for the tumultuous events of the 20th century, Vietnam found itself divided in two throughout much of the 17th and 18th centuries. The powerful Trinh Lords were later Le kings who ruled the North. To the South were the Nguyen Lords. The Trinh failed in their persistent efforts to subdue the Nguyen, in part because their Dutch weaponry was matched by the Portuguese armaments supplied to the Nguyen. By this time, several European nations were interested in Vietnam's potential and were jockeying for influence. For their part, the Nguyen expanded southwards again, absorbing territories in the Mekong Delta.

Tay Son Rebellion

In 1765 a rebellion erupted in the town of Tay Son near Qui Nhon, ostensibly against the punitive taxes of the Nguyen family. The Tay Son Rebels, as they were known, were led by the brothers Nguyen, who espoused the sort of Robin Hood–like philosophy of take from the rich and redistribute to the poor. It was clearly popular and in less than a decade they controlled the whole of central Vietnam. In 1783 they captured Saigon and the South, killing the reigning prince and his family. Nguyen Lu became king of the South, while Nguyen Nhac was crowned king of central Vietnam.

Continuing their conquests, the Tay Son Rebels overthrew the Trinh Lords in the North, while the Chinese moved in to take advantage of the power vacuum. In response, the third brother, Nguyen Hue, proclaimed himself Emperor Quang Trung. In 1789 Nguyen Hue's armed forces overwhelmingly defeated the Chinese army at Dong Da in another of the greatest hits of Vietnamese history.

In the South, Nguyen Anh, a rare survivor from the original Nguyen Lords – yes, know your Nguyens if you hope to understand Vietnamese history! – gradually overcame the rebels. In 1802 Nguyen Anh proclaimed himself Emperor Gia Long, thus beginning the Nguyen dynasty. When he captured Hanoi, his work was complete and, for the first time in two centuries, Vietnam was united, with Hue as its new capital city.

Dynasties of Vietnam

Ngo AD 939–965
Dinh 968–980
Early Le 980–1009
Ly 1010–1225
Tran 1225–1400
Ho 1400–1407
Post-Tran 1407–1413
Chinese rule 1414–1427
Later Le 1428–1524
Mac 1527–1592
Trinh Lords of the North 1539–1787
Nguyen Lords of the South 1558–1778
Tay Son 1788–1802
Nguyen 1802–1945

1427
Le Loi triumphs over the Chinese, declaring himself emperor, the first in the long line of the Le dynasty. He is revered as one of the nation's greatest heroes.

1471
The Vietnamese inflict a humbling defeat on the kingdom of Champa, killing more than 60,000 Cham soldiers and capturing 36,000, including the king and most of the royal family.

1516
Portuguese traders land at Danang, sparking the start of European interest in Vietnam. They set up a trading post in Faifo (present-day Hoi An) and introduce Catholicism.

1524
A period of instability and warfare ensues as feudal conflicts rage between the Trinh from the north (Thang Long) and the Nguyen from the South (based around Hue).

The Traditionalists Prevail

Emperor Gia Long returned Vietnam to Confucian values in an effort to consolidate his precarious position, a calculated move to win over conservative elements of the elite.

Gia Long's son, Emperor Minh Mang, worked to strengthen the state. He was profoundly hostile to Catholicism, which he saw as a threat to Confucian traditions, and extended this antipathy to all Western influences.

The early Nguyen emperors continued the expansionist policies of the preceding dynasties, pushing into Cambodia and Lao territory. Clashes with Thailand broke out in an attempt to pick apart the skeleton of the fractured Khmer empire.

The return to traditional values may have earned support among the elite at home, but the isolation and hostility to the West ultimately cost the Nguyen emperors as they failed to modernise the country quickly enough to compete with the well-armed Europeans.

> Buddhism flourished during the 17th and 18th centuries and many pagodas were erected across the country. However, it was not pure Buddhism, but a peculiarly Vietnamese blend mixed with ancestor worship, animism and Taoism.

The French Takeover

France's military activity in Vietnam began in 1847, when the French Navy attacked Danang harbour in response to Emperor Thieu Tri's imprisonment of Catholic missionaries. Saigon was seized in early 1859 and, in 1862, Emperor Tu Duc signed a treaty that gave the French the three eastern provinces of Cochinchina (the southern part of Vietnam during the French-colonial era). However, over the next four decades the French colonial venture in Indochina faltered repeatedly and, at times, only the reckless adventures of a few mavericks kept it going.

In 1872 Jean Dupuis, a merchant seeking to supply salt and weapons via the Red River, seized the Hanoi Citadel. Captain Francis Garnier, ostensibly dispatched to rein in Dupuis, instead took over where Dupuis left off and began a conquest of the North.

A few weeks after the death of Tu Duc in 1883, the French attacked Hue and the Treaty of Protectorate was imposed on the imperial court. A struggle then began for royal succession that was notable for its palace coups, the death of emperors in suspicious circumstances and heavy-handed French diplomacy.

The French colonial authorities carried out ambitious public works, such as the construction of the Saigon–Hanoi railway and draining of the Mekong Delta swamps. These projects were funded by heavy government taxes which had a devastating impact on the rural economy. Such operations became notorious for the abysmal wages paid by the French and the appalling treatment of Vietnamese workers.

1651	17th century
The first *quoc ngu* (Romanised Vietnamese) dictionary, the *Dictionarium Annamiticum Lusitanum et Latinum*, is produced, following years of work by Father Alexandre de Rhodes.	Ethnic Vietnamese settlers arrive in the Mekong Delta and Saigon region, taking advantage of Khmer weaknesses, who are torn apart by internal strife and Siamese invasions.

OLIVIER CIRENDINI / GETTY IMAGES ©

➡ The Mekong Delta today in Vinh Long

Independence Aspirations

Throughout the colonial period, the desire of many Vietnamese for independence simmered below the surface. Nationalist aspirations often erupted into open defiance of the French. This ranged from the publishing of patriotic periodicals to a dramatic attempt to poison the French garrison in Hanoi.

The imperial court in Hue, although allegedly quite corrupt, was a centre of nationalist sentiment and the French orchestrated a game of musical thrones, as one emperor after another turned against their patronage. This culminated in the accession of Emperor Bao Dai in 1925, who was just 12 years old at the time and studying in France.

Leading patriots soon realised that modernisation was the key to an independent Vietnam. Phan Boi Chau launched the Dong Du (Go East) movement which planned to send Vietnamese intellectuals to Japan for study with a view to fomenting a successful uprising in the future. Phan Tru Chinh favoured the education of the masses, the modernisation of the economy and working with the French towards independence. It was at this time that the Roman script of *quoc ngu* came to prominence, as educators realised this would be a far easier tool with which to educate the masses than the elaborate Chinese-style script of *nom*.

Rise of the Communists

The most successful of the anti-colonialists were the communists, who were able to tune into the frustrations and aspirations of the population – especially the peasants – and effectively channel their demands for fairer land distribution.

The story of Vietnamese communism, which in many ways is also the political biography of Ho Chi Minh, is convoluted. The first Marxist grouping in Indochina was the Vietnam Revolutionary Youth League, founded by Ho Chi Minh in Canton, China, in 1925. This was succeeded in February 1930 by the Vietnamese Communist Party. In 1941 Ho formed the Viet Minh, which resisted the Vichy French government, as well as Japanese forces, and carried out extensive political activities during WWII. Despite its nationalist platform, the Viet Minh was, from its inception, dominated by Ho's communists. However, as well as being a communist, Ho appeared pragmatic, patriotic and populist and understood the need for national unity.

HISTORY INDEPENDENCE ASPIRATIONS

Between 1944 and 1945, the Viet Minh received funding and arms from the US Office of Strategic Services (OSS; today the CIA). When Ho Chi Minh declared independence in 1945, he had OSS agents at his side and borrowed liberally from the American Declaration of Independence.

1765	1802	1862	1883
The Tay Son Rebellion erupts near Quy Nhon, led by the brothers Nguyen, and they take control of the whole country over the next 25 years.	Emperor Gia Long takes the throne and the Nguyen dynasty is born, ruling over Vietnam until 1945. The country is reunited for the first time in more than 200 years.	Following French attacks on both Danang and Saigon, Emperor Tu Duc signs a treaty ceding control of the Mekong Delta provinces to France, renaming them Cochinchina (Cochinchine).	The French impose the Treaty of Protectorate on the Vietnamese, marking the start of 70 years of colonial control, although active resistance continues throughout this period.

WWII & Famine

When France fell to Nazi Germany in 1940, the Indochinese government of Vichy France–collaborators acquiesced to the presence of Japanese troops in Vietnam. The Japanese left the French administration in charge of the day-to-day running of the country and, for a time, Vietnam was spared the ravages of Japanese occupation. However, as WWII drew to a close, Japanese rice requisitions, combined with floods and breaches in the dykes, caused a horrific famine in which perhaps two million North Vietnamese people starved to death. The only force opposed to both the French and Japanese presence in Vietnam was the Viet Minh, and Ho Chi Minh received assistance from the US government during this period. As events unfolded in mainland Europe, the French and Japanese fell out and the Viet Minh saw its opportunity to strike.

UNCLE OF THE PEOPLE

Father of the nation, Ho Chi Minh (Bringer of Light) was the son of a fiercely nationalistic scholar-official. Born Nguyen Tat Thanh near Vinh in 1890, he was educated in Hue and adopted many pseudonyms during his momentous life. Many Vietnamese affectionately refer to him as Bac Ho ('Uncle Ho') today.

In 1911 he signed up as a cook's apprentice on a French ship, sailing to North America, Africa and Europe. While odd-jobbing in England and France as a gardener, snow sweeper, waiter, photo retoucher and stoker, his political consciousness began to develop.

Ho Chi Minh moved to Paris, where he mastered a number of languages (including English, French, German and Mandarin) and began promoting Indochinese independence. He was a founding member of the French Communist Party in 1920 and later travelled to Guangzhou in China, where he founded the Revolutionary Youth League of Vietnam.

During the early 1930s the English rulers of Hong Kong obliged the French government by imprisoning Ho for his revolutionary activities. After his release he travelled to the USSR and China. In 1941 he returned to Vietnam for the first time in 30 years, and founded the Viet Minh, the goal of which was the independence of Vietnam. As Japan prepared to surrender in August 1945, Ho Chi Minh led the August Revolution, and his forces then established control throughout much of Vietnam.

The return of the French compelled the Viet Minh to conduct a guerrilla war, which ultimately led to victory against the colonists at Dien Bien Phu in 1954. Ho then led North Vietnam until his death in September 1969 – he never lived to see the North's victory.

The party has worked hard to preserve Bac Ho's reputation. His image dominates contemporary Vietnam – no town is complete without a Ho statue, and most cities have a museum in his name. This cult of personality is in stark contrast to the simplicity with which Ho lived his life. For more Ho, check out the excellent biography *Ho Chi Minh* by William J Duiker.

late 1800s	1925	1930s	1940
The Romanised *quoc ngu* alphabet for Vietnamese grows in popularity as a means of eradicating illiteracy and promoting education. Traditional Chinese-style scripts are phased out.	Ho Chi Minh moves towards organised political agitation, establishing the Revolutionary Youth League of Vietnam in southern China, an early incarnation of the Vietnamese Communist Party.	Marxism gains in popularity with the formation of three communist parties, which later unite to form the Vietnamese Communist Party with Tran Phu as the first Secretary General.	The Japanese occupation of Vietnam begins, as the pro–Vichy France colonial government offers the use of military facilities in return for the continued control over administration.

A False Dawn

By the spring of 1945 the Viet Minh controlled large swathes of the country, particularly in the north. In mid-August, Ho Chi Minh called for a general uprising, later known as the August Revolution. Meanwhile in central Vietnam, Bao Dai abdicated in favour of the new government, and in the South the Viet Minh soon held power in a shaky coalition with non-communist groups. On 2 September 1945, Ho Chi Minh declared independence at a rally in Hanoi. Throughout this period, Ho wrote eight letters to US president Harry Truman and the US State Department asking for US aid, but received no replies.

A footnote on the agenda of the Potsdam Conference of 1945 was the disarming of Japanese occupation forces in Vietnam: Chinese Kuomintang would accept the Japanese surrender north of the 16th Parallel and the British would do so in the south.

When the British arrived in Saigon, anarchy ruled with private militia, the remaining Japanese forces, the French, and Viet Minh competing for hegemony. When armed French paratroopers reacted to Ho's declaration of independence by attacking civilians, the Viet Minh began a guerrilla campaign. On 24 September, French general Jacques Philippe Leclerc arrived in Saigon, declaring: 'We have come to reclaim our inheritance'.

In the north, Chinese Kuomintang troops were fleeing the Chinese communists and making their way southward towards Hanoi. Ho tried to placate them, but as the months of Chinese occupation dragged on, he decided to accept a temporary return of the French, deeming them less of a long-term threat than the Chinese. The French were to stay for five years in return for recognising Vietnam as a free state within the French Union.

War with the French

The French had managed to regain control of Vietnam, at least in name. However, following the French shelling of Haiphong in November 1946, which killed hundreds of civilians, the détente with the Viet Minh began to unravel. Fighting soon broke out in Hanoi, and Ho Chi Minh and his forces fled to the mountains to regroup, where they would remain for the next eight years.

In the face of determined Vietnamese nationalism, the French proved unable to reassert their control. Despite massive US aid to halt communism throughout Asia, for the French it was ultimately an unwinnable war. As Ho said to the French at the outset: 'You can kill 10 of my men for every one I kill of yours, but even at those odds you will lose and I will win'.

In May 1954 the Viet Minh dug a tunnel network under French defences on Hill A1 at Dien Bien Phu and rigged it with explosives. Comrade Sapper Nguyen Van Bach volunteered himself as a human fuse in case the detonator failed. Luckily for him it didn't and he is today honoured as a national hero.

1941	mid-1940s	1945	1946
Ho Chi Minh forms the Viet Minh (short for the League for the Independence of Vietnam), a liberation movement seeking independence from France and fighting the Japanese occupation.	The combination of Japanese rice requisitions and widespread flooding leads to a disastrous famine in which 10% of North Vietnam's population dies, around two million people.	Ho Chi Minh proclaims Vietnamese independence on 2 September in Ba Dinh Square in central Hanoi, but the French aim to reassert their authority and impose colonial rule once more.	Strained relations between the Viet Minh forces and the French colonialists erupt into open fighting in Hanoi and Haiphong, marking the start of the eight-year Franco–Viet Minh War.

After eight years of fighting, the Viet Minh controlled much of Vietnam and neighbouring Laos. On 7 May 1954, after a 57-day siege, more than 10,000 starving French troops surrendered to the Viet Minh at Dien Bien Phu. This defeat brought an end to the French colonial adventure in Indochina.

The following day, the Geneva Conference opened to negotiate an end to the conflict, but the French had no cards left to bring to the table. Resolutions included an exchange of prisoners; the 'temporary' division of Vietnam into two zones at the Ben Hai River (near the 17th Parallel) until nationwide elections could be held; the free passage of people across the 17th Parallel for a period of 300 days; and the holding of nationwide elections on 20 July 1956. In the course of the Franco–Viet Minh War, more than 35,000 French fighters had been killed and 48,000 wounded; there are no exact numbers for Vietnamese casualties, but they were certainly higher.

In Hanoi and the North, Ho Chi Minh created a very effective police state. The regime was characterised by ruthless police power, denunciations by a huge network of secret informers, and the blacklisting of dissidents, their children and their children's children.

A Separate South Vietnam

After the Geneva Accords were signed and sealed, the South was ruled by a government led by Ngo Dinh Diem, a fiercely anti-communist Catholic. His power base was significantly strengthened by 900,000 refugees, many of them Catholics, who had fled the communist North during the 300-day free-passage period.

Nationwide elections were never held, as the Americans rightly feared that Ho Chi Minh would win with a massive majority. During the first few years of his rule, Diem consolidated power fairly effectively, defeating the Binh Xuyen crime syndicate and the private armies of the Hoa Hao and Cao Dai religious sects.

During Diem's 1957 official visit to the USA, President Eisenhower called him the 'miracle man' of Asia. As time went on Diem became increasingly tyrannical, closing Buddhist monasteries, imprisoning monks and banning opposition parties. He also doled out power to family members (including his sister-in-law Madame Nhu, who effectively became First Lady).

In the early 1960s the South was rocked by anti-Diem unrest led by university students and Buddhist clergy, which included several highly publicised self-immolations by monks that shocked the world. The US began to see Diem as a liability and threw its support behind a military coup. A group of young generals led the operation in November 1963. Diem was meant to go into exile, but the generals executed both Diem and his brother. Diem was succeeded by a string of military rulers who continued his policies.

late 1940s	1954	1955	1960
While the Viet Minh retreat to the mountains to regroup, the French attempt to forge a Vietnamese government under Emperor Bao Dai, last ruler of the Nguyen dynasty.	French forces surrender to Viet Minh fighters as the siege of Dien Bien Phu comes to a dramatic close on 7 May, marking the end of colonial rule in Indochina.	Vietnam is 'temporarily' divided at the 17th Parallel into North Vietnam and South Vietnam and people are given 300 days to relocate to either side of the border.	The National Liberation Front (better known as the Viet Cong) launch a guerrilla war against the Diem government in the South, sparking the 'American War'.

A New North Vietnam

The Geneva Accords allowed the leadership of the Democratic Republic of Vietnam to return to Hanoi and assert control of all territory north of the 17th Parallel. The new government immediately set out to eliminate those elements of the population that threatened its power. Tens of thousands of landlords, some with only tiny holdings, were denounced to security committees by their neighbours and arrested. Hasty trials resulted in between 10,000 and 15,000 executions and the imprisonment of thousands more. In 1956, the party, faced with widespread rural unrest, recognised that things had spiralled out of control and began a Campaign for the Rectification of Errors.

The North–South War

The communists' campaign to liberate the South began in 1959. The Ho Chi Minh Trail reopened for business, universal military conscription was implemented and the National Liberation Front (NLF), later known as the Viet Cong (VC), was formed.

As the NLF launched its campaign, the Diem government quickly lost control of the countryside. To stem the tide, peasants were moved into fortified 'strategic hamlets' in order to deny the VC potential support.

For the South it was no longer just a battle with the VC. In 1964 Hanoi began sending regular North Vietnamese Army (NVA) units down the Ho Chi Minh Trail. By early 1965 the Saigon government was on its last legs. Desertions from the Army of the Republic of Vietnam (ARVN) had reached 2000 per month. The South was losing a district capital each week, yet in 10 years only one senior South Vietnamese army officer had been wounded. The army was getting ready to evacuate Hue and Danang, and the central highlands seemed about to fall.

Enter the Cavalry

The Americans saw France's war in Indochina as an important element in the worldwide struggle against communist expansion. Vietnam was the next domino and could not topple. In 1950, US advisers rolled into Vietnam, ostensibly to train local troops – but American soldiers would remain on Vietnamese soil for the next 25 years. As early as 1954, US military aid to the French topped US$2 billion.

A decisive turning point in US strategy came with the August 1964 Gulf of Tonkin incident. Two US destroyers claimed to have come under unprovoked attack off the North Vietnamese coast. Subsequent research suggests that there was a certain degree of provocation: one ship was assisting a secret South Vietnamese commando raid, and according to

> The USA closed its consulate in Hanoi on 12 December 1955 and would not officially reopen an embassy in the Vietnamese capital for more than 40 years.

> Viet Cong and VC are both abbreviations for Viet Nam Cong San, which means Vietnamese communist. American soldiers nicknamed the VC 'Charlie', as in 'Victor Charlie'.

1962	1963	1964	1965
Cuc Phuong National Park, just west of the city of Ninh Binh is declared Vietnam's first national park as Ho Chi Minh declares 'forest is gold.'	South Vietnam's president Ngo Dinh Diem is overthrown and killed in a coup backed by the USA, which brings a new group of young military commanders into power.	Although the US is not officially at war, it launches Operation Pierce Arrow and bombs North Vietnam for the first time in retaliation for the Gulf of Tonkin incident.	To prevent the total collapse of the Saigon regime, US President Lyndon Johnson intensifies bombing of North Vietnam and approves the dispatch of American combat troops to the South.

an official National Security Agency report in 2005, the second attack never happened.

However, on US president Lyndon Johnson's orders, 64 sorties unleashed bombs on the North – the first of thousands of such missions that would hit every single road and rail bridge in the country, as well as 4000 of North Vietnam's 5788 villages. A few days later, the US Congress overwhelmingly passed the Tonkin Gulf Resolution, which gave the president the power to take any action in Vietnam without congressional control.

As the military situation of the Saigon government reached a new nadir, the first US combat troops splashed ashore at Danang in March 1965. By December 1965 there were 184,300 US military personnel in Vietnam and 636 Americans had died. By December 1967 the figures had risen to 485,600 US soldiers in the country and 16,021 dead. There were 1.3 million soldiers fighting for the Saigon government, including the South Vietnamese and other allies.

> The Tet Offensive was a long-term success for the Viet Cong and ensured that North Vietnamese soldiers would play a decisive role in the future of the war, but in the short-term it fundamentally weakened their military capacity .

US Strategies

By 1966 the buzz words in Washington were 'pacification', 'search and destroy' and 'free-fire zones'. Pacification involved developing a pro-government civilian infrastructure in each village, and providing the soldiers to guard it. To protect the villages from VC raids, mobile search-and-destroy units of soldiers moved around the country hunting VC guerrillas. In some cases, villagers were evacuated so the Americans could use heavy weaponry such as napalm and tanks in areas that were declared free-fire zones.

These strategies were only partially successful: US forces could control the countryside by day, while the VC usually controlled it by night. Even without heavy weapons, VC guerrillas continued to inflict heavy casualties in ambushes and through extensive use of mines and booby traps. Although free-fire zones were supposed to prevent civilian casualties, plenty of villagers were nevertheless shelled, bombed, strafed or napalmed. These attacks turned out to be a fairly efficient recruiting tool for the VC.

> **The War in Numbers**
>
> 3689 US fixed-wing aircraft lost
>
> 4857 US helicopters downed
>
> 15 million tonnes of US ammunition expended
>
> Four million Vietnamese killed or injured

The Turning Point

In January 1968 North Vietnamese troops launched a major attack on the US base at Khe Sanh in the Demilitarised Zone (DMZ). This battle, the single largest of the war, was in part a massive diversion from the Tet Offensive.

The Tet Offensive marked a decisive turning point in the war. On the evening of 31 January, as the country celebrated the Lunar New Year, the VC broke an unofficial holiday ceasefire with a series of coordinated strikes in more than 100 cities and towns. As the TV cameras rolled, a VC commando team took over the courtyard of the US embassy in

1967	1968	1969	1970
By the end of the year, there are 1.3 million soldiers fighting for the South – nearly half a million of these are from the US.	The Viet Cong launches the Tet Offensive, a surprise attack on towns and cities throughout the South. Hundreds of Vietnamese civilians are killed in the My Lai Massacre.	After a lifetime dedicated to revolution, Ho Chi Minh dies in Hanoi in September 1969, of heart failure. He's succeeded by a 'collective leadership,' headed by Le Duan.	Nixon's national security advisor, Henry Kissinger, and Le Duc Tho, for the Hanoi government, start talks in Paris as the US begins a reduction in troop numbers.

central Saigon. However, the communists miscalculated the mood of the population, as the popular uprising they had hoped to provoke never materialised. In cities such as Hue, the VC were not welcomed as liberators and this contributed to a communist backlash against the civilian population.

Although the US were utterly surprised – a major failure of military intelligence – they immediately counter-attacked with massive firepower, bombing and shelling heavily populated cities. The counter-attack devastated the VC, but also traumatised the civilian population. In Hue, a US officer bitterly remarked that they 'had to destroy the town in order to save it'.

The Tet Offensive killed about 1000 US soldiers and 2000 ARVN troops, but VC losses were more than 10 times higher.

The VC may have lost the battle, but were on the road to winning the war. The US military had long been boasting that victory was just a matter of time. Watching the killing and chaos in Saigon beamed into their living rooms, many Americans stopped swallowing the official line. While US generals were proclaiming a great victory, public tolerance of the war and its casualties reached breaking point.

Simultaneously, stories began leaking out of Vietnam about atrocities and massacres carried out against unarmed Vietnamese civilians, including the infamous My Lai Massacre. This helped turn the tide and a coalition of the concerned emerged.

Nixon & His Doctrine

Once elected president, Richard Nixon released a doctrine that called on Asian nations to be more 'self-reliant' in matters of defence. Nixon's strategy advocated 'Vietnamisation' – making the South Vietnamese fight the war without the support of US troops.

Meanwhile the first half of 1969 saw the conflict escalate further as the number of US soldiers in Vietnam reached an all-time high of 543,400. While the fighting raged, Nixon's chief negotiator, Henry Kissinger, pursued peace talks in Paris with his North Vietnamese counterpart Le Duc Tho.

In 1969 the Americans began secretly bombing Cambodia in an attempt to flush out Vietnamese communist sanctuaries. In 1970, US ground forces were sent into Cambodia and the North Vietnamese moved deeper into Cambodian territory. By summer 1970 they (together with their Khmer Rouge allies) controlled half of Cambodia, including Angkor Wat.

This new escalation provoked violent anti-war protests in the US and elsewhere. A peace demonstration at Kent State University in Ohio resulted in four protesters being shot dead. The rise of organisations such

HISTORY NIXON & HIS DOCTRINE

The American War in Vietnam claimed the lives of countless journalists. For a look at the finest photographic work from the battlefront, *Requiem* is an anthology of work from fallen correspondents on all sides of the conflict and a fitting tribute to their trade.

1971	1972	1973	1975
The ARVN's Operation Lam Son, aimed at cutting the Ho Chi Minh trail in Laos, ends in calamitous defeat as half its invading troops are either captured or killed.	The North Vietnamese cross the Demilitarized Zone (DMZ) at the 17th parallel to attack South Vietnam and US forces in what became known as the Easter Offensive.	All sides put pen to paper to sign the Paris Peace Accords on 27 January 1973, stipulating an end to hostilities, but the conflict rumbles on.	On 30 April 1975 Saigon falls to the North Vietnamese, as the last Americans scramble to leave the city.

as Vietnam Veterans Against the War demonstrated that it wasn't just those fearing military conscription who wanted the USA out of Vietnam. It was clear that the war was tearing America apart.

In the spring of 1972 the North Vietnamese launched an offensive across the 17th Parallel; the USA responded with increased bombing of the North and by laying mines in North Vietnam's harbours. The 'Christmas bombing' of Haiphong and Hanoi at the end of 1972 was calculated to wrest concessions from North Vietnam at the negotiating table. Eventually, the Paris Peace Accords were signed by the USA, North Vietnam, South Vietnam and the VC on 27 January 1973, which provided for a ceasefire, the total withdrawal of US combat forces and the release of 590

TRACKING THE AMERICAN WAR

The American War in Vietnam was the story for a generation. Follow in the footsteps of soldiers, journalists and politicians on all sides with a visit to the sites where the story unfolded.

China Beach The strip of sand near Danang where US soldiers dropped in for some rest and relaxation.

Cu Chi Tunnels The Vietnamese dug an incredible and elaborate tunnel network to evade American forces, just 30km from Saigon and right under the noses of a US base.

Demilitarised Zone (DMZ) The no-man's land at the 17th Parallel, dividing North and South Vietnam. After 1954 it became one of the most heavily militarised zones in the world.

Ho Chi Minh Trail The supply route for the South; the North Vietnamese moved soldiers and munitions down this incredible trail through the Truong Son Mountains in an almost unparalleled logistical feat.

Hue Citadel The ancient Citadel was razed to the ground during street-to-street fighting in early 1968 when the Americans retook the city from the communists after a three-week occupation.

Khe Sanh This was the biggest smokescreen of the war, as the North Vietnamese massed forces around this US base in 1968 to draw attention away from the coming Tet Offensive.

Long Tan Memorial The Australian contingent who fought in Vietnam, mostly based near Vung Tau in the south, is remembered here with the Long Tan Memorial Cross.

My Lai The village of My Lai is infamous as the site of one of the worst atrocities in the war, when American GIs massacred hundreds of villagers in March 1968.

Vinh Moc Tunnels The real deal: these tunnels haven't been surgically enlarged for tourists and they mark yet another feat of infrastructural ingenuity.

1976
The Socialist Republic of Vietnam is proclaimed as Saigon is re-named Ho Chi Minh City. Hundreds of thousands flee abroad, including many boat people.

1978
Vietnamese forces invade Cambodia on Christmas Day 1978, sweeping through the shattered country and later overthrowing the Khmer Rouge government on 7 January 1979.

CHRISTER FREDRIKSSON / GETTY IMAGES ©

Ho Chi Minh portrait in the Central Post Office, HCMC

American POWs. The agreement failed to mention the 200,000 North Vietnamese troops still in South Vietnam.

US teams continue to search Vietnam, Laos and Cambodia for the remains of their fallen comrades. In more recent years, the Vietnamese have been searching for their own MIAs in Cambodia and Laos.

Other Foreign Involvement

Australia, New Zealand, South Korea, the Philippines and Thailand also sent military personnel to South Vietnam as part of what the Americans called the 'Free World Military Forces', whose purpose was to help internationalise the American war effort in order to give it more legitimacy.

Australia's participation in the conflict constituted the most significant commitment of its military forces since WWII. Of the 46,852 Australian military personnel who served in the war, casualties totalled 496, with 2398 soldiers wounded.

Most of New Zealand's contingent, which numbered 548 at its highest point in 1968, operated as an integral part of the Australian Task Force, which was stationed near Baria, just north of Vung Tau.

The Fall of the South

Most US military personnel departed Vietnam in 1973, leaving behind a small contingent of technicians, advisors and CIA agents. The bombing of North Vietnam ceased and the US POWs were released. Still the war rumbled on, only now the South Vietnamese were fighting alone.

In January 1975 the North Vietnamese launched a massive ground attack across the 17th Parallel using tanks and heavy artillery. The invasion provoked panic in the South Vietnamese army, which had always depended on US support. In March, the NVA occupied a strategic section of the central highlands at Buon Ma Thuot. South Vietnam's president, Nguyen Van Thieu, decided on a strategy of tactical withdrawal to more defensible positions. This was to prove a spectacular military blunder.

Whole brigades of ARVN soldiers disintegrated and fled southward, joining hundreds of thousands of civilians clogging Hwy 1. City after city – Hue, Danang, Quy Nhon, Nha Trang – were simply abandoned with hardly a shot fired. The ARVN troops were fleeing so quickly that the North Vietnamese army could barely keep up.

Nguyen Van Thieu, in power since 1967, resigned on 21 April 1975 and fled the country, allegedly carting off millions of dollars in ill-gotten wealth. The North Vietnamese pushed on to Saigon and on the morning of 30 April 1975 their tanks smashed through the gates of Saigon's Independence Palace (now called Reunification Palace). General Duong Van Minh, president for just 42 hours, formally surrendered, marking the end of the war.

The poignant wartime diaries of a young doctor who volunteers for the Viet Cong, *Last Night I Dreamed of Peace: The Diary of Dang Thuy Tram* were only published 35 years after her death.

1979	1980s	1986	1989
China invades northern Vietnam in February in a retaliatory attack against Vietnam's overthrow of the Khmer Rouge, but the Vietnamese emerge relatively unscathed. Thousands of ethnic Chinese flee Vietnam.	During the decade Vietnam receives nearly $3 billion a year in economic and military aid from the Soviet Union and trades mostly with the USSR and eastern bloc nations.	*Doi moi* (economic reform), Vietnam's answer to *perestroika* and the first step towards re-engaging with the West, is launched with a rash of economic reforms.	Vietnamese forces pull out of Cambodia in September as the Soviet Union scales back its commitment to its communist partners. Vietnam is at peace for the first time in decades.

THE COST OF WAR

In total, 3.14 million Americans (including 7200 women) served in Vietnam. Officially, 58,183 Americans were killed in action or listed as missing in action (MIA). The direct cost of the war was officially put at US$165 billion, though its real cost to the economy was likely to have been considerably more.

By the end of 1973, 223,748 South Vietnamese soldiers had been killed in action; North Vietnamese and VC fatalities have been estimated at one million. Approximately four million civilians (or 10% of the Vietnamese population) were injured or killed during the war. At least 300,000 Vietnamese and 2200 Americans are still listed as MIA.

Just a few hours before the surrender, the last Americans were evacuated by helicopter from the US embassy roof to ships stationed just offshore. Harrowing images of US Marines booting Vietnamese people off their helicopters were beamed around the world. And so more than a quarter of a century of American military involvement came to a close. Throughout the entire conflict, the USA never actually declared war on North Vietnam.

The Americans weren't the only ones who left. As the South collapsed, 135,000 Vietnamese also fled the country; over the next five years, at least half a million of their compatriots would do the same. Those who left by sea would become known to the world as 'boat people'. These refugees risked everything to undertake perilous journeys on the South China Sea, but eventually some of these hardy souls found new lives in places as diverse as Australia and France.

Reunification of Vietnam

Neil Sheehan's account of the life of Colonel John Paul Vann, *Bright Shining Lie*, won the Pulitzer Prize and is the portrayal of one man's disenchantment with the war, mirroring America's realisation it could not be won.

On the first day of their victory, the communists changed Saigon's name to Ho Chi Minh City (HCMC). This was just for starters.

The sudden success of the 1975 North Vietnamese offensive surprised the North almost as much as it did the South. Consequently, Hanoi had no detailed plans to deal with the reintegration of the North and South, which had totally different social and economic systems.

The party faced the legacy of a cruel and protracted war that had fractured the country. There was bitterness on both sides, and a daunting series of challenges. Damage from the fighting was extensive, including anything from unmarked minefields to war-focused, dysfunctional economies; from a chemically poisoned countryside to a population who were physically or mentally scarred. Peace may have arrived, but the struggle was far from over.

1991	1992	1994	1995
Vietnam, a hard currency–starved nation, opens its doors to tourism in a bid to boost its finances. The first backpackers arrive, though tough restrictions apply to travel.	A new constitution is drawn up which allows selective economic reforms and freedoms. However, the Communist Party remains the leading force in Vietnamese society and politics.	The US trade embargo on Vietnam, in place in the North since 1964 and extended to the reunified nation since 1975, is revoked as relations begin to normalise.	Vietnam joins the Association of South-East Asian Nations (ASEAN), an organisation originally founded as a bulwark against the expansion of communism in the region.

Until the formal reunification of Vietnam in July 1976, the South was ruled by the Provisional Revolutionary Government. The Communist Party did not trust the South's urban intelligentsia, so large numbers of Northern cadres were sent southward to manage the transition. This fuelled resentment among Southerners who had worked against the Thieu government and then, after its overthrow, found themselves frozen out.

The party opted for a rapid transition to socialism in the South, but it proved disastrous for the economy. Reunification was accompanied by widespread political repression. Despite repeated assurances to the contrary, hundreds of thousands of people who had ties to the previous regime had their property confiscated and were rounded up and imprisoned without trial in forced-labour camps, euphemistically known as re-education camps. Tens of thousands of businesspeople, intellectuals, artists, journalists, writers, union leaders and religious leaders – some of whom had opposed both the Southern government and the war – were held in terrible conditions.

Contrary to its economic policy, Vietnam sought a rapprochement with the USA, and by 1978 Washington was close to establishing relations with Hanoi. But the China card was ultimately played: Vietnam was sacrificed for the prize of US relations with Beijing, and Hanoi moved into the orbit of the Soviet Union, on whom it was to rely for the next decade.

China & the Khmer Rouge

Relations with China to the north and its Khmer Rouge allies to the west were rapidly deteriorating. War-weary Vietnam felt encircled by enemies. An anti-capitalist campaign was launched in March 1978, seizing private property and businesses. Most of the victims were ethnic Chinese – hundreds of thousands soon became refugees or 'boat people', and relations with China soured further.

Meanwhile, repeated attacks on Vietnamese border villages by the Khmer Rouge forced Vietnam to respond. Vietnamese forces entered

> The Paris Peace Accords of 1973 included a provision for US reparations to Vietnam totalling US$3.5 billion, and this became the main stumbling block to normalising relations in 1978. No money has ever been paid to Vietnam.

'WE WERE WRONG'

Commentators and historians have since observed that if Washington had allowed Vietnam's long history of successfully repelling invaders to deter it, the extensive tragedy of this war might have been averted, and likewise the resulting social disruption in America, as people sought to come to terms with what had happened in Vietnam. An entire generation of Americans had to assess its conduct. Years later, one of the architects of the war, former Defense Secretary Robert NcNamara, stated in his memoir: 'We were wrong, terribly wrong. We owe it to future generations to explain why'.

2000	2003	2004	2006
Bill Clinton becomes the first American president to set foot in Hanoi, cementing a new chapter in Vietnamese-US relations. It was the last scheduled foreign visit of his presidency.	Crime figure Nam Can is sentenced to death for corruption, embezzlement, kidnap and murder; the case implicates dozens of police and politicians, rocking the reputation of the government.	The first US commercial flight since the end of the American War touches down in Ho Chi Minh City, as US-Vietnamese business and tourism links mushroom.	Vietnam plays host to the glitzy APEC summit, welcomes US president George W Bush, and prepares to join the WTO.

Cambodia on Christmas Day 1978. They succeeded in driving the Khmer Rouge from power on 7 January 1979 and set up a pro-Hanoi regime in Phnom Penh. China viewed the attack on the Khmer Rouge as a serious provocation. In February 1979 Chinese forces invaded Vietnam and fought a brief, 17-day war before withdrawing.

Liberation of Cambodia from the Khmer Rouge soon turned to occupation and a long civil war, which exacted a heavy toll on Vietnam. The command economy was strangling the commercial instincts of Vietnamese rice farmers. Today one of the world's leading rice exporters, Vietnam was a rice importer back in the early 1980s. War and revolution had brought the country to its knees and a radical change in direction was required.

Opening the Door

In 1985 President Mikhael Gorbachev came to power in the Soviet Union. *Glasnost* (openness) and *perestroika* (restructuring) were in, radical revolutionaries were out. Vietnam followed suit in 1986 by choosing reform-minded Nguyen Van Linh to lead the Vietnamese Communist Party. *Doi moi* (economic reform) was experimented with in Cambodia and introduced to Vietnam. As the USSR scaled back its commitments to the communist world, the far-flung outposts were the first to feel the pinch. The Vietnamese decided to unilaterally withdraw from Cambodia in September 1989, as they could no longer afford the occupation. The party in Vietnam was on its own and needed to reform to survive.

However, dramatic changes in Eastern Europe in 1989 and the collapse of the Soviet Union in 1991 were not viewed with favour in Hanoi. The party denounced the participation of non-communists in Eastern bloc governments, calling the democratic revolutions 'a counter-attack from imperialist circles' against socialism. Politically, things were moving at a glacial pace, but economically the Vietnamese decided to embrace the market. Capitalism has since taken root and it is unlikely that Ho Chi Minh would recognise the dynamic Vietnam of today.

Relations with Vietnam's old nemesis, the USA, have also vastly improved. In early 1994 the USA lifted its economic embargo, which had been in place against the North since the 1960s. Full diplomatic relations were restored and presidents Bill Clinton and George W Bush have subsequently visited Hanoi.

The majority of Vietnamese 'boat people' who fled the country in the late 1970s were ethnic Chinese whose wealth and business acumen, to say nothing of their ethnicity, made them an obvious target for the revolution.

2009	2010	2012	2013
Pro-democracy activists are jailed for 'spreading propaganda against the government' by actions including hanging pro-democracy banners on a road bridge and publishing articles on the internet.	Hanoi celebrates its 1000th birthday in October with exhibitions, and wild celebrations grip the capital; its imperial Citadel is declared a Unesco World Heritage site.	Despite Vietnam's bureaucratic visa procedures and a recession in the West, tourist arrivals hit 6.8 million, a growth of 13.9% over 2011. Chinese, Korean, Japanese and Americans are the top visitors.	General Giap, architect of the victory at Dien Bien Phu and military commander during the American War, dies at the age of 102. Millions pay their respects across the nation.

People & Culture

Industrious, proud, stubborn and yet mischievous, quick to laugh and fond of a joke, the Vietnamese are a complicated bunch. For Westerners the national character can be difficult to fathom: direct questions are frequently met with evasive answers. A Vietnamese person would never tell a relative stranger their life story or profound personal thoughts the way people sometimes share feelings in the West. Their deep respect for tradition, family and the state reflects core Confucian principles.

The National Psyche

Historically the national mentality has been to work as a team, in harmony rather than in conflict; but times are changing. If you're on the highway or doing business it's everyone for themselves. It's these attitudes (towards traffic and commerce) that many outsiders, not just Westerners, find most alien. 'Face' is vital, and Vietnamese people hate giving way, often employing elaborate tactics of bluster and bluff (and cunning) to ensure they get where they want to go.

My Generation

In many ways Vietnam is still a traditional, conservative society, particularly for the older generation, who remember the long, hard years and every inch of the territory for which they fought. Brought up on restraint and moderation, many remain unmoved by 21st-century consumer culture. For the new generation, Vietnam is very different: a place to succeed and to ignore the staid structures set by the Communists. And yes, to show off that gleaming new motorbike, sharp haircut or iPhone.

North–South Divide

The north–south divide lingers on. It's said that southerners think, then do; while northerners think, then think some more. Southerners typically reckon northerners have 'hard faces', that they take themselves too seriously and don't know how to have fun. Northerners are just as likely to think of southerners as superficial, frivolous and business-obsessed. Caricatures these may be, but they shed light on the real differences between north and south that reach beyond the (very different) regional dialects.

Shadows and Wind (1999), by journalist Robert Templer, is a snappily written exploration of contemporary Vietnam, from Ho Chi Minh personality cults to Vietnam's rock-and-roll youth.

BROTHERS OR MATES?

There are few places on earth where terms of address are as important as Vietnam. To use the wrong term can be a gross insult, disrespectful, or just a little too casual depending on the circumstances. Age and status are key factors.

Three men, all strangers, get chatting in a bar. Dzung is in his mid-twenties, Vinh is in his mid-thirties, Huong is in his forties. They quickly work out they have broadly similar social backgrounds. The correct way for Dzung to refer to Vinh is *anh* (big brother), but he should call Huong *chu* (uncle). He should also refer to himself as *em* (little brother) when speaking to Vinh but *chau* (nephew) to Huong.

Unless they are being very modern (or very merry!) and all decide to use the term *ban* (friend).

Climate plays its part too. Life is easier in the south, where the fertile Mekong Delta allows three rice harvests a year. The north endures a long winter of grey skies, drizzle, mist and cool winds. Think of the differences between northern and southern Europe (or Maine and Alabama) and you have a snapshot of how one people can become two. Don't forget that the north has also lived with communism for more than half a century, while the south had more than two decades of free-wheelin' free-for-all with the Americans.

Vietnamese who have emigrated are called Viet Kieu. They have traditionally been maligned by locals as cowardly, arrogant and privileged. However the official policy is now to welcome them, and their money, back to the motherland.

Face

Face is all important in Asia, and in Vietnam it is above all. Having 'big face' is synonymous with prestige, and prestige is particularly important. All families, even poor ones, are expected to have elaborate wedding parties and throw their money around like it's water in order to gain face. This is often ruinously expensive, but far less distressing than 'losing face'. And it is for this reason that foreigners should never lose their tempers with the Vietnamese; this will bring unacceptable 'loss of face' to the individual involved and end any chance of a sensible solution to the dispute.

Lifestyle

Traditionally, Vietnamese life has revolved around family, fields and faith, with the rhythm of rural existence continuing for centuries at the same pace. All this has been disrupted by war, the impact of communism and globalisation. While it's true that several generations may still

WHEN IN NAM... DO AS THE VIETS

Take your time to learn a little about the local culture in Vietnam. Not only will this ensure you don't inadvertently cause offence or, worse, spark an international incident, but it will also endear you to your hosts. Here are a few tips to help you go native.

Dress Code

Respect local dress standards: shorts to the knees, women's tops covering the shoulder, particularly at religious sites. Always remove your shoes before entering a temple. Nude sunbathing is considered totally inappropriate, even on beaches.

It's on the Cards

Exchanging business cards is an important part of even the smallest transaction or business contact. Get some printed before you arrive in Vietnam and hand them out like confetti.

Deadly Chopsticks

Leaving a pair of chopsticks sitting vertically in a rice bowl looks very much like the incense sticks that are burned for the dead. This is a powerful sign and is not appreciated anywhere in Asia.

Mean Feet

Like the Chinese and Japanese, Vietnamese strictly maintain clean floors and it's usual to remove shoes when entering somebody's home. It's rude to point the bottom of your feet towards other people. Never, ever point your feet towards anything sacred, such as a Buddha image.

Hats Off to Them

As a form of respect to elderly or other esteemed people, such as monks, take off your hat and bow your head politely when addressing them. In Asia, the head is the symbolic highest point – never pat or touch a person on the head.

share the same roof, the same rice and the same religion, lifestyles have changed immeasurably.

Vietnam is experiencing its very own '60s swing, which is creating feisty friction as sons and daughters dress as they like, date who they want and hit the town until all hours. But few live on their own and they still come home to Mum and Dad at the end of the day, where arguments might arise, particularly when it comes to marriage and settling down.

Some things never change. Most Vietnamese despise idleness and are early risers. You'll see parks full of t'ai chi devotees as dawn breaks, and offices are fully staffed by 7am. Indeed the whole nation seems super-charged with energy and vitality, no matter how hot and humid it is.

Family

In Vietnam the status of your family is more important than your salary. A family's reputation commands respect and opens doors.

Extended family is important to the Vietnamese and that includes second or third cousins, the sort of family that many Westerners may not even realise they have. The extended family comes together during times of trouble and times of joy, celebrating festivals and successes, mourning deaths or disappointments. This is a source of strength for many of the older generation.

Business Practices

Western visitors regularly complain about the business practices of many Vietnamese they encounter, which can range from mild price hiking to outright scamming. For many foreigners it's the most off-putting aspect of their time in the nation. At times it seems impossible to get the local price for anything. A little background is important.

Most of these rapacious individuals work in tourism; chronic over-charging is rare once you're off the main gringo trail. The mentality is that Westerners do not bother to learn the real price, don't learn any Vietnamese and are only in the country for a week or two. For years, many Vietnamese have only thought about the short term – about making a fast buck. As they've become more experienced in tourism, the concept has grown that good service will bring repeat business (and bad service will be all over internet forums immediately).

It's not an excuse, but Vietnam is a unique country. Famine killed two million in the 1940s, and the country was among the poorest of the poor following the American War. Vietnam's tourism industry is still very young and the Vietnamese state actually helped forge this overcharging mentality – until relatively recently the government set separate local and foreign rates (which were four to 10 times more) for everything from train fares to hotel rooms.

The People of Vietnam

Vietnamese culture and civilisation have been profoundly influenced by the Chinese, who occupied the country for 1000 years and whose culture deeply permeates Vietnamese society.

History has, of course, influenced the mix of Vietnamese minorities. The steady expansion southwards in search of cultivable lands absorbed first the Kingdom of Champa and later the eastern extent of the Khmer empire, and both the Chams and the Khmers are sizeable minorities today.

Traffic was not only one-way. Many of the 50 or more minority groups that inhabit the far northwest only migrated to these areas from Yunnan (China) and Tibet in the past few centuries. They moved into the mountains that the lowland Vietnamese considered uncultivable, and help make up the most colourful part of the ethnic mosaic that is Vietnam today.

Failing businesses often call in a geomancer (feng shui expert). Sometimes the solution is to move a door or a window. If this doesn't do the trick, it might be necessary to move an ancestor's grave.

Young Western travellers, depending on their dress, are often greeted with 'tay balo!' (literally, 'Westerner backpack'), an unflattering term for scruffy-looking foreigners.

The largest minority group in Vietnam has always been the ethnic-Chinese community, which makes up much of the commercial class in the cities. The government has traditionally viewed them with suspicion, and drove many of them out of the country as 'boat people' in the late 1970s. But today they play a major part in driving economic development.

Minorities

Mahayana Buddhists believe in bodhisattvas (Quan Am in Vietnam) or Buddhas that attain nirvana but postpone their enlightenment to stay on earth to save their fellow beings.

Vietnam's hill-tribe minorities have some autonomy and, though the official national language is Vietnamese, children can still learn their local languages, although this has been a sensitive issue in parts of the southwest highlands, where tensions remain high.

Prejudices against hill-tribe people endure. Attitudes are changing slowly but the Vietnamese media can still present them as primitive and exotic. It's not uncommon for Vietnamese people to still see minorities as subversive (some sided with the USA during the American War).

The reality is that minorities remain at the bottom of the educational and economic ladder. Despite improvements in rural schooling and regional healthcare, many hill-tribe people marry young, have large families and die early. They remain the poorest section of Vietnamese society: according to World Bank figures 46% live in poverty, compared to 8% of ethnic Vietnamese.

Religion

Many Vietnamese are not very religious and some surveys indicate that only 20% of the population consider themselves to have a faith. That said, over the centuries, Confucianism, Taoism and Buddhism have fused with popular Chinese beliefs and ancient Vietnamese animism to create the Tam Giao (Triple Religion) that many Vietnamese identify with. When discussing religion, Vietnamese people are likely to say that they are Buddhist, but when it comes to family or civic duties they are likely to follow the moral and social code of Confucianism, and turn to Taoist concepts to understand the nature of the cosmos.

Although the majority of the population has only a vague notion of Buddhist doctrines, they invite monks to participate in life-cycle ceremonies, such as funerals. Buddhist pagodas are seen by many Vietnamese as a physical and spiritual refuge from an uncertain world.

Christianity, present in Vietnam for 500 years, and Cao Daism (unique to the region) are other important religions.

Buddhism

To learn about Vietnamese Buddhism, check out leading Buddhist magazine and website Shambhala Sun (www.shambhalasun.com), and the informative UK-based Buddhist Society (www.thebuddhistsociety.org).

The predominant school of Buddhism in Vietnam is Mahayana Buddhism (Dai Thua, or Bac Tong, meaning 'From the North'). The largest Mahayana sect in the country is Zen (Dhyana, or Thien), also known as the school of meditation. Dao Trang (the Pure Land school), another important sect, is practised mainly in the south.

Theravada Buddhism (Tieu Thua, or Nam Tong) is found mainly in the Mekong Delta region, and is mostly practised by ethnic Khmers.

Taoism

Taoism (Lao Giao, or Dao Giao) originated in China and is based on the philosophy of Laotse (Old One), who lived in the 6th century BC.

Understanding Taoism is not easy. The philosophy values contemplation and simplicity. Its ideal is returning to the Tao (the Way, or the essence of which all things are made), and it emphasises *am* and *duong*, the Vietnamese equivalents of yin and yang.

Confucianism

More a philosophy than an organised religion, Confucianism (Nho Giao, or Khong Giao) has been an important force in shaping Vietnam's social system and the lives and beliefs of its people.

Confucius (Khong Tu) was born in China around 550 BC. His code laid down a person's obligations to family, society and the state, which remain the pillars of the Vietnamese nation today.

Cao Daism

Cao Daism is an indigenous Vietnamese religion founded in the 1920s that fuses the secular and religious philosophies of both East and West. Its prophets include Buddha, Confucius, Jesus Christ, Moses and Mohammed, and some wacky choices, such as Joan of Arc, William Shakespeare and Victor Hugo.

There are thought to be between two and three million followers of Cao Daism in Vietnam. Its colourful headquarters are in Tay Ninh, 96km northwest of Ho Chi Minh City.

Hoa Hao Buddhism

The Hoa Hao Buddhist sect (Phat Giao Hoa Hao) was founded in the Mekong Delta in 1939 by Huynh Phu So. His Buddhist philosophies involve simplicity in worship and no intermediaries between humans and the Supreme Being. Hoa Hao Buddhists are thought to number approximately 1.5 million.

In recent years vast new Buddhist temples have been constructed, including Chua Bai Dinh (near Ninh Binh), while giant new Buddha statues now define the coastline of Danang and Vung Tao.

TET: THE BIG ONE

Tet is Christmas, New Year and birthdays all rolled into one. Tet Nguyen Dan (Festival of the First Day) ushers in the Lunar New Year and is the most significant date in the Vietnamese calendar. It's a time when families reunite in the hope of good fortune for the coming year, and ancestral spirits are welcomed back into the family home. And the whole of Vietnam celebrates a birthday; everyone becomes one year older.

The festival falls between 19 January and 20 February, the same dates as Chinese New Year. The first three days after Tet are the official holidays but many people take the whole week off.

Tet rites begin seven days before New Year's Day. Altars, laden with offerings, are prepared to ensure good luck in the coming year. Cemeteries are visited and the spirits of dead relatives invited home for the celebrations. Absent family members return home. It's important that the new year is started with a clean slate; debts are paid and cleaning becomes the national sport. A New Year's tree (cay neu) – kumquat, peach or apricot blossom – is displayed to ward off evil spirits.

At the stroke of midnight on New Year's Eve, all problems are left behind and mayhem ensues. The goal is to make as much noise as possible: drums and percussion fill the night air.

The events of New Year's Day are crucial as it's believed they affect the year ahead. People take extra care not to be rude or show anger. Other activities that are believed to attract bad spirits include sewing, sweeping, swearing and breaking things.

It's crucial that the first visitor of the year to each household is suitable – a wealthy married man with several children is ideal. Foreigners may not be considered auspicious!

Apart from New Year's Eve itself, Tet is a quiet family affair – banh chung (sticky rice with pork and egg) is eaten at home. Shops are closed, and virtually all transport ceases to run. It's a troublesome time to travel in Vietnam. However, it is a special time of year and you're sure to be invited to join in the celebrations. Just remember this phrase: chuc mung nam moi – Happy New Year!

Christianity

Catholicism was introduced in the 16th century by missionaries. Today Vietnam has the second-highest concentration of Catholics (8% to 10% of the population) in Asia. Under the Communist government, Catholics faced severe restrictions on their religious activities. Since 1990, the government has taken a more liberal line and Catholicism is making a comeback.

Protestantism was introduced to Vietnam in 1911 and most of the 200,000 or so followers today are hill-tribe people in the central highlands.

Islam

Around 70,000 Muslims, mostly ethnic Chams, live in Vietnam, mainly in the south of the country. Traditionally most Cham Muslims followed a localised adaptation of Islam (praying only on Fridays), though more orthodox Muslim practices have now been adopted.

Hinduism

There are around 60,000 Cham living in Vietnam who identify themselves as Hindus. They predominantly live in the same region as Cham Muslims, concentrated around Phan Rang on the south-central coast.

Women in Vietnam

As in many parts of Asia, Vietnamese women take a lot of pain for little gain, with plenty of hard work to do but little authority at the decision-making level. Vietnamese women were highly successful as guerrillas in the American War. After the war, their contributions were given much fanfare, but most of the government posts were given to men. In the countryside, you'll see women doing backbreaking jobs, such as crushing rocks at construction sites and carrying heavy baskets.

Today more women are delaying marriage to get an education: around 50% of university students are female.

As in many Southeast Asian countries, substantial numbers of Vietnamese women (estimated at up to two million) end up in prostitution of some sort or another, working in massage parlours, karaoke clubs or dubious bars.

Beauty

The Vietnamese consider pale skin to be beautiful. On sunny days Vietnamese women can often be seen strolling under the shade of an umbrella in order to keep from tanning. Women who work in the fields will go to great lengths to preserve their pale skin by wrapping their faces in towels and wearing long-sleeved shirts, elbow-length silk gloves and conical hats. To tell a Vietnamese woman that she has white skin is a great compliment; telling her that she has a 'lovely suntan' is a grave insult.

Arts & Architecture

Vietnam has a fascinating artistic and architectural heritage. Historically, the nation has absorbed influences from China, India and the Khmer kingdoms and fused them with indigenous traditions. Then the French, Americans and Soviets left their mark. Today contemporary artists and architects look across the globe for inspiration.

Arts

Traditional Music

Vietnam's traditional music uses the five note (pentatonic) scale of Chinese origin. Folk tunes are usually sung without any instrumental accompaniment (and have been adapted by the Communist Party for many a patriotic marching song).

Indigenous instruments include the *dan bau*, a single-stringed zither that generates an astounding array of tones, and the *trung*, a large

Above Gate, Hue Citadel (p171)

bamboo xylophone. Vietnam's minorities use distinctive instruments: reed flutes, gongs and stringed instruments made from gourds.

Dance

Traditionally reserved for ceremonies and festivals, Vietnamese folk dance is again mainstream thanks to tourism. The conical hat dance is visually stunning: women wearing *ao dai* (the national dress of Vietnam) spin around, whirling their classic conical hats.

Theatre

Vietnamese theatre fuses music, singing, recitation, dance and mime into an artistic whole. Classical theatre is very formal, employing fixed gestures and scenery, and has an accompanying orchestra (dominated by the drum) and a limited cast of characters.

Popular theatre *(hat cheo)* expresses social protest through satire. The singing and verse include many proverbs and sayings, accompanied by folk melodies. Modern theatre *(cai luong)* shows strong Western influences. Spoken drama *(kich noi* or *kich),* with its Western roots, appeared in the 1920s and is popular among students and intellectuals.

Vietnamese theatre is performed by dozens of state-funded troupes and companies around the country.

A Good Scent from a Strange Mountain by Robert Olen Butler is a compelling collection of short stories focusing on the struggles of Vietnamese emigrants in America.

Puppetry

Conventional puppetry *(roi can)* and the uniquely Vietnamese art form of water puppetry *(roi nuoc)* draw their plots from the same legendary and historical sources as other forms of traditional theatre.

Water puppetry was first developed by farmers in northern Vietnam, who manipulated wooden puppets and used rice paddies as a stage. There are water-puppet theatres in both Hanoi and Ho Chi Minh City (HCMC).

Painting

Painting on frame-mounted silk dates from the 13th century. It was originally the preserve of scholar-calligraphers, who painted grand works inspired by nature and realistic portraits for use in ancestor worship.

During the past century, Vietnamese painting has been influenced by Western trends. Much recent work has had political rather than aesthetic or artistic motives – some of this propaganda art is now highly collectable. Many young artists now concentrate on producing commercial paintings. Some have gone back to the traditional-style silk or lacquer paintings, while others experiment with contemporary subjects. Hanoi and Hoi An have some great galleries.

Literature

One of Vietnam's literary masterpieces, *Kim Van Kieu* (The Tale of Kieu) was written during the first half of the 19th century by Nguyen Du (1765–1820), a poet, scholar, mandarin and diplomat.

Contemporary writers include Nguyen Huy Thiep, who articulates the experiences of Vietnamese people in *The General Retires and Other Stories,* and Duong Van Mai Elliot, whose memoir *The Sacred Willow: Four Generations in the Life of a Vietnamese Family* was nominated for a Pulitzer Prize.

Cinema

One of Vietnam's earliest cinematographic efforts was a newsreel of Ho Chi Minh's 1945 Proclamation of Independence. Later, parts of the battle of Dien Bien Phu were restaged for the benefit of movie cameras. Prior to reunification, the South Vietnamese movie industry produced a string of sensational, low-budget flicks. Conversely, North Vietnamese film-making efforts were very propagandist.

Interior art, Assembly Hall of the Cantonese Chinese Congregation (p201), Hoi An

Contemporary films span a wide range of themes, from warfare to modern romance. In Nguyen Khac's *The Retired General* (1988), the central character copes with adjusting from his life as a soldier during the American War to life as a civilian family man.

Dang Nhat Minh is perhaps Vietnam's most prolific film-maker. In *The Return* (1993), he homes in on the complexities of modern relationships, while *The Girl on the River* (1987) tells the stirring tale of a female journalist who joins an ex-prostitute in search of her former lover, a Viet Cong soldier.

Young overseas-Vietnamese film directors are steadily carving a niche for themselves in the international film industry and snapping up awards. Tran Anh Hung's touching *The Scent of Green Papaya* (1992) celebrates the coming of age of a young servant girl in Saigon. *Cyclo* (1995), his visually stunning masterpiece, cuts to the core of HCMC's gritty underworld and its violent existence.

Vietnamese-American Tony Bui made a splash with his exquisite feature debut *Three Seasons* (1999); it was set in HCMC and featured Harvey Keitel.

Architecture

Traditional Vietnamese architecture is unusual, as most important buildings are single-storey structures with heavy tiled roofs based on a substantial wooden framework (to withstand typhoons).

In rural parts houses are chiefly constructed from timber and built in stilted style, so that the home is above seasonal floods (and away from snakes and wild animals). Bamboo and palm leaves (for roofing) are also well suited to the tropical monsoon climate. Homes are usually divided into sections for sleeping, cooking and storage, while livestock live below the house.

Soviet architectural influence is deeply evident in Vietnam. Key buildings include Ho Chi Minh's Mausoleum in Hanoi and the Reunification Palace in Ho Chi Minh City.

Temple of Literature (p58), Hanoi

Quirky Vietnamese styles include the narrow tube houses of Hanoi's Old Quarter – the government collected tax according to the width of the commercial space, so the slimmer the cheaper. The Nung minority people's homes are also unusual, sometimes built with mud walls and with only one part elevated on stilts.

Consider the Vietnamese saying 'land is gold' as you survey a typical townscape today. Skinny concrete blocks of dubious architectural merit, many up to seven storeys high, soar above empty lots or loom above paddy fields. Planning laws (or the virtual lack of them) allow land owners to build whatever they like. Cement constructions painted lime green or pink, kitted out with mirror windows, and built with vaguely French-inspired ornate balconies or Chinese details are the flavour of the day in many places – the seafront in Cat Ba Town is one such example.

Colonial Buildings

Vietnam's French legacy is pronounced in the nation's architecture. Stately neoclassical buildings reinforced notions of European hegemony in the colonial era, and many still line grand city boulevards.

After the 1950s, most of these were left to rot as they symbolised an era many Vietnamese wished to forget. However, recent renovation programs have led to structures, such as the former Hôtel de Ville (People's Committee Building) in HCM City and the Sofitel Metropole Hotel in Hanoi, being restored to their former glory. If you have a postcard to send in HCMC, stop to admire the spectacular halls and vaulted ceiling of the central post office – designed by no less than Gustave Eiffel of tower fame. Haiphong is another city with wonderful French designs.

Colonial Style

Balconies
Elegant colonnaded balconies grace important municipal buildings.

Louvered windows *Usually green or brown, these allow air to circulate.*

Stucco features *A decorative flourish.*

Colour *Classy ochre or pale mustard.*

Terracotta roof tiles *Evoke memories of the Mediterranean.*

In Hanoi's French Quarter many grand villas have fallen on hard times and are today worth a fortune to developers. Meanwhile in Dalat, French villas have been converted into hotels; these include the classy Ana Mandara Villas, stately Dalat Hotel du Parc with its grand facade and the shock-and-awe colonial magnificence of the Dalat Palace Hotel.

Colonial churches were built in a range of architectural styles. In Hanoi the sombre neo-Gothic form of St Joseph Cathedral is enhanced by dark grey stone, whereas all the bricks used to construct HCMC's cathedral were imported from France.

Art deco curiosities built under French rule include Dalat's wonderful train station, with its multicoloured windows, and the sleek La Residence hotel in Hue.

Pagodas & Temples

Unlike other Asian nations, Vietnamese religious structures do not follow a specific national prototype. Pagoda styles echo the unique religious make-up of the nation, with strong Chinese content (including Confucian, Tao and Mahayana Buddhist elements), while southern Cham temples reflect influences from India, Hindu culture and the Khmer empire.

Pagodas *(chua)* incorporate Chinese ornamentation and motifs and follow a similar design, with buildings grouped around garden courtyards and adorned with plenty of statues and stelae. Most have single or double roofs with elevated hip rafters, though there are some with multi-tiered towers *(thap)* like Hue's Thien Mu Pagoda.

Vietnamese pagodas are designed according to feng shui (locally called *dia ly*) to achieve harmony of surroundings. They're primarily Buddhist places of worship, even though they may be dedicated to a local deity. Most are single-storey structures, with three wooden doors at the front. Inside are a number of chambers, usually filled with statues of Buddhas, bodhisattvas and assorted heroes and deities (Thien Hau, Goddess of the Sea, is popular in coastal towns). Flashing fairy lights, giant smoking incense spirals, gongs and huge bells add to the atmosphere. Garden courtyards, many with sculptures and some with a sacred pond (perhaps filled with turtles), connect to other temple structures, and there's often accommodation for monks at the rear.

Check out Hanoi's Temple of Literature for a superb example of a traditional Vietnamese temple or the wonderful pagodas in Hue's Imperial City.

Cham Style

The Cham primarily practised the Hindu religion, though some elements of Buddhism were also introduced. Temple-building commenced as early as the 4th century.

Most Cham temples were built from brick, with decorative carvings and detailing probably added later. Principal features included the *kalan* (tower; the home of the deity), saddle-roofed *kosagrha* temples (which housed valuables belonging to the gods) and the *gopura* gateway. Dotting the temple sites are stone statues of deities and numerous stelae with inscriptions listing important events.

Important Cham sights include My Son, Po Nagar, Po Klong Garai and Po Shanu.

ARTS & ARCHITECTURE ARCHITECTURE

Pagoda Features

Bodhisattvas
Enlightened earthly figures usually depicted as royals.

Cheung Huang Yeh *Greatly feared God of the City, akin to the grim reaper.*

Quan Am *Goddess of Mercy – a pale figure or statue with multiple arms.*

Swastika *Ancient Asian sacred symbol that signifies the heart of the Buddha.*

Thien Hau *Goddess who provides protection at sea.*

Food & Drink

Prepare to be amazed by Vietnam's cuisine. From traditional street stalls to contemporary big-city temples of upscale dining, the country serves up an endless banquet of exquisite eating.

Diverse landscapes – fertile highlands, waterlogged rice paddies, forest-cloaked mountains and sandy coasts – lend the cuisine variety, while a long history of contact with outsiders brings complexity. Over the centuries locals have adapted Chinese, Indian, French and Japanese techniques and specialities to their own palates.

The country's vast range of excellent edibles invites experimentation. Though Vietnam's well-known classics – *pho* (noodle soup), spring rolls and shrimp paste grilled on sugar cane – are all good and tasty, it pays to venture into the backstreets and markets and chow down on the street with the locals, as that's where you'll often find the most authentic food.

Flavours

Vietnamese palates vary from north to south, but no matter where they are, local cooks work to balance hot, sour, salty and sweet flavours in each dish.

Saltiness

> The best way to tackle Vietnamese cuisine head-on is to sign up for a cooking course during your stay. Courses have really taken off in recent years; see the destination chapters for recommendations.

Vietnamese food's saltiness comes from, well, salt, but also from the fermented seafood sauces that grace the shelves of every Vietnamese pantry. The most common is *nuoc mam* (fish sauce), which is so elemental to the cuisine that, sprinkled over a bowl of rice, it's considered a meal. *Nuoc mam* is made from small fish (most often anchovies) that are layered with salt in large containers, weighted to keep the fish submerged in their own liquid, and left in a hot place for up to a year. As they ferment the fish release a fragrant (some might say stinky) liquid. The first extraction, called *nuoc mam cot*, is dark brown and richly flavoured – essentially an 'extra virgin' fish sauce reserved for table use. The second extraction, obtained by adding salted water to the already fermented fish is used for cooking. Phu Quoc Island is famous for its *nuoc mam*, though some cooks prefer the milder version made around coastal Phan Thiet.

Sweetness

Sugar's centrality to the cuisine is best illustrated by the ever popular *kho*, a sweet-savoury dish of fish or meat simmered in a clay pot with fish sauce and another oft-used seasoning – bitter caramel sauce made from cane sugar. Vietnamese cooks also use sugar to sweeten dipping sauces, desserts and, of course, coffee.

Sourness

Sweetness is countered with fruity tartness, derived from lime (to squeeze into noodle soups and dipping sauces) and from *kalamansi* (a small, green-skinned, orange-fleshed citrus fruit), the juice of which is combined with salt and black pepper as a delicious dip for seafood, meats and omelettes. In the south, tamarind is added as a souring agent to a fish-and-vegetable soup called *canh chua*, and to a delectable dish of whole prawns coated with sticky, sweet-and-sour sauce called *tom rang me*. Northern cooks who seek sourness are more likely to turn to vinegar. A clear, yellowish vinegar mixed with chopped ginger is often served alongside snail specialities such as *bun oc* (rice noodle and snail soup).

Herbs

Vietnamese food is often described as 'fresh' and 'light' owing to the plates heaped with gorgeous fresh herbs that seem to accompany every meal. Coriander, mint and anise-flavoured Thai basil will be familiar to anyone who's travelled in the region. Look also for green-and-garnet *perilla* leaves; small, pointy, pleasantly peppery, astringent *rau ram* leaves; and *rau om* (rice-paddy herb), which has delicate leaves that hint of lemon and cumin. *Rau om* invariably shows up atop bowls of *canh chua*. Shallots, thinly sliced and slowly fried in oil until caramelised, add a bit of sweetness when sprinkled on salad and noodle dishes.

Chilli & Pepper

Vietnamese cooking uses less hot chilli than Thai cuisine, though it's a key ingredient in central Vietnamese meals. Local chillies vary from the mild-flavoured, long, red, fleshy variety that appears in many southern dishes and is served chopped to accompany noodles, to the smallish pale-chartreuse specimen served as an accompaniment in restaurants specialising in Hue cuisine. Beware: the latter really packs a punch. Dried ground chillies and spicy chilli sauces are table-top condiments in many a central Vietnamese eatery.

Vietnam is a huge peppercorn exporter, and ground black and white peppercorns season everything from *chao* (rice porridge) to beef stew. Wonderfully pungent, Vietnamese black peppercorns put what's sold in supermarkets back home to shame; if your country will allow it in, a half-kilogram bag makes a fine edible souvenir.

Fish Flavours

When it comes to fermented fish products, *nuoc mam* is only the tip of the iceberg. *Mam tom* is a violet (some would also say violent!) paste of salted, fermented shrimp. It's added to noodle soups, smeared onto rice-paper rolls, and even serves as a dip for sour fruits like green mango. It also lends a pungent salty backbone to specialities like *bun mam* (a southern fish-and-vegetable noodle soup). *Mam tom* has many versions in Vietnam, including ones made from crabs, shrimp of all sizes and various types of fish. Try to get past the odour and sample a range of dishes made with it: the flavour it lends to food is much more subtle than its stench might imply.

HABITS & CUSTOMS

Enter the Vietnamese kitchen and you'll be convinced that good food comes from simplicity. Essentials consist of a strong flame, basic cutting utensils, a mortar and pestle, and a well-blackened pot or two. The kitchen is so sacred that it is inhabited by its own deity, Ong Tao (Kitchen God). Offerings are always left in the kitchen for the spiritual guardian of the hearth, and every kitchen has an Ong Tao altar, considered to be the most important object in the room.

When ordering from a restaurant menu don't worry about the succession of courses. All dishes are placed in the centre of the table as soon as they're ready and diners serve themselves. If it's a special occasion, the host may drop a morsel or two into your bowl.

Fish flavours also come from dried seafood. Vietnamese cooks are quite choosy about dried shrimp, with market stalls displaying up to 15 grades. You'll also find all sorts and sizes of dried fish, both whole and in fillets, and dried squid. The latter is often barbecued and sold from roving stalls.

Sauces, Spices & Curries

Vietnamese cooks use quite a few sauces, such as soy, oyster and fermented soybean – culinary souvenirs of China's almost 1000-year rule over the country's north. Warm spices like star anise and cinnamon are essential to a good *pho*.

Curries were introduced to Vietnam by Indian traders; now they're cooked up using locally made curry powder and paste packed in oil. Vietnamese curries, such as *ca ri ga* (chicken curry cooked with coconut milk and lemongrass) and *lau de* (curried goat hotpot), tend to be more aromatic than fiery.

Kim Fay's *Communion: A Culinary Journey Through Vietnam* offers a real insight into Vietnam's wonderful food scene as the author travels the nation, shifting from street-food stalls to exquisite seafood restaurants. Engaging text is accompanied by recipes and photographs.

Staples

Rice

Com (rice) is the very bedrock of Vietnamese cuisine. In imperial Hue, rice with salt was served to distinguished guests by royal mandarins; these days locals eat at least one rice-based meal every day and offer a bowl of rice to departed ancestors.

If a Vietnamese says '*an com*' (literally 'let's eat rice'), it's an invitation to lunch or dinner. You can also get your fill of the stuff, accompanied by a variety of stir-fried meat, fish and vegetable dishes, at specialised, informal eateries called *quan com binh dan*.

Cooked to a soupy state with chicken, fish, eel or duck, rice becomes *chao* (rice porridge); fried in a hot wok with egg, vegetables and other ingredients, it's *com rang;* and 'broken' into short grains, steamed, topped with barbecued pork, an egg, and sliced cucumber, and accompanied by *nuoc cham* (a dipping sauce of sweetened fish sauce), it's *com tam*. Tiny clams called *hen* are sautéed with peppery Vietnamese coriander and ladled over rice to make *com hen*.

Sticky or glutinous rice (white, red and black) is mixed with pulses or rehydrated dried corn, peanuts and sesame seeds for a filling breakfast treat called *xoi* (*ngo* in central Vietnam). It can also be mixed with sugar and coconut milk then moulded into sweet treats, or layered with pork and steamed in bamboo or banana leaves for *banh chung,* a Tet speciality.

Soaked and ground into flour, rice becomes the base for everything from noodles and sweets to crackers and the dry, round, translucent 'papers' that Vietnamese moisten before using to wrap salad rolls and other specialities.

VEGETARIANS & VEGANS

The good news is that there is now more choice than ever before when it comes to vegetarian dining. The bad news is that you have not landed in Veg Heaven, for the Vietnamese are voracious omnivores. While they dearly love veggies, they also adore much of what crawls on the ground, swims in the sea or flies in the air.

However, all is not lost, as there are vegetarian *(com chay)* establishments in most towns. Often these are very local, simple places popular with observant Buddhists. Many use 'mock meat', tofu and gluten, to create meat-like dishes that can be quite delicious.

In keeping with Buddhist precepts, many vendors and eateries go vegetarian on the 1st and 15th days of each lunar month; this is a great time to scour the markets and sample dishes that would otherwise be off-limits. Otherwise, be wary. Any dish of vegetables may well have been cooked with fish sauce or shrimp paste.

REBECCA SKINNER / GETTY IMAGES ©

Regional Specialities

By Andrea Nguyen

Vietnam's cuisine is as multifaceted as its lengthy coastline. Travelling north to south is a journey that, geographically and gastronomically, begins in China and ends in Southeast Asia. The differences in history, culture and geography have resulted in a fascinating spectrum of techniques, ingredients and tastes, all linked by the Vietnamese love for vibrant flavours, fresh herbs, noodles and seafood.

Contents

➡ **Northern Vietnam**
➡ **Central Vietnam**
➡ **Southern Vietnam**

Above *Banh mi* (filled baguette; p456)

452

1. Fresh produce 2. *Pho bo* (beef noodle soup) 3. *Bun cha* (barbecued pork) with *nuoc mam* (fish sauce) 4. *Banh cuon* (rice crêpes filled with minced pork, mushrooms and shrimp)

Northern Vietnam

Northern Vietnamese food most clearly bears the imprint of the centuries of Chinese occupation. Comforting noodle dishes, generally mild flavours and rustic elegance are all hallmarks of the region's cuisine. The dishes tend to be mild and somewhat rustic. Soy is used as frequently as fish sauce, vinegar is more likely to add sourness than lime juice or tamarind, chillies give way to black pepper, and long cooking is used to coax maximum flavour from unpretentious ingredients.

Banh Cuon

These rolls are made from rice-flour batter that's poured onto a piece of muslin cloth stretched over a steamer; once firm, the noodle sheet is scattered with chopped pork, mushrooms and dried shrimp, then rolled up, sprinkled with crispy shallots, and served alongside a tangle of bean sprouts, slivered cucumber and chopped fresh herbs, with a saucer of *nuoc cham* (dipping sauce) for drizzling.

Bun Cha

This street favourite features barbecued sliced pork or pork patties served with thin rice vermicelli, a heap of fresh herbs and green vegetables, and a bowl of lightly sweetened *nuoc mam* (fish sauce) with floating slices of pickled vegetables. The Hanoi version combines sliced pork belly and pork patties formed from chopped pork shoulder.

Pho Bo

A culinary highlight of the north is *pho bo* (beef noodle soup). A good *pho* hinges on the broth, which is made from beef bones boiled for hours in water with shallot, ginger, fish sauce, black cardamom, star anise and cassia. Hardcore northern *pho* lovers frown upon adding lime, basil and bean sprouts to their bowls.

454

1. *Banh khoai* (shrimp crêpe) 2. Fish market 3. *Com hen* (rice with clams) 4. Chillies

TIM BARKER / GETTY IMAGES ©

Central Vietnam

Positioned between culinary extremes, the food of central Vietnam seems to be the product of moderation and balance – except where it concerns the locals' love of chilli. People cook from the land, turning their modest resources into fare fit for an emperor. Everything seems smaller here; baguettes and herbs are miniature versions of their southern selves, while Hue's imperial cuisine is a procession of dainty, delicate dishes. One edible legacy of the royal court is easily found on the street: *banh beo*, delicate steamed cakes made from rice flour. The central Vietnamese like gutsy and spicy flavours, and briny shrimp sauce and spritely lemongrass add to the cornucopia of flavours.

Banh Khoai

These hearty, dessert-plate-sized crêpes are made with rice-flour batter and cooked with copious amounts of oil in special long-handled pans. They feature a spare filling of shrimp, pork, egg and bean sprouts, are encased with fresh herbs in lettuce, and then dunked in a sauce based on earthy fermented soybeans.

Bun Bo Hue

This punchy rice-noodle soup with beef and pork exemplifies the central Vietnamese proclivity for spicy food. Tinged yellow-orange by chillies and annatto, the broth is laden with lemongrass notes and anchored by *mam tom* (savoury shrimp sauce). Like most Vietnamese noodle soups, it's accompanied by a riot of herbs and leafy greens.

Com Hen

Room-temperature rice is served with the flesh of tiny clams, their cooking broth, and myriad garnishes that include roasted rice crackers, crisp pork crackling, peanuts, sesame seeds, fresh herbs and vegetables. Add the broth and sauce to the other ingredients in your bowl; the liquid components moisten, season and harmonise.

Banh xeo (crispy pork and shrimp pancakes)

Southern Vietnam

Southern cuisine plays up the region's abundance and tends to be on the sweet side. No matter the season, vendors at southern markets display heaps of lush, big-leafed herbs, fruits in every colour and the freshest fish possible. Dishes are bigger, colourful and attractive. Coconut milk is the base for mild curries and also lends richness to sweets. The southern love of fresh herbs, fruit and vegetables comes to the fore in refreshing *goi* (salads) of green papaya, grapefruit-like pomelo or lotus stems.

Canh Chua Ca

This soup is the Mekong Delta in a bowl: plentiful fish, usually snakehead or catfish; fruits like tomato and pineapple; and vegetables including bean sprouts, okra and *bac ha* (taro stem), all in a broth that's tart with tamarind and salty with *nuoc mam*. Topped with vivid green herbs and golden fried garlic, it's as lovely to look at as it is to taste.

Banh Mi

This sandwich is a legacy of French and Chinese colonialism, but it's 100% Vietnamese. The baguette merely encases the filling, which might be a smearing of pâté or a few slices of silky sausage and a sprinkling of pepper. Mayonnaise moistens the bread and a sprinkling of soy sauce imparts *umami* (savoury) goodness.

Banh Xeo

This giant crispy, chewy rice crêpe is made in 12in or 14in skillets or woks and amply filled with pork, shrimp, mung beans and bean sprouts. Take a portion and encase it in lettuce or mustard leaf, add some fresh herbs, then dunk in the *nuoc cham*.

Noodles

Noodles are an anytime-of-day Vietnamese meal or snack. *Pho* is made with *banh pho* (flat rice noodles), and though this northern dish gets all the culinary press, the truth is that truly fine versions, featuring a rich, carefully made broth, are hard to come by. Other northern-style noodle dishes worth seeking out include *bun cha*, barbecued sliced pork or pork patties served with thin rice vermicelli, and *banh cuon*, stuffed noodle sheets that recall Hong Kong–style noodle rolls.

If you're a noodle lover look for dishes featuring *bun*, the round rice noodles that are a central element in *bun bo Hue*, a spicy, beef speciality from central Vietnam. Other characteristically central Vietnamese noodle dishes include *my quang*, a dish of rice noodles tinted yellow with annatto seeds or pale pink (if made from red rice flour) topped with pork, shrimp, slivered banana blossoms, herbs and chopped peanuts, and doused with just enough broth to moisten. It's eaten with rice crackers (crumbled over to add crunch) and sweet hot chilli jam.

Cao lau, a noodle dish specific to the ancient port town of Hoi An, features thick, rough-textured noodles that are said to have origins in the soba noodles brought by Japanese traders. It's moistened with just a smidge of richly flavoured broth, then topped with slices of stewed pork, blanched bean sprouts, fresh greens and herbs, and crispy square 'croutons' made from the same dough as the noodles.

Southerners lay claim to a number of noodle specialities as well, such as the cool salad noodle *bun thit nuong* and *bun mam*, a strong fish-flavoured rice-noodle broth that includes tomatoes, pineapple and *bac ha* (a thick, spongy plant stem). (An identically named but significantly more challenging dish of cool rice noodles, bean sprouts and herbs dressed with straight *nuoc mam* is found in central Vietnam.)

Across Vietnam, keep an eye open also for *banh hoi*, very thin rice-flour noodles that are formed into delicate nests and eaten rolled with grilled meat in leafy greens. Chinese-style egg noodles *(mi)* are thrown into soups or fried and topped with a stir-fried mixture of seafood, meats and vegetables in gravy for a dish called *mi xao*. *Mien* (bean-thread noodles) made from mung-bean starch are stir-fried with *mien cua* (crab meat) and eaten with steamed fish.

Rice-Paper Rolls

Vietnamese will wrap almost anything in crackly rice paper. Steamed fish and grilled meats are often rolled at the table with herbs, lettuce and slices of sour star fruit and green banana, and dipped in *nuoc cham*. Fat *goi cuon*, a southern speciality popularly known as 'salad' or 'summer' rolls, contain shrimp, pork, rice noodles and herbs and are meant to be dipped in bean paste or hoisin sauce. *Bo pia*, thin rice-paper cigars filled with slices of Chinese sausage, dried shrimp, cooked *jicama* (a crisp root vegetable), lettuce and chilli paste, are usually knocked up to order by street vendors with mobile carts.

Hue has its own version of the spring roll: soft, fresh *nem cuon Hue,* filled with sweet potato, pork, crunchy pickled prawns, water spinach and herbs. And then there's *nem ran ha noi,* northern-style, crispy, deep-fried spring rolls.

Meat, Fish & Fowl

Chicken and pork are widely eaten. In the mornings the tantalising aroma of barbecuing *nuoc-mam*-marinated pork, intended to fill breakfast baguette sandwiches and top broken rice, fills the air of many a city street. Beef is less frequently seen but does show up in bowls of *pho*, in *kho bo* (beef stew with tomato), in *thit bo bit tet* (Vietnamese pan-seared

FOOD & DRINK STAPLES

BANH MI

A legacy of the French, *banh mi* refers to the crackly crusted rice- and wheat-flour baguettes sold everywhere (eaten plain or dipped in beef stew and soups), and the sandwiches made with them, stuffed with meats, veggies and pickles. If you haven't tried stuffed *banh mi*, you haven't eaten in Vietnam.

beefsteak), and wrapped in *la lot* (wild pepper leaves) and grilled. Other sources of protein include goat (eaten in hotpots with a curried broth) and frogs.

Thanks to Vietnam's long coastline and plentiful river deltas, seafood is a major source of protein. From the ocean comes fish such as tuna, pomfret, red snapper and sea bass, as well as prawns, crabs and clams. In Vietnam seafood restaurants always keep their catch live in tanks or bowls, so you can be assured it's ocean fresh.

Flooded rice paddies yield minuscule crabs and golf-ball-sized snails called *oc*. In northern Vietnam the former go into *bun rieu cua,* thin rice noodles in a crimson-hued broth made from tomatoes and pulverised crab shells; on top floats a heavenly layer of crab fat sautéed with shallots.

Snails can be found in *bun oc* (rice noodle and snail soup), or chopped with lemongrass and herbs, stuffed into the snail shells and steamed, for *oc nhoi hap la xa* (a sort of Vietnamese escargot). A length of lemongrass leaf protrudes from each snail shell – give it a tug to pull out the meat.

Other favourite freshwater eats include the well-loved *ca loc* (snake-head fish), catfish, and, along the central coast, *hen* (small clams). The latter are eaten with rice in *hen com*, in broth with noodles, or scooped up with rice crackers *(banh da).*

Vegetables & Fruit

Keep an eye out for *sinh to* stalls stocked with a variety of fruits (including avocado, which the Vietnamese treat as a fruit rather than a vegetable) and a blender, where you can treat yourself to a refreshing blended-to-order iced fruit smoothie. It doesn't get much fresher than that.

Vegetables range from the mundane – tomatoes, potatoes, eggplants (delicious grilled and topped with ground pork and *nuoc mam*), cucumbers, asparagus – to the exotic. Banana blossoms and lotus stems are made into *goi* (salads); a thick, spongy plant stem called *bac ha* is added to soups; and *thien ly,* a wild plant with tender leaves and fragrant blossoms, is eaten stir-fried with garlic. Bunches of sunshine-yellow squash blossoms are a common sight in southern markets – locals like them simply stir-fried with garlic.

All sorts of delicious wild mushrooms sprout on forest floors during the rainy season, and if you're off the beaten track then you might also be treated to tender fern tips, which, like the more common *rau muong* (water spinach), get the stir-fry treatment. Especially loved are leafy greens such as lettuce, watercress and mustard, which Vietnamese use to wrap *banh xeo* (crispy pork and shrimp pancakes) into bite-sized parcels suitable for dipping in *nuoc mam.*

If you're a fruit lover you've come to the right place. Depending on when you're travelling you'll be able to gorge on mangoes, crispy and sour green or soft and tartly floral pink guavas, juicy lychees and longans, and exotic mangosteen, passionfruit and jackfruit. Hue cooks treat young jackfruit as a vegetable, boiling the flesh (which tastes like a cross between artichoke and asparagus), shredding it, dressing it with fish sauce, scattering the lot with sesame seeds, and serving the dish (called *nom mit non)* with rice crackers. Tamarind is a typically southern ingredient; it also sauces shelled or unshelled prawns in *tom rang me* – a messy but rewarding sweet-tart dish.

Sweets

Do ngot (Vietnamese sweets) and *do trang mieng* (desserts) are popular everywhere, and are especially prevalent during festivals when you'll encounter sweet varieties of *banh* (traditional cakes). Rice flour is the base for many desserts, sweetened with sugar and coconut milk and enriched with lotus seeds, sesame seeds and peanuts. Yellow mung beans are also used, while the French influence is evident in crème caramel. Cold sweets, like *kem* (ice cream), *thach* (lovely layered agar-agar jellies in flavours like pandan and coffee-and-coconut), and locally made sweetened yoghurt sold in small glass pots, hit the spot on steamy days.

VIETNAMESE COFFEE CULTURE

A Vietnamese coffee is a tradition that can't be rushed. A glass tumbler, topped with a curious aluminium top is placed before you while you crouch on a tiny blue plastic chair. A layer of condensed milk on the bottom of the glass is gradually infused with coffee lazily drop, drop, dropping from the aluminium top. Minutes pass, and eventually a darker caffeine-laden layer floats atop the condensed milk. Stir it together purposefully – maybe pouring it over ice in a separate glass – and it's definitely an energising ritual worth waiting for. And while you're waiting, consider the *caphe* variations usually on offer in a Vietnamese cafe.

Caphe sua da Iced coffee with condensed milk

Caphe da Iced coffee without milk

Caphe den Black coffee

Caphe sua chua Iced coffee with yoghurt

Caphe trung da Coffee topped with a beaten egg white

Che are sweet 'soups' that combine ingredients like lotus seeds or tapioca pearls and coconut milk. They're also a scrumptious shaved-ice treat, for which a mound of ice crystals with your choice of toddy palm seeds, bits of agar-agar jelly, white or red beans, corn, and other bits is doused with coconut milk, condensed milk, sugar syrup or all three. The combination of beans, corn and sweet liquid might sound strange, but in addition to being delicious, *che* is surprisingly refreshing.

Drinks

You're unlikely to go thirsty in Vietnam where, thanks to a healthy drinking culture, there exists all manner of beverages, including plenty of beer. Sooner or later every traveller succumbs to *bia hoi* (fresh draught beer) – local brands are served straight from the keg by the glass for a pittance from specialist stands on street corners. If you're looking to pay a little more, Saigon and Huda are decent, and La Rue, brewed on the central coast is quite good.

While imported liquor can be expensive, Vietnam brews a number of its own spirits, including a drinkable, dirt-cheap vodka called Ha Noi. Distilled sticky-rice wine called *ruou* is often flavoured with herbs, spices, fruits and even animals. Travel to the northern highlands and you may be offered *ruou can,* sherry-like rice wine drunk through long bamboo straws from a communal vessel. And you'll undoubtedly encounter *ruou ran* (snake wine), supposedly a cure-all elixir. Cobras and many other snakes in Vietnam are officially listed as endangered, a fact that producers rarely heed.

In Vietnam the preparation, serving and drinking of tea (*tra* in the south and *che* in the north) has a social importance seldom appreciated by Western visitors. Serving tea in the home or office is more than a gesture of hospitality; it is a ritual.

Vietnam is also a major coffee producer, and whiling away a morning or an afternoon over endless glasses of iced coffee, with or without milk (*caphe sua da* or *caphe da*), is something of a ritual for Vietnam's male population.

Other liquid options in Vietnam include *mia da,* a freshly squeezed sugar-cane juice that's especially refreshing served over ice with a squeeze of *kalamansi; sinh to* (fresh-fruit smoothies blended to order); and soy milk.

Northerners favour hot green tea, while in the south the same is often served over big chunks of ice. Chrysanthemum and jasmine infusions are also popular. Particularly delicious is a fragrant non-caffeinated tea made from lotus seeds.

Environment

Vietnam is one of the most diverse countries on earth, with tropical lowlands, intensely cultivated rice-growing regions, a remarkable coastline and karst mountains. But due to population pressure, poverty and a lack of environmental protection, many regions, and the nation's wildlife, are under threat.

The Landscape

As the Vietnamese are quick to point out, their nation resembles a *don ganh,* the ubiquitous bamboo pole with a basket of rice slung from each end. The baskets represent the main rice-growing regions of the Red River Delta in the north and the Mekong Delta in the south. The country bulges in the north and south and has a very slim waistline – at one point it's only 50km wide. Mountain ranges define most of Vietnam's western and northern borders.

Coast & Islands

Vietnam's extraordinary 3451km-long coastline is one of the nation's biggest draws and it doesn't disappoint, with sweeping sandy beaches, towering cliffs, undulating dunes and countless offshore islands. The largest of these islands is Phu Quoc in the Gulf of Thailand; others include Cat Ba and Van Don, the 2000 or so islets of Halong Bay, a spattering of dots off Nha Trang and the fabled Con Dao Islands way out in the South China Sea.

River Deltas

The Red River and Mekong River Deltas are both pancake-flat and prone to flooding. Silt carried by the Red River and its tributaries, confined to their paths by 3000km of dykes, has raised the level of the river beds

Tram Chim National Park in the Mekong Delta is one of Vietnam's most important wetland reserves, and home to the giant sarus crane, which can measure up to 1.8m in height.

ON THE BRINK

Vietnam's native elephant species has been listed as endangered since 1976. The government announced the creation of three conservation areas to help protect wild elephants (in Pu Mat, Cat Tien and Yok Don National Parks) in June 2013, but as the Forestry department estimates that only 75 to 130 elephants remain in the wild, many see the action as too little, too late.

Not discovered until 1992, the saola is a large antelope-like wild ox found only in the Annamite Mountains of Vietnam and Laos. Surviving numbers are thought to be in the hundreds. Conservation groups are working with minority people in the area to remove tens of thousands of snares from their forest habitat. For more information, consult www.savethesaola.org.

It's estimated that around 350 Indochinese tigers remain in the region, of which between 30 and 70 are in Vietnam. As they are in isolated pockets, their long-term chances are not great. Tigers are particularly vulnerable because of their value in the illegal trade in tiger parts for 'traditional' medicine.

KARST YOUR EYES

Karsts are eroded limestone hills, the result of millennia of monsoon rains that have shaped towering tooth-like outcrops pierced by fissures, sinkholes, caves and underground rivers. Northern Vietnam contains some of the world's most impressive karst mountains, with stunning landscapes at Halong Bay, Bai Tu Long Bay, around Ninh Binh and in the Phong Nha region. At Halong and Bai Tu Long Bays, an enormous limestone plateau has dramatically eroded so that old mountain tops stick out of the sea like bony vertical fingers pointing towards the sky. Phong Nha's cave systems are on an astonishing scale, stretching for tens of kilometres deep into the limestone land mass.

above the surrounding plains. The Mekong Delta has no such protection, so when *cuu long* ('the nine dragons', ie the nine channels of the Mekong in the delta) burst their banks, it creates havoc for communities and crops.

Highlands

Three-quarters of the country consists of rolling hills (mostly in the south) and mighty mountains (mainly in the north), the highest of which is 3143m Fansipan, close to Sapa. The Truong Son Mountains, which form the southwest highlands, run almost the full length of Vietnam along its borders with Laos and Cambodia. The coastal ranges near Nha Trang and those at Hai Van Pass (Danang) are composed of granite, and the giant boulders littering the hillsides are a surreal sight. The western part of the southwest highlands is well known for its fertile, red volcanic soil. However, northern Vietnam's incredible karst formations are probably the nation's most iconic physical features.

Wildlife

We'll start with the good news. Despite some disastrous bouts of deforestation, Vietnam's flora and fauna is still incredibly exotic and varied. Intensive surveys by the World Wildlife Fund along the Mekong River (including the Vietnamese section) found a total of 1068 new species from 1997 to 2007, placing this area on Conservation International's list of the top five biodiversity hot spots in the world. Numerous areas inside Vietnam remain unsurveyed or poorly known, and many more species are likely to be found.

The other side of the story is that despite this outstanding diversity, the threat to Vietnam's remaining wildlife has never been greater due to poaching, hunting and habitat loss. Three of the nation's iconic animals – the elephant, saola and tiger – are on the brink. It's virtually certain that the last wild Vietnamese rhino was killed inside Cat Tien National Park in 2010.

And for every trophy animal there are hundreds of other less 'headline' species that are being cleared from forests and reserves for the sake of profit (or hunger). Many of the hunters responsible are from poor minority groups who have traditionally relied on the jungle for their survival.

Vietnam: A Natural History, a collaboration between American and Vietnamese experts, is the best book for those wanting to learn about Vietnam's extraordinary flora and fauna.

Animals

Vietnam has plenty to offer those who are wild about wildlife, but in reality many animals live in remote forested areas and encountering them is extremely unlikely.

With a wide range of habitats – from equatorial lowlands to high, temperate plateaus and even alpine peaks – the wildlife of Vietnam is enormously diverse. One recent tally listed 275 species of mammals, more than 800 birds, 180 reptiles, 80 amphibians, hundreds of fish and tens of thousands of invertebrates, but new species are being discovered at such a rapid rate that this list is constantly being revised upward.

Rare and little-known birds previously thought to be extinct have been spotted and no doubt there are more in the extensive forests along the Lao border. Edwards' pheasant, previously believed to be extinct, was found on a scientific expedition, and other excursions have yielded the white-winged wood duck and white-shouldered ibis.

Even casual visitors will spot a few bird species: swallows and swifts flying over fields and along watercourses; flocks of finches at roadsides and in paddies; and bulbuls and mynas in gardens and patches of forest. Vietnam is on the east-Asian flyway and is an important stopover for migratory waders en route from Siberian breeding grounds to their Australian winter quarters.

Fauna & Flora International (www.fauna-flora.org) produces the excellent Nature Tourism Map of Vietnam, which includes detailed coverage of all the national parks in the country. All proceeds from sales of the map go towards supporting primate conservation in Vietnam.

Endangered Species

Vietnam's wildlife has been in significant decline as forest habitats are destroyed, waterways polluted and hunting continues with minimal checks. Captive-breeding programs may be the only hope for some, but rarely are the money and resources available for such expensive efforts.

Officially, the government has recognised 54 species of mammal and 60 species of bird as endangered. Larger animals at the forefront of the country's conservation efforts include elephant, tiger, leopard, black bear, honey bear, snub-nosed monkey, flying squirrel, crocodile and turtle. In the early 1990s a small population of Javan rhinoceroses, the world's rarest rhino, was discovered in Cat Tien National Park. Twenty years later they've all been wiped out.

However, there have been some successful stories. The Siamese crocodile, extinct in the wild due to excessive hunting and cross-breeding, has been reintroduced to Cat Tien and is now thriving. Wildlife populations have also re-established themselves in reforested areas, and birds, fish and crustaceans have reappeared in replanted mangroves.

National Parks

Vietnam has 31 national parks, from Hoang Lien in the far north to Mui Ca Mau on the very southern tip of Vietnam, plus 148 nature reserves. Officially, 9% of the nation's territory is now protected. Levels of infrastructure and enforcement vary widely but every park has a ranger station. You can hire a ranger to guide you in most parks.

ENV (Education for Nature-Vietnam; www.envietnam.org) works to foster greater understanding in Vietnam about wildlife, and the illegal consumption of products from endangered animals. If you see endangered animals for sale or listed on a restaurant menu, call its toll-free hotline (☎1800 1522).

The management of national parks is a continuing source of conflict because Vietnam is still figuring out how to balance conservation with the needs of the adjoining rural populations (many of them minority people). Rangers are often vastly outnumbered by villagers who rely on forests for food and income. Some parks now use high-tech mapping software to track poaching and logging activity.

If you can, try to visit the more popular parks during the week. For many locals a trip to a park is all about having a good time, and noise and littering can be a part of the weekend scene.

Many parks have accommodation and a restaurant; you should always call ahead and order food in advance though.

Environmental Issues

Vietnam's environment is not yet in intensive care, but it's reaching crisis level on several fronts. As a poor, densely populated country, the government's main priorities are job creation and economic growth. There's minimal monitoring of pollution and dirty industries, while loggers and animal traffickers are all too often able to escape trouble through bribery and official inaction. Quite simply, the environment is a low priority despite the government signing up to key conservation treaties.

Deforestation

Deforestation is a key issue. While 44% of the nation was forested in 1943, by 1983 only 24% was left and in 1995 it was down to 20%. Recent reforestation projects have increased cover since then, but these mostly consist of monocultural plantations of trees (like acacia for furniture) in straight rows that have little ecological merit. Plantations accounted for around 15% of all forest cover by 2013.

Vietnam banned unprocessed timber exports in 1992, which has produced a rise in the amount of forest cover. However, this has been bad news for its neighbours, because it simply means Vietnam buys its timber from Laos and Cambodia, where environmental enforcement is lax.

Hunting

Wildlife poaching has decimated forests of animals; snares capture and kill indiscriminately, whether animals are common or critically endangered. Figures are very difficult to ascertain, but a 2007 survey by wildlife trade monitoring organisation Traffic estimated that a million animals were illegally traded each year in Vietnam.

Some hunting is done by minority people simply looking to put food on the table, but there's a far bigger market (fuelled by domestic and Chinese traders) for *dac san* (bush meat) and traditional medicine. For many locals, a trip to the country involves dining on wild game – the more exotic the better – and there are bush-meat restaurants on the fringes of many national parks. A 2010 survey by the Wildlife Conservation Society found that 57 out of 68 restaurants in Dalat were offering wild game (including civet, porcupine and wild pig).

Twitchers with a serious interest in the birdlife of Vietnam should carry a copy of *Birds of Southeast Asia* (2005) by Craig Robson, which includes thorough coverage of Vietnam.

ENVIRONMENT ENVIRONMENTAL ISSUES

TOP 10 NATIONAL PARKS

PARK	FEATURES	ACTIVITIES	BEST TIME TO VISIT
Ba Be	lakes, rainforest, waterfalls, towering peaks, caves, bears, langurs	hiking, boating, bird-watching	Apr-Nov
Bach Ma	waterfalls, tigers, primates	hiking, bird-watching	Feb-Sep
Bai Tu Long	karst peaks, tropical evergreen forest, caves, hidden beaches	swimming, surfing, boating, kayaking, hiking	Apr-Nov
Cat Ba	jungle, caves, trails, langurs, boars, deer, waterfowl	hiking, swimming, bird-watching	Apr-Aug
Cat Tien	primates, elephants, birdlife, tigers	jungle exploration, hiking	Nov-Jun
Con Dao	dugongs, turtles, beaches	bird-watching, snorkelling, diving	Nov-Jun
Cuc Phuong	jungle, grottoes, primates, bird-watching centre, caves	endangered-primate viewing, hiking	Nov-Feb
Hoang Lien	mountains, birdlife, minority communities	hiking, cycling, bird-watching, mountain climbing	Sep-Nov, Apr-May
Phong Nha-Ke Bang	caves, karsts	boat trips, caving, kayaking, hiking	Apr-Sep
Yok Don	stilt houses, minority communities	elephant rides, hiking	Nov-Feb

RHINO HORN & VIETNAM

The international pressure around the use of rhino horn is growing; in 2013 the World Wildlife Fund and Traffic (the wildlife trade monitoring network) launched a campaign in Vietnam to counter its sale and consumption, declaring that the country needed to 'clean up its act'.

Demand for rhino horn has increased in recent years in Vietnam, spurred by superstitions and old wives' tales about rhino horn doing everything from increasing libido to curing cancer. Using rhino horn is also considered something of a status symbol for some of the emerging wealthy class.

Even the tragic news about the extinction of the rhino in Vietnam has failed to curb demand. With tens of thousands of dollars being paid per kilo of horn, traffickers have simply switched their attention elsewhere.

Vietnamese gangs have stolen dozens of antique rhino horns from museum displays across Europe, sometimes at gunpoint. And in South Africa, home to 73% of all the world's rhinos, there's been a rhino-poaching crisis. In 2012, authorities reported that 668 rhinos were killed. According to the Environmental Investigation Agency, groups including Al-Shabaab are selling rhino horn to fund terrorism.

A media campaign – public-service announcements on national TV and internet lobbying – was launched in 2013 to try to change mindsets and make the consumption of rhino horn unacceptable in Vietnam. **ENV** (Education for Nature-Vietnam; www.envietnam. org) is coordinating the efforts, which have included engaging popular comedian Nguyen Xuan Bac to speak out against the trade and educate people about the fact that rhino horn has no beneficial medical properties. Similar campaigns in other Asian countries, including China and Korea, have successfully reduced demand.

Rhino horn actually consists of a form of keratin, similar to fingernails.

For more information consult **Save the Rhino** (www.savetherhino.org) and the **Rhinose Foundation** (www.rhinoseday.com).

Attempts to curtail this trade at local and national level are thwarted by bribery, corruption and understaffing of the Forest Protection Department. ENV (Education for Nature-Vietnam) is a local NGO combating the illegal wildlife trade by lobbying politicians and providing educational programs in schools. It maintains files on restaurants offering bush meat and campaigns against the bear bile trade.

PanNature (www. nature.org.vn) is a Vietnamese NGO promoting solutions to environmental problems. It occasionally offers volunteer opportunities.

Industry & Pollution

Vietnam has a serious pollution problem. In HCMC the air quality is punishing, while Hanoi is the most contaminated city in Southeast Asia. Motorbikes are the main culprits, all running on low-quality fuel that has choking levels of benzene, sulphur and microscopic dust (PM10). Particulate (dust, grime) matter in Hanoi is around 150 micrograms per cu metre, whereas the World Health Organization recommends a limit of 20.

Water pollution affects many regions, particularly the cities and coastal areas (where groundwater has become saline due to over-exploitation). Manufacturers have flooded into Vietnam to build clothing, footwear and food-processing plants, but most industrial parks have no wastewater treatment plants. The result is that discharge has caused biological death for rivers like the Thi Van near Vung Tau. Nationwide only 14% of all city waste water is treated.

Toxic and industrial waste is illegally imported along with scrap for use as raw materials for production and for re-export. Enforcement is lax, though some violators have been fined.

Global Warming

Vietnam is ranked as one of the most vulnerable countries in the world in the face of climate change, because rising tides, flooding and hurricanes will likely inundate low-lying areas.

The National Centre for Hydro-Meteorology Forecasting reported that 246 tropical storms affected Vietnam between 1961 and 2010. While there were three storms in 1961, the number was 10 in 2008.

A sea-level rise of only a metre would flood more than 6% of the country and affect up to 10 million people. HCMC already experiences serious flooding every month, and the Saigon River only has to rise 1.35m for its dyke defences to be breached. If monsoons worsen, similar flooding will create havoc in the vast deltas of the Red River.

In the Mekong Delta, the nation's rice bowl, rivers up to 50km inland are seeing increased salinity. Near the mouth of the delta, salination of water supplies has been such that many families have switched from rice cultivation to shrimp farming.

Ecocide: The Impact of War

The American War witnessed the most intensive attempt to destroy a country's natural environment the world has ever seen. Forty years later Vietnam is still in recovery mode, such was the devastation caused. American forces sprayed 72 million litres of defoliants (including Agent Orange, loaded with dioxin) over 16% of South Vietnam to destroy the Viet Cong's natural cover.

Enormous bulldozers called 'Rome ploughs' ripped up the jungle floor, removing vegetation and topsoil. Flammable melaleuca forests were ignited with napalm. In mountain areas, landslides were deliberately created by bombing and spraying acid on limestone hillsides. Elephants, useful for transport, were attacked from the air with bombs and napalm. By the war's end, extensive areas had been taken over by tough weeds (known locally as 'American grass'). The government estimates that 20,000 sq km of forest and farmland were lost as a direct result of the American War.

Scientists have yet to conclusively prove a link between the dioxin residues of chemicals used by the USA and spontaneous abortions, stillbirths, birth defects and other human health problems. Links between dioxin and other diseases including several types of cancer are well established.

Ho Chi Minh, taking time off from the war in 1963 to dedicate Cuc Phuong National Park, said: 'Forest is gold. If we know how to conserve it well, it will be very precious. Destruction of the forest will lead to serious effects on both life and productivity.'

PARADISE IN PERIL

Unesco World Heritage site Halong Bay is one of Vietnam's crown jewels. A dazzling collection of jagged limestone karst islands emerging from a cobalt sea, its beauty is breathtaking.

This beauty has proved a blessing for the tourist industry, yet cursed Halong with an environmental headache. In 2012, 1.7 million people cruised the karsts. In order to accommodate everyone, the authorities have ripped up mangroves to build coastal roads and new docks. Inadequate toilet-waste facilities and diesel spills from cruise boats contaminate once-pristine seas.

A deep-water port in Hon Gai draws hundreds of container ships a year through an international shipping channel that cuts through the heart of Halong. The resulting silt and dust has cloaked the sea grasses and shallow sea bottom, making it a struggle for sea life to survive and putting the entire marine ecosystem in peril.

Even more alarming are the gargantuan Cam Pha coal mines and cement factory, just 20km east of Halong City, from which tonnes of coal dust and waste leak into the bay. Until 2012 untreated water was dumped into rivers and ended up in the bay, but a new treatment plant on the Vang Dang River has eased the flow of pollutants.

DOING YOUR BIT

➡ Vietnam has a low level of environmental awareness and responsibility, and many people remain unaware of the implications of littering. Try to raise awareness of these issues by example and dispose of your litter as responsibly as possible.

➡ Vietnam's fauna populations are under considerable threat from domestic consumption of 'bush meat' and the illegal international trade in animal products. Though it may be 'exotic' to eat muntjac deer, bat, sea horse, shark fin and so on, doing so will indicate your support or acceptance of such practices and add to the demand for them.

➡ When snorkelling or diving, or simply boating around coral reefs, be careful not to touch live coral or anchor boats on it, as this hinders the coral's growth. Boat operators should use buoys, or anchor in sandy areas – indicate your willingness to swim to the coral. Be aware that buying coral souvenirs supports the destruction of the very reefs you've come to see.

➡ When visiting limestone caves, be aware that touching the formations hinders growth and turns the limestone black.

➡ Refill plastic water bottles when possible.

Chemical manufacturers that supplied herbicides to the US military paid US$180 million to US war veterans, without admitting liability. However, the estimated four million Vietnamese victims of dioxin poisoning in Vietnam have never received compensation. Court cases brought by the pressure group Vietnamese Association of Victims of Agent Orange (VAVA) have so far been rejected in the USA.

Many journalists and other commentators have concluded that the Vietnamese government has been reluctant to pursue compensation claims for Agent Orange poisoning through the international courts because it has placed a higher priority on normalising relations with the USA.

Survival Guide

Directory A–Z

Accommodation

Accommodation in Vietnam is superb value for money. Big cities and the main tourism centres have everything from hostel dorm beds to luxe hotels. In the countryside and visiting provincial towns there's less choice; you'll usually be deciding between guesthouses and basic-but-decent hotels.

Cleanliness standards are generally good and there are very few real dumps – even remote rural areas have some excellent budget places. Communication can often be an issue (particularly off the beaten path where few staff speak English), but it's usually possible to reach an understanding. Perhaps because of this, service standards in Vietnam can be a little haphazard.

Prices are quoted in dong or US dollars based on the preferred currency of the particular property. Most rooms fall into a budget price category and dorm bed prices are given individually. Discounts are often available at quiet times of year.

Passports are almost always requested on arrival at a hotel. It is not absolutely essential to hand over your passport, but at the very least you need to provide a photocopy of the passport details, visa and departure card.

Guesthouses & Hotels

Hotels are called *khach san* and guesthouses *nha khach* or *nha nghi*. Many hotels have a wide variety of rooms (a spread of between US$20 and US$60 is not unusual). Often the cheapest rooms are at the end of several flights of stairs or lack a window.

Budget hotels Guesthouses (usually family run) vary enormously depending on the standards of the owner; often the newest places are in the best condition. Most rooms in this category are very well equipped, with US$12 to US$15 often bagging you in-room wi-fi, air-con, hot water and a TV. Some places even throw in a free breakfast, too. Towards the upper end of this category, mini-hotels (small, smart private hotels) usually represent excellent value for money. Few budget places have lifts (elevators), however.

Midrange hotels At the lower end of this bracket, many of the hotels are similar to budget hotels but with bigger rooms or balconies. Flash a bit more cash and the luxury factor rises exponentially, with contemporary design touches and a swimming pool and massage or spa facilities becoming the norm.

Top-end hotels Expect everything from faceless business hotels to colonial places resonating with history and chic boutique hotels in this bracket. Resort hotels are dotted along the coastline. Top beach spots such as China Beach, Nha Trang and Mui Ne all have a range of sumptuous places. Villa-hotels (where your accommodation has a private pool) are becoming popular, while others even include complimentary spa facilities. You'll find ecolodges in the mountains of the north and around the fringes of national parks.

Homestays

Homestays are a popular option in parts of Vietnam. As the government imposes strict rules about registering

---

SLEEPING PRICE RANGES

The following price ranges refer to a double room with bathroom in high season. Unless otherwise stated, tax is included, but breakfast excluded, from the price.

$ less than US$25 (525,000d) a night

$$ US$25 (525,000d) to US$75 (1,575,000d)

$$$ more than US$75 (1,575,000d)

HOTELS FROM HELL

There are a lot of hotel scams in Vietnam, mostly, but not exclusively, happening in the budget sector in Hanoi. A hotel will get a good reputation and recommendation in a guidebook and before you know it a copycat place with exactly the same name opens down the road. Dodgy taxi drivers work in tandem with these copycat hotels, ferrying unsuspecting visitors to the fake place. Check out your room before you check in if you have any concerns. Some Hanoi hotels will also harass you to book tours with them. That said, most guesthouse and hotel operators are decent and honest folk.

foreigners who stay overnight, all places have to be officially licensed.

Areas that are well set up include the Mekong Delta (p359); the White Thai villages of Mai Chau, Ba Be, Moc Chau; parts of the central highlands; the Cham Islands; and the Bho Hoong village near Hoi An (p212).

Some specialist tour companies (p485) and motorbike touring companies (p486) have developed excellent relations with remote villages and offer homestays as part of their trips.

Taxes

Most hotels at the top end levy a tax of 10% and a service charge of 5%, displayed as ++ ('plus plus') on the bill. Some midrange (and even the odd budget place) also try to levy a 10% tax, though this can often be waived.

Children

Children get to have a good time in Vietnam, mainly because of the overwhelming amount of attention they attract and the fact that almost everybody wants to play with them. However, this attention can sometimes be overwhelming, particularly for blonde-haired, blue-eyed babes. Cheek pinching, or worse still (though rare),

groin grabbing for boys, are distinct possibilities, so keep them close.

Big cities have plenty to keep kids interested, though in most smaller towns and rural areas boredom may set in from time to time. There are some great beaches, but pay close attention to any playtime in the sea, as there are some big rip tides along the main coastline. Some popular beaches have warning flags and lifeguards, but at quieter beaches parents should test the current first. Seas around Phu Quoc Island are more sheltered.

Kids generally enjoy local cuisine, which is rarely too spicy: the range of fruit is staggering and spring rolls usually go down very well. Comfort food from home (pizzas, pasta, burgers and ice cream) is available in most places too.

Pack plenty of high-factor sunscreen before you go as it's not that widely available in Vietnam (and costs more than in many Western countries).

Babies & Infants

Baby supplies are available in the major cities, but dry up quickly in the countryside. You'll find cots in most midrange and top-end hotels, but not elsewhere. There are no safety seats in rented cars or taxis, but some restaurants can find a high chair.

Breastfeeding in public is quite common in Vietnam, but there are few facilities for changing nappies (diapers) other than using toilets and bathrooms. For kids who are too young to handle chopsticks, most restaurants also have cutlery.

The main challenge throughout Vietnam is keeping an eye on what strange things infants are putting into their mouths. Their natural curiosity can be a lot more costly in a country where dysentery, typhoid and hepatitis are commonplace. Antibacterial hand gel (bring from home) is a great idea.

Keep their hydration levels up and slap on the sunscreen.

Customs Regulations

Enter Vietnam by air and the procedure usually takes a few minutes. If entering by land, expect to attract a bit more interest, particularly at remote borders. Duty limits:

➡ 400 cigarettes

➡ 1.5 litres of spirit

➡ Large sums of foreign currency (US$7000 and greater) must be declared.

BOOK YOUR STAY ONLINE

For more accommodation reviews by Lonely Planet authors, check out http://lonelyplanet.com/hotels/Vietnam. You'll find independent reviews, as well as recommendations on the best places to stay. Best of all, you can book online.

Electricity

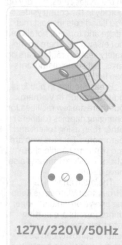

127V/220V/50Hz

The usual voltage is 220V, 50 cycles, but you'll (very rarely) encounter 110V, also at 50 cycles, just to confuse things. Electrical sockets usually accommodate plugs with two round pins.

Embassies & Consulates

Generally speaking, embassies won't be that sympathetic if you end up in jail after committing a crime. In genuine emergencies you might get some assistance, but only if other channels have been exhausted.

If you have your passport stolen, it can take some time to replace it as some embassies in Vietnam do not issue new passports, which have to be sent from a regional embassy.

Australian Embassy (☑04-3774 0100; www.vietnam. embassy.gov.au; 8 Đ Dao Tan, Ba Dinh District, Hanoi)

Australian Consulate (Map p299; ☑08-3521 8100;

5th fl, 5B Đ Ton Duc Thang, HCMC)

Cambodian Embassy (Map p64; camemb.vnm@mfa.gov.kh; 71A P Tran Hung Dao, Hanoi)

Cambodian Consulate (Map p302; ☑08-3829 2751; 41 Đ Phung Khac Khoan, HCMC)

Canadian Embassy (Map p62; www.canadainternational. gc.ca/vietnam; 31 Đ Hung Vuong, Hanoi)

Canadian Consulate (Map p299; ☑08-3827 9899; www. canadainternational.gc.ca/ vietnam; 10th fl, 235 Đ Dong Khoi, HCMC)

Chinese Embassy (Map p62; ☑04-8845 3736; http:// vn.china-embassy.org/chn; 46 P Hoang Dieu, Hanoi)

Chinese Consulate (Map p304; ☑08-3829 2457; 39 Đ Nguyen Thi Minh Khai, HCMC)

French Embassy (Map p64; ☑04-3944 5700; www. ambafrance-vn.org; P Tran Hung Dao, Hanoi)

French Consulate (Map p302; 27 Đ Nguyen Thi Minh Khai, HCMC)

German Embassy (Map p62; ☑04-3845 3836; www. hanoi.diplo.de; 29 Đ Tran Phu, Hanoi)

German Consulate (Map p302; ☑08-3829 1967; www. hanoi.diplo.de; 126 Đ Nguyen Dinh Chieu, HCMC)

Japanese Embassy (☑☑3846 3000; www.vn.emb-japan.go.jp; 27 P Lieu Giai, Ba Dinh District, Hanoi)

Japanese Consulate (Map p299; ☑08-3822 5341; 13-17 ĐL Nguyen Hue, HCMC)

Laotian Embassy (Map p64; ☑04-3942 4576; www.embal-aohanoi.gov.la; 22 P Tran Binh Trong, Hanoi)

Laotian Consulate (Map p299; ☑08-3829 7667; 93 Đ Pasteur, HCMC)

Netherlands Embassy (☑04-3831 5650; www. netherlands-embassy.org; 6th

fl, Daeha Office Tower, 360 Kim Ma St, Ba Dinh, Hanoi)

Netherlands Consulate (Map p302; ☑08-3823 5932; Saigon Tower, 29 ĐL Le Duan, HCMC)

New Zealand Embassy (Map p58; ☑04-3824 1481; www.nzembassy.com/vietnam; Level 5, 63 P Ly Thai To, Hanoi)

New Zealand Consulate (Map p299; ☑08-3827 2745; 8th fl, The Metropolitan, 235 Đ Dong Khoi, HCMC)

Philippine Embassy (Map p64; ☑04-3943 7948; www. hanoipe.org; 27B P Tran Hung Dao, Hanoi)

Singaporean Embassy (Map p62; ☑04-3848 9168; www.mfa.gov.sg/hanoi; 41-43 Đ Tran Phu, Hanoi)

Swedish Embassy (☑04-3726 0400; www.swedena-broad.com; 2 Đ Nui Truc, Hanoi)

Thai Embassy (Map p62; ☑04-3823 5092; www.thaiem-bassy.org; 3-65 P Hoang Dieu, Hanoi)

Thai Consulate (Map p304; ☑08-3932 7637; 77 Đ Tran Quoc Thao)

UK Embassy (Map p58; ☑04-3936 0500; http://ukinvietnam. fco.gov.uk; Central Bldg, 31 P Hai Ba Trung, Hanoi)

UK Consulate (Map p302; ☑08-3829 8433; 25 ĐL Le Duan, HCMC)

US Embassy (☑04-3850 5000; http://vietnam.usem-bassy.gov; 7 P Lang Ha, Ba Dinh District, Hanoi)

US Consulate (Map p302; ☑08-3822 9433; http:// hochiminh.usconsulate.gov; 4 ĐL Le Duan, HCMC)

Food

Eating out is a real highlight of travel in Vietnam. See the boxed text opposite for information on the price ranges used in this guide. For more information on cuisine and eating out in Vietnam, see p41 and p448.

EATING PRICE RANGES

The following price ranges refer to a typical meal (excluding drinks). Unless otherwise stated, taxes are included in the price.

Budget less than US$5

Midrange US$5 to US$15

Top-end more than US$15

Gay & Lesbian Travellers

Vietnam is a relatively hassle-free place for homosexuals. There are no official laws prohibiting same-sex relationships in Vietnam, nor is there much in the way of individual harassment. Hanoi's first Gay Pride march was held in 2012. Indeed, in 2013 the government started a consultation process about legalising same-sex marriages.

Hanoi and Ho Chi Minh City have healthy gay scenes, but gay venues keep a very low profile. Most gay Vietnamese have to hide their sexuality from their families and friends and a lot of stigma remains.

Gay travellers shouldn't expect any problems in Vietnam. Checking into hotels as a same-sex couple is perfectly acceptable, though it's prudent not to flaunt your sexuality. As with heterosexual couples, passionate public displays of affection are considered a basic no-no.

Utopia (www.utopia-asia.com) has useful gay travel information and contacts in Vietnam.

Insurance

Insurance is a must for Vietnam, as the cost of major medical treatment is prohibitive (p488). A travel-insurance policy to cover theft, loss and medical problems is the best bet.

Some insurance policies specifically exclude such 'dangerous activities' as riding motorbikes, diving and even trekking. Check that your policy covers an emergency evacuation in the event of serious injury.

Worldwide travel insurance is available at www.lonelyplanet.com/travel_services. You can buy, extend or claim anytime – even if you're already on the road.

Internet Access

Internet and wi-fi is widely available throughout Vietnam. However, be aware that the government regularly blocks access to social-networking sites, including Facebook.

The cost of internet access generally ranges from 3000d to 8000d per hour in cybercafes. Something like 98% of hotels and guesthouses have wi-fi. Only in very remote places (such as national parks) is it not standard. It's almost always free of charge, except in some five-star places.

Connection speeds in towns and cities are normally quite good, though not usually fast enough for gaming or streaming.

Language Courses

Vietnamese-language courses are offered in Ho Chi Minh City (HCMC), Hanoi and elsewhere. Note that the northern and southern dialects are quite different.

Legal Matters

Civil Law

On paper it looks good, but in practice the rule of law in Vietnam is a fickle beast. Local officials interpret the law as it suits them, often against the wishes of Hanoi. There is no independent judiciary. Not surprisingly, most legal disputes are settled out of court.

Drugs

The drug trade has made a comeback in Vietnam. The country has a very serious problem with heroin these days and the authorities clamp down hard.

Marijuana and, in the northwest, opium are readily available. However, there are many plain-clothes police in Vietnam and if you're arrested, the result might be a large fine, a long prison term or both.

Police

Few foreigners experience much hassle from police and demands for bribes are very rare. That said, police corruption is an everyday reality for locals. If something does go wrong, or if something is stolen, the police can't do much more than prepare an insurance report for a negotiable fee – take an English-speaking Vietnamese with you to translate.

Maps

The road atlas *Tap Ban Do Giao Thong Duong Bo Viet Nam* is the best available, but the latest roads are not included. It's available in bookstores including Fahasa and costs 220,000d.

Vietnamese street names are preceded by the words Pho, Duong and Dai Lo – on maps they appear respectively as P, Đ and ĐL.

It's also worth picking up a copy of the highly informative *Xin Chao Map of Hanoi*, which has tips and recommendations.

PLANET OF THE FAKES

You'll probably notice a lot of cut-price Lonely Planet *Vietnam* titles available as you travel around the country. Don't be deceived. These are pirate copies, churned out on local photocopiers. Sometimes the copies are OK, sometimes they're awful. The only certain way to tell is the price. If it's cheap, it's a copy.

Money

The Vietnamese currency is the dong (abbreviated to 'd'). US dollars are also widely used – less so in rural areas.

For the last few years the dong has been fairly stable at around 21,000d to the dollar. For more on exchange rates, see p19.

Where prices on the ground are quoted in dong, we quote them in dong. Likewise, when prices are quoted in dollars, we follow suit.

There's no real black market in Vietnam.

ATMs

ATMs are widespread in Vietnam and present in virtually every town in the country. You shouldn't have any problems getting cash with a regular Maestro/ Cirrus debit card, or with a Visa or MasterCard debit or credit card. Watch out for stiff withdrawal fees, however (typically 20,000d to 30,000d), and withdrawal limits – most are around 2,000,000d; Agribank allows up to 6,000,000d.

Bargaining

Some bargaining is essential in most tourist transactions. Remember that in Asia 'saving face' is important, so bargaining should be good-

natured. Smile and don't get angry or argue. In some cases you will be able to get a 50% discount or more, at other times this may only be 10%. And once the money is accepted, the deal is done.

Cash

The US dollar remains king of foreign currencies and can be exchanged and used widely. Other major currencies can be exchanged at banks including Vietcombank and HSBC.

Check that any big dollar bills you take do not look too tatty, as no one will accept them in Vietnam.

You cannot legally take dong out of Vietnam but you can reconvert reasonable amounts of it into US dollars on departure.

Most land border crossings now have some sort of official currency exchange, offering the best rates available in these remote parts of the country.

Credit Cards

Visa and MasterCard are accepted in major cities and many tourist centres, but don't expect budget guesthouses or noodle bars to take plastic. Commission charges (around 3%) sometimes apply. Some merchants also accept Amex, but the surcharge is typically 4%.

If you wish to obtain a cash advance, this is possible at Vietcombank branches in most cities. Banks generally charge at least a 3% commission for this service.

Tipping

Tipping is not expected in Vietnam, but it is enormously appreciated. For a person who earns US$100 per month, a US$1 tip is significant. Upmarket hotels and some restaurants may levy a 5% service charge, but this may not make it to the staff.

Consider tipping drivers and guides. Typically, travellers on minibus tours will pool together to collect a communal tip to be split

between the guide and driver (roughly US$10 per day).

It is considered proper to make a small donation at the end of a visit to a pagoda (roughly US$2), especially if a monk has shown you around; most pagodas have contribution boxes for this purpose.

Travellers Cheques

Travellers cheques can be a real pain to cash in Vietnam. Few banks will touch them these days and expect a long wait if one agrees to. In towns popular with tourists, readers report more success – try Vietcombank. **Sinh Tourist** (☎08-3838 9597; www.thesinh tourist.com) offices also cash travellers cheques.

Travellers cheques in currencies other than US dollars can be next to useless.

Opening Hours

Vietnamese people rise early and consider sleeping in to be a sure indication of illness. Lunch is taken very seriously and virtually everything shuts down between noon and 1.30pm. Government workers tend to take longer breaks, so figure on getting nothing done between 11.30am and 2pm. Many government offices are open till noon on Saturday, but closed Sunday. In this book, opening hours are only included when they differ from these standard hours.

Banks 8am to 3pm weekdays, to 11.30am Saturday

Offices and museums 7am or 8am to 5pm or 6pm; museums generally close on Monday

Restaurants 11.30am to 9pm

Shops 8am to 6pm

Temples and pagodas 5am to 9pm

Photography

Memory cards are pretty cheap in Vietnam, which is fortunate given the visual feast awaiting even the amateur photographer. Most internet cafes can also burn photos on to a CD or DVD to free up storage space. It's worthwhile bringing the attachment for viewing your files on the big screen, as many hotels come equipped with televisions.

Colour print film is widely available and prices are pretty reasonable at about US$3 for a roll of 36 print film. Slide film can be bought in Hanoi and HCMC, but don't count on it elsewhere.

Cameras are reasonably priced in Vietnam but the selection is limited. All other camera supplies are readily available in major towns.

Sensitive Subjects

Avoid snapping airports, military bases and border checkpoints. Don't even think of trying to get a snapshot of Ho Chi Minh in his glass sarcophagus!

Photographing anyone, particularly hill-tribe people, demands patience and the utmost respect for local customs. Photograph with discretion and manners.

It's always polite to ask first and if the person says no, don't take the photo. If you promise to send a copy of the photo, make sure you do.

For a comprehensive guide to all aspects of travel photography, check out Lonely Planet's *Travel Photography* book.

Post

Every city, town and village has some sort of buu dien (post office).

Vietnam has a quite reliable postal service. For anything important, express-mail service (EMS), available in the larger cities, is twice as fast as regular airmail and everything is registered.

Private couriers such as FedEx, DHL and UPS are reliable for transporting documents or small parcels.

Public Holidays

If a public holiday falls on a weekend, it is observed on the Monday.

New Year's Day (Tet Duong Lich) 1 January

Vietnamese New Year (Tet) January or February – a three-day national holiday

Founding of the Vietnamese Communist Party (Thanh Lap Dang CSVN) 3 February – the date the party was founded in 1930

Hung Kings Commemorations (Hung Vuong) 10th day of the 3rd lunar month (March or April)

Liberation Day (Saigon Giai Phong) 30 April – the date of Saigon's 1975 surrender is commemorated nationwide

International Workers' Day (Quoc Te Lao Dong) 1 May

Ho Chi Minh's Birthday (Sinh Nhat Bac Ho) 19 May

Buddha's Birthday (Phat Dan) Eighth day of the fourth moon (usually June)

National Day (Quoc Khanh) 2 September – commemorates the Declaration of Independence by Ho Chi Minh in 1945

Safe Travel

All in all, Vietnam is an extremely safe country to travel in. The police keep a pretty tight grip on social order and we rarely receive reports about muggings, armed robberies or sexual assaults. Sure there are scams and hassles in some cities, particularly in Hanoi and Nha Trang. But perhaps the most important thing you can do is to be extra careful if you're travelling on two wheels on Vietnam's anarchic roads – traffic accident rates are woeful and driving standards are pretty appalling.

Sea Creatures

If you plan to spend your time swimming, snorkelling and scuba diving, familiarise yourself with the various hazards. The list of dangerous sea creatures includes jellyfish, stonefish, scorpion fish, sea snakes and stingrays. However, there is little cause

GOVERNMENT TRAVEL ADVICE

The following government websites offer travel advisories and information on current hot spots:

Australian Department of Foreign Affairs (☎1300 139 281; www.smarttraveller.gov.au)

British Foreign Office (☎0845-850-2829; www.fco.gov.uk/en/travel-and-living-abroad)

Canadian Department of Foreign Affairs (☎800-267 6788; www.dfait-maeci.gc.ca)

New Zealand Ministry of Foreign Affairs & Trade (☎04-439 8000; www.safetravel.govt.nz)

US Bureau of Consular Affairs (☎888-407 4747; http://travel.state.gov)

for alarm as most of these creatures avoid humans, or humans avoid them, so the number of people injured is very small.

Jellyfish tend to travel in groups, so as long as you look before you leap into the sea, avoiding them should not be too hard. Stonefish, scorpion fish and stingrays tend to hang out in shallow water along the ocean floor and can be very difficult to see. One way to protect against these nasties is to wear plastic shoes in the sea.

Undetonated Explosives

For more than three decades, four armies expended untold energy and resources mining, booby-trapping, rocketing, strafing, mortaring and bombarding wide areas of Vietnam. When the fighting stopped, most of this ordnance remained exactly where it had landed or been laid; American estimates at the end of the war placed the quantity of unexploded ordnance (UXO) at 150,000 tonnes.

Since 1975 more than 40,000 Vietnamese have been maimed or killed by this leftover ordnance. While cities, cultivated areas and well-travelled rural roads and paths are safe for travel, straying from these areas could land you in the middle of danger. *Never* touch any rockets, artillery shells, mortars, mines or other relics of war you may come across. Such objects can remain lethal for decades. And don't climb inside bomb craters – you never know what undetonated explosive device is at the bottom.

You can learn more about the issue of landmines from the Nobel Peace Prize–winning **International Campaign to Ban Landmines** (ICBL; www.icbl.org), or visit the website of the **Mines Advisory Group** (MAG; www.maginternational.org), which specialises in clearing landmines and UXO. Cluster munitions were outlawed in a 2008 treaty signed by more than 100 countries, the usual suspects declining to sign: visit www.stopclustermunitions.org.

Telephone

A mobile phone with a local SIM card and a Skype account will allow you to keep in touch economically with anyone in the world.

International Calls

It's usually cheapest to use a mobile phone to make international phone calls; rates can be as little as US$0.10 a minute.

Otherwise you can webcall from any phone in the country. Just dial ☎17100, the country code and your number – most countries cost a flat rate of just US$0.50 per minute. Many budget hotels now operate even cheaper web-call services, as do post offices.

Of course, using services such as Skype (especially Skype to Skype) cost next to nothing; many budget and midrange hotels now have Skype and webcams set up for their guests.

Reverse charges or collect calls are possible to most, but not all, Western countries including Australia, Canada, France, Japan, New Zealand, the UK and the USA.

Local Calls

Phone numbers in Hanoi, HCMC and Hai Phong have eight digits. Elsewhere around the country phone numbers have seven digits. Telephone area codes are assigned according to the province.

Local calls can usually be made from any hotel or restaurant phone and are often free. Domestic long-distance calls are also quite reasonably priced.

Mobile (Cellular) Phones

Vietnam has an excellent, comprehensive cellular network. The nation uses GSM 900/1800, which is compatible with most of Asia, Europe and Australia but not with North America.

SIM cards It's well worth getting a local SIM card if you're planning to spend any time in Vietnam. A local number will enable you to send texts (SMS) anywhere in the world for 500d to 2500d per message. If you don't want to bring your flash handset from home, you can buy a cheap phone in Vietnam for as little as US$30, often with US$15 of credit included. Get the shop owner (or someone at your hotel) to set up your phone in English or your native language. Three main mobile-phone companies (Viettel, Vinaphone and Mobifone) battle it out in the local market, and they all have offices and branches nationwide.

Roaming If your phone has roaming, it is easy enough to use your handset in Vietnam, though it can be outrageously expensive, particularly if you use the internet.

Time

Vietnam is seven hours ahead of Greenwich Mean Time/ Universal Time Coordinated (GMT/UTC). Because of its proximity to the equator, Vietnam does not have daylight-saving or summer time.

Toilets

The issue of toilets and what to do with used toilet paper causes some confusion. In general, if there's a waste-paper basket next to the toilet, that is where the toilet paper goes, as many sewage systems cannot handle toilet paper. If there's no basket, flush paper down the toilet.

Toilet paper is usually provided, except in bus and train stations, though it's wise to keep a stash of your own while on the move.

There are still some squat toilets in public places and out in the countryside.

The scarcity of public toilets is more of a problem for women than for men. Vietnamese men often urinate in public. Women might find roadside toilet stops easier if wearing a sarong. You usually have to pay a few dong to an attendant to access a public toilet.

Tourist Information

Tourist offices in Vietnam have a different philosophy from the majority of tourist offices worldwide. These government-owned enterprises are really travel agencies whose primary interests are booking tours and turning a profit. Don't come

here hoping for independent travel information.

Vietnam Tourism and Saigon Tourist are old examples of this genre, but nowadays every province has at least one such organisation. Travel agents, backpacker cafes and your fellow travellers are a much better source of information than any so-called 'tourist office'.

There are privately operated, fairly helpful tourist offices in Hanoi and Ho Chi Minh City.

Travellers with Disabilities

Vietnam is not the easiest of places for travellers with disabilities, despite the fact that many Vietnamese are disabled as a result of war injuries. Tactical problems include the chaotic traffic and pavements that are routinely blocked by parked motorbikes and food stalls.

That said, with some careful planning it is possible to enjoy a trip to Vietnam. Find a reliable company to make the travel arrangements and don't be afraid to double-check things with hotels and restaurants yourself.

Some budget and many midrange and top-end hotels have lifts. Note that bathroom doorways can be very narrow; if the width of your wheelchair is more than 60cm you may struggle to get inside.

Train travel is not really geared for travellers with wheelchairs, but open tour buses are doable. If you can afford to rent a private vehicle with a driver, almost anywhere becomes instantly accessible. As long as you are not too proud about how you get in and out of a boat or up some stairs, anything is possible, as the Vietnamese are always willing to help.

The hazards for blind travellers in Vietnam are pretty acute, with traffic coming at you from all directions. Just getting across the road in cities such as Hanoi and HCMC

is tough enough for those with 20:20 vision, so you'll definitely need a sighted companion!

The Travellers With Disabilities forum on Lonely Planet's **Thorn Tree** (www.lonelyplanet.com/thorntree) is a good place to seek the advice of other travellers. Or check out the following:

Accessible Journeys (☏610-521 0339; www.disabilitytravel.com)

Mobility International USA (☏54-1343 1284; www.miusa.org)

Royal Association for Disability Rights (Radar; ☏020-7250 3222; http://disabilityrightsuk.org)

Society for Accessible Travel & Hospitality (SATH; ☏212-447 7284; www.sath.org)

Visas

Most nationalities have to endure the hassle of arranging a visa (or approval letter) to enter Vietnam. Entry and exit points include Hanoi, HCMC and Danang airports or any of Vietnam's plentiful land borders, shared with Cambodia, China and Laos (p479).

Tourist visas are valid for a 30- or 90-day stay (and can be single or multiple entry). Online visa agents provide a more efficient, cheaper and quicker service than Vietnamese embassies for those flying into Vietnam.

In Asia the best place to pick up a Vietnamese visa is Cambodia, where it costs US$55 to US$60 and can be arranged the same day. Bangkok is also a popular place, as many agents offer cheap packages with an air ticket and visa thrown in.

If you plan to exit Vietnam and enter again from Cambodia or Laos, arrange a 90-day multiple-entry visa (around US$110). (We've also heard of occasional 180-day visas being issued in Cambodia, though nowhere else.)

In our experience, personal appearance influences

the reception you'll receive from airport immigration – if you wear shorts or scruffy clothing, or look dirty or unshaven, you can expect problems. Try your best to look 'respectable'.

Multiple-Entry Visas

It's possible to enter Cambodia or Laos from Vietnam and then re-enter without having to apply for another visa. However, you must hold a multiple-entry visa before you leave Vietnam.

If you arrived in Vietnam on a single-entry visa, multiple-entry visas are easiest to arrange in Hanoi or HCMC, but you will have to ask a visa or travel agent to do the paperwork for you. Agents charge about US$45 for the service and visa fees are charged on top of this – the procedure takes up to seven days.

Visa Extensions

If you've got the dollars, they've got the rubber stamp. Tourist visa extensions officially cost as little as US$10, and have to be organised via agents. The procedure can take seven days and you can only extend the visa for 30 or 90 days depending on the visa you hold.

You can extend your visa in any provincial capital, but if it's done in a different city from the one you arrived in (oh the joys of Vietnamese bureaucracy!) it'll cost you around US$30. In practice,

extensions work most smoothly in major cities, such as HCMC, Hanoi, Danang and Hue.

Volunteering

Opportunities for voluntary work are quite limited in Vietnam as there are so many professional development staff based here.

For information, chase up the full list of nongovernment organisations (NGOs) at the **NGO Resource Centre** (☑04-3832 8570; www.ngocentre.org.vn; Room 201, Building E3, 6 Dang Van Ngu, Trung Tu Diplomatic Compound, Dong Da, Hanoi), which keeps a

database of all of the NGOs assisting Vietnam. **Service Civil International** (www.sciint.org) has links to options in Vietnam, including the **SOS Village** (www.sos-childrensvillages.org) in Viet Tri, north of Hanoi, and the **Friendship Village** (www.vietnamfriendship.org), established by veterans from both sides to help victims of Agent Orange. Or try contacting the following organisations if you want to help in some way.

You can donate your skills, time or money to **KOTO** (www.koto.com.au), which helps give street children career opportunities in its restaurants in Hanoi or HCMC; a three-month minimum commitment is required.

Volunteers for Peace (www.vpv.vn) is always looking for volunteers to help in an orphanage on the outskirts of Hanoi.

International organisations offering placements in Vietnam include **Voluntary Service Overseas** (VSO; www.vso.org.uk) in the UK, **Australian Volunteers International** (AVI; www.australianvolunteers.com) and **Volunteer Service Abroad** (VSA; www.vsa.org.nz) in New Zealand. The UN's volunteer program details are available at www.unv.org. Other volunteer sites include www.globalvolunteernetwork.org, which has a teaching program in Vietnamese orphanages, www.idealist.org and www.goabroad.com.

Women Travellers

Vietnam is relatively free of serious hassles for Western women. There are issues to consider of course, but thousands of women travel alone through the country each year and love the experience. Most Vietnamese women enjoy relatively free, fulfilled lives and a career; the sexes mix freely and society does not expect women to behave in a subordinate manner. That said, Vietnamese women take their appearance very seriously and femininity is still defined by beauty, slimness and grace.

East Asian women travelling in Vietnam may want to dress quite conservatively, especially if they look Vietnamese. Things have improved as more Vietnamese people are exposed to foreign visitors, but very occasionally some ill-educated locals may think an Asian woman accompanying a Western male could be a Vietnamese prostitute.

Many Vietnamese women dress modestly and expose as little body flesh as possible (partly to avoid the sun). Be aware that exposing your upper arms (by wearing a sleeveless top) can attract plenty of attention away from the beach.

Work

There's some casual work available in Western-owned bars and restaurants throughout the country. This is of the cash-in-hand variety; that is, working without paperwork. Dive schools and adventure-sports specialists will always need instructors, but for most travellers the main work opportunities are teaching a foreign language.

Looking for employment is a matter of asking around – jobs are rarely advertised.

Teaching

English is by far the most popular foreign language with Vietnamese students. There's some demand for Mandarin and French too.

Private language centres (US$10 to US$18 per hour) and home tutoring (upwards of US$15 per hour) are your best bet for teaching work. You'll get paid more in HCMC or Hanoi than in the provinces.

Government-run universities in Vietnam also hire some foreign teachers. Pay is generally around US$7 to US$12 per hour, but benefits such as free housing and unlimited visa renewals are usually thrown in.

Transport

GETTING THERE & AWAY

Most travellers enter Vietnam by plane or bus, but there are also train links from China and boat connections from Cambodia via the Mekong River. Flights, tours and rail tickets can be booked online at lonelyplanet.com/bookings.

Entering Vietnam

Formalities at Vietnam's international airports are generally smoother than at land borders. That said, crossing overland from Cambodia and China is now relatively stress free. Crossing the border between Vietnam and Laos can be slow.

Passport

Your passport must be valid for six months upon arrival in Vietnam. Most nationalities need to arrange a visa in advance.

Air

Airlines

Vietnam Airlines (www.vietnamairlines.com.vn), the state-owned carrier, has flights to 28 international destinations, mainly in east Asia, but also to the UK and Australia. There are plans to start connections to the USA in the future.

The airline has a modern fleet of Airbuses and Boeings, and has a good recent safety record.

Airports

There are four established international airports in Vietnam. Others including Phu Quoc and Hue are officially classified as 'international' but at the time of writing had no overseas connections (apart from the odd charter).

Cam Ranh International Airport (058-398 9913) Located 30km south of Nha Trang, with international connections to Moscow with Vietnam Airlines and Seoul with Asiana.

Danang Airport (Map p193; 0511-383 0339) International flights to Nanning (China) with China Southern Airlines, to Hong Kong with Dragonair, to Siem Riep (Cambodia) and Singapore with Silk Air, and to Pakse, Savannakhet and Vientiane (all in Laos) with Lao Airlines.

Noi Bai Airport (04-3827 1513; www.hanoiairportonline.com) Noi Bai Airport serves the capital.

Tan Son Nhat International Airport (08-3848 5383; www.tsnairport.hochiminhcity.gov.vn/vn; Tan Binh District) For Ho Chi Minh City.

Tickets

It's hard to get reservations for flights to/from Vietnam during holidays, especially Tet, which falls between late January and mid-February.

Land

Vietnam shares land borders with Cambodia, China and Laos and there are plenty

---

CLIMATE CHANGE & TRAVEL

Every form of transport that relies on carbon-based fuel generates CO_2, the main cause of human-induced climate change. Modern travel is dependent on aeroplanes, which might use less fuel per kilometre per person than most cars but travel much greater distances. The altitude at which aircraft emit gases (including CO_2) and particles also contributes to their climate change impact. Many websites offer 'carbon calculators' that allow people to estimate the carbon emissions generated by their journey and, for those who wish to do so, to offset the impact of the greenhouse gases emitted with contributions to portfolios of climate-friendly initiatives throughout the world. Lonely Planet offsets the carbon footprint of all staff and author travel.

of border crossings open to foreigners with each neighbour: a big improvement on a decade ago. The downside is that it is still not possible to get a Vietnamese **visa** (www.visatovietnam.org) on arrival at any of these borders.

Border Crossings

Standard times that foreigners are allowed to cross are usually 7am to 5pm daily.

There are now legal money-changing facilities on the Vietnamese side of these border crossings, which can deal with US dollars and some other key currencies, including Chinese renminbi, Lao kip and Cambodian riel. Avoid black marketeers, as they have a well-deserved reputation for short-changing and outright theft.

Travellers at border crossings are occasionally asked for an 'immigration fee' of a dollar or two.

CAMBODIA

Cambodia and Vietnam share a long frontier with seven (and counting) border crossings. One-month Cambodian visas are issued on arrival at all border crossings for US$20, but overcharging is common at all borders except Bavet.

Cambodian border crossings are officially open daily between 8am and 8pm.

CHINA

There are currently three borders where foreigners are permitted to cross between Vietnam and China: Huu Nghi Quan (the Friendship Pass), Lao Cai and Mong Cai. It is necessary to arrange a Chinese visa in advance.

China time is one hour ahead.

LAOS

There are seven (and counting) overland crossings between Vietnam and Laos. Thirty-day Lao visas are available at all borders.

The golden rule is to try to use direct city-to-city bus connections between the countries, as potential hassle will be greatly reduced. If you travel step by step using local buses, expect hassle and transport scams (eg serious overcharging) on the Vietnamese side. Devious drivers have even stopped in the middle of nowhere to renegotiate the price.

Transport links on both sides of the border can be hit and miss, so don't use the more remote borders unless you have plenty of time, and patience, to spare.

Bus

Bus connections link Vietnam with Cambodia, Laos and China. The most popular way to/from Cambodia is the international buses via the

VIETNAM BORDER CROSSINGS

Cambodia

CROSSING	VIETNAMESE TOWN	CONNECTING TOWN	MORE INFORMATION
Le Thanh–O Yadaw	Pleiku	Ban Lung	p291
Moc Bai–Bavet	Ho Chi Minh City	Phnom Penh	p336
Vinh Xuong–Kaam Samnor	Chau Doc	Phnom Penh	p391
Xa Xia–Prek Chak	Ha Tien	Kep, Kampot	p386
Tinh Bien–Phnom Den	Ha Tien	Phnom Penh	p391

China

CROSSING	VIETNAMESE TOWN	CONNECTING TOWN	MORE INFORMATION
Lao Cai–Hekou	Lao Cai	Kunming	p137
Mong Cai–Dongxing	Mong Cai	Dongxing	p115
Dong Dang–Pingxiang	Dong Dang	Pingxiang	p116

Laos

CROSSING	VIETNAMESE TOWN	CONNECTING TOWN	MORE INFORMATION
Bo Y–Pho Keau	Kon Tum, Pleiku	Attapeu	p293
Cau Treo–Nam Phao	Vinh	Lak Sao	p151
Lao Bao–Dansavanh	Dong Ha	Sepon, Savannakhet	p166
Nam Can- Nong Haet	Vinh	Phonsavan	p151
Na Meo–Nam Xoi	Thanh Hoa	Sam Neua	p151
Dien Bien Phu–Muang Khua	Dien Bien Phu	Muang Khua	p127

Vietnam Border Crossings

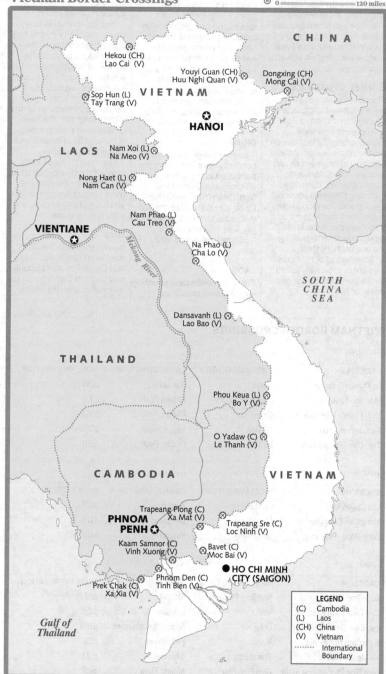

0
200 km
120 miles

CHINA

Hekou (CH)
Lao Cai (V)

Youyi Guan (CH)
Huu Nghi Quan (V)

Dongxing (CH)
Mong Cai (V)

VIETNAM

Sop Hun (L)
Tay Trang (V)

★ HANOI

LAOS

Nam Xoi (L)
Na Meo (V)

Nong Haet (L)
Nam Can (V)

Nam Phao (L)
Cau Treo (V)

VIENTIANE ★

Na Phao (L)
Cha Lo (V)

Mekong River

SOUTH
CHINA
SEA

Dansavanh (L)
Lao Bao (V)

THAILAND

Phou Keua (L)
Bo Y (V)

O Yadaw (C)
Le Thanh (V)

CAMBODIA

VIETNAM

Trapeang Plong (C)
Xa Mat (V)

PHNOM
PENH ★

Trapeang Sre (C)
Loc Ninh (V)

Kaam Samnor (C)
Vinh Xuong (V)

Bavet (C)
Moc Bai (V)

● HO CHI MINH
CITY (SAIGON)

Prek Chak (C)
Xa Xia (V)

Phnom Den (C)
Tinh Bien (V)

Gulf of
Thailand

LEGEND

(C)	Cambodia
(L)	Laos
(CH)	China
(V)	Vietnam
....	International Boundary

Moc Bai–Bavet border crossing. When it comes to Laos, many travellers take the nightmare bus between Vientiane and Hanoi via the Cau Treo crossing, or the easier route from Savannakhet in southern Laos to Hue in central Vietnam via the Lao Bao border crossing. Twice-daily buses also link Hanoi with Nanning in China.

Passengers always have to get off buses at borders to clear immigration and customs.

Car & Motorcycle

It is theoretically possible to travel in and out of Vietnam by car or motorbike, but only through borders shared with Cambodia and Laos. However, bureaucracy makes this a real headache. It is generally easy enough to take a Vietnamese motorbike into Cambodia or Laos but very difficult in the other direction (and the permits are costly). It's currently not possible to take any vehicle into China.

Consult the forums on www.gt-rider.com for the latest cross-border biking information.

Drivers of cars and riders of motorbikes will need the vehicle's registration papers, liability insurance and an International Driving Permit, in addition to a domestic licence. Most important is a *carnet de passage en douane,* which is effectively a passport for the vehicle and acts as a temporary waiver of import duty.

Train

Several international trains link China and Vietnam. A daily train connects Hanoi with Nanning (and on to Beijing!). The most scenic stretch of railway is between Hanoi and Kunming via Lao Cai; however, there's currently only one daily train from the Chinese border town of Hekou to Kunming. There are no railway lines linking Vietnam with Cambodia or Laos.

CHINA GUIDEBOOKS CONFISCATED

Travellers entering China from Vietnam have reported that Lonely Planet *China* guidebooks have been confiscated by border officials. The guidebook's maps show Taiwan as a separate country and this is a sensitive issue. If you're carrying a copy of Lonely Planet's *China* guide, consider putting a cover on the book, removing any potentially offensive maps and burying it deep in your bag.

River

There's a river border crossing between Cambodia and Vietnam on the banks of the Mekong. Regular fast boats ply the route between Phnom Penh in Cambodia and Chau Doc in Vietnam via the Vinh Xuong–Kaam Samnor border. Several luxury riverboats with cabins run all the way to the temples of Angkor at Siem Reap in Cambodia.

GETTING AROUND

Air

Airlines in Vietnam

Vietnam has good domestic flight connections, with new routes opening up all the time, and very affordable prices (if you book early). Airlines accept bookings on international credit or debit cards. Note, however, that cancellations are quite common. It's safest not to rely on a flight from a regional airport to make an international connection the same day – travel a day early if you can.

Jetstar Airways (☑1900 1550; www.jetstar.com) This budget airline has very affordable fares, but serves a limited number of destinations.

Vasco (☑038 422 790; www.vasco.com.vn) Connects HCMC with the Con Dao Islands and the Mekong Delta. Owned by, and code-shares with, Vietnam Airlines.

VietJet Air (☑1900 1886; www.vietjetair.com) A new,

---

privately owned airline with an expanding number of internal flights.

Vietnam Airlines (☑04-3832 0320; www.vietnamairlines.com.vn) The leading local carrier is the most reliable and has the most comprehensive network.

Bicycle

Bikes are a great way to get around Vietnam, particularly when you get off the main highways. In the countryside, Westerners on bicycles are often greeted enthusiastically by locals who don't see many foreigners pedalling around.

Long-distance cycling is popular in Vietnam. Much of the country is flat or only moderately hilly, and the major roads are in good shape. Safety, however, is a considerable concern. Bicycles can be transported around the country on the top of buses or in train baggage compartments if you run out of puff (usually US$1 for a short trip or US$1.50 per hour for longer trips).

Bicycle Types

Decent bikes can be bought at a few speciality shops in Hanoi and HCMC, but it's better to bring your own if you plan to cycle long distances. Basic cycling safety equipment and authentic spare parts are also in short supply, so bring all this from home. A bell or horn is mandatory – the louder the better.

Rentals

Hotels and some travel agencies rent bicycles for US$1 to

FARE'S FAIR?

For most visitors one of the most frustrating aspects of travelling in Vietnam is the perception that they are being ripped off. Here are some guidelines to help you navigate the maze.

Airfares Dependent on when you book and what dates you want to travel. No price difference between Vietnamese and foreigners.

Boat fares Ferries and hydrofoils have fixed prices, but expect to pay more for the privilege of being a foreigner on smaller local boats around the Mekong Delta and to places like the Cham Islands.

Bus fares More complicated. If you buy a ticket from the point of departure (ie the bus station), then the price is fixed and very reasonable. However, should you board a bus along the way, there's a good chance the driver or conductor will overcharge. In remote areas drivers may ask for four, or even 10, times what the locals pay. Local bus prices should be fixed and displayed by the door, but foreigners are sometimes overcharged on routes such as Danang–Hoi An.

Rail fares Fixed, although naturally there are different prices for different classes.

Taxis Mostly metered and very cheap, but very occasionally some taxis have dodgy meters that run fast.

Xe oms and cyclos Fares are definitely not fixed and you need to bargain. Hard.

While this is all very frustrating, in many ways it's a legacy of the early days of tourism in Vietnam, when all hotels were government-owned and charged foreigners five times the local rate. A similar fare structure existed for rail travel until quite recently too.

US$3 per day, better-quality models cost around US$10. Cycling is the perfect way to explore smaller cities such as Hoi An, Hue or Nha Trang (unless it's the rainy season!). There are innumerable bicycle-repair stands along the side of the road to get punctures fixed and the like.

Boat

Vietnam has an enormous number of rivers that are at least partly navigable, but the most important by far is the Mekong and its tributaries. Scenic day trips by boat are possible on rivers in Hoi An, Danang, Hue, Tam Coc and even HCMC.

Boat trips are also possible on the sea. Cruising the islands of Halong Bay is a must for all visitors to northern Vietnam. In central Vietnam the lovely Cham Islands (accessed from Hoi An) are a good excursion, while in the south, trips to the islands off Nha Trang and around Con Dao are also popular.

Bus

Vietnam's extensive network of buses reach the far-flung corners of the country. Modern buses, operated by myriad companies, run on all the main highways. Out in the sticks expect seriously uncomfortable local services.

Many travellers (perhaps the majority) never visit a Vietnamese bus station at all, preferring to stick to the convenient, tourist-friendly open-tour bus network.

Whichever class of bus you're on, bus travel in Vietnam is never speedy – reckon on just 50km/h on major routes (including Hwy 1) due to the sheer number of motorbikes, trucks and pedestrians competing for space.

Bus Stations

Cities can have several bus stations, and responsibilities can be divided according to the location of the destination (whether it is north or south of the city) and the type of service (local or long distance, express or non-express).

Bus stations can look chaotic but many now have ticket offices with official prices and departure times clearly displayed.

Deluxe Buses

Modern air-con buses operate between the main cities. This is the deluxe class and you can be certain of an allocated seat and enough space.

Some offer comfortable reclining seats, others have padded flat beds for really long trips. These sleeper buses can be a good alternative to trains, and costs are comparable.

Deluxe buses are non-smoking. On the flipside, most of them are equipped with TVs (expect crazy kung fu videos) and some with dreaded karaoke machines. Ear plugs and eye patches are recommended.

Deluxe buses stop at most major cities en route, and for meal breaks.

Reliable, punctual **Mai Linh Express** (☎ 098 529 2929; www.mailinhexpress.vn) operates clean, comfortable deluxe buses across Vietnam. Destinations covered include all main cities along Hwy 1 between Hanoi and HCMC, Hanoi to Haiphong, HCMC to Dalat, and cities in the central highlands.

Local Buses

Short-distance buses depart when full (jam-packed with people and luggage). Don't count on many leaving after about 4pm.

These buses and minibuses drop off and pick up as many passengers as possible along the route, so the frequent stops make for a slow journey.

Conductors tend to routinely overcharge foreigners on these local services so they're not popular with travellers.

Be aware that luggage is easily pilfered at toilet stops unless it's looked after.

Open Tours

In backpacker haunts throughout Vietnam, you'll see lots of signs advertising 'Open Tour' or 'Open Ticket'. These are bus services catering mostly to foreign budget travellers. The air-con buses run between HCMC and Hanoi (and other routes) and passengers can hop on and hop off the bus at any major city along the route.

Prices are reasonable. A through ticket from Ho Chi Minh City to Hanoi costs between US$25 and US$45, depending on the operator and exact route. Try to book the next leg of your trip at least a day ahead.

The downside is that you're herded together with other backpackers and there's little contact with locals. Some open-tour operators also depend on kickbacks from sister hotels and restaurants along the way. On the plus side, the

buses depart from central places (often hostels popular with travellers), avoiding an extra journey to the bus station. Some open-tour buses also stop at sights along the way (such as the Cham ruins of Po Klong Garai).

Buying shorter point-to-point tickets on the open-tour buses costs a bit more but you achieve more flexibility, including the chance to take a train, rent a motorbike or simply change your plans.

Nevertheless, cheap open-tour tickets are a temptation and many people go for them. Aside from the main north–south journey, the HCMC–Mui Ne–Dalat–Nha Trang route is being increasingly popular.

If you are set on open-tour tickets, look for them at budget cafes in HCMC and Hanoi. **The Sinh Tourist** (☎ 08-3838 9597; www.thesinhtourist.com) has a good reputation, with computerised seat reservations, but there are other companies.

Reservations & Costs

Reservations aren't required for most of the frequent, popular services between towns and cities, but it doesn't hurt to purchase the ticket the day before. Always buy a ticket from the office, as bus drivers are notorious for overcharging.

On rural runs foreigners are typically charged anywhere from twice to 10 times the going rate. As a benchmark, a typical 100km ride *should be* between US$2 and US$3.

Car & Motorcycle

Having your own set of wheels gives you maximum flexibility to visit remote regions and stop where you please. Car hire always includes a driver. Motorbike hire is good value and this can be self-drive or with a driver.

Driving Licence

In order to drive a car in Vietnam, you need a Vietnamese licence and an International Driving Permit (IDP), usually issued by an automobile association back home. You have to be resident in Vietnam for three months to apply for a Vietnamese licence.

When it comes to renting motorbikes, the whole situation is a grey area. An IDP and motorbike licence (which includes a test in the Vietnamese language) is officially required but the reality on the ground is that foreigners are never asked for it by police, and no rental places ever ask to see one.

Fuel

Fuel costs around 24,500d per litre of unleaded gasoline. Even isolated communities usually have someone selling petrol by the roadside. Some sellers dilute fuel to make a quick profit – try to fill up from a proper petrol station.

Hire

The major considerations are safety, the mechanical condition of the vehicle, the

ROAD DISTANCES (KM)

	Dalat	Hoi An	Sapa	Hue	Halong City	Hanoi
Hoi An	716					
Sapa	1868	1117				
Hue	830	138	1038			
Halong City	1653	911	545	823		
Hanoi	1488	793	380	658	165	
HCMC	310	942	2104	1097	1889	1724

reliability of the rental agency, and your budget.

CAR & MINIBUS

Self-drive rental cars are unavailable in Vietnam, which is a blessing given traffic conditions, but cars with drivers are popular and plentiful. Renting a vehicle with a driver-cum-guide is a realistic option even for budget travellers, if there are enough people to share the cost.

Hanoi, HCMC and the main tourist centres have a wide selection of travel agencies that rent vehicles with drivers for sightseeing trips. For the rough roads of northwestern Vietnam you'll definitely need a 4WD.

Approximate costs per day are US$70 and US$100 for a standard car, or US$115 and US$135 for a 4WD.

MOTORBIKE

Motorbikes can be rented from virtually anywhere, including cafes, hotels and travel agencies. Some places will ask to keep your passport until you return the bike. Try to sign some sort of agreement, clearly stating what you are renting, how much it costs, the extent of compensation and so on.

To tackle the mountains of the north, it is best to get a slightly more powerful model such as a road or trail bike. Plenty of local drivers are willing to act as chauffeur and guide for around US$20 per day.

The approximate costs per day without a driver are between US$4 and US$6 for a semi-auto moped, between US$7 and US$10 for a fully automatic moped, or US$20 and up for trail and road bikes.

Insurance

If you're travelling in a tourist vehicle with a driver, it is almost guaranteed to be insured. When it comes to motorbikes, many rental bikes are not insured and you will have to sign a contract agreeing to a valuation for the bike if it is stolen. Make sure you always leave it in guarded parking where available.

Do not even consider renting a motorbike if you are daft enough to be travelling in Vietnam without insurance. The cost of treating serious injuries can be bankrupting for budget travellers.

Road Conditions & Hazards

Road safety is definitely not one of Vietnam's strong points. The intercity road network of two-lane highways is becoming more and more dangerous. High-speed, head-on collisions are a sickeningly familiar sight on main roads.

In general, the major highways are paved and reasonably well maintained, but seasonal flooding can be a problem. A big typhoon can create potholes the size of bomb craters. In some remote areas, roads are not surfaced and transform themselves into a sea of mud when the weather turns bad – such roads are best tackled with a 4WD vehicle or motorbike. Mountain roads are particularly dangerous: landslides, falling rocks and runaway vehicles can add an unwelcome edge to your journey.

EMERGENCIES

Vietnam does not have an efficient emergency-rescue system, so if something happens on the road, it could be some time before help arrives and a long way to even the most basic of medical facilities. Locals might help in extreme circumstances, but in most cases it will be up to you (or your guide) to get you to the hospital or clinic.

Road Rules

Basically, there aren't many or, arguably, any. Size matters and the biggest vehicle wins by default. Be particularly

HIRING A VEHICLE & DRIVER

Renting a car with a driver gives you the chance to design a tailor-made tour. Seeing the country this way is almost like independent travel, except that it's more comfortable, less time-consuming and allows for stops along the way.

Most travel agencies and tour operators can hook you up with a vehicle and driver (most of whom will *not* speak English). Try to find a driver/guide who can act as a translator and travelling companion and offer all kinds of cultural knowledge, opening up the door to some unique experiences. A bad guide can ruin your trip. Consider the following:

➡ Try to meet your driver/guide before starting out and make sure that this is someone you can travel with.

➡ What languages do they speak, and how fluently?

➡ Drivers usually pays for their own costs, including accommodation and meals, while you pay for the petrol. Check this is the case.

➡ Settle on an itinerary and get a copy from the travel agency. If you find your guide is making it up as they go along, use it as leverage.

➡ Make it clear you want to avoid tourist-trap restaurants and shops.

➡ Tip them if you've had a good experience.

HELMET LAW

It is compulsory to wear a helmet when riding a motorbike in Vietnam, even when travelling as a passenger. Consider investing in a decent imported helmet if you are planning extensive rides on busy highways or winding mountain roads, as the local eggshells don't offer much protection. Better-quality helmets are available in major cities from US$25.

careful about children on the road. Livestock is also a menace; hit a cow on a motorbike and you'll both be hamburger.

The police almost never bother stopping foreigners on bikes. However, speeding fines are imposed and the police now have speed 'guns'. In any area deemed to be 'urban' (look out for the blue sign with skyscrapers), the limit is just 50km/h. In cities, there is a rule that you cannot turn right on a red light.

Honking at all pedestrians and bicycles (to warn them of your approach) is not road rage but an essential element of safe driving – larger trucks and buses might as well have a dynamo-driven horn. There is no national seat-belt law.

Legally, a motorbike can carry only two people, but we've seen up to six on one vehicle, plus luggage! This law is enforced in major cities, but wildly ignored in rural areas.

Spare Parts

Vietnam is awash with Japanese (and increasingly Chinese) motorbikes, so it is easy to get spare parts for most bikes. But if you are driving something obscure, bring substantial spares.

Local Transport

Bus

Few travellers deal with city buses due to communication issues and the cheapness of taxis, cyclos and xe om. That said, the bus systems in Hanoi and HCMC are not impossible to negotiate – get your hands on a bus map.

Cyclo

The cyclo is a bicycle rickshaw. This cheap, environmentally friendly mode of transport is steadily dying out, but is still found in Vietnam's main cities.

Groups of cyclo drivers always hang out near major hotels and markets, and many speak at least broken English. To make sure the driver understands where you want to go, it's useful to bring a city map. Bargaining is imperative. Settle on a fare before going anywhere or you're likely to get stiffed.

Approximate fares are between 10,000d and 15,0000d for a short ride, between 20,000d and 35,000d for a longer or night ride, or around 40,000d per hour.

Travellers have reported being mugged by cyclo drivers in HCMC so, as a general rule, hire cyclos only during the day in that city. When leaving a bar late at night, take a metered taxi.

Taxi

Taxis with meters, found in most major cities, are very cheap by international standards and a safe way to travel around at night. Average tariffs are about 10,000d to 15,000d per kilometre. However, dodgy taxis with go-fast meters do roam the streets of Hanoi and HCMC; they often hang around bus terminals. Only travel with reputable or recommended companies.

Two nationwide companies with excellent reputations are **Mai Linh** (www.mailinh.vn) and **Vinasun** (www.vinasuntaxi.com).

Xe Om

The xe om (zay-ohm) is a motorbike taxi. Xe means 'motorbike', om means 'hug' (or 'hold'), so you get the picture. Getting around by xe om is easy, as long as you don't have a lot of luggage.

Fares are comparable with those for a cyclo, but negotiate the price beforehand. There are plenty of xe om drivers hanging around street corners, markets, hotels and bus stations. They will find you before you find them...

Tours

The quality of bottom-end budget tours being peddled in HCMC and Hanoi is often terrible. You tend to get what you pay for.

Handspan Adventure Travel (www.handspan.com) Expert locally owned company that offers a wide range of innovative, interesting tours to seldom-visited regions including Moc Chau and alternative destinations like Cao Bang in the north. Other options include jeep tours, mountain biking, trekking and kayaking.

Ocean Tours (www.oceantours.com.vn) Well-organised tour operator with Halong Bay and Ba Be National Park options, and 4WD road trips around the northeast.

Buffalo Tours (Map p54; www.buffalotours.com) Offers diverse and customised trips, from a nine-day Gourmet Vietnam tour to a 14-day Vietnam Beach Break.

Exotissimo (www.exotissimo.com) Runs a wide range of tours, including cycling, trekking and golfing. The 10-day Flavors of Vietnam tour has a strong culinary emphasis.

Sinhbalo Adventures (www.sinhbalo.com) Specialises in cycling tours to the Mekong Delta and beyond, plus trips to the central and northern highlands.

Motorbike Tours

Specialised motorbike tours through Vietnam are a brilliant way to experience the nation and get off the main highways. Two wheels can reach the parts that four wheels sometimes can't, by traversing small trails and traffic-free back roads. A little experience helps, but many leading companies also offer tuition for first-timers. Mounting a bike to take on the peaks of the north is one of Vietnam's defining moments and should not be missed.

Foreign guides charge considerably more than local guides. Based on a group of four people, you can expect to pay from US$100 per person per day for an all-inclusive tour that provides motorbike rental, petrol, guide, food and accommodation. Some of the best companies running trips include the following:

Hoi An Motorbike Adventure (www.motorbiketours-hoian.com; tours US$40-1050) Terrific tours, mainly shortish rides around along beautiful backroads in Hoi An area (from US$40) but longer trips up Son Tra, to the Demilitarised Zone (DMZ) and Hue are also offered. Well-maintained classic-looking Minsk bikes are used.

Explore Indochina (Map p58; www.exploreindochina. com; per day US$175-235) Expertly arranged motorbike tours, with a great range of trips, including an epic Border Trails tour that shadows the frontier with China. All trips are on vintage Urals or modified Minsks. Jeep tours are also offered.

Offroad Vietnam (www. offroadvietnam.com; self-guided per day from US$17) This professional company offers three types of trips: fully guided (all-inclusive), semi-guided (you and a guide), and self-guided (DIY) across northern Vietnam, mainly using Honda bikes. Owner Anh is a fluent English-speaker and excellent source of advice.

Cuong's Motorbike Adventure (http://cuongs-motorbike-adventure.com) Well-planned, adventurous tours across the northeast, northwest and beyond organised by experts with decades of experience. Daily all-inclusive rates cost US$170 for Minsk bikes, or US$230 for Urals.

Free Wheelin' Tours (www. freewheelin-tours.com) Offers some excellent eight-day trips to Ha Giang, as well as custom-made tours in northern Vietnam.

Voyage Vietnam (www.voya-gevietnam.net; per day from US$90) A locally run outfit with a good reputation for its trips in the north, Mekong and HCMC highway. Uses Royal Enfields and Honda bikes.

Train

Operated by national carrier **Vietnam Railways** (Duong Sat Viet Nam; ☑3747 0308; www.vr.com.vn) the Vietnamese railway system is an ageing but pretty dependable service, and offers a relaxing way to get around the nation. Travelling in an air-con sleeping berth sure beats a hairy overnight bus journey along Hwy 1. And of course, there's some spectacular scenery to lap up too.

Classes

Trains classified as SE are the smartest and fastest, while those referred to as TN are slower and older.

There are four main ticket classes: hard seat, soft seat, hard sleeper and soft sleeper. These are also split into air-con and non air-con options. Presently, air-con is only available on the faster express trains. Hard-seat class is usually packed and tolerable for day travel, but expect plenty of cigarette smoke.

PRIVATE CARRIAGES

Comfortable, even luxurious private carriages tagged onto the back of trains offer a classy way of travelling between Lao Cai and Hanoi: those offered by Victoria Hotels are renowned and very pricey, but there are many others, including **Livitrans** (www.livitrans.com), which charges US$45 to US$85.

Livitrans also offers luxury carriages between Hanoi and Hue (US$70) and Danang (US$80), as do several other companies. **Golden Trains** (☑08-3825 7636; www.golden-train.com) connect HCMC with Nha Trang (US$39 to US$44 soft sleeper) and Phan Tiet, for Mui Ne (US$15 soft seat).

SLEEPERS

A hard sleeper has three tiers of beds (six beds per compartment), with the upper berth cheapest and the lower berth most expensive. Soft sleeper has two tiers (four beds per compartment) and all bunks are priced the same. Fastidious travellers will probably want to bring a sleeping sheet, sleeping bag and/or pillow case, although linen is provided.

Costs

Ticket prices vary depending on the train; the fastest trains are more expensive. Children under two travel free; those aged between two and nine years pay 50% of the adult fare. There are no discounts on the Hanoi–Lao Cai route.

REUNIFICATION EXPRESS

Construction of the 1726km-long Hanoi–Saigon railway, the Transindochinois, began in 1899 and was completed in 1936. In the late 1930s the trip from Hanoi to Saigon took 40 hours and 20 minutes at an average speed of 43km/h.

During WWII the Japanese made extensive use of the rail system, resulting in Viet Minh sabotage on the ground and US bombing from the air. After WWII, efforts were made to repair the Transindochinois, major parts of which were either damaged or overgrown.

During the Franco–Viet Minh War (1946–54), the Viet Minh again engaged in sabotage against the rail system. At night the Viet Minh made off with rails to create a 300km network of tracks (between Ninh Hoa and Danang) in an area wholly under their control – the French quickly responded with their own sabotage.

In the late 1950s the South, with US funding, reconstructed the track between Saigon and Hue, a distance of 1041km. But between 1961 and 1964 alone, 795 Viet Cong (VC) attacks were launched on the rail system, forcing the abandonment of large sections of track (including the Dalat spur).

By 1960 North Vietnam had repaired 1000km of track, mostly between Hanoi and China. During the US air war against the North, the northern rail network was repeatedly bombed. Even now, clusters of bomb craters can be seen around virtually every rail bridge and train station in the north.

Following reunification in 1975, the government immediately set about re-establishing the Hanoi–Ho Chi Minh City rail link as a symbol of Vietnamese unity. By the time the Reunification Express trains were inaugurated on 31 December 1976, 1334 bridges, 27 tunnels, 158 stations and 1370 shunts (switches) had been repaired.

Today the Reunification Express chugs along only slightly faster than the trains did in the 1930s, at an average speed of 50km/h. Chronic underinvestment means that it's still mainly a single-track line, and carries less than 1% of all north–south freight.

Plans for a massive overhaul of the rail system to create a high-speed network have been shelved, but a gradual upgrade of the network is planned. The aim is to reduce travel time between Hanoi and HCMC from around 30 hours to 24 hours by 2017.

Freight

Bicycles and motorbikes must travel in freight carriages, which will cost around 350,000d for a typical overnight trip. Sometimes it's not possible to travel on the same train as your bike so remember to make a note of the train it's on and when it is expected to arrive.

Reservations

You cannot buy tickets in advance from Vietnam Railways, but agencies can make bookings for you. Reservations for all trips should be made at least one day in advance. For sleeping berths, it's wise to book several days before the date of departure.

Schedules, fares, information and advance bookings are available at **Vietnam Railway** (https://vietnam-railway.com/) and **Vietnam Impressive** (www.vietnamimpressive.com), two dependable private booking agents. They'll deliver tickets to your hotel in Vietnam, free of charge (or can send them abroad using DHL for a fee).

Many travel agencies, hotels and cafes will also buy you train tickets for a small commission.

Routes

Aside from the main HCMC–Hanoi run, three rail-spur lines link Hanoi with the other parts of northern Vietnam. One runs east to the port city of Haiphong. A second heads northeast to Lang Son and continues across the border to Nanning, China. A third runs northwest to Lao Cai and on to Kunming, China.

The train journey between Hanoi and HCMC takes from 30 to 41 hours, depending on the train.

Safety

Petty crime can be a problem on Vietnamese trains. Thieves occasionally try to grab stuff as trains pull out of stations. Always keep your bag nearby and lock or tie it to something, especially at night.

Schedules

Several Reunification Express trains depart from Hanoi and HCMC every day. Train schedules change frequently, so check departure times on the Vietnam Railway website (if working), Vietnam Impressive's website or www.seat61.com, the international train website.

A bare-bones train schedule operates during the Tet festival, when most trains are suspended for nine days, beginning four days before Tet and continuing for four days afterwards.

Health

Health issues (and the quality of medical facilities) vary enormously depending on where you are in Vietnam. The major cities are generally not high risk and have good facilities, though rural areas are another matter.

Travellers tend to worry about contracting infectious diseases in Vietnam, but serious illnesses are rare. Accidental injury (especially traffic accidents) account for most life-threatening problems. That said, a bout of sickness is a relatively common thing. The following advice is a general guide only.

BEFORE YOU GO

→ Pack any medications that you'll need to take in clearly labelled containers.

→ Bring a letter from your doctor describing your medical conditions and medications.

→ If carrying syringes or needles, have a physician's letter documenting their medical necessity.

→ If you have a heart condition, bring a copy of a recent electrocardiogram (ECG).

→ Bring extra supplies of any regular medication that you take (in case of loss or theft).

Insurance

Even if you are fit and healthy, don't travel without health insurance – accidents do happen. If your health insurance doesn't cover you for medical expenses abroad, get extra insurance – check our website (www.lonelyplanet.com) for more information. Emergency evacuation is expensive – bills of US$100,000 are not unknown – so make sure your policy covers this.

Recommended Vaccinations

The only vaccination required by international regulations is yellow fever. Proof of vaccination will only be required if you have visited a country in the yellow-fever zone within six days of entering Vietnam.

Most vaccines don't produce immunity until at least two weeks after they're given, so visit a doctor four to eight weeks before departure.

Medical Checklist

Recommended, but not exhaustive, items for a personal medical kit:

→ antibacterial cream, eg mupirocin

→ antihistamines for allergies, eg cetirizine for daytime and promethazine for night

→ antiseptic for cuts and scrapes, eg iodine solution such as Betadine

→ DEET-based insect repellent

→ diarrhoea 'stopper', eg loperamide

→ first-aid items, such as scissors, plasters (such as Band-Aids), bandages, gauze, safety pins and tweezers

→ paracetamol for pain

→ steroid cream for allergic/itchy rashes, eg 1% hydrocortisone

→ sunscreen

→ antifungal treatments for thrush and tinea, eg clotrimazole or fluconazole

Websites

There's a wealth of travel-health advice on the internet.

World Health Organization (WHO; www.who.int/ith) Publishes a superb book called *International Travel & Health*, which is revised annually and is available free online.

MD Travel Health (www.mdtravelhealth.com) Provides complete travel-health recommendations.

Centers for Disease Control and Prevention (CDC; www.cdc.gov) Good general information.

IN VIETNAM

Availability & Cost of Health Care

The significant improvement in Vietnam's economy has brought with it some major advances in public health. However, in remote parts, local clinics will only have basic supplies – if you become seriously ill in rural Vietnam, get to Ho Chi Minh City (HCMC), Danang or Hanoi as quickly as you can. For surgery or other extensive treatment, don't hesitate to fly to Bangkok, Singapore or Hong Kong.

Private Clinics

These should be your first port of call. They are familiar with local resources and can organise evacuations if necessary. The best medical facilities – in Hanoi, HCMC and Danang – have health-facility standards that come close to those in developed countries.

State Hospitals

Most are overcrowded and basic. In order to treat foreigners, a facility needs to obtain a special licence and so far only a few have been provided.

Self-Treatment

If your problem is minor (eg travellers' diarrhoea), this is an option. If you think you may have a serious disease, especially malaria, do not waste time – travel to the nearest quality facility to receive attention.

Buying medication over the counter is not recommended, as fake medications and poorly stored or out-of-date drugs are common. Check expiry dates on all medicines.

Infectious Diseases

Bird Flu

The bird flu virus rears its head from time to time in Vietnam. It occurs in clusters, usually among poultry workers. It's rarely fatal for humans, though a child did die in August 2013. When outbreaks do occur, eggs and poultry are banished from the menu in many hotels and restaurants.

Dengue

This mosquito-borne disease is becoming increasingly problematic in Southeast Asia. Several hundred thousand people are hospitalised with dengue haemorrhagic fever in Vietnam every year, but the fatality rate is less than 0.3%. As there is no vaccine available, it can only be prevented by avoiding mosquito

---

REQUIRED & RECOMMENDED VACCINATIONS

The World Health Organization (WHO) recommends the following vaccinations for travellers to Southeast Asia:

Adult diphtheria and tetanus Single booster recommended if you've had none in the previous 10 years.

Hepatitis A Provides almost 100% protection for up to a year; a booster after 12 months provides at least another 20 years' protection.

Hepatitis B Now considered routine for most travellers. Given as three shots over six months. A rapid schedule is also available, as is a combined vaccination with Hepatitis A. Lifetime protection occurs in 95% of people.

Measles, mumps and rubella Two doses of MMR are required unless you have had the diseases. Many young adults require a booster.

Typhoid Recommended unless your trip is less than a week and only to developed cities. The vaccine offers around 70% protection and lasts for two or three years.

Varicella If you haven't had chickenpox, discuss this vaccination with your doctor.

Long-Term Travellers

These vaccinations are recommended for people travelling for more than one month, or those at special risk:

Japanese B encephalitis Three injections in all. A booster is recommended after two years. A sore arm and headache are the most common side effects reported.

Meningitis Single injection.

Rabies Three injections in all. A booster after one year will provide 10 years of protection.

Tuberculosis Adults should have a TB skin test before and after travel, rather than the vaccination.

bites. The mosquito that carries dengue bites throughout the day and night, so use insect-avoidance measures at all times. Symptoms include a high fever, a severe headache and body aches (dengue was once known as 'breakbone fever'). Some people develop a rash and experience diarrhoea. There is no specific treatment, just rest and paracetamol – do not take aspirin as it increases the likelihood of haemorrhaging. See a doctor to be diagnosed and monitored.

Hepatitis A

A problem throughout the region, this food- and waterborne virus infects the liver, causing jaundice (yellow skin and eyes), nausea and lethargy. There is no specific treatment for hepatitis A – you just need to allow time for the liver to heal. All travellers to Vietnam should be vaccinated against hepatitis A.

Hepatitis B

The only serious sexually transmitted disease that can be prevented by vaccination, hepatitis B is spread by body fluids, including sexual contact. In some parts of Southeast Asia up to 20% of the population are carriers of hepatitis B, and usually are unaware of this. The long-term consequences can include liver cancer and cirrhosis.

HIV

The official figures on the number of people with HIV/AIDS in Vietnam are vague, but they are on the rise. Health-education messages relating to HIV/

AIDS are visible all over the countryside, but the official line is that infection is largely limited to sex workers and drug users. Condoms are widely available throughout Vietnam.

Japanese B Encephalitis

This viral disease is transmitted by mosquitoes. It's very rarely caught by travellers but vaccination is recommended for those spending extended time in rural areas. There is no treatment; a third of infected people will die while another third will suffer permanent brain damage.

Malaria

For such a serious and potentially deadly disease, there is an enormous amount of misinformation concerning malaria. You must get expert advice as to whether your trip actually puts you at risk. Many parts of Vietnam, particularly city and resort areas, have minimal to no risk of malaria. For most rural areas, however, the risk of contracting the disease far outweighs the risk of any tablet side effects. Travellers to isolated areas in high-risk regions such as Ca Mau and Bac Lieu provinces, and the rural south, may like to carry a treatment dose of medication for use if symptoms occur. Remember that malaria can be fatal. Before you travel, seek medical advice on the right medication and dosage for you.

Malaria is caused by a parasite transmitted by the

bite of an infected mosquito. The most important symptom of malaria is fever, but general symptoms such as headache, diarrhoea, cough or chills may also occur. Diagnosis can only be made by taking a blood sample.

Two strategies should be combined to prevent malaria – mosquito avoidance and antimalarial medications.

MALARIA PREVENTION

➡ Choose accommodation with screens and fans (if not air-conditioned).

➡ Impregnate clothing with permethrin in high-risk areas.

➡ Sleep under a mosquito net.

➡ Spray your room with insect repellent before going out for your evening meal.

➡ Use a DEET-containing insect repellent on all exposed skin, particularly the ankle area. Natural repellents such as citronella can be effective but must be applied frequently.

➡ Use mosquito coils.

➡ Wear long sleeves and trousers in light colours.

MALARIA MEDICATION

There are various medications available.

Chloroquine and Paludrine The effectiveness of this combination is now limited in Vietnam. Generally not recommended.

Doxycycline A broad-spectrum antibiotic that has the added benefit of helping to prevent a variety of tropical diseases, including leptospirosis, tick-borne disease, typhus and melioidosis. Potential side effects include a tendency to sunburn, thrush in women, indigestion and interference with the contraceptive pill. It must be taken for four weeks after leaving the risk area.

Lariam (mefloquine) Receives a lot of bad press, some of it justified, some not. This weekly

TAP WATER

Be very careful of what you drink. Tap water is heavily chlorinated in urban areas, but you should still avoid it. Stick to bottled water, which is available everywhere. Ice is generally safe in the cities and resorts, and is often added to drinks and coffee.

tablet suits many people. Serious side effects are rare but include depression, anxiety, psychosis and seizures. It's around 90% effective in Vietnam.

Malarone Side effects are uncommon and mild, most commonly nausea and headaches. It is the best tablet for scuba divers and for those on short trips to high-risk areas. A final option is to take no preventive medication but to have a supply of emergency medication (Malarone is usually recommended: four tablets once daily for three days) should you develop the symptoms of malaria. This is less than ideal, and you'll still need to get to a good medical facility within 24 hours of developing a fever.

Measles

Measles remains a problem in Vietnam, including the Hanoi area. Many people born before 1966 are immune as they had the disease in childhood. Measles starts with a high fever and rash but can be complicated by pneumonia and brain disease. There is no specific treatment.

Rabies

This uniformly fatal disease is spread by the bite or lick of an infected animal – most commonly a dog or monkey. Seek medical advice immediately after any animal bite and start post-exposure treatment. Having a pre-travel vaccination means the post-bite treatment is greatly simplified. If an animal bites you, gently wash the wound with soap and water, and apply an iodine-based antiseptic. If you are not vaccinated, you will need to receive rabies immunoglobulin as soon as possible.

Schistosomiasis

Schistosomiasis (also called bilharzia) is a tiny parasite that enters your skin after you've been swimming in contaminated water. If you

are concerned, you can be tested three months after exposure. Symptoms are coughing and fever. Schistosomiasis is easily treated with medications.

Sexually Transmitted Diseases

Condoms, widely available throughout Vietnam, are effective in preventing the spread of most sexually transmitted diseases (STDs). However, they may not guard against genital warts or herpes. If after a sexual encounter you develop any rash, lumps, discharge or pain when passing urine, seek immediate medical attention.

Tuberculosis

Tuberculosis (TB) is very rare in short-term travellers. Medical and aid workers, and long-term travellers who have significant contact with the local population should take precautions. Vaccination is usually only given to children under the age of five, but it is recommended that at-risk adults have pre- and post-travel TB testing. The main symptoms are fever, cough, weight loss, night sweats and tiredness.

Typhoid

This serious bacterial infection is spread via food and water. It gives a high, slowly progressive fever and headache. Vaccination is recommended for all travellers spending more than a week in Vietnam, or travelling outside of the major cities. Be aware that vaccination is not 100% effective so you must still be careful with what you eat and drink.

Typhus

Murine typhus is spread by the fleas of rodents whereas scrub typhus is spread via a mite. These diseases are rare in travellers. Symptoms include fever, muscle pains and

a rash. You can avoid these diseases by following general insect-avoidance measures. Doxycycline will also help prevent them.

Travellers' Diarrhoea

Travellers' diarrhoea is by far the most common problem affecting travellers. Between 30% and 50% of people will suffer from it within two weeks of starting their trip. In over 80% of cases, travellers' diarrhoea is caused by a bacteria, and therefore responds promptly to treatment with antibiotics. It can also be provoked by a change of diet, and your stomach may settle down again after a few days.

Treatment consists of staying hydrated, or you could take rehydration solutions.

Loperamide is just a 'stopper' and doesn't get to the cause of the problem. It is helpful if you have to go on a long bus ride, but don't take loperamide if you have a fever or blood in your stools.

Amoebic Dysentery

Amoebic dysentery is very rare in travellers. Symptoms are similar to bacterial diarrhoea (eg fever, bloody diarrhoea and generally feeling unwell). Treatment involves two drugs: tinidazole or metronidazole to kill the parasite and a second drug to kill the cysts.

Giardiasis

Giardia lamblia is a parasite that is relatively common in travellers. Symptoms include nausea, bloating, excess gas, fatigue and intermittent diarrhoea. 'Eggy' burps are often attributed solely to giardiasis, but they are not specific to this infection. The treatment of choice is tinidazole.

Environmental Hazards

Air Pollution

Air pollution, particularly vehicle pollution, is severe in Vietnam's major cities. If you have severe respiratory problems consult your doctor before travelling.

Food

Eating in restaurants is the biggest risk factor for contracting travellers' diarrhoea. Ways to avoid it include eating only freshly cooked food, and avoiding shellfish and buffets. Peel all fruit and try to stick to cooked vegetables. Eat in busy restaurants with a high turnover of customers.

Heat

Many parts of Vietnam are hot and humid throughout the year. Take it easy when you first arrive. Avoid dehydration and excessive activity in the heat. Drink rehydration solution if required.

Heat exhaustion Symptoms include feeling weak, headache, irritability, nausea or vomiting, sweaty skin and a fast, weak pulse. Cool down in a room with air-conditioning and rehydrate with water containing a quarter of a teaspoon of salt per litre.

Heatstroke This is a serious medical emergency. Symptoms come on suddenly and include weakness, nausea, a temperature of over 41°C, dizziness, confusion and eventually collapse and loss of consciousness. Seek medical help and start reducing body temperature by applying cooling treatment.

Prickly heat A common skin rash in the tropics. Stay in an air-conditioned area for a few hours and take cool showers.

Bites & Stings

Bedbugs These don't carry disease but their bites are very itchy. Move hotel, and treat the itch with an antihistamine.

Jellyfish In Vietnamese waters most are not dangerous, just irritating. Pour vinegar (or urine) onto the affected area. Take painkillers, and seek medical advice if you feel ill in any way. Take local advice if there are dangerous jellyfish around and keep out of the water.

Leeches Found in humid forest areas. They do not transmit any disease but their bites can be intensely itchy. Apply an iodine-based antiseptic to any leech bite to help prevent infection.

Snakes Both poisonous and harmless snakes are common in Vietnam, though very few travellers are ever bothered by them. Wear boots and avoid poking around dead logs and wood when hiking. First aid in the event of a snakebite involves pressure immobilisation via an elastic bandage firmly wrapped around the affected limb, starting at the bite site and working up towards the chest. The bandage should not be so tight that the circulation is cut off, and the fingers or toes should be kept free so the circulation can be checked. Immobilise the limb with a splint and carry the victim to medical attention. Do not use tourniquets or try to suck the venom out. Antivenom is available only in major cities.

Ticks Contracted during walks in rural areas. If you have had a tick bite and experience symptoms such as a rash (at the site of the bite or elsewhere), fever or muscle aches you should see a doctor. Doxycycline prevents tick-borne diseases.

Skin Problems

Fungal rashes Common in humid climates. Moist areas that get less air, such as the groin, armpits and between the toes,

are often affected. Treatment involves using an antifungal cream such as clotrimazole. Consult a doctor.

Cuts and scratches Minor cuts and scratches can become infected easily in humid climates and may fail to heal because of the humidity. Take meticulous care of any wounds: immediately wash in clean water and apply antiseptic.

Sunburn

➡ Even on a cloudy day sunburn can occur rapidly.

➡ Always use a strong sunscreen (at least factor 30).

➡ Reapply sunscreen after swimming.

➡ Wear a hat.

➡ Avoid the sun between 10am and 2pm.

Women's Health

Supplies of sanitary products are readily available in urban areas. Birth-control options may be limited, so bring adequate stocks.

Pregnant women should receive specialised advice before travelling. The ideal time to travel is in the second trimester (between 16 and 28 weeks), during which the risk of pregnancy-related problems is at its lowest. Some advice:

Rural areas Avoid remote areas with poor transportation and medical facilities.

Travel insurance Ensure you're covered for pregnancy-related possibilities, including premature labour.

Malaria None of the more effective antimalarial drugs are completely safe in pregnancy.

Travellers' diarrhoea Many diarrhoea treatments are not recommended during pregnancy. Azithromycin is considered safe.

Language

Vietnamese, or *tiếng Việt* dee·úhng vee·uht, is the official language of Vietnam and spoken by about 85 million people worldwide, both in Vietnam and among migrant communities around the world. It belongs to the Mon-Khmer language family and has Muong (a hill-tribe language) as its closest relative.

Vietnamese pronunciation is not as hard as it may seem at first as most Vietnamese sounds also exist in English. With a bit of practice and reading our coloured pronunciation guides as if they were English, you shouldn't have much trouble being understood. Note that the vowel a is pronounced as in 'at', aa as in 'father', aw as in 'law', er as in 'her', oh as in 'doh!', ow as in 'cow', u as in 'book', uh as in 'but' and uhr as in 'fur' (without the 'r'). Vowel sounds can also be combined in various ways within a word – we've used dots (eg dee·úhng) to separate the different vowel sounds to keep pronunciation straightforward. As for the consonants, note that the ng sound, which is also found in English (eg in 'sing') can also appear at the start of a word in Vietnamese. Also note that d is pronounced as in 'stop', đ as in 'dog' and ğ as in 'skill'.

You'll notice that some vowels are pronounced with a high or low pitch while others swoop or glide in an almost musical manner. This is because Vietnamese uses a system of tones. There are six tones in Vietnamese, indicated in the written language (and in our pronunciation guides) by accent marks above or below the vowel: mid (ma), low falling (mà), low rising (mả), high broken (mã), high rising (má) and low broken (mạ). Note that the mid tone is flat. In the south, the low ris-

ing and the high broken tones are both pronounced as the low rising tone. Vietnamese words are considered to have one syllable, so word stress is not an issue.

The variation in vocabulary between the Vietnamese of the north and that of the south is indicated in this chapter by (N) and (S).

BASICS

Hello.	*Xin chào.*	sin jòw
Goodbye.	*Tạm biệt.*	daạm bee·uht
Yes.	*Vâng.* (N)	vuhng
	Dạ. (S)	yạ
No.	*Không.*	kawm
Please.	*Làm ơn.*	laàm ern
Thank you	*Cảm ơn.*	ğaảm ern
You're welcome.	*Không có chi.*	kawm ğó jee
Excuse me./ Sorry.	*Xin lỗi.*	sin lỗy

How are you?
Có khỏe không?   ğáw kwả kawm

Fine, thank you. And you?
Khỏe, cảm ơn.   kwá ğaảm ern
Còn bạn thì sao?   kwá ğòn bạan teè sow

What's your name?
Tên là gì?   den laà zeè

My name is ...
Tên tôi là ...   den doy laà ...

Do you speak English?
Bạn có nói được   bạan ğó nóy duhr·erk
tiếng Anh không?   díng aang kawm

I (don't) understand.
Tôi (không) hiểu.   doy (kawm) heẻ·oo

WANT MORE?

For in-depth language information and handy phrases, check out Lonely Planet's *Vietnamese Phrasebook* and *Hill Tribes Phrasebook*. You'll find them at **shop. lonelyplanet.com**, or you can buy Lonely Planet's iPhone phrasebooks at the Apple App Store.

ACCOMMODATION

Where is a ...?	*Đâu có ... ?*	doh ğó ...
hotel	*khách sạn*	kaák saạn
guesthouse	*nhà khách*	nyaà kaák

I'd like (a) ...	Tôi	doy
	muốn ...	moo·úhn ...
single room	phòng đơn	fòm dern
double room (big bed)	phòng giường đôi	fòm zuhr·èrng doy

How much is it per night/person?
Giá bao nhiêu một đêm/người? zaá bow nyee·oo mawt dem/nguhr·eè

air-con	máy lạnh	máy laạng
bathroom	phòng tắm	fòm dúhm
fan	quạt máy	gwaat máy
hot water	nước nóng	nuhr·érk nóm
mosquito net	màng	maàng
sheet	ra trải giường	zaa chaỉ zuhr·èrng
toilet	nhà vệ sinh	nyaà vẹ sing
toilet paper	giấy vệ sinh	záy vẹ sing
towel	khăn tắm	kúhn dúhm

DIRECTIONS

Where is ...?
... ở đâu ? ... ẻr đoh

What is the address?
Địa chỉ là gì? đee·ụh cheẻ laà zeè

Could you write it down, please?
Xin viết ra giùm tôi. sin vee·úht zaa zùm doy

Can you show me (on the map)?
Xin chỉ giùm (trên bản đồ này). sin jeẻ zùm (chen baản dàw này)

Go straight ahead.
Thẳng tới trước. tủhng der·eé chuhr·érk

at the corner	ở góc đường	ẻr góp đuhr·èrng
at the traffic lights	tại đèn giao thông	dại đèn zow tawm
behind	đằng sau	đùhng sow
in front of	đằng trước	đùhng chuhr·érk
near (to)	gần	gùhn
opposite	đối diện	đóy zee·ụhn
Turn left.	Sang trái.	saang chaí
Turn right.	Sang phải.	saang faỉ

EATING & DRINKING

I'd like a table for ...	Tôi muốn đặt bàn cho ...	doy moo·úhn dụht baàn jo ...
(two) people	(hai) người	(hai) nguhr·eè
(eight) o'clock	vào lúc (tám) giờ	vòw lúp (dúhm) zèr

KEY PATTERNS

To get by in Vietnamese, mix and match these simple patterns with words of your choice:

When's (the next bus)?
Khi nào là (chuyến xe buýt tới)? kee nòw laà (jwee·úhn sa bwéet der·eé)

Where's (the station)?
(Nhà ga) ở đâu? (nyaà gaa) ẻr đoh

Where can I (buy a ticket)?
Tôi có thể (mua vé) ở đâu? doy gỏ tẻ (moo·uh vá) ẻr đoh

I'm looking for (a hotel).
Tôi tìm (khách sạn). doy dìm (kaát saạn)

Do you have (a map)?
Bạn có (bản đồ) không? baạn gỏ (baản dàw) kawm

Is there (a toilet)?
Có (vệ sinh) không? gỏ (vẹ sing) kawm

I'd like (the menu).
Xin cho tôi (thực đơn). sin jo doy (tụhrk đern)

I'd like to (hire a car).
Tôi muốn (xe hơi). doy moo·úhn (sa her·ee)

Could you please (help me)?
Làm ơn (giúp đỡ)? laàm ern (zúp đẻr)

I have (a visa).
Tôi có (visa). doy gỏ (vee·saa)

Do you have a menu in English?
Bạn có thực đơn bằng tiếng Anh không? baạn káw tụhrk đern bùhng díng aang kawm

What's the speciality here?
Ở đây có món gì đặc biệt? ẻr day kó món zeè dụhk bee·ụht

I'd like ...
Xin cho tôi ... sin jo doy ...

Not too spicy, please.
Xin đừng cho cay quá. sin dùrng jo gay gwaá

I'm a vegetarian.
Tôi ăn chay. doy uhn jay

I'm allergic to (peanuts).
Tôi bị dị ứng với (hạt lạc). doy beẹ zẹ úhrng ver·eé (haạt laạk)

Can you please bring me ...?
Xin mang cho tôi...? sin maang jo doy ...

Can I have a (beer), please?
Xin cho tôi (chai bia)? sin jo doy (jai bee·uh)

Cheers!
Chúc sức khoẻ! júp súhrk kwả

Thank you, that was delicious.
Cảm ơn, ngon lắm. ğaám ern ngon lúhm

The bill, please.
Xin tính tiền. sin díng dee·ùhn

Key Words

bottle	*chai*	jai
bowl	*bát/ chén* (N/S)	baát/ jén
breakfast	*ăn sáng*	uhn saáng
chopsticks	*đôi đũa*	doy·ee đoõ·uh
cold	*lạnh*	laạng
dessert	*món tráng*	món chaáng
dinner	*ăn tối*	uhn dóy
fork	*cái đĩa/ nĩa* (N/S)	ğaí deẽ·uh/ neẽ·uh
glass	*cốc/ly* (N/S)	káwp/lee
hot (warm)	*nóng*	nóm
knife	*con dao*	ğon zow
lunch	*ăn trưa*	uhn chuhr·uh
plate	*đĩa*	đeẽ·uh
restaurant	*nhà hàng*	nyaà haàng
snack	*ăn nhẹ*	uhn nyạ
spicy	*cay*	ğay
spoon	*cái thìa*	ğaí tee·ùh
with	*với*	ver·eé
without	*không có*	kawm ğó

Meat & Fish

beef	*thịt bò*	tịt bò
chicken	*thịt gà*	tịt gaà
crab	*cua*	ğoo·uh
eel	*lươn*	luhr·ern
fish	*cá*	kaá
frog	*ếch*	ék
goat	*thịt dê*	tịt ze
pork	*thịt lợn/ heo* (N/S)	tịt lẹrn/ hay·o
prawns/shrimp	*tôm*	dawm
snail	*ốc*	áwp
squid	*mực*	mụhrk

Fruit & Vegetables

apple	*táo/bơm* (N/S)	dów/berm
banana	*chuối*	joo·eé
cabbage	*bắp cải*	búhp ğaỉ
carrot	*cà rốt*	ğaà záwt
coconut	*dừa*	zuhr·ùh
corn	*ngô/bắp* (N/S)	ngow/búp
cucumber	*dưa leo*	zuhr·uh lay·o
eggplant	*cà tím*	ğaà dím
grapes	*nho*	nyo

green beans	*đậu xanh*	đọh saang
green pepper	*ớt xanh*	ért saang
lemon	*chanh*	chaang
lettuce	*rau diếp*	zoh zee·úhp
lychee	*vải*	vai
mandarin	*quýt*	gweét
mango	*xoài*	swaì
mushrooms	*nấm*	núhm
orange	*cam*	ğaam
papaya	*đu đủ*	doo đỏo
peas	*đậu bi*	đọh bee
pineapple	*dứa*	zuhr·úh
potato	*khoai tây*	kwai day
pumpkin	*bí ngô*	beé ngaw
strawberry	*dâu*	zoh
sweet potato	*khoai lang*	kwai laang
tomato	*cà chua*	ğaà joo·uh
watermelon	*dưa hấu*	zuhr·uh hóh

Other

chilli sauce	*tương ớt*	duhr·erng ért
eggs	*trứng*	chúhrng
fish sauce	*nước mắm*	nuhr·érk múhm
flat rice noodles	*phở*	fẻr
fried rice	*cơm rang thập cẩm* (N) *cơm chiên* (S)	ğerm zaang tụhp ğủhm ğerm jee·uhn
rice	*cơm*	ğerm
salad	*sa lát*	saa laát
soup	*canh*	ğaang
steamed rice	*cơm trắng*	ğerm chaáng
ice	*đá*	đaá
pepper	*hạt tiêu*	haạt dee·oo
salt	*muối*	moo·eé
sugar	*đường*	dur·èrng
thin rice noodles	*bún*	bún
yellow egg noodles	*mì*	meè

Drinks

beer	*bia*	bi·a
coffee	*cà phê*	ğaà fe
iced lemon juice	*chanh đá*	jaang đaá
milk	*sữa*	sũhr·uh
mineral water	*nước khoáng* (N) *nước suối* (S)	nuhr·érk kwaáng nuhr·érk soo·eé

Numbers

1	*một*	mạwt
2	*hai*	hai
3	*ba*	baa
4	*bốn*	báwn
5	*năm*	nuhm
6	*sáu*	sóh
7	*bảy*	bảy
8	*tám*	dúhm
9	*chín*	jín
10	*mười*	muhr·eè
20	*hai mươi*	hai muhr·ee
30	*ba mươi*	ba muhr·ee
40	*bốn mươi*	báwn muhr·ee
50	*năm mươi*	nuhm muhr·ee
60	*sáu mươi*	sów muhr·ee
70	*bảy mươi*	bảy muhr·ee
80	*tám mươi*	daám muhr·ee
90	*chín mươi*	jín muhr·ee
100	*một trăm*	mạwt chuhm
1000	*một nghìn* (N)	mạwt ngyìn
	một ngàn (S)	mọt ngaàn

orange juice	*cam vắt*	ğaam vúht
red wine	*rượu vang đỏ*	zee·oọ vaang đỏ
soy milk	*sữa đậu nành*	sũhr·uh dọh naàng
tea	*chè/trà* (N/S)	jà/chaà
white wine	*rượu vang trắng*	zee·oọ vaang chaáng

EMERGENCIES

Help!
Cứu tôi! ğuhr·oó doy

There's been an accident!
Có tai nạn! ğó dai nạạn

Leave me alone!
Thôi! toy

I'm lost.
Tôi bị lạc đường. doi bẹẹ lạạk đuhr·èrng

Where is the toilet?
Nhà vệ sinh ở đâu? nyaà vẹ sing ér doh

Please call the police.
Làm ơn gọi công an. laàm ern gọy ğawm aan

Please call a doctor.
Làm ơn gọi bác sĩ. laàm ern gọy baák seẽ

I'm sick.
Tôi bị đau. doy bẹẹ đọh

It hurts here.
Chỗ bị đau ở đây. jãw bẹẹ đoh ér đay

I'm allergic to (antibiotics).
Tôi bị dị ứng với (thuốc kháng sinh). doy bẹẹ zẹẹ úhrng vér·eé (too·úhk kaáng sing)

SHOPPING & SERVICES

I'd like to buy ...
Tôi muốn mua ... doy moo·úhn moo·uh ...

Can I look at it?
Tôi có thể xem được không? doy ğó tẻ sam đuhr·ẹrk kawm

I'm just looking.
Tôi chỉ ngắm xem. doy jeẻ ngúhm sam

I don't like it.
Tôi không thích nó. doy kawm tík nó

How much is this?
Cái này giá bao nhiêu? ğaí này zaá bow nyee·oọ

It's too expensive.
Cái này quá mắc. ğaí này gwaá múhk

Do you accept credit cards?
Bạn có nhận thẻ tín dụng không? bạạn kó nyụhn tả dín zụm kawm

There's a mistake in the bill.
Có sự nhầm lẫn trên hoá đơn. ğó sụhr nyùhm lũhn chen hwaá đern

I'm looking for a/the ...	*Tôi tìm ...*	doy dìm ...
bank	*ngân hàng*	nguhn haàng
market	*chợ*	jẹr
tourist office	*văn phòng hướng dẫn du lịch*	vuhn fòm huhr·érng zũhn zoo lịk

TIME & DATES

What time is it?
Mấy giờ rồi? máy zèr zòy

It's (eight) o'clock.
Bây giờ là (tám) giờ. bay zèr laà (dúhm) zèr

morning	*buổi sáng*	boó·ee saáng
afternoon	*buổi chiều*	boó·ee jee·oò
evening	*buổi tối*	boó·ee dóy
yesterday	*hôm qua*	hawm ğwaa
today	*hôm nay*	hawm nay
tomorrow	*ngày mai*	ngày mai

Monday	*thứ hai*	túhr hai
Tuesday	*thứ ba*	túhr baa
Wednesday	*thứ tư*	túhr đuhr
Thursday	*thứ năm*	túhr nuhm
Friday	*thứ sáu*	túhr sóh

Saturday	thứ bảy	túhr bảy
Sunday	chủ nhật	jóo nhụht
January	tháng giêng	taáng zee·uhng
February	tháng hai	taáng hai
March	tháng ba	taáng baa
April	tháng tư	taáng tuhr
May	tháng năm	taáng nuhm
June	tháng sáu	taáng sóh
July	tháng bảy	taáng bảy
August	tháng tám	taáng dúhm
September	tháng chín	taáng jín
October	tháng mười	taáng muhr·eè
November	tháng mười một	taáng muhr·eè mạwt
December	tháng mười hai	taáng muhr·eè hai

TRANSPORT

Public Transport

When does the (first)... leave/arrive?	Chuyến ... (sớm nhất) chạy lúc mấy giờ?	jwee·úhn ... (sérm nyúht) jạy lúp máy zèr
boat	tàu/ thuyền	dòw/ twee·ùhn
bus	xe buýt	sa beét
plane	máy bay	máy bay
train	xe lửa	sa lúhr·uh

I'd like a ... ticket.	Tôi muốn vé ...	doy moo·úhn vá ...
1st class	hạng nhất	haạng nyúht
2nd class	hạng nhì	haạng nyeè
one way	đi một chiều	đee mạt jee·oò
return	khứ hồi	kúhr haw·eè

I want to go to ...
Tôi muốn đi ...   doy moo·úhn đee ...

How long does the trip take?
Chuyến đi sẽ   jwee·úhn đee sã
mất bao lâu?   múht bow loh

What time does it arrive?
Mấy giờ đến?   máy zèr dén

bus station	bến xe	bén sa
railway station	ga xe lửa	gaa sa lúhr·uh
the first	đầu tiên	dòw dee·uhn

the last	cuối cùng	ğoo·eé ğùm
the next	kế tiếp	ğé dee·úhp
ticket office	phòng bán vé	fòm baán vá
timetable	thời biểu	ter·eè beẻ·oo

Driving & Cycling

I'd like to hire a ...	Tôi muốn thuê ... (N)	doy moo·úhn twe ...
	Tôi muốn muốn ... (S)	doy moo·úhn muhr·érn ...
car	xe hơi	sa her·ee
bicycle	xe đạp	sa đạp
motorbike	xe moto	sa mo·to

Is this the road to ...?
Con đường nầy   ğon đuhr·èrng này
có dẫn đến ...?   ğó zũhn đén ...

How many kilometres to ...?
... cách đây bao   ... ğaák đay bow
nhiêu ki-lô-mét?   nyee·oo kee·law·mét

Where's a service station?
Trạm xăng ở đâu?   chaạm suhng ér doh

Please fill it up.
Làm ơn đổ đầy bình.   laàm ern đỏ đày bìng

I'd like ... litres.
Tôi muốn ... lít.   doy moo·úhn ... léet

diesel	dầu diesel	zòh dee·sel
highway	xa lộ	saa law
leaded petrol	dầu xăng có chì	zòh suhng ğó jeè
map	bản đồ	baán đàw
unleaded petrol	dầu xăng	zòh suhng

(How long) Can I park here?
Chúng tôi có thể đậu   júm doy ğó tẻ dọh
xe được (bao lâu)?   sa đuhr·ẹrk (bow loh)

I need a mechanic.
Chúng tôi cần thợ   júm doy ğùhn tẹr
sửa xe.   súhr·uh sa

The car/motorbike has broken down (at ...)
Xe bị hư (tại ...).   sa bẹẹ huhr (dại ...)

The car/motorbike won't start.
(Xe hơi/Xe moto)   (sa her·ee/sa mo·to)
không đề được.   kawm đề đuhr·ẹrk

I have a flat tyre.
Bánh xe tôi bị xì.   baáng sa doy bẹẹ seè

I've run out of petrol.
Tôi bị hết dầu/xăng.   doy bẹẹ hét zòh/suhng

I've had an accident.
Tôi bị tai nạn.   doy bẹẹ dai naạn

GLOSSARY

A Di Da – Buddha of the Past

Agent Orange – toxic, carcinogenic chemical herbicide used extensively during the American War

am duong – Vietnamese equivalent of Yin and Yang

American War – Vietnamese name for what is also known as the Vietnam War

Annam – old Chinese name for Vietnam, meaning 'Pacified South'

ao dai – Vietnamese national dress worn by women

apsaras – heavenly maidens

ARVN – Army of the Republic of Vietnam (former South Vietnamese army)

ba mu – midwife. There are 12 'midwives', each of whom teaches newborns a different skill necessary for the first year of life: smiling, sucking, lying on their stomachs, and so forth

ban – mountainous village

bang – congregation (in the Chinese community)

bar om – literally 'holding' bars associated with the sex industry. Also known as 'karaoke om'.

buu dien – post office

cai luong – Vietnamese modern theatre

Cao Daism – indigenous Vietnamese religion

Cham – ethnic minority descended from the people of Champa

Champa – Hindu kingdom dating from the late 2nd century AD

Charlie – nickname for the Viet Cong, used by US soldiers

chua – pagoda

chu nho – standard Chinese characters (script)

Cochinchina – the southern part of Vietnam during the French-colonial era

com pho – rice and rice-noodle soup

crémaillère – cog railway

cyclo – pedicab or bicycle rickshaw

Dai The Chi Bo Tat – an assistant of *A Di Da*

dan bau – single-stringed zither that generates an astounding magnitude of tones

dan tranh – 16-stringed zither

den – temple

Di Lac Buddha – Buddha of the Future

dikpalaka – gods of the directions of the compass

dinh – communal meeting hall

DMZ – Demilitarised Zone, a strip of land that once separated North and South Vietnam

doi moi – economic restructuring or reform, which commenced in Vietnam in 1986

dong – natural caves. Also Vietnamese currency.

dong son – drums

ecocide – term used to describe the devastating effects of the herbicides sprayed over Vietnam during the American War

fléchette – experimental US weapon. An artillery shell containing thousands of darts.

Funan – see *Oc-Eo*

garuda – half human-half bird

gom – ceramics

hai dang – lighthouse

hat boi – classical theatre in the south

hat cheo – Vietnamese popular theatre

hat tuong – classical theatre in the north

ho ca – aquarium

Ho Chi Minh Trail – route used by the North Vietnamese Army and Viet Cong to move supplies to the south

Hoa – ethnic Chinese, one of the largest single minority groups in Vietnam

hoi quan – Chinese congregational assembly halls

huong – perfume

huyen – rural district

Indochina – Vietnam, Cambodia and Laos. The name derives from Indian and Chinese influences.

kala-makara – sea-monster god

kalan – a religious sanctuary

khach san – hotel

Khmer – ethnic Cambodians

Khong Tu – Confucius

kich noi – spoken drama

Kinh – Vietnamese language

Kuomintang – Chinese Nationalist Party, also known as KMT. The KMT controlled China between 1925 and 1949 until defeated by the communists.

li xi – lucky money distributed during the Vietnamese Lunar New Year

liberation – 1975 takeover of the South by the North. Most foreigners call this 'reunification'.

Lien Xo – literally, Soviet Union. Used to call attention to a foreigner

linga – stylised phallus which represents the Hindu god Shiva

manushi-buddha – Buddha who appeared in human form

moi – derogatory word meaning 'savages', mostly used by ethnic Vietnamese to describe hill-tribe people

Montagnards – term meaning highlanders or mountain people, sometimes used to refer to the ethnic minorities who inhabit remote areas of Vietnam

muong – large village unit made up of *quel* (small stilt-houses)

naga – Sanskrit term for a mythical serpent being with divine powers; often depicted forming a kind of shelter over the Buddha

nam phai – for men

napalm – jellied petrol (gasoline) dropped and lit from aircraft; used by US forces during devastating repercussions during the American War

nguoi thuong – the current government's preferred term for highland people

nha hang – restaurant

nha khach – hotel or guesthouse

nha nghi – guesthouse

nha rong – large stilt house, used by hill tribes as a kind of community centre

nha tro – dormitory

NLF – National Liberation Front, the official name for the VC

nom – Vietnamese script, used between the 10th and early 20th centuries

nu phai – for women

nui – mountain

nuoc mam – fish sauce, added to almost every main dish in Vietnam

NVA – North Vietnamese Army

Oc-Eo – Indianised Khmer kingdom (also called Funan) in southern Vietnam between the 1st and 6th centuries

Ong Bon – Guardian Spirit of Happiness and Virtue

OSS – US Office of Strategic Services. The predecessor of the CIA.

pagoda – traditionally an eight-sided Buddhist tower, but in Vietnam the word is commonly used to denote a temple

phong thuy – literally, 'wind and water'. Used to describe geomancy. Also known by its Chinese name, feng shui.

PRG – Provisional Revolutionary Government, the temporary Communist government set up by the VC in the South. It existed from 1969 to 1976.

quan – urban district

Quan Cong – Chinese God of War

Quan The Am Bo Tat – Goddess of Mercy

quoc am – modern Vietnamese literature

quoc ngu – Latin-based phonetic alphabet in which Vietnamese is written

rap – cinema

Revolutionary Youth League – first Marxist group in Vietnam and predecessor of the Communist Party

roi can – conventional puppetry

roi nuoc – water puppetry

ruou (pronounced xeo) – rice wine

RVN – Republic of Vietnam (the old South Vietnam)

salangane – swiftlet

sao – wooden flute

saola – antelope-like creature

shakti – feminine manifestation of Shiva

song – river

SRV – Socialist Republic of Vietnam (Vietnam's official name)

Strategic Hamlets Program – program (by South Vietnam and the USA) of forcibly moving peasants into fortified villages to deny the VC bases of support

sung – fig tree

Tam Giao – literally, 'triple religion'. Confucianism, Taoism and Buddhism fused over time with popular Chinese beliefs and ancient Vietnamese animism.

Tao – the Way. The essence of which all things are made.

Tay ba lo – backpacker

Tet – Vietnamese Lunar New Year

thai cuc quyen – Vietnamese for t'ai chi

Thich Ca Buddha – the historical Buddha Sakyamuni, whose real name was Siddhartha Gautama

thong nhat – reunification. Also a commonly used term for the Reunification Express train.

thuoc bac – Chinese medicine

toc hanh – express bus

Tonkin – the northern part of Vietnam during the French-colonial era. Also the name of a body of water in the north (Tonkin Gulf).

truyen khau – traditional oral literature

UNHCR – UN High Commissioner for Refugees

VC – Viet Cong or Vietnamese Communists

Viet Kieu – overseas Vietnamese

Viet Minh – League for the Independence of Vietnam, a nationalistic movement that fought the Japanese and French but later became communist dominated

VNQDD – Viet Nam Quoc Dan Dang. Largely middle -class nationalist party.

xang – petrol

xe Honda loi – wagon pulled by a motorbike

xe lam – tiny three-wheeled trucks used for short-haul passenger and freight transport

xe loi – wagon pulled by a motorbike in the Mekong Delta region

xe om – motorbike taxi, also called *Honda om*

xich lo – *cyclo*, from the French *cyclo-pousse*

Behind the Scenes

SEND US YOUR FEEDBACK

We love to hear from travellers – your comments keep us on our toes and help make our books better. Our well-travelled team reads every word on what you loved or loathed about this book. Although we cannot reply individually to postal submissions, we always guarantee that your feedback goes straight to the appropriate authors, in time for the next edition. Each person who sends us information is thanked in the next edition – the most useful submissions are rewarded with a selection of digital PDF chapters.

Visit **lonelyplanet.com/contact** to submit your updates and suggestions or to ask for help. Our award-winning website also features inspirational travel stories, news and discussions.

Note: We may edit, reproduce and incorporate your comments in Lonely Planet products such as guidebooks, websites and digital products, so let us know if you don't want your comments reproduced or your name acknowledged. For a copy of our privacy policy visit lonelyplanet.com/privacy.

OUR READERS

Many thanks to the travellers who used the last edition and wrote to us with helpful hints, useful advice and interesting anecdotes:

A Aimee Clark, Andre Sypkens, Andrew Chong, Andrew Kay, Andrew Singer, Ann Charlesworth, Anna Bartle, Anna Downing **B** Bart Lauran, Bas Nieuwesteeg, Belinda King, Bernard Boixière, Bod Hopkins, Boris Katz, Brian Clayton, Brian Cox, Bryan Carvill **C** Caralin Fleet, Carol Godden, Celia North, Chris Urbasic, Christina Scerbo, Christina Thompson, Cristina Ribosa, Cuiling Su **D** David Beame, David Gustavsen, David Shanks, David Tognarini, Debra Dorn, Derek Hirst, Dionne Findley **E** Eran Friedlander, Eric Yu, Estibaliz Castrillo **F** Fabrice Simonin, Felix O Wagner, Fiona Rosemarine, Fiona Woodley **G** Gemma Mellides, George Nelis, Gerold Seibert, Graeme Dawson, Greg de Malherbe, Guillaume Duclouet **H** Hannah Logan, Hans van der Broek **I** Iris Brummans **J** James Stuart Armitage, Jan Cullen, Janet Liddle, Jason Bonney, Jens Werzner, Jeroen Bakker, Jim Hollander, Joan Ng, Jodie Horton, Joel Richer, Johan Coopman, Jolanda Spoelstra, Jolijn Vannuffelen, Jonathan G, Joyce van den Oever, Julia Pehl, Julie Pichon **K** Karan Khetan, Kennet Fischer, Koen van Delft, Krystyna Deuss **L** Laura Boutevillain, Le Van Phong Uy, Lea Champoux, Liesbeth Langerak, Luc Frans, Lyn Fawcett **M** Maria Krüger, Mario Knape, Marky Enriquez, Martin Hellwagner, Matthias Kläy, Matthias Kranke, Melissa Calderisi, Michael Schuetz, Michael Vanmechelen, Mick Flood, Mike Musil, Mike Rinowski, Monique Saegesser **N** Nagore Saiz Menchaca, Nicola Cammisa **O** Orly Flax **P** Patrick Bernard, Peter Ackoff, Peter Bowert, Peter Madsen, Peter McIver, Peter Rossi **R** Ralph Schwer, Randy Grasser, Renae Lodo, Robbert Barends, Robert Costabile, Roberta Gorgone, Robin Blench, Ruben Mooijman, Ruth Rosant **S** Sabrina Desprats, Samantha Lush, Sander Brasser, Sandra Doennhoff, Sapa O'Chau, Sarah Attwell, Sarah Jensen, Scott Fletcher, Scott Lang, Shirley Sim, Sophie Galharret, Stefan Recksiegel **T** Tamara Dekum, Thomas Beaven, Thomas Rye, Thuy Nguyen, Tim Samuelson, Tlaloc Tokuda, Tom Abbott, Tony Harman, Tony James Slater, Torben Giesselmann, Trena Kennedy **W** Werner Bruyninx, William M Worden **X** Xie Yang **Y** Yannick Arnaud, Yvette Walsh

AUTHOR THANKS

Iain Stewart

It was a remarkable trip, thanks to the kindness and help of Vinh Vu, Chien, Dzung, Neil and Caroline in Hoi An, Mark Wyndham, Ben and Bich, Howard and Deborah Limbert, the

Nha Trang boys, Tam in Dong Ha and Mark and Jason in Ho Chi Minh City. And thanks to all the Lonely Planet people in Melbourne (and beyond) for sterling work and support behind the scenes.

Brett Atkinson

Thanks to Kien and family in Hanoi and on the road, and to the always stylish Mr Hai for negotiating a smooth path through challenging north Vietnamese landscapes. In Sapa, thanks to Shu and Peter – keep up the great work – and cheers to Mr Tung, Jim and Graeme on Cat Ba. Finally thanks to Carol and my family back home in Auckland for their love and support through interesting times.

Damian Harper

Thanks to everyone who helped: Iain Stewart for invaluable pointers, Nguyen Linh, Mark Zazula, Jason Donovan, Steph Akhurst, Tim Doling, Walter Pearson, Sophie Hughes, Stu, Rohan Barker, Su-Su, Hung, Thanh and of course the magnificent and warm-hearted people of Vietnam, who made my journey a joy every step of the way. Thanks also to the ever-useful and well-thumbed Hoa–Viet Chinese–Vietnamese Dictionary and immense gratitude as always to Dai Min, Timothy Jiafu and Emma Jiale.

Nick Ray

A huge and heartfelt thanks to the people of Cambodia, whose warmth and humour,

stoicism and spirit make it a happy yet humbling place to be. Biggest thanks are reserved for my lovely wife Kulikar Sotho and our children Julian and Belle, as without their support and encouragement the adventures would not be possible. Thanks to fellow travellers and residents, friends and contacts in Cambodia who have helped shaped my knowledge and experience in this country. There is no room to thank everyone, but you all know who you are, as we meet for anything from beers to ecotourism conferences regularly enough. Thanks also to my co-authors in Vietnam for going the extra mile to ensure this is a worthy new edition. Finally, thanks to the Lonely Planet team who have worked on this title. The author may be the public face, but a huge amount of work goes into making this a better book behind the scenes and I thank everyone for their hard work.

ACKNOWLEDGMENTS

Climate map data adapted from Peel MC, Finlayson BL & McMahon TA (2007) 'Updated World Map of the Köppen-Geiger Climate Classification', Hydrology and Earth System Sciences, 11, 163344.

Cover photograph: Traditional fisher, Hoi An / HNH Images, Getty Images.

Illustrations pp172–3 and pp410–11 by Michael Weldon.

THIS BOOK

This 12th edition of Lonely Planet's *Vietnam* guidebook was researched and written by Iain Stewart, Brett Atkinson, Damian Harper and Nick Ray. The previous edition was written and researched by Iain, Brett and Nick, along with Peter Dragicevich. This guidebook was commissioned in Lonely Planet's Melbourne office, and produced by the following:

Commissioning Editor Ilaria Walker

Coordinating Editors Elin Berglund, Kate Mathews

Senior Cartographer Diana Von Holdt

Book Designer Mazzy Prinsep

Managing Editors Sasha Baskett, Bruce Evans

Assisting Editors Alison Barber, Michelle Bennett, Penny Cordner, Adrienne Costanzo, Helen Koehne, Charlotte Orr, Gabrielle Stefanos, Ross Taylor

Assisting Cartographers Jeff Cameron, Corey Hutchison, James Leversha

Cover Research Naomi Parker

Language Content Branislava Vladisavljevic

Thanks to Anita Banh, Brendan Dempsey, Ryan Evans, Larissa Frost, Genesys India, Catherine Naghten, Lorna Parkes, Chad Parkhill, Trent Paton, Martine Power, Dianne Schallmeiner, Gerard Walker

Index

Map Legend

Sights
- Beach
- Bird Sanctuary
- Buddhist
- Castle/Palace
- Christian
- Confucian
- Hindu
- Islamic
- Jain
- Jewish
- Monument
- Museum/Gallery/Historic Building
- Ruin
- Sento Hot Baths/Onsen
- Shinto
- Sikh
- Taoist
- Winery/Vineyard
- Zoo/Wildlife Sanctuary
- Other Sight

Activities, Courses & Tours
- Bodysurfing
- Diving
- Canoeing/Kayaking
- Course/Tour
- Skiing
- Snorkelling
- Surfing
- Swimming/Pool
- Walking
- Windsurfing
- Other Activity

Sleeping
- Sleeping
- Camping

Eating
- Eating

Drinking & Nightlife
- Drinking & Nightlife
- Cafe

Entertainment
- Entertainment

Shopping
- Shopping

Information
- Bank
- Embassy/Consulate
- Hospital/Medical
- Internet
- Police
- Post Office
- Telephone
- Toilet
- Tourist Information
- Other Information

Geographic
- Beach
- Hut/Shelter
- Lighthouse
- Lookout
- Mountain/Volcano
- Oasis
- Park
- Pass
- Picnic Area
- Waterfall

Population
- Capital (National)
- Capital (State/Province)
- City/Large Town
- Town/Village

Transport
- Airport
- Border crossing
- Bus
- Cable car/Funicular
- Cycling
- Ferry
- Metro/MRT station
- Monorail
- Parking
- Petrol station
- Skytrain/Subway station
- Taxi
- Train station/Railway
- Tram
- Underground station
- Other Transport

Routes
- Tollway
- Freeway
- Primary
- Secondary
- Tertiary
- Lane
- Unsealed road
- Road under construction
- Plaza/Mall
- Steps
- Tunnel
- Pedestrian overpass
- Walking Tour
- Walking Tour detour
- Path/Walking Trail

Boundaries
- International
- State/Province
- Disputed
- Regional/Suburb
- Marine Park
- Cliff
- Wall

Hydrography
- River, Creek
- Intermittent River
- Canal
- Water
- Dry/Salt/Intermittent Lake
- Reef

Areas
- Airport/Runway
- Beach/Desert
- Cemetery (Christian)
- Cemetery (Other)
- Glacier
- Mudflat
- Park/Forest
- Sight (Building)
- Sportsground
- Swamp/Mangrove

Note: Not all symbols displayed above appear on the maps in this book

OUR STORY

A beat-up old car, a few dollars in the pocket and a sense of adventure. In 1972 that's all Tony and Maureen Wheeler needed for the trip of a lifetime – across Europe and Asia overland to Australia. It took several months, and at the end – broke but inspired – they sat at their kitchen table writing and stapling together their first travel guide, *Across Asia on the Cheap*. Within a week they'd sold 1500 copies. Lonely Planet was born.

Today, Lonely Planet has offices in Melbourne, London and Oakland, with more than 600 staff and writers. We share Tony's belief that 'a great guidebook should do three things: inform, educate and amuse'.

OUR WRITERS

Iain Stewart

Coordinating Author, Central Vietnam, Southeast Coast, Southwest Highlands
Iain's been visiting Vietnam for over two decades, and has written numerous guides for Lonely Planet, including three editions of this title. He's been to virtually every province in the nation but has a weakness for beaches and great ocean roads. Highlights on this trip were eating the best food in the world, travelling virtually the entire coastline with mate Vinh and his family, visiting the swim-through caves of Phong Nha, mountain biking around Dalat, hanging out in Hoi An, bar-hopping in Ho Chi Minh City (HCMC) and savouring the silence of Con Dao.

Brett Atkinson

Hanoi, Northern Vietnam Brett's been travelling to Vietnam from his hometown of Auckland for two decades, and continues to explore new areas of one of his favourite countries. In his second Lonely Planet *Vietnam* research trip he devoured Hanoi street food atop tiny blue plastic stools, got way off the beaten track in Ha Giang province and rested road-weary limbs in a restorative Red Dzao herbal bath near Sapa. See www.brett-atkinson.net for details of his latest travels and writing.

Damian Harper

Ho Chi Minh City, Mekong Delta After graduating with a degree in Chinese in the days when it was still an exotic choice, Damian relocated to Hong Kong to see out the last year of British rule. He has also lived in Beijing and Shanghai and today calls London home. He has worked on over 30 books for Lonely Planet since 1997, including *China*, *Shanghai, Beijing* and *Malaysia, Singapore & Brunei*. Damian's Vietnam journey took him from the roaring streets of HCMC to the dirt roads and idyllic beaches of Phu Quoc, via a choice of lip-smacking Vietnamese restaurants and unforgettable views of the Mekong waters.

Read more about Damian at:
lonelyplanet.com/members/damianharper

Nick Ray

Siem Reap & the Temples of Angkor A Londoner of sorts, Nick comes from Watford, the sort of town that makes you want to travel. He lives in Phnom Penh with his wife Kulikar and his young children Julian and Belle. He has contributed to countless guidebooks on the Mekong region, including Lonely Planet's *Cambodia, Laos, Myanmar* and *Vietnam* guides. When not writing, Nick is often exploring remote parts of Indochina as a location scout and manager for the world of television and film, including everything from *Tomb Raider* to *Top Gear*.

Contributing Authors

Andrea Nyugen wrote the Regional Specialities feature. Andrea is the acclaimed author of *Into the Vietnamese Kitchen* and *Asian Tofu*. She also publishes Vietworldkitchen.com.

Published by Lonely Planet Publications Pty Ltd
ABN 36 005 607 983
12th edition – July 2014
ISBN 978 1 74220 582 3
© Lonely Planet 2014   Photographs © as indicated 2014
10 9 8 7 6 5 4 3 2 1
Printed in China